Seam in Action

Seam in Action

DAN ALLEN

MANNING

Greenwich
(74° w. long.)

To my wife Sarah, without whom this book would not have been possible.
Thanks for giving up everything.
I love you forever.

Manning Publications Co.
Sound View Court 3B
Greenwich, CT 06830

Development Editor: Cynthia Kane
Copyeditor: Liz Welch
Typesetter: Gordan Salinovic
Cover designer: Leslie Haimes
Proofreader: Katie Tennant

ISBN 1933988401
Printed in the United States of America
1 2 3 4 5 6 7 8 9 10 – MAL – 13 12 11 10 09 08

brief contents

v

contents

vii

foreword

The most challenging part of being a developer on the Seam project isn't writing the code—it's trying to explain Seam to new users. There's a large gap that a Seam neophyte must cross to really "get" what Seam is about. The problem isn't that Seam is overly complex, or that it requires an esoteric skill set. Seam puts together a number of ideas that are unfamiliar to mainstream Java developers. Many of those ideas challenge the common wisdom of enterprise Java development.

To start with, Seam fills a gap not many Java developers realize exists. We are so accustomed to working with a half dozen disintegrated technologies that a truly integrated application framework seems foreign to us. This disintegration is most painfully clear at the persistence layer. Where ineffective caching and lazy instantiation issues plague most applications, Seam actually gets it right. When you consider that the creators of Seam were the brains behind Hibernate, that's not hard to believe!

Then you've got Seam's dynamic bidirection injection (bijection), which is radically different from the static injection offered by the popular dependency injection frameworks. And we haven't even mentioned the clever stateful components in a world where the prevailing technologies force all applications into a multilayered stateless architecture regardless of whether that architecture suits the application being developed.

We're just scratching the surface, and already we can see that Seam offers a vision that's so different from the status quo that guiding a new Seam user becomes a huge challenge. As a result, few introductions to Seam go beyond the basics, presenting the ABCs of the technology without showing how to put the letters together to make words and sentences. *Seam in Action* is the first Seam book to capture the spirit of Seam and show you how to put those words and sentences together the way we on the Seam team intended the technology to be used.

What impresses me most about the book you're holding in your hands is that it doesn't blindly toe the Seam party line. Dan Allen has painstakingly broken Seam down to its core concepts and reassembled them in a way that is fresh and unique. *Seam in Action* isn't a simple-minded regurgitation of the Seam reference documentation. Instead, it's a perfect companion to it, showing how to understand Seam and best apply it to your own applications.

Seam can help you code better, more functional applications. It can help you work faster, and it can help you code your applications with a simpler, easier-to-manage architecture. But you'll only reap those benefits if you take the time to learn how to best apply the technology. *Seam in Action* is the perfect guide to get you to the point where you can apply Seam to its full potential.

If you're up to the challenge, then, to shamelessly borrow the analogy of the book, I invite you to step up to the first tee—and take a swing.

NORMAN RICHARDS
Senior Engineer, Red Hat

preface

We can't solve problems by using the same kind of thinking we used when we created them.

—Albert Einstein

As I write this passage, I'm flying over the Atlantic Ocean on my way back from Europe to the United States for the second time in a month. This trip was to Tuscany for a meeting to discuss Seam's future; the previous trip had been to Zurich, where I spoke about Seam at the Jazoon '08 conference. The first trip was especially significant to me because it marked the first time in the 30 years of my life that I've traveled outside of North America. I was beginning to think that day would never come, but it did, thanks to Seam. (And because my brother purchased the ticket to get me there. Thanks, Kevin!)

You might think I'm ridiculous for attributing this milestone to Seam. After all, how can a framework motivate a person to embark on an unprecedented trip? Before you call me crazy, let me explain how I got involved in Seam and how it influenced me to expand my horizons.

Around the time Seam was being developed, I was spending my days banging my head on a project built using Spring and JSF. For more than a year, I felt stuck in a rut trying to manage the application's state, wrestling with irrelevant decisions such as whether to name a business object a *Manager* or a *Service*, and rationalizing how many layers to use and which layer should take ownership of a given task. All of these distractions held back the project and my growth. I kept looking for some way out.

The spark that attracted me to Seam is the fine-grained control it provides over JSF requests through its page descriptor. The reason I stuck with Seam (and ultimately decided to write about it) goes well beyond the voids it filled for me at the time.

Seam has clout because it follows a consistent approach without imposing arbitrary restrictions. It leverages annotations, interceptors, XHTML-based templates, and JSF components to give you the most bang for your keystroke. It provides access to objects when and where you need them and manages them so you don't have to. It also helps establish continuity from one page request to the next. Above all, it gives you freedom to organize the application as it suits you and to choose the tools you want to use to build it: Java or Groovy, XML or annotations, JavaScript or rich widgets, built-in or custom components, and so on.

But we have a tendency to get caught up in the word *framework* and forget the real reason we're writing software: to serve the needs of our users or our clients' users. That's the angle you have to take going into learning one of these tools.

Users don't want to spend their days paging through endless result sets and could care less if you're having a problem with lazy initialization exceptions in the view. They want mature software. They want advanced searches, reports in PDF or Excel, charts, emails, file uploads, dynamic graphics, wizards, workspaces, and so on. Basically, they want the stuff that's really hard to develop, or at least harder than feeding the database through a CRUD generation tool. Seam gives you the CRUD generation tool, which gets you developing immediately, and it also provides the extra stuff.

Seam is worth knowing because it touches on nearly every aspect of Java EE. Sure, you have a lot to learn, but Seam makes every facet of the platform remarkably accessible and gets you working on the advanced parts of your application early in the project. You no longer have to dread those wild and crazy requirements that the user dreams up. Instead, you feel empowered to write applications—and you'll get to the feature wish lists.

As an integration framework, Seam keeps a vast number of technologies close at hand and accessible. As a result, you find yourself trying out technologies you never thought you'd use, and you witness your application and skill set maturing quickly. You also start introducing new styles of interaction into your application, such as the event-observer model or something as revolutionary as Ajax Push. You get used to venturing into new territory, without having to abandon the familiar, and it affects your general attitude toward life.

That brings me back to my original statement. Seam is the driver that finally launched me out of North America. It also kick-started my writing and consulting career, got me involved in a successful open source project, and allowed me to meet interesting and talented people. How will Seam change your career? How will it change your life?

Somewhere over the Atlantic, July 2008

acknowledgments

While writing this book, I made many promises to myself and others about what I'd do when I finished. The most important of those promises was to acknowledge everyone who made this book possible. Of course, I'm grateful to have you as a reader. But you should appreciate those people who got this book out on the shelves and into your hands.

The first and last person I want to thank is my wife, Sarah. If it weren't for her help, you wouldn't be holding this book. I have no idea where to even begin thanking her. She pushed me to believe in myself, kept me motivated when the end kept moving further away, tolerated being inundated with Seam and my relentless questioning about how to structure the book, edited drafts, assembled the index, provided therapy, made sure I ate, and took care of countless chores I let slip. What meant the most is that she put my project before her own, something I look forward to doing for her now. Please help me in thanking her.

Writing a book puts a tremendous strain on relationships. I would like to thank all my friends and family for supporting me in this endeavor and having faith that I would eventually come out of my hole and once again answer phone calls, hang out, and talk about something other than writing a book. I am forever indebted to my parents, James and Mary Allen, for extending me every opportunity in my life to be successful. You only get one childhood and they made it both a rewarding and a memorable one. Mom and Dad, thanks for passing on to me your relentless perseverance and strong desire to learn and for always being there to support me in my endeavors.

Rewinding to the origin of this book, I want to thank Andrew Glover for introducing me to Jennifer Aloi from IBM developerWorks, who in turn launched my technical writing career by sponsoring the *Seamless JSF* series. Much of the credit for that series' success goes to Athen O'Shea for doing a superb job of editing and helping me find the right words. Little did I know that I would soon be buried deep in turning those ideas into a book.

I want to thank Marjan Bace and Michael Stephens for taking a chance on me and trusting that I would finish as I blew past one deadline after the next. Something tells me they had the real schedule hidden in a drawer and had already anticipated the 15 months that would elapse over the course of this project. I'm also grateful to Andy Kapit and Andrew Van Etten of CodeRyte, Inc., for endorsing this book in its early stages.

Moving along chronologically, I'd like to acknowledge Cynthia Kane for helping me see the big picture and for reminding me that I had a book to write when I started to daydream. I was fortunate to have an ambitious and talented set of reviewers who donated their time and insight to help make this the best Seam resource available: Peter Johnson, Doug Warren, Peter Pavlovich, Devon Hillard, Nikolaos Kaintantzis, Hung Tang, Michael Smolyak, Benjamin Muschko, Kevin Galligan, Judy Guglielmin, Valentin Crettaz, Carol McDonald, Ara Abrahamian, Horaci Macias, Norman Richards, Ted Goddard, Costantino Cerbo, Mark Eagle, Carlo Bottiglieri, and Jord Sonneveld. Thanks to Karen Tegtmeyer for seeking out the reviewers, conducting the reviews, and scaring the volunteers into actually sending back their comments. Special thanks to Benjamin Muschko, Pete Pavlovich, and Ray Van Eperen for thoroughly reading the book and giving me line-by-line edits and advice; thanks to Michael Youngstrom for reviewing chapter 15; thanks to Ted Goddard and Judy Guglielmin for their help with chapter 12 and the development of the source code for the ICEfaces example; and thanks to Valerie Griffin and Daniel Hinojosa for providing last-minute corrections and feedback. I also want to thank all my loyal MEAP readers and forum participants, especially those who were there from the very beginning, patiently waiting for this book to materialize into print.

The heroes of this project are the production team, under the leadership of Mary Piergies, who coaxed me out of rewriting hell and worked in overdrive to get this book into print. The person who took on the biggest burden in this transition was Liz Welch, my copy editor. I want to extend enormous thanks to Liz for weeding out all the inconsistencies in the book and tolerating my pursuit of perfection. I also want to thank Norman Richards, my technical editor, for challenging me to get all my facts about Seam straight and steering me away from giving readers impractical advice. I'd like to recognize the tremendous work done by the remaining members of the production and postproduction team: Katie Tennant for proofreading the manuscript, squashing all of those "writing bugs"; Dottie Marsico and Gordan Salinovic for morphing the chapters from office document format into the professional layout that you see in front of you in record time; Leslie Haimes for making the book look eye-catching on the shelves and enticing readers, like yourself, to dive into it; Tiffany Taylor for maintaining the document templates; Gabriel Dobrescu for handling the book's web presence on manning.com; and Steven Hong for continued support in publicizing the book and preparing marketing materials.

Join me in thanking Gavin King for sharing his vision of Seam and its contextual component model with the world as an open source project and to all the Seam developers that matured his vision into the robust integration framework that it is today.

I would like to thank Panera Bread in Laurel, MD, for serving as my retreat/second office when my house was trying to stifle my writing. I am grateful for the bottomless tea and free wireless internet. I wish more companies were as progressive as yours.

I'm happy to say that each and every person mentioned in this passage, and sadly those I overlooked, helped me complete the most ambitious goal of my life. Thanks again to my wife for standing by me during this project.

about this book

If you're ready to become an expert on Seam, I can guarantee you that this book will get you there. I don't use terms that confuse you just to make myself feel smart. I don't say "trust me on this; it will all work out." I don't distract you with an outline of the next chapter when you're trying to focus on the current material. And especially, I don't sprinkle @In and @Out annotations over a class and expect that you'll know what they will do. Nope. I lay down the facts. I show you the steps. I reveal the logic. I diagram the flow. What I like most about programming is that each thing happens for a reason. The exciting challenge is learning what that reason is and then turning around and discovering how to make practical use of it. Some areas of Seam are hard to get, I'll admit. But trust that with guidance, you will get it. Never settle for less than the facts, and don't give up!

Not only do I teach you how Seam works, I also teach you the *how* and the *why* so you can go off and teach Seam to others. I've traveled into each and every corner of Seam, and I want to share with you what I've experienced to motivate you to travel there yourself. I want to give you what Seam gave me: the ability to reach my true potential as a developer. This is the best resource to help you understand Seam without gaps.

Roadmap

The goal of this book is to get you started with Seam quickly. It's divided into four parts. The first part does a flyover of Seam and gets you ready to learn about it. The second part focuses in on the core concepts until you can see the blades of grass. The third part studies Seam's state-management solution and Java persistence support.

The last part teaches you to make your application secure and stand above the competition. Best of all, you get to have fun.

Chapter 1 answers three questions: *What is Seam? Why was Seam created? What does a Seam application look like?* The chapter explains how Seam fits into the Java EE landscape and enumerates ways it extends the platform to make it more accessible and pertinent. You see a basic Seam application, which provides an overview of what is to come.

Rather than diving directly into the fundamentals of Seam, chapter 2 steps you through setting up a Seam project. Not only does this give you an environment for testing the Seam concepts covered in the remainder of the book, it leaves you with a complete CRUD application that supports incremental hot deployment of changes.

Because JSF is the primary view framework in Seam, chapter 3 provides a glimpse of it, identifies its weaknesses, and shows how Seam improves it. You study the page-oriented enhancements to JSF that Seam provides and get a high-level overview of how Seam involves itself in the JSF life cycle. By the chapter's end, you should appreciate that the only reasonable way to develop using JSF is with Seam.

Chapter 4 explores the heart of Seam: the contextual container. You learn what a Seam component is, how it differs from a component instance, the palette of scopes in which you can store instances and other context variables, and how Seam manages the component life cycle. You get a feel for using annotations to control the application. You also learn ways to access components and when they are instantiated.

Seam's central switchboard, the component descriptor, is introduced in chapter 5. You learn about its two main functions: defining a component in XML as an alternative to annotations and assigning initial property values, either to control the behavior of a component or to build object prototypes. Although the metadata in this file is XML, Seam leverages namespaces to make the configuration *type-safe*. You even learn to develop your own namespace. Tucked away at the end of the chapter is an introduction to Seam's simple, yet powerful, approach to managing message bundles.

Chapter 6 is paramount because it presents Seam's most compelling and progressive feature, bijection. The key benefit bijection provides is to allow component instances in different scopes to safely collaborate without risk of scope impedance or concurrency violations. The other theme in this chapter is how Seam initializes objects on demand.

Chapter 7 covers Seam's *conversation*, another vital feature. Java-based web applications have always lacked a scope that correlates with the user's activity. You discover that the conversation fits this need, overcomes the shortcomings of the HTTP session, and provides a way for the user to manage parallel activities. The most important use of the conversation is to manage the persistence context.

To appreciate how Seam improves Java persistence, you have to learn what it is. Chapter 8 gives you an introductory view of Java persistence and points you to valuable resources on the topic; explains how Java persistence is managed in a pure Java EE environment; and helps you distinguish between Hibernate and JPA.

Chapter 9 presents Java persistence under the stewardship of Seam and demonstrates how Seam gets persistence right, where Java EE falls short. You learn that the conversation-scoped persistence context frees you from lazy initialization errors and dirty merge operations. You also learn that Seam blankets the request in a series of transactions, extending the guarantees they provide to all operations in a request. The chapter concludes by examining the most important feature of a multiuser web application: the *application transaction*, which makes persistence operations in a conversation atomic.

Chapter 10 is round two of developing a CRUD application—only this time, you do everything yourself. Well, not everything. You learn how to leverage the classes in the Seam Application Framework to handle most of the boilerplate code, so all you have to do is design and customize the user interface. After reading chapter 2 and chapter 10, you should be able to do CRUD in your sleep.

An application wouldn't be much use without security. In three strokes, chapter 11 gets you authenticating users and then proceeds to teach you how to implement basic role-based and contextual rule-based authorization to protect your application in powerful ways.

One of the things Seam does well is make other technologies look good. In chapter 12, you learn how to add Ajax to your application using RichFaces or ICEfaces components without touching a line of JavaScript. Seam manages state to ensure these Ajax interactions don't bog down the server resources. You also learn to enhance the capabilities of JavaScript by giving it direct access to server-side components and learn to integrate Seam with a rich user interface technology such as GWT.

Chapter 13 lets you escape the humdrum of HTML by teaching you to create a wide variety of content types, such as PDFs, emails, charts, graphics, and binary documents. You also learn to style your application and give the user control over the user interface.

I had so much to talk about that the last two chapters wouldn't fit in the book. On this book's website (www.manning.com/SeaminAction), you can check out Seam's business process management solution in chapter 14 and Seam's Spring integration in chapter 15.

Appendix A shows you how to set up Seam and the supporting environment and prepares you to follow along with the source code for this book.

Who should read this book?

Seam in Action was described by one reviewer as "written by an expert for experts." If you've picked up this book hoping it has the breadth of knowledge you seek, that quote should satisfy you. A second reviewer claimed that "experienced Seam developers are likely to get something out of reading the book." Another stated that "even if you are already an expert in the underlying technologies, you will not be disappointed." If you want to master Seam, it's well worth having this book in your backpack.

Where does that leave the rest of you, who are just getting started with Seam? You won't be disappointed either. If you're a Seam newbie or a manager, you'll get plenty of value out of just the first two chapters. If you want to go further, you have to ask yourself if you're committed to learning about this technology and if you're willing to put some effort into it. Are you ready to become an expert? If not, it might be best for you to start with the Seam reference documentation or perhaps an introductory book. Chances are, you'll be back when you're ready to know all the details about how Seam works.

If you're still with me, be aware that you need some prior experience before you take on this book. I've been able to go into detail in the book because I've left out introductory material that's readily available elsewhere. At the very least, I expect that you have experience developing with Java, using the Java Servlet API, and deploying to application servers or servlet containers. I move quickly through JSF and ORM technologies, assuming that you've at least read about them. You should also have some awareness of method interceptors and how they work, although this knowledge can be inferred from the text. Finally, if you're interested in the parts of the book that cover the EJB 3 integration or Spring integration, you need some prior experience with these technologies. That sounds like a lot of prerequisites, but if you're dedicated, you can pick up this information from the book and the resources I recommend as you read.

If you're worried about the requirement to understand JSF, the next section provides a brief introduction that should get you by. I also suggest a couple of additional resources if you feel you need more explanation. Honestly, though, basic JSF is straightforward, and Seam hides a lot of complexity beyond that point.

What you need to know about JSF to use Seam

JSF is a component-oriented user interface (UI) framework as opposed to an action-based framework like Struts. Struts requires that you write a custom action handler that processes the request and then forwards control to a JSP page, which renders the HTML response. JSF, on the other hand, resolves a view template—typically a JSP page—automatically from a request and transfers control directly to it. The lack of a front controller may appear to be a step backward. The enhancement comes in the way the view template is processed.

JSF reads the view template, which contains custom JSP or Facelets tags, and constructs a UI component tree, effectively deferring the rendering process. The UI component tree is a hierarchical graph of Java objects that represents the structure of the page. Rendering is only a secondary concern and occurs when the component tree is "encoded" to the client (that is, the browser). The renderer attached to each component produces the markup.

The main concern of the UI component tree is to act as a server-side representation of the view and listen for events that occur in the UI. There is a one-to-one mapping between the elements in the component tree and the elements on the page (with the exception of literal HTML). For instance, if the page contains a form with inputs and buttons, a corresponding form and nested input and button components exist in the UI component tree. Because the processing of the view template is separate from the encoding of the UI component tree, you can build the component tree using an alternate view technology, such as Facelets or pure Java. The component tree can also produce markup other than HTML.

The design of JSF goes beyond separating the view definition and view rendering with an intermediary object graph. JSF uses the component tree to capture events and allow programmatic, server-side manipulation of the view. In this regard, it's similar to Swing, except that it operates in the context of the web environment. Any event performed by the user results in an HTTP request. During this request, or *postback*, the component tree is "restored" from its previous state. The events are processed, and the component tree is once again encoded to the client (the HTML response).

A simple example of the event mechanism is when the user clicks a button—a UICommand component—in a JSF form. As a result, the method bound to the action of the button is executed. You don't have to worry about how the request is handled or how this mapping is prepared. If the form has inputs—UIInput components—the values in those inputs are assigned to the JavaBean properties to which they're bound. The properties are then available to the action method when it executes. The objects that are bound to UI components are called *managed beans*. As you learn later, JSF does the managing.

How is a managed bean bound to a UI component? This binding is done using expression language (EL) notation, also found in JSP. There are both value- and method-binding expressions, although the latter are unique to JSF. JSF can use a value expression to capture a property value, in addition to outputting it, unlike in JSP. A method expression is used to bind a method to a UI component so that the method is invoked when the component is activated.

In the button example, a method on a managed bean might be bound to the action of the button through the expression #{beanName.methodName}. This expression resolves to the methodName() method on an instance of a JSF managed bean named beanName. Managed beans are defined in the JSF descriptor, faces-config.xml, using the <managed-bean> element. JSF automatically creates instances of these managed beans as needed.

Value expressions appear identical to method expressions, although they have a vastly different purpose. The value of an input component might be bound to a property on a managed bean using the expression #{beanName.propertyName}. JSF reads the value from the JavaBean getter method, getPropertyName(), when the page is rendered and writes the new value captured in the input to the setter method, setPropertyName(), after the button is clicked. Again, you don't have to worry about reading request values from the HttpServletRequest object. The assignment happens automatically, and you can focus on implementing the business logic.

The EL is an important part of JSF and Seam, and you should be sure to understand it. Two resources I recommend are the article "Unified Expression Language for JSP and JSF," published on java.net,[1] and the FAQs about the EL on seamframework.org.[2]

The example just presented appears simple enough, but what goes on during each JSF request, especially the postback, is quite a bit more sophisticated. Each request activates the JSF life cycle, which consists of six phases:

1 Restore View
2 Apply Request Values
3 Process Validations (and conversions)
4 Update Model Values
5 Invoke Application
6 Render Response

If the request is a postback, the UI component tree is restored during the *Restore View* phase. If this is an initial request, meaning the URL was requested from the browser's location bar or a regular link, the life cycle skips directly to the *Render Response* phase.

---

[1] http://today.java.net/pub/a/today/2006/03/07/unified-jsp-jsf-expression-language.html
[2] http://seamframework.org/Documentation/WhatIsAnExpressionLanguageEL

A postback continues through the life cycle. In the three phases that follow *Restore View*, the form values are captured, converted, validated, and assigned to the JavaBean properties on the managed beans to which they are bound. Validations and conversions get assigned to an input component either as nested tags or correlated with the property's type in the JSF descriptor.

The *Invoke Application* phase is where the action methods are executed. There can be at most one primary action and any number of secondary action listeners. The difference between the two types is that only the primary action can trigger a navigation rule. The navigation rules, also defined in the JSF descriptor, dictate the next view to render and are consulted once the *Invoke Application* phase completes.

Finally, in the *Render Response* phase, the UI component tree is built from the view template and subsequently encoded to HTML (or alternate output) and sent to the browser (or client).

That's all there is to JSF. If you're a newcomer to the framework, this brief explanation may leave you wanting. In that case, I'll point you to several excellent resources on JSF that should get you up to speed. If you read nothing else, check out the *JSF for nonbelievers* series[3] on IBM developerWorks. While you're there, also check out the article titled "Facelets fits JSF like a glove"[4] to learn about Facelets, the alternate view technology used in Seam applications. If you're willing to invest in your JSF knowledge, you should pick up a copy of either *JavaServer Faces in Action* (Manning, 2004) or *Pro JSF and Ajax* (Apress, 2006). When reading these resources, keep in mind that you're studying JSF to learn how to use Seam, not necessarily to buy into JSF by itself. In chapter 3, you learn about the many enhancements Seam brings to JSF, a combination that is sure to please.

Next, because this book makes numerous references to golf, I want to give you some background to help you understand it as well.

The game of golf

The objective of golf is simple. You must get your ball into a hole in the ground using the fewest strokes possible, beginning from an area paired with that hole known as a *tee box*—or *tee* for short. A regulation golf course has 18 such holes. Each hole has a *par*, which is a guideline for how many strokes you should expect to take to get the ball into the hole; this number is significant in calculating your score.

The term *hole* refers to both the hole in the ground and its pairing with a tee box. A hole has a fixed number of tee boxes, each identified by a color. The tee boxes are set various distances from the hole and represent different experience levels, to make the game more challenging for those who are better at it. You pick one color and start from the designated area for that color on each hole. Those starting points are known as your *tee set*. In a golf round, you play each hole in sequence for a given tee set.

To advance the ball, you use a set of golf clubs. Each golf club consists of a shaft and a head. The angle of the head determines the loft of the ball when you hit it. The

---

[3] http://www.ibm.com/developerworks/views/java/
libraryview.jsp?sort_order=asc&sort_by=Date&search_by=nonbelievers%3A&search_flag=true

[4] http://www-128.ibm.com/developerworks/java/library/j-facelets/

lower the loft, the further the ball is *supposed* to go (realizing this difference requires some skill). To hit the ball, you swing the club much like you would a baseball bat, but don't tell the golf pro I said that! You use a special club called a *putter* to advance the ball on the green—the area that surrounds the hole. When using the putter, you tap the ball rather than swing at it. Each time you make contact with the ball, regardless of which club you use, it counts as one stroke.

When you start each hole, you're permitted to elevate your ball using a golf tee. The first shot on a hole is the only time you're allowed to use this aid. The tee is intended to accommodate the swing of a driver, the club in your bag with the lowest loft. Once you take your first stroke on a given hole, you advance the ball using a club until the ball lies at rest in the hole. You then pick up your ball and walk—or ride—to the next tee. At the end of the round, you add up all your strokes to calculate your raw score (I won't get into the concept of a *handicap*, but just know that it is used to weight your score.) The lower that number, the better you played.

I chose golf as the topic of the example application because, like programming, it's challenging. In golf, you're only as good as your next round. Sounds a lot like the programming world, doesn't it? As soon as we master a technology, there's one right behind it to learn. Fortunately, lots of books are available to help us keep on top of our game.

Code conventions

The book provides copious examples, which include all the Seam application artifacts: Java code, XML-based descriptors, Facelets templates, and Java property files. Source code in listings or in text is in a `fixed-width font like this` to separate it from ordinary text. If there is part of the example I want to draw your attention to, it will be emphasized using bolded code font. Additionally, Java method names, Java class names, Seam component names and context variable names, event names, request parameter names, Java keywords, object properties, EL expressions, Java 5 annotations and enum constants, XML elements and attributes, and commands in text are also presented using `fixed-width` font. When an annotation appears in the text, the @ symbol is treated as silent.

Java, XHTML, and XML can all be verbose. In many cases, the original source code (available online) has been reformatted; I've added line breaks and reworked indentation to accommodate the available page space in the book. In some cases, even this was not enough, and the listings include line-continuation markers (➡).

I apply several other space optimizations. Comments in the source code have been omitted from the listings, and the code is instead described in the text. Class imports in Java classes also tend to take up a lot of space, so I omit those in cases when the code editor can easily resolve them for you. The complete set of imports can be found in the source code. When an implementation of a method isn't important or remains unchanged from a previous listing, you will see { ... }, which is a code fold. Often, I place Java 5 annotations inline with the properties or methods to which they apply to conserve space. Personally, I prefer to use a newline after each Java 5 annotation in my own code.

Code annotations accompany some of the source code listings, highlighting important concepts. In some cases, numbered bullets link to explanations that follow the listing.

The location of individual applications will be referred to throughout the book using a variable notion. For instance, the JBoss AS directory is tokenized as ${jboss.home}.

Source code downloads

Seam is an open source project released under the Lesser GNU Public License (LGPL). Directions for downloading the Seam distribution, which includes both the source and binaries, are available from the Seam community site, http://seamframework.org/Download/SeamDownloads.

The source code for the Open 18 examples in this book is available from http://code.google.com/p/seaminaction and released under the LGPL. Because Seam is constantly evolving, I decided to make the source code available as an open source project so that I can keep the code up to date for readers as needed. You can also download the code for the examples in the book from the publisher's website, http://www.manning.com/SeaminAction. Details about how to use the source code can be found in the README.txt file at the root of the source code and also on the project wiki.

Organizing the software

To help you keep the software in order so that you can follow along with the source code examples, I recommend a directory structure that I adhere to throughout the book. But it's just a recommendation. Only you have a say in where your files are placed, and these conventions are by no means a prerequisite to using Seam.

THE DIRECTORY YOU CALL "HOME"

Your *home directory* is where your personal files live. The last path in the directory is typically the same as your username. The book uses the home directory of a fictional developer, whose username is *twoputt*, whenever an absolute path must be referenced. Table 1 shows the home directory for twoputt as it would appear on several different operating systems. Whenever you see twoputt's home directory used in the book, replace it with your own home directory.

The home area on several operating systems

Operating system	Home area
Linux	/home/twoputt
Mac OSX	/Users/twoputt
Windows	C:\Documents and Settings\twoputt

The terminal output included in the listings has been generated on a Linux system, but you can look beyond this detail because it makes no difference which operating system you use for developing Seam applications.

STRUCTURING YOUR HOME

Table 2 lists several folders, along with their purpose, that I like to set up when doing development. You'll recognize these directories from the book's source code.

Folders in the development area

Folder	What it contains
databases	File-based databases and database schemas
lib	JAR files not included with Seam, such as the H2 driver
opt	Java applications, such as JBoss AS and Seam
projects	Development projects

Appendix A shows you how to install the software you need to use the examples in this book and Seam, with references to this structure.

About the author

DAN ALLEN is an independent software consultant, author, and open source advocate. After graduating from Cornell University with a degree in materials science and engineering in 2000, Dan became captivated by the world of free and open source software, which is how he got his start in software development. He soon discovered the combination of Linux and the Java EE platform to be the ideal blend on which to build his professional career. In his search for a robust web framework, Dan discovered Seam, which was quickly granted this most coveted spot in his development toolbox. Excited about Seam, Dan decided to share his thoughts with the world. This project is a (rather extensive) continuation of his three-part series on Seam published by IBM developerWorks. Dan continues to write articles on Seam and related technologies. Dan is a member of the Seam project, an active participant in the Seam community, and a Java blogger. You can keep up with Dan's development experiences by subscribing to his blog at http://mojavelinux.com.

Author Online

Purchase of *Seam in Action* includes free access to a private web forum run by Manning Publications where you can make comments about the book, ask technical questions, and receive help from the author and from other users. To access the forum and subscribe to it, point your web browser to http://www.manning.com/SeaminAction. This page provides information on how to get on the forum once you are registered, what kind of help is available, and the rules of conduct on the forum.

Manning's commitment to our readers is to provide a venue where a meaningful dialogue among individual readers and between readers and the authors can take place.

It is not a commitment to any specific amount of participation on the part of the author, whose contribution to the AO remains voluntary (and unpaid). We suggest you try asking the author some challenging questions, lest his interest stray! Since authors are busy people, like most people in the technology field, there is a chance your question will not be answered as quickly as you would like. In that case, you are encouraged to try your question on the Seam community website, http://seamframework.org, where you will find a much larger pool of people reading and answering Seam-related posts.

The Author Online forum and the archives of previous discussions will be accessible from the publisher's website as long as the book is in print.

about the cover illustration

The figure on the cover of *Seam in Action* is captioned "La Béarnaise," or a woman from the former Béarne province, a mountainous region in southwest France. The illustration is taken from the 1805 edition of Sylvain Maréchal's four-volume compendium of regional dress customs. Each illustration is finely drawn and colored by hand.

The colorful variety of Maréchal's collection reminds us vividly of how culturally apart the world's towns and regions were just 200 years ago. Isolated from each other, people spoke different dialects and languages. In the streets or the countryside, they were easy to place—sometimes with an error of no more than a dozen miles—just by their dress.

Dress codes have changed since then and the diversity by region, so rich at the time, has faded away. It is now hard to tell apart the inhabitants of different continents, let alone different towns or regions. Perhaps we have traded cultural diversity for a more varied personal life—certainly for a more varied and fast-paced technological life.

At a time when it is hard to tell one computer book from another, Manning celebrates the inventiveness and initiative of the computer business with book covers based on the rich diversity of regional life of two centuries ago, brought back to life by Maréchal's pictures.

Part 1

Teeing off with Seam

Many excellent frameworks exist to support the development of web-based Java applications. Chapter 1 presents Seam and explains how it manages to stand above this crowd by incorporating all of your existing Java Enterprise experience into an innovative and modernized rendition of the Java EE platform. You learn how Seam uncovers the platform's tremendous capabilities, buried underneath layers of complexity for more than a decade, through the use of annotations, interceptors, and configuration by exception. EJB 3 components, Groovy scripts, and anything in between can participate in this lightweight, POJO-based programming model. After this introduction, you are taken through a Seam example, emphasizing how Seam removes infrastructure code and allows components to focus on pure business logic. The chapter also highlights ways in which Seam improves the development process, getting you to your target sooner.

In today's fast-paced world, we often have to show results before completely understanding what we are doing. To help you get started, chapter 2 highlights Seam's project generator tool and shows you how to use it to create a functional, database-oriented application without any coding involved. You are given a glimpse of a Seam project's structure and get a chance to feel out the development cycle by making a few customizations. While you won't have a lot of opportunity to write code in part 1, it will build up enough anticipation to prepare you to take on the commitment of learning a new framework. The best part is, you will have plenty of time to do so since your boss will be drooling over the application you create in the second chapter. That same application also serves as a working model for you as you explore Seam.

Seam unifies Java EE

This chapter covers

- Lightweight Enterprise Java
- Seam as an application stack
- Simplified configuration using annotations
- Tools that enable agile development

Is JSF worth a second look? Is EJB really fixed? Is it worth sticking with Java rather than jumping ship for Ruby on Rails?

With the release of Seam 2.0, you can now confidently answer *yes* to all of these questions. Seam is a progressive application framework for the Java Platform, Enterprise Edition (Java EE) that makes writing web-based applications simple by finally delivering on the promise of a unified component architecture. Seam builds on the innovative changes in Java EE 5 brought about primarily by the Enterprise JavaBeans (EJB) 3 specification. These changes include favoring annotations over container interfaces and relying on configuration by exception rather than verbose and laborious XML descriptors. Seam tears down Java EE's remaining heavyweight legacy by spreading EJB 3's pivotal changes across the platform. Seam also extends the platform as designed by weaving additional functionality into the JavaServer Faces (JSF) life cycle and taps into the unified Expression Language (EL) to allow a wide range of technologies to communicate. With Seam, the pain typically associated with using

Java EE has vanished and JSF, in particular, appears completely revamped and worthy of attention.

In this chapter, you discover why Seam is the most exciting technology in Java right now and the reasons why you should make Seam your framework of choice. I demonstrate how Seam solves your current problems with the Java EE platform by blending innovation with existing standards. In a world inundated with frameworks, Seam is the *unframework*. It does not prescribe a new programming model that you must adopt. Seam simply pulls together the standard Java EE APIs, most notably EJB 3, JSF, Java Persistence API (JPA)/Hibernate, and Java Authentication and Authorization Service (JAAS), and makes them more accessible, functional, and attractive. Seam finishes off these improvements with modern upgrades such as conversations, page flows, business processes, rule-based security, JavaScript (Ajax) remoting, PDF rendering, email composition, charting, file uploads, and Groovy integration. Like a classic car, Seam sports the muscle of Java EE under the hood, but on the surface it appears stunning and elegant.

Putting Seam's strengths aside, the fact remains that you can choose among many qualified frameworks. In the next section, I provide you with advice that can hopefully put an end to your search and move you toward developing your application. Despite the fact that no one can tell you what framework is right for you, you're probably going to ask anyway, right? Don't worry—I came prepared.

1.1   Which framework should I use?

In a world full of framework options, how do you choose one? There are so many frameworks available for the Java platform, some proven, some promising, that the decision is downright agonizing! Does figure 1.1 speak to you?

The choice is so bewildering that the framework inquiry is now the dominant greeting exchanged between developers at conferences. While the question "What do you do?" may

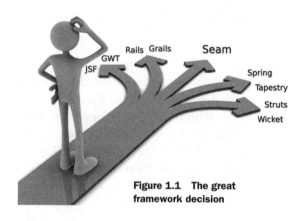

Figure 1.1   The great framework decision

have traditionally served in the role of sizing up a person's abilities, these days you are judged based on the merit of what framework you use for software development (or the advice that you can give pertaining to that choice). Just when you've made a decision, a new framework arrives on the scene promising to bury its predecessors.

These choices can be harmful, especially to productivity. Barry Schwartz argues in *The Paradox of Choice* (Ecco, 2003) that having a bewildering array of options floods our already exhausted brains. The result is that your ability to write a quality application stalls. You keep believing that the best framework is the one you haven't tried yet. As a consequence, you spend more time researching frameworks than you do designing functional applications. The search *consumes* you. You develop a false sense of how busy you are.

If any of these choices were truly satisfying, then you probably would not be reading this book. You would already have a set of tools that you know, beyond all doubt, allows you to be highly productive. But you don't, do you? You're still searching for a framework that is new, yet familiar. Lightweight, yet powerful. You are in need of a platform that integrates the vast landscape of Java technologies into a unified stack. Seam might be just the framework you are looking for.

1.2 Choosing Seam

You might be tempted to think that Seam is just another web framework, competing in an already flooded market. In truth, to tag Seam as a web framework is quite unfitting. Seam is far broader than a traditional web framework, such as Struts, and is better described as an *application stack*.

1.2.1 A complete application stack

Let's consider the distinction between an *application stack* and a *web framework*. Web frameworks are analogous to the guests who show up just in time for dinner and then leave immediately after eating. They entertain and soak up the limelight, but they are mostly unhelpful. They go out the same way they arrived: with lots of flair. An application stack, in contrast, is like the people who help to plan the dinner party, shop for the groceries, cook, set up, serve, make the coffee, and then ultimately clean up when it is all over. They are steadfast and resourceful. Sadly, their work goes mostly unrecognized.

In a world where everyone wants to be a rock star (i.e., web framework), Seam is your practical sidekick, your sous-chef. The Seam application stack includes the framework, the libraries, the build script and project generator, the IDE integration, a base test class, the Embedded JBoss container, and integrations with many technologies. Seam is certainly a hard worker. Figure 1.2 gives a sample cross section of the technologies that Seam is capable of pulling together in a typical application.

While this stack gives you an idea of the technologies used in a Seam application, it does not give you a clear picture of Seam's purpose and

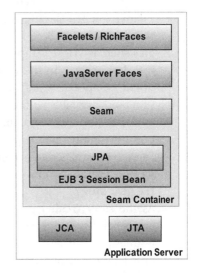

Figure 1.2 A cross section of the technologies incorporated in the Seam stack

why it exists. To understand why Seam was created, you have to recognize the challenge that it faced. Although the Java EE 5 release took a gigantic step toward establishing an agile platform for enterprise Java development, it left behind a rather significant gap between the component-based web tier managed by JSF and the component-based business-tier managed by EJB 3. A bridge was needed.

1.2.2   *Why Seam was created*

The Java EE 5 specification incorporates two key component architectures (specifications for creating reusable objects) for creating web-based business applications: Java-Server Faces (JSF) 1.2 and Enterprise JavaBeans (EJB) 3. JSF is the standard presentation framework for the web tier that provides both a user interface (UI) component model and a server-side event model. EJB 3 is the standard programming model for creating secure and scalable business components that access transactional resources. EJB 3 also encompasses the Java Persistence API (JPA), which defines a standard persistence model for translating data between a relational database and Java entity classes.

Aside from their residence in the Java EE 5 specification, the two architectures just mentioned share little resemblance, their backs facing each other like two sides of a coin. This communication barrier casts a shadow on the tremendous potential of each technology. While it's true that developers are able to get these two Java EE tiers to work together, it requires a lot of "glue" code. Seam absorbs that responsibility and fits JSF and EJB 3 together, thus ironing out one of the roughest spots in the Java EE 5 specification and completing the missing link in the evolution of the Java EE platform. As such, Seam has positioned itself as the prototype for future Java EE specifications. So far, three Java Specification Requests (JSRs) have been accepted: JSR 299 (Web Beans), JSR 314 (JavaServer Faces 2.0), and JSR 303 (Bean Validation). Seam isn't married to JSF or EJB 3, as figure 1.2 suggests. You can swap in alternative view technologies such as Wicket, Tapestry, GWT, and Flex in place of JSF, though understandably with less accord. In the business tier, Seam supports the use of JavaBeans as transactional components and also boasts integration with the Spring container, both of which are arguably better choices than EJB 3.

With that said, becoming an important part of Java EE's future and an integration point for many open source technologies is not what sparked Seam. That's just what Seam has managed to accomplish. As with most software projects, Seam was started to scratch a single developer's itch.

THE REAL STORY

As the story (really) goes, Gavin King was fed up with developers using Hibernate improperly by trapping it inside of the stateless design proliferated by the Spring Framework. Recognizing that the missing integration between JSF and EJB 3 would only lead to further abuse of Hibernate as a JPA provider, he decided to step up and build a foundation that would allow the persistence context (Hibernate `Session` or JPA `EntityManager`) to transcend layers and would permit stateful session beans to respond directly to JSF UI components. To support this vision, Seam encourages the adoption of a stateful, yet efficient, architecture. As a result, applications built on Seam have effortless continuity from one user interaction (or event) to the next, a feature that is labeled a web conversation. The keen focus on variable scoping is what makes Seam contextual.

The name *Seam* was chosen for the project because it provides a foundation that brings JSF and EJB 3 together and teaches them to play nicely together in the same sandbox. In the process of solving the mismatch between JSF and EJB 3, the Seam architects broadened the solution to include any Plain Old Java Object (POJO) acting as a business component, not just the EJB 3 variety. Seam's universal component model brings the implicit and declarative services provided by the EJB 3 programming model, such as transactions, interceptors, threading, and security, to non-EJB components such as JavaBeans and Spring beans. For non-EJB components, Seam takes on the role of processing the Java EE 5 annotations—or synonyms of these annotations from the Seam API—and weaves in the managed services. What this means is that you *do not* have to rely on an EJB 3 container to leverage the benefits that EJB 3 provides. You may even want to reconsider the use of EJB 3 unless you have a specific need for it, choosing to go with JavaBeans instead. Regardless of your choice, you aren't required to deploy a Seam application to the JBoss Application Server, despite what you may have heard.

1.2.3 Debunking the "vendor lock-in" myth

I don't want to be shy about addressing the myth that Seam is a JBoss-focused technology or that by using Seam, you get locked into JBoss. The Seam development team isn't hesitant about making recommendations against the JBoss party line. The Seam application stack is an aggregation of best-of-breed technologies known to work well together. Seam is no more a JBoss technology than Struts is an Apache technology or Spring is a SpringSource technology. An examination of the most successful complex projects in enterprise Java outside of JBoss, such as Spring, Hibernate, Eclipse, and the Java EE platform itself, reveals that these projects are supported by organizations with paid developers. Seam is open source and can be whatever you, the community,[1] drive it to be. Although the projects may be hosted in the JBoss Labs under the roof of JBoss/Red Hat, the source code is yours to copy, share, and modify. Specifically, JBoss Seam is licensed under the Lesser GNU Public License (LGPL), which is considered one of the more flexible options.

Seam was designed to be container agnostic and much effort has gone into ensuring that Seam is compatible with all major application servers, including BEA WebLogic, IBM WebSphere, Oracle Containers for Java EE (OC4J), Apache Tomcat, and GlassFish. But the compatibility runs deeper than deployment. The improvements that Seam has introduced into Java EE are being contributed back into the platform as standards using

---

[1] http://www.seamframework.org is the main community site for Seam.

the Java Community Process (JCP) as a vehicle and captured in JSR 299: Web Beans, as mentioned earlier. The goal of this JSR is to unify the JSF managed bean component model with the EJB component model, resulting in a significantly simplified programming model for web-based application development. The effect of this JSR is that it will foster alternative implementations of Seam's innovations.

With an understanding of why Seam exists, and faith that you are not getting locked into JBoss by choosing this technology, you now need to consider whether Seam is the right framework for you based on technical merit. After all, Seam may have saved Java EE, but can it fit the bill as your development framework of choice?

1.2.4 *Making the case for Seam*

Is there really a need for another application framework? Wasn't Spring supposed to be the one framework to rule them all? I'll let the success of Ruby on Rails, and the wave of Java developers flocking to it, prove that the need for a suitable Java application framework—or, in some developers' minds, an entire programming environment—remains. So, should you follow the crowd? My advice is to look before you leap.

Promising that a framework will make the job of developing applications simpler is lip service. Just because you are able to create a throwaway blog application with a framework doesn't make it viable. To earn the right to be called enterprise software, the framework has to stand up to the challenges of the real world, warts and all, and help the developer create well-designed, robust, and readable code. That is Seam's goal. Seam eliminates complexity and makes proven libraries more accessible. Seam doesn't turn its back on the pervasive Java EE platform, but rather serves as the glue that makes it truly integrated. Rather than encourage you to forget everything you know, Seam finds a way to allow you to use the Java EE services in a more agile way, while also providing enough new toys, in the form of extensions and third-party integrations, to make using it fun and interesting.

Here is a small sampling of the many improvements that Seam brings to the Java EE platform, all of which succeed in making the platform simpler:

- Eliminates the shortcomings in JSF that have been the subject of countless rants
- Mends the communication between JSF and transactional business components
- Collapses unnecessary layers and cuts out passive middle-man components
- Offers a solution for contextual state management, discouraging the use of the stateless architecture (i.e., procedural business logic)
- Manages the persistence context (Hibernate `Session` or JPA `EntityManager`) to avoid lazy initialization exceptions in the view and subsequent requests
- Provides a means for extending the persistence context for the duration of a use case
- Connects views together with stateful page flows
- Brings business processes to the web application world

- Plugs in a POJO-based authentication and authorization mechanism backed by JAAS that is enforced at the JSF view ID level, accessible via the EL, and can be extended using declarative rules and ACLs
- Provides an embedded container for testing in non-Java EE environments
- Delivers more than 30 reference examples with the distribution

As you can see, Seam isn't shy about addressing problems in the platform, particularly those with JSF. For existing JSF developers, the first bullet point is enough to justify the need for this framework. They can attest to that fact that JSF can be quite painful at times. That is no longer true with Seam's aid. The second point justifies Seam's usefulness in standards-based environments, where Seam fits in quite naturally. But Seam doesn't stop there. It encourages developers to collapse unnecessary layers to achieve simpler architectures and promotes the use of long-running contexts to relieve the burden of state management. Aside from improving the programming model, Seam provides a tool that prepares the scaffolding of a Seam-based project; generates a create, read, update, delete (CRUD) application from an existing database schema; makes integration testing easy; and serves up Ajax in a variety of ways.

1.3 Seam's approach to unification

Seam revitalizes the standard Java EE platform by putting an end to its divergence and unifying its components, filling in the voids for which it is often criticized, making it more accessible, extending its reach to third-party frameworks and libraries, and form-fitting them all together as a well-integrated and consistent stack. While the features of Seam are vast, Seam's core mission is getting JSF, JPA, and POJO components to work together so that the developer's focus can be placed on building the application, not on integrating unallied technologies.

1.3.1 Seam integrates JSF, JPA, and POJO components

Getting technologies to work with one another is more than just having them pass messages back and forth. It's about creating an interaction that blurs the boundary between them, making them act as a single, unified technology. Seam achieves this integration by fitting EJB 3 up against the web tier, finding a place for JPA, and scrapping the ineffectual JSF managed bean container. After reviewing how Seam tackles these challenges, you get a chance to determine which Seam stack is right for you.

HELPING OUT A WEB-CHALLENGED EJB 3

By design, EJB components cannot be bound directly to a JSF view. It's great that EJB components are scalable, transactional, thread-safe, and secure, but it doesn't do much good if they are completely isolated from the web tier, accessible only through a JSF backing bean acting as an intermediary. This isolation makes them of limited use in web applications because of the complexity involved to integrate them. They are not able to access data stored in any of the web-tier scopes (request, session, and application) or the JSF component tree, thus impairing their insight into essential parts of the application. (The goal here is really just to give EJB 3 components access to Seam's stateful scopes.) Also, it's easy to get into trouble with concurrency when using EJB components from the web tier. For instance, the Java EE container is not required to serialize access to the same stateful session bean, leaving it up to the developer to take care of this task or catch the exception that can result. Also, complexities arise when dealing with non-thread-safe resources such as the JPA EntityManager. The only way the developer can safely use EJB components in the web tier is by interfacing with an adapter layer.

Seam gives EJB 3 components access to web-tier scopes, offers a way to manage the state of EJB 3 components so that they can be used safely in the web tier, and even serializes access to stateful components to make concurrency issues a responsibility of the infrastructure and not the developer. Also, there is never a question about accessing non-thread-safe resources since Seam handles the scoping properly.

Turning the tables, JSF faces equivalent challenges accessing business-tier components.

HOOKING JSF TO A BETTER BACK END

JSF has its own "managed" bean container that is configured using a verbose XML descriptor, as opposed to the annotation-based configuration in EJB 3, and has a limited dependency injection facility. While JSF managed beans can be stored in the web-tier contexts, they are barren objects, lacking scalability, transaction atomicity, and security (probably why they are termed beans and not components). They must reach out to an EJB 3 component to attain these business services. What you find is that you're stuck creating this façade layer to bridge EJB 3 components to the UI that acts on them.

To correct this mismatch, Seam enables JSF UI components to tap right into the EJB layer by allowing EJB 3 components to stand in as JSF "backing" beans and action listeners. There's no longer a need for the managed bean façade layer and its verbose XML descriptor. By eliminating the complexity caused by the mismatch, it encourages developers to relax stringent mandates on overarchitected designs.

WHICH SEAM ARE YOU?

Seam is not just a collection of classes and artifacts that get dropped on your desk with the disclaimer "Some assembly required." The key to Seam's success is that it offers a handful of well-tested bundles that operate fluently. These bundles include compatible versions of many third-party libraries. You can liken the offering to the simplicity of buying a Mac when compared to buying a Dell. When you buy a Dell, you can customize the assembly down to the last stick of RAM. You get a product customized exactly to your needs, but getting there requires a lot of thought and effort on your part. Buying a Mac is much simpler in comparison. You choose between a laptop and a notebook, and then you select a screen size. Everything else is just details that Apple works out for you. Seam has a comparable set of options. You choose a state provider and a persistence provider (and, down the road, a web framework). Everything else is just details that the Seam developers work out for you. By removing the burden of too many choices, Seam can make life for the developer simpler.

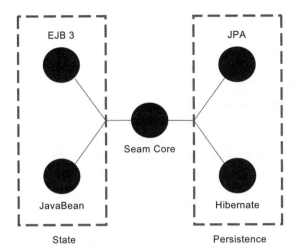

Figure 1.3 Seam's stack matrix, with options for a state and persistence provider

The two main technology choices in a Seam application, summarized in figure 1.3, are the state provider and the persistence provider. The state provider is the technology that handles the application logic and responds to events in the UI. The persistence provider transports data to and from persistence storage. Seam manages the persistence provider to allow for the persistence context to be extended across a series of pages and shared among multiple components.

As mentioned earlier, Seam does not require you to use EJB 3. You have the option of using basic JavaBeans along with Hibernate without fear that you are losing out on functionality. The term *JavaBean* broadly encompasses all non-EJB components, so Spring beans apply here as well. Another popular choice is to partially adopt EJB 3 by combining JPA with JavaBeans, which is the bundle used by the example application in this book.

Prior to Seam, getting these technologies to work together meant integrating the containers that manage them. EJB 3 has its container. JSF has one too. Spring is yet another. Once again, the task of writing this glue code fell on the shoulders of the developer. The need for a central integration point gave rise to Seam's contextual component model.

1.3.2 *The contextual component model*

At the heart of Seam is the contextual component model. Before your eyes gloss over, give me three short sentences to make this term meaningful to you. (1) Seam is a factory that constructs objects according to component definitions. (2) After creation, each object is stored in the container under one of several contexts (i.e., variable scopes) with varying lifetimes, making the objects contextual and capable of holding state (i.e., stateful). (3) Seam promotes the interaction of these stateful objects across contexts, assembling them together according to metadata associated with their respective classes. Chapter 4 explores components and contexts in depth and gives you an opportunity to learn how they are used in an application.

In this section, you learn how this model provides the basis for the unification of the technologies previously discussed. The unification is facilitated by a combination of the component registry, annotations, configuration by exception, method interceptors, and the unified Expression Language (EL).

A CENTRAL COMPONENT REGISTRY

Seam rakes in all of the Java EE components into a central registry, whether they are EJB session beans, JavaBeans, Spring beans, or JPA entities. Any technology incorporated into the Seam stack can look to the Seam container to retrieve instances of the components by name and collaborate with the container to exchange state. Technologies that have access to the container include Seam components, JSF view templates, Java Business Process Management (jBPM) process definitions, Java Process Definition Language (jPDL) page flow definitions, Drools rules, Spring beans, JavaScript, and more. Seam's container also unifies the variable scopes of the Servlet API while introducing two of its own stateful scopes, conversation and business process, that are better suited to support user interactions.

Of course, components aren't just going to fall into this registry; they have to be recruited. Seam scours the classpath and enlists any class that contains a marker annotation, discussed next, that identifies it as a Seam component.

ANNOTATIONS OVER XML

One way that Seam cuts down on the configuration overhead of Java EE is by eliminating needless XML. Although once thought to be desirable because of is flexibility, XML is external configuration and quickly becomes out of sync (and out of touch) with the application logic. Seam brings configuration back in line with the code where it is easier to locate and can be refactored.

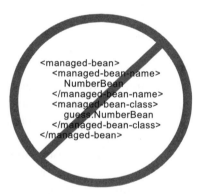

When the temptation arises to define JSF managed beans in XML, Seam just says "No!," a tenet that is captured in figure 1.4. Seam reduces the declaration of a component to a single annotation, `@Name`, placed above the class definition. Seam components can take the place of JSF managed beans.

Figure 1.4   Seam cuts down on superfluous XML configuration that's difficult to keep in sync with the source code.

With enough dedication, you can avoid the use of XML in Seam altogether, which is quite surprising given the number of places it *could* be warranted. Seam only resorts to XML when annotations do not suffice or to isolate deployment overrides. If you are not a fan of annotations, don't go running for the door just yet. Seam still allows you to define components using XML, which is the main topic of chapter 5. Annotations are just more concise and easier to maintain, in my opinion.

Moving to annotations is more than just improving the efficiency of keystrokes. Annotations are the central piece of Seam's configuration by exception strategy, conserving keystrokes until they are really necessary.

CONFIGURATION BY EXCEPTION

A good way to describe configuration by exception is by saying that the software is "opinionated." The general idea is that the framework happily prefers to operate as designed. The more you embrace the defaults, the less work you have to do. You are only required to step in and play a part when the software needs to do something different than the typical behavior.

In Seam, configuration by exception goes hand in hand with annotations. The annotations give Seam a hint to apply behavior and Seam tries to assume as much as possible about the declaration by relying on sensible defaults and standard naming conventions to keep your load light. In this way, Seam offers a nice balance between explicit declarations and assumed functionality.

While annotations cut down on keystrokes, there's more to annotations than just the elimination of XML. Annotations supply extra metadata to the class definition, where it is easier to find and refactor than metadata stored in external descriptors.

DECORATING COMPONENTS WITH SERVICES

Since components are requested through the Seam container, Seam has an opportunity to manage the instances throughout their life cycle. Seam wires the object with interceptors, wrapping it in a shell known as an object proxy, before handing down the newly created instance. This allows Seam to act as the object's puppeteer, pulling on its strings during each method call to add behavior, as depicted in figure 1.5. Interceptors account for much of the implicit logic in Seam that makes it "just work." Examples include beginning and committing transactions, enforcing security, and getting objects to socialize with one another. Annotations on the class definition give the interceptors a hint of how to apply the extra functionality, if for some reason it can't be implied or needs to be different than the default behavior.

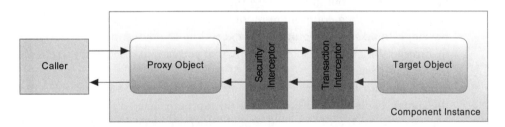

Figure 1.5   Interceptors trap method calls and perform cross-cutting logic around a method invocation.

The final piece to the unification puzzle is to give the application a way to access components in the container using a universal syntax. That's the role of the unified EL.

EXTENDING THE REACH OF THE UNIFIED EL

The unified EL is an expressive syntax used to resolve variables and bind components to properties and methods on JavaBeans. It was first introduced to better integrate JSF with JavaServer Pages (JSP), to look up managed beans and other objects stored in web-tier scopes, and to serve as the basis for the JSF binding mechanism. Its impact, however, is far more widespread, thanks to its pluggable design.

The EL is an open API that allows custom resolvers to be registered, thus turning the EL into a variable hub. Consequently, any layer of the code that wants to tap into the EL unified variable context can do so using the public API. Thus, the EL frees you from having to develop a custom bridge between the variable contexts used by the different technologies in your application. Although you're used to seeing the EL only in the view, there isn't anything web specific about it.

Seam takes advantage of the EL in two ways. First, it registers a custom EL resolver that is aware of the Seam container. This allows Seam components to be accessed using EL notation from anywhere in the application where the EL is available (which is pretty much everywhere). Second, Seam makes heavy use of the EL under the covers, allowing EL notation to be used in annotations, configuration descriptors, log and message strings, Java Persistence Query Language (JPQL) queries, page flow definitions, and even business processes. With Seam, the EL truly is unified.

Despite all that has been said about Seam, nothing speaks to a programmer like lines of code. To help demonstrate why Seam is a sound choice and how it saves you valuable development time, I am going to whet your appetite with a brief example. In chapter 2, you'll get a chance to sink your teeth into Seam by building an entire application with just a couple of commands.

1.4   *Your first swings with Seam*

To demonstrate some of the core principles of Seam, I'm going to step you through a basic application that manages a collection of golf tips. Don't worry about trying to understand everything that you see here. Instead, focus on how Seam relies on annotations to define components, how the layers of the application are pulled together through the unified component model, and the high signal-to-noise ratio in the business logic thanks to configuration by exception. I demonstrate a densely packed set of features in this example, so don't think that you have to use all of these techniques in order to use Seam.

We all want to be better golfers (at least, those of us who torture ourselves with the sport). Focusing on a simple golf tip can help shave off a couple of strokes from your round. To keep track of the tips that you collect from the pros, buddies, and articles, you're going to slap together a Seam application that reads and writes these tips to a database. Aside from the deployment artifacts, which aren't considered in this example, there are only a handful of files that you need to produce a functional application.

1.4.1   *Entity classes serving as backing beans*

I'll start by discussing the `GolfTip` JPA entity class, shown in listing 1.1. In a Seam application, entity classes serve two purposes. Their primary role is to carry data to and from the database. The object-relational mapping (ORM) mechanism, as this is called, is not part of Seam per se. That work is handled either by JPA (the standard Java persistence framework) or Hibernate, though you discover in chapter 8 how Seam can bootstrap the ORM runtime and regulate the lifetime of the ORM's persistence manager.

The second role of entity classes in a Seam application is to serve as form "backing" beans (akin to a Struts `ActionForm`) to capture input from the user, thus replacing the need for a shallow "backing" bean class. An entity class becomes a candidate for use in a JSF view if it has a `@Name` annotation on its class definition, a condition that is satisfied by the `GolfTip` class in listing 1.1. You then bind the form inputs directly to properties on the entity class and JSF handles the necessary conversions and validations.

Listing 1.1 The JPA entity class that represents a golf tip

```
@Entity          ❷
@Name("tip")          ❶
public class GolfTip implements Serializable {
    @Id @GeneratedValue          ❸
    protected Long id;

    protected String author;

    protected String category;

    protected String content;

    // getters/setters for author, category and content not shown
}
```

The keywords prefixed with the @ symbol are Java 5 annotations. The `@Name` annotation ❶, shown in bold, is a Seam annotation that registers the `GolfTip` class as a Seam component named `tip`. Whenever the context variable `tip` is requested from the Seam container, Seam creates a new instance of the `GolfTip` class, binds the instance to the `tip` context variable in the conversation context (the default scope for entity classes), and returns the instance to the requester.

The remaining annotations in this class pertain to JPA. The `@Entity` annotation ❷ associates the `GolfTip` class with a database table by the same name. The `@Id` annotation ❸ indicates to JPA which property is to be used as the primary key. The `@GeneratedValue` annotation ❸ enables automatic surrogate key generation in the database. All of the other properties on the class (`author`, `category`, and `content`) are automatically mapped to columns with the same name as the respective property in the `GolfTip` table, following configuration by exception semantics.

As you can see, using the `@Name` annotation gives you one less file to worry about (that of the JSF managed bean facility and its verbose XML dialect). Staying away from the managed bean configuration is one of the early benefits of moving to Seam components. Another compelling advantage of adopting Seam is being able to bind the action of the UI command component to a method on a transactional business object.

1.4.2 *An all-in-one component*

As with entity classes, there's no need to create a dedicated managed bean to act as a mediator between the JSF page and the service object in Seam. Instead, the service object can respond directly to an action invoked in the UI. At first, that might sound like a bad idea because it appears to cause tight coupling between the UI and the application logic. Seam prevents this coupling by acting as the mediator. As a result, the action component does not have to contain a single reference to a JSF resource. In fact, in chapter 3 you discover that the return value of the method need not serve as a logical outcome for a navigation rule—a typical requirement of JSF managed beans—since Seam can evaluate an arbitrary EL value expression for this purpose. This example relaxes the separation from JSF to keep the number of classes to a minimum.

In the golf tips application, the `TipAction` class, shown in listing 1.2, is declared as a Seam component using the `@Name` annotation and is thus capable of having its methods bound to UI controls. It handles the add and delete operations in the golf tips interface.

Listing 1.2   The action listener for the JSF view

```
@Name("tipAction")                      ❶
public class TipAction {
   @In
   private EntityManager entityManager;        ◁─┐
                                              ❷  │
   @In                                    ◁──────┘
   private FacesMessages facesMessages;

   @DataModel(scope = ScopeType.PAGE)        ◁──┐
   private List<GolfTip> tips;                   │
                                                 │
   @DataModelSelection                       ❸   │
   @Out(required = false)          ❹             │
   private GolfTip activeTip;                    │
                                                 │
   @Factory("tips")                          ◁───┘
   public void retrieveAllTips() {
      tips = entityManager.createQuery("select t from GolfTip t")
        .getResultList();
   }

   public void add(GolfTip tip) {
      entityManager.persist(tip);
      activeTip = tip;
      facesMessages.add(                                 ┐
        "Thanks for the tip, #{activeTip.author}!");     │
      retrieveAllTips();                                 │
   }                                                     │
                                                         │
   public void delete() {                          ❺     │
      activeTip = entityManager.find(                    │
        GolfTip.class, activeTip.getId());               │
      entityManager.remove(activeTip);                   │
      facesMessages.add("The tip contributed by " +     │
        "#{activeTip.author} has been deleted.");        │
      retrieveAllTips();                                 │
   }                                                     ┘
}
```

Like the `GolfTip` entity class, the `@Name` annotation ❶ marks the `TipAction` class as a Seam component, this time scoped to the event context (the default scope for Java-Bean components). What sets this component apart from the `GolfTip` entity class is that it is capable of having other components "wired" into it because the `@In` annotation is placed above certain fields of the class ❷, a mechanism known as bijection. In this example, the two dependent components are the JPA `EntityManager` and Seam's built-in JSF messages manager. This component also prepares a collection of `GolfTip` objects for use in the JSF view ❸; captures the `GolfTip` that the user selects from that collection, making it available to both the method handling the event and the subsequent view ❹; and interpolates the active `GolfTip` in the JSF status messages ❺.

The `TipAction` component packs a lot of functionality in a limited amount of space. What I want you to recognize is that, aside from the annotations, there's practically no evidence of infrastructure code in this class. Apart from creating the status messages, the only code that you're required to write is code that reads, persists, and removes tips from the database using the JPA `EntityManager` instance. It's probably best to push this code into a data access object (DAO), which may also be a Seam component, but Seam doesn't impose this architectural requirement on you. Seam's focus is on frugality, as demonstrated in this example. Absent are any Servlet API calls that read request parameter values or set request or session attributes. Instead, the component consists solely of business logic.

1.4.3 Binding components to the view

Seam bridges the layers in the golf tips application by binding both the properties of the entity class and the methods of the action component to elements in the JSF view. Figure 1.6 shows the golf tips user interface. Behind this rendered page is a Facelets

Share your golf wisdom!

ⓘ Thanks for the tip, Jack Nicklaus!

Golf tips

Tiger Woods on The Swing

Shake hands with the target.   🗑

Tommy Twoputt on Putting

Use one basic motion around the green.   🗑

Jack Nicklaus on The Swing

The single most important maneuver in golf is the set-up.   🗑

Do you have golf wisdom to share?   «

Author *   [   ]

Category *   [-- Select -- ▾]

Content *   [   ]
                [   ]
                [   ]

* required fields

[**Submit Tip**]

Figure 1.6 The golf tips page, which renders the collection of tips at the top and a form for contributing a new tip at the bottom

template, golftips.xhtml, which associates value- and method-binding expressions to elements on this page to output data, capture form input, and respond to user actions. Use this figure to follow along with the discussion of how the JSF view interacts with the Seam components in the server.

NOTE   The file extension .xhtml indicates that this file is a Facelets template. Facelets is an alternative view handler for JSF that was created to escape the mismatch between the JSF and JSP life cycles. Facelets is the preferred view technology for Seam applications and is used throughout the book.

Start by focusing your attention on the form that is used to submit a new tip at the bottom of the page. Each input element is bound to properties on the GolfTip entity class using EL notation (e.g., #{tip.author}). When used in the value attribute of an input element, the EL notation acts as a value-binding expression. It captures the form value and transfers it to an instance of the GolfTip entity class as part of the JSF life cycle. Here's the (slightly trimmed-down) fragment of the JSF template that renders the form:

```
<h:form>
  <h3>Do you have golf wisdom to add?</h3>
  <div class="field">
    <h:outputLabel for="author">Author:</h:outputLabel>
    <h:inputText value="#{tip.author}"/>
  </div>
  <div class="field">
    <h:outputLabel for="category">Category:</h:outputLabel>
    <h:selectOneMenu value="#{tip.category}">
      <f:selectItem itemValue="The Swing"/>
      <f:selectItem itemValue="Putting"/>
      <f:selectItem itemValue="Attitude"/>
    </h:selectOneMenu>
  </div>
  <div class="field">
    <h:outputLabel for="content">Advice:</h:outputLabel>
    <h:inputTextarea value="#{tip.content}"/>
  </div>
  <div class="actions">
    <h:commandButton action="#{tipAction.add(tip)}"
      value="Submit Tip"/>
  </div>
</h:form>
```

Seam makes the association between the value-binding expressions used by the input fields and the GolfTip entity class through the context variable tip. The @Name annotation on the GolfTip class binds the class to the tip context variable. When the tip context variable is referenced by a value expression in the JSF template (#{tip.*}), Seam instantiates the GolfTip class and stores the instance in the Seam container under the variable name tip. All the value expressions that reference the tip context variable are bound to that same instance of the GolfTip class. When the form is submitted, the input values are transferred to the properties of the unsaved entity instance.

Let's consider what happens when the form is submitted. With Seam working in conjunction with JSF, any interaction with the Servlet API is abstracted away. Instead, you work through declarative bindings. The method-binding expression specified in the action attribute of the submit button, #{tipAction.add(tip)}, indicates that the TipAction component serves as the action component for this form and that when the button is activated, the add() method is invoked. Notice that this method expression actually passes the GolfTip instance associated with the tip context variable directly into the action method as its sole argument, which effectively makes the form data available to the method. Seam provides parameterized method-binding expressions as an enhancement to JSF. When the method completes, the list of tips is refreshed and the page is once again rendered.

1.4.4 *Retrieving data on demand*

What makes Seam so powerful is that it includes a mechanism for initializing a variable on demand. The top half of the screen in figure 1.6 renders the collection of tips in the database using the following markup:

```
<rich:dataGrid var="_tip" value="#{tips}" columns="1">
  <rich:panel>
    <f:facet name="header">
     <h:outputText value="#{_tip.author} on #{_tip.category}"/>
    </f:facet>
    <h:outputText value="#{_tip.content}"/>
    <h:commandLink action="#{tipAction.delete}">
     <h:graphicImage value="/images/delete.png" style="border: 0;"/>
    </h:commandLink>
  </rich:panel>
</rich:dataGrid>
```

The focal point of this markup is the #{tips} value expression. Notice that tips is not the name of one of the Seam components in the golf tips application. However, it is referenced in the value attribute of the @Factory annotation above the retrieveAllTips() method of the TipAction class from listing 1.2. The purpose of this method is to initialize the value of the tips context variable when it's requested. Subsequent requests for the same variable return the previously retrieved value rather than triggering the method to execute again.

But hold on a minute! The retrieveAllTips() method doesn't return a value. How is the value passed back to the view renderer? That's where things get a little tricky. After executing this method, Seam exports properties of the component that are annotated with either @Out or @DataModel to the view. Seam notices that the @DataModel annotation is assigned to the tips property on the TipAction component. That tells Seam not only to export its value to the tips context variable, but also to wrap the value in a JSF DataModel instance. The view iterates over this wrapped collection to render the data grid. The reason the collection is wrapped in a DataModel is to enable clickable lists to support the delete functionality.

1.4.5 *Clickable lists*

The scope specified on the annotation is ScopeType.PAGE, which instructs Seam to store the collection of tips in the JSF component tree. Since the data model is being stored in the JSF component tree, it is made available to any JSF action that is invoked from that page (resulting in a "postback").

The #{tipAction.delete} method expression, bound to the delete link adjacent to each golf tip, benefits from the propagation of the tips data model through the JSF component tree. When the user clicks one of the delete buttons, the data model is restored along with the JSF component tree. When JSF processes the event, the internal pointer of the data model is positioned to the index of the activated row. This is where the complement to the @DataModel annotation, the @DataModelSelection annotation, is used. This annotation reads the current row data (the instance of GolfTip) from the data model and injects it into the property over which the annotation resides. All the action method has to do is pass the instance of the selected GolfTip to the JPA EntityManager to have it removed from the underlying database. Once again, the action component remains void of infrastructure code. Compare that to the JSF blueprints.[2]

All that's left is to write a quick end-to-end test to ensure that we can save a new tip and that it can be subsequently retrieved.

1.4.6 *Integration tests designed for JSF*

The area of development that has routinely slowed down Java EE developers most often is testing. Even if you've never written a test, you're still testing. You test your code every time you redeploy your application or restart the application server to view the result of your latest modifications. It's just slow and boring to do it that way. These days, testing is an integral part of any application development, and no framework is complete without an environment that allows you to test "outside of the container." Seam once again demonstrates its simplicity by exposing a single test class that can handle all of the integration testing needs in a Seam-powered application.

To make integration testing of JSF actions a breeze, Seam provides a base test class that sets up a stand-alone Java EE environment and executes the JSF life cycle within the test cases. The test infrastructure is driven by TestNG,[3] a modern unit-testing framework that can be configured using annotations. Although TestNG doesn't require you to inherit from a base test class, Seam's testing framework uses this approach to set up the fixture needed to bootstrap the embedded Java EE environment and the JSF context.

The test class GolfTipsTest in listing 1.3 simulates the initial request for the golf tips page and the subsequent form submission to add a new tip. The code in the test is invoked nearly identical to when it's used in the deployed application.

> **Listing 1.3   An end-to-end test of the golf tips application using the Seam test framework**

```
public class GolfTipsTest extends SeamTest {

    @Test                                          Designates a
    public void testAddTip() throws Exception {    TestNG test method
```

2   https://bpcatalog.dev.java.net/nonav/webtier/index.html
3   http://www.testng.org

```
    new NonFacesRequest("/golftips.xhtml") {
        protected void renderResponse() throws Exception {
            assert (Boolean) getValue("#{tips.rowCount eq 0}");
        }
    }.run();
```
Asserts number of matched tips

```
    new FacesRequest("/golftips.xhtml") {
        protected void updateModelValues() throws Exception {
            setValue("#{tip.author}", "Ben Hogan");
            setValue("#{tip.category}", "The Swing");
            setValue("#{tip.content}",
                "Good golf begins with a good grip.");
        }
```
Emulates user filling out form

```
        protected void invokeApplication() throws Exception {
            invokeMethod("#{tipAction.add(tip)}");
        }
```
Emulates user clicking submit button

```
        protected void renderResponse() throws Exception {
            assert (Boolean) getValue("#{tips.rowCount eq==1}");
            List<FacesMessage> messages =
              FacesMessages.instance().getCurrentMessages();
            assert messages.size() == 1;
            assert messages.get(0).getSummary()
              .equals("Thanks for the tip, Ben Hogan!");
        }
    }.run();
    }
}
```
Asserts number of matched tips

Listing 1.3 tests both the initial rendering of the JSF view and the subsequent JSF action triggered from the rendered page. The first request is an HTTP GET request, which simulates the user requesting the golf tips page in the browser. This part of the test verifies that when the tips are retrieved in the *Render Response* phase, Seam properly resolves a DataModel, but the collection underlying that model is empty. The second part of the test simulates the user submitting the form to create a new tip. The *Update Model Values* phase performs the work JSF does to bind the input values to the value expressions. The method expression that is bound to the submit button is then explicitly invoked. Because Seam automatically wraps the *Invoke Application* phase in a transaction, there is no need to worry about beginning and committing the transaction. Finally, in the *Render Response* phase, the test verifies that when the tips are retrieved this time, exactly one tip is found and that the author's name has been interpolated properly in the message displayed to the user. This test is intentionally terse. There are, of course, many other scenarios that could be verified. Focus instead on how easy it is to exercise a Seam application using this simple test framework and how you can leverage EL notation to perform assertions.

Hopefully the golf tips application has given you a general understanding of how Seam simplifies your application and saves you time by relying on a centralized container, annotations, configuration by exception, and the unified EL. That's the essence of Seam. I now want to give you an idea of what else Seam offers before you begin your journey down the road to becoming a Seam master.

1.5   Seam's core competencies

Throughout this chapter, there has been a lot of discussion about how Seam resolves issues in Java EE. I want to leave you with an understanding of how Seam is going to help your development process. Given how much Seam has to offer, this was a challenging exercise, but I've been able to summarize its benefits into three core competencies. Seam offers a better JSF, allows you to get rich quick, and fosters an agile environment.

1.5.1   Turns JSF into a pro

Although JSF isn't without flaws, it was selected as the main presentation framework in Seam because of its extensible request life cycle and strong UI component model. Realizing its potential, Seam taps into this design to strengthen JSF, making it a compelling and modern technology for creating web-based interfaces. While it's true that Seam supports alternative view technologies, this book primarily focuses on using Seam with JSF. Much of this coverage comes in chapter 3, which covers Seam's extension to the JSF life cycle.

ENHANCING JSF

Seam's most recognizable improvement to JSF is eliminating the requirement to declare managed beans in the JSF descriptor. In addition, Seam adds a rich set of page-oriented functionality, covered in chapter 3, that makes the navigation rules in the JSF descriptor obsolete as well. These features include

- Prerender page actions
- Managed request parameters (for a given page)
- Intelligent stateless and stateful navigation
- Transparent JSF data model and data model selection handling
- Fine-grained exception handling
- Page-level security (per view ID)
- Annotation-based form validation
- Bookmarkable command links (solving the "everything is a POST" problem)
- Entity converter for pick lists
- Conversation controls
- Support for preventing lazy initialization exceptions and nontransactional data access in the view

Part of the cleaning-out process of JSF involves purging passive connector beans that do nothing more than adapt UI events to back-end business components.

ELIMINATING CONNECTOR BEANS

Any Seam component can be connected to a JSF view using EL bindings. Figure 1.7 shows the design of an interaction between a UI form and an EJB 3.0 session bean (or regular JavaBean) that completely eliminates the need for the legacy connector bean. The form inputs are bound directly to the entity class and the session bean is bound to the Save button to handle the action of persisting the data.

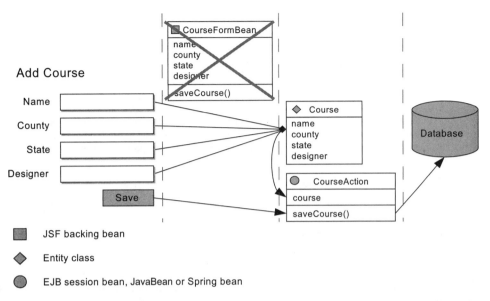

Figure 1.7 **Seam cuts out the middleman by eliminating the need for a JSF backing bean. Instead, the entity class and the EJB 3.0 session bean work together to capture data from the UI and handle the event to persist the data.**

By cutting out the middleman, not only does Seam allow you to eliminate a class that you have to write and maintain, but it allows you to cut back on the number of layers, thus allowing your applications to become more lightweight.

Aside from providing universal access to components, the Seam container augments the coarsely grained scopes in the Java servlet specification—request, session, and application—to include scopes that make more sense from the perspective of the application user. Seam offers two "stateful" contexts that are used to support single and multiuser pages flows in an application.

INTRODUCING STATEFUL VARIABLE SCOPES

One of the main challenges with developing applications that are delivered over the web is learning how to efficiently propagate data from one page to the next—so-called *state management.* The two go-to options are hidden form fields or the HTTP session. The first is cumbersome for the developer, and the second eventually eats through precious server resources and hurts an application's ability to scale.

Seam addresses need for stateful variable scopes whose lifetime aligns with user interactions by adding the conversation context and business process context to the standard web scopes. The conversation scope, covered in chapter 7, maintains data for a single user across a well-defined series of pages while the business process scope, covered in chapter 14 (online), is used to manage data that supports multiuser flows complete with wait states. The relationship between the lifetime of the scopes managed by the Seam container is illustrated in figure 1.8.

Figure 1.8   The lifetimes of the six scopes in a Seam application. The standard scopes are represented by dashed lines. The scopes that Seam contributes appear as solid lines. The business process scope is persisted to a database and can thus outlive the application scope across server restarts.

The conversation context is tremendously important in Seam not only because it is so unique and gives the user a better experience, but because it makes working with an ORM tool easy on the developer.

EXTENDING THE PERSISTENCE CONTEXT

When you talk to the database using ORM, you use a persistence manager (i.e., JPA `EntityManager` or Hibernate `Session`). Each instance of a persistence manager maintains an internal persistence context, which is an in-memory cache of entity instances that have been unmarshaled from the database. Given that databases are among the most expensive and heavily used resources in your server room, you want to leverage this in-memory cache as much as possible to avoid redundant queries. Extending the persistence context across the entire request is a step in the right direction (the so-called Open Session in View Pattern), but having it extend across multiple page requests is even better. Prior to Seam, there was just no good place to stick it, and as a result, each request reset the persistence context to a blank slate.

Seam takes control of the persistence manager and stores it in the conversation context. As a result, Seam is able to carry it, along with its persistence context, across the duration of an entire use case, potentially spanning more than one request, as shown in figure 1.9. Extending the persistence context across the three operations in this feature allows the entity instance to remain managed by the persistence context

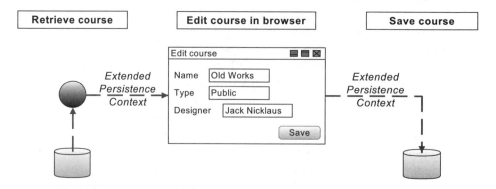

Figure 1.9   Using the extended persistence context to keep an object in scope for an entire use case, even across multiple page views. The extended persistence context avoids the need to merge detached entity instances.

and monitored for changes that need to be written to the database. This ensures object identity and can guarantee atomicity of the operation.

With Seam in control of the persistence manager, lazy initialization exceptions (LIEs) are also a thing of the past since the persistence manager remains open throughout the use case and can thus load additional records as needed. The conversation and persistence context fit together so naturally that the conversation has been dubbed Seam's unit of work. You learn all about the interaction between the two in part 3.

1.5.2 Gets you rich quick

Seam gives you tools to build rich, Web 2.0 applications or to gently weave this richness into an existing page-oriented application. Lately, the term "rich" has become synonymous with a desktop-like experience in the web browser driven by Ajax. There are two approaches you can take to incorporate Ajax into a Seam application. You can use Ajax-enabled JSF components, such as RichFaces or ICEfaces, or you can invoke server-side components directly from the browser using JavaScript remoting. Seam extends the meaning of rich to incorporate media such as PDFs, charts, and graphics.

TAPPING INTO THE JSF ECOSYSTEM

Web user interfaces are getting more and more sophisticated, and it is unreasonable to think that you can code the XHTML and JavaScript from scratch and get the job done cheaply. You need to build on what others have done. That is one of the primary goals of JSF and why Seam went with JSF as the primary UI framework.

JSF is all about putting widgets on the screen. It decouples the design of a UI component from its use. Similar to widgets in Swing, JSF components are general solutions to common controls. This time, the vendors really did come through. There are loads of component libraries for JSF that range from basic data tables, to tree structures, to drag-and-drop targets.

Historically one of the most entangled parts of an enterprise application is the UI (let's share hideous JSP files). By moving to JSF, the UI becomes a much simpler place. You don't even need a WYSIWYG IDE because visualizing what these components render is quite reasonable. They are human-friendly, rather than tool-friendly. With JSF, the UI finally has an API too.

While JSF has its place, if you are looking for a lighter way to communicate with the server, Seam's JavaScript remoting library is a great alternative.

JAVASCRIPT REMOTING

Invoking server-side components from JavaScript in Seam couldn't be easier, as chapter 12 proves. You simply add the @WebRemote annotation to the Seam component method that you want to call from JavaScript, import the JavaScript remoting library into the web page, and then invoke the component method using a JavaScript client stub of the component. Seam handles the rest. The punchline of this feature is that it opens the door to creating single-page applications with Seam.

Although Ajax gets most of the attention these days when web applications are discussed, there are other ways to make your application rich. These fall under the heading of *rich media*.

CREATING RICH MEDIA

Seam is adept at generating a variety of rich media, which you learn to incorporate into your application in chapter 13. Seam uses the Facelets view library to support alternate output based on XHTML templates, including PDF documents, RTF documents, charts, and multipart emails with attachments that include the previous items. With the addition of two JSF component tags, Seam can accept file uploads without any custom, low-level coding and can render dynamic graphics. All of these tasks are typically passed off by web frameworks to third-party libraries. While it's true that Seam leverages functionality provided by libraries such as iText and JFreeChart, the delegation is abstracted away. You are provided with a consistent approach, based on Facelets composition templates, that allows these features to be a native part of your Seam application.

1.5.3   *Fosters an agile environment*

In addition to being a framework, Seam provides a collection of tools that help you set up a project, generate code, and develop in an incremental manner.

PROJECT GENERATOR

One of the main highlights of Seam is its project generator, seam-gen. This tool serves two main functions. It sets up the structure of a Seam-based project, complete with a build script, environment profiles, a compatible set of libraries, and the configurations required to start developing your application. It's the best way to get started with Seam if you are new to the framework. The seam-gen tool can also create an application prototype by reverse-engineering a database schema and generating all of the necessary artifacts to create, read, update, and delete (CRUD) data in that database. In chapter 2, you learn all about seam-gen and use it to create a complete golf course directory web application.

HOT DEPLOYMENT

Seam makes preparations to enable "instant change" in the development cycle, which you learn to take advantage of in chapter 2. Seam's strategy is to initialize a hot deploy classloader capable of detecting and dynamically reloading changed Java class files, just as if they were JSP pages.[4] The project build script compiles any source files that have changed and ships them off to a special path in the server's hot deployment directory, where Seam picks them up and incorporates them into its runtime. Because the modified files remain isolated, they do not cause the application server to restart nor do they cause the application to reload. That means you can make a change to a Java file and have it take effect in the application immediately. This feature applies to Seam page descriptors and uncompiled Groovy scripts as well. You can finally match the change-view-change-view cycle that was previously only available with scripting languages such as PHP and Ruby!

---

[4] Java EE containers support dynamic reloading of JSP pages when they're moved into the deployment directory for the application or web module.

SEAM DEBUG PAGE

While developing your application, bad stuff happens. As a result, you get exceptions. Rather than always having to race to the log file to find the cause, Seam gives you a head start. When you run Seam in debug mode, any exception that occurs will be caught and summarized on a special debug page, accessible at the servlet path /debug.seam. In addition to the exception, this page gives you a snapshot of the JSF component tree and any Seam component instances that are present at the time of the exception.

You don't have to wait for an exception to occur to use this page. When the debug page is accessed directly, it renders a list of all conversations and sessions that are currently active. From there, you can drill down on any of the active contexts to inspect the component instances that are stored in them.

TESTING WITHOUT DEPLOYING

The primary reason developers grew wary of the standard Java EE platform was because of its inability to operate in isolation. Testing an application meant packaging it up and shipping it off to a Java EE–compliant application server, a costly process.

To work around this problem, developers adopted the POJO programming model, which encourages you to design code in such a way that it can be tested in isolation from the container and its services. While POJOs are definitely a good thing and encourage proper unit testing, there is no replacement for integrating your components in a real environment to ensure that they work together. Previously, that meant deploying to the application server once again. Seam has a better solution.

To support integration test environments (and also deployment to non-Java EE containers, such as Tomcat), Seam ships with the Embedded JBoss container. This portable container bootstraps a Java EE environment to support services such as JNDI, JTA, JCA, and JMS in a stand-alone environment. With these services up and running, you can test your application in place without having to deploy to a container. Seam supports this testing scenario by bootstrapping the Embedded JBoss container as part of its single class integration test framework, demonstrated back in section 1.4.6. This test infrastructure should prevent you from having to deploy over and over again to verify that your action components talk properly to your persistence layer and so on.

Between the incremental hot deployment support and the in-place testing infrastructure, your valuable time should rarely be wasted when working on a Seam application. If it's your business logic that is hanging you up, unfortunately there is not much Seam can do to help you there. That's all you.

1.6 *Summary*

The enthusiasm for Ruby on Rails was a real wake-up call for the Java EE platform. It enlightened developers to the fact that sacrifice is not a prerequisite for creating a successful application. Developers no longer wanted to tolerate the burden of "XML situps"[5] and overengineered flexibility. In response, the Seam developers assembled an

---

[5] A term coined by the Ruby on Rails camp that equates XML authoring to strenuous exercise

agile platform, comprised of best-of-breed Java EE technologies, that takes a bold stance against the formalities of the Java EE specifications, cutting back the XML descriptor overgrowth, accentuating the platform's recent adoption of annotations and configuration by exception, and embracing the expressive syntax embodied by the EL, Facelets, and Groovy. With Seam, creating applications in Java becomes exciting again, whether you are a front-end designer, back-end developer, or jack-of-all-trades. Best of all, you can be confident that applications built with Seam are scalable because the Java EE platform has proven itself in this regard, giving you productivity without sacrificing performance.

First and foremost, Seam makes the task of defining and accessing stateful business-logic components simple, regardless of whether they are EJB or non-EJB components. A basic `@Name` annotation atop a class gains it admission into Seam's contextual container. The container wraps these components in method interceptors, enabling enterprise services, such as transactions, security, and component assembly, to be declared with equivalent ease by applying an annotation at the class, method, or field level. Seam grants the technologies that it integrates access to the components in this container, primarily through the use of the unified EL. This arrangement facilitates the use of JPA entity classes as "backing" beans in a JSF form, EJB session beans or transactional JavaBeans as action listeners on a JSF UI component, and variables to be resolved on demand using Seam's factory or manager mechanism.

An important aspect of Seam's container is its state management capabilities. It consolidates the variable scopes in JSF with two of its own business-oriented scopes. Seam understands variable scoping and helps components from different scopes to work with one another without violating thread safety. Of particular note, Seam can extend the lifetime of the persistence manager across multiple page requests to reduce load on the database and eliminate complexities of using ORM in web applications.

If you picked up this book because you believe that there is a better framework choice out there for you (and you are not yet using Seam), my promise to you is that Seam is worth checking out and that the time you spend reading this book will be worthwhile. But merely knowing what framework someone recommends is not enough to decide to use it. You have to know *why* a person prefers a particular framework.[6] In this book, I share with you my extensive knowledge of Seam and explain to you why I find it to be a compelling technology choice. As you read along, I encourage you to develop your own reason for choosing Seam.

The key to agile development with Seam begins with the project generator, seam-gen. In the next chapter, I show you how to use this tool to develop an entire application from scratch, how to get the application set up in your IDE, and how to take advantage of incremental hot deployment. While you must turn over some control when you opt to go with seam-gen, you'll quickly find that you don't miss the work.

---

[6] Scott Davis' talk, given during the No Fluff, Just Stuff 2007 tour, entitled "No, I Won't Tell You Which Framework to Use: or The Truth (With Jokes)" inspired this perspective.

Putting seam-gen to work

This chapter covers

- Setting up a project with seam-gen
- Reverse engineering a database schema
- Hot-deploying incremental changes
- Choosing an IDE for development

Learning a new framework can be challenging, risky, and time consuming. You must leave the comfort of your current tool set and venture into unknown territory. To justify your research, you seek out early victories in the form of trivial "Hello World" examples. After completing one, you celebrate your accomplishment. Sadly, few others will be so impressed.

Thanks to seam-gen, Seam's rapid development tool, you can skip the putt-putt course and come out swinging on your first day with Seam. seam-gen creates for you a functional, database-oriented application that is ready for show and tell without requiring you to write a single line of code. The seam-gen tool first gathers information about your application, such as the project name and database connection properties. It then uses that information to put in place the scaffolding of a Seam-based project. Finally, you point seam-gen at your database, which it reverse-engineers to create artifacts that serve dynamic web pages used to create, read, update, and delete (CRUD) records in the database tables. The result? An achievement that's sure to impress even the toughest crowd. How's that for *in Action*?

In this chapter, I demonstrate how seam-gen can get you set up quickly to start developing with the Seam framework. By the end of this chapter, you'll have a working golf course directory application that you can deploy to various JBoss Application Server environments. A cookie-cutter process is going to fall short in some areas, so I also show you ways to customize the application that seam-gen kicks out, a process that's carried forth throughout the book. What you're left with is an achievement that is far more functional and rewarding than what a typical "Hello World" has to offer. Don't you know? For judging the merit of a web-oriented framework, CRUD is the new "Hello World."

2.1   The Open 18 prototype

In this book, you'll be developing an application named Open 18, a community site oriented towards golf. Golf is a tremendously rich domain model and offers a nice opportunity to demonstrate Seam's features. You'll start by reverse engineering an existing database schema to create a prototype of the application. I chose this scenario because it demonstrates how you can use seam-gen to escape the dreaded unproductive phase when starting a new project. You may also find these techniques useful for producing applications that don't aspire to be more than a CRUD front end for a database. The remainder of the book takes a primarily free-formed approach when incorporating additional functionality. Some of the enhancements you'll see later in the book include a data entry wizard, side-by-side course comparison, score tracker, favorite courses, registration emails, and PDF scorecards.

If you want to follow along with the development of the project as you read, you'll need Seam and its prerequisites extracted on your hard drive. You can find instructions on how to set up your software in appendix A. I encourage you to scan this supplementary material before continuing so that you can take a hands-on approach to this tutorial.

Let's start by taking a look at the initial requirements for our prototype application and see how seam-gen can help us fulfill them.

2.1.1   Consider yourself tasked

It's 1:30 PM on Wednesday, two days before your summer vacation. Your boss taps you on the shoulder just as you finish reserving tee times for your annual golf getaway in "Golf Heaven." You can't wait. You've practiced all summer at the driving range so you can top last year's scores. Actually, let's be honest. You seasoned your swing so that you can look like a pro in front of your fans (*cough* friends).

You look up and realize that your boss is still standing there, waiting for you to break out of your daze and return to the real world. He looks serious. Obviously, this conversation is not going to be spent reminiscing about golf. With a sobering tone, he informs you that he just ducked out of a management meeting in which he was reminded of a web application that was supposed to have been completed months ago. The anxiety begins to build in you.

The sales team is expecting to present an application that provides access to the company's extensive database of golf courses at the biggest trade show of the year, which happens to be this coming weekend. Without this application, they won't have anything new to demonstrate. Showing up empty-handed would hurt the company image and jeopardize its credibility. In truth, your manager should be sacked for letting the situation get to this point. The sad reality is that it won't happen. Besides, turnover isn't going to help you now. The deed has been done; the promise has been made. Someone is going to have to reach into the hat and yank the rabbit out by the scruff of its neck. That someone is you.

If this were any other week, these antics would barely register on your annoyance meter. But this week is different. The mercury is rising. If things don't go well, it may put your much anticipated vacation at risk. The thought of not standing on the first tee at the break of dawn, in complete Zen with the dew-laden landscape all around you, is just killing you. But you also get a kick out of being a hero, so you decide to crank out a prototype by the end of the week and save the company before seeking your leisure.

The question is, do you have something in your toolbox that can get you out of this time crunch? A solution that you can live with when you return? You've read about how quickly you can create a functional Java EE 5–based application using seam-gen, so you decide to put it to the test. For that, you need requirements; they come from your boss in an email:

> *You must build a web-based directory for the company's extensive database of golf facilities and courses. The application's users should be able to browse, paginate, sort, and filter all of the entities in the schema. By selecting one of the facilities, they should be presented with its details, as well as a list of its courses. From there, they should be able to drill down again to see the holes and tee sets for each course. An administrative user should be able to modify the database records. The marketing department also has some verbiage that you need to place on the home page.*

There you have it: the only task standing between you and 18 holes of serenity. The first step in building the prototype is getting your hands on the database. You and the database administrator (DBA) need to sit down and have a chat to settle the age-old debate between developers and DBAs for this application: *Which comes first, the entity or the schema?*

2.1.2 *Mapping entities to the database schema*

In this book, you'll encounter two development scenarios used by the sample application: *bottom-up* and *top-down*. The difference is a matter of which one comes first: the database schema or the Java entity classes.

If the database schema arrives into the world first, that is bottom-up development. The schema dictates, to a large degree, how the Java entity classes are formed. On the other hand, if the Java entity classes show up first, that is top-down development. The classes have free rein over how the database schema is designed. Object-relational mapping (ORM) tools, such as Hibernate, give you some wiggle room in how the Java entity classes are mapped to the database. For instance, it's possible to change the name of a column mapped to a property of a Java entity class without having to alter the property's name. However, there are limits to how much the schema and the entity classes can deviate. The one that shows up first is the master and the follower must adapt. As a developer, you have to be familiar with how to work in both cases.

NOTE   Technically speaking, there is a third scenario, *meet-in-the-middle*, where you have existing Java entity classes and an existing database. In this case, you're at the mercy of the mapping tool's capabilities. If you have stretched it to its limit and still can't cover the mismatch, you have to refactor the Java class or the database table, bringing you back to bottom-up or top-down semantics.

seam-gen has tasks that support both bottom-up and top-down development. In this chapter, we take the bottom-up approach by using seam-gen to reverse-engineer the database schema. In chapter 4, we reverse the process, taking the top-down approach to extend the schema to include golfer profiles.

BOTTOMS UP!

You'll be performing *bottom-up* development to create the golf course directory outlined earlier. Using *bottom-up* development, as illustrated in figure 2.1, you will convert the five

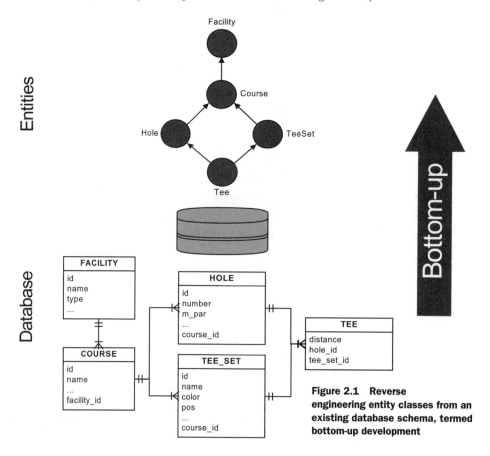

Figure 2.1   Reverse engineering entity classes from an existing database schema, termed bottom-up development

tables in the golf course directory schema (FACILITY, COURSE, HOLE, TEE_SET, and TEE) into the five Java entity classes (`Facility`, `Course`, `Hole`, `TeeSet`, and `Tee`)[1] that map to them. Mapping tables to Java classes sounds like it requires a lot of effort. Don't worry; working with existing database tables is where seam-gen really shines. Before running seam-gen, though, you need to get your hands on the schema and put the database in place.

You bug the DBA (perhaps yourself in another role) to prepare you a Hypersonic 2 (H2) database loaded with the golf course directory schema and some sample data. H2 bootstraps from a directory on the file system and thus the entire H2 database can be handed to you as a compressed archive. You'll use H2 in embedded mode, which allows the database to be started with the application, linked to the application's runtime. The embedded mode of H2 is ideal for rapid prototyping since it requires no installation and you don't need to run a separate server. Having one less server to worry about is a good thing, especially for the sales team.

Section A.3 of appendix A introduces the H2 database further and explains where to find the database archive used for creating the prototype. Once you have the database in place, you can use the H2 administration console to poke around in the schema. This step isn't required to generate a CRUD application with seam-gen, but it's important for understanding the application you're building.

INSPECTING THE SCHEMA

You can connect to the provided database using the H2 administration console that's included with the H2 JDBC driver JAR. Start the admin console by executing the `Console` class from the H2 JAR file:

```
java -cp /home/twoputt/lib/h2.jar org.h2.tools.Console
```

This command instructs you to visit the H2 console URL in your browser, http://localhost:8082. That URL brings up the database connection screen in figure 2.2. Enter the connection URL and credentials shown in this figure and click Connect.

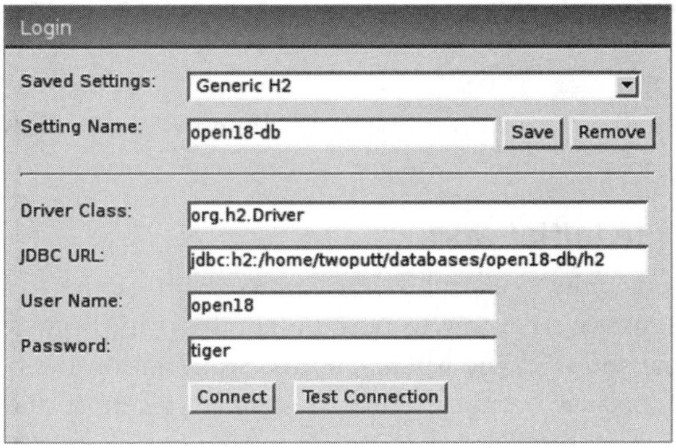

Figure 2.2 The database connection screen for the H2 admin console

---

[1] An introduction to the game of golf and the roles these entities play in it can be found in the beginning of this book.

TIP   The connection screen lets you save your connection profiles, useful when you are managing multiple databases. To create a new profile, replace the setting name "Generic H2" with a name for your connection and click Save. The H2 administration console is capable of connecting to any database with JDBC support. To use another database, you must add the appropriate JDBC driver (JAR file) to the classpath argument of the `java` command that starts the console. Refer to the H2 manual for more information.

Once the connection is established, a schema browser/query console appears, as shown in figure 2.3. This database console should explain why I chose to use the H2 database for the example application: it packs a lot of functionality in a surprisingly small JAR file.

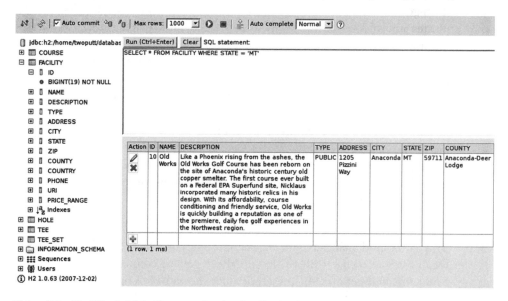

Figure 2.3   The H2 administration console, showing the database schema on the left and a query console on the right. The result set viewer can be used to modify records.

Now that you know the database is set up properly, it's time to turn the job over to seam-gen. Let's discover why I recommend using seam-gen to get started.

2.2   *Letting seam-gen do the initial work*

seam-gen gives you the opportunity to learn how the Seam creators prefer to organize a Seam-based project. It's also a great way to become familiar with Seam's moving parts so that you know what you're doing when you take Seam out on the course. If you are a do-it-yourselfer, you may be uneasy about letting seam-gen do the work. I recommend that you leave your reservations at the door, step out of your "working" environment if necessary, and observe Seam in its "natural" environment at least once. From the words of Seam's founder, Gavin King:

There really are a LOT of advantages to starting with the seam-gen structure. I did a lot of work on things that will take you a while to reproduce if you try to do it all from scratch (like, weeks of work!). However, there's nothing magical about it, and other structures can work just as well.

—Gavin King, JBoss Seam Forums[2]

I, too, was hesitant to use seam-gen at first. I viewed the tool as handholding for a novice developer. After spending a lot of time using Seam (like, months of time!) I have found seam-gen to be a huge timesaver; I strongly encourage you to give it a try.

2.2.1 *seam-gen's specialty*

seam-gen is an application factory, as depicted in figure 2.4. At the very basic level it creates a skeleton project, allowing you to focus on application development with little time spent doing setup. From there, it can take you all the way to a functional application using its code-generation tasks. The code that it lays down can also serve as a demonstration for how to use several of Seam's features.

I'll admit that I haven't been a huge fan of code generation in the past, mainly because it leaves behind lots of code that's scary to touch. With seam-gen, I have come to realize that creating the initial ORM mappings and CRUD screens is something I'm willing to delegate, precisely the tasks that seam-gen handles. I find that the code seam-gen produces is quite workable and likely equivalent to what I'd have written as a first cut anyway. Don't assume, though, that seam-gen is for "green-field" projects only. You can generate code in a sandbox project and then steal the code for use in other applications. In that regard, think of seam-gen as a tool that you can call upon when needed. If you don't like the output that seam-gen produces, you can even tailor it by modifying its templates.

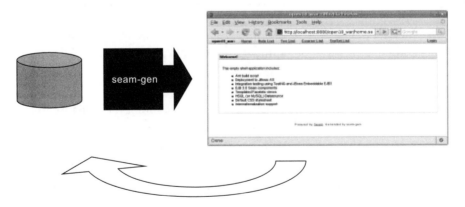

Figure 2.4   The seam-gen application generator examines an existing database and creates a CRUD application to manage the entities stored in the database tables.

---

2   The forum post can be found at http://www.jboss.com/index.html?module=bb&op=viewtopic&p=4030018.

TIP   seam-gen produces Java classes and Facelets view templates from Free-
          Marker templates, which can be found in the seam-gen folder of the
          Seam distribution. If you plan to customize the generated application,
          you may want to consider making changes to these templates. This
          approach allows you to customize the code without losing the ability to
          reverse-engineer.

seam-gen has also proved to be immensely helpful in figuring out how to define the JPA
mappings for an existing database schema. Setting up the associations between entities
can be an extremely tedious task. Just the other day I got stumped trying to remember
how to map a complex table relationship. Is it one-to-many or many-to-one? Do I need
a composite key? To avoid wasting time, I pointed seam-gen at my database and
inspected the result. seam-gen bailed me out and helped get me back on the right page.
If you've spent any length of time poring through the JPA or Hibernate reference documentation in search of a solution to these questions, seam-gen can help.

That's just the beginning of what a seam-gen project is capable of. Let's look at
what other features it sets up for you.

2.2.2   *Features that seam-gen provides*

In addition to producing CRUD applications from an existing database schema, seam-
gen can work from an existing set of entity classes. In that case, the database schema can
be created retroactively by Hibernate when the application starts, thus making seam-
gen attractive even when an existing database hasn't been dropped on your desk.

seam-gen goes far beyond creating a CRUD prototype application. It sets up an
extensive set of configurations and resources that are important as you begin customizing the application. Here's a combined list of features, many of which are covered in
this chapter:

- Incremental hot deployment of static resources, view templates, and page
  descriptors
- Incremental hot deployment (dynamic reloading) of JavaBean and Groovy
  components (excludes entity classes and EJB components)
- Ready-made project files for quick import into Eclipse, NetBeans, and IntelliJ
  IDEA
- Facelets view templates (a JSF-centric view technology; alternative to JSP)
- RichFaces or ICEfaces UI components (panels, tables, and menus)
- A custom stylesheet that reinforces the look and feel of the rich UI components
- Bookmark-friendly search and pagination of records on the entity listing pages
- RESTful entity detail screens; includes tabs showing the parent and child
  entities
- A lookup routine for establishing a link to a related entity in the entity editor
- Entity model validations enforced in the UI with instant feedback using Ajax
  (Ajax4jsf)

- Basic page-level authorization that requires users to authenticate before performing write operations (the default authentication is a stub that accepts any credentials)
- A component debug page, developer-friendly error page, and user-friendly error page
- JCA data source, JPA persistence unit, and JPA entity manager configured for target database (Hibernate 3.2 is the default JPA provider)
- Seeding of database from the `import.sql` script on classpath (Hibernate feature)

While seam-gen does crank out a working application, by no means is it going to put you out of a job. Although the CRUD application it creates is very capable, which you'll see later, it's no replacement for hand-crafted work. You have to take it for what it is: *a prototype*. It lacks the business knowledge necessary to properly categorize the entities, instead treating every entity with equal significance. This limitation is especially noticeable if you have a large schema with lots of lookup tables. seam-gen also falls short on rendering binary data properly in the user interface because there's no way for seam-gen to know if that data represents an image, a document, or an encrypted stream of data. But these shortcomings just give you room to add your personal touch—and give you a job.

The point to take away from this section is that seam-gen eliminates all the tedious work that you don't want to do anyway. It sets you up with a foundation and turns the project over to you, letting you rapidly develop and customize the application as you see fit. Let's now follow Gavin's advice and use seam-gen as the starting point for the example application. At last, we put seam-gen to the test.

2.3   *Kick off your project with seam-gen*

There are two versions of seam-gen, a command-line script and an IDE plugin. The command-line version, which is a wrapper around Ant, has the advantage that both it and the project it produces can be driven from the command line or from an IDE. The prominent IDE version of seam-gen is an Eclipse plug-in that's part of the JBoss-Tools suite. The JBossTools project hosts a variety of standalone Eclipse plug-ins that support Java EE development. These plug-ins get bundled with the JBoss Developer Studio (JBDS),[3] a set of Eclipse-based development tools preconfigured for the JBoss Enterprise Middleware Platform and Red Hat Enterprise Linux. This section primarily focuses on the command-line version of seam-gen, with a brief discussion of the Eclipse plug-in. I don't go into much detail about the IDE version since user interfaces tend to fall out of date quickly. You can find references to tutorials for using the Eclipse plug-in on the book's online companion resources.

I begin by giving you an overview of the seam-gen command-line script; then we plunge into executing the seam-gen commands.

---

[3] http://www.jboss.com/products/devstudio

2.3.1 *A look at the seam-gen commands*

You should have already downloaded the Seam distribution. If you haven't, please refer to appendix A, section A.2. You should also have the example H2 database prepared as described in section 2.1.2. Once you have all of the prerequisites, change into the directory where you extracted Seam. In that directory you'll find two scripts, seam and seam.bat. The former is used on Linux/Unix platforms and the latter on the Windows platform. To perform seam-gen operations, you type seam followed by the name of a command from the root directory of the Seam distribution.[4]

Let's begin by asking the seam script what it can do. The script's capabilities are provided by the help command. In your console, type seam help and press the Enter key. The output of this command gives a brief description of seam-gen and a long list of all the commands it supports. That description is shown here:

```
seam (aka seam-gen) - Execute seam code generation.

The seam.bat (Windows) and seam (Linux/Unix) scripts support
commands that use Ant build targets to set up a Seam project and
generate source code. Ant is not required to be on your path to
use this script.

JBoss AS must be installed to deploy the project. If you use EJB3
components, the JBoss server must have EJB 3 capabilities.
(JBoss AS 4.2 is strongly recommended)
```

The list of commands that the help command spits out can be divided into two categories. The first set of commands, shown in table 2.1, are used to set up, manage, and deploy a seam-gen project.

Table 2.1 The setup, create, and deployment commands that can be provided to the seam-gen script

Command	Description
setup	Generates the seam-gen/build.properties used to create projects. The key-value pairs are taken from the responses to the questionnaire conducted by this command. Information gathered includes the project directory, Java package names, database connection information, and the location of JBoss AS. You can hand-edit seam-gen/build.properties after completing the questionnaire.
create-project	Creates a Seam project complete with a build script, library dependencies, and basic Seam component configurations. Uses the values in seam-gen/build.properties to customize the project.
update-project	Updates the generated project with the latest library dependencies.
delete-project	Undeploys and deletes the generated project.

---

[4] If you're using a Unix platform (Linux, Unix, Mac OSX), you need to make sure the seam script is executable. You also need to prefix the seam command with dot-slash (./). See appendix A for more details.

Table 2.1 The setup, create, and deployment commands that can be provided to the seam-gen script *(continued)*

Command	Description
deploy	Deploys the project archive (packaged Web Archive [WAR] or Enterprise Archive [EAR]) and data source to JBoss AS.
undeploy	Undeploys the project archive and data source.
explode	Deploys the project archive (exploded Web Archive [WAR] or Enterprise Archive [EAR]) and data source to JBoss AS. Also performs incremental hot deployment of web artifacts and Java classes (excludes EJB 3 components and JPA entity classes).
restart	Restarts the project previously deployed as an exploded archive. Does not restart JBoss AS.
unexplode	Undeploys the exploded archive and data source.
archive	Creates a project archive (packaged Web Archive [WAR] or Enterprise Archive [EAR]) and puts it in the dist folder at the root of the project.
clean	Removes all compiled files and staging directories in the generated project.
test	Runs the tests in the generated project.
settings	Displays the current settings as defined in seam-gen/build.properties.
reset	Removes the seam-gen/build.properties to start the process over from scratch.

The second set of commands, shown in table 2.2, is used for generating code for a project that seam-gen is currently managing.

Table 2.2 Code-generation commands that can be provided to the seam-gen script

Command	Description
new-action	Creates a new Java interface and stateless session bean with key Seam/EJB3 annotations. Also creates a test case and TestNG launch configuration for simulating a JSF request/response.
new-form	Create a new Java interface and stateful session bean with key Seam/EJB3 annotations. Also creates a test case and TestNG launch configuration for simulating a JSF request/response.
new-conversation	Creates a new Java interface and stateful session bean with key Seam/EJB3 annotations. Adds annotations and stub methods for @Begin and @End.
new-entity	Creates a new entity bean with key Seam/EJB3 annotations.
new-query	Creates a new class that extends EntityQuery to manage a custom JPA query and a view template to display the results of the query.
generate	Generates JPA entity classes from an existing database schema and a CRUD user interface to view and manage them.

Table 2.2　Code-generation commands that can be provided to the seam-gen script *(continued)*

Command	Description
`generate-ui`	Generates a CRUD user interface to view and manage an existing set of JPA entity classes.
`generate-model`	Generates JPA entity classes from an existing database schema.

Don't worry right now about understanding each and every command. You're going to get an opportunity to study most of the commands individually throughout the course of the book. These two tables should give you a feel for the capabilities of seam-gen before we take it into battle.

TIP　If you're super shell savvy, you can source the bash completion script in seam-gen/contrib/seam-completion to get tab completion for the seam-gen commands in Unix.

Table 2.3 lists the steps that you will take to create the Open 18 prototype application.

Table 2.3　The steps to create and deploy a prototype application

Command	Purpose
1. `seam setup`	Enters information about the Open 18 prototype and the H2 database
2. `seam create-project`	Instructs seam-gen to create the open18 project
3. `seam generate`	Reverse-engineers the Open 18 database to create a CRUD application to manage the tables
4. `seam explode`	Deploys the application to JBoss AS as an exploded Java EE archive

Once you've completed the steps in table 2.3 and started JBoss AS, you'll be ready to show the Open 18 prototype to your boss. If he asks for changes, you won't be at a loss for words. Customizing a seam-gen application is very straightforward. Later in the chapter you learn how to get your hands dirty with the application by checking out the "instant change" development environment that seam-gen sets up and by deploying to multiple environments. Before you can do any of that, you have to inform seam-gen about your project so that it knows what to create for you.

2.3.2　A Q&A session with seam-gen

Enough watercooler talk. Let's get to work! You begin by running the `seam setup` command. When you run this command, it launches a series of questions that allow seam-gen to gather the information it needs to create your project. Each line consists of three parts: the question, the current value, and a list of valid responses (if applicable). For each question, enter a response and press the Enter key to continue to the next question. To create a working application, this is the only real work that you have to do: seam-gen takes over once it has the information it needs.

Listing 2.1 shows the full seam-gen setup questionnaire along with the responses used for creating the Open 18 prototype in the WAR archive format. Anytime you see /home/twoputt in a response, replace it with your development folder (according to the layout explained in the README.txt file of the book's source code).

NOTE If you're using a Windows OS, use the forward slash (/) when entering file paths (e.g., C:/twoputt) in the seam-gen interview, particularly when entering the path to the H2 database. The default file separator in Windows is the backslash, which in Java is the escape character. For Java to accept a literal backslash, you have to escape it with another backslash (\\). You can avoid this whole issue by always using forward slashes in file paths, regardless of the operating system. Java is smart enough to convert the forward slash to the correct file separator for the host platform.

Let's start the interview by typing the following:

```
seam setup
```

Listing 2.1 Responding to the seam-gen setup questionnaire

```
    [echo] Welcome to seam-gen :-)
    [input] Enter your Java project workspace (the directory that contains
➥your Seam projects) [C:/Projects] [C:/Projects]
/home/twoputt/projects
    [input] Enter your JBoss home directory [C:/Program Files/jboss-4.2.2.GA]
    ➥ [C:/Program Files/jboss-4.2.2.GA]
/home/twoputt/opt/jboss-as-4.2.2.GA
    [input] Enter the project name [myproject] [myproject]        Applies only to
open18                                                                RichFaces
    [echo] Accepted project name as: open18
    [input] Do you want to use ICEfaces instead of RichFaces [n] (y, [n])
n
    [input] Select a RichFaces skin [blueSky] ([blueSky],
    ➥classic, ruby, wine, deepMarine, emeraldTown, japanCherry, DEFAULT)
emeraldTown
    [input] Is this project deployed as an EAR (with EJB            Selects
    ➥components) or a WAR (with no EJB support) [ear] ([ear], war)  Java EE
war                                                                  archive
    [input] Enter the Java package name for your session           type
    ➥beans [com.mydomain.open18] [com.mydomain.open18]
org.open18.action                                                  Sets
    [input] Enter the Java package name for your entity beans      package
    ➥ [org.open18.action] [org.open18.action]                      of hot
org.open18.model                                                   deployed
    [input] Enter the Java package name for your test cases        classes
    ➥ [org.open18.action.test] [org.open18.action.test]
org.open18.test
    [input] What kind of database are you using? [hsql] ([hsql], mysql,
    ➥oracle, postgres, mssql, db2, sybase, enterprisedb, h2)
```

```
h2
   [input] Enter the Hibernate dialect for your database
 ➥[org.hibernate.dialect.H2Dialect] [org.hibernate.dialect.H2Dialect]
Hit Enter key
   [input] Enter the filesystem path to the JDBC driver jar [lib/h2.jar]
 ➥[lib/h2.jar]
/home/twoputt/lib/h2.jar
   [input] Enter JDBC driver class for your database [org.h2.Driver]
 ➥[org.h2.Driver]
Hit Enter key
   [input] Enter the JDBC URL for your database [jdbc:h2:.] [jdbc:h2:.]
jdbc:h2:file:/home/twoputt/databases/open18-db/h2        ◄──┐
   [input] Enter database username [sa] [sa]                │    Specifies file
open18                                                 ◄─┐  │    location of H2
   [input] Enter database password [] []         Supplies custom │ database
tiger                                             H2 credentials │
                                                       ◄─┘
   [input] Enter the database schema name (it's OK to leave it blank) [] []
PUBLIC                                                                    ◄───┐
   [input] Enter the database catalog name (it's OK to leave it blank) [] []  │
H2                                                                        ◄───┘
   [input] Are you working with tables that already exist in the database?
 ➥[n] (y, [n])
y
   [input] Do you want to drop and re-create the database tables and data in
 ➥import.sql each time you deploy? [n] (y, [n])
n                                                    Keeps values out of
[propertyfile] Creating new property file:          @Table annotation
 ➥/home/twoputt/opt/jboss-seam-2.0.3.GA/seam-gen/build.properties
   [echo] Installing JDBC driver jar to JBoss server
   [copy] Copying 1 file to
 ➥/home/twoputt/opt/jboss-as-4.2.2.GA/server/default/lib

   [echo] Type 'seam create-project' to create the new project

BUILD SUCCESSFUL
```

The goal of the seam setup command is to populate seam-gen/build.properties—overwriting it if it already exists—with the settings used to create the seam-gen project, which is the next step. The build.properties file stores your responses in the typical Java properties file format, using key-value pairs separated by an equals sign (=). If you mess up any of the questions, don't fret—you can always run through the setup again. Seam will remember the responses from your previous run through, as long as you ran it to completion. You accept your previous response for a question by pressing Enter. If you'd rather not use the setup wizard, you can just edit the seam-gen/build.properties file manually. The wizard just makes the task more user-friendly.

The responses in listing 2.1 prepare seam-gen to create a WAR project. You choose the WAR format if you plan on developing JavaBean components rather than EJB 3 components and you want to take advantage of incremental hot deployment. If you want to create EJB 3 components, the EAR format is the required choice. You'll learn about both of these archive formats, as well as incremental hot deployment, later in the chapter.

Choosing ICEfaces over RichFaces

ICEfaces and RichFaces are JSF component libraries for building rich, Web 2.0 user interfaces based on Ajax. seam-gen is capable of generating projects that use either ICEfaces or RichFaces, made possible by two equivalent sets of view templates that are maintained under the seam-gen folder of the Seam distribution. seam-gen selects the appropriate template folder based on your response in the setup questionnaire and caters the application to that JSF component library.

If you choose ICEfaces, seam-gen automatically uses the bundled version, thus requiring no setup on your part. If you'd like to have seam-gen use the version of your choosing, you specify the root folder of the ICEfaces binary distribution when you're prompted for it in the seam-gen setup.

Because RichFaces is a JBoss project, you can understand why RichFaces is the default choice in seam-gen, but the ICEfaces contributors ensure that the generated application works equally well in ICEfaces. I encourage you to give both a try and decide for yourself.

In addition to creating and populating the seam-gen/build.properties file, the setup command copies the JDBC driver to JBoss AS to allow the database connection to be defined as a JCA data source. In our case, the H2 JDBC driver, h2.jar, is copied to ${jboss.home}/server/default/lib. The JCA data source is registered in the Java Naming and Directory Interface (JNDI) upon deployment of the project, where the JPA persistence unit can access it. The configuration of the data source and the persistence unit are tasks handled by the create-project command, covered next.

2.3.3 Creating a basic project structure

The setup command merely prepares seam-gen to create a project. To actually have Seam transform its templates into a newly forged project, you must execute

```
seam create-project
```

When you execute this command, Seam will create a new project in your Java workspace directory and populate it with everything you need to start developing a Seam-based project, complete with an Ant-based build for compiling, testing, packaging, and deploying the application. Listing 2.2 shows the output of the create-project command. You'll see a lot of other output fly by, which you can ignore.

Listing 2.2 Creating a new project with seam-gen

```
create-project:
    [echo] A new Seam project named 'open18' was created in the
  ➡/home/twoputt/projects directory
    [echo] Type 'seam explode' and go to http://localhost:8080/open18
    [echo] Eclipse Users: Add the project into Eclipse using File >
  ➡New > Project and select General > Project (not Java Project)
```

```
[echo] NetBeans Users: Open the project in NetBeans
BUILD SUCCESSFUL
```

The project is now ready. As you can see in this output, seam-gen provides instructions to keep you moving right along. It tells you to run `create-project` after running the setup command and `seam explode` after running the `create-project` command. However, you'll likely agree that setting up a project, particularly filling out the questionnaire shown here, is best suited for a windowing environment. If you're turned off by the command-line interface, I have good news for you. The JBossTools plug-in for Eclipse wraps these steps into the Seam project creation wizard, which allows you to create a seam-gen project just like you would any other Eclipse project. One of the screens from this wizard is shown in figure 2.5. This wizard provides a much more interactive experience and lets you leverage existing servers, runtimes, and database connection profiles that you have set up in Eclipse.

A step-by-step tutorial of the JBoss-Tools plug-in won't be covered here. If you're interested in using it, you should be able to apply the foundation knowledge that you have learned in this chapter to that wizard. Be aware that the project the JBossTools wizard creates is not exactly the same as a project created by the command-line script. It's designed to be used with an IDE (i.e., Eclipse) and only an IDE—meaning it doesn't have a universal build script. My preference is to stick with the the command-line script (herein referred to as seam-gen) because it allows me to use the generated project from the command line or in the IDE of my choice (any IDE that can drive an Ant build). This flexibility is demonstrated repeatedly throughout the rest of this chapter.

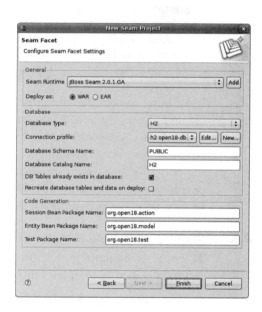

Figure 2.5   The Seam project creation wizard that is included with the JBossTools Eclipse plug-in. This wizard performs the same work as the `seam-gen` command-line tool but offers a more interactive experience.

2.3.4   *Generating the CRUD*

You now have a basic project scaffolding that's ready to deployed. But let's keep the code generation going by doing some reverse engineering first. That is the function that the `seam generate` command[5] performs. This command generates JPA entity classes from

---

[5] Prior to Seam 2.0.1.GA, this command was named **generate-entities**. Both names are supported as of 2.0.1.GA.

an existing database schema and a CRUD user interface to manage these entities rendered from Facelets view templates and supported by JavaBean action classes.

NOTE   By supplying values for the schema and catalog in seam setup, we ensure that the @Table annotation placed on each JPA entity class remains agnostic to these data-specific settings. The schema and the catalog are more likely to change than the table and column names, so it's best not to tie your entity classes to these values. If necessary, the default schema and catalog can be set in the Hibernate or JPA configuration using the properties hibernate.default_schema and hibernate.default_catalog.

Next, kick off the reverse engineering:

```
seam generate
```

The output for the generate command is quite extensive as Hibernate feels the need to keep us informed of its reverse-engineering progress every step of the way. A truncated version of that output is shown in listing 2.3.

Listing 2.3   Reverse engineering the database to create entities and session beans

```
...
generate-model:

  [echo] Reverse engineering database using JDBC driver
  ➥/home/twoputt/lib/h2.jar
  [echo] project=/home/twoputt/projects/open18
  [echo] model=org.open18.model
[hibernate] Executing Hibernate Tool with a JDBC Configuration (for reverse
  ➥engineering)
[hibernate] 1. task: hbm2java (Generates a set of .java files)
...
[hibernate] INFO: Hibernate Tools 3.2.0.CR1
[javaformatter] Java formatting of 8 files completed. Skipped 0 files(s).

generate-ui:
  [echo] Building project 'open18' to generate views and controllers

...
[hibernate] Executing Hibernate Tool with a JPA Configuration
[hibernate] 1. task: generic exporter... view/list.xhtml.ftl
...
[hibernate] 2. task: generic exporter... view/view.xhtml.ftl
[hibernate] 3. task: generic exporter... view/view.page.xml.ftl
[hibernate] 4. task: generic exporter... view/edit.xhtml.ftl
[hibernate] 5. task: generic exporter... view/edit.page.xml.ftl
[hibernate] 6. task: generic exporter... src/EntityList.java.ftl
[hibernate] 7. task: generic exporter... view/list.page.xml.ftl
[hibernate] 8. task: generic exporter... src/EntityHome.java.ftl
[hibernate] 9. task: generic exporter... view/layout/menu.xhtml.ftl
[javaformatter] Java formatting of 15 files completed. Skipped 0 files(s).
  [echo] Type 'seam restart' and go to http://localhost:8080/open18

generate:

BUILD SUCCESSFUL
```

Believe it or not, that's it! The prototype application is built. Ah, but we aren't quite ready for deployment. If you were to run `seam restart` now, as the `generate` command instructs, you would find that unless you already had JBoss AS running, the request for the URL http://localhost:8080/open18 would simply give you a 404 error page. To put the application in motion, you need to boot up JBoss AS. In the next section, you learn about the two options you have for deploying the application, how it affects development, and finally how to start JBoss AS so that you can see the application that seam-gen has prepared for you.

2.4   *Deploying the project to JBoss AS*

As I mentioned earlier, seam-gen produces projects that are configured to deploy to JBoss AS out of the box. For now, let's stick with the convention to keep the effort of getting the application running to a minimum. Once you're comfortable with that, you can explore alternatives.

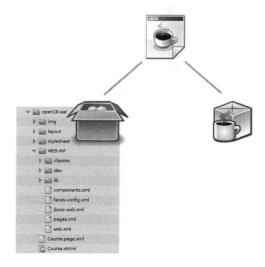

You can take one of two paths when deploying your application to JBoss AS. You can either deploy it as a packaged archive:

```
seam deploy
```

or you can deploy it as an exploded archive:

```
seam explode
```

These two alternatives are illustrated in figure 2.6.

Figure 2.6   The two deployment scenarios offered by seam-gen. On the left, an exploded WAR (or EAR) directory. On the right, a packaged WAR (or EAR) file. Incremental hot deployment is not available when using a packaged archive.

NOTE   Despite its alarming name, the `explode` command will not perform a destructive process on your project. It simply copies the deployable files to the application server without packaging them. The name is meant to indicate that the archive is broken open as if it had been "exploded." A more reassuring name for this command might have been "unfurl" (like a sail). But `explode` just sort of stuck.

Let's weigh the attributes of each command and decide which one is best to use.

2.4.1   *To deploy...*

If you use the `deploy` command, the build will create an archive that uses one of two standard Java EE package formats, Web Archive (WAR) or Enterprise Archive (EAR), depending on which one you chose during the seam-gen setup routine. If you plan to use only JavaBean components, like the example application presented in this chapter, your best choice is the WAR format. In this case, the `deploy` command packages the application into the WAR file open18.war. If you intend to use EJB components in your application, you must use the EAR format. In that case, the deploy command will create the EAR file open18ee.ear for an application named open18ee. The sample code that accompanies the book includes projects for both archive formats. Note, however, that once you make a choice between WAR and EAR, you're stuck with it. There is no built-in seam-gen command to toggle a project between the two archive formats.

Packaging Java EE applications

There are three prominent archive types that can be used to deploy components to a Java EE–compliant application server. A Web Archive (WAR) is the format with which most people are familiar. A WAR bundles servlets, JSPs, the archive is static resources, and supporting classes for the purpose of serving dynamic web pages. EJBs are deployed in the pervasive Java Archive (JAR) format, except that the archive is augmented with a special XML deployment descriptor that identifies it as an EJB JAR. Both the WAR and JAR formats are Java EE modules that can be bundled inside an Enterprise Archive (EAR), which deploys the containing modules under the same classloader, presenting them as a single application. The EAR is the standard packaging unit for a Java EE application. Basic servlet containers, such as Tomcat, can only handle WAR packages.

Once the archive has been packaged, seam-gen moves it to the deployment directory in the default domain of the JBoss server, located at ${jboss.home}/server/default/deploy. The JBoss server monitors this directory for changes. When a new or changed archive is detected, the application is "reloaded." This feature is known as "hot deploy," but it's not just about deployment. The server also recognizes when an archive has been removed from this directory and subsequently unloads the application. You can remove the deployed archive by running

```
seam undeploy
```

The downside to using a packaged archive is that every change you want to apply requires a complete build, package, and deploy cycle. At the end of this cycle, a fresh version of the archive is shipped off to the server, the old application is unloaded, and finally, the new application is loaded. In this case, we're talking about hot-deploying the application as a whole rather than incremental changes, which is covered later. It's all or nothing. During a reload, the JBoss server shuts down all the services that were started by your application. These services include the database connection, the JPA `EntityManagerFactory` (or Hibernate `SessionFactory`), the Seam container, and perhaps others. When the new application is deployed, all of these services are started again under the new deployment. This process can be *very* time consuming—and that time increases as your project grows and more services have to be stopped and started.

To make matters worse, reloading an application terminates all of its active HTTP sessions. If the page you're testing requires you to be authenticated, or otherwise holds state, you'll be forced to reestablish your place. Needless to say, the packaged deployment isn't recommended for development. The good news is that there's a better way.

2.4.2 ...or to explode

The alternative to a packaged deployment is an exploded archive. An exploded archive is a WAR or EAR that has been extracted into a directory that has the same name as the archive. You can deploy the application as an exploded archive using the `seam explode` command.

The `explode` command is a slight variation on the `deploy` command. Like the `deploy` command, the `explode` command assembles the deployable files into the structure of the archive in the build directory. But the `explode` command skips the bundling step and just copies the build directory in its raw form to the server. Subsequent calls to `seam explode` synchronize the changed files to the exploded archive directory on the server, thus supporting incremental updates. How the application deals with its changes is determined by its hot deployment capabilities. Section 2.5.1 examines incremental hot deployment and what it means in terms of development.

To force a reload of the application when using an exploded archive deployment, mimicking the behavior that occurs when a package archive is dropped into the hot deployment directory of JBoss AS, you use the `restart` command. As its name may imply, this command doesn't restart the JBoss AS—it just reloads the application.

The `restart` command begins by mirroring the work done by the `explode` command. As a final step, it updates the timestamp of the application deployment descriptor, which is application.xml, in the case of an EAR deployment, or web.xml, in the case of a WAR deployment. When the application server detects that the timestamp of the application deployment descriptor has changed, it triggers a reload. To remove an exploded archive, and have it undeployed, you execute

```
seam unexplode
```

The `explode` command is best suited for development. With support for incremental updates, it gives you the "instant change" capabilities that you may be familiar with if you've ever developed in a scripting language like PHP. The degree to which a Seam application supports instant change will be put to the test later.

To summarize your options, you can use the `deploy` command to deploy a package archive or you can use the `explode` command to deploy an exploded archive. The `undeploy` and `unexplode` commands serve as their complements by removing the archive from the server. That covers the deployment life cycle to a single environment. seam-gen sets up your project with additional deployment profiles, which allow you to tune the archive based on environment, possibly even deploying it to a different server instance. Let's take one more tangent to learn about deployment profiles before we move on to starting JBoss AS.

2.4.3   *Switching between environments*

The build that seam-gen creates for your project supports the concept of deployment profiles. Profiles can be used to customize deployment descriptors and configuration settings for different environments. To cite a common case, you may need to use a different database in production than the one used in development. You certainly don't want to be burdened with having to switch the database connection settings every time you cut a production release. Instead, you can set up a profile for that environment, which you can activate with a single flag when executing the production build. The appropriate database settings, and any other settings specific to that environment, will then be applied.

Seam configures three profiles out of the box: dev, prod, and test. The test profile is a special case, which we look at next. By default, Seam uses the dev profile when commands are executed. You can enable a different profile by changing the value of the Ant `profile` property. Adding the following key-value pair to the build.properties file in the root of the project activates the prod profile, effectively deactivating the dev profile:

```
profile=prod
```

Having to change the build.properties file feels too manual for my taste. As another option, you can set the `profile` property from the `seam` command:

```
seam clean deploy -Dprofile=prod
```

TIP   When you switch profiles, it's a good idea to run `clean`—and possibly even `undeploy` or `unexplode`—prior to running `deploy` or `explode` to be sure that settings from the previous profile do not linger.

As I mentioned, the test profile is handled as a special case. It's not activated using the `profile` property. Instead, there are special Ant targets for running tests that know to use the test versions of the environment-specific files. Writing and executing tests will be covered in chapter 4.

Table 2.4 itemizes the files that are selected according to the active profile, indicating whether the file is used in the case of the test profile. These files contain settings and configurations that you have control over between environments. You can introduce your own profile, such as qa, by creating each of the files listed in table 2.4. When naming the file, replace the token %PROFILE% with the name of the profile. For instance, the build properties file for the qa profile would be build-qa.properties.

Table 2.4   Files that are selected based on the profile property value

File selected based on profile value	Purpose of file	Used in test profile?
build-%PROFILE%.properties	Used to set Ant build properties, such as the location of the JBoss AS deploy directory and the debug mode flag	No
resources/META-INF/persistence-%PROFILE%-war.xml	The JPA persistent unit configuration file	Yes

Table 2.4   Files that are selected based on the profile property value *(continued)*

File selected based on profile value	Purpose of file	Used in test profile?
resources/import-%PROFILE%.sql	A SQL script that will be used to load seed data into the database when the application starts if the database is being re-created each time	Yes
resources/open18-%PROFILE%-ds.xml[a]	The data source configuration file for JBoss AS	No

a. Named according to the application, which in this case is open18.

If you want to change the location of the JBoss AS deploy directory for a production build, you can set the `jboss.home` property in build-prod.properties. You probably want to disable debug mode as well, since it's only desirable in development:

```
jboss.home=/opt/jboss-production
debug=false
```

You now know how to deploy and undeploy the application to the JBoss AS deployment directory, both as a packaged archive and an exploded directory structure. You can also control the settings and configurations for the target environment, such as development, QA, or production, by toggling the value of the profile property. Without further ado, let's fire up JBoss AS and see what the application looks like.

2.4.4   *Launching JBoss AS*

Without any customization, JBoss AS runs on port 8080, so first ensure this port isn't already in use (be aware that Apache Tomcat also runs on port 8080 by default). In your console, navigate to the JBoss AS installation directory, ${jboss.home}, and then descend into the bin directory. If you're using a Unix platform, execute the command:

```
/run.sh
```

If you're on Windows, execute the command:

```
run
```

These scripts start the default domain of the JBoss AS server. As an alternative to using the console, you may also choose to launch JBoss AS from your IDE. Eclipse, NetBeans, and IntelliJ IDEA all support launching the JBoss Application Server.

Keep an eye on the console while the server is starting to watch for any exceptions that may occur. When the console output settles down, the final line should give you the thumbs up that JBoss AS is running:

```
00:00:00,426 INFO [Server] JBoss (MX MicroKernel) [4.2.2.GA (build:
   [CA]SVNTag=JBoss_4_2_2_GA date=200710221139)] Started in 17s:14ms
```

If you're using the Sun JVM, I can almost guarantee that when you start hot-deploying applications to JBoss AS, you're going to get out-of-memory errors using the default JVM

Sun JVM options when running JBoss AS

While you're on the task of setting up the JBoss AS runtime, I recommend a set of JVM options to use when running JBoss AS with the Sun JVM. The default memory allocation settings in Java are extremely conservative. On top of that, Sun's JVM has a concept of PermGen space, a separate allocated memory region from the heap.[6] Even though the JVM garbage collector frees up memory automatically, there are certain objects (such as class and method objects) that can evade removal because they are in this isolated memory region. A flag must be provided that enables garbage collection for the PermGen space. In addition, the garbage collector has trouble keeping up when memory is tight. The limited resources quickly become a problem when running a hefty application like JBoss AS that has high memory demands.

To avoid an untimely death of the JVM, and in turn, JBoss AS, you should supply the following parameters in the VM options of the JBoss AS runtime configuration in your IDE (or bin/run.conf in the JBoss AS home directory). I have **never** experienced an out-of-memory error when using these settings.[7]

```
-Xms128m -Xmx512m -Dsun.rmi.dgc.client.gcInterval=3600000
  ➥-Dsun.rmi.dgc.server.gcInterval=3600000
  ➥-XX:+UseConcMarkSweepGC -XX:+CMSPermGenSweepingEnabled
  ➥-XX:+CMSClassUnloadingEnabled -XX:MaxPermSize=512m
  ➥-Xverify:none
```

There are ramifications of using the Concurrent Mark Sweep (CMS) garbage collector, such as a longer startup time, so I wouldn't blindly apply these settings to production. However, I have found them to be sufficient for development purposes. The other solution is to switch to the IBM JVM, which doesn't experience this problem.

options. I strongly urge you to follow the advice in the accompanying sidebar. These settings can be applied to the JBoss AS runtime configuration either by adding them to the ${jboss.home}/bin/run.conf or by using the configuration screen in the IDE.

If JBoss AS started cleanly, you can open your browser and point it to http://localhost: 8080/open18 to see the result of your work. In the next section, I walk you through the application and point out the work seam-gen has done for you. I then demonstrate how you can continuously make changes to the application without having to suffer the wait of restarting either the application or the server.

2.5 Show and tell, change, and repeat

You might recall the activity of "show and tell" from your school days. In today's show and tell, I will be demonstrating the Open 18 prototype application that you have

---

[6] For more information on the design of the garbage collection mechanism in Sun's JVM, please see http://java.sun.com/javase/technologies/hotspot/gc/gc_tuning_6.html or a more abbreviated list at http://performance.netbeans.org/howto/jvmswitches/index.html.

[7] If you would like to know more about these settings and why they were chosen, please see http://my.opera.com/karmazilla/blog/2007/03/13/good-riddance-permgen-outofmemoryerror.

created thus far using seam-gen, both from outside and the inside. This exercise is important because it's necessary to know how seam-gen assembled the application so that you're familiar with how to make modifications to it. In this section, you learn how you can alter the application by controlling the reverse-engineering process. In the next section, you learn how to make changes after the fact. Before we get to that, it's time for the unveiling.

Ta-da! The opening screen of the Open 18 application is shown in figure 2.7.

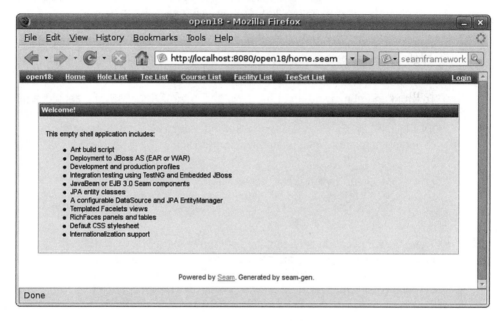

Figure 2.7   The splash page of an application created by seam-gen. The links in the upper menu bar represent each of the entities that seam-gen extracted from the database schema.

I'll admit, the home page isn't all that interesting. At the very least, it's clear that the application has a nice look and feel, courtesy of RichFaces, which is typically rare for starter applications. The folks on the floor of the trade show pavilion probably don't care to read about the benefits of seam-gen, though. Thankfully, there is an email from the marketing team waiting for you in your inbox with flashier markup for this page. You'll soon learn how changes such as these can be deployed in real time during development, as if you were editing the page live.

Notice at the top of the page there are links for each of the entities in the data model and another link encouraging you to authenticate. Clearly there is some substance behind this curtain. Let's dig deeper to find out what's inside.

2.5.1   *Walking the course*

From the top-level menu in figure 2.7, you can verify that seam-gen produced five entities: Facility, Course, Hole, TeeSet, and Tee. The List suffix on each link indicates that these pages are listings. We'll focus on these pages first and then see where else they take us.

ENTITY LISTINGS

Clicking one of the entity links at the top of the page brings up the listing for that entity. In this walkthrough, we'll focus on the course listing, shown in figure 2.8. However, the tour I am about to give applies to the other entities as well.

The listing screen has two parts. The featured content is a table of all the courses found in the database, seen in the bottom half of the screen. This table has two key features. It can be sorted and paginated. The result set is broken into pages, truncated at a page size of 25 by default. Links at the bottom of the screen allow you to flip through the pages in the result set. The columns of the table are also sortable. The heading of each column is rendered as a link, allowing you to sort the table by that column. Now, tell me, how much time have you burned implementing sortable and paginated tables in an application in your career? If you winced at that question, you should be happy to see that seam-gen takes care of all that for you. So go ahead and revel in it by clicking on a couple of the column headers and flipping through the pages. You should notice that the sort is not lost when you paginate, the offset is not lost when you sort, and every page can be bookmarked. Another seam-gen special.

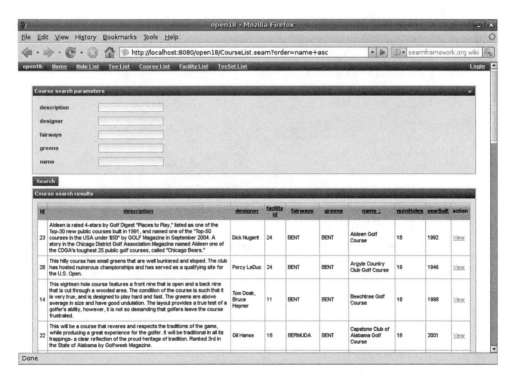

Figure 2.8 The Course List screen as created by seam-gen. This page includes a collapsible search form in the top half and a pageable, sortable result set of courses in the bottom half.

The page also includes a search feature. The search form, shown in the top half of figure 2.8, includes an input field for every string property of the Course entity class. You can type text in any of the fields that appear above the table and Seam will use that text to perform a search to filter the rows displayed in the table. The best part is that when you sort and paginate, your search filter is not reset. In the next chapter you learn the technique that powers this functionality.

From the course list page, you can either create a course or you can view the details of a particular course. Let's drill down to see the details of one of the courses.

DRILL-DOWNS

In the last column of the course listing is a link to view the course. When you click this link, it brings up a page showing the details of the course, shown in figure 2.9.

The course detail screen shows all the properties of the course at the top of the screen and each of the course's related entities at the bottom. Since each course has 18 holes,

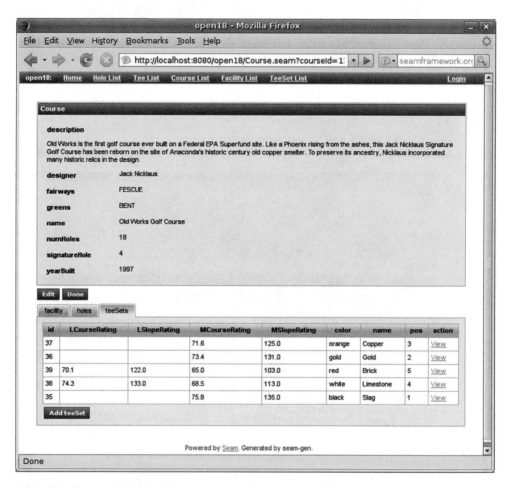

Figure 2.9 The course detail screen as generated by seam-gen. This page displays all the data for a given course and also uses a tabbed pane to show the associated facility, tee sets, and holes.

there are 18 rows in the table in the holes tab pane. The teeSets tab pane shows a table with rows for each set of tees (the colored markers at the start of each hole). Each course is also associated with a golf facility, the details of which are shown in the facility tab pane. You can continue to drill down further by clicking the View link in the row of any related entity. But the application really gets interesting when you add a new record or edit an existing one.

ENTITY EDITORS

There are buttons for both editing and adding entities. However, pages that alter the state of the database require you to be logged in. When you click one of these buttons, you'll be directed to the login screen, shown in figure 2.10. The login requirement is enforced in the page descriptor that coincides with the JSF page. For the Course entity, the editor page is CourseEdit.xhtml and its page descriptor is CourseEdit. page.xml. You'll learn about page descriptors in chapter 3.

Any credentials will do since the authentication module is just a stub. You learn how to tie authentication to the database and how to further lock down pages in chapter 11.

Once you authenticate, you're taken to the course editor, shown in figure 2.11. If you're updating an existing record, Seam will apply the changes to it when you click Save. Otherwise, a new record will be inserted into the database.

At first glance, the forms for editing an entity appear straightforward, perhaps even a bit dull. A closer look reveals that they are enriched with subtle features that would be very time consuming to prepare. The * in figure 2.11 indicates a required field or relationship. At the bottom half of the page is a button that lets you select a facility to satisfy

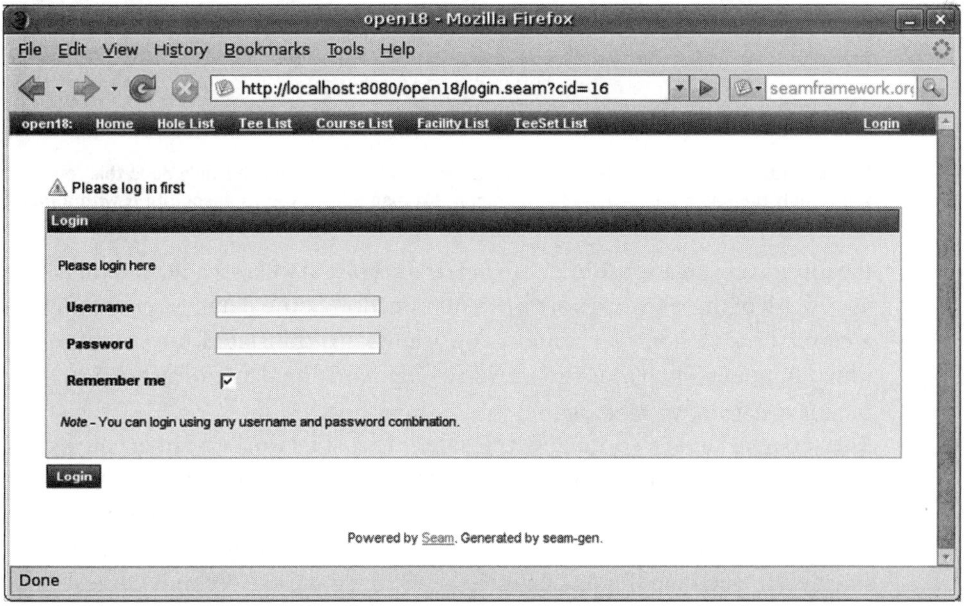

Figure 2.10   The login screen of an application created by seam-gen. The authentication provider is just a stub, so any username/password combination is accepted in the default configuration.

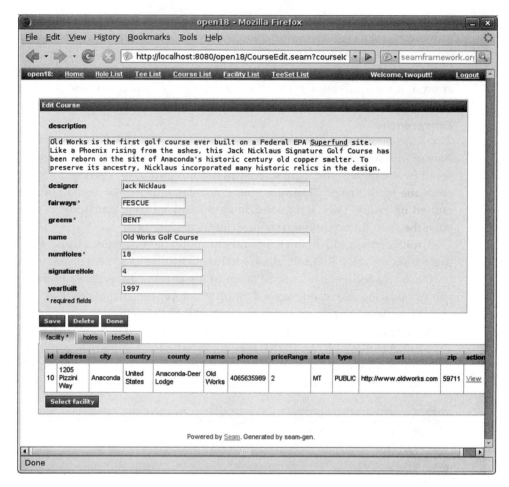

Figure 2.11 The course editor screen as generated by seam-gen. Not only does this form allow you to edit the basic properties of a course, but it also allows you to associate it with a facility.

the foreign key relationship. If you delete a record, it will cascade, deleting child records as well. All of these features are a direct reflection of the database constraints. Let's take a closer look at how the column constraints are translated into form requirements, which happens when seam-gen reverse-engineers the database schema.

DATABASE COLUMN TO FORM FIELD

The seam `generate` command delegates most of its work to Hibernate's reverse-engineering tool. In that step, the database tables are translated into entity classes and the columns become properties on the respective classes. The properties on the entity class manifest as form fields in the entity's editor during the creation of the CRUD screens. To get from the database to the UI, the database column names are converted into entity property names, which become the form field labels in the UI.

seam-gen is fairly intelligent about creating form fields that adapt to the type accepted by the corresponding database columns. To start, the Java type chosen for each property is derived from the SQL type of the corresponding column. If the column type is numeric, the editor will only accept numbers in the input field. Even better, the validation is performed in real time using Ajax. If you try entering letters into the `yearBuilt` field on the course editor, then click somewhere else on the page, you'll see that you get a validation error, as shown in figure 2.12. You'll learn how to configure the form field to enforce validations in the next chapter. Chapter 5 shows you how to customize messages in Seam, since clearly this error message could stand to be improved.

seam-gen also picks up on non-nullable column constraints in the database and enforces them as required fields in the editor as indicated by the star (*) after the field label in figure 2.11. Where appropriate, the property on the entity class is defined using a primitive type in this case. If a primitive type can't be used, such as when the column type is a string, then the `@NotNull` annotation from the Hibernate Validator library is added to the property on the entity class. If the column allows null values, then a nullable Java type is used for the property and the field isn't required in the UI. There are a number of other Hibernate Validator annotations that seam-gen applies to the entity classes and in turn enforces in real time in the UI. One such example is maximum character length, defined using the `@Length` annotation and reflecting the constraint on the database column.

seam-gen can also identify foreign key relationships between tables and use them to establish associations between the corresponding entities. On the one hand, these relationships are used to display child collections on the detail screens, such as the set of holes associated with a course. The entity editor also supports the selection of a parent entity when adding or updating a record. For instance, the `Course` entity has a foreign key relationship to the `Facility` entity. At the bottom of the editor screen is a tab pane that shows the current facility selection—if one has been selected—and provides a button to allow you to select a different facility. Clicking this button takes you to the facility listing page. In the table of facilities, the action in the last column has changed from *View* to *Select*. Clicking one of these links takes you back to the course editor, which now reflects your selection. Being able to satisfy the entity relationships in the editor is critical. Without this feature, the edit functionality would be severely crippled.

I don't know about you, but I'm pretty impressed. This application satisfies just about every requirement for the golf course directory and you haven't touched a line of code. With all of the extra time, you may be tempted to start daydreaming about your golf weekend again or head out for one last round at the range. Well, don't head out just yet. You have some work to do to clean up the application so that it's presentable. The reverse engineering does a pretty good job, but it isn't always perfect. To take the prototype the last mile, you're going to customize seam-gen so that it produces an application that is ready for the sales team to start gawking over.

Figure 2.12   The course editor enforcing a number value for the `yearBuilt` field. Validations occur in real time using Ajax.

2.5.2 *Guiding the reverse-engineering process*

Hibernate's reverse-engineering tool is very capable of interpreting what the database schema has to say about the entity relationships. But it can't read what is not there and it can't do much about poorly named columns. For example, the property for men's par on the `Hole` entity is `mPar`, which is a rather cryptic name. The relative position of a tee set is represented by the `pos` property on the `TeeSet` entity, another name lacking clarity. These names are a reflection of abbreviated column names. As the saying goes, "garbage in, garbage out." What's worse is the situation where the information isn't in the database at all. If a foreign key is missing in the table, seam-gen can't make the leap that the table is related to another. Thus, the corresponding entities won't be linked and that means you won't get any of the support in the UI that you observed during the walkthrough.

   Both of the shortcomings just cited can be corrected by tuning the Hibernate reverse-engineering configuration. Despite its long, foreboding name, the configuration is quite straightforward. Its purpose is to tweak the decisions made by seam-gen when generating the entity classes. These adjustments then affect all the downstream UI code generation. Using the reverse-engineering configuration, you can make any of the following adjustments:

- Customize a property name on an entity class
- Customize the Java type of a property on an entity class
- Change the mapping between SQL column type and Java property type globally
- Exclude tables from participating in code generation
- Establish an entity relationship that isn't represented by a foreign key
- Exclude the reverse mapping of an entity relationship
- Enable generation of the `toString()` and `hashCode()` methods
- Add extra code and imports to the generated class

Let's apply customization to clean up the prototype application using the `<table>` element. This element can be used to fix the problematic property names as well as add some convenience methods to the entity classes that will be useful later on. The reverse-engineering configuration file that seam-gen uses is resources/seam-gen.reveng.xml inside the generated project. Listing 2.4 shows the contents of this file populated with the customizations just mentioned.

Listing 2.4   Customizes property names of entity classes and adds extra methods

```
<?xml version="1.0" encoding="UTF-8"?>
<!DOCTYPE hibernate-reverse-engineering SYSTEM
  "http://hibernate.sourceforge.net/hibernate-reverse-engineering-3.0.dtd">
<hibernate-reverse-engineering>
  <table name="HOLE">                          ⟵── Customizes the HOLE table mapping
    <column name="M_PAR" property="mensPar"/>        ⟵
    <column name="L_PAR" property="ladiesPar"/>            Maps
    <column name="M_HANDICAP" property="mensHandicap"/>    nonabbreviated
    <column name="L_HANDICAP" property="ladiesHandicap"/>  property name
  </table>
```

```
  <table name="TEE_SET">
    <meta attribute="extra-import">        Adds imports to
      javax.persistence.Transient          support custom code
    </meta>
    <meta attribute="class-code">          Appends custom code
@Transient                                 to generated class
public int getFrontNineDistance() {
    int distance = 0;
    for (Tee tee : tees) {
        if (tee.getHole().getNumber() &lt;= 9) {
            distance += tee.getDistance();
        }
    }
    return distance;
}

@Transient
public int getBackNineDistance() {
    int distance = 0;
    for ( Tee tee : tees ) {
        if ( tee.getHole().getNumber() > 9 ) {
            distance += tee.getDistance();
        }
    }
    return distance;
}
    </meta>
    <column name="POS" property="position"/>
    <column name="M_SLOPE_RATING" property="mensSlopeRating"/>
    <column name="M_COURSE_RATING" property="mensCourseRating"/>
    <column name="L_SLOPE_RATING" property="ladiesSlopeRating"/>
    <column name="L_COURSE_RATING" property="ladiesCourseRating"/>
  </table>
</hibernate-reverse-engineering>
```

When you're done customizing, you can run `seam generate restart` to apply the changes. Please note that running `generate` will clobber any changes you previously made to the generated files. Thus, you need to be cautious about enhancing the application if you plan on executing the reverse engineering again. One way to avoid losing the customizations to entity classes is to define the extra class code in the reverse-engineering configuration, as shown in listing 2.4. You also have the option of tweaking the seam-gen templates to achieve the output you desire.

Instead of running the code generation full scale, you can split the code generation into two steps. As of Seam 2.0.1.GA, the `generate` command is a combination of the `generate-model` and `generate-ui` commands. You can run `generate-model` to incrementally develop the JPA entity classes and then run `generate-ui` once you've tweaked the domain model to your liking. You can even skip `generate-model` altogether and simply use `generate-ui` to build a CRUD user interface from an existing set of JPA entity classes[8] that reside under the src/model tree.

---

[8] If you're working without an existing database schema, you can set the Hibernate flag **hibernate. hbm2ddl.auto** to **create-drop**, **create**, or **update** to have the database schema autogenerated when the application starts. The first two options will also execute custom SQL in the import.sql file.

DEALING WITH LEGACY DATABASES

Code generation customization is useful when you find yourself having to reverse-engineer a much larger, perhaps more loosely defined database than the one prepared for the Open 18 prototype application. Faced with this task, you may need to use only portions of the schema or simply exclude temporary tables. The reverse-engineering tool offers the `<table-filter>` element to satisfy this requirement. The `<table-filter>` accepts a schema name and a table name, which it uses in a `LIKE` clause to locate tables in the database. You can use the string `.*` in the name, which is replaced with `%` when the lookup is executed to allow for a fuzzy search. If you set the `exclude` attribute on `<table-filter>` to false, then the filter works by including tables from an empty set. Otherwise, the table filter excludes tables from the full set of tables.

Legacy databases tend to lack consistent naming. For instance, you may encounter the need to specify a name for the generated entity class if the table name is abbreviated or includes an unnecessary prefix. It's also possible that the database is missing foreign keys, in which case you must specify the entity relationship explicitly. These two changes can be made using additional elements within the `<table>` node.

The configuration in listing 2.5 presents an example of how to work around the challenges just described for a hypothetical golf equipment database.

Listing 2.5   Filters tables and establishes missing relationships

```xml
<?xml version="1.0" encoding="UTF-8"?>
<!DOCTYPE hibernate-reverse-engineering SYSTEM
  "http://hibernate.sourceforge.net/hibernate-reverse-engineering-3.0.dtd">
<hibernate-reverse-engineering>

  <table-filter
    match-schema="EQUIPMENT" match-name="PRDCT" exclude="false"/>
  <table-filter
    match-schema="EQUIPMENT" match-name="MFR" exclude="false"/>
  <table-filter
    match-schema="EQUIPMENT" match-name="EQ_TYP" exclude="false"/>

  <table name="EQ_TYP" class="org.open18.model.EquipmentType"/>

  <table name="PRDCT" class="org.open18.model.Product">
    <foreign-key foreign-table="MFR">
      <column-ref local-column="MFR_ID" foreign-column="ID"/>
    </foreign-key>
    <foreign-key foreign-table="EQ_TYP">
      <column-ref local-column="EQ_TYP_ID" foreign-column="ID"/>
    </foreign-key>
  </table>

  <table name="MFR" class="org.open18.model.Manufacturer"/>

</hibernate-reverse-engineering>
```

The goal of this section was not to cover the reverse engineering exhaustively, but to introduce you to it and inform you of the fact that it can help you fine-tune your application. There are a handful of features that were not highlighted here, so I encourage you to do some more digging, starting with the Hibernate tools reference documentation.[9] Even then, there are still some areas where the reverse engineering comes up short when handling advanced mappings such as embeddable entities, enums, and entity inheritance.

If you're still not pleased with the classes that the reverse-engineering tool creates, you can further customize them by modifying the FreeMarker templates used to construct them. Hibernate includes an entire reverse-engineering API that you can tap into during this process. The templates it uses reside in the seam-gen/pojo directory. There, you'll find a small set of customizations to support the seam-gen tasks. Hibernate falls back on its own default template if the one it's looking for is not present in this directory. Chapter 2 of Java Persistence with Hibernate has an excellent section covering reverse engineering customizations.

Once you're satisfied with the entity model that seam-gen creates, you're ready to move into the development phase. Because you don't know anything about the structure of the project that seam-gen has created, you may feel uneasy about this task. Rest assured that seam-gen has prepared a well-organized source tree for you. I'll now help you become acquainted with that structure.

2.5.3 *Exploring the structure of the generated project*

One of the difficult parts of starting with a project-generation tool is becoming familiar with the layout that it leaves behind. A period of adjustment is to be expected. It's akin to inheriting someone else's code. In this section, we explore the code that seam-gen leaves you with and how the generated project can stand on its own without seam-gen's reigns.

PROJECT LAYOUT

The layout of a seam-gen project isn't what you might consider standard, nor does it follow the popular Maven 2 structure. However, the structure does strike a nice balance between the multiple masters that it serves. It is capable of

- Building from the command line
- Hooking into the IDE build cycle
- Running integration tests in an embedded Java EE environment
- Performing incremental hot deployment to the application server

A select set of files and directories in a seam-gen WAR project are shown in table 2.5. This table will help you become better acquainted with the project structure that seam-gen creates for you, but there's still much to learn, so don't get caught up trying to understand every file and directory right now. Note that several of the paths use a wildcard (*) to indicate the presence of multiple files of the same type.

I want to draw your attention to the persistence-*-war.xml and open18-*-ds.xml file sets, because they will be most relevant in the early stages of working with the project. There's an instance of each file per deployment profile. At build time, the file from the persistence-*-war.xml set that matches the current deployment profile is

---

[9] http://www.hibernate.org/hib_docs/tools/reference/en/html/reverseengineering.html

Table 2.5   Select files and directories in a seam-gen WAR project

File or directory in project	Purpose
bootstrap/	Embedded JBoss configuration for tests
deployed-jars.list	Specifies which JAR files to package in the archive
exploded-archives/	Exploded Java EE archive assembly area
lib/	Library dependencies for build and deployment
lib/test	Embedded JBoss libraries for tests
nbproject/	NetBeans project files
resources/META-INF/persistence-*-war.xml	JPA persistence unit descriptors
resources/WEB-INF/components.xml	Seam component descriptor
resources/WEB-INF/pages.xml	Seam page descriptor
resources/components.properties	Replacement properties for Ant-style tokens
resources/import-*.sql	Database build scripts and seed data
resources/messages_*.properties	Internationalization messages
resources/open18-*-ds.xml	JBoss data source descriptor (database connection)
resources/seam-gen.reveng.xml	Hibernate reverse-engineering configuration
resources/seam.properties	Component configuration properties
resources/security.drl	Drools security rules
src/action/	Classes that can be hot-deployed at runtime
src/model/	Classes that cannot be hot-deployed at runtime
src/test/	Test classes and test suite configurations
view/*.page.xml	Fine-grained Seam page descriptors
view/*.xhtml	Facelets composition templates (JSF views)
.classpath | explode.launch | .project | .settings/	Eclipse project files
build.properties, build-*.properties	Ant build properties and overrides per profile
build.xml	Ant build file
hibernate-console.properties | open18.launch	JBossTools Hibernate Console configuration

renamed to persistence.xml and moved to the classpath of the exploded archive. This file is the JPA persistence unit descriptor, but also hosts various Hibernate settings since Hibernate is the default JPA provider used in seam-gen projects. You'll learn about Java persistence in chapter 8. Accordingly, the file from the open18-*-ds.xml set that matches the current deployment profile is renamed to open18-ds.xml and moved to the JBoss AS deployment folder. This file is the JCA DataSource descriptor and is where the database connection profiles for the various deployment environments are specified.

An EAR project differs from the WAR structure by only a couple of files. The most notable differences appear in the exploded-archives directory during packaging of the archive, which is not evident by looking at the project structure alone. To aid in the packaging of an EAR, the following four additional files appear in an EAR project:

- resources/META-INF/application.xml
- resources/META-INF/ejb-jar.xml
- deployed-jars-war.list (used in place of deployed-jars.list)
- deployed-jars-ear.list (used in place of deployed-jars.list)

The second file is important to Seam because it registers the Seam interceptor on EJB 3 components. You may also notice that the JBoss AS descriptor for a web application, resources/WEB-INF/jboss-web.xml, is replaced with the equivalent descriptor for an enterprise application, resources/WEB-INF/jboss-app.xml.

Although the WAR and EAR project structures are nearly identical, the logic in the build script that packages the archives varies widely. Thus, once you choose a Java EE archive type for a seam-gen project, there's no automated step to switch. If it were necessary for you to perform this migration, you'd have to replace the build.xml with the build.xml from the other project type and add or remove the extra files just described.

BOOTSTRAPPING THE DATABASE

Before moving on, I want to mention an important Hibernate configuration setting, `hibernate.hbm2ddl.auto`, which controls whether Hibernate will attempt to create or modify the database schema when initialized. The default value is `validate`. Table 2.6 shows all the possible values for this property. If the database is slated to be created when Hibernate initializes, the seed data in the import.sql at the root of the classpath is loaded into the database automatically. The import.sql file is derived from the import-<profile>.sql file according to the build profile. The Open 18 application works with an existing database, so we want to be sure not to destroy it. In our scenario, the best choice is `update` since it allows the database to evolve as we add new entities to the application.

Table 2.6   Possible values for hibernate.hbm2ddl.auto, set in the persistence-*.xml files

Value	Affect on startup	Affect on shutdown	Imports seed data from import.sql?
create	Creates database (destroys it if it exists)	None	Yes
create-drop	Creates database (destroys it if it exists)	Destroys database	Yes
update	Updates database to reflect changes to mappings	None	No
validate	Validates database from mappings	None	No
none	None	None	No

Getting to know the project structure is going to take some time, but don't worry. You have the whole book to become familiar with how to use and enhance a seam-gen project. Regardless of whether you use an EAR project or a WAR project, the project is built and deployed the same way. That brings us to our next topic: how seam-gen projects are built.

ANT BUILD TARGETS

Ant has been mentioned throughout this chapter, but I haven't provided definitive information on how it is being used. The seam command operates using Ant. Projects that seam-gen creates are also built using Ant. Once the project is generated, seam-gen remotely controls the project's build script to compile, test, and deploy the application. Two Ant scripts are at work here: the one used by the seam-gen script and the one in the root of the project directory.

Project-specific seam-gen commands are passed down to the project's Ant build, where they are executed, as shown in the left side of figure 2.13. This arrangement works as long as seam-gen is still "connected" to the project—meaning the settings in seam-gen/build.properties haven't been modified since the project was generated. seam-gen becomes "disconnected" from the project the minute you use it to create a different project. When you do, it switches its control to the new project. Once you alter the seam-gen settings, the path on the left side can no longer be used.

As it turns out, the Ant build script in the root of the project can stand on its own. It supports all the same project-specific commands as seam-gen. Thus, you can call the build script directly, as shown in the right side of figure 2.13.

You must have Ant available on your path in order to execute the project's Ant targets without the assistance of the seam script. Appendix A has information about how to install Ant. By moving to the project's build, you can execute all of the build-related targets that were available with the seam script. These targets include test, deploy, undeploy, explode, restart, unexplode, clean, and archive. The only change in how you run these targets is that you prefix the command with ant rather than seam. For instance, to deploy the application as an exploded archive, you run ant explode. You cannot, however, run any of the code-generation commands. You have to complete all

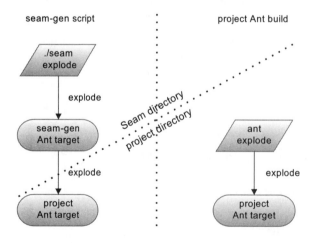

Figure 2.13 The seam-gen script invokes Ant targets in the project's build. This image shows the difference between executing the explode command from seam-gen and executing the explode target directly from the project.

of that work using the seam script before you remove its reigns on your project. Just remember, you use seam when you're in the Seam distribution directory and ant when you're in the project directory.

2.6   Rapidly developing a seam-gen project

One of the best features of seam-gen is that sets up a build that supports a continuous development cycle. By that, I mean that you can make changes to the application and have them immediately swept away to the server. If you choose the exploded archive format, you can take advantage of seam-gen's incremental hot deployment to JBoss AS. This feature publishes the changes to the project source files so they take effect immediately in the application, which is the focus of this section.

> ### What about other application servers?
>
> Out of the box, seam-gen is set up to deploy incrementally to JBoss AS. Other application servers feature incremental hot deployment to an exploded archive as well, and there is nothing preventing you from modifying the build script to support those servers. In fact, several initiatives are under way to improve seam-gen's application server support. You can find instructions on how to use seam-gen with alternative application servers in the Seam reference documentation and on the Seam community site.

This section begins by clarifying what is meant by incremental hot deployment, how it can speed up development, and how to get the IDE to handle the last remaining bit of manual work necessary to make development truly continuous.

2.6.1   Incremental hot deployment

The term *incremental hot deployment* means that the deployed application can be updated while it's running with the latest changes from development. However, what this term doesn't tell you is what types of files can be redeployed and what effect they will have on the application—meaning, what really qualifies for "instant change"?

The reason that support for incremental hot deployment is so different from one application server to the next is because the Java EE specification doesn't address this feature, resulting in no real standard. Essentially, it's an extension to Java EE; even then it only applies to development. Unfortunately, that's what is most important to us developers. What I find most frustrating is that because there are no clear bounds on what can be called incremental hot deployment, the term is often thrown around as marketing jargon to draw you to a vendor. Let's expose the frauds and see if seam-gen deploying to JBoss AS can meet our agile development demands.

This section clarifies which files participate in incremental hot deployment in a seam-gen project, when and under what conditions, and what happens when the files get deployed. We're looking for the answers to two questions: *How hot is "hot"?* and *Does Seam deliver the promise of "instant change"?*

SYNCHRONIZING STATIC RESOURCES

Anytime you're working with an exploded archive, regardless of whether you're using the EAR or WAR package format, you can push out changes made to static resources —stylesheets, graphics, and JavaScript—by running `seam explode`. The Ant build properly detects which files have been added or modified since the last run and copies them to the exploded archive directory on the server.

When working with static resources, the application server is merely acting as a web server. It reads the contents of the static resource from the file system and serves it to the browser in response to an incoming request for the resource. The application doesn't have to reload to serve a static resource that has changed. If the server supports runtime JSP compilation, which JBoss AS enables by default, the server will also recompile JSP files that have changed without causing the application to reload.

While synchronization of static resources and JSP files is certainly nice, I don't consider it enough to warrant the label *incremental hot deployment* as some application server vendors like to think. To me, it's just a baseline. If a build cannot, at the very least, handle this scenario, then it isn't much of a build. The absence of this feature puts an exploded archive on par with a packaged archive.

Let's take it a step further and look at two additional web resources that can be hot deployed in seam-gen projects.

INSTANT JSF

A majority of your time working in the view will be spent developing JSF pages. You certainly want those changes to be picked up as well. If you're using JSP for your JSF pages, you're already covered. However, projects created by seam-gen use Facelets as the JSF view technology. Facelets will not read a view template more than one time unless it's running in development mode. This mode is the complement to runtime JSP compilation. To enable development mode, you just need to ensure that the build-<profile>.properties file for your profile has the `debug` property set to true:

```
debug=true
```

When the build is run, this property will be applied to the web.xml descriptor, setting the `facelets.DEVELOPMENT` servlet context parameter in the web.xml descriptor to true:

```
<context-param>
  <param-name>facelets.DEVELOPMENT</param-name>
  <param-value>true</param-value>
</context-param>
```

To test that this works, use your file explorer to locate the project directory. Open the view/home.xhtml page in a text editor. With the file open, replace the bulleted list of Seam benefits with a description of the Open 18 application (you can make it up). When you're done, run `seam explode`, and confirm that the change was picked up by refreshing the home page. You should also be able to verify that the server log is silent and doesn't report a reload of the application. Feel free to try out other changes.

The debug property has another affect. It controls whether Seam is running in debug mode. When debug mode is active, Seam will detect changes to the page descriptor files (pages.xml and *.page.xml) and reload their definitions while the application is still running. Page descriptors are a substitute for most of faces-config.xml. They provide navigation, page-oriented actions, exception handling, security, and conversation controls for JSF requests. Since they are capable of being hot deployed, all of the aforementioned features can be modified without having to restart the application. You'll learn about page descriptors in chapter 3.

Even with the incremental hot deployment of static resources, Facelets view templates, and page descriptors, an important piece is still missing: Java classes.

THE HOLY GRAIL: HOT REDEPLOYMENT OF JAVA CLASSES

Seam doesn't draw the line at web resources. The Seam developers recognized that it's highly unlikely that you'll make a change to a JSF page without also needing to make a change to the Java class or classes used by the page. There is a strong bond between the two. Thus, only being able to deploy web resources offers a false promise of "instant change."

Seam goes the extra mile to enable live development by using an isolated development classloader that supports incremental hot deployment of JavaBean components. This classloader is used if the following conditions are satisfied:

- Seam is running in debug mode.
- jboss-seam-debug.jar is on the runtime classpath.
- SeamFilter is registered in web.xml.
- The application is using the WAR archive format.

The first two conditions are controlled by the debug flag just covered. You learn how the SeamFilter gets registered in the next chapter. Java classes eligible for hot deployment must reside in the src/action directory of the project. The classes in the src/model directory don't participate in this classloader and thus can't be hot deployed. Seam supports hot deployment of both Java and Groovy classes, though with a slightly different approach.

The seam explode command compiles Java classes in the src/action directory of the project and moves them to WEB-INF/dev in the exploded WAR archive, the root of the development classloader. Seam leverages the Groovy classloader to load Groovy scripts dynamically, so the explode command copies Groovy scripts in src/action to the development classpath directly, without compiling them. When Seam detects that a file has been changed or added to WEB-INF/dev, it initiates a new component scan on this directory. During the scan, components that were previously loaded from this directory are removed and the new components are instantiated. Any component properties defined in components.xml or seam.properties are then applied to the new components, which you learn about in chapter 5.

Seeing is believing, so let's give this feature a try. Referring back to the course listing screen, notice that the courses are listed in the order that they are fetched from the database, which isn't very intuitive. How about we change the default sort property? To do that, we need to add an order clause to the query that's used to back this table.

Once again, use your file explorer to navigate to the project directory. Open src/action/org/open18/action/CourseList.java in your editor and add the getOrder() method shown in listing 2.6. This method contributes the order clause to the Java Persistence Query Language (JPQL) query that's constructed by this class. If an order hasn't been specified explicitly, we instruct the query to sort the courses by name, in ascending order. CourseList inherits from EntityQuery, a parent class in the Seam Application Framework that acts as a data provider. You'll learn more about the Seam Application Framework in chapter 10.

Listing 2.6 Method that sets the sort order for the course list

```
public String getOrder() {
    if (super.getOrder() == null) {
        setOrder("name asc");
    }
    return super.getOrder();
}
```

Save the CourseList class file and run seam explode to migrate your changes to JBoss AS. Reload the page in your browser and you should see that the list is sorted based on the name of the course. If you take a look at your JBoss AS server log, you should see messages appearing similar to listing 2.7. Note that JBoss AS doesn't reload the application. What you see here is Seam dumping the classes in the development classloader and rereading the components into memory.

Listing 2.7 Incremental redeployment as reported by the development classloader

```
00:00:00,385 INFO  [Initialization] redeploying
00:00:00,395 INFO  [Scanner] scanning:
/home/twoputt/opt/jboss-as-4.2.2.GA/server/default/deploy
  ➥/open18.war/WEB-INF/dev
00:00:00,424 INFO  [Initialization] Installing components...
...
00:00:00,720 INFO  [Component] Component: courseList, scope: EVENT,
type: JAVA_BEAN, class: org.open18.action.CourseList
...
00:00:00,491 INFO  [Initialization] done redeploying
```

Pretty cool, huh? The best part is that the application experiences minimal disruption. Your HTTP session remains intact and therefore you should be able to continue testing the interface without starting over from the beginning.

I'll agree that we still haven't quite achieved "instant change," if you count from the time you saved the file, because it's still necessary to run the command seam explode. You'll soon learn how to get the IDE to handle this task for you. Assuming we have the IDE integration setup, the development classloader delivers on the promise of instant change for *Java* files to complement the instant change already available for *non-Java* resources. Few Java web frameworks offer such comprehensive incremental hot deployment capabilities. It is by far one of the coolest, and competitive, features of Seam. (Grails is an alternative framework that offers incremental hot deployment.)

There are some limits to the hot deployment feature. Seam cannot hot-deploy any of the following:

- Classes outside of the src/action directory
- JPA entity classes
- EJB session bean components
- Seam components defined in components.xml

After making changes to any of the files just listed, you must run the following command to see the changes take effect:

```
seam restart
```

In addition, hot deployable components can't be used by classes outside of the development classloader, nor can they be referenced in the components.xml descriptor.

The incremental hot deployment features discussed in this section are summarized in table 2.7. This table lists the conditions that must be true for the resource to be eligible for redeployment.

Table 2.7 Incremental hot deployment resources when using an exploded archive

Resource	Available with WAR	Available with EAR	Debug mode required?
Images, CSS, JavaScript, static HTML, JSP	✓	✓	No
Facelets view templates, page descriptors (pages.xml or *.page.xml)	✓	✓	Yes
Java classes in src/action	✓		Yes
Groovy scripts in src/action	✓		Yes
Java classes or Groovy script in src/model or components defined in component descriptors (components.xml or *.component.xml)	No	No	N/A

Seam developers are working on expanding the capability of the development classloader to be able to handle all Java types. It's just a matter of time before all changes in the Java code can be seen immediately in the running application. But even without these improvements, the incremental hot deployment feature puts the productivity of Seam development on a par with PHP and Ruby development.

The multitude of command-line tasks that you have to perform are likely taking their toll on you. Having to navigate the file system in order to edit the project files hasn't been fun either. The goal of the next section is to show how to bring the project into an IDE so that you can leverage the IDE to customize your application without having the burden of executing the seam-gen commands manually.

2.6.2 *Accelerating development by using an IDE*

Importing a preexisting project into an IDE can be like trying to force a square peg into a round hole. It takes time to enlighten the IDE about the structure of the project. seam-gen removes this hurdle by generating ready-made project files for the two most popular open source Java IDEs: Eclipse and NetBeans. As a result, importing the project becomes an effortless task.

Although seam-gen generates the IDE project files automatically, the Ant build is the key to IDE portability. seam-gen hooks the Ant targets into the build life cycle of the IDE to leverage the auto-build feature to make the instant change feature even more instant. Let's start by importing the project into Eclipse and exploring how the Ant targets are hooked into Eclipse's build.

IMPORTING THE PROJECT INTO ECLIPSE

seam-gen lays down the very same project files that Eclipse creates when you use the New Project wizard, as well as a handful of additional configurations, shown here:

- ❶ .project
- ❷ .classpath
- ❸ explode.launch
- ❹ debug-jboss.launch
- ❺ open18.launch

When you point Eclipse at the project folder, Eclipse immediately recognizes it as one of its own projects. Eclipse is blissfully unaware of that fact that it was not the originator.

If you've explored the contents of a project managed by Eclipse, you should recognize the main Eclipse project file ❶ and the classpath definition file ❷. The explode launch configuration ❸ hooks the execution of Ant targets into the Eclipse build cycle, thus allowing Eclipse to assume all responsibility of executing the Ant targets as part of its automatic, continuous compilation cycle. You see this integration in action once you pull the project into your Eclipse workspace. A launch configuration for attaching the debugger to an external instance of JBoss AS ❹ and a launch configuration for using the Hibernate Console from the JBossTools Eclipse plug-in ❺ are also created. I don't cover these last two configurations here, but you can find additional information about them in the Hibernate Tools reference documentation.[10]

To perform the import, start Eclipse and choose File > Import. When the Import dialog box appears, select the Existing Projects into Workspace option, which you can quickly find if you filter the options by typing the first few characters of the option name into the Select an Import Source field. Click Next to begin the import process.

---

[10] http://www.hibernate.org/hib_docs/tools/reference/en/html_single/

In the dialog box that appears, click the Browse button adjacent to the Select Root Directory radio button. When the native file selection window appears, locate the project directory. If you're following along with the example, the location of the project is /home/twoputt/projects. Figure 2.14 shows the Import dialog box acknowledging open18 as a valid project. To edit the project in place, ensure that the Copy Projects into Workspace check box remains unselected. If you were to enable this option, Eclipse would make a copy of the project and put it in the Eclipse workspace directory—typically ${user.home}/.eclipse/workspace.

Figure 2.14 The Eclipse import wizard identifying the seam-gen project as an existing Eclipse project and a candidate for import

When you click Finish, Eclipse incorporates the project into your Eclipse workspace and lists it in the Project Navigator view. In the console, you should notice a flurry of activity as the project builds for the first time. If you don't, then you likely have the auto-build feature disabled and you'll need to run the build manually.

That's it! You have the project running in Eclipse. Now you can get serious about developing the source code. To aid in development, the Seam source code has been attached to the Seam library in the Eclipse project. That means for any class in the Seam API you get context-sensitive JavaDoc, you can view the class source, and you can step into the class during a debug session. The other benefit of having the project in Eclipse is the integration between the Ant build script and Eclipse's build life cycle. Let's explore how that works and what it means for development.

HOOKING INTO ECLIPSE'S AUTO-BUILD

Before launching into a technical discussion, I want to give you a feel for how Eclipse lightens the development load by initiating the project's incremental hot deployment facility. In the process, we'll add some color to the application.

Golf scorecards are filled with color. In particular, each tee set has a color associated with it. Yet our golf course directory is looking pretty monotone. It's time to give it some flair. In the tee sets table on the course detail page, shown back in figure 2.9, the color column simply displays the name of the color. A nice improvement would be to have this column render a colored boxed instead.

In Eclipse, navigate to the view/Course.xhtml file and open it. You can also get there by using the Ctrl+Shift+R key combination and typing in the name of the file in the input box. When the file opens, look for the component tag `<rich:tab label="teeSets">`. Next, find the `<h:outputText>` component tag that uses the #{teeSet.color} expression. You should expect to find this tag in the third `<h:column>` of the `<rich:dataTable>` that is contained in that teeSets tab. You're going to change this column to render a colorized box rather than the name of the color, but still use the color in the title attribute for Section 508 compliance:

```
<rich:tab label="teeSets">
...
  <rich:dataTable id="teeSetsTable" var="teeSet"
  value="#{courseHome.teeSets}"
  rendered="#{not empty courseHome.teeSets}"
  rowClasses="rvgRowOne,rvgRowTwo">
    ...
  <h:column>
    <f:facet name="header">color</f:facet>
    <div title="#{teeSet.color}"
      style="background-color: #{teeSet.color}; height: 1em;
➥width: 1em; outline: 1px solid black; margin: 0 auto;"/>
  </h:column>
    ...
  </rich:dataTable>
...
</rich:tab>
```

NOTE A better approach is to create CSS for the colorized box and then reference the class in the template, but that goes beyond the point of this exercise.

When you save the file, you should be able to immediately check it in your browser, thanks to incremental hot deployment. You don't even have to refresh the page for the change to take effect. Just click the facility tab and then the teeSets tab again. The contents of the tab are retrieved from the server using an Ajax request. Ladies and gentlemen, we have color! The colorized tee boxes are shown in figure 2.15.

Notice that you did not have to execute ant explode for your change to take effect. How is it that Eclipse knows to run this Ant target? As mentioned earlier, seam-gen configures Eclipse to fire Ant targets during various stages in the Eclipse build life cycle. The configuration of Eclipse's build is shown in figure 2.16.

The screen on the left confirms that the Ant launch configuration, identified by the Ant icon next to the name, is activated after Eclipse's native Java Builder. The screen on the right shows the details of the Ant launch configuration. The Targets tab

id	color	ladiesCourseRating	ladiesSlopeRating	mensCourseRating	mensSlopeRating	name	position	action
39	■	70.1	122.0	65.0	103.0	Brick	5	View
37	■			71.6	125.0	Copper	3	View
38	□	74.3	133.0	68.5	113.0	Limestone	4	View
35	■			75.8	135.0	Slag	1	View
36	■			73.4	131.0	Gold	2	View

Add teeSet

Figure 2.15 The list of tee sets for a course. The value of the color property is being used to display a colorized box.

shows the Ant targets that are executed during each stage of the Eclipse build life cycle. You can use this screen to change the targets as you see fit.

Notice that the combination of `explode` and `buildtest` is executed whenever Eclipse issues an auto-build—also referred to as an incremental build. When the Eclipse auto-build runs, it performs the equivalent work of running `ant explode buildtest` from the command line in the project directory. The auto-build runs whenever a file in the editor is saved. All you have to do is save the file to have your changes carried to the exploded archive on the JBoss server. Eclipse won't slack off while you're editing. When you really get going, you can keep Eclipse in a constant build loop. I'm sure you'll agree that keeping Eclipse busy is better than having to switch to the command line and repeatedly type `ant explode`.

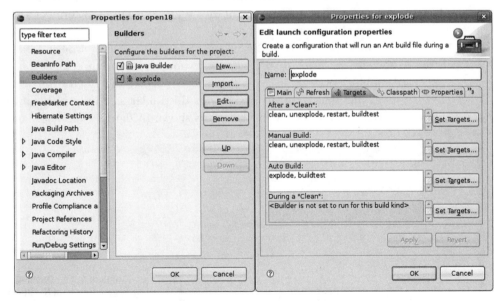

Figure 2.16 The external tool build configuration for Eclipse that seam-gen installs to execute Ant targets during the Eclipse build process. On the left is the list of Eclipse builders. The right screen shows the details of the Ant builder.

Earlier, I promised to relieve you of your command-line duties and fully deliver on the promise of instant change. There you have it! Eclipse is doing your dirty work. Change, save, view in browser, and repeat. That goes for web resources and JavaBean components. No marketing jargon here. The only thing you need now is for Eclipse and seam-gen to write the business logic for you. Of course, if that were true, we'd be out of a job.

Eclipse isn't the only way to achieve instant build. NetBeans works just as well, if not better. Let's give NetBeans a try to contrast it with Eclipse and help you decide which environment you prefer.

IMPORTING THE PROJECT INTO NETBEANS

seam-gen also generates project files for NetBeans. The steps for importing the project into NetBeans do not differ all that much from Eclipse, though the way the project build is integrated is quite different. NetBeans has native Ant integration, which means that the Ant build *is* the NetBeans build. You'll witness the benefits of this as you step through this section. The screenshots in this section were taken using Net-Beans 6, but NetBeans 5.5 will work just as well.

The NetBeans project files that get put into the nbfolder of the project are as follows:

❶ project.xml

❷ ide-file-targets.xml

❸ debug-jboss.properties

The file project.xml ❶ is the main NetBeans project file. It manages the classpath and the mapping between NetBeans build targets and Ant targets from the project build. The other two files, ❷ and ❸, augment the build with a target to connect a debug session to a running JBoss server.

To begin the import, start NetBeans and choose File > Open Project. When the file browser appears, navigate to the /home/twoputt/projects directory. You'll notice either an emblem or a different colored icon (depending on the version of Net-Beans), indicating that NetBeans recognizes this folder as a valid NetBeans project. Select the folder and click Open Project, as shown in figure 2.17. There are added

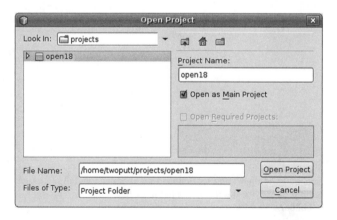

Figure 2.17 Opening a seam-gen project in NetBeans. The icon color indicates that NetBeans recognizes the folder as a valid project.

benefits if you make this the main project, so go ahead and leave the Open as Main Project option checked.

Notice that I've avoided using the word "import" when describing how to bring the project into NetBeans. Unlike Eclipse, NetBeans does not maintain a "workspace" of projects. Therefore, opening a project is similar to opening a document in a word processor.

AUTHOR The NetBeans strategy for opening projects makes more sense to me.
NOTE The Eclipse workspace quickly becomes littered with projects and I feel like a bad owner when I have to kick them out. Closing a project folder in NetBeans just seems more humane, making me feel comfortable with keeping my project navigator in order.

You can now work with the project in NetBeans.

LEVERAGING NETBEANS' NATIVE ANT INTEGRATION

As I mentioned, NetBeans uses the Ant build script as its build life cycle. NetBeans is just a UI wrapper that can execute the build targets. Thus, the project created by seam-gen is right at home in the NetBeans environment.

To dig into the extensiveness of this integration, begin by right-clicking on the open18 node in the Project view and selecting Properties. The Build Script property in the Java Source pane, shown in figure 2.18, acknowledges that the Ant build script is a first-class citizen in the NetBeans project. The Build and Run pane, also shown in figure 2.18, reveals how the Ant targets are mapped to each stage of the build cycle in NetBeans. Contrast this approach with the custom builder that's required to tie Ant into the Eclipse build cycle. My feeling is that the NetBeans integration makes managing a seam-gen project more straightforward.

The integration goes one level deeper. The Ant targets that are configured in the Build and Run pane in figure 2.18 are included directly in the context menu, shown in

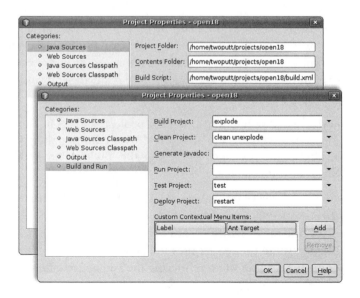

Figure 2.18 The NetBeans Project Properties screens showing the direct integration of the Ant targets from the seam-gen project build

figure 2.19. In the same figure, you see the targets of the build.xml file are shown as child elements of the file node. Although build.xml is not a directory, NetBeans understands the parent-child relationship between the Ant script and its targets.

Notice the Debug item on the context menu. If you have the JBoss server running in debug mode, this target allows you to attach the NetBeans debugger to it. This is interesting because NetBeans uses the same target to debug a remote JBoss server as it does to debug one started from within NetBeans. Eclipse requires two different configurations to accomplish the same set of scenarios.

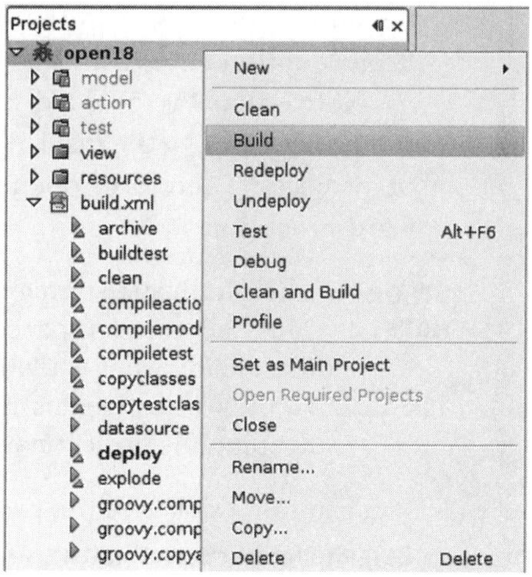

There's an important difference between Eclipse and NetBeans in how the two integrate with Ant. Eclipse ties Ant into its auto-build life cycle, so it fires off the Ant build *every time you save any file* (assuming you have auto-build enabled). If you have an idle computer, Eclipse can give it plenty to chew on while operating in this mode. NetBeans, on the other hand, waits for your instruction to run the Ant targets. I prefer the NetBeans approach. Eclipse, in its auto-build configuration, is just wasting processor cycles with its constant build activity. Watch out when you start Eclipse too, since it will immediately deploy all of your seam-gen projects to JBoss AS. You can remedy these problems in Eclipse by disabling auto-build, but that goes too far because it eliminates all automatic build tasks, including incremental Java compilation.

In NetBeans, if the project is set as the main project, you can build and rebuild using either the build buttons on the main build toolbar or the build keybindings. You'll likely find the keybinding to be the fastest because it avoids use of the mouse. Then it's just a matter of hitting the build key when you're ready to send your changes off to the application server.

TIP The default keybinding for building the main project is F11. On Linux, this keybinding is reserved by the GNOME desktop for toggling full-screen mode. Therefore, you need to remap the Build Main Project action to an alternative key, such as F10.

Let's make a change to the application to see what it is like to develop with this setup. Look back to figure 2.15. Notice that the list of holes and tee sets at the bottom of the course detail screen have one major flaw: they are out of order. For holes, the number property dictates the order, while the tee set uses the position property to maintain order. We need to honor those values when rendering the respective tables.

Figure 2.19 The context menu of a project in NetBeans, which includes items that map directly to Ant targets in the build file created by seam-gen. The build.xml node can also be expanded to reveal all of the available Ant targets.

You can track down the backing value expression of these two tables in view/ Course.xhtml. The list of holes is provided by #{courseHome.teeSet} and the list of tee sets is provided by #{courseHome.holes}. Both of these collections, which reside on the CourseHome class, are converted from a java.util.Set to a java.util.List and then returned. This conversion is necessary since UIData components, such as <h:dataTable>, can't iterate over a java.util.Set. These methods provide a good opportunity to use a Comparator to sort the collections before they are returned.

Fortunately, CourseHome is a Seam component in the src/action directory, which means that it can be hot deployed. Listing 2.8 shows the modified version of the property getter methods that sort the collections before returning them.

Listing 2.8   TeeSet and Hole collections ordered according to golf regulation

```java
public List<Hole> getHoles() {
    if (getInstance() == null) {
        return null;
    }

    List<Hole> holes =
        new ArrayList<Hole>(getInstance().getHoles());
    Collections.sort(holes, new Comparator<Hole>() {
            public int compare(Hole a, Hole b) {
                return Integer.valueOf(a.getNumber())
                    .compareTo(Integer.valueOf(b.getNumber()));
            }
    });

    return holes;
}
public List<TeeSet> getTeeSets() {
    if (getInstance() == null) {
        return null;
    }

    List<TeeSet> teeSets =
        new ArrayList<TeeSet>(getInstance().getTeeSets());
    Collections.sort(teeSets, new Comparator<TeeSet>() {

        public int compare(TeeSet a, TeeSet b) {
            return a.getPosition() == null ||
                b.getPosition() == null ? 0 :
                a.getPosition().compareTo(b.getPosition());
        }

    });

    return teeSets;
}
```

NOTE   A better solution is to specify the sort order globally by adding the @OrderBy JPA annotation to the collection property on the parent entity, Course. The @OrderBy annotation instruments the sort as part of the query so that when the collection is retrieved from the database, it's already sorted. The modification of CourseHome is simply to demonstrate the hot-redeploy feature. A change to an entity class would require an application restart.

Once you've made those changes, hit the build keybinding or right-click on the project's root node and select Build. Behind the scenes, NetBeans will run the `explode` Ant target. To give you a taste of the fruits of your labor, figure 2.20 shows the course detail page with the teeSets tab selected.

facility	holes	teeSets							
id	color	ladiesCourseRating	ladiesSlopeRating	mensCourseRating	mensSlopeRating	name	position	action
35	■			75.8	135.0	Slag	1	View
36	□			73.4	131.0	Gold	2	View
37	■			71.6	125.0	Copper	3	View
38	□	74.3	133.0	68.5	113.0	Limestone	4	View
39	■	70.1	122.0	65.0	103.0	Brick	5	View

Add teeSet

Figure 2.20   The list of tee sets for a course sorted according to the value of the `position` property

Having the project set up in both Eclipse and NetBeans allows it to stand on its own and puts you right where you need to be to start developing significant enhancements to the application and applying refactorings to the code. I chose these two IDEs because seam-gen generates their respective project files, allowing you to import the project into either IDE without having to apply any force. To take a different approach, you could have used the JBossTools plug-in for Eclipse to create a seam-gen project from within the IDE. Unfortunately for NetBeans users, the equivalent plug-in for NetBeans has fallen quite a bit out of date and lacks the true depth of what JBoss-Tools offers. That may make you wonder which IDE is best for you.

CHOOSING AN IDE
You may find it helpful to know which IDE I recommend. As you observed in this section, you can get started using either IDE very quickly. But, if you're on the fence, I find NetBeans easier to get into if you're a new user. It has less clutter and it is geared specifically toward Java EE development out of the box. However, if you're a power user who wants to take advantage of the JBossTools plug-in, you're not afraid to spend time installing various other plug-ins for the better part of a day, and you want every feature under the sun, then Eclipse is the IDE for you. It was once true that Eclipse had much better refactoring support than NetBeans, but even that gap is closing as of NetBeans 6.

There is nothing limiting you from using another IDE to develop a seam-gen project, such as IntelliJ IDEA. You can use IDEA's Eclipse project importer to get started. From there, the knowledge that you gained in this chapter about the Ant-based build will allow you to make the leap to this alternative IDE environment, as well as others.

If you had started from scratch, it could have taken a week or more to get the application to where it is now. Instead, you can start a prototype in the second half of the week and have it done in time to hit the road for your weekend getaway!

2.7 Summary

The Open 18 prototype developed in this chapter is the start of the example application used throughout this book. At the beginning of this chapter, you had an overdue project dropped on your lap just before your vacation. You decided to transfer the burden to seam-gen because of its ability to quickly produce Seam projects, helping you out the door in time for your vacation. This decision paid off, as seam-gen was able to build a working prototype from an existing database schema, complete with JPA entities and a UI capable of listing, sorting, paginating, filtering, persisting, updating, and deleting these entities, in just a couple of hours. It's also good that the interface has a nice look and feel. Even better, you discovered that the project scaffolding and build script are suitable to be used as the foundation of the project long term, most notably because of the instant change feature and its ability to prepare the application for multiple environments. In chapter 4, you'll continue using seam-gen to build new modules from scratch, starting with golfer registration.

This chapter also gave you an overview of the standard Java EE archive formats and how the two options offered by seam-gen affect development. The most compelling feature of the generated project is the incremental hot deployment of static web resources, JSF views (JSP or Facelets) and page descriptors, *and* JavaBean components. Java development can be as productive as any scripting environment. While taking a look around the Open 18 prototype, you saw that not only is it able to read and write database records, it can also display entity relationships. You also learned that validations are interpreted from the database schema and enforced in real time.

Having felt out the prototype, we took a look under the hood to see how it is laid out. We demystified the `seam` script, revealing that it's actually a branded Ant build. You learned that the Ant build is the key to IDE portability. You had the opportunity to import the project into both Eclipse and NetBeans, contrasting the approach that each takes to managing the project.

By far, the best part of seam-gen is not what it creates, but what it enables you to create: a project that you can use to learn about Seam *in action*. While seam-gen prepares you to start developing in Seam, it cannot teach you how to use Seam itself, other than by providing a few examples. You are now ready to begin your journey into the core of Seam: its components, contexts, declarative services, and life cycle.

Part 2

Seam fundamentals

Golf is challenging to players of all skill levels, but it's especially unforgiving to beginners. If you expect to stop by the sporting goods store to pick up a set of clubs, a bag, and a collared shirt, then ride up to the first tee in your golf cart to begin your golfing career, you are in for a big surprise. So are the worms whose heads you try to take off on your first shot, which in golf lingo we call a "worm burner." After barely breaching the boundaries of the tee box, you still have 300-plus yards to travel minus the benefit of using that little wooden tee.

To have a fighting chance at making it to the target, it's essential that you learn the fundamentals of golf. Getting started with a new framework, like Seam, must be handled in the same manner. The prototype application you built in chapter 2 made you look good, but seam-gen carried you most of the way. Without a deeper knowledge of how Seam functions, you aren't going to travel far from the starting point, nor will your application make it off the ground. It's time to step back and take some lessons.

This part gives you a firm understanding of how Seam works. Chapter 3 provides insight into how Seam participates in each request and what Seam does to enhance the JSF life cycle. Seam's essential offering, though, is its contextual component model, which you are introduced to in chapter 4. You learn how a component is born, what it means for a component to be contextual, and how you instantiate and access component instances. Seam encourages the use of annotations to define components, but also allows you to define them in XML, which is covered in chapter 5. You'll discover how to initialize the properties of a component once it's instantiated. With components and contexts down, chapter 6 explains how components interact and communicate through Seam's two inversion of control mechanisms: bijection and events. After reading this part of the book, you'll be perfectly comfortable extending a Seam application. You'll feel empowered by the ease with which you can quickly define components, wire them together, bind them to JSF views, and have complete control over page requests.

The Seam life cycle 3

This chapter covers

- Using Seam to improve JSF
- Navigating between JSF views
- Mapping requests to page actions
- Handling exceptions

There is a stark difference between hitting balls at the driving range and taking your shot out on a golf course. The driving range offers a nice, level surface that's perfect for making square contact with the ball. The golf course surfaces are rarely so ideal. Surface variations include the tee box, the fairway, the rough, the sand trap, from behind a tree, in a creek, and—if you are my brother—on top of a warehouse. The point is, the real world is not as manageable as the practice area.

The JavaServer Faces (JSF) specification lives in the ideal world with driving ranges, where everything works by design. As long as your application doesn't need to pass data across redirects, call EJB 3 session beans from a JSF page, execute actions on an initial request, or execute contextual navigation—to cite several problem cases—JSF appears to be a pro. The JSF component model and event-driven design conveniently mask the underlying HTTP communication between the browser and the server-side logic. Where JSF comes up short is in catering to nonconforming use cases. Unfortunately, the real world is full of nonconformity. To adapt JSF to these less-than-ideal situations, Seam taps into the extension points in the JSF life cycle, putting shape to a more sophisticated request-handling facility known as the Seam life cycle. Seam provides a front controller, advanced page navigation, support for RESTful URLs, and exception handling, which are so integrated with JSF that it's hard to know where JSF ends and where Seam begins.

This chapter sorts out which aspects of JSF Seam keeps and which parts are tossed to the side. By the end of the chapter, you'll have an understanding of the difference between an initial JSF request and a subsequent postback and how Seam weaves its enhancements into both styles of request to form the Seam life cycle. You'll then be ready to learn about Seam components—those are beans for you Spring fans—which are used to control the user interface and respond to actions triggered from it.

NOTE   If you aren't familiar with JSF, you may be concerned that you can't use Seam without JSF experience. Seam doesn't depend on JSF, but you aren't going to appreciate Seam's JSF enhancements, which is the focus of this chapter, without a basic understanding of how JSF works. After all, Seam was developed to provide integration between JSF and EJB 3, and happened to solve shortcomings in JSF along the way. If you aren't familiar with JSF, or its problems, I recommend that you read through the JSF introduction provided in the front of this book before continuing. If you're a quick learner, or have spent enough time in the Java enterprise landscape, you should pick up on JSF in no time. Given that Seam extends beyond the user interface, you can boldly skip this chapter and advance to learning about Seam components and contexts in chapter 4.

Since this chapter focuses on the Seam life cycle, let's begin by looking at how Seam registers itself to participate in both JSF and basic servlet requests.

3.1   *Exploring how Seam participates in a request*

For us to use Seam in an application server environment, it must be hooked into the life cycle of the servlet container. When the application starts, the servlet container bootstraps Seam, at which time Seam loads its contextual container, scans for components, and begins serving out component instances. Once running, the servlet container also notifies Seam when HTTP sessions are opened and closed. Seam also enrolls itself in servlet requests by registering a servlet filter, a servlet, and a JSF phase listener. It is through these servlet and JSF phase events that Seam manages its container and enhances the default JSF life cycle.

Before getting knee-deep into configurations, I want to provide context to the phrase *life cycle*, as it's being thrown around quite casually. I've referred to a servlet context life cycle, a request life cycle, a JSF life cycle, and a Seam life cycle. Let's sort them out.

The *servlet context life cycle* represents the entire lifespan of the web application. It is used to bootstrap services, such as the Seam container. The *request life cycle*, on the other hand, is the overarching life cycle for a single request. It envelops the JSF and Seam life cycles. It lasts from the time the browser requests a URL handled by the application to the time the server finishes sending the request to the browser. The *JSF life cycle* is fairly limited in scope. It's confined to the `service()` method of the JSF servlet and doesn't concern itself with non-JSF requests. The *Seam life cycle* is broader. On the one hand, it works alongside the JSF life cycle, weaving in extra services at strategic extension points. On the other hand, it extends beyond the JSF life cycle, both vertically, capturing events that occur outside the scope of the JSF servlet, and horizontally, by participating in non-JSF requests. You can think of the Seam life cycle as an evolution of the JSF life cycle.

In this section, you learn how to register Seam to participate in servlet requests. The configurations covered here are simply a review of what seam-gen has already prepared for you. However, if you're starting an application from scratch without seam-gen, you'll have to perform these steps in order to use Seam. Let's begin by learning how to "turn on" Seam.

3.1.1 Flipping Seam's switch

A servlet life cycle listener is notified as soon as the application with which it is registered is initialized. Seam uses this life-cycle event to bootstrap itself. You register the `SeamListener` by adding the following XML stanza to the application's web.xml descriptor, located in the WEB-INF directory:

```
<listener>
  <listener-class>org.jboss.seam.servlet.SeamListener</listener-class>
</listener>
```

As soon as Seam is called into action, it begins scanning the classpath for components. The component scanner places the definition for components that it locates into the Seam container. Any components marked as application-scoped startup components (i.e., annotated with both `@Startup` and `@Scope(ScopeType.APPLICATION)`) are automatically instantiated by Seam at this time. Startup components are ideal for performing "bootstrap" logic, such as updating the database or registering modules.

The `SeamListener` also captures notifications when new HTTP sessions are started, at which time it instantiates startup components that reside in the session scope (i.e., annotated with both `@Startup` and `@Scope(ScopeType.SESSION)`). All other components are instantiated on demand during the processing of an HTTP request. You'll learn all about components and how Seam locates, starts, and manages them in the next chapter.

Once Seam is running, it's ready to lend a hand with incoming requests. A majority of that work is done in the JSF servlet, so let's see how Seam ties in with JSF.

3.1.2 The JSF servlet, the workhorse of Seam

Given that Seam is so deeply invested in JSF (though not tied to JSF), it should come as no surprise to you that the main servlet in a Seam application is the JSF servlet. This servlet could easily be named the Seam servlet because of how much Seam-related activity occurs within it. If you're using JSF in your project, or you started with seam-gen, then your web.xml descriptor already has the necessary servlet configuration. If not, add the following two XML stanzas to your application's web.xml descriptor to enable the JSF servlet:

```
<servlet>
  <servlet-name>Faces Servlet</servlet-name>
  <servlet-class>javax.faces.webapp.FacesServlet</servlet-class>
</servlet>
<servlet-mapping>
  <servlet-name>Faces Servlet</servlet-name>
  <url-pattern>*.seam</url-pattern>
</servlet-mapping>
```

Notice that the mapping pattern is defined as *.seam rather than the default for JSF requests, *.jsf. Applications created by seam-gen are configured to this Seam-branded extension for the JSF servlet mapping. You are free to use the extension of your choosing. The change to the servlet pattern is, for the most part, cosmetic. However, the choice of which view technology to use with JSF is far more significant.

A COMMITMENT TO FACELETS

There is an important change that you should consider making to your JSF technology stack if you haven't done so already. Seam developers *strongly* recommend using Facelets as the JSF view handler in place of JavaServer Pages (JSP). JSF and JSP have an inherant mismatch that causes a great deal of pain for the developer. The purpose of JSP is to produce dynamic output, while JSF component tags are intended to produce a UI component model capable of rendering itself. These vastly different goals clash at runtime.

Facelets is a lightweight, XML-based view technology that parses valid XML documents with the sole intent of producing the JSF UI component tree. It provides component tags that are translated natively into UI components and dually wraps non-JSF markup, including inline EL, into JSF text components (meaning you no longer need `<f:verbatim>`[1] for outputting HTML or `<h:outputText>` for outputting a value expression). As a result, the need for the JSP tag layer, as well as the entire overhead of JSP compilation, is eliminated.

Facelets accommodates the same familiar XML-based tags as JSP, making its adoption very easy, but it purges the problems that seek to complicate JSP, such as its pseudo, non-validating XML syntax and the permitted use of Java scriptlets. Originally, Facelets was attractive because it delivered JSF 1.2 features before the JSF 1.2 implementations were ready and capable of being run on servlet containers such as Tomcat. The value of Facelets extends beyond its early utility because it removes the coupling between JSF and JSP and, more importantly, the variance of JSP versions across containers.

Facelets is more than just a view parser. It offers an extensible templating system akin to Struts Tiles. You create templates, known in Facelets as compositions, to define page layouts. A page inherits the template's layout by extending it and contributing unique content to specially marked regions. Compositions can also serve as reusable page fragments. In fact, a composition can act as a UI component itself.

---

[1] This tag is necessary in JSP to wrap plain HTML markup as a JSF UI component or else it is skipped.

Using this feature, you can build new JSF components without having to write a line of Java.

To use Facelets, you have to register the Facelets view handler in the faces-config.xml descriptor, which is located in the WEB-INF directory:

```
<faces-config>
  <application>
      <view-handler>com.sun.facelets.FaceletViewHandler</view-handler>
  </application>
</faces-config>
```

Next, you need to get JSF to look for Facelets templates rather than JSPs, the default.

Using Facelets with Ajax4jsf/RichFaces

At one time the Facelets view handler had to be registered using a web.xml context parameter, org.ajax4jsf.VIEW_HANDLERS, when Facelets was used in combination with Ajax4jsf/RichFaces. This requirement is no longer necessary. You only need this context parameter if you're using more than one view handler and you want to set the order in which they are called. Otherwise, you can simply register the Facelets view handler in the faces-config.xml descriptor.

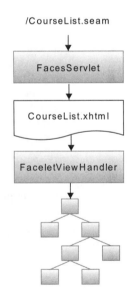

Figure 3.1   Translation from servlet path to UI component tree, which is built by Facelets

Examining the project tree created by seam-gen, you should recognize an abundance of files ending in .xhtml in the view directory. The .xhtml extension is the default suffix for Facelets view templates. However, the default behavior of JSF is to map the incoming request for a JSF view identifier, or view ID for short, to a JSP file with the file extension .jsp. To get JSF to look for a Facelets template instead, you must register the .xhtml extension as the default suffix for JSF views in the web.xml descriptor using a servlet context parameter:

```
<context-param>
  <param-name>javax.faces.DEFAULT_SUFFIX</param-name>
  <param-value>.xhtml</param-value>
</context-param>
```

Figure 3.1 illustrates how an incoming JSF request is processed and translated into a UI component tree. The JSF servlet mapping extension (e.g., .seam) tells the servlet container to direct the request to the JSF servlet, FacesServlet. The servlet mapping extension is stripped and replaced with the javax.faces.DEFAULT_SUFFIX value to build the view ID. The JSF servlet then hands the view ID to the registered view handler, FaceletViewHandler. Facelets uses the view ID to locate the template. It then parses the document and builds the UI component tree.

NOTE   One of the pitfalls of JSF is that the file extension of the view template is hard-coded as part of the view ID. The view ID not only determines what template is to be processed, but is also used to match against navigation rules. Therefore, a change to `javax.faces.DEFAULT_SUFFIX` affects all places where the view ID is referenced.

Seam goes beyond just swapping in the Facelets view handler—it leverages Facelets compositions to keep the JSF views DRY (Don't Repeat Yourself).

FACELETS COMPOSITIONS

JSF is clumsy when it comes to including dynamic markup in a page, something Facelets addresses as a primary feature. Facelets is founded on the idea of compositions. A composition is a branch of a UI component tree, defined using the `<ui:composition>` tag. Unlike JSF subviews, a composition fuses the branch into the component tree without leaving a trace of itself. A composition tag also has templating abilities, which means that it can accept markup as a parameter and incorporate that markup into the fused branch.

Seam's UI component library (see the accompanying sidebar) includes the tag `<s:decorate>` that extends the functionality of `<ui:composition>`, adding to it predefined template facets and features that cater to the rendering of form input fields. Let's consider an example of how the `<s:decorate>` tag helps minimize redundant markup in a form-based JSF view.

> ### Seam's UI component library for JSF
>
> Seam bundles a UI component library for JSF (in the jboss-seam-ui.jar file). The component tags fall under the `http://jboss.com/products/seam/taglib` namespace and are usually written with the prefix "s". The aim of this component set is to further extend JSF in areas where it is deficient, serving as controls rather than rich widgets. There are tags for creating RESTful command links and buttons, templating, custom validators and converters, and page fragment caching, to cite several examples. Note that several of these tags may only be used in conjunction with Facelets (not JSP).

As you'd expect, every form has fields and those fields must have labels. But to do it right, you also need to have a marker to indicate required fields (often represented as a "*") and a place for an error message when validation fails. To round things off, you want to centralize the HTML used to lay out the label and input for each field so that the look is consistent and can be easily changed. Listing 3.1 shows typical markup that you need for each field. It's certainly a lot of typing (or will lead to a lot of copy-paste).

Listing 3.1 A field in a JSF form using standard markup

```
<div class="prop">
  <h:outputLabel for="name" styleClass="name">      ❶
    Name: <span class="required">*</span>      ❷
  </h:outputLabel>
  <span class="value">
```

```
  <h:inputText id="name" required="true"        ❸
    value="#{courseHome.instance.name}">
    <f:validateLength minimum="3" maximum="40"/>    ❹
  </h:inputText>
</span>
<span class="error">
  <h:message for="name" styleClass="errors"/>      ❺
</span>
</div>
```

The main problem with this markup is not so much that it is verbose, but that there's a lot of repetition. And this is just a single field! The identifier (id) of the field appears three times: at ❶, ❸, and ❺. The required symbol ❷ has to be consistent with the required attribute on the field ❸. There's no easy way to add an error icon that's rendered only if an error occurs on the field ❺ because JSF doesn't make that flag available on a per-field basis. Each field must be validated explicitly using nested validation tags ❹. Finally, the layout and associated CSS classes are hard-coded into each field, which makes them difficult to change or augment later on a page-wide or site-wide basis.

In contrast, you'll find the form field declaration in listing 3.2 to be far more reasonable. This substitute markup uses <s:decorate> to push most of the aforementioned work to the Facelets composition template view/layout/edit.xhtml, shown in listing 3.3. Now, instead of laying out and formatting the field, the focus of the markup is on providing the template with what it needs to do this work. Every character typed is providing vital information with minimal repetitive elements. In addition, a change to the template is propagated to all fields.

Listing 3.2 A JSF form field decorated by the layout/edit.xhtml composition template

```
<ui:composition xmlns="http://www.w3.org/1999/xhtml"
  xmlns:ui="http://java.sun.com/jsf/facelets"
  xmlns:h="http://java.sun.com/jsf/html"                    Imports Seam UI
  xmlns:s="http://jboss.com/products/seam/taglib"  ◁───┘   component set
  xmlns:a="http://richfaces.org/a4j">
  ...
                                                                 Defines named
                                                                 template
  <s:decorate id="nameField" template="layout/edit.xhtml">       parameter
    <ui:define name="label">Name:</ui:define>            ◁────┘
    <h:inputText id="name" size="50" required="true"  ◁───┐
      value="#{courseHome.instance.name}">                 Defines unnamed
      <a:support event="onblur" reRender="nameField"       template
        ajaxSingle="true" bypassUpdates="true"/>           parameter
    </h:inputText>
  </s:decorate>
  ...
</ui:composition>
```

Although not a feature provided by the template, the input field has been augmented to perform instant validation upon losing focus, instrumented by the Ajax4jsf <a:support> tag. But what about the <f:validateLength> tag? Its absence doesn't mean that the validation requirement has been lifted. Instead, this common bit of functionality has been pushed into the input field template, shown in listing 3.3. There, the validations are applied to the input component automatically using another custom

Seam UI component, `<s:validateAll>`, which enforces validation rules declared using Hibernate Validator annotations on the corresponding entity class property.

Listing 3.3   The layout/edit.xhtml composition template for input fields

```
<ui:composition xmlns="http://www.w3.org/1999/xhtml"          ❶
  xmlns:ui="http://java.sun.com/jsf/facelets"
  xmlns:h="http://java.sun.com/jsf/html"
  xmlns:f="http://java.sun.com/jsf/core"
  xmlns:s="http://jboss.com/products/seam/taglib">

  <div class="prop">
    <s:label styleClass="name #{invalid ? 'errors' : ''}">
      <ui:insert name="label"/>          ❷
      <s:span styleClass="required" rendered="#{required}">*</s:span>
    </s:label>
    <span class="value #{invalid ? 'errors' : ''}">
      <s:validateAll>          ❸
        <ui:insert/>          ❹
      </s:validateAll>
    </span>
    <span class="error">
      <h:graphicImage value="/img/error.gif"
        rendered="#{invalid}" styleClass="errors"/>
      <s:message styleClass="errors"/>
    </span>
  </div>

</ui:composition>
```

Although this template appears complex, it isolates all of that complexity into a single document. The root of the template is `<ui:composition>` ❶, which indicates that the markup should be fused into the parent JSF tree. Tag libraries are declared as XML namespaces on the root element, similar to the XML-based JSP syntax. The composition accepts two insertions. The first is a named insertion for supplying a label ❷, and the second is an unnamed insertion for supplying any number of input fields ❹. The `<s:decorate>` tag sets two implicit variables, `required` and `invalid`, which indicate if the input field is required and whether it has an outstanding validation error, respectively.

You may notice that this template doesn't use standard JSF component tags for the field label and error message. Instead, they are replaced with equivalent Seam component tags, `<s:label>` and `<s:message>`. The benefit of using the Seam tags is that they are automatically correlated with the adjacent input component, a feature of `<s:decorate>`.

The `<s:validateAll>` tag ❸ enveloping the unnamed insertion activates the Hibernate Validator for any input components it passes in. The Hibernate Validator can also be registered by nesting `<s:validate>` within the component tag. For the field in listing 3.2, the following annotation on the `name` property of the `Course` entity would ensure that the number of characters entered is greater than 3 but doesn't exceed 40:

```
@Length(min = 3, max = 40)
public String getName() { return this.name; }
```

The Hibernate Validator validations are applied twice, once in the UI to provide the user feedback, thanks to the Hibernate Validator-JSF validator bridge registered by the `<s:validateAll>` component tag, and once before the entity is persisted to ensure no bad data ends up in the database. The model validations are applied alongside other validators registered with the input component.

seam-gen includes a similar template for displaying field values, view/layout/display.xhtml, and a master composition template, view/layout/template.xhtml, that provides the layout for each page. The master template accepts a single named insertion, body, which injects primary page content into the template. Any markup outside of the `<ui:define>` tag is ignored. This example page uses the master template:

```
<ui:composition xmlns="http://www.w3.org/1999/xhtml"
  xmlns:ui="http://java.sun.com/jsf/facelets"
  xmlns:f="http://java.sun.com/jsf/core"
  xmlns:h="http://java.sun.com/jsf/html"
  template="layout/template.xhtml">
  {this text is ignored}
  <ui:define name="body">
    main context goes here
  </ui:define>
  {this text is ignored}
</ui:composition>
```

Facelets offers additional features that you may find helpful for defining your JSF views. One of the most enticing features is the ability to create JSF components purely using XHTML markup (no Java code). Given that the task of creating a JSF component in the standard way is so involved, this can save you a lot of time. It's also a great way to prototype a JSF component before you commit to creating it. To learn more about what Facelets has to offer, consult the Facelets reference documentation.[2]

Most of the calls in a JSF application go through the JSF servlet. However, in some cases you need to send other types of resources to the browser that are not managed by the JSF life cycle. Seam uses a custom servlet to handle this task.

3.1.3 Serving collateral resources via the Seam resource servlet

The JSF specification doesn't provide guidance on how to push supporting resources, such as images, Cascading Style Sheets (CSS), and JavaScript files, to the browser. The most common solution is to serve them from a custom JSF phase listener that traps requests matching designated path names. Rather than getting mixed up in the JSF life cycle, Seam uses a custom servlet to serve such resources, sidestepping the life cycle and thus avoiding the unnecessary overhead. Using a separate servlet is justifiable since the steps involved in serving a resource are inherently different from those of processing an application page, eliminating the need for a comprehensive life cycle.

To configure the resource servlet, place the following servlet stanzas above or below the JSF servlet configured earlier. The URL pattern for this servlet must be different than the pattern used for the JSF servlet:

---

[2] https://facelets.dev.java.net/nonav/docs/dev/docbook.html

```
<servlet>
  <servlet-name>Seam Resource Servlet</servlet-name>
  <servlet-class>
    org.jboss.seam.servlet.SeamResourceServlet
  </servlet-class>
</servlet>
<servlet-mapping>
  <servlet-name>Seam Resource Servlet</servlet-name>
  <url-pattern>/seam/resource/*</url-pattern>
</servlet-mapping>
```

The `SeamResourceServlet` uses a chaining model to minimize the configuration you perform in the web.xml descriptor. Seam uses this servlet to

- Serve JavaScript files for the Ajax Remoting library
- Handle Ajax Remoting requests
- Serve CAPTCHA images (visual-based challenges to circumvent bots)
- Serve dynamic images
- Integrate with Google Web Toolkit (GWT) (and other RPC view technologies)

Keep in mind that Seam operates just fine without this servlet, but these extra features listed won't be available. Seam may use this servlet for other purposes in the future. If you have it installed, you won't have to worry about changing your configuration to take advantage of new features that rely on it.

In addition to the resource servlet, which allows Seam to process non-JSF requests, Seam offers a servlet filter, which it uses to operate beyond the reach of both the JSF servlet and the custom resource servlet. Let's see how the servlet filter is registered and what it can do for you.

3.1.4   *Seam's chain of servlet filters*

Servlet filters wrap around the entire request, executing logic before and after the servlet handling the request. Seam uses a single filter to wrap the JSF servlet in order to trap scenarios that fall outside of the JSF life cycle—or that JSF fails to capture. But Seam's filter isn't limited to JSF requests. It canvases all requests, allowing non-JSF requests to access the Seam container as well. Seam can function without relying on filters, but the services it adds are worth the small effort of getting them installed.

The Seam filter must be positioned as the *first* filter in the web.xml descriptor. By not putting this filter first, you run the risk of some features not functioning properly. To register it, place the following two stanzas above all other filters in the web.xml descriptor:

```
<filter>
  <filter-name>Seam Filter</filter-name>
  <filter-class>org.jboss.seam.servlet.SeamFilter</filter-class>
</filter>
<filter-mapping>
  <filter-name>Seam Filter</filter-name>
  <url-pattern>/*</url-pattern>
</filter-mapping>
```

Although there's only a single filter definition shown here, I've alluded to the existence of more than one filter. Seam uses a chaining model, trapping all requests and delegating to any filter registered with the Seam container. This delegation model[3] minimizes the configuration that you need in web.xml descriptor. Once the `SeamFilter` is installed, the remaining configuration of Seam-controlled filters occurs in the Seam component descriptor.

SEAM'S BUILT-IN FILTERS

Filters registered in the Seam component descriptor (e.g., /WEB-INF/components.xml) are managed by the master `SeamFilter` using a chain delegation model. Every filter supports two properties, `url-pattern` and `disabled`, to control which incoming requests are trapped. By default, Seam applies all of the filters in the chain to all requests captured by the filter. You can reduce the matched set of requests by providing an override pattern in the `url-pattern` attribute of the servlet configuration. It's also possible to disable a filter outright by setting the `disabled` attribute to true. The component configuration syntax used to configure these filters is covered in section 5.3.3 of chapter 5.

The filters that are included with Seam at the time of writing are summarized in table 3.1. The table explains the purpose of each filter, lists the additional configuration properties, and indicates under what conditions they are installed.

Table 3.1 The built-in Seam filters

Component/Purpose	Additional configuration	Installed?
`ExceptionFilter` Handles exceptions generated in the JSF life cycle; performs transaction rollbacks.	None	Yes
`RedirectFilter` Propagates conversations and page parameters across redirects for navigations defined in faces-config.xml.	None	Yes

`MultipartFilter`
 	
Processes file uploads from the Seam upload UI component.
	`create-temp-files`
	
	Controls whether a temporary file is used instead of holding the file in memory
	
	`max-request-size`
	
	Aborts request if file is used being uploaded is larger than this limit (in bytes)
		Yes

---

[3] The article "Follow the Chain of Responsibility" (http://www.javaworld.com/javaworld/jw-08-2003/jw-0829-designpatterns.html) gives a nice explanation of the chain of responsibility pattern that is employed by the `SeamFilter.`

Table 3.1   The built-in Seam filters *(continued)*

Component/Purpose	Additional configuration	Installed?
`LoggingFilter` Binds the username of the authenticated user to the Log4j Mapped Diagnostic Context (MDC),[a] referenced using the literal pattern %X{username}.	none	Yes, if Log4j is on the classpath; uses the Seam identity component

`CharacterEncodingFilter`
 	
Sets the character encoding for submitted form data.
	`encoding`
	The output encoding (i.e., UTF-8)
	`override-client`
	Ignores client preference
		No

`Ajax4jsfFilter`
 	
Configures the Ajax4jsf filter that ships with the Ajax4jsf library. Eliminates the need to have to set up this filter individually in the web.xml descriptor.
	`force-parser`
	Applies XML syntax checker to all requests, not just Ajax ones
	`enable-cache`
	Caches generated resources
		Yes, if Ajax4jsf is on the classpath

`ContextFilter` Enables Seam container and contexts for non-JSF requests. Should *not* be applied to JSF requests as it causes duplicate logic to be performed, leading to undefined results.	None	No

`AuthenticationFilter`
 	
Provides HTTP Basic and Digest authentication.
	`realm`
	The authentication realm
	`auth-type`
	Basic or digest
	`key`
	Used as a salt for the digest
	`nonce-validity-seconds`
	Length of time the security token is valid, helping to prevent replay attacks
		No

a.The MDC is a thread-bound map that allows third-party libraries to contribute to the log message. The MDC is described in this wiki page: http://wiki.apache.org/logging-log4j/NDCvsMDC.

These filters each offer specific features that contribute to enhancing the narrowly scoped JSF life cycle. For instance, the `ExceptionFilter` allows Seam to capture all exceptions that are thrown during request processing, something that servlets alone cannot encompass. I cover exception handling in Seam near the end of this chapter. As fine-grained as the JSF life cycle is, its scope is limited to the JSF servlet alone. The `ContextFilter` opens access to the Seam container and its context variables to non-JSF servlets, such as Struts, Spring MVC, and Direct Web Remoting (DWR). Although a majority of Seam's work is done in the JSF servlet, these additional filters allow Seam to extend the boundaries of its life cycle above and beyond the reach of the JSF servlet.

That covers the configurations necessary to hook Seam into the servlet life cycle. But wait a minute; aren't we missing the JSF phase listener configuration? After all, that's how Seam is able to tap into the JSF life cycle.

3.1.5 *The Seam phase listener*

Considering that many of Seam's enhancements to JSF are performed in a JSF phase listener, `SeamPhaseListener`, it would appear as if there's one more configuration to put in place. But there isn't—at least, it isn't necessary. Seam leverages a design feature of JSF that allows for any faces-config.xml descriptor available on the classpath to be loaded automatically. In Seam 2.0, the Seam phase listener is declared in a faces-config.xml descriptor that's included in the core Seam JAR file, jboss-seam.jar. Thus, the phase listener is available as soon as you include this JAR file in your application. The stanza that registers the Seam phase listener is as follows:

```
<lifecycle>
  <phase-listener>
    org.jboss.seam.jsf.SeamPhaseListener
  </phase-listener>
</lifecycle>
```

Although you aren't required to add this declaration to your faces-config.xml descriptor, that doesn't mean you can't adjust how it operates. Configuration settings that affect this phase listener are adjusted in the Seam component descriptor (using `<core:init>`). You can control such things as transaction management, debug mode, and the JNDI pattern used to locate EJB components. I explain component configuration in chapter 5.

If the Seam debug JAR file, jboss-seam-debug.jar, is included on the classpath, and Seam is running in debug mode, Seam registers an additional JSF phase listener, `Seam-DebugPhaseListener`. The sole purpose of this phase listener is to trap requests for the servlet path /debug.seam (assuming the JSF servlet extension mapping .seam) and render a developer debug page. This debug page introspects various Seam contexts (conversation, session, application, business process) and lets you browse the objects stored in them. Information about the long-running conversations in the current session is displayed and conversations can be selected to reveal the objects stored in them. The debug page is also used to display the exception summary when the application faults.

That wraps up the configuration necessary to allow Seam to partake in requests. From here on, I'll refer to the combination of the Seam servlet filter and the JSF life cycle, which Seam now has a hand in, as the *Seam life cycle*. Figure 3.2 illustrates the two paths that a request can take as it enters the Seam life cycle. The `SeamFilter` can also wrap additional servlets such as Struts, Spring MVC, or DWR, allowing you to tap into the Seam container from these third-party frameworks as needed.

With the configuration of Seam out of the way, let's take a step back and consider what the JSF life cycle is like without Seam. The goal of this exercise is to gain an appreciation for the assumptions made by the JSF specification and where those

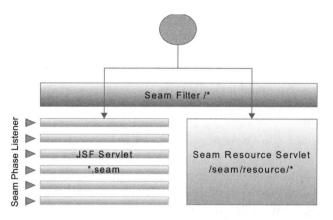

Figure 3.2   Requests are preprocessed by the Seam filter, proceeding to the JSF servlet or the Seam resource servlet.

assumptions come up short. Contrasting the native JSF life cycle with the version enhanced by Seam helps you understand why Seam is relevant and clarifies when you should choose the Seam facilities over the JSF equivalents that they replace. I'll start by reviewing the general principles of JSF and then walk you through the JSF life cycle.

3.2   *The JSF life cycle sans Seam*

It's certainly possible to learn how to develop a JSF application while remaining naive of the fact that there's an underlying life cycle that processes each request. Figure 3.3 shows the leap the JSF designers want you to make between the click of a command button (e.g., <h:commandButton>) and the invocation of an action method on a server-side component that's registered with the command button using an EL method binding expression.

This event-driven relationship is one of the fundamental ways that JSF is *supposed* to make web development easy. The direct binding between the command button and the server-side component weeds out most, if not all, of the low-level details of the HTTP request that you would otherwise have to address, instead getting you right down to the business logic. There is no HttpServletRequest, HttpServletResponse, or ActionForm (for you Struts developers) to have to concern yourself with. It's perfect... too perfect.

JSF developers often fall victim to the leaky abstraction.[4] When the use case fits, life is grand and you don't need to know how the request is handled by JSF. You just know that your action method is executed when a certain button is clicked. However, when

Figure 3.3   A rudimentary look at event-driven behavior in JSF. Method-binding expressions on command buttons trigger methods on server-side components— in this case a Seam component—when activated.

---

[4] http://www.joelonsoftware.com/articles/LeakyAbstractions.html: According to Joel Spolsky, all nontrivial abstractions are, to some degree, leaky.

things get messy, as they often do in the real world in which our applications live, you need to know what's going on inside. That means it's time to hit the books and learn the phases of the JSF life cycle. Since this book focuses on Seam, we're only looking at the life-cycle phases as a means to better understand what Seam does to improve on them. To study the JSF life cycle in greater depth, consult the JSF resources recommended in the introduction of this book (The *JSF for Nonbelievers* series published by IBM developerWorks, *JavaServer Faces in Action* [Manning, 2005], and *Pro JSF and Ajax* [Apress, 2006]).

3.2.1 *The JSF life-cycle phases*

The JSF life cycle decomposes a single servlet request—typically sent over HTTP—into six distinct phases. Each phase focuses on one task in a progressive chain that ultimately results in sending a response back to the browser. By executing these steps incrementally, it gives frameworks, such as Seam, the ability to get intimately involved in the life cycle (in contrast to servlet filters, which only get the before and after picture). Each phase raises an event both before and after it executes. Classes that want to be notified of these phase transition events, perhaps to execute arbitrary logic or weave in additional services, are called phase listeners. Phase listeners must implement the `PhaseListener` interface and be registered with the JSF application, just like the `SeamPhaseListener`. The phase listener serves as the backbone of Seam's life cycle.

The six phases of the JSF life cycle are shown in figure 3.4. Execution occurs in a clockwise manner. We have not yet activated the life cycle, which is why there are no arrows in this initial diagram. In the next two sections, you'll discover the path that a request takes through this life cycle as we put it into motion.

The JSF life cycle phases perform their work on a component hierarchy. This tree of components is similar to the Document Object Model (DOM) that's built for an HTML page (typically exposed through JavaScript). Each node of the component tree is responsible for an element in the rendered page. JSF uses this tree to keep track of events that are triggered from those components. Having an object representation of the rendered view makes it easy to apply partial page updates using Ajax (Ajax4jsf is one library that provides this feature).

JSF can handle two types of requests: an *initial request* and a *postback*. Let's start by looking at how an initial request is processed.

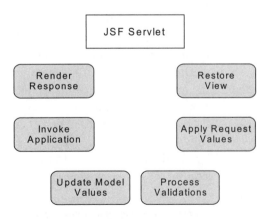

Figure 3.4   The six phases of the JSF life cycle are executed in a clockwise manner.

3.2.2 *The initial request*

Every user interaction in a web application starts with an initial request for a URL. The source may be a bookmark, a link in an email or on another web page, or as a result of the user typing in the URL directly. However it occurs, there is no prior saved state. That means there are no actions and thus no form data to process. Initial requests to the JSF servlet use an abbreviated life cycle of only two phases, as shown in figure 3.5.

In the first phase, *Restore View*, the only activity that occurs is the creation of an empty component tree. The request then proceeds immediately to the *Render Response* phase, skipping most of the life cycle. It does not pass Go, it does not collect the proverbial $200.[5] An initial request isn't designed to handle any events or process form data.[6]

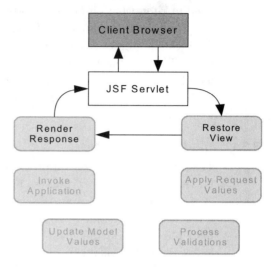

Figure 3.5   The life cycle phases used on an initial request for a JSF page

The main activity on an initial request happens in the *Render Response* phase. In this phase, the request URL is examined to determine the value of the view ID. Next, the template associated with this view ID is passed to the view handler, parsed, and converted into a UI component tree, which was illustrated in figure 3.1.

While the template is being read, two things happen. The component hierarchy is built and the response to the client is prepared by "encoding" each component. Encoding is a way of saying that the component spits out generated markup, typically XHTML, though JSF can accommodate any type of output. The generated response includes elements that are "bound" to server-side components. Input and output elements bind to properties on *backing bean* components, while links and buttons bind to methods on *action bean* components. A single component can serve in both roles. In the absence of Seam, components must be defined in the faces-config.xml descriptor as managed beans. When an event is triggered on the page, it launches JSF into a postback, which we'll get to next.

Once the entire response has been rendered, the UI component tree is serialized and either stuffed into the response sent to the client or saved in the HTTP session under a unique key. The state of the UI component tree is stored so that on a

---

[5] This reference is to the game of Monopoly by Parker Brothers. When you get sent to Jail, you pass by the payday square on the board.

[6] It's possible to implement a phase listener to perform this work, but as you'll see, Seam handles these tasks without any work on your part.

subsequent postback, changes to the form input values can be applied to the properties bound to them and any events can be enqueued and subsequently invoked.

Server-side vs. client-side state saving in JSF

No technology platform would be complete without a vanilla versus chocolate debate. For JSF, that debate is whether to store the UI component tree on the server or on the client. Let's consider the two options.

In server-side state saving, the UI component tree is stored in the user's HTTP session. A token is sent along with the response and stored in a hidden form field. The token value is used to retrieve the component tree from the session on a postback. Server-side state saving is good for the client but bad for the server (because it increases the size of the HTTP session).

In client-side state saving, the UI component tree is serialized (using the standard Java serialization mechanism), compressed, encoded, and sent along with the response. The whole process is reversed on a postback to reinstate the component tree. Client-side state saving is bad for the client (because it increases the size of the exchanged data) but good for the server.

So which should you choose? In my opinion, the choice is clear. Never make your customer or your web server suffer. If you have an opportunity to reduce bandwidth usage, take it. The connection to the client is often unpredictable. While some customers may be able to take the large pages in stride, others may experience significant lag. There is an even more compelling reason to use server-side state saving. JSF-based Ajax requests must reinstate the component tree, so if you use client-side state saving, what was once a trickle of information going from the browser to the server on an Ajax request is now a massive exchange. Server-side state saving limits the extra overhead to the value of the token. The one benefit to client-side state saving is that it's not affected by session expiration. However, if the session expires, there could be a deeper impact.

The state-saving method is set using a top-level context parameter named `javax.faces.STATE_SAVING_METHOD` in the web.xml descriptor. The web.xml descriptor installed by seam-gen doesn't include this context parameter, so the setting falls back to the JSF default, which is server-side state saving.

```
<context-param>
    <param-name>javax.faces.STATE_SAVING_METHOD</param-name>
    <param-value>server</param-value>
</context-param>
```

Each JSF implementation offers ways to tune the memory settings for state saving. seam-gen projects use Sun's JSF implementation (code-named Mojarra), so consult the Mojarra FAQ[7] to learn about the available settings.

---

[7] http://wiki.glassfish.java.net/Wiki.jsp?page=JavaServerFacesRI

Before moving on to postback, let's consider a couple of the assumptions made by this abbreviated life cycle. The initial request assumes that

- No logic needs to happen before the response is generated
- The user has permission to view this page
- The page requested is an appropriate place to begin within the application flow

I'm sure you can think of a handful of situations from the applications that you have developed in which these assumptions don't hold true. The initial request is the Achilles' heel of JSF. You'll soon discover that, thanks to Seam, there's a better way.

As bad as JSF is at handling the initial request, it does a pretty good job of handling a postback. After all, that's what JSF was primarily designed to do. Let's check it out!

3.2.3 *The postback*

Unless a condition occurs that short-circuits the process, a postback exercises the full JSF life cycle, illustrated in figure 3.6. The ultimate goal of a postback is to invoke an action method during the *Invoke Application* phase, though various ancillary logic may accompany this primary activity. During a postback, a short-circuit may happen as the result of a validation or conversation error, an event designated as "immediate," or a call to the renderResponse() method on the FacesContext. In the event of a short-circuit, control is passed to the *Render Response* phase to prepare the output to be sent to the browser. If a call is made to the responseComplete() method on the FacesContext at some point during the life cycle, even the *Render Response* phase is skipped.

The *Restore View* phase of a postback restores the component hierarchy from the state information stored in the client or server, rather than just creating an empty shell. In the *Apply Request Values* phase, each input component retrieves its value from the submitted form data and any events (such as a button click or a notification of a changed value) are queued. The next two phases deal with massaging the submitted values and, if all validations and conversions are successful, assigning the values to the properties on the object (or objects) to which the form inputs are bound (the *Update Model Values* phase).

The life cycle hands control back over to the application during the *Invoke Application* phase, which triggers the method bound to the action of the command component that initiated the postback. If any

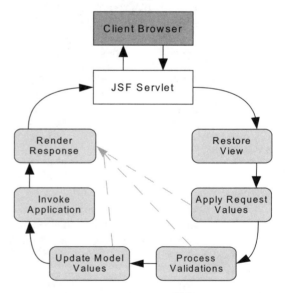

Figure 3.6 During a postback, the full JSF life cycle is used unless short-circuited by an error.

action listeners have been registered with the command component, they are executed first. However, only the action method affects navigation.

Following the execution of the action method, the navigation rules defined in faces-config.xml are consulted to decide where to go next. If the return value of the action method is null or the method return type is void, and there are no rules that match the EL signature of the method (the method-binding expression), then the same view is rendered again. If the return value of the action method is a non-null string value, or there is a rule that matches the method's EL signature, then the rule dictates the next view to be rendered. The presence of the `<redirect/>` element in the rule indicates that a redirect should be issued prior to rendering the next view, rather than rendering the view immediately in the same request, which is the default. A redirect results in a new initial request. An example of a navigation rule is shown here:

```
<navigation-rule>
  <from-view-id>/register.xhtml</from-view-id>
  <navigation-case>
    <from-action>#{registerAction.register}</from-action>
    <from-outcome>success</from-outcome>
    <to-view-id>/welcome.xhtml</to-view-id>
    <redirect/>
  </navigation-case>
</navigation-rule>
```

That concludes your crash course in JSF. Let's reflect on what you just learned and address several holes in the aforementioned life cycle. This discussion will lead us into Seam's most targeted improvement to JSF: advanced page orchestration.

3.2.4 *Shortcomings of the JSF life cycle*

As I've mentioned a number of times in this chapter, JSF is well designed, but there's no denying that it has some quirks. In this section I want to enumerate them so that it's clear what problem Seam is attempting to solve. I am hard on JSF in this section, perhaps unnecessarily so, because I want to emphasize that Seam addresses the concerns people have with JSF so that the Seam/JSF combination is an attractive choice as a web framework. The weaknesses in JSF begin with the initial request. So, let's start there.

LIFE BEFORE THE FIRST ACTION

The two styles of request in JSF are very lopsided. On the one hand, you have an anemic initial request that hardly does more than serve the page. On the other, you have a robust and sophisticated postback that exercises the entire life cycle and triggers all sorts of activity. There are times when you need the services of a postback on an initial request.

Frameworks like Struts allow you to invoke an action as soon as a page is requested. JSF, in contrast, assumes that the first activity will come *after* a page has been rendered. Lack of a front controller makes it difficult to implement functionality such as RESTful URLs, security checks, and prerender navigation routing (unless you're willing to place this logic in a phase listener or at the top of the view template). It also makes it tough for other frameworks to interact with a JSF application since JSF doesn't expose a mechanism for invoking action methods from a regular link. You'll see in the next section that Seam allows page actions, and navigation events that result from them, to occur on an initial request.

NOTE   Savvy JSF readers may point out that a custom `PhaseListener` can be used to execute code prior to the *Render Response* phase. However, doing so requires a lot of redundant work on your part to achieve what Seam gives you right out of the box. Not only do you have to instrument a lot of boilerplate code, you end up hard-coding the view IDs—easily the most irresolute component of the application—into your compiled Java code. Seam allows you to externalize these mappings in a configuration file.

The back-loaded design of JSF leads us into the next problem: the postback becomes the predominate means of navigation in JSF.

EVERYTHING IS A POST

The critics of JSF often point to its reliance on POST requests (i.e., submitting a form) as its biggest downfall. On the surface, this may appear to be just a cosmetic problem, but in fact it is more severe. The browser is very boorish when dealing with POST requests. If users click the browser Refresh button after invoking a JSF action, the browser might prompt them to make a decision about whether to allow the form to be resubmitted. That might not be frightening to you and me, but it may cause customers a great deal of stress and paranoia. Consider the fact that the customer just submitted a large order and the browser is now asking them if they want to resubmit the form. If I were a paranoid customer, I'd just force-quit my browser at that point to prevent any damage from being done. How would I know that the developer was smart enough to check for a duplicate response (and that the QA team confirmed that the logic works)?

Here's an example of a navigation rule, as defined in the faces-config.xml descriptor, that would direct users back to the course detail page once they click the save button on the course editor page:

```
<navigation-rule>
  <from-view-id>/CourseEdit.xhtml</from-view-id>
  <navigation-case>
    <from-action>#{courseHome.update}</from-action>
    <to-view-id>/Course.xhtml</to-view-id>
  </navigation-case>
</navigation-rule>
```

Submitting the editor form issues a POST request. When the browser comes to rest after rendering the Course.xhtml, the location bar will still end in /CourseEdit.seam, appearing as if it is behind by one page. This situation happens because JSF posts back to the same URL that rendered the form and then selects a different template to render. If this navigation rule were changed to perform a redirect instead of a render by adding a nested `<redirect/>` tag with the `<navigation-case>` element, the URL bar would reflect the new page. However, in the process, all of the request parameters and attributes would get dropped.

If keeping the state of the browser location bar in sync with the current page is a requirement, then JSF's behavior puts the developer in a difficult place. One work-around is to make heavy use of the session, to avoid lost data, and perform a redirect on every navigation event, to keep the location bar updated and make bookmarking pages possible. However, using the session precariously is dangerous because it can lead to memory leaks, concurrency problems, multiwindow complications, and over-eager state retention.

RUDIMENTARY NAVIGATION RULES

The other problem with the JSF life cycle is that the navigation model is rudimentary. Navigation rules defined in the faces-config.xml descriptor assume the use of a controller layer whose methods are capable of returning declarative navigation outcomes. The rules match against an originating view ID, the outcome of the action method (i.e., its return value), and the action method's EL signature. The rule dictates the navigation event that should take place, but the rule itself has no access to the general context, such as the value of other scoped variables. You end up having to mix application logic with UI logic in your component. You find that many applications struggle with this model.

AN OVERLY COMPLEX LIFE CYCLE

Some people consider the JSF life cycle to be overly complex. This issue I will actually defend in JSF's favor. I don't believe the problem is being accurately represented. The JSF life cycle is a good decomposition of the logical phases that occur in just about any web request, written in any programming language, and run on any platform. The problem is that the life cycle is *missing* some areas of coverage. The lack of an action-based front controller, like Struts, is a perfect example. As a result of these oversights, developers have been forced to use the framework in ways for which it wasn't intended or to bolt on haphazard solutions that seek to fill these voids.[8] Having to constantly compensate for these problems is where the pretense of complexity manifests itself.

The vast majority of JSF's limitations come down to the fact that JSF fails to provide strong page-oriented support, coming up short on features such as page-level security, prerender actions, intelligent navigation, and RESTful URLs. Seam focuses heavily on strengthening these weak areas by adding advanced page controls to the JSF life cycle, remedying the shortcomings just mentioned and stretching JSF's capabilities beyond these expectations. Let's explore these page-oriented enhancements.

3.3   *Seam's page-oriented life-cycle additives*

In this section, you discover the page orchestration that Seam weaves into the JSF life cycle, saving you from having to patch JSF with the missing page-related functionality yourself. This section introduces Seam's page descriptor, pages.xml, which gives you a way to configure Seam's page-oriented enhancements, namely, more advanced

---

[8] The On-Load module of the jsf-comp project (http://jsf-comp.sourceforge.net/components/onload/index.html) is a perfect example of a haphazard solution to JSF's lack of a front controller.

navigation and page actions. By the end of this section, you'll have all but forgotten about faces-config.xml and the pain it may have caused you.

3.3.1   *Advanced orchestration with pages.xml*

For as much control as the JSF life cycle gives to Seam, the JSF descriptor, faces-config.xml, offers no support for extended elements. For that reason, Seam introduces a new configuration descriptor to support its advanced page orchestration.

Seam's page descriptor offers a much wider range of navigation controls than what the faces-config.xml descriptor is capable of supporting. Describing the page descriptor as a navigation configuration, though, doesn't do it justice. It's really about the page and everything that happens around it—hence the term page orchestration. The page descriptor can be used to

- Define contextual navigation rules
- Generate messages and pass parameters on a redirect
- Invoke actions before rendering a view
- Enforce security restrictions and other prerequisites
- Control conversation boundaries
- Control page flow boundaries
- Control business process and task boundaries
- Map request parameters to EL value bindings
- Bind context variables to EL value bindings and vice versa
- Raise events
- Handle exceptions

The default global page descriptor is /WEB-INF/pages.xml, though its location can be changed, as shown in section 5.3.3 of chapter 5. This descriptor is used to configure an unbounded set of pages, each represented by a <page> element, as well as a handful of non-page-specific configurations. The page-oriented configuration can also be divided into fine-grained configuration files. These individual files serve a single JSF page. They are named by replacing the suffix of the JSF view ID with .page.xml. For example, the fine-grained configuration file for Facility.xhtml is Facility.page.xml.

WARNING   The same page cannot be configured in both the global page descriptor and the fine-grained descriptor. In fact, there can be only be a single page configuration per view ID.

In seam-gen projects, a fine-grained page descriptor accompanies each page that's generated by the seam generate command. Given that Seam boasts about avoiding the use of XML, the abundance of page descriptor files in a seam-gen CRUD application may seem contradictory to this goal. The fine-grained configurations could have been crammed into one file using multiple <page> elements. Even then, you may wonder why you need XML at all. The reason is that seam-gen projects are designed to support RESTful behavior, which is best implemented through the use of page descriptors. It's certainly possible to design a Seam application that works without these page-oriented features. What you'll discover, though, is that the page descriptors give you the best control over the incoming request and are worth the XML you have to endure to get that control.

> ## Making the switch to Seam's navigation rules
>
> Seam's page descriptor is a stand-in replacement for the navigation rules defined in the faces-config.xml file. The main difference is that the `<navigation-rule>` node from faces-config.xml becomes `<navigation>` in the Seam page descriptor and the nested `<navigation-case>` nodes become `<rule>` nodes. The page descriptor supports additional navigation conditions that extend beyond what faces-config.xml offers. Seam also uses its own navigation handler that is capable of folding Seam-specific functionality into the execution of the navigation rule. For instance, it will append the conversation id to the redirect URL to ensure that the conversation propagates across a redirect.

Seam's page descriptor offers a plethora of additional features beyond what the faces-config.xml descriptor has to offer. While the added palette of XML tags is important, the real benefit is its awareness of context, emphasized in the first bullet point. Context—the current state of the system—is a common thread in Seam. By leveraging context, navigation rules defined in Seam's page descriptor are cognizant of the big picture. In other words, they are intelligent.

3.3.2 Intelligent navigation

Seam gives you an intelligent mechanism for orchestrating the transition between pages, more so than what is available with faces-config.xml. When defining navigation rules, you can take advantage of the following extra page descriptor controls:

- Use an arbitrary value binding to determine the outcome of an action rather than using the return value of the action method
- Make navigation cases conditional using a value-binding expression
- Indicate how the conversation should be propagated through the transition
- Control page flows and business processes through the transition
- Add JSF messages before rendering or redirecting
- Add parameters to a redirect
- Raise an event at a transition

The rules defined in Seam's page descriptor make decisions not just based on where the request is coming from, or what action was executed, but on what the objects in context—or scope—have to tell.

NEGOTIATING WHERE TO GO NEXT

Let's consider a hypothetical conversation that may occur between the navigation handler and the navigation rules when taking the user through a basic wizard for adding a new golf facility to the directory (if only code could speak):

- Navigation handler: *The user wants to register a new facility.*
- Navigation rule: *Take the user to the /FacilityEdit.xhtml page.*
- Navigation handler: *The* `#{facilityHome.persist}` *method was called from the /FacilityEdit.xhtml page and it returned an outcome of "persisted."*
- Navigation rule: *Does the user want to enter a course?*
- Context variable `#{facilityHome.enterCourse}`: *Yes.*
- Navigation rule: *Take the user to the /CourseEdit.xhtml page.*
- Navigation handler: *The* `#{courseHome.persist}` *method was called from the /CourseEdit.xhtml page and it returned an outcome of "persisted."*
- Navigation rule: *Does the user want to enter a tee set?*
- Context variable `#{courseHome.enterTeeSet}`: *No.*
- Navigation rule: *Is there somewhere that we need to return the user?*
- Context variable `#{courseFrom}`: *Facility.*
- Navigation rule: *Take the user to the /Facility.xhtml page and display a message to the effect that the user has finished registering the facility.*

The critical piece of this negotiation consists of the context variables. They are used to make the navigation rules conditional. You'll learn about context variables in the next chapter. For now, you can attribute them to the request- and session-scoped attributes with which you are familiar, though they go well beyond the limits of these two scopes. Using context variables in conjunction with the extensive set of controls in the pages.xml descriptor gives you fine-grained control of page-specific handling and transitions between pages.

PUTTING WORDS INTO ACTION

Let's attempt to translate some of the previous example into JSF navigation rules. Unfortunately, using rules defined in faces-config.xml, we can only make a decision based on the EL signature of the action method and the outcome of that method:

```
<navigation-rule>
  <from-view-id>/FacilityEdit.xhtml</from-view-id>
  <navigation-case>
    <from-action>#{facilityHome.persist}</from-action>      Matches action
    <from-outcome>persisted</from-outcome>                   method and
    <to-view-id>/Facility.xhtml</to-view-id>                 return value
    <redirect/>
  </navigation-case>                    Issues redirect
</navigation-rule>                       before rendering
```

The trouble with this rule is that it can't make a complex decision as to where to go next, such as whether to return to the Facility.xhtml or move on to the CourseEdit.xhtml page. It's blind to the larger context. You could have the action method return finer-grained outcomes, but that forces it to be more specialized merely to accommodate navigation. These rules also require that action methods return string outcomes, making them less business-like (they are tied to the requirements of the framework).

Seam's page descriptor uses a similar, yet abbreviated syntax for defining navigation rules than does the faces-config.xml descriptor. The `<rule>` node in Seam's page descriptor, which is the equivalent of the `<navigation-case>` node from faces-config.xml, can draw on the larger context. In listing 3.4, the negotiation with the navigation handler presented earlier has been translated into page descriptor configuration. The value of the `#{facilityHome.enterCourse}` expression is consulted to determine the next page, assuming this value is captured by a checkbox in the facility editor. The user is also kept informed about why the redirect is occurring through the use of a JSF message.

Listing 3.4 Contextual navigation rule consulted after persisting a facility

```
<page view-id="/FacilityEdit.xhtml">
  <navigation from-action="#{facilityHome.persist}">        Matches request
    <rule if-outcome="persisted"                            to add course
      if="#{facilityHome.enterCourse}">                 ◁
      <redirect view-id="/CourseEdit.xhtml"/>               Tracks where
        <param name="courseFrom" value="Facility"/>   ◁──── user came from
        <message severity="INFO">
          Enter course information for #{facilityHome.instance.name}.
        </message>
      </redirect>
    </rule>
    <rule if-outcome="persisted" if="#{!facilityHome.enterCourse}">
      <redirect view-id="/Facility.xhtml"/>
    </rule>
  </navigation>
</page>
```

During a redirect, Seam can add both request parameters and JSF messages. The `courseFrom` parameter is added explicitly to track how we arrived at the course editor. Seam adds additional request parameters based on page parameter configuration. One such parameter is `facilityId`, which is added to the redirect for the purpose of associating the facility just entered with the new course about to be entered. You'll learn about page parameters in the next section. In the JSF message that's added, you can see that it's possible to use an EL value expression. In this case, the message includes the name of the facility, read from the component named `facilityHome`. The EL is commonly used to reference Seam components, which you'll learn about in the next chapter.

A similar set of navigation rules is added for the /CourseEdit.xhtml page to continue the progression. The navigation rules decide whether to return the user to the course editor or to the facility detail page after saving a course according to the value of the `#{courseFrom}` context variable. Notice that EL notion is being used in the `view-id` attribute:

```
<page view-id="/CourseEdit.xhtml">
  <navigation from-action="#{courseHome.persist}">
    <rule if-outcome="persisted" if="#{courseFrom != null}">
      <redirect view-id="/#{courseFrom}.xhtml">
        <message severity="INFO">
          The data entry for #{courseFrom} is complete.
```

```
      </message>
    </redirect>
  </rule>
  <rule if-outcome="persisted" if="#{courseFrom == null}">
    <redirect view-id="/Course.xhtml"/>
  </rule>
</navigation>
</page>
```

If you're getting the sense that the navigation rules in this example could be better written as a page flow, you are right. In addition to declarative navigation rules demonstrated here, Seam supports stateful page flows. Page flows are tied closely with conversations. You'll study both in chapter 7. The purpose of this example is to show that you can consult EL value expressions to determine which navigation rule to apply. You might want to direct users to a special page if they entered a private golf facility versus a public facility. The actual use case is going to depend heavily on the requirements for your application.

FINDING THE OUTCOME ANOTHER WAY

Up to this point, you have relied on the action method to return a logical outcome value. There are two problems with this approach, depending on how you look at it. For rapid prototyping, this level of indirection is inconvenient since it forces you to a define navigation rule even if you don't require the flexibility yet. To simplify matters, Seam lets you specify the target view ID in the return value of the action method. If the return value begins with a forward slash (/), Seam assumes it's a valid view ID and immediately issues a redirect to the view ID:

```
public String goToCourse() {
    return "/Course.xhtml";
}
```

At the other extreme, using the action method return value as the navigation outcome imposes a requirement on business methods to assist with navigation decisions. The declarative return value likely won't make sense in the context of the business logic. This coupling becomes especially noticeable when you start attaching EJBs to your JSF pages. EJB components are supposed to be business components. Using return values for the purpose of driving navigation is just wrong. A far better way is to expect the business object to maintain state that can be consulted by the navigation rule to determine the appropriate maneuver.

> ### Catchall navigation rules in the page descriptor
> Instead of matching against a specific outcome (action method return value), you can define a generic navigation rule to match against either a non-null or null outcome. A `<rule>` node without any attributes will match any non-null outcome (including a void return value). A null outcome is matched by placing either a `<redirect>` or `<render>` node as a direct child of the `<navigation>` node. In Seam, null is often considered an "exceptional" outcome, canceling the normal behavior, such as beginning a conversation.

Let's ignore the return value of the persist() method, assuming that it doesn't tell us anything particular about navigation. Instead, the entity state (persisted, deleted, updated) will be exposed via the property lastStateChange. The evaluate attribute on the element, which is an EL value expression, is consulted to obtain an outcome value rather than the return value of the action method. The resolved expression is matched against the if-outcome attribute on the <rule> nodes to select the navigation to follow:

```
<page view-id="/FacilityEdit.xhtml">
  <navigation from-action="#{facilityHome.persist}"
    evaluate="#{facilityHome.lastStateChange}">
    <rule if-outcome="persisted" if="#{facilityHome.enterCourse}">
      ...
    </rule>
    <rule if-outcome="persisted" if="#{!facilityHome.enterCourse}">
      ...
    </rule>
  </navigation>
</page>
```

In simple terms, the pages.xml steps the navigation capabilities of JSF up a notch. Before we get into the other features of the page descriptor, I want to briefly mention two UI components that Seam introduces that complement the page-oriented controls.

3.3.3 *Seam UI command components*

I mentioned earlier that one of the main criticisms of JSF is that "everything is a POST." This means that any link or button slated to execute an action method when activated does so by submitting a POST request (i.e., a form post). While this design is suitable for accepting form data, it's not so ideal for creating bookmarkable links. Seam offers two UI command components, one for creating links, <s:link>, and one for creating buttons, <s:button>, that stand in for the corresponding command components, <h:commandLink> and <h:commandButton>, from the standard JSF component set. The Seam UI command components can perform all the same functions as the standard command components, with one exception: they can't submit form data. But then again, if you're submitting form data, you likely aren't concerned with the fact that a POST request is being issued; in fact, that's what you want.

You're going to see <s:link> and <s:button> used a lot in this book. Of the two, <s:link> is probably the most attractive because it allows a user to right-click and open the link in a new tab or window, something that isn't possible with JSF command links. In addition to being able to execute an action method, the Seam UI command components can navigate directly to a specific view ID, eliminating the need for a navigation rule:

```
<s:link view="/CourseList.xhtml" value="Course List"/>
```

The value of the view attribute can either use the servlet extension (.seam) or the view ID suffix (.xhtml) to reference the view ID (the real secret is that the extension doesn't matter at all). What <s:link> has over <h:outputLink> in this case is that

Seam will prepare page parameters associated with the target view ID as part of the URL, which you'll learn about next. As you move to the next section, pay attention to how Seam frees JSF from the grips of postbacks and allows it to behave more like an action-based framework.

3.3.4 *Page parameters*

In the native JSF life cycle, value-binding expressions are only passed to the underlying model during the *Update Model Values* phase on a JSF postback. Seam brings this feature to initial requests by introducing a feature known as page parameters.

Page parameters are a truly unique feature in Seam. They're used to bind request parameters to model properties through the use of value expressions. The request parameter can either be form POST data or a query-string parameter. The "model" can be any Seam component (or JSF managed bean), whether it be a presentation model or a business domain model. Again, Seam doesn't force your hand. When a request for a given JSF view is received, as identified by its view ID, each page parameter associated with that view ID is evaluated upon entering the page—just prior to the *Render Response* phase. That value is then assigned to the model property using its Java-Bean setter method as mapped by the value expression.

Let's consider the course detail page, Course.xhtml, from the Open 18 directory application generated in the previous chapter. Assume there's an incoming request for the Course entity with an identifier of 1:

```
http://localhost:8080/open18/Course.seam?courseId=1
```

The component responsible for providing data for the course page is named course-Home. (A component is the Seam equivalent of a JSF managed bean.) Prior to the rendering of the Course.xhtml page, the value of the courseId query string parameter must be assigned to the courseId property on the courseHome component. That assignment occurs as a result of the following page parameter assignment in pages.xml:

```
<page view-id="/Course.xhtml">
  <param name="courseId" value="#{courseHome.courseId}"/>
</page>
```

The name attribute specifies the name of the request parameter and the value attribute specifies the value expression to which the value of the request parameter gets bound. The courseHome component then retrieves the instance from the database to be rendered. Alternatively, you could specify this mapping in the fine-grained configuration file, Course.page.xml, which sits adjacent to the Course.xhtml view template. The fine-grained configuration file is intended to serve only a single view ID. Therefore, the view-id attribute can be excluded in the declaration:

```
<page>
  <param name="courseId" value="#{courseHome.courseId}"/>
</page>
```

For the remainder of the chapter, I'll always include the view-id attribute for clarity.

The `<page>` node is used to designate which pages the configurations apply to. In a global page descriptor, the `view-id` attribute can either be an exact match or it can match multiple view IDs by using a wildcard character (*).

Home and Query components

Throughout this chapter, you have seen a lot of references to components that end in either Home (e.g., courseHome) or List (e.g., facilityList). Components ending in Home extend from the `EntityHome` class and components ending in List extend from the `EntityQuery` class, both of which are part of the Seam Application Framework. The `EntityHome` class is used for managing the persistent state of a single entity instance, while the `EntityQuery` component manages a JPQL query result set. Chapter 10 provides comprehensive coverage of the Seam Application Framework and explains how to take advantage of these two components.

Page parameters aren't limited to accepting values—they are bidirectional. In addition to taking request parameters, they're used to rewrite links by reading the value of the mapped value bindings and appending name-value pairs to the query string. In this way, page parameters automatically take care of decomposing server-side objects into string values, passing them along with the request, and then reconstructing the objects on the other side by mapping the parameters to value binding expressions. For instance, the course editor page includes a link to cancel and return to the course detail page, `<s:link view="/CourseList.xhtml" value="Cancel"/>`. The courseId parameter is automatically appended to the page by reversing the page parameter declaration shown earlier:

```
/Course.seam?courseId=1
```

This rewriting happens in the following cases:

- The URL generated by Seam command components (`<s:link>` and `<s:button>`)
- JSF postbacks from `UICommand` components (i.e., `<h:commandLink>`)
- Navigation redirects defined in the page descriptor (pages.xml or *.page.xml)

For links and redirects, the parameters that are applied to the URL are read from the configuration for the *target* view ID. JSF forms post back to the same page, so the target view ID is the same as the page that rendered the form. It's a bit trickier with `<s:link>` and `<s:button>` since the target page can be different than the current page. For example, consider the following link:

```
<s:link view="/Course.xhtml" value="View course"/>
```

The page parameters will be read from the Course.page.xml page descriptor, even if this link is included on the CourseList.xhtml page.

Let's explore how the page parameters and the Seam UI component exchange request parameters.

THE SEARCH FORM PARADOX

When would you want to use page parameters to pass on values? Consider the paradox of providing both search capabilities and sorting for a data set. I can almost guarantee you have been in this seat before. When the user searches, you need to retain the sort and pagination, and when the user sorts or paginates, you have to retain the search. This leads to heavy use of hidden form elements within a form that wraps the entire page or a liberal use of JavaScript to move values between forms. One way or another, it becomes a tangled mess and leads to many headaches.

Page parameters in Seam make this situation trivial. Consider the golf course facility listing page in the same application. The `facilityList` component is the action class that manages the collection of courses. The page parameters are defined as follows:

```
<page view-id="/FacilityList.xhtml">
  <param name="firstResult" value="#{facilityList.firstResult}"/>
  <param name="order" value="#{facilityList.order}"/>
  <param name="from"/>
  <param name="name" value="#{facilityList.facility.name}"/>
  <param name="type" value="#{facilityList.facility.type}"/>
  <param name="address" value="#{facilityList.facility.address}"/>
  <param name="city" value="#{facilityList.facility.city}"/>
  <param name="state" value="#{facilityList.facility.state}"/>
  <param name="zip" value="#{facilityList.facility.zip}"/>
</page>
```

For any Seam command component on the page (`<s:link>` or `<s:button>`), the expressions are evaluated during page rendering and the resolved value and corresponding parameter name are combined and added to the query string of the link. If you searched for PUBLIC facilities and then sorted on the name of the facility, the URL would look like this:

```
/FacilityList.seam?zip=&phone=&state=&type=PUBLIC&uri=&cid=25&country=
    &city=&order=name+asc&county=&address=&description=&name=
```

The sort link is built using the link component tag from the Seam UI component set (trimmed down for clarity):

```
<s:link value="name">
  <f:param name="order"
    value="#{facilityList.order=='name asc' ? 'name desc' : 'name asc'}"/>
</s:link>
```

Note that the `<s:link>` tag automatically targets the current view ID if one is not explicitly provided. Both the `type` and `order` request parameters are maintained in the URL generated by this link. The order clause is divided into property name and sort direction and both clauses are sanitized by the `FacilityList` component to protected against SQL query injection vulnerabilities. When you submit the search form, you don't see these parameters in the browser's location bar because they're passed through the UI component tree instead. Since page parameters transcend forms—propagated because of their association with a given view ID—it doesn't matter where the links that use them are located. When a search is executed, the sort order is maintained; when a sort is issued, the search parameters are maintained. All of this happens without any custom URL rewriting on your part. Another place page parameters are extremely valuable is on a navigation redirect.

SURVIVING REDIRECTS

As I pointed out earlier, JSF normally drops request-scoped data when issuing a redirect. Page parameters offer a way to retain these values across the redirect. When the redirect is prepared, the data mapped to the view ID using page parameters is automatically appended to the redirect URL. You'll learn in chapter 7 that Seam automatically carries conversation-scoped data over a redirect as well, even in the absence of a long-running conversation.

PARAMETER PEACE OF MIND

By now you are probably getting excited about these page parameters. But here's the real kicker: page parameters can also register converters and validators. That means you aren't blindly stuffing request parameters into properties on your model. You get the peace of mind of the JSF conversion and validation process just as you would on a postback.

In JSF, validators and converters operate at the field level. A validator is a class that implements the `javax.faces.validator.Validator` interface and a converter is a class that implements the `javax.faces.convert.Converter` interface. Validators and converters can be defined as managed beans (or Seam components) or they can be registered under a lookup id in faces-config.xml. If defined as a managed bean, the class instance is referenced using a value expression. When the lookup id is used, JSF is responsible for instantiating the class.

Let's assume that we need to perform some conversions and validations for our facility search to give the user a better chance of locating a facility without getting tripped up over errant symbols or confused when no results are found because of an invalid parameter value. In the following excerpt, the phone number parameter is converted to the storage format used in the database using a custom converter registered under the id `org.open18.PhoneConverter`. The value of the state parameter is checked using a custom validator registered under the id `org.open18.StateValidator`. (You declare validators and convertors in faces-config.xml or by adding `@Validator` and `@Converter` annotations to a Seam component, respectively.) The validator for the facility type is retrieved from a value expression, `#{facilityTypeValidator}`, which resolves to a JSF managed bean or Seam component implementing the `javax.faces.Validator` interface:

```
<page view-id="/FacilityList.xhtml">
  <param name="phone" value="#{facilityList.facility.phone}"
    converterId="org.open18.PhoneConverter"/>
  <param name="state" value="#{facilityList.facility.state}"
    validatorId="org.open18.StateValidator"/>
  <param name="type" value="#{facilityList.facility.type}"
    validator="#{facilityTypeValidator}"/>
</page>
```

What about model validations defined using Hibernate Validator? Good news. Seam enforces model validations on any property referenced by a page parameter as long as the parameter value is non-null. Speaking of null values, it's possible to declare a page parameter as required. Though not the friendliest approach, such a feature does comes in handy for enforcing the presence of a request parameter. For instance, an error can be thrown if the user attempts to request for the facility detail page without the `facilityId` parameter:

```
<page view-id="/Facility.xhtml">
  <param name="facilityId" value="#{facilityHome.facilityId}"
    required="true"/>
</page>
```

The downside of adding the required flag is that Seam throws a `ValidatorException` when the parameter is missing or empty rather than directing the user to a proper page. There are other ways to handle this problem, which are explored later.

Page parameters essentially emulate a form submission on an initial request. But what makes them especially valuable is that they are also propagated transparently through a JSF postback, making them bidirectional.

FROM QUERY STRING TO PAGE SCOPE AND BACK

Here's something easy to overlook the first time you encounter page parameters: they don't necessarily have to refer to a value-binding expression. When the value is left off the declaration, the request parameter is simply placed into the page scope under the same name. Valueless page parameters are useful when you just need to carry values around but don't want to map them into a model object or use hidden form fields. You can sort of think of them as JSF hidden fields. For instance, you can track the page from where the user came using the following valueless page parameter:

```
<page>
  <param name="returnTo"/>
</page>
```

You can then make a decision based on this value when creating navigation buttons:

```
<s:button value="Cancel"
  view="/#{empty returnTo ? 'FacilityList' : returnTo}.xhtml"/>
```

Please note that this example is conceptual. You probably want to filter the `returnTo` variable through a preprocessor to ensure that its value is legitimate given the context.

What about when you need to execute an action on an initial request, not just apply request parameters to the model? Executing code prior to rendering a page is the forte of Seam's page actions.

3.3.5   *Page actions: execute me first!*

Page actions are what drew me to Seam and encouraged me to stick with JSF. In my mind, they are the saving grace of JSF. More times than not, information is retrieved by pulling up a URL in the browser, or following a link from another site, not from clicking a button in the application. However, the JSF specification focuses heavily on the latter use case. Seam adds the ability for JSF to accommodate RESTful URLs (i.e. "bookmarkable" links).

RESTFUL URLs

Without page actions, you have to think about the world in terms of form submissions. That is a stark contrast with the direction the world is actually taking, which is to rely on a REST architecture style—or the more pertinent term, RESTful URLs. [9] Once you have the power of page actions at your fingertips, any request can be made to perform prerender logic to retrieve and prepare data *before* the component tree of the next view is built and ultimately rendered. You may even decide to serve a different view than what was requested by the browser. In this case, there isn't an automatic mapping between the URL that's requested and the page template that's to be rendered, like the default behavior of JSF.

> ### What is a RESTful URL?
>
> A RESTful URL is one that permanently represents a resource that is returned by the server when that URL is requested by a client, typically a browser. A resource is any item of interest, such as information about a golf course or a golfer's profile. The URL contains all the information necessary to pull up a unique resource (citing the read operation). REST is an acronym for Representational State Transfer. The state is the resource (the golf course information or golfer's profile) as it exists on the server, typically stored in a database. The representation of that state is the document returned. When the URL is requested, the state is transferred from the server to the client. [10]

In essence, page actions tack a front controller onto the JSF life cycle. Page actions behave similarly to Struts actions. In either framework, the action is selected by the controller based on a URL-to-action mapping and subsequently invoked prior to any view processing or page rendering. The front controller is the design pattern used by action-based frameworks, including Struts, WebWork (Struts 2), and Spring MVC. You can take comfort in the fact that, with Seam at the helm, you don't have to abandon your action-based way of thinking or the ability to serve RESTful URLs when you make the move to JSF.

Page actions are specified using method-binding expressions. There are two ways to associate a page action with a view ID. The action can be defined on a page node in Seam's page orchestration descriptor, pages.xml, either in the `action` attribute on the `<page>` node or in a nested `<execute>` node. The action can also be specified in the `action` attribute on a Seam UI command component, `<s:button>` or `<s:link>`. You may wonder how the latter can be considered a page action since it's triggered by a user action, just as the `UICommand` components work. It's because the Seam command components construct URLs that issue an initial request (not a postback) and therefore

---

[9] Admittedly, I am using the term RESTful URL with great liberty in this section. I cannot claim that a GET request is enough to qualify it as a RESTful URL. However, the point here is that prerender page actions are a prerequisite to implementing a complete REST solution.

[10] http://www.xfront.com/REST-Web-Services.html

contain all the information necessary to trigger an action method. If the URL created by one of these components is bookmarked, the action is executed just as if the user had activated the component.

One of the most common use cases for page actions is preloading data prior to rendering a view. To satisfy this use case, it's most appropriate to use the pages.xml descriptor to associate the action method with the view ID since the idea is to handle all requests for the resource, even invalid ones.

PRELOADING DATA

Suppose you wanted to preload the list of golf courses before rendering the directory listing. Doing so would allow you to trap possible errors that might occur when retrieving the results from the database before the page begins rendering.

To execute an action before rendering, you specify a method-binding expression in the `action` attribute of the `<page>` node in any page descriptor. The page parameters are applied to the model before the page action executes. So, just as form element bindings are used to populate the model for actions executing in the *Invoke Application* phase of a JSF postback, page parameters are used to populate the model for page actions. Here, the `Facility` result list is fetched in the page action, perhaps eagerly fetching lazy associations on the `Facility` entity as part of the query:

```
<page view-id="/FacilityList.xhtml"
  action="#{facilityList.preloadFacilities}">
  ...
</page>
```

Now let's assume that you want to bring up the list of facilities that are in the home state of the user, if the user is authenticated. You'll learn how to implement authentication with Seam in chapter 11. Assuming that there's a mechanism available to access the current user's information, the `#{facilityList.applyRegionalFilter}` method will apply it to the search parameters, but only if an active search isn't detected (to avoid interfering with it). The facilities will then be preloaded as before since the actions are executed in the order they appear in the page node. To apply multiple page actions to a single page node, you use nested `<action>` nodes:

```
<page view-id="/FacilityList.xhtml">
  <action execute="#{facilityList.applyRegionalFilter}"
    if="#{identity.loggedIn and !facilityList.searchActive}"/>
  <action execute="#{facilityList.preloadFacilities}"/>
  ...
</page>
```

Having the ability to execute a method prior to rendering is only half the benefit. The true value of page actions is their ability to trigger declarative navigation. This is one feature you don't get by putting the prerender logic in the `beforePhase()` method of a JSF `PhaseListener`.

3.4   *Combining page actions with navigation*

The navigation that follows a page action works just like the navigation used after the *Invoke Application* phase on a JSF postback. Thus, Seam's page actions can be combined with its intelligent navigation capabilities in order to make decisions about how to direct the user in the event that a page action needs to divert the user from the requested page. If you perform a redirect—not a <render>—in the navigation rule, then the ensuing page may also use a page action. Thus, chaining actions prior to rendering a page is possible. A view ID that participates in this chain does not need to correspond to an view template (i.e., it's a pseudo-page).

The most obvious use for combining a page action with navigation is to validate that the URL being requested is legitimate and that the page can be rendered successfully.

3.4.1 Sanity checking a request

Consider what happens when a user requests the course detail screen directly, perhaps from a bookmark. The course is looked up by id using the value supplied in the courseId request parameter. What happens when the requested courseId is empty or no such id exists in the course table? JSF is notoriously awful at handling this situation. Because the JSF controller works in a passive manner, it doesn't figure out that the request is missing information until halfway through the rendering process. Once the page begins rendering, you can't reroute the user to a more appropriate page, even when it becomes apparent that the target data is absent—unless you throw an exception. You end up displaying a page with blank values and other potential rendering glitches.

Page actions to the rescue! Let's implement a method validateEntityFound() that verifies that a course can be found before rendering begins:

```
public String validateEntityFound() {
    try {
        this.getInstance();
    }
    catch (EntityNotFoundException e) {
        return "invalid";
    }
    return this.isManaged() ? "valid" : "invalid";
}
```

Behind the scenes, the getInstance() method is using the courseId value that's assigned to the courseHome component by the page parameter to look up the corresponding entity instance in the database. The isManaged() method tells us whether the entity was found in the database, as opposed to a new, transient instance being created.

Of course, if things don't go well, and the outcome value is "invalid," then we need to perform navigation. Navigation rules are invoked after executing a page action just as they are when an action is invoked on a JSF postback. Here, we redirect users to the /CourseList.xhtml JSF view if the course cannot be successfully loaded, letting them know with a warning message why they were redirected:

```
<page view-id="/Course.xhtml" action="#{courseHome.validateEntityFound}">
  <navigation from-action="#{courseHome.validateEntityFound}">
    <rule if-outcome="invalid">
      <redirect view-id="/CourseList.xhtml">
```

```
      <message severity="WARN">
        The course you requested does not exist.
      </message>
    </redirect>
  </rule>
</navigation>
</page>
```

Your Course.xhtml page is now protected from bogus requests. You may be wondering about the CourseEdit.xhtml page, which also needs to be protected. You could apply the same logic to that page as well by registering equivalent configuration with the /CourseEdit.xhtml view ID. However, just to demonstrate additional capabilities of the <page> node, let's combine the two view IDs together and use a complex conditional expression to determine when the validation should be applied. First, a <page> node is defined that matches all view IDs that begin with /Course. Then, by consulting the implicit JSF expression #{view.viewId}, which resolves to the current view ID, the validation can be applied to the detail page and, if the courseId property on course-Home is non-null, the editor page:

```
<page view-id="/Course*">
  <action execute="#{courseHome.validateEntityFound}"
    if="#{view.viewId == '/Course.xhtml' or
      (view.viewId == '/CourseEdit.xhtml' and
      courseHome.courseId != null)}"/>
  <navigation from-action="#{courseHome.validateEntityFound}">
    <rule if-outcome="invalid">
      <redirect view-id="/CourseList.xhtml">
        <message severity="WARN">
          The course you requested does not exist.
        </message>
      </redirect>
    </rule>
  </navigation>
</page>
```

Note that the navigation rules are consulted after each action is executed. If the outcome of a page action matches a navigation rule, the remaining page actions will be short-circuited. So for all page actions to execute, only the last one can trigger navigation.

As you can see, it's possible to create fairly sophisticated rules about when to invoke page actions. However, they do require some setup. To handle the more common cases of prerender functionality, Seam provides a couple of built-in page actions to secure a view.

3.4.2   *Built-in page actions*

Every application needs certain page-oriented features, such as the ability to restrict unauthenticated or unauthorized users from accessing protected pages. Rather than forcing you to invest time in a solution for every application, Seam offers a handful of built-in page actions for handling this work.

If you've ever tried to use a servlet filter-based security mechanism, such as Spring Security, to secure JSF pages, you were likely frustrated by the fact that it doesn't do a good job of securing JSF pages because it's not granular enough. Securing JSF pages is easy if done at the proper level, just prior to the *Render Response* phase. Page actions are the perfect fit. To restrict access to users that aren't authenticated, you simply add the `login-required` attribute to the page definition:

```
<page view-id="/CourseEdit.xhtml" login-required="true"/>
```

You can also enforce custom security rules using a nested `<restrict>` element. If you're using a Java Authentication and Authorization Service (JAAS) principle (we cover its configuration in chapter 11), and you want to enforce role-based security according to the return value of `isUserInRole()`, then you can do so using the built-in EL function named `s:hasRole` in the `<restrict>` element. Let's assume that there's a role named "edit" that is used to grant privileges to modify records. You can prevent anyone who isn't assigned the edit role from modifying a course with the following page declaration:

```
<page view-id="/CourseEdit.xhtml" login-required="true">
  <restrict>#{s:hasRole('edit')}</restrict>
</page>
```

In a fashion similar to how you require the user to be authenticated, you can enforce that a conversation already be in effect by adding the `conversation-required` attribute to the page declaration. Both of these tags can also be added to the root `<pages>` node if you want either of them to apply to all pages. If either of these two conditions fails, Seam provides the `login-view-id` and `no-conversation-view-id` attributes that indicate where to direct the user. We'll look at security and conversations in much greater depth later in this book. Just note that these are features of Seam that you can configure using pages.xml.

There is another built-in page action that is capable of loading a message bundle for a set of pages. The keys are added to the unified message bundle that's prepared by Seam. You learn how to configure and use the Seam message bundle in section 5.5.2 of chapter 5. The following declaration loads the message bundle defined in the admin.properties file on the classpath for the administration section of the website:

```
<page view-id="/admin/*" bundle="admin"/>
```

It's also possible to enforce that a page be requested via an HTTPS request using a built-in action. The `scheme` attribute on the page declaration checks the current scheme and redirects the user to the appropriate scheme if it's not the correct one:

```
<page view-id="/secure/*" scheme="https"/>
```

I could fill a book trying to cover every last detail of Seam's page-oriented functionality. Since there's plenty more in Seam to cover, I need to move on rather than itemize the entire page descriptor schema. I encourage you to consult the Seam reference documentation if you're curious about a lesser-used page descriptor configuration element that I haven't covered here.

The prerender logic discussed so far is transparent to the user. However, a URL that makes sense to the developer doesn't always make sense to the end user or a search engine. Specifically, URLs that have a lot of query string parameters appear rather cryptic. The next section shows you how to create friendlier-looking URLs in Seam.

3.4.3   *Search engine–friendly URLs*

Using a layer of abstraction between the URL and the rendered view can accommodate a more logical, prettier, and RESTful URL strategy. The goal is to turn URLs that look like /Course.seam?courseId=15 into /course/view/15. JSF wasn't designed with the REST concept in mind, so we must look elsewhere. Although it's possible to preprocess the request using page actions, as we did in the previous example, it's far easier to accomplish this task using a third-party rewrite filter, aptly named `UrlRewriteFilter`. If you're familiar with Apache's `mod_rewrite` filter, the premise is the same.

> ### Why are search engine–friendly URLs desirable?
>
> To help people find information on your site, you want to ensure that search engines understand your website or application. One way to optimize a site for search engines is by making the links that point to other pages of the site self-describing. The URL should contain words and characters that provide clues as to what resource will be displayed when the URL is requested. Search engines can then learn this pattern and provide search results that associate a direct link to a resource that matches the search terms.
>
> All the relevant information should also be in the URL path. Putting information in the query string makes it difficult for the search engine to sort between essential and nonessential information and may even cause important information about the resource to be truncated. Statistics engines are notorious for wreaking such havoc on URLs. So having search engine–friendly URLs also means having *statistics engine–friendly* URLs. The statistics generated are also more accurate since you get the granularity of showing the requests for resources rather than just the servlet path that serves them.
>
> Search engine–friendly URLs are desirable because they are simple and they are technology agnostic. Suppose you implement your application in Struts and spread around links that ended in .do. Then, if you later switch to JSF, all of the existing links instantly become invalid, likely resulting in a 404 error for the user. You now have the job of publicizing the new links that end in .jsf (or .seam). Instead, what you want to do is make the URL about the resource, not about the framework that's serving it.

At the time of this writing, Seam doesn't include a filter in its filter chain for enabling and configuring the `UrlRewriteFilter`, though it's expected to be in the Seam 2.1 release. Until then, it needs to be configured in the web.xml descriptor. Add the following XML stanza anywhere below the `SeamFilter` in that file:

```
<filter>
  <filter-name>UrlRewriteFilter</filter-name>
  <filter-class>
    org.tuckey.web.filters.urlrewrite.UrlRewriteFilter
  </filter-class>
</filter>
<filter-mapping>
  <filter-name>UrlRewriteFilter</filter-name>
  <url-pattern>/*</url-pattern>
</filter-mapping>
```

You'll also need to modify the build to include the urlrewritefilter.jar file in the deployment archive. Please see appendix A for details on how to add a library to the deployment archive.

The rewrite rules are defined in the /WEB-INF/urlrewrite.xml descriptor. The rules are defined using either Perl 5 regular expressions or wildcards. It's possible to capture match references and pass them on to the new URL that's constructed. Listing 3.5 shows the configuration for friendly course URLs.

Listing 3.5   URL rewrite configuration for friendly URLs

```
<?xml version="1.0" encoding="UTF-8"?>
<!DOCTYPE urlrewrite PUBLIC
  "-//tuckey.org//DTD UrlRewrite 3.0//EN"
  "http://tuckey.org/res/dtds/urlrewrite3.0.dtd">
<urlrewrite>
  <rule>                                              Matches URLs like
    <from>^/course/view/([0-9]+)$</from>        ◄──  /course/view/I5
    <to last="true">/Course.seam?courseId=$1</to>
  </rule>
  <rule>                                              Matches URLs like
    <from>^/course/edit/([0-9]+)$</from>        ◄──  /course/edit/I5
    <to last="true">/CourseEdit.seam?courseId=$1</to>
  </rule>
  <rule>
    <from>^/$</from>          ◄──  Matches
    <to>/home.seam</to>            root URL
  </rule>
</urlrewrite>
```

Friendly URLs can cause relative paths to break since the servlet path is no longer representive of the rendered view. A reference to a stylesheet may stop working because the browser thinks that the friendly URL is the base URL of the resource. To solve this problem, you should use absolute references to such resources, such as

```
#{facesContext.externalContext.request.contextPath}/stylesheet/theme.css
```

It's also possible to create friendly URLs using the inverse mechanism. If you use regular HTML links, links created with <h:outputLink>, or Seam UI command components in your view, you can define outbound rules that convert link targets to friendly URLs before they are sent along with the response. Here's an example of an outgoing rewrite rule that produces friendly course URLs for the course detail page:

```
<outbound-rule>
  <from>^(/.+)?/Course.seam\?courseId=(\d+)$</from>
  <to>$1/course/view/$2</to>
</outbound-rule>
```

When defining outbound rules with strict matching (the leading caret), the context path (in this case /open18) must be captured in the `<from>` expression and passed on to the target URL. You also have to consider all the possible query parameters that may appear in the URL for the rule to be matched. A common parameter to watch out for is the conversation id parameter, thus requiring a more complex expression.

The `UrlRewriteFilter` is quite capable of slicing and dicing the URL in whatever creative ways you can think of to write regular expressions. Not only is it useful for creating friendly URLs, but it can also help when you want to migrate a site to a new structure, serve custom resources based on the user agent (browser), or trim long or complicated URLs. You can see more examples of the `UrlRewriteFilter` in action in the example projects (under the examples directory) that come with the Seam distribution.

Now that you are well versed in Seam's pages.xml configuration, it's time to see how Seam ties this functionality into the JSF life cycle and what else it adds in the process.

3.5   *The JSF life cycle with Seam*

The JSF life cycle under the direction of Seam is more well balanced than its intrinsic counterpart. By that, I mean that in Seam's version of the JSF life cycle, the initial request processing is just as full-featured as the postback processing. You've seen many of the ways in which Seam expands the activity in the initial request by applying page-oriented features. These new features include parameter mappings, front controllers, and request routing. In this section, we're going to (quickly) step through the JSF life cycle again, this time observing the points where Seam adds its enhancements.

3.5.1   *Phase listeners versus servlet filters*

Seam is able to work closely with JSF thanks to the granularity offered by a phase listener. Few other frameworks offer such a deep view into the execution processes. You'll often see frameworks using servlet filters to perform such tasks, such as Spring Security. The problem with filters is that they work at too high a level and lack the intimate knowledge of what's going on inside the request. Without this context, it becomes difficult to make the correct decision. Under some circumstances, it's impossible for a filter to influence the execution path. Seam's phase listener, `SeamPhaseListener`, is low-level enough to alter the execution flow of the life cycle as dictated by the page-oriented functionality or to get it involved in supplemental business. Let's examine when these activities take place.

3.5.2   *Stepping through the augmented life cycle*

Before we get started with the revamped JSF life cycle, let me warn you that the amount of activity that happens in the Seam life cycle is daunting. Trying to cover it all on a single walkthrough would be difficult. Therefore, I'll give you a general idea of what happens, emphasizing key points. Think of this run-through as the highlights reel: it's going to give you a broad overview and plenty to be excited about. Are you ready to roll the tape?

THE INITIAL REQUEST, SEAM-STYLE

Once again, we'll examine the life cycle as it processes the initial request. I promise that the story is far more interesting this time around. Table 3.2 walks through the tasks that Seam wraps around the JSF phases on the initial request.

Table 3.2 **A general overview of the tasks that Seam incorporates into the JSF life cycle on an initial request (JSF phases shown in bold; horizontal line signifies transition from *Restore View* to *Render Response*)**

Step	Task	Description
1	Initial request	The life cycle begins with a GET request captured by the JSF servlet.
2	Begin JTA transaction	If transaction management is enabled and JTA transactions are being used, a JTA transaction is opened.
3	**Restore View**	On an initial request, the *Restore View* phase merely creates an empty component hierarchy.
4	Restore or initialize conversation	Restore the long-running conversation if requested. If there's a problem restoring it due to a timeout or concurrent access and authentication isn't required, advance to the no-conversation view. If a long-running conversation doesn't exist, initialize a temporary conversation.
5	Handle conversation propagation	Determine from the request parameters if a long-running conversation is to begin, end, be joined, or remain untouched.
6	Validate page flow	If a stateful page flow is in use, it is validated to ensure the user isn't attempting to request a page out of sequence. If the request isn't compliant, appropriate action is taken.
7	Process page parameters	The parameters associated with this view ID are read from the request, converted, validated, and stored in the view root.
8	Enforce login, long-running conversation, and permissions	If the user must be authenticated to view this page, the nonauthenticated user is redirected to the login page. Once authenticated, the process of rendering this page is resumed. If a long-running conversation is required to view this page and one doesn't exist, the user is forwarded to the no-conversation view. If the user doesn't have appropriate permissions to view this page, a security error is raised.
9	Apply page parameters	If all validations and conversations pass, the page parameters are applied to the model via the value bindings or stored in the page context (no value binding).
10	Begin non-JTA transaction	If transaction management is enabled and resource-local (non-JTA) transactions are being used, the remaining response is wrapped in a resource-local transaction (through interaction with the persistence manager).
11	Emulate the *Invoke Application* phase	The life cycle temporarily takes on the signature of the *Invoke Application* phase to accommodate postback features on an initial request.

Table 3.2   **A general overview of the tasks that Seam incorporates into the JSF life cycle on an initial request (JSF phases shown in bold; horizontal line signifies transition from *Restore View* to *Render Response*) *(continued)***

Step	Task	Description
12	Enforce login, long-running conversation, and permissions	The restrictions are once again applied. This step occurs twice because some execution paths will skip steps 1–9 when rendering a given view ID after a navigation event.
13	Select data model row	If request was initiated by a Seam UI command component within a `UIData` component, advance the index of `DataModel` to the corresponding row.
14	Execute page actions	Each page action associated with the view ID is executed. This includes actions that are passed through a Seam UI command component. Navigation rules are applied after each execution. If more than one navigation rule is applicable, the one with the highest priority is used.
15	Commit transaction	If transaction management is enabled and a transaction is active, it is committed. A new transaction is opened to prepare for the rendering of the response.
16	Migrate JSF messages	Interpolate then migrate Seam-managed `FacesMessages` stored in the conversation to the `FacesContext`, having now survived any redirects.
17	Prepare conversation switching	Conversations can be selected through a UI component. This step remembers the description and view ID for the current page. The stack must be prepared at this point in the event the life cycle is short-circuited before the *Render Response* phase.
18	Store conversation	The conversation is stored in the session until the next request.
19	**Render Response**	The response is rendered by reading the JSF view template and encoding it to the generated markup (typically XHTML). The UI component hierarchy is stored in either the client or the server to be restored on a postback.
20	Commit transaction	If transaction management is enabled, commit the transaction that was active during the rendering of the response.
21	Prepare conversation switching	Conversations can be selected through a UI component. This step remembers the description and view ID for the current page, and updates the stack prepared prior to the *Render Response* phase.
22	Clean up conversation	Either end the temporary conversation or update the last request time of the long-running conversation.

You can breathe again; the process is over. Table 3.2 doesn't cover every last detail of the steps added by Seam in the JSF life cycle, but it comes pretty close. If you had to abbreviate this list, the most notable improvements made to the initial request are

- Transactions are started and stopped automatically (if they are enabled).
- Page parameters, actions, and restrictions defined in the page descriptor are applied.

The global transaction that Seam wraps around each request is an important part of what makes Seam applications so practical. You can safely perform persistence operations in your page actions and action methods without having to worry about beginning and committing a transaction. Seam takes care of it for you. If you prefer to push your persistence logic to other layers, you are still able to take advantage of the global transaction since it spans the entire action method call stack. Global transactions are addressed in chapters 8, 9, and 10, which cover transactions and persistence in depth.

Lazy associations in the view

One of the key benefits of Seam is how it properly scopes the persistence manager (JPA `EntityManager` or Hibernate `Session`) to allow uninitialized proxies and entity associations to be traversed in the view without fear of encountering a `Lazy-InitializationException` (LIE). In short, they just work. In the past, developers have relied on the Open Session in View pattern to extend the lifetime of the persistence manager across a single request. Seam takes a smarter approach by binding the persistence manager to the conversation scope and dually wrapping a transaction around the request. In chapter 9, you learn about Seam's conversation-scoped persistence manager and how it contrasts with the Open Session in View pattern.

After seeing nearly two dozen steps on the initial request, you may be dreading the postback. Well, fear not, because there isn't much to cover. Seam performs most of its work around the *Restore View* and *Render Response* phases.

LESS PATCHING ON POSTBACK

This section is extremely short because a postback in the Seam life cycle is simply a combination of Seam's page-oriented additives and the standard JSF postback mechanism. The most notable enhancement is that Seam wraps a transaction around the *Invoke Application* phase, committing the transaction once the phase is complete. This parallels how page actions are managed. Once again, Seam takes the tedium of dealing with transactions out of the picture until we're absolutely ready to start fine-tuning them. One thing to watch out for is that page actions get executed on a postback, something you might not think about at first. To ensure that a page action only executes during an initial request, you can apply the following conditional logic to the page action declaration:[11]

```
<page>
  <action execute="#{actionBean.executeOnInitialRequestOnly}"
    if="#{empty param['javax.faces.ViewState']}"/>
</page>
```

The Seam life cycle introduces quite a number of new features on top of what was already available with the JSF life cycle by hooking into its phase listener architecture. The most blatant deficiencies in JSF are the initial request handling and the navigation

---

[11] In JSF 1.2, this check is performed by the ResponseStateManager#isPostback(FacesContext) method.

capabilities, both of which Seam corrects, making it possible to create more sophisticated JSF applications. All too often, though, things go wrong. When they do, the application should handle itself just as well as it does when things go as planned. In the next section, you'll learn that Seam helps out in this area by tacking an exception-handling facility onto JSF.

3.6   A try-catch block around the life cycle

The ability to handle exceptions is just as important as all the other cool and exciting things that a framework such as Seam can do. Unfortunately, exception handling is often overlooked. This is true of JSF. The faces-config.xml descriptor doesn't allow exception handlers to be defined. Fortunately, Seam taps into the JSF life cycle to trap and handle exceptions gracefully.

3.6.1   Failing gracefully or with intentional crudeness

Seam handles failures by catching a thrown exception that occurs during the processing of the request and offers you a chance to deal with it from within the same execution of the life cycle. By catching the exception as part of its life cycle, Seam can retain page parameters, the temporary or long-running conversation, and any JSF messages that may have been added before the exception occurred. Seam will also ensure that any transactions are rolled back before delegating to the exception handler if deemed appropriate.

When dealing with an exception, you can take one of two actions:

- Redirect
- Send HTTP error code

In the process of handling an exception, you may also

- Add a JSF message
- End a conversation
- Add parameters to a redirect

There are two ways you can define how an exception is handled. You can either define exception matching rules in the page descriptor that watch and act on exceptions when they are thrown, or you can go straight to the exception class and configure how the exception should be handled when it is raised.

3.6.2   Registering an exception handler

To configure an exception handler, you again leverage the page descriptor. Using the code in listing 3.6, we capture a Seam authorization exception in a graceful manner. When Seam catches the exception, it first stores the original exception in the conversation-scoped variable named org.jboss.seam.caughtException.[12] It then looks through the exception hierarchy for an exception handler. If it finds one, it stores the

---

[12] Prior to Seam 2.1 the original exception was stored in the variable named **org.jboss.seam.exception.**

handled exception in the conversation-scoped variable named `org.jboss.seam.`
`handledException`. The exception handler can then add a message to the request and
issue navigation to an error page. The message is a standard JSF `FacesMessage` and is
thus displayed in the user interface using the `<h:messages>` component tag.

Listing 3.6   Configuration for capturing authorization exceptions

```
<exception class="org.jboss.seam.security.AuthorizationException">
  <redirect view-id="/error.xhtml">
    <message severity="WARN">
      Sorry, you do not have access to the requested resource.
      This message may explain why:
      #{org.jboss.seam.handledException.message}      <-- Inner exception
      or
      #{org.jboss.seam.caughtException.message}       <-- Outermost exception
    </message>
  </redirect>
</exception>
```

NOTE   If you're using Facelets, you have to ensure that both Facelets development mode and Seam debug mode are disabled in order for the exception handler to kick in all cases. Otherwise, you may be presented with a
special debug page that displays the exception. The instructions for toggling Seam debug mode and Facelets development mode can be found
in section section 2.6.1 of chapter 2.

3.6.3   Handling the exception at the source

You can also configure exception handling through annotations by adding either an
`@HttpError` annotation or a `@Redirect` annotation to the exception class (but not
both). You can supplement either of these with the `@ApplicationException` annotation to control how the active transaction or long-running conversation is handled.

The `@Redirect` annotation, summarized in table 3.3, allows you to render a pretty
error page and kindly inform the user what went wrong.

Table 3.3   The `@Redirect` annotation

Name:	Redirect
Purpose:	Indicates that an HTTP redirect should be issued when this exception is raised.
Target:	TYPE (exception class)

Attribute	Type	Function
`message`	`String (EL)`	The message used to register an info-level `FacesMessage`. Default: the exception message.
`viewId`	`String (EL)`	The JSF view ID to redirect to when this exception is thrown. Default: the current view ID.

The `@HttpError` annotation, on the other hand, is typically used to generate a fatal
and ungraceful response to the client. I think of it as screaming at an unwelcome

guest. When an exception class annotated with @HttpError is thrown, Seam will send the specified HTTP status code to the browser along with the message in the exception. The @HttpError annotation is summarized in table 3.4.

Table 3.4   The @HttpError annotation

Name:	HttpError
Purpose:	Indicates that an HTTP error response should be sent when this exception is raised.
Target:	TYPE (exception class)

Attribute	Type	Function
message	String (EL)	The message used to register an info-level FacesMessage. Default: the exception message.
errorCode	int	One of the HTTP error code constants in the Java Servlet API. Default: 500, an internal server error.

The @ApplicationException annotation, summarized in table 3.5, is used to end a long-running conversation or immediately roll back the active transaction. When an exception class annotated with @ApplicationException is thrown, Seam determines from this annotation how to handle the conversation and the transaction. Note that unhandled exceptions always force a rollback. The @ApplicationException just forces the rollback to happen *immediately*.

Table 3.5   The @ApplicationException annotation

Name:	ApplicationException
Purpose:	Controls how the long-running conversation and transaction are handled when this exception is raised. A synonym to javax.ejb.ApplicationException for use in non-EJB environments.
Target:	TYPE (exception class)

Attribute	Type	Function
rollback	boolean	If true, this flag indicates that the transaction should roll back immediately. If false, the transaction is rolled back at the end of the request. Default: false.
end	boolean	If true, this flag indicates the long-running conversation should be ended. If false, the conversation is left untouched. Default: false.

As an example, suppose you've implemented an exception specific to your application:

```
@Redirect(viewId = "/penaltyStrokeWarning.xhtml"
    message = "You're ball is out of play. That will cost you one stroke.")
public class OutOfBoundsException extends Exception {}
```

With exceptions handled properly, and the user having received the appropriate slap on the wrist for foul play, the coverage of the Seam life cycle comes to a close. Seam is a tremendous web-oriented framework because it has taken JSF and extended it to give you all the control you need over the pages in your application.

3.7   *Summary*

In this chapter, you learned how Seam hooks into the Java Servlet and JSF life cycles to provide services for both JSF and non-JSF requests. You witnessed the multifaceted nature of this integration, which leverages a servlet listener to bootstrap Seam and listen for HTTP session events, a JSF phase listener to tap into the JSF life cycle, a servlet to generate and serve supporting resources, and a servlet filter to provide services beyond the reach of the JSF servlet. With this integration in place, focus turned toward Seam's JSF enhancements.

This chapter dedicated a section to reviewing the JSF life cycle, presenting the stark contrast between an initial request and a postback and identifying which of the six life-cycle JSF phases play a role in each scenario. You discovered that the notification of each phase transition, captured using a JSF phase listener, is how Seam weaves in many of its JSF enhancements, giving rise to the Seam life cycle. The steps of the Seam life cycle were explained.

Most of Seam's enhancements affect the initial request, in the form of page-oriented controls, which were covered in detail. The controls are configured in Seam's page descriptor, which you learned acts as a stand-in replacement for navigation rules defined in the JSF configuration file. I encouraged you to move to Seam's navigation rules to gain more intelligent navigation. You also learned that committing to Seam's page descriptor gives you the ability to accomplish tasks that JSF has been criticized for lacking in the past, such as a front controller, advanced page navigation, RESTful URLs, and exception handling. In short, by extending JSF, Seam delivers features of an action-based framework like Struts without ditching the many benefits of a component-based model.

Having gained the big picture of a Seam request, you are now ready to turn to the other essential aspects of Seam: components and contexts. In the next chapter, you'll learn about Seam components, those classes in a seam-gen project decorated with the @Name annotation. You'll discover that Seam components can effectively replace the managed bean facility in JSF. But what makes Seam stand apart is that Seam components can serve many roles, ranging from presentation to business to persistence. In fact, a single component can serve in all three roles. Read on to discover how Seam's contextual container is used to support the Seam life cycle and how Seam's liberal architecture gives Seam components tremendous utility.

Components and contexts

This chapter covers
- Defining Seam components using annotations
- Hooking into component life-cycle events
- Using EJB session beans as Seam components
- Accessing instances of Seam components

This chapter introduces the components and contexts that Seam manages. If you've worked with the Spring Framework, the idea of declaring managed objects should be familiar to you. In Seam, however, you replace all uses of the word *bean* with the word *component*. Like Spring, Seam boasts similar capabilities to define, configure, and instantiate *components*. In one regard, you can think of Seam as a lightweight container. It doesn't force you to code to container-specific interfaces, require you to adopt a special programming model, or mandate that your components even live in a container. Instead, components are just plain old Java objects (POJOs). What makes Seam unique is that it leverages existing containers and contexts to *host* the objects it instantiates, so it's more accurately classified as a meta-container. After obtaining an instance of a component, Seam decorates it with enterprise services that are applied transparently through the use of method interceptors. The main advantage that Seam has over other managed containers such as Spring is that Seam treats a component's context with equal importance as the component itself. Thus, the focus of this chapter is not just components, but rather *contextual components*.

Chapter 2 provided the opportunity to get an application up and running and observe *Seam in Action*. I am sure those exercises, as well as references from the previous chapter, have spawned *loads* of questions about components. I can assure you that your questions will be addressed in this chapter. To learn about Seam components, you're going to use top-down development to add member registration to the Open 18 application. You'll first use seam-gen to create a new entity and the supporting view and action bean component. Hibernate then takes care of adding the corresponding table to the database when the application starts based on the information in the JPA annotations on the entity class. You then study how the view, the action bean component, and the entity interact with one another. Before doing all that, though, you must understand Seam's very essence: the contextual container.

4.1 Seam's contextual naming container

At its core, Seam is a container that holds names, or rather, variable names. But Seam doesn't just let all of these variable names clump together at the bottom of the barrel. Instead, Seam divides container into compartments and disperses the variables into each one accordingly. Each compartment represents a scope, or in Seam terminology, a *context*. A context defines where a variable name can be found and for how long it hangs around.

To be precise, the Seam container holds *context variables*. A context variable can hold a reference to any type of object. But, as you'll soon discover, the real divas of the Seam container are the components. When the application interacts with a context variable holding a reference to a component instance, lots of exciting things happen. From this point forward, when I use the term *context variable*, I'm referring to a variable in the Seam container that stores a value in a distinct context.

NOTE   In the text, I'll often switch between the terms *scope* and *context*. Don't let this confuse you; these two terms are interchangeable. Technically, the context is the bucket and the scope is the marker that identifies the bucket, but that's really splitting hairs.

Before advancing with your lesson on Seam components and getting the lowdown on where they hang out, I first need to briefly introduce you to Seam's contexts and show you what sets them apart from the traditional contexts in the Java Servlet API.

4.1.1 Seam's context model

You have a set of contexts for storing variables for the same reason that you have multiple golf clubs in your bag. In golf, you choose a club depending on how far you want the ball to go. In a web application, you choose a context depending on how long you want a variable to stick around. You're likely familiar with the three scopes defined in the Java Servlet API: application, session, and request. The problem with this abridged set of scopes is that they are too few. It's like trying to play a round of golf with a driver, a five-iron, and a putter. You can make it work, but there are times when you're going to have to make each club do something for which it wasn't designed.

The vast chasms that lie between the coarse-grained servlet scopes have claimed the lives of many applications. In addition, each servlet scope requires that you use a different API to access its variables, letting unnecessary complexity slip into the code. The Seam developers solved these two obstacles by introducing the contextual naming container, which provides a single interface to access all variables, regardless of the context in which they are stored, and introduces several new contexts that fill in the gaps between the existing ones.

4.1.2   Unifying the Java servlet contexts

Seam delivers a much needed technology update to the Java web environment by establishing a *unified* context model. Seam takes all contexts under the wings of its container, allowing the existing contexts to fit naturally with the new set of contexts that it contributes. By controlling the contexts, Seam provides one-stop shopping for context variables and adds useful enhancements to the existing servlet contexts.

The list of contexts Seam adds to the existing options are the stateless context, the page context, the conversation context, and the business process context. The complete set of contexts Seam supports are represented by the names in the Java 5 enum `Scope-Type`, which you'll see used in a couple of Seam annotations later in the chapter. Table 4.1 identifies these contexts, the associated name in the enum type, and a brief description of the context's life span. Note that the stateless and unspecified scopes aren't real contexts, but rather directives that instruct Seam how to handle a variable lookup.

Table 4.1   Seam's contexts, ordered from the shortest to the longest lifespan

Context name	Enum name in org.jboss.seam.ScopeType	Description
Stateless	STATELESS	A nonstoring context. Forces a component to be instantiated each time the component name is resolved. Equivalent to Spring's prototype scope.
Event	EVENT	Analogous to the servlet request scope. Exists from the beginning of the *Restore View* phase until the end of the *Render Response* phase in the JSF life cycle or until a redirect occurs.
Page	PAGE	Begins at the start of the JSF *Render Response* phase and carries on with each adjoining JSF postback until a redirect or a navigation to another page occurs. The storage mechanism for this context is the JSF component tree.
Conversation	CONVERSATION	Lasts from at least the *Restore View* phase until the end of the *Render Response* phase, even in the event of a redirect. If converted to a long-running conversation, it spans multiple requests for a single user until terminated. Conversations are propagated by the use of a special request parameter for non-JSF postback requests and through the JSF component tree on a JSF postback.
Session	SESSION	Analogous to the servlet session scope. Access to session-scoped component instances are serialized.

Table 4.1 Seam's contexts, ordered from the shortest to the longest lifespan *(continued)*

Context name	Enum name in org.jboss.seam.ScopeType	Description
Application	APPLICATION	Analogous to the servlet application scope.
Business process	BUSINESS_PROCESS	Spans multiple conversations for multiple users as controlled declaratively by start and end states in the business process definition file.
Unspecified	UNSPECIFIED	A directive to indicate that the scope should be implied. Depending on the circumstance, it tells Seam to either use the scope of the current component or to performing a hierarchical search across all scopes.

Let's briefly explore the storing contexts and the relevance of each, starting with the stateful contexts contributed by Seam.

4.1.3 *Seam's new stateful contexts*

Seam makes a big deal about providing *stateful* contexts. As the user interacts with the application, state is accumulated and that state needs to be tracked. In traditional web applications, long-term state would be stored in the HTTP session, the de facto stateful context. However, Seam encourages you to store long-term state in a context whose lifetime aligns better with a user's interaction. In support of this recommendation, Seam's stateful context stack includes two new contexts, conversation and business process, that model a use case, rather than being fixed to predetermined boundaries like the HTTP session scope. Seam also exposes JSF's view root attributes as the page context, solidifying them as a legitimate stateful context. Having these new stateful contexts is important because they help reduce load on the server while also staving off bugs caused by inadvertent sharing of state. But what's most important about Seam's array of stateful contexts is that they prevent misuse of the HTTP session. Let's consider the purpose and duration of each context.

JSF has always supported a page scope, which is an unofficial classification of the attributes stored in the view root of the JSF UI component tree. Seam recognizes these attributes as first-class context variables and exposes them via the Seam page context. The page context is capable of propagating data from the *Render Response* phase of the JSF life cycle through at least the ensuing *Invoke Application* phase on a postback, then on to the *Render Response* phase if the same view is rendered again without a redirect. This cycle continues for as many times as the same UI component tree is restored (as a result of a postback), and is only terminated by a navigation event that occurs prior to the *Render Response* phase. You may have used this scope in a less formal way if you have ever included the <t:saveState> component tag from the MyFaces Tomahawk component set[1] in your application. The benefit of using Seam's page context is that you don't tie the state logic to the view.

---

[1] http://myfaces.apache.org/tomahawk/uiSaveState.html

The conversation and business process scopes are for managing long-running processes. Their boundaries are controlled declaratively using annotations or page descriptor tags. A conversation is a drop-in replacement for most uses of the session scope. The business process is a variation on the conversation scope, but can pass state between multiple users of the application, backed by persistence storage. You'll learn more about conversations in chapter 7 and business processes in chapter 14 (online).

4.1.4   *Seam's enhanced servlet contexts*

Seam doesn't turn its back on the traditional Java servlet contexts—it just fixes them. Seam even uses the Java Servlet API as the underlying storage mechanism for these particular contexts, though not blindly. By taking control of these scopes, Seam is able to generalize their purpose and address flaws in how they are handled by the native container.

For instance, the event context wraps the servlet request scope. This abstraction generalizes a web request as an event so that the Java Servlet API is abstracted from Seam's core. This generalization opens the door for Seam to support the event construct as defined in alternate environments. For typical web development, the event context and request scope are one and the same.

There are times when variables need to be retained throughout a logical request—defined as the time between when a page is requested and when it is rendered. A logical request differs from a servlet request when it involves one or more interim redirects. An example is the Redirect-After-Post pattern.[2] Unfortunately, the request scope is useless in this case since it doesn't survive a redirect. Developers who have used the Redirect-After-Post pattern on a JSF postback know that it causes all request-scoped data prepared in the *Invoke Application* phase to be dropped. The data that is most often missed is the JSF status messages. So what does Seam do to help? In the absence of a long-running conversation, which you'll learn about in chapter 7, Seam's conversation scope propagates context variables across a logical request—what Seam terms a temporary conversation. A temporary conversation covers the purpose of a Ruby on Rails flash hash. Seam's conversation-scoped `FacesMessages` component can be used, for instance, to ensure that JSF status messages survive redirects. Problem solved.

KEEPING COMPONENTS @SYNCHRONIZED

Seam improves the session context as well by protecting session-scoped components from concurrent access. Multiple requests scheduled to be handled by the same servlet (i.e., `FacesServlet`) may arrive at the server at the same time. These requests run in different threads but are serviced by the same servlet instance. If the application logic executed by both requests accesses the same session-scoped variable, it may result in the object referenced by that variable being altered in conflicting ways. This scenario is said to violate thread safety. To avoid it, you'd need to add the `synchronized` keyword to the region of code accessing the variable. Seam addresses this

---

[2] Redirect-After-Post is a workaround that prevents double posts as a result of the user clicking refresh after submitting a form. An explanation can be found in the Redirect After Post article on the ServerSide.com: http://www.theserverside.com/tt/articles/article.tss?l=RedirectAfterPost.

long-standing pitfall in web-based applications by automatically synchronizing session-scoped variables for you, and doing so with optimal efficiency. You can apply this synchronization logic to components in other scopes by adding the @Synchronized annotation to the class definition, summarized in table 4.2. This annotation allows the timeout period of the synchronization to be tuned using the timeout attribute.

Table 4.2 The @Synchronized annotation

Name:	Synchronized	
Purpose:	Protects a component against concurrent access	
Target:	TYPE (class)	

Attribute	**Type**	**Function**
timeout	long	The duration of time in milliseconds that a thread should be made to wait before an IllegalStateException is thrown. Default: 1000.

The important point to remember about the contextual container is that it provides access to *all* context variables through a consistent interface, regardless of the underlying storage mechanism. You'll learn how to use the context API in section 4.7. With contexts covered, let's turn the focus of our discussion to the components associated with them.

4.2   *Sorting out components*

The term *component* has been used to mean many things. In my attempts to describe it to you, I found it difficult to locate a universal definition, likely because one doesn't exist. In theory, a component is supposedly a module that can be plugged into an application in the same way that one Lego piece is attached to another Lego piece to form a larger structure. As a person who makes a living developing software, I'm sure you'll agree that software components are a bit more complicated than Legos.

Definitions and intentions don't matter anyway. What matters is what the word means to you as a software developer. Up to now, we've assumed that a component is equivalent to a JSF managed bean. Although a Seam component can stand in for a JSF managed bean, the definition of a component is broader. A component is a set of instructions, stored in a container, that is used to create objects whose life cycle is managed by the container. After taking a deeper, but brief dive into this somewhat abstract term, I promise that this *component* jargon will make sense. It's all in the naming.

4.2.1   *Components vs. component instances*

A component is a set of instructions, or a blueprint, for creating an object. It supplements the Java class definition. Each component is assigned a name, which is used to address the component. Table 4.3 lists several containers and how the components they manage are declared.

When a class becomes a component, it gains access to whatever services the container has to provide. For instance, methods on EJB session beans are automatically wrapped in transactions; servlet components and JSF managed beans have access to

Table 4.3   A sampling of component containers and how components are defined in each one

Container	How classes become components
Seam	Annotated with @Name or declared in components.xml
EJB	Annotated with @Stateful, @Stateless, @MessageDriven or declared in ejb-jar.xml (annotations only relevant for EJB 3)
JSF	Declared as managed beans in faces-config.xml
Spring	Declared as a Spring bean in applicationContext.xml
Servlet container	Servlets, filters, and listeners declared in web.xml

web-tier resource injections; Spring beans are injected with other Spring beans when instantiated. As you can see, being a component gives a class special privileges.

Great, so now you know what a component is. But since this book is about Seam, let's focus on Seam components. A Seam component holds

- Metadata pertaining to the creation of an instance
- Life-cycle methods
- Initial property values or object references

Seam creates component instances from the component definition, as figure 4.1 illustrates. When your application interacts with a component, what it's really invoking is an *instance* of that component.

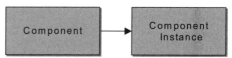

Figure 4.1   Component instances are created from components by the Seam container

---

Component vs. component instance: making the distinction

The relationship between a component and a component instance parallels the relationship between a Java class and a Java object, respectively. Seam even uses the Component type to describe a component definition in the same way that Java uses the Class type to describe a class definition.

Once an instance of a component is created, it's stored as an attribute in its designated context under the name of the component, forming what is known as a context variable. An instance of a component is just a Java object, with one exception. It is strung with interceptors that allow Seam to keep tabs on it and manage its life cycle. Once in control, Seam is able to transparently weave behavior into the object when it is invoked. You may recognize this technique as Aspect-Oriented Programming (AOP). The idea of AOP is to handle cross-cutting concerns that would otherwise appear as boilerplate code or tie the code to a particular environment. With AOP at work, a method call isn't just a method call. More goes on around each invocation, and that means you get more for less work.

Seam determines how to handle the object based on the instructions provided in annotations. The behavior that Seam applies includes injecting dependencies, managing transactions, enforcing security constraints, invoking life-cycle methods, and handling events triggered by the component, to mention a few. That should sound similar to how EJB works as it inspired this design.

4.2.2 Seam manages components

There's another important characteristic of a component: a component is managed by the Seam container. The container hands out an instance of a component when the name assigned to the component is requested, as shown in figure 4.2. When this request comes in, Seam first tries to locate an existing instance. If one can't be found, Seam will create one (if asked to do so). The instance is then returned to the requester.

With Seam in control, you no longer have to create instances by instantiating the Java class explicitly using the Java `new` operator. That isn't to say that you can't—but to get all of the enhancements that Seam applies to the object via AOP (which happens during the `newInstance()` routine in figure 4.2), you must allow Seam to create the instance for you. In that regard, the Seam container is a factory for component instances, which uses the component definitions as the schematics for how to create those instances.

The translation from component to component instance happens more often in a Seam application than it does in other lightweight containers such as Spring. That's because context is so important in Seam. In Seam, component instances come and go along with the life cycle of the contexts in which they are stored. As you learned earlier, Seam's contexts have varying life spans (one with no life span at all). More often than not, components in Seam are associated with stateful contexts, which means they don't invariably hang around for the lifetime of the application.

Instance creation takes place in the Spring container just as it does in Seam, but you typically don't give it much thought. That's because Spring primarily uses singleton beans, whose lifetime is tied to that of the application. What's so interesting about Seam is that it's perfectly natural to create an object and inject dependencies into it at an arbitrary point in time, rather than when the application starts.

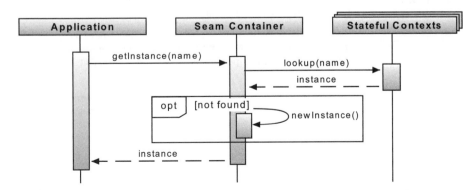

Figure 4.2 Sequence diagram of a component instance being requested from the Seam container

NOTE   Spring does provide prototype beans that are created each time they're referenced, but they are arguably more difficult to use than Seam's contextual components.

We haven't yet addressed how Seam components are defined. To be more concise, how do the components get *into* the Seam container? Read on to find out.

4.3   *Defining components using annotations*

In Seam, you can define components in one of two ways: you can use either annotations or XML. The goal of Seam is to reduce as much XML coding as possible. Therefore, annotations are the preferred mechanism for defining a Seam component. Two common alternatives are the XML-based Seam component descriptor, covered in chapter 5, and Seam's pluggable container mechanism—the integration that allows Spring beans to serve as Seam components—which is explored in chapter 15 (online). This chapter focuses on the annotation approach. The annotations that dictate how a component is defined are listed in table 4.4. As the chapter develops, I'll introduce you to each one in detail.

Table 4.4   Seam annotations that define components and declare how they are instantiated

Annotation	What it does
@Name	Declares a class as a Seam component and assigns it a name. When the component name is requested, Seam instantiates a new instance of the class and binds it to the context variable with the same name.
@Scope	Specifies the default scope in which the context variable is stored when an instance of the component is instantiated.
@Role (@Roles)	Defines alternate name and scope pairings for the component that can be used to instantiate parallel instances of the same component for different purposes. Multiple @Role declarations are wrapped in a @Roles annotation.
@Startup	Instructs Seam to instantiate the component automatically when its assigned context starts (only applies to application-scoped and session-scoped components).
@Namespace	Binds a URI to a Java package and used to define custom XML namespaces in the Seam component descriptor.
@Install	Used to make installation of a component conditional or to provide a precedence to override another component definition. Conditions include the presence of a class on the classpath, the presence of another component, or the debug mode setting.
@AutoCreate	Tells Seam to create a new instance of the component when the component name is first requested, even if the calling code doesn't request for it to be created.

This section concentrates on @Name and @Scope, which together form an integral component definition. The remaining annotations are auxiliary and affect how the component is processed or behaves at runtime.

4.3.1   Giving a component a @Name

It all starts with a @Name. The most fundamental way of creating a Seam component is by adding the @Name annotation to the class declaration. This annotation is summarized in table 4.5. Given that every Seam component must be assigned a name, you must provide one using the value attribute of the @Name annotation.

Table 4.5   The @Name annotation

Name:	Name
Purpose:	Marks a Java class as a Seam component and assigns the component a unique name
Target:	TYPE (class)

Attribute	Type	Function
value	String	The name of the component. This value is used as the name of the context variable to which instances are bound in the component's scope. Default: none (required).

You can place a @Name annotation on any class that you'd like to dress up as a Seam component. Keep in mind, though, that annotations are obviously only useful for classes that you can modify. See the accompanying sidebar describing the syntax of annotations if you're unfamiliar with how to use them.

The syntax of annotations

Annotations are markers. They consist of a Java type—a name prefixed with an at sign (@)—and a set of attributes associated with that type. Annotations can be placed on interfaces, class definitions (types), methods, fields, parameters, and packages. The acceptable locations are defined by the annotation.

The attribute assignments for an annotation appear as a list of name-value pairs placed between a set of parentheses and separated by commas. There's an exception to this syntax rule, though. If you're defining exactly one attribute, and the name of that attribute is value, then the attribute name and the equals sign (=) can be omitted. If the name of the attribute is not value, or you're defining multiple attributes on a single annotation, then both the attribute name and value are required for every attribute. If you're not declaring any attributes, the parentheses can be omitted.

Attribute values can be primitives, Java types, annotations, or arrays of the former. When defining an array value, the items are placed between a set of curly braces and separated by commas. Again, there is an exception to this syntax rule. If the multi-valued attribute has exactly one item, the curly braces can be omitted.

The coolest part of Seam is its ability to normalize the nonsemantic differences among components' native types. The list of candidates for a Seam component includes

- JavaBean (POJO)
  - JavaBean
  - Groovy class (Groovy Bean)
  - Spring bean[3]
- EJB component
  - Stateless session bean
  - Stateful session bean
  - Message-driven bean
- JPA entity class (treated differently than JavaBean components)

Seam decorates JavaBean components with functionality equivalent to what is provided by the EJB container, such as container-managed transaction management and security, shielding the rest of the application from being affected by the underlying type. What sets components in Seam apart from those in other containers is the attention to the context of a component instance—the scope of its existence.

4.3.2   *Putting a component in @Scope*

The @Name annotation is only half of the component story in Seam. The component instance has to be put somewhere once it's created. That's where the @Scope annotation comes in. The @Scope annotation dictates the contextual scope in which an instance of the component will be stored after it's instantiated by the Seam container. You can, of course, put the component instance anywhere you want using a manual assignment. The @Scope annotation just determines the *default* scope where Seam stores the instance. Table 4.6 lists the scope that is used for each type of component if one is not specified in the component definition.

Component type	Default scope assignment
EJB stateful session bean	Conversation
JPA entity class	Conversation
EJB stateless session bean	Stateless
EJB message driven bean	Stateless
JavaBean (POJO)	Event

Table 4.6   Seam component classifications and default scopes

You can override these default scope assignments by adding the @Scope annotation, summarized in table 4.7, to the class definition.

Let's consider an example of how to put the @Name and @Scope annotations together to develop a new module for the Open 18 application.

---

[3] Spring beans are classes that are managed by the Spring container. Seam can "borrow" a bean from the Spring container and decorate it with Seam services, just like it can with EJB components.

Table 4.7   The @Scope annotation

Name:	Scope
Purpose:	Overrides the default scope for a Seam component
Target:	TYPE (class)

Attribute	Type	Function
value	ScopeType	The Seam context in which instances of this component are stored. Table 4.6 lists the default value according to component type. Default: none (required).

4.4   A comprehensive component example

To add member registration to the Open 18 application, we first need to create an entity that holds a member's details. Thus, we're going to make a JPA entity class our first Seam component. Because members who register with the Open 18 application are golfers, we'll name the corresponding entity Golfer.

4.4.1   Creating the entity components

To create the Golfer entity, navigate to the Seam distribution directory and run the seam new-entity command using the following responses:

```
Entity class name: Golfer
Master page name: golferList
Detail page name: golfer
```

The new-entity command generates the Golfer JPA entity class containing a base set of properties, a page to list the golfers (golferList.xhtml) and corresponding page controller (GolferList), and a page to display the details of a golfer (golfer.xhtml) and corresponding page controller (GolferHome). The action beans components that support the CRUD operations are covered in depth in chapter 10. For now, let's focus on using the Golfer entity class for the registration page.

The @Entity annotation added to the class declaration marks this class a JPA entity and the @Table annotation customizes the database table mapping. Whenever you add a new entity to the application, you also need to add a corresponding table to the database. Fortunately, Hibernate takes care of this task for you when the application is deployed as long as the value of the Hibernate property hibernate.hbm2ddl.auto in the resources/META-INF/persistence-dev-war.xml descriptor is update. Note that this is a change from the default value of validate set by seam-gen. Hibernate will also add additional table columns for any new entity properties that it detects.

I've decided to enhance the Golfer class, shown in listing 4.1, by making it a subclass of Member, shown in listing 4.2. The use of entity inheritance sets the stage for a more flexible and realistic application. However, don't concern yourself too much with the JPA annotations, such as @PrimaryKeyJoinColumn, if they aren't familiar to you, because the primary focus here is on using this class as a form "backing" bean in a JSF page. In order for that to happen, it needs to be declared as a Seam component.

To make `Golfer` a Seam component, you simply add the `@Name` and `@Scope` annotations alongside the JPA annotations, shown in bold in listing 4.1. The component name `newGolfer` has been chosen since the component will be called on to instantiate a fresh instance of a golfer for use in the registration form. The `@Scope` annotation is present to explicitly bind the component to the event scope for demonstration, overriding the default scope assignment for entity classes, which is the conversation scope. Several bean properties have been added to support the use case, which map to columns in the `GOLFER` table. Also note the use of the Hibernate Validator annotations which, as you learned in the previous chapter, help enforce validations in the UI.

AUTHOR NOTE   An alternative to adding `@Name` and `@Scope` to a JPA entity class is to declare the component in the Seam component descriptor using XML, which you'll learn about in the next chapter. For now, appreciate that the use of annotations keeps things simple by eliminating XML configuration. Given that annotations are merely class metadata, they don't affect the execution of the code (unless consulted using reflection). I confess that I prefer to limit the use of the `@Name` annotation to action beans and business components. Entity classes are the most frequently shared components, so conflicts can occur between teams over how to define the Seam annotations. Besides, entity classes instantiated by the persistence manager aren't decorated with Seam interceptors. The primary use of a Seam entity component is to serve as a prototype—a new, transient (not yet persisted) instance. The prototype typically requires additional configuration that can only be defined in the component descriptor.

Listing 4.1   The `Golfer` entity class as a Seam component

```
package org.open18.model;

import java.util.Date;
import javax.persistence.*;
import org.hibernate.validator.*;
import org.jboss.seam.annotations.*;
import org.jboss.seam.ScopeType;

@Entity
@PrimaryKeyJoinColumn(name = "MEMBER_ID")
@Table(name = "GOLFER")
@Name("newGolfer")
@Scope(ScopeType.EVENT)
public class Golfer extends Member {
    private String firstName;
    private String lastName;
    private Gender gender;
    private Date dateJoined;
    private Date dateOfBirth;
    private String location;

    @Column(name = "last_name", nullable = false)
    @NotNull @Length(max = 40)
    public String getLastName() { return lastName; }
    public void setLastName(String lastName) {
```

```
        this.lastName = lastName;
    }

    @Column(name = "first_name", nullable = false)
    @NotNull @Length(max = 40)
    public String getFirstName() { return firstName; }
    public void setFirstName(String firstName) {
        this.firstName = firstName;
    }

    @Transient
    public String getName() { return firstName + ' ' + lastName; }

    @Enumerated(EnumType.STRING)
    public Gender getGender() { return gender; }
    public void setGender(Gender gender) {
        this.gender = gender;
    }

    @Temporal(TemporalType.TIMESTAMP)
    @Column(name = "joined", nullable = false, updatable = false)
    @NotNull
    public Date getDateJoined() { return dateJoined; }
    public void setDateJoined(Date dateJoined) {
        this.dateJoined = dateJoined;
    }

    @Temporal(TemporalType.DATE)
    @Column(name = "dob")
    public Date getDateOfBirth() { return dateOfBirth; }
    public void setDateOfBirth(Date dateOfBirth) {
        this.dateOfBirth = dateOfBirth;
    }

    public String getLocation() { return this.location; }
    public void setLocation(String location) {
        this.location = location;
    }
}
```

Member is an abstract entity class that holds the username, passwordHash, and emailAddress inherited by the Golfer entity. The Member entity, shown in listing 4.2, uses a joined-inheritance strategy. This design makes it possible to have different types of members that are represented in separate tables. For the purpose of this registration example, we assume that a golfer is the only type of member. Again, don't get bogged down in this design if you're new to JPA. Appreciate that the goal here is to establish a JavaBean that can be used to capture data from the registration form.

Listing 4.2   The Member entity class, a superclass for application user types

```
package org.open18.model;

import java.io.Serializable;
import javax.persistence.*;
import org.hibernate.validator.*;

@Entity
@Inheritance(strategy = InheritanceType.JOINED)
```

```
@Table(name = "MEMBER", uniqueConstraints = {
    @UniqueConstraint(columnNames = "username"),
    @UniqueConstraint(columnNames = "email_address")
})
public abstract class Member implements Serializable {
    private Long id;
    private String username;
    private String passwordHash;
    private String emailAddress;

    @Id @GeneratedValue
    public Long getId() { return id; }
    public void setId(Long id) {
        this.id = id;
    }

    @Column(name = "username", nullable = false)
    @NotNull @Length(min = 6)
    public String getUsername() { return username; }
    public void setUsername(String username) {
        this.username = username;
    }

    @Column(name = "password_hash", nullable = false)
    @NotNull
    public String getPasswordHash() { return passwordHash; }
    public void setPasswordHash(String passwordHash) {
        this.passwordHash = passwordHash;
    }

    @Column(name = "email_address", nullable = false)
    @NotNull @Email
    public String getEmailAddress() { return emailAddress; }
    public void setEmailAddress(String emailAddress) {
        this.emailAddress = emailAddress;
    }
}
```

The registration form needs to capture a plain-text password from the user as well as a password confirmation. Corresponding properties aren't found on either the Golfer or the Member entity since these fields aren't to be persisted. Rather than dirtying the entity classes with transient fields, we'll put these fields on a reusable JavaBean, PasswordBean, defined in listing 4.3. The PasswordBean also contains a business method for verifying that the two passwords entered are equivalent. This class is created under the src/model directory of the seam-gen project along with the entity classes.

Listing 4.3 A Seam JavaBean component that holds and verifies a new password

```
package org.open18.auth;

import org.jboss.seam.annotations.Name;

@Name("passwordBean")
public class PasswordBean {
    private String password;
    private String confirm;

    public String getPassword() { return password; }
```

```
        public void setPassword(String password) { this.password = password; }

        public String getConfirm() { return confirm; }
        public void setConfirm(String confirm) { this.confirm = confirm; }

        public boolean verify() {
            return confirm != null && confirm.equals(password);
        }
    }
```

To give you a true appreciation of how easy Seam is making your life, I want to now show you how @Name and @Scope provide everything necessary to design a JSF form and action bean component to process the form submission. No XML is required.

4.4.2 *Preparing an action bean component*

Return once again to the Seam distribution directory. Execute the command seam new-action to create the RegisterAction component using the following responses:

```
Seam component name: registerAction
Bean class name: RegisterAction
Action method name: register
Page name: register
```

This command generates the RegisterAction JavaBean class shown in listing 4.4. The @Name annotation above this class makes it a Seam component. Since the @Scope annotation is excluded, and this is a regular JavaBean, instances of it are bound to the event context. (The Seam annotations @In and @Logger are described later in this chapter.) This component will serve as an action bean component—a component that provides action methods used by UI command components. A Seam component used for this purpose completely replaces the need for a JSF managed bean.

The RegisterAction component contains a single method, register(), that will be used as the target of the form on the register.xhtml page, also generated by the new-action command. Although the register() method is just a stub, it will suffice for now. You'll develop the RegisterAction component and register.xhtml page further as you progress through the chapter.

Listing 4.4 The Seam component that handles the member registration

```
package org.open18.action;

import org.jboss.seam.annotations.*;
import org.jboss.seam.log.Log;
import org.jboss.seam.faces.FacesMessages;

@Name("registerAction")
public class RegisterAction {

    @Logger private Log log;

    @In private FacesMessages facesMessages;

    public void register() {
        log.info("registerAction.register() action called");
        facesMessages.add("register");
    }
}
```

Before taking another step down the development path, we need to safeguard our-selves by creating a test. Fortunately, seam-gen has already done the legwork for us.

4.4.3   Integration testing components

To practice good agile development techniques, you always want to create a test either before or while you're developing a new component. Conveniently, the `new-action` command also generated an integration test class, `RegisterActionTest`, in the src/test directory. The test class, shown in listing 4.5, has been renamed to `RegisterGolfer-IntegrationTest` to better represent its function as an integration test.

Listing 4.5   A TestNG-based Seam integration test

```
package org.open18.test;

import org.jboss.seam.mock.SeamTest;
import org.testng.annotations.Test;

public class RegisterGolferIntegrationTest extends SeamTest {

    @Test
    public void test_register() throws Exception {
        new FacesRequest() {                          Indicates method
            @Override                          ◁───── override (Java 5)
            protected void invokeApplication() {
                invokeMethod("#{registerAction.register}");
            }
        }.run();
    }
}
```

The test class in listing 4.5 extends `SeamTest`, which bootstraps the Embedded JBoss to provide a Java EE–compliant environment in which to test your components. The `FacesRequest` anonymous inner class is used to emulate the JSF life cycle, shown here passing through the *Invoke Application* phase. seam-gen projects use the testing frame-work TestNG. A TestNG configuration file, RegisterActionTest.xml, is created along with this class to configure the test runner. A modified version that takes into account the renamed test class is shown here:

```
<!DOCTYPE suite SYSTEM "http://beust.com/testng/testng-1.0.dtd">
<suite name="RegisterAction Tests" verbose="2" parallel="false">
  <test name="RegisterAction Test">
      <class name="org.open18.test.RegisterGolferIntegrationTest"/>
    </classes>
  </test>
</suite>
```

The Ant target named `test` in the project's build.xml file looks for files ending in Test.xml and feeds them into the TestNG test runner to execute. You should be able to run `ant test` from the root of the project to verify that the test passes, producing the output shown here:

```
test:
   [testng] [Parser] Running:
```

```
[testng]    /home/twoputt/projects/open18/test-build/
➥RegisterAction.xml
[testng]
[testng] INFO  [org.open18.action.RegisterAction] registerAction.
➥register() action called
[testng] PASSED: test_register
[testng]
[testng] ===============================================
[testng]     RegisterAction Test
[testng]     Tests run: 1, Failures: 0, Skips: 0
[testng] ===============================================
[testng]
[testng]
[testng] ===============================================
[testng] RegisterAction Tests
[testng] Total tests run: 1, Failures: 0, Skips: 0
[testng] ===============================================
[testng]

BUILD SUCCESSFUL
Total time: 12 seconds
```

You can adjust the log levels used during a test run by editing the Log4j configuration bootstrap/log4j.xml. The file src/test/readme.txt contains instructions on how to run a Seam integration test from Eclipse (it requires that you have Embedded JBoss on the test classpath).

NOTE The Embedded JBoss bundled with Seam 2.0 only works with a Java 5 runtime (not a Java 6 or 7 runtime). Until a version of Seam is released with a Java 6–compatible Embedded JBoss container, you must run tests using Java 5.

What about unit tests?

Seam favors the use of integration tests, not unit tests, for validating the behavior of action bean components. This approach aligns with Seam's goal to eliminate unnecessary layers. These integration tests are necessary if your action bean component works with an ORM or JSF directly. You can use Seam to create a well-layered application, thus allowing you to create unit tests at the boundaries of every layer. Seam just helps you get an application up and running quickly, and for that, integration tests are the tests that matter the most.

If you believe strongly in the fact that your unit tests should run without any external dependencies—such as the Embedded JBoss runtime—and your action bean component depends on functionality provided by the Seam container, it's possible to bootstrap a mock Seam container. Refer to the Seam test suite for examples of how this is done. If you venture down that path, I encourage you to have a framework like EasyMock handy to mock built-in Seam components that are harder to make work in isolation.

The action bean component `RegisterAction` is just a stub at this point, but it's good enough to turn to the task of creating the JSF template that renders the registration form. Using test-driven development (TDD) principles, we'll complete the implementation of the `register()` method when we need it—not a minute sooner.

4.4.4   *Hooking components into JSF*

Now we need to set up JSF so that it can access the Seam components. Guess what? There's nothing to do! Believe it or not, any Seam component is accessible to JSF as is (see the accompanying sidebar). The `@Name` annotation can be compared to defining a JSF managed bean in the faces-config.xml descriptor, except that the resulting component is far more capable. While you may look back and see that you've entered quite a bit of code, you haven't had to write a single line of XML. And there's no need to mess with glue code, either. `Golfer` and `PasswordBean` can serve as backing beans, and `RegisterAction` can provide the action method for the registration page. All you need to do is write a JSF view to use them. Let's enhance the registration view generated by seam-gen to capture the input necessary to register a new member.

Resolving Seam components from JSF

Seam establishes a bridge between JSF and its own container by registering a custom expression language (EL) resolver with the JSF 1.2 application runtime. The configuration for this resolver is defined in the faces-config.xml descriptor in the Seam core JAR file:

```
<faces-config>
  <application>
   <el-resolver>org.jboss.seam.el.SeamELResolver</el-resolver>
  </application>
</faces-config>
```

When a Seam component name is used as the root—the first segment—of an EL expression, Seam either locates or creates a component instance and makes it available to the variable resolver. For instance, the EL resolver divides the expression `#{passwordBean.password}` into the method `getPassword()` on a Seam component named `passwordBean`. If the custom resolver cannot find a matching Seam component, it passes the torch back to the default JSF variable resolver.

JSF VIEWS, SEAM-STYLE

The register.xhtml page was created with a basic JSF form when you ran the `new-action` command, but we need to add input fields to it. The augmented form is shown in listing 4.6. The `register()` method on the `RegisterAction` component serves as the form's action, as defined by the method-binding expression `#{registerAction.register}` in the `action` attribute of the UI command button. This method-binding expression is derived by combining the component name of the action bean component, `register-Action`, with the name of the action method, `register` (minus the parentheses). Seam also prepares an instance of the `Golfer` entity class, binding it to the context variable `newGolfer`, and an instance of the `PasswordBean` JavaBean class, binding it to the context variable `passwordBean`, which are both used to capture data from the input fields.

Listing 4.6   The golfer registration form

```
<h:form id="registerActionForm">
  <rich:panel>
    <f:facet name="header">Open 18 Member Registration</f:facet>
    <s:decorate id="firstNameField" template="layout/edit.xhtml">
      <ui:define name="label">First name</ui:define>
      <h:inputText id="firstName"
        value="#{newGolfer.firstName}" required="true"/>
    </s:decorate>
    <s:decorate id="lastNameField" template="layout/edit.xhtml">
      <ui:define name="label">Last name</ui:define>
      <h:inputText id="lastName"
        value="#{newGolfer.lastName}" required="true"/>
    </s:decorate>
    <s:decorate id="emailField" template="layout/edit.xhtml">
      <ui:define name="label">Email address</ui:define>
      <h:inputText id="emailAddress"
        value="#{newGolfer.emailAddress}" required="true"/>
    </s:decorate>
    <s:decorate id="usernameField" template="layout/edit.xhtml">
      <ui:define name="label">Username</ui:define>
      <h:inputText id="username"
        value="#{newGolfer.username}" required="true"/>
    </s:decorate>
    <s:decorate id="passwordField" template="layout/edit.xhtml">
      <ui:define name="label">Password</ui:define>
      <h:inputSecret id="password"
        value="#{passwordBean.password}" required="true"/>
    </s:decorate>
    <s:decorate id="confirmField" template="layout/edit.xhtml">
      <ui:define name="label">Confirm password</ui:define>
      <h:inputSecret id="confirm"
        value="#{passwordBean.confirm}" required="true"/>
    </s:decorate>
    <s:decorate id="dateOfBirthField" template="layout/edit.xhtml">
      <ui:define name="label">Date of birth</ui:define>
      <rich:calendar id="dateOfBirth"
        value="#{newGolfer.dateOfBirth}"/>
    </s:decorate>
    <s:decorate id="genderField" template="layout/edit.xhtml">
      <ui:define name="label">Gender</ui:define>
      <h:selectOneRadio id="gender" value="#{newGolfer.gender}">
        <s:convertEnum/>
        <s:enumItem enumValue="MALE" label="Male"/>
        <s:enumItem enumValue="FEMALE" label="Female"/>
      </h:selectOneRadio>
    </s:decorate>
    <s:decorate id="locationField" template="layout/edit.xhtml">
      <ui:define name="label">Location</ui:define>
      <h:inputText id="location" value="#{newGolfer.location}"/>
```

```
      </s:decorate>
      <div style="clear:both">
        <span class="required">*</span> required fields
      </div>
    </rich:panel>
    <div class="actionButtons">
      <h:commandButton id="cancel" value="Cancel"
        action="home" immediate="true"/>
      <h:commandButton id="register" value="Register"
        action="#{registerAction.register}">
        <s:defaultAction/>
      </h:commandButton>
    </div>
  </h:form>
```

This form should appear familiar to you since the markup, particularly <s:decorate>, was covered in the previous chapter. Let's focus on how the form data is exchanged with our components. Value-binding expressions that take the form #{newGolfer. username} are a two-way street. They're used to output a component property to the screen as well as capture a value to be assigned to the property when the form is submitted. This form captures data from the user and assigns the values to the properties of the Seam components bound to the newGolfer and passwordBean context variables.

This JSF template takes advantage of several UI components not yet covered. The <s:convertEnum> and <s:enumItem> Seam UI component tags translate Java 5 enum type properties to and from string values. The <rich:calendar> component tag from RichFaces lets the user select a date using a pop-up calendar. The <s:defaultAction> Seam UI component tag sets which button is activated when the user presses the Enter key. This overrides the default browser behavior of associating the first submit button in the form with the Enter key, which in this case would be the Cancel button. For a complete list of component tags that Seam adds to JSF, consult the Seam reference documentation.

As you can see, annotations and Seam UI component tags dramatically reduce the amount of work necessary to pull together a JSF application. While we still need to provide an implementation for the register() action method, the @Name annotation is the only link needed to get JSF working with your Seam components.

A component lives a busy life outside of these moments in the limelight. In the next section, you'll get a glimpse behind the scenes of the life of a component: how it's discovered, selected, groomed, and managed by the Seam container.

4.5 *A component's life*

Before a component definition can be used to spawn component instances, the definition of the component must be discovered by the Seam container. Even upon discovery, the component may not be loaded into the Seam container if its prerequisites aren't satisfied. Once loaded, Seam will create an instance from the definition immediately if it's a startup component or wait for it to be requested if not. Regardless of when instance creation occurs, its life-cycle callback methods are invoked before the instance is returned to the requester. Finally, when the component is destroyed or goes out of scope, it has one last opportunity to perform work before being cast away. That's a component's life; let's start from the birth.

4.5.1 *Loading component definitions*

In order for the components to get into the container, Seam has to find them. This happens during the Seam initialization process. The means by which Seam is bootstrapped is covered in the previous chapter. During initialization, a deployment scanner scours the classpath looking for classes that host the @Name annotation. In addition to Java classes, Seam accepts both compiled and noncompiled Groovy classes. Seam also looks for classes that are identified as components in the XML-based component descriptor and loads them into the container. The component descriptor is covered in depth in the next chapter.

For each class declared as a component, Seam creates a component definition and stashes it away in the application scope. The name of the attribute under which the component definition is stored is derived by appending .component to the component name (e.g., registerAction.component). For your purposes, you'll *always* address the component by its component name (e.g., registerAction).

Many XML configurations were devised because the Java language lacked a common syntax for adding class metadata that is detectable by the classloader. That changed when annotations were introduced. The component scanner frees you from having to declare every Seam component in an XML descriptor because it's capable of seeking out classes that host the @Name annotation. The result is that you have one less XML file to juggle (and no unnecessary layer of abstraction).

Ah, but there's a catch! Seam only considers qualified classpath entries (class directories and JAR files). A classpath entry is considered qualified if it contains a seam.properties file at its root or the META-INF directory contains a component descriptor (i.e., components.xml). In the next chapter, you'll discover that the seam.properties file has another use: to initialize the properties of Seam components.

Figure 4.3 shows the presence of the seam.properties file at the root of classpath for the open18.jar. If you have Seam components deployed and they aren't being picked up, the first thing to verify is that a seam.properties file is present on the classpath where your Seam components reside.

Requiring the presence of a marker file is a JVM classloader optimization that works to pare down the number of classpath entries that must be scanned for components. Though it may seem annoying to have to ensure that a marker file is present, this annoyance pays off in that it helps Seam figure out which classpath entries are relevant. Without this optimization, Seam would go looking all over the classpath for components, possibly even stepping into the application server classpath, an expensive and potentially

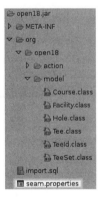

Figure 4.3 Seam will scan this classpath entry since it contains the seam.properties marker file.

error-prone operation. By using the classpath markers, Seam knows exactly where to look.

It is possible that even though a class is in a qualified classpath entry and has a @Name annotation, or it's declared as a component in the component descriptor, it still won't be recognized as a Seam component. The next section details how to define prerequisites on a class that make its installation conditional.

4.5.2   *When to @Install a component*

When the component scanner finds a class annotated with @Name, the default behavior is to make it a component. While the automatic discovery of components is a powerful mechanism, you lose a degree of flexibility over which classes are turned into components. That's where the @Install annotation comes into play. This @Install annotation, summarized in table 4.8, tells Seam the conditions under which to honor a component declaration. It can also be used to allow a second definition of the same component to override the first. Both cases will be considered in detail.

You have a wide range of prerequisites for controlling the condition under which a component is installed. The most clear-cut is the value attribute on the @Install annotation, which is a boolean that can be used to switch the component on or off.

Table 4.8   The @Install annotation

Name:	Install	
Purpose:	Used to define a set of prerequisite conditions necessary for a component declaration to be accepted and the component registered with the Seam container (i.e., installed).	
Target:	TYPE (class)	

Attribute	Type	Function
value	boolean	A flag indicating whether to install the component. Subsequent conditions may still prevent the component from being installed. Default: true.
dependencies	String[]	The names of other components that must be installed for this component to be installed. Default: none.
classDependencies	String[]	Classes that must be available on the classpath for this component to be installed. Classes are provided as strings to avoid unnecessary compilation requirements. Default: none.
genericDependencies	Class[]	Classes that must be acting as components for this component to be installed. Default: none.
precedence	int	A weighted value used to compare against other components assigned the same name. The component of higher precedence will be installed. Default: 20.
debug	boolean	Indicates that this component should only be installed when Seam is operating in debug mode. Default: false.

You can further control whether the component is installed by enforcing any of the following prerequisites:

- The presence of other component definitions, looked up by component name
- The presence of other component definitions, looked up by class name
- Classes available on the classpath
- A weighted precedence value (selects one definition over another for the same component name and precedence combination)
- The Seam debug mode setting

If the prerequisites are not satisfied, that doesn't mean that its future as a component is entirely bleak, though. You can still place it back into the ranks of the other components by declaring it in the component descriptor. Several built-in Seam components are declared using `@Install(false)`, allowing you to enable them as needed. A sampling of components include

- Seam managed persistence context
- jBPM session factory
- POJO cache
- Asynchronous dispatcher (Quartz, EJB 3, Spring)
- Non-JTA transaction manager
- JMS topic publisher
- Spring context loader

Aside from limiting the set of component definitions, conditional installation can be useful for selecting between alternate implementations of a component.

ALTERNATE IMPLEMENTATIONS

There are times when you need to perform different logic to support different implementations of the same API, such as the JSF specification or application server environment. To keep your component clean, void of conditional logic that checks for the presence of an implementation class, you may choose to separate the logic for each implementation into different components and have the appropriate component selected by Seam according to the prerequisites defined in the `@Install` annotation.

To make use of the `@Install` annotation in this case, you create two implementation classes and one interface. Then you give the two implementations the same component name, and let the `@Install` annotation handle which one will be configured based on the presence of a particular JSF implementation class.

You can create a component for the Sun JSF implementation:

```
@Name("jsfAdapter")
@Install(classDependencies = "com.sun.faces.context.FacesContextImpl")
public class SunJsfAdapter implements JsfAdapter {...}
```

and another for the MyFaces JSF implementation:

```
@Name("jsfAdapter")
@Install(classDependencies =
```

```
        "org.apache.myfaces.context.servlet.ServletFacesContextImpl")
public class MyFacesJsfAdapter implements JsfAdapter {...}
```

You can then request the component named `jsfAdapter` from the Seam container and Seam will return the appropriate implementation for you depending on which `FacesContext` implementation class is available on the classpath.

How many frameworks completely overlook this type of functionality, forcing you to devise your own solution? Conditional installation is a fundamental part of defining components.

NOTE Seam doesn't allow EL value expressions to be used in the `value` attribute of the `@Install` annotation. However, you can put a replacement token (a name surround by a pair of @ symbols) in the `installed` attribute on the `<component>` element and then have your build supply an environment-specific value for that token in the components.properties file. You'll learn how to use replacement tokens in the next chapter.

There is another facet to alternate implementations: you can define components that should only be available during development mode, possibly ones that override equivalently named production components.

DEBUG MODE COMPONENTS

Another way to control the installation of a component is to tie it to Seam's debug mode flag. You do so by setting the `debug` attribute on the `@Install` annotation to `true`. Seam's debug mode is controlled by the `debug` property on the `org.jboss.seam.core.init` component. You enable the debug mode flag by adding the following declaration to the component descriptor:

```
<core:init debug="true"/>
```

You'll learn how to configure built-in Seam components using XML in the next chapter. For now, let's focus on the effect of this setting. When it's set to `true`, Seam activates components that are marked with `@Install(debug=true)`. You can use this flag to swap in components that return canned data or otherwise stub out back-end logic. In debug mode, the debug component has higher priority. When it comes time to deploy to a production environment, the debug component is disabled, and if a non-debug component with the same component name exists, it becomes activated.

Speaking of priority, one component definition can be selected over another based on its precedence. A precedence value is required any time you have two components assigned to the same component name. Let's see how Seam handles the curve ball of conflicting component definitions.

INSTALLATION PRECEDENCE

Precedence defines which component definition wins when two components try to occupy the same space—in other words, they have the same component name. A precedence is an integer value assigned to a component using the precedence attribute on the `@Install` annotation. The higher the value, the more clout it has. All built-in

Seam components have a precedence of `Install.BUILT_IN` (0), so they can easily be overridden. If a precedence isn't defined, it defaults to `Install.APPLICATION` (20). With precedence in the picture, the rule is that two components can't be defined with the same name and precedence value. If this situation occurs, it will cause an exception to be thrown at startup when the component scanner discovers it.

If all the prerequisites are satisfied, the component gets the gig. It has made it into the container. A single class can also produce multiple component definitions with different component names and potentially different scopes. These alternate definitions are known as component roles.

4.5.3 Giving a component multiple @Roles

As you know, a component must be assigned a name. But that doesn't mean it can't be assigned more than one name. Alternate name and scope combinations are assigned to a component using the `@Role` annotation, summarized in table 4.9. To define multiple `@Role` annotations for a single component, you nest them within the `@Roles` annotation.

Table 4.9 The `@Role` annotation

Name:	Role
Purpose:	Associates the component with an alternate name and scope. Multiple roles are nested within the `@Roles` annotation.
Target:	TYPE (class)

Attribute	Type	Function
name	String	An alternate name for this component. A new instance of this component is created when this alternate name is requested, independent of any instance bound to its primary name. Default: none (required).
scope	ScopeType	The Seam context in which an instance of this component is stored for this role. Table 4.6 lists the default value according to component type.

The idea behind roles is to allow the same component to be instantiated and managed by Seam for different purposes. A scope is assigned to a role in order to relieve the code that uses the role name from making the decision of where to store the new instance. You'll often see this technique used in *outjection*, covered in chapter 6.

Multiple roles also allow you to use multiple instances of the same component class simultaneously in the same scope. Let's consider a simple example when such dualism is needed. The registration form is using an instance of the `Golfer` component, named `newGolfer`, to capture the new member information. Suppose that we want to use an example query, fed with another instance of the `Golfer` class, that allows the registering member to locate the member that referred them to the website. To implement this feature, the `Golfer` component needs to be accessed under two different names, `newGolfer` and `golferExample`. When the user clicks the lookup button, the search criteria get applied to the auxiliary `Golfer` instance bound to the `golferExample` context variable and passed on to the back end to perform the example query. The alternate name is assigned to the `Golfer` class using a `@Role` annotation, shown here in bold:

```
@Name("newGolfer")
@Scope(ScopeType.EVENT)
@Role(name = "golferExample", scope = ScopeType.EVENT)
public class Golfer extends Member { ... }
```

Example queries are supported natively in Hibernate but not in JPA. Here's how an example query is conducted using Hibernate:

```
List<Golfer> existingGolfers = (List<Golfer>) session
    .createCriteria(Golfer.class)
    .add(Example.create(golferExample)).list();
```

Later in this chapter, you'll learn how to access a component instance populated from a UI form in your action bean component. For now, keep in mind that the role lets you isolate the instance of `Golfer` used for the example query from the instance used to back the registration form.

  Returning to the component scanner, once it finishes addressing all the component definitions and role assignments, the Seam container is left with a bunch of component definitions. But there aren't yet any component instances. Typically, a component definition has to wait until its component name is requested in order to be instantiated. There's one condition when the instance of the component is created even though it's not explicitly requested: if the component is a startup component.

4.5.4   *Instantiating components at @Startup*

The `@Startup` annotation, summarized in table 4.10, instructs Seam to take the initiative of creating an instance of the component when the component's scope is initialized. At the time of this writing, only application- and session-scoped components can be flagged as startup components, though other scopes may be added in the future.

  If you add the `@Startup` annotation to the class definition of a component, and the component is scoped to the application context, Seam automatically creates an

Table 4.10   The `@Startup` annotation

Name:	Startup
Purpose:	Instructs the container to eagerly instantiate a component at system initialization for application-scoped components or when the session starts for session-scoped components.
Target:	TYPE (class)

Attribute	Type	Function
depends	String[]	The names of other components that should be started before this one, if they're available. Dependencies must be in the same scope as the component itself. Default: none.

instance of the component *when the application starts.* This eager instantiation is consistent with the default behavior of singleton Spring beans. The instance is available as a context variable for the lifetime of the container and thus doesn't have to be instantiated when requested. The @Startup annotation is well suited for components that use the singleton design pattern.

WARNING   Application-scoped components aren't well suited as business objects. Because they're shared among all threads and synchronizing them would be *extremely* expensive, storing client-specific information in them is out of the question. Without state, their use in a long-running business use case is limited. Despite this general rule, the @Startup hook is useful for thread-safe resources such as a Hibernate SessionFactory or JPA EntityManagerFactory that you do want in the application scope because they are expensive to initialize.

If the component flagged with the @Startup annotation is scoped to the session context, Seam automatically creates an instance of the component *when the HTTP session starts.* This functionality is a unique Seam feature. It enables you to have components that are automatically instantiated on a per-user basis.

The depends attribute on the @Startup annotation can be used to control the order in which other startup components are instantiated (though as a side effect it can also result in components being started even if they aren't defined as startup components). The dependent components are supplied as a list of component names in the order that you want them to start.

Regardless of whether the component is instantiated eagerly by the container or it waits for the component name to be requested by the application, Seam handles instance creation. While it is nice to have Seam handle these details for you, there are times when you need to be there to help out with the creation of the instance or to perform custom cleanup when the instance is being destroyed. Component life-cycle callback methods give you that chance.

4.5.5   *Component life-cycle callbacks*

At the beginning of this chapter, I mention that one of the benefits of using the Seam container to instantiate your classes is that it manages the life cycle of the instance. You can add code that participates in the life cycle by registering two special life-cycle methods. One method is invoked when the component instance is created and another when it's destroyed. These methods are identified through the use of annotations (the method name is therefore irrelevant). Note that there can only be a single create method and a single destroy method per component.

The method on a component annotated with @PostConstuct is called after an instance has been created and initialized (meaning after the initial property values have been applied). The @PreDestroy method is called before the component instance is removed from the context in which it resides. Both of these annotations are part of the Java EE 5 API. When working with a non-EJB component, you can use

either the standard Java EE annotations or their synonyms from the Seam API. The
`@Create` annotation stands in for the `@PostConstruct` annotation and the `@Destroy`
annotation stands in for the `@PreDestroy` annotation in non-Java EE 5 environments,
as explained in table 4.11.

Table 4.11 The component life-cycle methods per environment

When called	Java EE environment	Non-Java EE environment
After initialization of the component instance	`@PostConstruct`	`@Create`
Before component instance is removed from the Seam context	`@PreDestroy`	`@Destroy`

Note that Seam takes care of invoking the create and destroy methods on JavaBean
components while the EJB container handles this task for EJB 3 components. It's just
that with Seam JavaBean components, you have a choice as to which annotation set
to use.

NOTE   Any of the life-cycle methods called by Seam can be a no-argument
method or accept the Seam component definition—an instance of
`org.jboss.seam.Component`—as its sole parameter. The `getName()`
method on the component definition provides access to the name of the
component, which may be useful during an initialization routine.

Let's consider a simple example of when the create and destroy life-cycle methods are
used. In the following code, the `RegisterAction` component writes to the log file
whenever it's created and destroyed:

```
@Name("registerAction")
public class RegisterAction {
    ...
    @PostConstruct                        ⟵——— @Create also
    public void onCreate(Component self) {      works here
        log.debug("Created " + self.getName() + " component");
    }
    @PreDestroy                                ⟵——— @Destroy also
    public void onDestroy() {                        works here
        log.debug("Destroyed registerAction component");
    }
}
```

You can also have collaborator components tap into the life cycle of a component by
observing events raised by the container when an instance is created and destroyed.
Events are also raised when the instance is bound to and unbound from a context variable. You'll learn about component events in the next chapter.

The create method is the component way of writing a constructor. It's especially
useful for performing postinitialization logic on the component, such as validating
its state or loading auxiliary resources that it needs. If you add the `@Startup` annotation to the component, the create method becomes a way to perform logic when the

application starts or when the user's session begins, depending on whether the component is application- or session-scoped. Startup logic is useful for performing tasks such as

- Starting an in-memory database and loading it with seed data
- Applying a database upgrade script
- Running an indexing service (i.e., Lucene)
- Starting up a third-party container, library, or service (i.e., Spring, JMS, jBPM)

The @Install(debug=true) combined with @Startup can be useful for seeding a database in a test environment, as an alternative to Hibernate's import.sql. You can also have a non-startup component execute logic when the application starts by observing the Seam container postinitialization event (org.jboss.seam.postInitialization).

JavaBean components also support the Java EE standard @PrePassivate and @PostActivate annotations. Methods on a JavaBean marked with these annotations are invoked by Seam when the HTTP session is migrated between nodes in a cluster.[4] If these annotations are used on an EJB component, Seam has no say in the matter and the EJB container takes on the task of invoking these methods.

Although components are the divas of the Seam container, even rock stars need agents. Let's look at how components get connected to one another.

4.5.6 *Wiring components together*

Since Seam is a lightweight, dependency injection facilitator, you may be eager to know how components are wired together. I hate to disappointment you, but this is going to be a short section. Dependency injection is one of Seam's biggest features and there's too much to get into right now. This brief introduction will give you a glimpse of what you need to know.

The primary means of wiring Seam components together in Seam is a mechanism called *bijection*, which is explained in detail in chapter 6. Bijection is controlled using annotations. The @In annotation placed on a field or JavaBean property of a component tells Seam to assign to that property the value of a component instance whose component name matches the name of the recipient property, commonly referred to as *injection*. The *bi* prefix is used in the name because in addition to injecting components, the inverse is possible. The @Out annotation placed on a field or JavaBean property of a component declares that the value of that property is to be bound to a context variable of the same name.

Bijection is a new approach to inversion of control. Seam also supports the traditional dependency injection mechanism—dubbed static dependency injection, which is controlled using the component descriptor. You'll learn about static dependency injection in the next chapter. There's one case when Seam uses an annotation to perform static dependency injection: the @Logger annotation injects a logger instance at component creation time.

---

[4] http://wiki.jboss.org/wiki/HttpSessionReplication

INJECTING A @LOGGER

Seam can automatically create a logger that's configured exclusively for a component. This feature should be a welcome relief for anyone who is tired of fiddling with mundane logger declarations. But Seam also offers some other nice enhancements. Just like Apache's commons-logging, Seam's logger implementation supports different logging providers. What makes Seam's logger unique is that it lets you use value expressions inline in the log messages. These smart log messages reduce the tedium of providing contextual information in the message (the name of the authenticated user, the account name, the order ID, and so on).

To have Seam inject a `Log` instance into a property of a component, simply place that `@Logger` annotation above the property whose type is `org.jboss.seam.log.Log`:

```
@Name("registerAction")
public class RegisterAction() {
    @Logger private Log log;
    ...
}
```

The `Log` instance is injected after the component is instantiated but before the `@Post-Construct` method is invoked. Table 4.12 summarizes the `@Logger` annotation.

Table 4.12   The @Logger annotation

Name:	Logger	
Purpose:	Injects a Seam `Log` instance into this field when the component is instantiated.	
Target:	FIELD (of type `org.jboss.seam.log.Log`)	

Attribute	**Type**	**Function**
category	String	A custom log category for this instance. Default: the fully qualified class name in which this annotation is used.

TIP   How do you configure the logging? There's no change in configuration if you're using Log4j or the standard JDK logging. Seam uses Log4j if it's available on the classpath, falling back to standard JDK logging if it's not. Seam's Log implementation is merely a wrapper around the existing logging frameworks, adding the convenience of injecting the `Log` instance via dependency injection and using EL notation in the message.

Here's an example of a log message that uses EL notation:

```
log.debug("Registering golfer #{newGolfer.username}");
```

The messages are considered contextual because they can access any Seam component that's "in context" at the time the log message is reported. This parallels the use of EL in JSF messages when added using the `FacesMessage` component.

In section 4.7, you'll learn how to access a component once it is loaded and ready to perform. For now, let's skip to the end of a component's life.

4.5.7   *Where all components go to die*

Just like any other Java objects, component instances die when they go out of scope. A component instance is destroyed when any of the following occurs:

- The context it occupies ends
- The context variable to which it is bound is assigned a null value
- The instance is explicitly removed using the Seam API

The instance is invoked one last time before it goes out of scope when its destroy method is called by the Seam container. The destroy method was covered in section 4.5.5.

That covers the life of a *JavaBean* component and the instances that it spawns. Seam is also capable of participating in the life of an EJB session bean component. However, in this case, Seam merely plays the role of collaborator to the EJB container. Let's see how Seam works with the EJB container to turn EJB session beans into Seam components.

4.6   *Using EJB 3 session beans in Seam*

After I made so much ado about how Seam stitches EJB 3 and JSF together in chapter 1, you may be wondering why I avoided the use of an EJB 3 session bean in the registration example. If you're waiting for the big unveiling, I'm sorry to disappoint you. There isn't much to show. The switch from a JavaBean to an EJB 3 session bean is just a matter of adding a couple of annotations and an interface and voilà, you have an EJB component. Of course, this migration isn't nearly as simple in EJB 2. Although Seam can work with EJB 2 components, all references to EJB in this book assume the use of EJB 3.

NOTE   In order to use an EJB session bean, your project must be deployed as an EAR. The EJB session beans are packaged as an EJB JAR and the web application is packaged separately as a WAR. These two archives are then bundled together to form an EAR. To create an EAR project, run seam setup again, this time choosing the EAR project option. Unfortunately, by using the EAR format you lose incremental hot deployment of JavaBean components.

Up to this point, I've presented several areas of Java EE that Seam replaces with its own solution. For instance, the page descriptor replaces the declarative JSF navigation and adds page-oriented features, the @Name annotation replaces the JSF managed bean facility, and the Seam container manages all variable contexts. Apart from these improvements, Seam leverages a great deal of the Java EE standard, which is most apparent in the area of EJB.

In this section, you'll learn that Seam can derive a component from an EJB 3 session bean—herein referred to as a Seam session bean component. The EJB 3 container does most of the work of managing it; Seam only steps in to bind the component to a context variable and apply its own set of method interceptors. While we are on the topic of ownership, let's consider who owns a Seam session bean component, the EJB container or Seam?

4.6.1   *Whose component is it, anyway?*

At first, you might not give the question of who owns a Seam session bean component much thought. The component scanner finds a class with a `@Name` annotation in an EJB JAR with a seam.properties file and creates a component for it. But the same class has already been picked up by the EJB container, either because it has a `@Stateless` or `@Stateful` annotation or it's declared as an EJB component in an XML descriptor. So, who owns the component, the EJB container or Seam?

The answer is: *The EJB container.* Still, session beans designated as Seam components have a sort of dual personality. They act as both Seam components and EJB 3 components, taking on the services of both containers. The EJB container manages the session bean, but Seam gets its hands on the session bean's life cycle, using interceptors to weave in additional services.

Seam session bean components differ from other Seam component types in one fundamental way: Seam doesn't create instances of session bean components using the default constructor of the class. Instead, the work of instantiating the class is delegated to the EJB container. The EJB container is responsible for managing session bean components in the same way that Seam manages JavaBean components.

When the Seam container determines that an instance of the component needs to be created, Seam asks the EJB container for a reference to the session bean instance using a JNDI lookup. Once Seam has a reference to the session bean instance, Seam adds additional services to it and then binds it to a context variable, just as Seam would do with a JavaBean component instance. The two containers are working together to create and initialize an instance of a session bean component.

NOTE   What about message-driven beans? I am purposefully not discussing message-driven beans (MDBs) in this section. Although an MDB can act as a Seam component, the dynamics are very different. Message-driven beans can't be instantiated by the application, which means they're never associated with a context. Instead, they listen for messages on a JMS topic or queue and get instantiated by the EJB container to handle a message when it arrives. They can, however, take advantage of bijection.

Let's take a closer look at how a session bean becomes a Seam component and what it means for the component's functionality.

4.6.2   *The making of a Seam session bean component*

A handful of differences exists between a JavaBean component and a Seam session bean component. One set of differences pertains to the requirements for creating an EJB 3 component. The other set of differences relates to how Seam treats these components when compared to other Seam components.

The EJB 3.0 specification requires session beans to implement either a local or remote interface (though this requirement is being removed in EJB 3.1). The interface must be annotated with either `@Local` or `@Remote` or must be declared as an EJB 3 interface in an XML descriptor. In order for a method on a session bean component to be accessible to the client (e.g., a Seam application), it must be defined on the EJB 3 interface. It's not enough just to declare the method as public on the implementing class.

There's one final requirement that only pertains to stateful session bean components. All stateful session beans acting as Seam components *must* define a no-arguments method marked with the EJB 3 @Remove annotation. The @Remove method is called when the context containing the session bean reference is destroyed. Seam uses this method to instruct the EJB container to destroy the session bean. If the @Remove method is invoked directly, it leads to an immediate removal of the session bean reference, unless a runtime or remote exception is thrown and the exception class is marked with @ApplicationException (it's not a system exception) or an exception is thrown that isn't a runtime or remote exception and the retainIfException attribute on the @Remove annotation is set to true.

NOTE   Note that there is a distinct difference between the @Remove and @Pre-Destroy annotations. The method marked with the @Remove annotation is called when Seam removes the *reference* to the instance, and the method marked with the @PreDestroy annotation is called when the EJB 3 container destroys the instance itself.

The action bean component for the registration page can be rewritten as a stateful Seam session bean component. Begin by renaming the implementation class to RegisterActionBean, annotating it with @Stateful, and implementing the Register-Action interface:

```
package org.open18.action;

import ...;
import javax.ejb.Stateful;

@Stateful
@Name("registerAction")
@Scope(ScopeType.EVENT)
public class RegisterActionBean implements RegisterAction {
    ...
    @Remove public void destroy() {}
}
```

Note that the rest of the class body remains as before since Seam session bean components can still use annotations handled by Seam, such as @Logger and @In.

The next, and final, step is to define the RegisterAction type as the EJB 3 interface and declare the methods that need to be accessible to clients, such as JSF. The method annotated with @Remove must also be defined on the interface. The result is shown here:

```
package org.open18.action;

import ...;
import javax.ejb.Local;

@Local
public interface RegisterAction {
    public void register();
    public void destroy();
}
```

EJB References

To access an EJB component via JNDI when deploying to a compliant Java EE server, you must register an EJB reference in the web.xml descriptor. The reference is declared using `<ejb-ref>` for a remote component and `<ejb-local-ref>` for a local component. The value of `<ejb-ref-name>`, which is arbitrary, is bound to the java:comp/env namespace in JNDI. Here's an example of a local reference for `RegisterActionBean`:

```
<ejb-local-ref>
  <ejb-ref-name>open18ee/RegisterActionBean/local</ejb-ref-name>
  <ejb-ref-type>Session</ejb-ref-type>
  <local>org.open18.action.RegisterAction</local>
</ejb-local-ref>
```

This step is not required on JBoss AS 4 since the component is automatically registered with JNDI using the pattern: application name/component name/client view type.

Unlike JavaBean components, the methods of an EJB component are automatically wrapped in a transaction, unless specified otherwise. You haven't had to worry about transactions up to this point since Seam automatically wraps each request in a global JTA transaction. However, if you were to disable Seam's transaction management, the transactional behavior of EJB 3 components would kick in.

Besides the difference in default scopes and which container handles transactions, the persistence context, concurrency, and security, the session bean components operate just like their JavaBean counterparts. Seam truly does make the use of EJBs a preference rather than a design decision. If you determine that you need an EJB feature, such as web services, you can make the switch when necessary. For in-depth coverage of EJB and the features it provides, consult *EJB 3 in Action* (Manning, 2007). The focus of this chapter is on the integration between Seam and EJB 3 components.

4.6.3   *The mechanics of the interaction*

Let's take a closer look at how Seam obtains session bean references from the EJB container and how it participates in the life cycle of the server-side component. There are several references in this section to features of Seam that are covered in chapter 6, such as bijection and interceptors. Feel free to come back to this section once you've learned that material. You can safely skip this section if you're only interested in the high-level view of Seam EJB components right now.

PLAYING A PART IN THE LIFE OF A SESSION BEAN COMPONENT

From the moment the Seam component scanner detects a Seam session bean component, Seam begins to participate in its life. Seam taps into the postconstruct logic of the EJB component to register additional server-side method interceptors that decorate the component with services such as bijection, conversation controls, and event handling. Seam brings these features to Seam session beans by registering an EJB interceptor using the following interceptor mapping in the EJB deployment descriptor, META-INF/ejb-jar.xml:

```
<ejb-jar xmlns="http://java.sun.com/xml/ns/javaee"
  xmlns:xsi="http://www.w3.org/2001/XMLSchema-instance"
  xsi:schemaLocation="http://java.sun.com/xml/ns/javaee
    http://java.sun.com/xml/ns/javaee/ejb-jar_3_0.xsd"
  version="3.0">
  <interceptors>
    <interceptor>
      <interceptor-class>
        org.jboss.seam.ejb.SeamInterceptor
      </interceptor-class>
    </interceptor>
  </interceptors>
  <assembly-descriptor>
    <interceptor-binding>
      <ejb-name>*</ejb-name>
      <interceptor-class>
        org.jboss.seam.ejb.SeamInterceptor
      </interceptor-class>
    </interceptor-binding>
  </assembly-descriptor>
</ejb-jar>
```

Obviously, you want this type of configuration to be set up automatically, which luckily seam-gen handles for you. As an alternative, you can skip the XML descriptor and install the interceptor on each session bean component individually using the EJB 3 `@Interceptors` annotation, as follows:

```
@Stateful
@Name("registerAction")
@Interceptors(SeamInterceptor.class)
public class RegisterActionBean implements RegisterAction { ... }
```

Intercepting session bean invocations is only part of the work Seam has to do to expose a session bean as a Seam component. The next step happens when the Seam component scanner comes across the session bean implementation class annotated with `@Name` (or declared in the component descriptor). The component scanner simply mines the class definition for information, looking for Seam annotations as it normally would for any other component, and then stores the component definition away in the Seam container. At this point, no interaction occurs with the EJB container.

OBTAINING A SESSION BEAN REFERENCE

The fusion with the EJB container occurs when the Seam container receives a request for an unassigned context variable that's associated with a session bean component. To resolve a value, Seam performs a JNDI lookup to get a reference to the corresponding session bean in the EJB container. This lookup is part of the standard EJB mechanism.

WARNING   In order to use an EJB session bean as a Seam component, you have to let Seam retrieve it from JNDI. The application should not perform the JNDI lookup itself.

There are two ways to declare the JNDI name that Seam should use to look up the session bean. You can either specify a name explicitly in the component class or you can define a template that Seam uses to compute the JNDI name for individual components. The first option is the most straightforward, yet also the most tedious. Here we supply the JNDI name on the session bean component explicitly using the @JndiName annotation:

```
@Stateful
@Name("registerAction")
@JndiName("open18ee/RegisterAction/local")
public class RegisterActionBean implements RegisterAction { ... }
```

A summary of the @JndiName annotation is provided in table 4.13.

Table 4.13   The @JndiName annotation

Name:	JndiName
Purpose:	Supplies the JNDI name that Seam uses to obtain a reference to an EJB component.
Target:	TYPE (class)

Attribute	Type	Function
value	String	The JNDI name of the EJB component. Default: none (required).

TUNING THE JNDI PATTERN

It's possible to have Seam resolve the JNDI name implicitly instead of having to declare the @JndiName annotation on every session bean component. However, Seam still needs assistance in dealing with the widely varying JNDI naming conventions across application servers. You provide Seam with a template, which you assign to the jndi-Pattern property on the built-in init component. You learn how to assign values to properties of a Seam component in the next chapter. For now, just know that the init component is configured in the component descriptor using the <core:init> element. Here's the template that's used when deploying to JBoss AS 4, where open18ee is the name of the application:

```
<core:init jndiPattern="open18ee/#{ejbName}/local"/>
```

Seam uses this template to construct the JNDI name for the EJB component. The #{ejbName} token is not interpreted as an EL expression. Rather, it gets replaced with the first nonempty value in the following list:

- The value of the name attribute on the @Stateful or @Stateless annotation
- The unqualified class name of the component
- The value of the <ejb-name> node in the EJB deployment descriptor or web.xml

Applying these rules to the example, the #{ejbName} is replaced with RegisterAction, making the entire pattern open18ee/RegisterAction/local. If the server uses a JNDI namespace, such as GlassFish, the pattern must include it:

```
<core:init jndiPattern="java:comp/env/open18ee/#{ejbName}/local"/>
```

In Java EE-compliant environments, EJB references are declared in the web.xml descriptor. The jndiPattern merely reflects the naming convention you use for those reference names.

Projects created by seam-gen use the property replacement token `@jndiPattern@` for specifying a value for the `jndiPattern` property in the test environment. The value for the token is defined in the components.properties file. The pattern found in that file is specific to the Embedded JBoss container:

```
jndiPattern=\#{ejbName}/local
```

Everything that happens after the lookup of the session bean reference up until the reference to the newly minted instance is returned to Seam is controlled by the EJB 3 container. Let's consider what happens after that point.

INFUSING SESSION BEAN COMPONENTS WITH SEAM FUNCTIONALITY

Once Seam has obtained a client-side reference to the session bean, it wraps the proxy in additional client-side interceptors and stores it as a context variable just like any other Seam component. Unless specified otherwise, the default scope for stateless session beans is the stateless context, and for stateful session beans the default scope is conversation context.

What makes Seam session bean components so unique is that they share a hybrid of functionality from the EJB container and the Seam container. For instance, all methods are, by default, automatically wrapped in a container-managed transaction, courtesy of the Java EE container. But the component can also take advantage of bijection, a service provided by the Seam container. Bijection allows other Seam component instances to be injected into session beans, something that's more cumbersome to do with EJB 3 alone (you have to pull in objects from JNDI using the Java EE `@Resource` annotation). You see this same type of crossover with Spring-Seam components in chapter 15 (online). Table 4.14 lists all of the core services available to a hybrid Seam-EJB 3 component (excluding Seam extensions).

The only catch is that by mixing services, your session beans are going to miss the features provided by Seam in a pure EJB 3 environment. You could stick to obtaining a reference to another EJB component using the `@EJB` resource injection annotation

Table 4.14   A list of the core annotations available on a hybrid Seam session bean component

Annotation	Provided by	When applied and condition
`@Resource`	Java EE (web tier, EJB 3 tier)	Postconstruct, static
`@EJB`	Java EE (EJB 3 tier)	Postconstruct, static
`@PersistenceContext`	Java EE (web tier, EJB 3 tier) proxied by Seam	Postconstruct, static
`@Interceptors`	Java EE (EJB 3 tier)	Around invoke, stateless
`@Interceptors` (on `@interface`)	Seam	Around invoke, stateless or stateful
`@AroundInvoke`	Java EE (EJB tier)	Around invoke
`@PreDestroy`	Java EE (EJB tier)	Predestroy

Table 4.14   A list of the core annotations available on a hybrid Seam session bean component *(continued)*

Annotation	Provided by	When applied and condition
`@PrePassivate`	Java EE (EJB tier)	Prepassivate
`@PostConstruct`	Java EE (EJB tier) enhanced by Seam	Postconstruct

`@In, @RequestParameter,`
`@DataModelSelection,`
`@DataModelSelectionIndex`
	Seam	Around invoke, dynamic

`@Out, @DataModel`	Seam	Around invoke, dynamic
`@Logger`	Seam	Postconstruct, static

rather than using bijection, for instance. But why? "Upgrading" your EJB 3 environment is just a matter of adding Seam to the classpath and configuring it, so I encourage you to let go of the purist flag and use Seam in combination with the Java EE services if at all possible.

You have now witnessed a day in the life of both JavaBean components and session bean components. It's time to learn how to get components to participate in your application.

4.7   *Accessing components*

Seam components are the key enablers for integrating technologies in a Seam application. Consequently, Seam's forte is providing unified access to those components across the board. There are three ways to ask for an instance of a Seam component from the Seam container. You can use

- The component name
- EL notation (binding expression) that references the component name
- The Java class of the component

Table 4.15 gives a preview of where component instances can be accessed.

In the previous chapter you saw some examples of Seam components being used in page orchestration logic. That's just the beginning. The EL is used in JSF views, page flows, business process definitions, annotations, and Java code. You'll begin learning

Table 4.15   Places where Seam components can be accessed

From where	How accessed
JSF view	EL notation
Seam annotation (e.g., `@In, @Out`)	Component name or EL notation
Java code: `Component.getInstance()`	Component name or component class
Java code: `Expressions.instance()`	EL notation
JPQL or HQL query	EL notation
JSF message (i.e., `FacesMessage`)	EL notation

Table 4.15 Places where Seam components can be accessed *(continued)*

From where	How accessed
Java properties (i18n bundle or component property)	EL notation
JavaScript using Seam Remoting	Component name, stub instance, or EL notation
Seam component descriptor (e.g., components.xml)	Component name, component class, or EL notation
Seam page descriptor (e.g., pages.xml)	EL notation
jPDL page flow descriptor	EL notation
jBPM business process descriptor	EL notation
Spring configuration file	Component name or EL notation

about these options in this section. Let's start by considering what happens when a component instance is requested.

4.7.1 Access modes

As it has probably been ingrained into you by now, a component is a recipe that describes how to create a Java object that is managed by the Seam container (a component instance). When you request a component, you're effectively asking the container to hand you back an instance of the component. This request operates in one of two modes:

- *Lookup only*—In this mode, Seam searches for a component instance that's bound to the requested context variable. It either looks for an instance in the specified scope, or, if a scope isn't provided, it uses a hierarchical search of all the contexts. If an instance cannot be found, a null value is returned—the non-conditional path in figure 4.2. This mode is the default for the @In annotation, covered in chapter 6.
- *Lookup with option to create*—In this mode, Seam performs the same search that's used in the lookup-only mode, but this time, if an instance can't be found, Seam instantiates an instance according to the component definition and stores it in the context specified by that definition. Instance creation is represented by the optional clause in figure 4.2. When a component is referenced via a value expression, this mode is always used to locate an instance.

There's one case when Seam creates a component instance when operating in lookup-only mode: if the requested component is an *autocreate* component and an instance hasn't already been forged. In this case, a new instance of the component is created, regardless of the mode. An autocreate component is formed by placing the @AutoCreate annotation on the component class (or by setting the auto-create attribute of the component definition declared in the component descriptor to true). Factory components, which you'll learn about in chapter 6, can also declare autocreate behavior.

Autocreate functionality eliminates the need to specify the create option on the context variable at the point of access, shifting the responsibility to the component definition. The @AutoCreate annotation is summarized in table 4.16.

Table 4.16   The @AutoCreate annotation

Name:	AutoCreate
Purpose:	Indicates that Seam should automatically instantiate the component when its component name is requested if an instance doesn't already exist
Target:	TYPE (class), PACKAGE

Several methods of accessing a Seam component are summarized in table 4.17. The final three examples involve the @In annotation, which allows the bijection mechanism to supply a component instance to a property of a Seam component. For now, you can think of the @In annotation as shorthand for looking up the component name explicitly using Component.getInstance() and then assigning it to a property of the component class. This table also indicates the conditions under which the instance will be created if it doesn't exist in the container.

Table 4.17   Ways to access a Seam component

Example usage	Create if doesn't exist?
Component.getInstance("componentName")	Yes
#{componentName}	Yes
Component.getInstance(ComponentClass.class)	Yes
@In("componentName")	No, unless an autocreate component
@In(value="componentName", create = true)	Yes
@In("#{componentName}")	Yes

That covers the conditions by which Seam will create component instances. Let's take a closer look at the strategies you can use to access these component instances.

4.7.2   Access strategies

In a Seam application, you'll find references to components in annotations, EL notation, and via the Seam API. Regardless of which access strategy you use, the lookup always trickles down to a Seam API call. Therefore, let's study this interaction.

SEAM API

Seam offers several static getInstance() methods on the Component class that are capable of locating and creating component instances. But it's important to understand this means of access because it's how instances are requested from the Seam container.

You access a component using the Seam API by passing either the component name (e.g., passwordManager) or the Java class object (e.g., PasswordManager.class) to the `Component.getInstance()` method. (The `PasswordManager` component, introduced in listing 5.3 in the next chapter, is responsible for hashing the new golfer's password.) When you supply a Java class, Seam resolves the component name automatically from the component definition and continues the lookup based on the resolved value. Here's an example of a lookup by component name:

```
PasswordManager passwordManager =
    (PasswordManager) Component.getInstance("passwordManager");
```

You can also access a context variable directly from the context where it is stored. To do so, you use the `Context.get*Context()` to retrieve the context—where the * is a placeholder for the name of the context—and then use the `get()` method to pull the component instance out of the context based on the context variable name:

```
PasswordManager passwordManager =
    (PasswordManager) Context.getEventContext().get("passwordManager");
```

The main difference between `Component.getInstance()` and accessing the instance directly from the context in which it's stored is that `Component.getInstance()` creates an instance if one doesn't exist (unless you pass `false` as the second argument), whereas accessing the instance using the `Context` API *never* creates a new instance. The context API merely gives you direct access to the storage location of context variables.

You can also search across all contexts using the `org.jboss.seam.contexts.Context.lookupInStatefulContexts()` method:

```
PasswordManager passwordManager = (PasswordManager)
    Contexts.lookupInStatefulContexts("passwordManager");
```

The `lookupInStatefulContexts()` method is used by Seam to locate a component instance in cases when a scope isn't explicitly provided.

Component names and context variables

Uses of the term *context variable* in this chapter have been in relation to component names. While it's true that a component instance is stored in a context variable according to its component name, a context variable can refer to an object not derived from a Seam component. In fact, any of the name-based access strategies discussed in this section happily return non-Seam objects along with those that are managed by Seam. The notable difference between a component name and plain context variable name is that Seam knows how to initialize a Seam component if the search by component name turns up empty, whereas Seam returns null (in this scenario) if the name isn't associated with a component.

Let's use the Seam API to look up the dependent components needed to complete the registration logic in the `register()` method of the `RegisterAction` component. The implementation is shown in listing 4.7. It needs to be paired with a navigation rule to direct the user to a success page when registration is complete, which is not shown here.

Listing 4.7   Using the Seam API to access dependent component instances

```
package org.open18.action;

import ...;
import org.jboss.seam.context.Contexts;

@Name("registerAction")
public class RegisterAction {
    @Logger private Log log;

    public String register() {
        log.debug(
            "Registering golfer #{newGolfer.username}");        Evaluates EL
                                                                immediately
        Context eventContext = Contexts.getEventContext();
        PasswordBean passwordBean = (PasswordBean)
            eventContext.get("passwordBean");
        if (!passwordBean.verify()) {
            FacesMessages.instance()
                .addToControl("confirm", "value does not match password");
            return null;              Forces page to
        }                             be rerendered
        Golfer newGolfer =
            (Golfer) Contexts.lookupInStatefulContexts("newGolfer");
        PasswordManager passwordManager = (PasswordManager)
            Component.getInstance(PasswordManager.class);
        newGolfer.setPasswordHash(
            passwordManager.hash(passwordBean.getPassword()));
        EntityManager entityManager = (EntityManager)
            Component.getInstance("entityManager");
        newGolfer.setDateJoined(new Date());
        entityManager.persist(newGolfer);
        FacesMessages.instance().add(                       Evaluates EL
            "Welcome to the club, #{newGolfer.name}!");      when phase ends
        return "success";
    }
}
```

This method is abnormally complex because it does not take advantage of bijection. You will appreciate the simplicity that bijection introduces when you see the refactored version of this component in chapter 6. However, there are perfectly justifiable reasons for using the Seam API directly as in this example, such as to reduce the overhead of method interceptors, to obtain a component instance in a test case, or when bijection isn't available.

Let's enhance the integration test from earlier to validate the newly implemented registration logic. The updated test case in listing 4.8 uses a mixture of the Seam API and the EL. The form backing beans are populated in the *Update Model Values* phase, emulating a form submission, and the register() method is invoked in the *Invoke Application* phase.

Listing 4.8   Using the Seam API and the EL in an integration test

```
package org.open18.action;

import ...;
```

```
public class RegisterActionIntegrationTest extends SeamTest {

    @Test public void registerValidGolfer() throws Exception {
        new FacesRequest("/register.xhtml") {
            @Override protected void updateModelValues() {
                Golfer g = (Golfer) Component.getInstance("newGolfer");
                g.setFirstName("Tommy");
                g.setLastName("Twoputt");
                g.setUsername("twoputt");
                g.setEmailAddress("twoputt@open18.org");
                setValue("#{passwordBean.password}","ilovegolf");
                setValue("#{passwordBean.confirm}","ilovegolf");
            }

            @Override protected void invokeApplication() {
                String result = invokeMethod("#{registerAction.register}");
                assert result != null && result.equals("success");
            }
        }.run();
    }
}
```

The test should once again succeed, this time accompanied by SQL statements in the log.

You often see the Seam API used to look up a component instance by calling a static instance() method on the component itself. This replaces the use of a static or thread local variable to maintain an instance of an object. Instead, you let the Seam container manage the instance in one of its scopes. I like to call this a *scoped singleton*, since it's accessed just as you would access a singleton, except it isn't necessarily scoped to the lifetime of the application. For instance, the following method can be used to obtain the event-scoped PasswordManager:

```
public static PasswordManager instance() {
    return (PasswordManager)
        Component.getInstance(PasswordManager.class, ScopeType.EVENT);
}
```

This technique is useful for retrieving an implementation class of an interface by component name. An example of this type of lookup is seen in the Seam transaction component. The instance() method on the org.jboss.seam.transaction.Transaction class returns a JTA UserTransaction subclass instance using Seam's alternate implementation selection logic described earlier (which installs one of several candidate components):

```
public static UserTransaction instance() {
    return (UserTransaction)
        Component.getInstance(Transaction.class, ScopeType.EVENT);
}
```

You'll learn about configuring transactions in Seam in chapter 9. If you're interested in how this lookup works, I encourage you to dive into the Seam source code.

You have to decide for yourself whether it's acceptable to interact directly with the Seam API in your business logic. It's certainly the most efficient way to access Seam components, but if POJO development is important to you, you may prefer the level of abstraction provided by bijection. Again, Seam doesn't force your hand.

A more ubiquitous and flexible means of component access is through EL notation. That's our next stop. You've already seen several examples of this syntax in this chapter's examples. Let's take a closer look.

EL NOTATION

Value- and method-binding expressions are the lingua franca of Seam. The reason EL notation is so appealing is because it cleanly separates component access from the container responsible for serving the component instance. It's also attractive because it is dynamic and untyped. EL notation is like having a sticker slapped on your code that says *Insert Component Here*. The rest is up to the EL resolver and, in turn, the container managing the instance. The EL is the key for being able to resolve components from anywhere and makes the references portable to any EL resolver, not just Seam's.

Value expressions are used for both resolving a component instance and binding to its properties. Value expressions can also be used in JSF messages and log messages if registered using Seam's `FacesMessages` and `Log` components, respectively. In addition to using value and method expressions in the usual places, you can call on the EL using the Seam API. Let's rewrite the portion of the `register()` method to use value and method expressions instead of looking up a component instance and acting on it directly. The following snippet shows two ways to interact with the `PasswordBean` component via the EL:

```
Boolean valid = (Boolean)
    Expressions.instance()
        .createMethodExpression("#{passwordBean.verify}")
        .invoke();
...
String password = (String)
    Expressions.instance()
        .createValueExpression("#{passwordBean.password}")
        .getValue();
```

You can also use a value expression to assign a value. For instance, say that you want to clear the confirm password when it's wrong. You can once again use a value-binding expression:

```
Expressions.instance()
    .createValueExpression("#{passwordBean.confirm}")
    .setValue(null);
```

We just covered good old-fashioned EL. But Seam offers so much more. Let's see what Seam does to make the EL even more powerful as an integrator.

SEAM'S ENHANCED EL

The EL is ideal for integrating technologies because it uses a simple, technology-agnostic syntax. It standardizes on the JavaBean property notation for value expressions and no-argument methods for method expressions. Unfortunately, its simplicity is also its downfall. Because it's at the intersection of so many technologies, you often find that if the EL supported that one additional feature, you'd be able to take the integration to the next level. This longing is especially strong when you're attempting to implement advanced layouts that require more sophisticated logic, which you encounter in later examples in the book.

Fortunately, Seam supports several enhancements to the EL, provided in part by the JBoss EL library and supplemented by the Seam EL resolver:

- Parameterized method-binding expressions
- Parameterized value-binding expressions
- No-argument event listener methods
- "Magic" bean properties (properties not present on the class)
- Projections

The first two enhancements allow you to use method arguments in an EL expression. The arguments are surrounded in parentheses and separated by commas, just like in Java. Each argument is interpreted as a context variable unless it is quoted or is a number. Before looking at examples of parameterized expressions, I want to highlight the fact that Seam goes in the other direction as well by making the `FacesEvent` argument on JSF event listener methods optional (e.g. `ActionEvent`, `ValueChangeEvent`, and so on). This feature lets you implement an action or event listener without tying your UI logic directly to the JSF API.

You can use a parameterized method binding to pass data to a method on a Seam component. Using the example from earlier in the chapter, you can change the `register()` action method to pass the `newGolfer` and `passwordBean` context variables as arguments:

```
<h:commandButton id="register" value="Register"
  action="#{registerAction.register(newGolfer, passwordBean)}"/>
```

Be aware that the context variable is resolved when the action method is invoked, not when the button in which it's used is rendered. Thus, the parameters should be names of proper Seam components that will be available on the next request.

You can also pass parameters to value-binding expressions. However, note that when doing so you have to use the full method name of the property (i.e., `getName()`), not the shorthand syntax (`name`). Say you're creating a page in which you want to display the collection of tees for a particular hole on the golf course. The following value expression gives you access to calculated data that otherwise wouldn't be attainable with standard EL:

```
#{teeSet.getTeesByHoleNumber(10)}
```

Parameterized method- and value-binding expressions allow Seam components to serve as a function library for use in a JSF view, circumventing the need to have to go through the formal process of registering EL functions. A prime example is custom string manipulation, perhaps to truncate a string, leaving a trailing ellipsis if it exceeds a maximum length:

```
#{stringUtils.truncate(facility.name, 10)}
```

You can also call a method on the model to execute domain-specific Boolean logic:

```
<h:graphicImage value="/img/signature.gif"
  rendered="#{course.isSignatureHole(hole)}"/>
```

The parameterized syntax also provides access to methods that don't follow the Java-Bean property syntax. For instance, that pesky `size()` method on collections and equally evasive `length()` method on strings aren't reachable using a standard value expression. But you can use the parameterized method syntax to get there:

```
#{course.holes.size()}
#{course.name.length()}
```

Recognizing that there are a handful of collection methods that are extremely useful but happen to not follow the JavaBean naming convention, Seam developers have weaved them into the Seam EL resolver as "magic" methods. These properties are summarized in table 4.18, which map to equivalently named no-argument methods on the Java type.

Table 4.18   The magic bean properties supported by the Seam EL resolver

java.util.Collection	java.util.Map	javax.faces.DataModel
size	entrySet keySet size values	empty size

The Seam EL resolver provides direct access to Seam context maps, which are referenced as the root of an EL expression. The name of the map for each context is derived by appending `Context` to the lowercase name of the context. For instance, `eventContext` is a map of variables in the event context. You can access the `PasswordBean` instance via EL using `#{eventContext.passwordBean}` or `#{eventContext["passwordBean"]}`.

The parameterized syntax for value and method expressions is only available if you're using JSP 2.1 (or later) or Facelets (another compelling reason for using Facelets). The optional `FacesEvent` argument on action and event listeners and magic methods are available across the board. Because of limitations in the JSP compiler, the final enhancement, projections, is only available for expressions appearing within strings in Java code, within component tag attributes in Facelets view templates, or in Seam descriptors.

Projections allow you to mine a collection for values. For instance, suppose you want to get all of the colors used for tee sets on a course:

```
#{course.teeSets.{ts|ts.color}}
```

The `ts` acts as the iterator variable for the `teeSets` collection, and the pipe character (|) separates the iterator variable from the nested expression. It's equivalent to the following pseudocode:

```
List result = new ArrayList()
for (ts : course.teeSets) {
    result.add(ts.color)
}
return result;
```

Projections work for any collection type (list or set), map (entries), or array. The resulting type is always a `java.util.List` (providing a convenient way to convert a `Set` to a `List`) Though not demonstrated in this example, the value expression used in the projection can use the parameterized syntax described earlier.

Projections can also be nested. This allows you to descend into collections returned by the collections, with each level of nesting using the same pattern of iterator variable and nested expression separated by the pipe character. Say you wanted to amass a collection of the distances of all the tees on the course:

```
#{course.teeSets.{ts|ts.tees.{t|t.distance}}}
```

To get access to all the tees, instead of the tee distances, you have to reference the iterator variable in the expression segment, highlighted in bold:

```
#{course.teeSets.{ts|ts.tees.{t|t}}}
```

Projections are convenient if you're trying to save typing and perform quick one-liners like you can do in languages such as Ruby and Groovy. Projections demonstrate how Seam stretches the limits of Java EE to offer next-generation efficiencies. Even if you don't take advantage of projections, you'll likely use the other EL enhancements quite often.

The final place you'll access Seam components is in annotations, which you'll get a heavy dose of in chapter 6. You should now have an appreciation for the various ways in which you can interact with Seam's contextual container for the purpose of retrieving component instances. Trust that you'll get plenty more practice at it as you progress through the book.

4.8   Summary

This chapter covered the two essential concepts in Seam: components and contexts. The chapter opened by introducing Seam's rich contexts, which provides a centralized storage mechanism for objects. You learned that objects stored in these buckets are known as context variables. Seam's contexts build on those available in the Java Servlet API, encouraging you to hold long-running state to support use cases without fear of memory leaks, expensive replication, or concurrency problems.

The term *component* was given meaning in the context of Seam, being defined as a blueprint for creating an object whose lifecycle is managed by Seam. You learned that creation happens when the name assigned to a component is requested and an instance doesn't already exist. In this sense, the Seam container is a simple object factory. But you discovered that Seam goes well beyond instantiating the component by wrapping it with method interceptors that allow Seam to weave functionality into the instance, provide life-cycle callbacks, and ultimately manage it throughout its lifetime. Many of the core interceptors are covered in chapter 6, and additional ones pertaining to conversations persistence, and security are explored in chapters 7, 9, and 11, respectively.

Throughout the chapter, examples were provided that demonstrate how to access components using the Seam API and EL notation. These examples serve merely as a warm-up for what's to come. Indeed, components are used in every remaining chapter in this book. If by some chance you don't feel comfortable with how to access them yet, you'll get plenty more practice, especially with how they're exchanged declaratively using annotations in chapter 6.

To balance the focus on annotations in this chapter, the next chapter presents an XML-based approach to defining components. You discover that this alternative approach is about more than just replacing @ symbols with angled brackets. You learn that XML gives you a way to configure components by assigning initial values. Component configuration, as this mechanism is termed, builds on the basic component knowledge that you learned about in this chapter. You have only seen the beginning of what you can do with a component.

The Seam
component descriptor

Seam embraces annotations to keep you out of the XML weeds. You are a Java (or Groovy) developer, darn it, and that's the language in which you should be allowed to program your application! Despite this pragmatic statement, it would be misleading to say that Seam eliminates XML entirely. It doesn't. If you're one of those XML enthusiasts, you'll be glad to know that you don't have to give up your angled brackets when you move to Seam. In fact, there are some areas of Seam where XML configuration is the best choice—or even the only choice. One example is Seam's page descriptor, covered in chapter 3, which administers Seam's page-oriented functionality.[1] Since views are defined in XML, it's only natural for page controls to be defined

---

[1] Java-based page configuration is in the pipeline, so this requirement may not hold true for long.

179

that way as well. The use of XML also ensures a quick turnaround by avoiding the compilation step, which is important given that views often require a lot of tinkering.

Component definitions are another example where XML proves useful. Annotations such as @Name are easy enough to add to classes under your control. However, if the class you intend to declare as a Seam component is sealed in a third-party JAR file or maintained by another team, annotations don't do you much good. There may also be situations where you need to alter an existing component definition—either one from your application or one of Seam's built-in components—or assign property values to that component. In these cases, you have to resort to external configuration, which this chapter covers.

In the previous chapter, you gained an appreciation for the simplicity that annotations bring to the development of Seam components. If you are content working with annotations, I encourage you to skip ahead to the next chapter to learn about another set of annotations that are used to wire components together and to initialize context variables. On the other hand, if you are interested in learning how to define and configure components in XML, this chapter shows how this task is accomplished using the Seam component descriptor. The component descriptor contains XML-based metadata that offers a way to keep the component definition separate from the class. You can also use this file to assign initial property values to component instances, wire components together, override the settings of existing components, and control built-in Seam functionality. The XML in Seam isn't all old-fashioned, though. Thanks to XML namespaces, you may almost mistake the XML for a real language. In addition to XML, you'll learn that Java properties files can be used to accomplish certain types of configuration in Seam. We'll look at Seam's internationalization (i18n) support as an example of configuring a built-in Seam component and how keys in a message bundle can in turn be used to supply locale-specific values to the properties of a Seam component. By the end of the chapter, you'll appreciate that both XML and Java properties serve as a valuable supplement to Seam's primarily annotation-based approach.

5.1   Defining components using XML

The last thing the world needs is another XML configuration file, right? After the debacle that was EJB 2, a major theme of the EJB 3 rework was to do away with required XML descriptors. That theme carries into Seam. As promised in the previous chapter, Seam components can be authored strictly using annotations. So, while Seam has an XML-based component descriptor, its use is entirely optional. Seam happily bootstraps in its absence.

Let's talk about those cases, though, when annotations are not well suited and XML *is* warranted. The component descriptor supplements annotations in the following cases:

- Declare a class, which you can't modify and that lacks a @Name annotation, as a Seam component (admittedly you could extend the class as an alternative)
- Install a class that's not installed by default (the class has an @Install annotation indicating that the component shouldn't be installed)

- Override a component definition setting, such as the scope or autocreate value (the value from the descriptor always takes precedence over the annotation)
- Configure bean properties of components that get applied to the component instance (perhaps to externalize deployment-specific information)

There's also the possibility that you simply prefer XML over annotations. In that case, you can use the component descriptor to define all of your Seam components. Seam affords you that flexibility, though I don't recommend that approach. Either way, Seam has a wealth of built-in functionality that is only an XML element away. Likewise, you can use the component descriptor to dress up your own components once they are set in stone (i.e., compiled).

I begin by providing an overview of the component descriptor; what it is, where it lives, and the syntax it uses. I then explain how to use it to define and configure components.

5.1.1 *Choosing your descriptor strategy*

Seam's XML-based component configuration can be partitioned across many files. The component descriptor is a general term for the combined sum of the configurations in all of the component descriptors on the classpath. Note that *descriptor* is a fancy term for XML file.

Seam supports both general descriptors and fine-grained descriptors. The general descriptor can hold an arbitrary number of component definitions, whereas the fine-grained descriptor is designed to govern the components for a single class. The name of the general descriptor is components.xml, whereas fine-grained descriptors are named using the file extension .component.xml.

The general descriptor is often placed in the WEB-INF directory of the web application, which is where seam-gen stashes it. However, this file need not be confined to the WEB-INF directory. Instead, it can be distributed across the classpath, allowing you to organize your configuration the way that's most suitable for you, rather than having to jam every last component definition into a single file. One recommendation is to partition your component descriptors by module so that each descriptor is centered on the classes within that artifact. You can narrow it even further by putting a general descriptor in each Java package. The most extreme solution to avoiding monolithic component descriptors is to define every component in a fine-grained descriptor adjacent to the subject class. The choice is up to you.

The rules regarding where the component descriptors can be placed are fairly loose. The locations that the Seam component scanner visits are summarized in table 5.1,

Table 5.1 The resource locations where Seam looks for XML-based component descriptors

Resource	Location details
WEB-INF/components.xml	Located in a web application archive (WAR)
META-INF/components.xml	Located in any classpath entry (root of JAR or WEB-INF/classes in WAR)
components.xml or *.component.xml	Located anywhere in a scanned classpath entry (a classpath entry is scanned if it has a marker file, as described in section 4.5.1 of chapter 4)

listed in the order that they're addressed by the scanner. Regardless of how you decide to divide up your XML-based component configuration, Seam collects them, combines them with the settings defined in annotations, and assembles a unified set of component definitions in memory. From that unified set is where instances are born, as you learned in the previous chapter.

TIP   Although seam-gen places the components.xml file in the WEB-INF directory, consider storing it in the META-INF directory instead, where it's accessible to unit and integration test environments that don't recognize the WEB-INF directory as part of the classpath.

That sums up where the component descriptor can be placed. Let's open up the file, have a look at its structure, and learn how to use it to create component definitions.

5.1.2   *The structure of the component descriptor*

The Seam component descriptor consists of one or more component definitions, declared using the `<component>` element and nested within the root `<components>` element. (In a fine-grained component descriptor, `<component>` can be the root element.) In addition to generic `<component>` elements, Seam supports extension elements through the use of XML namespaces to accommodate "type-safe" XML component declarations. The component descriptor also accommodates a handful of noncomponent elements, such as `<import>` and `<factory>`, that are covered later in this chapter and the next.

NOTE   If you've worked with the Spring configuration file, you should feel right at home using the Seam component descriptor. The main difference is that instead of having a root `<beans>` element and child `<bean>` elements, the Seam component descriptor has a root `<components>` element and child `<component>` elements. Both Seam and Spring support extension elements using XML namespaces.

Listing 5.1 shows a simple component descriptor with two components defined. For the components shown, it is assumed that the `@Name` and `@Scope` annotations are absent from the class definitions. Instead, these classes are declared to be components using XML. If the classes had `@Name` annotations equivalent to these definitions, an exception would result for reasons that are described in section 5.4 (which covers component definitions overrides).

Listing 5.1   A component descriptor with two component definitions

```
<components xmlns="http://jboss.com/products/seam/components"
 xmlns:xsi="http://www.w3.org/2001/XMLSchema-instance"
 xsi:schemaLocation="
   http://jboss.com/products/seam/components
   http://jboss.com/products/seam/components-2.0.xsd">

<component name="newGolfer"
  class="org.open18.model.Golfer" scope="event"/>
```

```
<component name="passwordBean"
  class="org.open18.auth.PasswordBean" scope="event" auto-create="true"/>

</components>
```

If Spring hasn't made you tired of XML yet, then these definitions don't look so bad. The `<component>` element defines a new Seam component for the class specified in the `class` attribute. The `name` attribute is equivalent to the `@Name` annotation and the `scope` attribute is equivalent to the `@Scope` annotation. The mappings between component definition annotations and the XML `<component>` element attributes are shown in table 5.2.

Table 5.2   The correlation between Seam annotations and the component descriptor

Class-level annotation or annotation attribute	XML attribute on `<component>`
Java class name	`class`
`@Name`	`name`
`@Scope`	`scope`
`@AutoCreate`	`auto-create`
`@Install(value)`	`installed`
`@Install(precedence)`	`precedence`
`@Startup`	`startup`
`@Startup(depends)`	`startupDepends` (Seam 2.1 or greater)
`@JndiName`[a]	`jndi-name`[a]

a. The `@JndiName` annotation and `jndi-name` attribute are only relevant for EJB session bean components.

You may notice that the XML equivalent of the `@Role` annotation is missing from this list. Actually, it's not. It's the `<component>` element itself. The component descriptor supports an arbitrary number of component definitions for a single class. The only requirement is that you assign a different component name to each definition using the `name` attribute. In effect, the `name` attribute *is* the role name. You may find the `<component>` declaration to be more suitable for defining roles than the `@Role` annotation, as I have.

Here, the role assigned to the `Golfer` entity in the previous chapter using the `@Role` annotation is defined using the `<component>` element instead:

```
<component name="golferExample"
  class="org.open18.model.Golfer" scope="event"/>
```

From the standpoint of the application, there's no difference in how the component is constructed when it's defined using annotations versus XML. Seam builds the same internal representation of a component definition in both cases and uses it to dish out component instances. But the XML version allows you to assign initial values to bean properties, which is covered in section 5.3. Right now, the XML stanza appears basic because all it's doing is declaring the component.

WARNING   You can't create XML-based component definitions for classes on the hot-deployment classpath (sourced from the src/action folder of WAR projects created by seam-gen). The component scanner that processes the component descriptors can't "see" classes in the hot-deploy classloader. This shortcoming may be resolved in a future release. Regardless, it defeats the purpose of using the hot-deploy classloader since components defined in component descriptors are not hot deployable (hot-deployable components can only be defined using @Name). The component descriptor can still be used to register initial property values for hot-deployable components.

Although the general component descriptor may seem simple enough to manage with just a few component definitions in it, the trouble is that its size can quickly get out of hand as you start relying on it more heavily. Narrowing in on a single configuration becomes as challenging as finding a matching sock in a laundry pile. To prevent this melting pot of configurations, let's consider how to segment declarations by component class using fine-grained component descriptors.

5.1.3   *Fine-grained component descriptors*

The fine-grained component descriptor is designed to make it more intuitive for the developer to locate the configuration for a class, since it's adjacent to the class it configures, and to make the content of that descriptor be "task-oriented" since it focuses on a single class. It also offers a nice alternative to using Seam component annotations—especially if you shiver at the thought of using a lot of annotations on your class—without losing the benefit of being in close proximity to the class.

Fine-grained descriptors are identified by the .component.xml file extension and are used to configure a neighboring Java (or Groovy) class as a Seam component. The name of the class to which the fine-grained descriptor corresponds is derived by stripping the .component.xml extension from the descriptor's resource path and converting slashes (/) to dots (.). For example, the fine-grained component descriptor whose resource path is org/open18/auth/PasswordBean.component.xml is used to configure the org.open18.auth.PasswordBean class. The reverse logic is used to derive the resource path of the fine-grained descriptor from the name of a class. Seam searches in both directions when preparing the component definition.

You saw this dispersed approach to XML-based configuration in chapter 3 when you were introduced to fine-grained page descriptors. They differ in that a fine-grained page descriptor only deals with a single <page> element, whereas the fine-grained component descriptor is capable of accepting one or more <component> elements, depending on whether the root tag is <component> or <components>. If you intend on declaring only a single component definition, you use `<component>` as the root element. A fine-grained descriptor with a single component definition need not declare the `class` attribute, as the class name is derived according to the conversion logic just described. The content of a fine-grained descriptor is shown here, which includes the optional XML namespace declarations:

```
<component xmlns="http://jboss.com/products/seam/components"
  xmlns:xsi="http://www.w3.org/2001/XMLSchema-instance"
  xsi:schemaLocation="
    http://jboss.com/products/seam/components
    http://jboss.com/products/seam/components-2.0.xsd"
  name="passwordBean" scope="event"/>
```

If you intend on using multiple declarations in the fine-grained descriptor, you make `<components>` the root element. However, by not using `<component>` as the root element, you lose the benefit of the implied value of the `class` attribute, which is now required. What you do gain is the full capacity of the component descriptor for configuring the class. You can assign one or more roles using multiple `<component>` elements, or you can use auxiliary elements like `<factory>` and `<event>`, which are both covered in the next chapter.

WARNING   There's nothing stopping you from putting arbitrary component definitions—definitions not related to the adjacent class—in a fine-grained descriptor that uses `<components>` as the root element. However, this practice is discouraged because it hides component definitions in unexpected places.

The downside of the fine-grained descriptor is that it is yet another XML file that you have to manage. You also lose the type safety that annotations afford you. Fortunately, there's a compromise. Seam offers "type-safe" XML elements through the use of XML namespaces and XML Schema, thus reducing the pain involved in working with XML.

5.2   *XML namespaces in the component descriptor*

You can hardly ignore the XML namespace declarations at the top of the component descriptors presented thus far. In fact, they account for more than half of the characters in the documents! Let's see what this gratuitous metadata is all about and what it buys you.

5.2.1   *The purpose of XML namespace declarations*

The namespace declarations that attach to the root element of the component descriptor import a vocabulary of XML elements and attributes defined in W3C XML Schema for creating and configuring components. The reason XML Schema is used is because it offers a rich typing system and allows the vocabulary to be extended through custom namespaces (akin to a Java package). That means the names, classes, and bean properties of components can be reflected in the names of the XML elements and attributes, and that strict validation of the markup can be enforced. It's for this reason that the XML is considered "type-safe."

DON'T BE SO GENERIC

The `http://jboss.com/products/seam/components` namespace represents the generic Seam component vocabulary, which provides the `<component>` element already covered. Aside from the root element, `<components>`, the other elements in this namespace are `<property>` (for setting a property value), `<import>` (which we examine later in this chapter), and `<factory>` and `<event>`, both of which are described in the next chapter. Using this namespace alone, you don't see much benefit from using XML Schema over a less verbose alternative like DTD because the property names in generic `<component>` definitions can't be validated. The benefit comes in the extensive set of component-specific namespaces that Seam provides that widen this vocabulary and make it type safe. You can also define your own XML namespaces, as you'll learn to do later in this section.

NOTE   Each namespace that you import provides an XML vocabulary that maps one-to-one with the names of component classes and their bean properties. Therefore, I'll refer to the namespaces from this point forward as component XML namespaces.

Let's look at an example where an element from a component XML namespace is used to replace a generic element. The built-in component named `org.jboss.seam.core.init` has a property named `debug` that controls Seam's debug mode. With the generic component namespace already declared, the debug mode property is set to true using the following stanza, which references this component by its name (not class):

```
<component name="org.jboss.seam.core.init">
  <property name="debug">true</property>
</component>
```

Instead of using generic elements to define or configure components, you can use custom elements and attributes imported from a component XML namespace. The vocabulary associated with the built-in `http://jboss.com/products/seam/core` namespace includes the XML element `<init>` (which maps to the Seam component class `org.jboss.seam.core.Init`) and a set of XML attributes (which fit to the properties of the class). By importing this namespace into the component descriptor and binding it to the namespace alias `core`, it's possible to use the qualified `<core:init>` element to set the `debug` property of the corresponding component to `true`, shown here in bold:

```
<components xmlns="http://jboss.com/products/seam/components"
  xmlns:core="http://jboss.com/products/seam/core"
  xmlns:xsi="http://www.w3.org/2001/XMLSchema-instance"
  xsi:schemaLocation="
    http://jboss.com/products/seam/components
    http://jboss.com/products/seam/components-2.0.xsd
    http://jboss.com/products/seam/core
    http://jboss.com/products/seam/core-2.0.xsd">
  <core:init debug="true"/>
</components>
```

This declaration assigns an initial value to the property of a built-in component, which you'll learn more about in section 5.3. The key point is that both the property name and value are validated by the schema. Although the namespace declarations are quite verbose, they help cut down on the number of characters needed throughout the remainder of the component descriptor.

INFO If you aren't accustomed to XML Schema-based configuration, you may be turned off by the clutter they introduce to the root element. However, these formalities are your ticket to a friendly development experience. The `xsi:schemaLocation` attribute maps the XML namespaces to XML Schema Documents (XSDs), which the IDE retrieves and interprets to provide you with XML tag completion, similar to what you get with Java syntax. If you don't need the IDE support, you can leave off the namespace declarations.

Most built-in Seam components are associated with a namespace, which we explore next. After a survey of the built-in namespaces, we tackle the mapping between XML elements in a component namespace and Java classes.

A SURVEY OF SEAM'S BUILT-IN COMPONENTS

An itemization of all of the built-in components in Seam would be in vain, as they are ever-changing. I want to at least give you a snapshot of the functional areas of Seam. Table 5.3 lists Seam's built-in namespaces along with a description of the components they include.

NOTE The version in the .xsd filename must match Seam's major version. Thus, if you're using Seam 2.1.0.GA, the version should be 2.1. Table 5.3 lists the 2.0 versions.

Table 5.3   Built-in component XML namespaces

Namespace URI / schema location	Purpose
http://jboss.com/products/seam/async http://jboss.com/products/seam/async-2.0.xsd	Asynchronous dispatchers
http://jboss.com/products/seam/bpm http://jboss.com/products/seam/bpm-2.0.xsd	jBPM integration
http://jboss.com/products/seam/components http://jboss.com/products/seam/components-2.0.xsd	Generic component definitions, factories, event observers, and context variable prefix imports
http://jboss.com/products/seam/core http://jboss.com/products/seam/core-2.0.xsd	Core Seam settings (debug mode, transaction management switch, etc.)
http://jboss.com/products/seam/drools http://jboss.com/products/seam/drools-2.0.xsd	Drools configuration and security rules
http://jboss.com/products/seam/framework http://jboss.com/products/seam/framework-2.0.xsd	Seam application (CRUD) framework

Table 5.3   Built-in component XML namespaces *(continued)*

Namespace URI / schema location	Purpose
http://jboss.com/products/seam/international http://jboss.com/products/seam/international-2.0.xsd	Locale and time zone selector components
http://jboss.com/products/seam/jms http://jboss.com/products/seam/jms-2.0.xsd	JMS integration
http://jboss.com/products/seam/mail http://jboss.com/products/seam/mail-2.0.xsd	E-mail integration and connection settings
http://jboss.com/products/seam/navigation http://jboss.com/products/seam/navigation-2.0.xsd	Global navigation rules and resource locations for global page descriptors
http://jboss.com/products/seam/pdf http://jboss.com/products/seam/pdf-2.0.xsd	PDF document storage and key-store configuration for signed PDFs (requires jboss-seam-pdf.jar)
http://jboss.com/products/seam/persistence http://jboss.com/products/seam/persistence-2.0.xsd	Persistence units and manager configurations
http://jboss.com/products/seam/remoting http://jboss.com/products/seam/remoting-2.0.xsd	JavaScript remoting settings
http://jboss.com/products/seam/security http://jboss.com/products/seam/security-2.0.xsd	Identity (authentication and authorization) configuration
http://jboss.com/products/seam/spring http://jboss.com/products/seam/spring-2.0.xsd	Spring integration (requires jboss-seam-spring.jar)
http://jboss.com/products/seam/theme http://jboss.com/products/seam/theme-2.0.xsd	UI theme selector and available themes
http://jboss.com/products/seam/transaction http://jboss.com/products/seam/transaction-2.0.xsd	Transaction providers
http://jboss.com/products/seam/web http://jboss.com/products/seam/web-2.0.xsd	Servlet filter configuration

To register a component namespace in your component descriptor, first choose a component namespace from table 5.3 and declare it as an XML namespace using an alias of your choice. Next, add the namespace URI and schema location to the xsi:schema-Location attribute on the root node. Then, you can use tag completion support in the IDE to discover the available components since all of Seam's built-in namespaces are backed by an XML Schema vocabulary. If you are the exploratory type, I encourage you to just add all of the namespaces from this table and see what your XML editor gives you.

While having fun with tag completion and exploring the built-in components that Seam offers through XML, you may be wondering what these elements have to do with Java classes and component definitions. The first step to understanding this relationship is learning how the namespaces are associated with Java packages.

NAMESPACES AND JAVA PACKAGES

An XML namespace is a URI—a fancy way of saying a unique name. A namespace looks like a URL, but it's not mandatory that it resolve to a public document. The namespace is mapped to an alias, such as core in the previous example. The name of the alias is arbitrary. It's used as a prefix on element names, such as `<core:init>`, to associate these elements with a particular namespace. The prefix isn't required for elements in the default namespace, which is set using the xmlns attribute. Typically, component descriptors declare `http://jboss.com/products/seam/components` as the default namespace. As such, the `<component>` element doesn't need a prefix.

Namespaces are similar to Java packages. In fact, Seam enforces a one-to-one relationship between namespaces in the component descriptor and Java packages. You'll soon learn that the elements are transformations of Java class names and the attributes the bean properties. The use of XML namespaces in the component descriptor is the closest you can get to writing Java without actually using the Java syntax.

Let's draft an XML namespace for the Open 18 application to replace the use of the generic `<component>` element. This lesson should also help you understand how elements in a component XML namespace are interpreted so that you can make sense of the syntax used to configure one of Seam's built-in components.

5.2.2 Defining an XML @Namespace for components in a package

An XML namespace URI can be associated with a Java package using the @Namespace annotation, summarized in table 5.4. @Namespace is a package-level annotation, which means it's placed above the package declaration in the package-info.java file.[2] When Seam encounters an XML element that's not in the generic component namespace, it looks for a @Namespace annotation to make the connection between the namespace URI of that element and a Java package. Seam 2.1 supports an implied mapping between namespace URI and Java package, making the @Namespace annotation just a formality. The mechanics of this mapping are addressed in the next section.

Table 5.4 The @Namespace annotation

Name:	Namespace
Purpose:	Maps a URI to a Java package. The URI can be used as an XML namespace in the component descriptor. The mapping tells Seam which Java package to look in to find components when processing an XML element in that namespace.
Target:	PACKAGE

Attribute	Type	Function
value	String	The XML namespace (URI) for this package. Default: none (required).
prefix	String	A qualifier used to derive the component name from the local name of the XML element, similar to how a Java package qualifies a class name. If this value is empty, a prefix is not used. Default: empty string.

---

[2] package-info.java was introduced in Java 5 for declaring package-level annotations and JavaDoc comments.

Let's create a namespace for the authentication package in the Open 18 application. The contents of the package-info.java file in the `org.open18.auth` package are shown here:

```
@Namespace(value="http://open18.org/components/auth")
@AutoCreate
package org.open18.auth;
import org.jboss.seam.annotations.AutoCreate;
import org.jboss.seam.annotations.Namespace;
```

Notice that in addition to the `@Namespace` declaration, other Seam component annotations can be added to the package-info.java file to set defaults for any component in that package. In this case, all components in the `org.open18.auth` package support the autocreate functionality.

WARNING   As of Seam 2.0, the component scanner does not pick up `@Namespace` annotations located on the hot-deploy classpath (sourced from the src/action directory of seam-gen WAR projects). They must be on the main classpath (e.g., the src/model directory).

You find similar declarations scattered throughout the Seam code base defining the namespaces shown in table 5.3. Having created a component namespace of our own, let's see how it's used to enable domain-specific markup in the component descriptor.

5.2.3   *How XML namespaces are interpreted*

The `@Namespace` declaration establishes a link between an XML namespace and a Java package. (Again, in Seam 2.1, this mapping can be implied.) This relationship is the key to extensible XML authoring of components. In other words, you can define your components using custom XML elements just like Seam does its built-in components.

   As with Seam's built-in namespaces, begin by adding the namespace from the `@Namespace` annotation to the component descriptor. Then choose a namespace alias for associating XML elements with this URI. Listing 5.2 shows the declaration of the `http://open18.org/components/auth` namespace bound to the `auth` namespace alias and a definition of a component in the associated Java package.

> **Listing 5.2   The `PasswordBean` defined using a component namespace**

```
<components xmlns="http://jboss.com/products/seam/components"
  xmlns:auth="http://open18.org/components/auth"
  xmlns:xsi="http://www.w3.org/2001/XMLSchema-instance"
  xsi:schemaLocation="
    http://jboss.com/products/seam/components
    http://jboss.com/products/seam/components-2.0.xsd">
  <auth:password-bean scope="event"/>
</components>
```

The `<auth:password-bean>` element is a type-safe way of declaring the `PasswordBean` class as a component. You don't actually have to declare the XML namespace in the root element. You have the option of using the namespace directly in the prefix of the element:

```
<http://open18.org/components/auth:password-bean scope="event"/>
```

The namespace alias is merely a shorthand syntax. Either way, the result is equivalent to what's achieved using the following generic component definition:

```
<component name="passwordBean"
  class="org.open18.auth.PasswordBean" scope="event"/>
```

Let's explore how Seam interprets the type-safe declaration to derive the same set of information provided by the generic component definition.

TRANSLATING XML INTO JAVA

The translation from the `<auth:password-bean>` element to a fully qualified Java class is shown in figure 5.1.

When Seam encounters an XML element in the `auth` namespace, it looks to see if there's a `@Namespace` annotation with a value that matches the XML namespace URI. Indeed, the namespace maps to a Java package as follows:

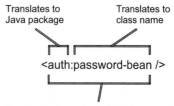

Figure 5.1 How Seam interprets an XML element in a component namespace

```
http://open18.org/components/auth -> org.open18.auth
```

As of Seam 2.1, there are two ways the Java packages can be derived from the XML namespace URI if a matching `@Namespace` annotation isn't defined. When the scheme of the URI is http://, Seam implies the package name by stripping the www prefix (if present), reversing the domain name, and appending the trailing paths as subpackages (converting slashes to dots):

```
http://www.open18.org/auth -> org.open18.auth
```

When the namespace scheme is java:, rather than http://, the part of the URI that follows the scheme is used as the package name:

```
java:org.open18.auth -> org.open18.auth
```

At this point, the namespace URI has served its purpose and Seam ceases to do anything more with it. It just helps put Seam in the right playing field. Next, the simple name of the class—the class name without the Java package—is derived from the local name of the XML element, which in this case is `password-bean`. This conversion occurs by making the first letter and any letter after a hyphen uppercase and dropping the hyphens:

```
password-bean -> PasswordBean
```

The package `org.open18.auth` and the simple class name `PasswordBean` are assembled to form the fully qualified Java class. The complete translation is as follows:

```
<auth:password-bean> -> org.open18.auth.PasswordBean
```

NOTE   The benefit of using a custom XML element is that it eliminates the need to specify the `class` attribute on the component definition. Instead, the class is derived by adjoining the Java package assigned to the element's namespace URL and a translation of the element's local name from the XML element. If a Java package can't be resolved from the XML namespace URI of the element, an exception is thrown during deployment that prevents the application from loading.

That takes care of the component class, but as you've learned, every Seam component must be associated with a name and scope. Let's see how they are assigned.

RESOLVING A COMPONENT NAME AND SCOPE

XML elements in a component namespace are treated as extensions to the `<component>` element. That means they inherit all of the standard attributes used to define a component that were listed in table 5.2. Because the standard attributes are inherited, the component name and scope can be specified as attributes on the custom element:

```
<auth:password-bean name="passwordBean" scope="event"/>
```

However, declaring the component name on a custom element isn't necessary. Seam uses the following search order to locate a name to assign to a component defined using a namespace element in the component descriptor:

- The `name` attribute on the custom XML element
- The `@Name` annotation on the associated Java class
- A value derived from the local name of the XML element

If a component name is not specified in the `name` attribute of the XML element or the `@Name` annotation, Seam gets its hands dirty and derives a name from the Java class. Seam begins by lowercasing the first letter of the simple name of the class to arrive at the unqualified component name:

```
PasswordBean -> passwordBean
```

This is where the `@Namespace` annotation comes back into play. The `@Namespace` annotation has a `prefix` attribute, whose value is used to qualify a component name just as a Java package qualifies a class name. If the `prefix` attribute on the `@Namespace` annotation is empty, then the unqualified component name is equivalent to the fully qualified component name. In this example, the `prefix` attribute is empty, so the component name remains `passwordBean`.

If the `prefix` attribute is not empty, the fully qualified component name is constructed by combining the value of the `prefix` attribute with the unqualified component name, separated by the dot (.) character. Assume for a moment that the namespace had been defined as follows:

```
@Namespace(value = "http://open18.org/components/auth",
    prefix = "org.open18.auth")
```

The component name derived from the `<auth:password-bean>` declaration becomes `org.open18.auth.passwordBean`. *Don't confuse this with the fully qualified class name.*

To locate a scope, Seam consults the `scope` attribute on the custom XML element, then checks the `@Scope` annotation on the class. If neither one is present, a scope is chosen automatically according to table 4.6 in chapter 4.

You should now understand how Seam gets from `<core:init>` to the built-in Seam component name `org.jboss.seam.core.init`, shown in an earlier example, knowing that there's a `@Namespace` annotation declared on the `org.jboss.seam.core` package with a prefix of the same name and namespace URI `http://jboss.com/products/seam/core`. Let's see how to get the IDE to make this type of association for our component namespace.

ENABLING VALIDATION AND IDE TAG COMPLETION

Declaring the `auth` namespace alias in your component descriptor isn't enough to get the XML to validate or to give the IDE the information it needs to provide tag completion. You still need to provide an XML Schema Document (XSD) for each of the component namespaces that you declare. The XML Schema vocabulary for the `auth` namespace, auth-1.0.xsd, is not shown here, but it's available in the book source code for this chapter. Once you've written that file, you add it to the `xsi:schemaLocation` attribute in the component descriptor, shown here in bold:

```
<components xmlns="http://jboss.com/products/seam/components"
 xmlns:auth="http://open18.org/components/auth"
 xmlns:xsi="http://www.w3.org/2001/XMLSchema-instance"
 xsi:schemaLocation="
   http://open18.org/components/auth
   http://open18.org/components/auth-1.0.xsd
   http://jboss.com/products/seam/components
   http://jboss.com/products/seam/components-2.0.xsd">
 ...
</components>
```

If the XSD isn't available at the URL provided, you need to make the correlation between the auth-1.0.xsd file and its namespace in your XML editor to achieve XML tag completion and validation. This works automatically for Seam's built-in namespaces since the XSD files are published to a public web server.

Although creating component XML namespaces may appear challenging, the good news is that you are more often a consumer than you are a creator. Most of the time you find yourself using the namespaces included with Seam to configure Seam's built-in components. Speaking of Seam's built-in components, you may notice that all of Seam's components have fully qualified component names to avoid naming conflicts. However, these long component names can be cumbersome to type. Let's see how to import context variable prefixes so it's possible to address component instances by their base names.

5.2.4 *Importing a context variable prefix*

Just as packages are used in Java to avoid naming conflicts between classes, prefixes are used to avoid naming conflicts between component names. A context variable prefix even uses the same dot (.) notation that you're familiar with from Java packages.

To make referring to these names more convenient, Seam offers a way to import a set of qualified context variable prefixes just like the import statement works in Java.

A context variable prefix is imported using the `<import>` element in the component descriptor so that you can reference the context variable according to its last segment—its unqualified name. Assume for a moment that we assigned the `org.open18.auth` prefix to the component namespace mapped to the `auth` XML namespace. The context variable prefix could be imported with the following declaration in the component descriptor:

```
<import>org.open18.auth</import>
```

This import statement applies globally across the application. It allows you to reference the context variable for the `PasswordBean` component as `passwordBean` rather than `org.open18.auth.passwordBean`.

TIP   I encourage you to use fully qualified context variable names for your application's components and then import the context variable prefixes using the `<import>` tag as needed. This becomes especially important if you are building reusable Seam libraries.

All built-in Seam components use qualified component names to be polite and avoid "stealing" context variable names you might need to use. You can find a complete list of Seam's built-in components in the Seam reference documentation. Given that many of these components are so commonly used, Seam imports their context variable prefixes automatically. At the time of this writing, that list includes the following:

- org.jboss.seam.bpm
- org.jboss.seam.captcha
- org.jboss.seam.core
- org.jboss.seam.faces
- org.jboss.seam.framework
- org.jboss.seam.international
- org.jboss.seam.jms
- org.jboss.seam.mail
- org.jboss.seam.pageflow
- org.jboss.seam.security
- org.jboss.seam.security.management (Seam 2.1 or greater)
- org.jboss.seam.security.permission (Seam 2.1 or greater)
- org.jboss.seam.theme
- org.jboss.seam.transaction
- org.jboss.seam.web

This set of imports is especially convenient for those often-used Seam components. One common component to reference in the UI is the `FacesMessages` class, bound to the `org.jboss.seam.faces.facesMessages` context variable. You can see that the namespace used by the context variable appears in the default list of imports, so you can instead reference it using the abbreviated context variable name `facesMessages`. You may use this component, for example, to iterate over the global JSF messages, without having to use `<h:messages>` with the `globalOnly` flag:

```
<rich:dataList var="msg" value="#{facesMessages.currentGlobalMessages}">
  #{msg.summary}
</rich:dataList>
```

Component names are used as context variables to access Seam components, which you learned about in the previous chapter. They also provide a means of configuring initial property values for a component, which are applied to an instance after it's created (either by Seam or by a collaborating container). In the next section, you'll learn how to set the initial state of an instance by supplementing its component definition with property values.

5.3   *Configuring component properties*

In the previous chapter you learned how a class enters into "component-hood" by way of annotations and, in this chapter, as a result of XML-based declarations. But alone, these definitions are just a fancy way of instantiating a class and weaving services into it. Oftentimes, a component becomes useful only once its state is initialized, which entails assigning initial values to its properties. This initialization comes in the form of a simple property value, such as a connection string, or as a reference to another component, effectively wiring components together. The property value assignments occur prior to the instance being put to work as a context variable.

NOTE   The `@Create` and `@PostConstruct` life-cycle callback methods are executed *after* the initial property values have been assigned to the component instance.

In this section, you'll learn how these initial property values are declared and what types of values can be supplied. Before we get into the mechanics, let's consider the benefit of establishing the initial state of a component and find out what is meant by a component property.

5.3.1   *Component definitions as object prototypes*

Where a component definition pays off is when it's used to produce an object prototype. As part of the component definition, you can store a set of property names and associated values, which Seam picks up on startup and subsequently transfers to the component instance after it's instantiated. The prototype might serve to prepopulate a form or to fill in fixed values that aren't modifiable by the user, such as the date a record is created. Let's see how these properties get mapped to the class.

A property name is mapped to either a JavaBean-style "setter" method or a field on the target object, herein referred to generally as a *bean property*. The field name shares the same name as the property, whereas the setter method is derived by capitalizing the property name and prefixing it with `set` (e.g., the `createdDate` property maps to the `setCreatedDate()` method). If a property name matches both a field and a setter method, the setter method takes precedence. The property value is then injected into the method or field using reflection. When the dependency being injected is a reference to another component instance, the mechanism is referred to as dependency injection (DI), or more informally "component wiring" to borrow from the Spring term "bean wiring."

NOTE   The access level of the method or field on the target object doesn't matter. Seam can assign a value to a method or field of any access level, even if it's private—a privilege granted to reflection.

Unlike other parts of the component definition, component properties must be defined in external configuration, rather than in annotations.[3] Although Seam tries to avoid unnecessary external configuration, namely XML, configurable properties is one case where it makes sense to take advantage of the decoupling. Declaring a property value outside of the Java source code allows you to achieve any of the following:

- Adjust the runtime behavior of the application without having to recompile (e.g., timeout period, debug mode, maximum number of query results)
- Define different property values for different component roles
- Declare references to other component instances, known as component wiring

It's up to you to decide when and where to use component properties in your application. The next choice to make is where to define that initial property value.

5.3.2   *Where component properties are defined*

You can add an initial property value to a component definition by declaring it in one of three places, listed in the order of increasing precedence:

- Component descriptor
- Servlet context parameter
- seam.properties

Chances are, you'll use the component descriptor a vast majority of the time, given that it's the most flexible and convenient. Earlier you learned to use the component descriptor to define Seam components with either a generic <component> element or an element bound to a component XML namespace. You can use the same elements to assign property metadata, to augment the component definition, or to configure an existing component. Section 5.4 clarifies this distinction.

As an alternative to using the component descriptor, you can configure component properties using the standard Java properties syntax, herein referred to as *external property settings*. External property settings can be defined in either the seam.properties file or as servlet context parameters. Seam employs a simple naming convention to determine how the property key is mapped to the bean property of a Seam component, which we'll go over when we look at this technique.

---

[3] There is one exception to this rule. The @Logger annotation instructs Seam to inject a log instance into the annotated method or field when the component is instantiated.

The remainder of this section takes a hands-on approach to explaining how to use the formats just mentioned, drawing on use cases from the Open 18 application. Given that you already have the component descriptor open, we'll start with the XML-based component configuration.

DEFINING PROPERTIES IN THE COMPONENT DESCRIPTOR

Properties can be associated with any component definition declared in the component descriptor. If you use the generic <component> element, the properties are configured using nested <property> elements. The name of the property being configured is specified in the name attribute of the <property> element, and the value to be assigned is specified in the body of the element (or within a nested <value> element).

To associate the configuration properties with an existing component definition, you specify the component's name in the name attribute of the <component> element. If you want the <component> declaration to also serve as a component definition, you must also supply the class attribute. To learn the distinction between the two, see section 5.4.

Let's assume that we want to configure the hashing algorithm and character set used in the PasswordManager component, shown in listing 5.3. The digestAlgorithm property determines the type of hash that's calculated from the plain-text password, and the charset property determines the encoding scheme applied to the password prior to hashing it.

Listing 5.3 A configurable component used to hash plain-text passwords

```
package org.open18.auth;

import java.security.MessageDigest;
import org.jboss.seam.annotations.Name;
import org.jboss.seam.util.Hex;

@Name("passwordManager")
public class PasswordManager {
   private String digestAlgorithm;
   private String charset;

   public void setDigestAlgorithm(String algorithm) {
      this.digestAlgorithm = algorithm;
   }

   public void setCharset(String charset) {
      this.charset = charset;
   }

   public String hash(String plainTextPassword) {
      try {
         MessageDigest digest =
            MessageDigest.getInstance(digestAlgorithm);
         digest.update(plainTextPassword.getBytes(charset));
         byte[] rawHash = digest.digest();
         return new String(Hex.encodeHex(rawHash));
      }
      catch (Exception e) {
```

```
            throw new RuntimeException(e);
        }
    }
}
```

Initial property values must be assigned to customize the behavior of the hash()
method for the current application (and to prevent a NullPointerException). The
following declaration configures the digestAlgorithm and charset values for a component named passwordManager using nested <property> elements:

```
<component name="passwordManager">
  <property name="digestAlgorithm">SHA-1</property>
  <property name="charset">UTF-8</property>
</component>
```

If there is no component named passwordManager in the Seam container, this configuration serves no purpose. When the passwordManager component name is
requested, Seam instantiates a new instance of the corresponding class and then
applies the property values using reflection. The net effect is equivalent to the following Java code:

```
PasswordManager passwordManager = new PasswordManager();
passwordManager.setDigestAlgorithm("SHA-1");
passwordManager.setCharset("UTF-8");
Contexts.getEventContext().set("passwordManager", passwordManager);
```

This snippet is intended to provide a general picture of how the property values affect
the instance. Of course, this is a generalization of what happens when a component is
instantiated. In actuality, there are a plethora of method interceptors that are wrapped
around the instance followed by execution of its life-cycle methods, if defined.

To make for a more concise declaration, properties can be defined as attributes on
the <component> element. The component configuration for PasswordManager has
been modified to take advantage of this shorthand:

```
<component name="passwordManager" digestAlgorithm="SHA-1" charset="UTF-8"/>
```

However, the attribute syntax comes with a very important disclaimer. You can't use
the attribute syntax to configure a property whose name is a reserved word in the
XML vocabulary of the <component> element. The reserved words follow; these attribute names are interpreted as part of the component definition:

- name
- class
- scope
- auto-create
- installed
- startupDepends (Seam 2.1 or greater)
- startup
- precedence
- jndi-name

Memorize this list or keep it close at hand. Otherwise, you'll be very confused as to why you get an error (or a silent failure) when you try to assign a value to a bean property whose name is in this reserved list using an attribute on the <component> element. One way to handle this case is to use a nested <property> (or namespace element). Another option is to use an external property setting, covered later.

The third syntax for registering an initial property value in the component descriptor is to use a nested element whose name is equivalent to the property that you're configuring. Once again, the component configuration for PasswordManager has been rewritten to reflect this syntax:

```
<component name="passwordManager">
  <digestAlgorithm>SHA-1</digestAlgorithm>
  <charset>UTF-8</charset>
</component>
```

If you've been following along with your XML editor, you know that the XML Schema validator is not happy with these last two variations—using an attribute on <component> or nested element that shares the name of the property. That's because the generic component XML vocabulary doesn't declare any attributes or elements with the names digestAlgorithm or charset.

So what good is this syntax if it doesn't validate? Well, it just doesn't validate *yet*. You simply need to educate the XML validator. As you learned, an element in a component XML namespace extends from the generic <component> element. You have to extend the XML Schema of the generic namespace and append any custom attributes or nested element names used by your component namespace. That requires that you create an XSD, as covered in section 5.2.3. Then you can use the element-based syntax to configure the property of a component and still have the document validate.

Granted, if you aren't concerned about the document validating and just want to make your XML cleaner without the overhead of creating an XSD, then there's nothing stopping you. Seam doesn't mandate that the document validate against the schema so as to avoid imposing an arbitrary restriction on you. Use of XSD is merely a best practice to get the type safety when developing. However, be warned that the XML editor may not be so forgiving and may complain loudly about the custom attribute and element names being invalid. Fortunately, all of the built-in Seam components already have corresponding XSDs, so you can use custom attribute and element names to define properties for these components and the document will validate.

Assuming that you've imported the appropriate XML vocabulary, then the configuration for the PasswordManager component can take advantage of the shorthand syntax, as shown in listing 5.4, and still validate.

Listing 5.4 Component configuration using custom XML attribute and element names

```
<components xmlns="http://jboss.com/products/seam/components"
  xmlns:auth="http://open18.org/components/auth"
  xmlns:xsi="http://www.w3.org/2001/XMLSchema-instance"
  xsi:schemaLocation="
```

```
    http://jboss.com/products/seam/components
    http://jboss.com/products/seam/components-2.0.xsd
    http://open18.org/components/auth
    http://open18.org/components/auth-1.0.xsd">
  <auth:password-manager>
    <auth:digest-algorithm>SHA-1</auth:digest-algorithm>
    <auth:charset>UTF-8</auth:charset>
  </auth:password-manager>
</components>
```

I threw a curve ball at you in that last excerpt. Can you tell what it is? I changed the name of the `<digestAlgorithm>` element to `digest-algorithm`. Seam *always* converts hyphenated element names, attribute names, and the value of the `name` attribute on the `<property>` element to their camel-case equivalents. This conversion is consistent with what's done to derive the simple name of the class from the element name, as you learned in section 5.2.3.

Thus, you could have written the `<property>` element for the `digestAlgorithm` property using the hyphenated form:

```
<property name="digest-algorithm">SHA-1</property>
```

or, if the namespace vocabulary supports it, written the attribute name as

```
<auth:password-manager digest-algorithm="SHA-1"/>
```

NOTE The XML namespace alias (e.g., `auth`) doesn't play a role in the processing of elements that map to properties as it does when top-level elements mapped to component classes are interpreted (in the latter case, the alias is used to resolve a Java package as described in section 5.2.3). In the previous example, you could have used the unqualified element `<digest-algorithm>` and, disregarding the whining from the XML editor, the property value would have been assigned properly.

To summarize, you can configure a component property using a nested `<property>` element, an attribute with the same name as the property on the component element, or a nested element with the same name as the property. The important question to ask is, "Does it validate?" In all cases, the nested `<property>` element validates, though without any guarantee of type safety. The component XML namespace vocabulary dictates the custom attributes and nested elements you can use to configure a component's properties. Seam's built-in component namespaces mostly rely on the syntax of attribute names in hyphenated form. See section 5.5 for more examples of this syntax. If you're defining your own XML Schema, you may choose to adopt Seam's style as your standard.

That covers the variety of syntaxes you can use to define component properties in XML. Let's move on to property configuration using external property settings.

EXTERNAL PROPERTY SETTINGS

The component descriptor allows you to declare a component and configure its properties. External property settings only allow you to configure the properties of existing

Seam components. That means the class must have a @Name annotation or it must be declared as a component in a component descriptor (it must also meet the conditions to be installed).

To define the property of a component using an external property, the property key is constructed by joining the name of the component with the name of the bean property on the component, separated by a dot (.) character. The value associated with that key is used as the value to assign to the bean property. Note that in this case the hyphenated form isn't acknowledged, so the key must reference the property name verbatim.

Let's return to our PasswordManager component. For the purpose of this example, we'll assume that the PasswordManager has been defined as a Seam component named passwordManager. To assign values to the digestAlgorithm and charset properties using external property settings, you add the following two lines to a seam.properties file:

```
passwordManager.digestAlgorithm=SHA-1
passwordManager.charset=UTF-8
```

If you assigned the fully qualified name org.open18.auth.passwordManager to the PasswordManager component, the assignments appear as follow:

```
org.open18.auth.passwordManager.digestAlgorithm=SHA-1
org.open18.auth.passwordManager.charset=UTF-8
```

The location of the seam.properties file is described in section 4.5.1 of chapter 4. When you define the property settings in the seam.properties file, you specify the value in the standard java.util.Properties syntax, separating the name of the configuration property from the value with either an equals sign (=) or a space. For more complex string values than what is shown here, see the JavaDoc for java.util.Properties for a more complete explanation of the standard rules.

WARNING In seam-gen projects, you must use the seam.properties from the resources folder, not the one from src/action or src/model. The latter two locations are ignored by the build.

Instead of registering initial property values in a seam.properties file, you can set them up as servlet context parameters in the web application's WEB-INF/web.xml file. The same java.util.Properties syntax applies. Note that these parameters aren't defined in the JSF servlet definition, but rather as context-wide initialization parameters using top-level <context-param> elements:

```
<context-param>
  <param-name>passwordManager.digestAlgorithm</param-name>
  <param-value>SHA-1</param-value>
</context-param>
<context-param>
  <param-name>passwordManager.charset</param-name>
  <param-value>UTF-8</param-value>
</context-param>
```

Using servlet context parameters is arguably less flexible since it requires a servlet environment for the properties to take effect. This limitation can make it difficult to create basic unit tests because it forces you to bootstrap the servlet environment.

WARNING   Keep in mind that the component name (the context variable name) is used as the first half of the property key, *not* the class name of the component. Many of the built-in Seam components have names that closely resemble the class that they represent, so don't confuse the two. In addition, don't confuse the dots in the component name with the final dot used to isolate the name of the bean property.

Just to get a taste for a more advanced property key, let's consider how you might set the property on one of Seam's built-in components. Figure 5.2 shows how to disable the transaction management in Seam by setting the `transactionManagementEnabled` property on the built-in `org.jboss.seam.init` component to `false`. Transaction management is covered in chapter 9. For now, we're merely playing around with the setting for demonstration purposes.

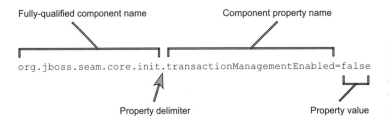

Figure 5.2   **How Seam interprets an external property setting in order to assign an initial value to the property of a component**

Assigning values to the bean properties of a component using external property settings is a simpler and more terse alternative than XML. In addition, if you define a value for a component property using an external property setting, it takes precedence over the configuration of the same property in the component descriptor. This override can be useful for adjusting property values for different deployment environments.

Those are the basics of configuring components, but your exposure has been limited to basic string properties. Let's step it up a notch and explore the more complex property types that Seam gives you the capability to configure.

5.3.3   *Property value types*

The values that are assigned to the properties of a component can be any of the following:

- Basic types (strings, numbers, Booleans, enums, characters, and class names)
- EL (value and method expressions)
- Collections (where each individual value can be any item in this list)
- Replacement tokens (a name surrounded by @ symbols)

Let's cover a couple more of the basic types before moving further down the list.

BASIC VALUE TYPES

The basic types are straightforward. A value begins its life as a string when it's read from the configuration file. Seam then determines the correct type for the value based on the target property's type and converts it before performing the assignment. If a converter isn't registered, an exception is thrown at startup. If the value can't be converted, an exception is thrown when the component is instantiated.

TIP   You can create your own property converter by implementing the Con-verter interface on `org.jboss.seam.util.Conversions` and registering it using the static `putConverter()` method on that class. However, right now you have to subclass `SeamListener` in order to install the converter before Seam initializes.

In the case of the `PasswordManager` component, no conversion occurs since both properties, `digestAlgorithm` and `charset`, are strings. But Seam can handle most of the common conversations that you'd expect to be supported. Let's look at a couple more examples.

Most golf courses have 18 holes (those that don't have nine holes). Let's use component configuration to set a sensible default value for the `numHoles` property on a transient `Course` instance:

```
<component name="newCourse" class="org.open18.model.Course">
  <property name="numHoles">18</property>
</component>
```

The property `numHoles` is a primitive integer. Seam performs a basic conversation in this case using `Integer.valueOf(String)`. You can expect the same conversion to be done for all types represented by primitive wrapper classes (and thus have the `valueOf(String)` method). Two additional types that Seam supports are `java.lang.Class` and `java.lang.Enum`. A class is derived from a string using `Class.forName(String)` and an enum is selected by matching the string against the literal value of the constant.

Let's assume that the `type` property on the `Facility` entity has been changed from a string to the `FacilityType` enum defined as follows:

```
public enum FacilityType {
    PUBLIC, PRIVATE, SEMI_PRIVATE, RESORT, MILITARY;
}
```

You could set the default `type` to `PUBLIC` on the `Facility` prototype as follows:

```
<component name="newFacility" class="org.open18.model.Facility">
  <property name="type">PUBLIC</property>
</component>
```

WARNING   The tricky conversion is that of Booleans, which Seam converts from a string using `Boolean.valueOf(String)`. This method only considers a value `true` if it matches the string "true," ignoring case. All other values are interpreted as `false`.

Component configuration gets interesting when the initial value is an EL expression since it's capable of injecting a dynamic, contextual value. The value may even be an instance of another Seam component. If the Spring-Seam bridge is configured, which is covered in chapter 15 (online), you can even inject a Spring bean into a Seam component using the EL. Let's dig into EL property values and review some examples.

EXPRESSION LANGUAGE VALUES

It's been pretty much hammered into your brain by this point that Seam relies heavily on the EL as a means of getting a handle on a component instance or other context variable. The EL's API agnostic syntax is the reason Seam is able to unify such a wide range of technologies in a straightforward way. So it should be no surprise that Seam turns to the EL again for assigning dynamic property values. Using the EL to define property values is a powerful concept for two reasons:

- You can leverage existing knowledge of the EL.
- Any value accessible via the EL can be assigned (not just component instances).

That's right. Rather than inventing yet another XML vocabulary for wiring Java objects together, Seam leverages the EL to establish references between components. You'll learn about component wiring in the next section. The EL can also be used for calculating a value and injecting the result. There's really nothing new here, which is a good thing. Let's explore the mechanics of how the EL is handled as an initial property value and when it is evaluated.

INFO   In Spring, you have to choose the appropriate XML element depending on what you're injecting. For instance, to inject a reference to another bean you use `<ref>` or `<bean>`. To assign a null value, you use `<null>`. In Seam, all of those details are handled beneath the EL. A reference to another component is written as #{componentName}, and to assign a null value you use #{null}.

When you declare a property value using a value expression, Seam doesn't evaluate the expression immediately, but instead stores it in the component definition in raw form. When the properties of a new component instance are being initialized, Seam evaluates the value expression, performs any necessary conversion on the resolved value (as described previously), and then assigns the value to the property.

Think about the possibilities that this introduces. You can theoretically have a component whose purpose is to provide a prepopulated contextual instance. For example, when the member registration page is brought up, the transient `Golfer` instance can be initialized with the current date and time assigned to the `dateJoined` property, saving the `register()` method from having to perform this work:

```
<component name="newGolfer" class="org.open18.model.Golfer" scope="event">
  <property name="dateJoined">#{currentDatetime}</property>
</component>
```

To set the value of the `dateJoined` property, you could supply any EL expression that generates a `java.util.Date`. Saving you a few keystrokes, Seam provides a built-in component named `currentDatetime` that supplies the current date and time—as produced by new java.sql.Timestamp()—when it's looked up. This component is one of several date-related components in the Seam Application Framework (the others are currentDate and currentTime). You'll learn about the Seam Application Framework in chapter 10.

Let's get a little fancier. Many golf facilities have only one golf course that bears the same name as the facility. Let's set the name of the new course to the facility name when creating a transient Course instance:

```
<component name="newCourse" class="org.open18.model.Course" scope="event">
  <property name="name">#{facilityHome.instance.name}</property>
</component>
```

There are several important points to be made about properties defined using value expressions:

- The component instance never sees the value expression, only the resolved value.
- The value expression is resolved when the component instance is created.
- The component instance won't be notified if the underlying value of the value expression changes after the component instance is created.

If you've used the JSF managed-bean facility, you should recognize that this is exactly how JSF deals with value expression injections. While the component configuration stores the expression, only the resolved value is passed on to the property.

There are two exceptions to these rules. If the target property's type is a Value-Expression or a MethodExpression, Seam won't evaluate the expression, even when the properties of the component instance are being initialized. Instead, the expression string is converted to an expression object (ValueExpression or MethodExpression) and assigned to the property. The evaluation of the expression is left up to the component. You can see an example of this scenario in the built-in Seam component org.jboss.seam.security.Identity. The authenticateMethod property is of type MethodExpression. The method expression is evaluated in the application logic to perform authentication against the credentials supplied in the login form. Assuming you've defined a Seam component named authenticator with the method authenticate() that handles authentication, you wire the authenticate method into the built-in component using the following declaration:

```
<security:identity authenticate-method="#{authenticator.authenticate}"/>
```

The other exception is a bit of an anomaly (perhaps even a bug). EL notation in a property value isn't interpreted unless the EL appears as the first character. Otherwise, Seam treats the value as a regular string, assigning it to the property unevaluated. It's the responsibility of the application logic to interpolate the string for any embedded EL expressions after that. For example, you might want to define a contextual message string:

```
<framework:created-message>
  You have successfully added #{course.name}.
<framework:created-message>
```

One of the main benefits of using the EL is that it's universal. You'll learn in section 5.3.4 how to use this exact syntax to perform static wiring of components. The point I want to make here is that you use a consistent approach for assigning any value, whether it be a simple type, a basic object (e.g., a date), or an EL expression. In fact, next you'll discover that the same is true for assigning collection and map values. While Seam does introduce elements for building a collection of values, you can alternatively use the EL to handle the assignment.

COLLECTIONS AND MAPS

There are two ways to assign a value to a property whose type is a collection, aside from using an EL value expression. You can either use a flat string value, which Seam will automatically slice and dice to extract the values, or you can specify each item explicitly using nested XML elements. Obviously, the second option only works when using the component descriptor. XML is also the only way to assign values to maps. The value of each item can be a basic value or an EL value expression.

WARNING   In order for you to use component configuration on a collection property, the property must be a parameterized collection or an array. Seam relies on the generic type information in the parameterized collection or the array type to convert the individual values.

Let's begin by looking at collections. Seam converts flat values into collections by splitting on all of the following characters:

- Comma
- Space or tab (\t)
- End of line (EOL) character (\n, \f, \r)

Seam uses the flat value converter if the property type is a collection (which includes both arrays and `java.util.Collection` types). The only time Seam doesn't perform this conversion is if the value is placed within a `<value>` element nested inside a `<property>` or custom namespace element. Let's try some examples, looking first at when the conversion is used and then how to use the `<value>` element to avoid the conversion.

Assume that the property `proStatus` has been added to the `Golfer` entity to capture the golfer's skill level—amateur, pro, or semi-pro. The available options are stored in the `proStatusTypes` property on the `RegisterAction` component:

```
@Name("registerAction")
public class RegisterAction {
   ...
   private String[] proStatusTypes;

   public String[] getProStatusTypes() { return this.proStatusTypes; }
   public void setProStatusTypes(String[] types) {
      this.proStatusTypes = types;
   }
}
```

The options can be registered using XML as before. However, now the value is split on the recognized delimiter characters before being assigned to the collection property on the component. Here's an XML-based example:

```
<component name="registerAction">
  <property name="pro-status-types">amateur pro semi-pro</property>
</component>
```

The property can also be assigned using an external property setting:

```
registerAction.proStatusTypes=amateur pro semi-pro
```

The options are converted into a list of JSF `SelectItem` objects in the registration form using Seam's `<s:selectItems>` component tag:

```
<h:selectOneMenu value="#{newGolfer.proStatus}">
  <s:selectItems var="_status" label="#{_status}" noSelectionLabel=""
    value="#{registerAction.proStatusTypes}"/>
</h:selectOneMenu>
```

The string-to-collection converter works great when the values don't contain any of the delimiter characters. But what happens when one of them does? Let's consider an example that demonstrates this problem and learn how to work around it.

Assume that the property `specialty` has also been added to the `Golfer` entity to capture the golfer's forte. An array property named `specialtyTypes` is added to `RegisterAction` to hold the available options. If any option contains a delimiter character, we'll have a problem using the flat property value syntax. To work around this situation, we must declare each value using a child `<value>` element in XML:

```
<component name="registerAction" class="org.open18.action.RegisterAction">
  <property name="pro-status-types">amateur pro semi-pro</property>
  <property name="specialtyTypes">
    <value>Driving</value>
    <value>Chipping</value>
    <value>Putting</value>
    <value>Iron play</value>
    <value>Lookin' good</value>
  </property>
</component>
```

Let's look at an example of configuring a multivalue property on one of Seam's built-in components. The following stanza registers a second page descriptor:

```
<components xmlns="http://jboss.com/products/seam/components"
  xmlns:navigation="http://jboss.com/products/seam/navigation"
  xmlns:xsi="http://www.w3.org/2001/XMLSchema-instance"
  xsi:schemaLocation="
    http://jboss.com/products/seam/navigation
    http://jboss.com/products/seam/navigation-2.0.xsd
    http://jboss.com/products/seam/components
    http://jboss.com/products/seam/components-2.0.xsd">
  <navigation:pages>
    <navigation:resources>
      <value>/WEB-INF/pages.xml</value>
```

```
      <value>/META-INF/pages.xml</value>
    </navigation:resources>
  </navigation:pages>
</components>
```

The nested `<value>` element syntax is used here since it's enforced by the XML Schema vocabulary. I show this example to make you aware of the fact that the XML Schema for Seam's built-in namespaces typically requires this formal syntax. The same configuration can be specified in a seam.properties file as follows:

```
org.jboss.seam.navigation.pages.resources=/WEB-INF/pages.xml \
/META-INF/pages.xml
```

What I really like about how Seam handles multivalue types is that it doesn't force you to use a special syntax for different types of collections, such as `<set>` and `<list>`. Collections are just collections. Maps do necessitate a special configuration element, though, because of the extra dimension.

Seam supports configuration of associative types—or to use the more familiar term, maps. To make this work, you have to use both a `<key>` element and a `<value>` element inside the `<property>` element. Unfortunately, maps can only be configured using XML. Let's assume that we want to associate codes to each of the specialties listed above. We first have to change the specialtyTypes property to a `java.util.Map`. Then we can define the key-value pairs using the following stanza:

```
<component name="registerAction"
  class="org.open18.action.RegisterAction">
  <property name="pro-status-types">amateur pro semi-pro</property>
  <property name="specialtyTypes">
    <key>DRIVE</key> <value>Driving</value>
    <key>CHIP</key>  <value>Chipping</value>
    <key>PUTT</key>  <value>Putting</value>
    <key>IRON</key>  <value>Iron play</value>
    <key>LOOKS</key> <value>Lookin' good</value>
  </property>
</component>
```

You can also make specialtyTypes a `java.util.Properties` type and the same declaration would work. Seam doesn't force you to use distinct elements for different types of associative types.

REPLACEMENT TOKENS

There's one more level of abstraction that you can use when supplying property values. Instead of using a value or value expression in the property declaration, you can use a replacement token. Tokens are names that are surrounded by @ symbols.[4] The value of a token is read from the components.properties file at the root of the classpath and applied to the component definition. The value of the token can even be an EL expression. Tokens make it easier to customize the values for different environments without having to modify the descriptor itself. Note that the token has to represent the whole property. It won't work if you try to put the token inline in a string property.

---

[4]   In Seam 2.0, using tokenized values in the component descriptor would cause it not to validate. That has been fixed in Seam 2.1 for commonly tokenized properties.

I cite the example that you'll see most often used in a Seam application: toggling debug mode. Assuming that you have the following property set in the components.properties file:

```
debug=true
```

you can then use this key as a token value in the component descriptor:

```
<core:init debug="@debug@"/>
```

The value of the token can be a value expression, which will be subject to further evaluation:

```
debug=#{facesContext.externalContext.request.serverName eq 'localhost'}
```

Although not as likely, the token could also represent a reference to another component. That brings us to the topic of component wiring. I introduced the EL as a means of assigning a property value, but let's now look at the implications of those values resolving to Seam component instances.

5.3.4   *Wiring components together*

The philosophy behind POJO (Plain Old Java Object) development is that components don't concern themselves with locating references to other components in the midst of a business method call. Instead, those references are provided during initialization of the component through a technique known as dependency injection, which Seam fully supports. You may choose to adopt this approach if you intend to use your components outside of Seam, perhaps in unit tests or because they're part of a shared model. In addition, it can be a performance optimization since this type of configuration is performed up front rather than recurring during the lifetime of the component.

In dependency injection, a component first declares that it has one or more dependencies by exposing them as bean properties. The bean property provides the type, name, and means of accepting the reference. The dependency may be another component instance or a regular Java object. You then use some mechanism of declaring how the reference is going to be found. The reference is then resolved and injected into the bean property at runtime. Seam supports two styles of component wiring, one that is static and one that is dynamic. Both styles use reflection to assign values to either the fields or properties—setter methods—of a bean. The difference is when it happens. Depending on the style of injection, the value is injected either when the component instance is created or when a method on the component is executed. Let's sort out the two cases.

STATIC VS. DYNAMIC DEPENDENCIES

When you use component configuration, you're performing static dependency injection. With static injection, Seam assigns a value to a field or property of a component instance when it's created. The value is specified using the EL variant of component configuration. This style of injection is analogous to that used by other lightweight containers, such as Spring and the JSF managed bean facility. The assignment happens once, drawing from resources available at the time the component is instantiated. After that point, the values of the fields and properties of the component instance aren't affected by this mechanism. What's done is done. The properties get their shot again when a new instance is created.

Seam also supports a style of dependency injection that's dynamic. This hook is activated by placing the @In annotation above a field or JavaBean-style property "setter" method. Annotation-based injections are resolved each time a method is invoked on a component. This mechanism is the key to Seam's inversion of control, which you'll learn about in depth in the next chapter.

A STATIC COMPONENT WIRING EXAMPLE

seam-gen applications include a static dependency injection for the purpose of assembling the components that create an EntityManager instance. You'll learn about Seam's persistence configuration in chapter 9. Right now, we're focusing on the mechanics of the wiring. The component descriptor from the Open 18 application includes the following two stanzas from the persistence namespace:

```
<persistence:entity-manager-factory name="open18EntityManagerFactory"    ❶
  persistence-unit-name="open18"/>
<persistence:managed-persistence-context name="entityManager"            ❷
  entity-manager-factory="#{open18EntityManagerFactory}"
  auto-create="true"/>
```

The EntityManagerFactory manager component ❶ is an application-scoped startup component that bootstraps a JPA EntityManagerFactory, maintains a reference to it, and closes it on application shutdown. The managed persistence context component ❷ manages a conversation-scoped extended persistence context (EntityManager instance) for the lifetime of the conversation. Here's how they're assembled. When the entityManager context variable is first resolved in a conversation, an instance of the managed persistence context component is created and the EntityManagerFactory component is wired into it, which is then used to create a new EntityManager instance. This wiring only happens once, which works in this case since the reference (a wider-scoped component) is only needed by the persistence manager context (a narrower-scoped component) while it's being initialized. Static injection is playing a configuration role here.

Using static injection, let's now wire dependent component instances into the RegisterAction component to remove the burden (and coupling) of it having to look up these references itself. The focus of the logic shifts to registering the user. It also makes the component more testable. In listing 5.5, the dependent components of RegisterAction are exposed as private fields. We leverage the ability of Seam to inject references into private fields to eliminate unnecessary getters and setters.

Listing 5.5   A component that relies on static injection of dependent components

```
package org.open18.action;

import javax.persistence.EntityManager;
import org.open18.auth.*;
import org.open18.model.Golfer;
```

```
@Name("registerAction")
public class RegisterAction {
   private EntityManager entityManager;
   private FacesMessages facesMessages;
   private PasswordManager passwordManager;
   private Golfer newGolfer;
   private PasswordBean passwordBean;

   public String register() {
      if (!passwordBean.verify()) {
         facesMessages.addToControl("confirm",
            "value does not match password");
         return "failed";
      }
      newGolfer.setPasswordHash(
         passwordManager.hash(passwordBean.getPassword()));
      entityManager.persist(newGolfer);
      facesMessages.add("Welcome to the club, #{newGolfer.name}!");
      return "success";
   }
}
```

The next step is to wire the dependent components to the properties of this component in the component descriptor:

```
<component name="registerAction">
  <property name="entity-manager">#{entityManager}</property>
  <property name="faces-messages">#{facesMessages}</property>
  <property name="password-manager">#{passwordManager}</property>
  <property name="new-golfer">#{newGolfer}</property>
  <property name="password-bean">#{passwordBean}</property>
</component>
```

While this refactoring drastically simplifies the component, there's still room for improvement. In the next chapter, you'll replace the XML configuration with annotations.

TIP If you're familiar with Spring, you might be tempted to use static injection as the primary means of wiring your components together. I don't recommend that you standardize on this approach. For one, it requires a ridiculous amount of XML. In general, XML should be reserved for infrastructure configuration. Although not applicable in this example, you also must ensure that you aren't injecting a component from a shorter-term scope into a component in a longer-term scope, as it results in scope impedance. It's much cleaner, safer, and Seam-esque to wire components together using dynamic injection, declared using the @In annotation, which you'll learn to do in the next chapter.

With all this great knowledge of how to configure the properties of a component, you're ready to dress up your component prototypes with initial state so that they'll come into the world mature. However, there's one more piece of information you need to know about configuring components; without it, you run the risk of creating a conflicting component definition.

5.4   *Component definitions vs. component configuration*

The component descriptor can be used to define a new component, configure the properties of an existing component, or define a new component and configure its properties simultaneously. You have to be aware of what constitutes a component definition and when the <component> element is merely interpreted as a means of assigning initial property values to a previously defined component. This section clarifies the distinction and gives you strategies to kept the two separated.

5.4.1   *Avoiding conflicts with an existing definition*

It's not permissible to have two components defined with the same name and precedence, which was touched on briefly in the previous chapter. For now, let's assume that the precedence value isn't being adjusted. Knowing that you can use the component descriptor to both define and configure components, you can get into trouble if Seam inadvertently tries to create a new component definition when your intention is to assign initial property values to an existing component. Here's the reasoning Seam uses when it processes the declaration. If the <component> element defines both a class attribute *and* a name attribute, it's treated as a new component definition. If the @Name annotation is also present on the class in this case, or there's an equivalent component definition in another descriptor, the following exception is thrown at application startup:

```
java.lang.IllegalStateException:
Two components with the same name and precedence
```

If either the class attribute or the name attribute is excluded from the <component> element, Seam treats that declaration as supplemental component configuration (for instance, to enable autocreate) or a contribution of initial property values.

   If you're configuring a class that isn't a Seam component (it doesn't have the @Name annotation or the value of the @Install annotation is false), no worries. You can define the component using the <component> element, specifying both name and class. However, if the class that you want to configure is already a Seam component (it has a @Name annotation and isn't disabled by an @Install annotation), then you have to make sure you don't collide with the existing definition.

   On the other hand, a component definition declared using a component namespace element is subject to different rules that protect it from conflicting with an existing definition. There is reasoning behind this special treatment, but it also gives motivation for using component namespaces. When Seam processes a namespace element, the class attribute is implied from the name of the XML element. The same goes for the name attribute if the @Name annotation is absent from the class. Since the developer can no longer prevent violation of the unique class and name constraint, Seam has to intelligently determine the intention of the declaration. If a component definition already exists, Seam assumes that the goal is to assign component properties, not to define a new component. This explains how you're able to safely configure a built-in Seam component using a custom namespace element without fear of conflicting with the existing component definition that Seam declares using annotations. In cases where a component definition doesn't already exist, the namespace element is considered a complete component definition.

Let's consider an example of how to resolve a conflicting component definition. Assume that the `PasswordManager` has the annotation `@Name("passwordManager")`. The following XML stanza defines a conflicting Seam component for this component name:

```
<component name="passwordManager" class="org.open18.auth.PasswordManager">
  <property name="digestAlgorithm">SHA-1</property>
  <property name="charset">UTF-8</property>
</component>
```

You can alter the root tag of this XML stanza so that it doesn't collide with the existing definition by making one of four changes:

1 You can use a custom element from the `auth` component namespace:
   ```
   <auth:password-manager>
   ```
2 You can remove the `class` attribute:
   ```
   <component name="passwordManager">
   ```
3 You can remove the `name` attribute:
   ```
   <component class="org.open18.auth.PasswordManager">
   ```
4 You can set a higher precedence:
   ```
   <component name="passwordManager" class="org.open18.auth.PasswordManager"
    precedence="25">
   ```

The last variation overrides the existing definition since its precedence (25) is higher than the default precedence (20). Precedence values were covered in section 4.5.2 of chapter 4.

Of course, if you place the `@Name` annotation on a class and also define a component for that class in the component descriptor using a different component name, the result is two separate component definitions. But then again, you're no longer configuring an existing component. All that you need to be aware of is that you can't have two components defined that use the same name and precedence.

5.4.2 *Dividing the configuration between annotations and XML*

In the event that the component definition is overridden in XML, any attribute from table 5.2 that isn't defined in the XML declaration is inherited from its annotation equivalent if present on the class. For instance, the XML definition can rely on the scope defined in the `@Scope` annotation on the class without having to define the scope in the XML. If the annotation `@Scope(ScopeType.APPLICATION)` were defined on the class (but not `@Name`), that value would be inherited by the XML component definition as if the `scope` attribute had been defined on the `<component>` element. Basically, not all attributes need to be specified in the same place. If a setting is defined both in the annotation and in the XML, the value in the XML always wins. This hybrid approach is one way to override the component definition in classes that you don't control.

Now that you have studied defining and configuring components in great detail and have been debriefed on how to avoid conflicts in component definitions when using the component descriptor, you should feel comfortable configuring built-in Seam components.

5.5   *Configuring and enabling built-in components*

The component descriptor is your primary means for configuring Seam. As much as I hate to say that the component descriptor allows you to "program in XML," the component descriptor allows you to program in XML. Seam provides a lot of glue code for solving common web application problems and for integrating disparate technologies. To take advantage of some of these features, you have to step in and *configure* that code. This section explores what areas of Seam can be controlled, focusing on Seam's language support as a case study.

5.5.1   *Using the component descriptor to control Seam*

The component descriptor allows you to control Seam to accomplish the following goals:

- *Configure Seam runtime settings*—Seam has a lot of switches and levers that you can use to control how it functions. To cite a couple of examples, you can enable debug mode, disable transaction management, define the authentication method, customize parameter names used to manage conversations and the conversation timeout period, specify the names of the resource bundles, or configure the available themes. These components act as the central switchboard in Seam.
- *Activate a feature that is disabled by default*—Some of the built-in components aren't useful to all applications (or may depend on an environment that isn't always available). Seam disables these components by default. The component descriptor gives you an opportunity to enable them. To provide some examples, you can enable jBPM, hook into the email service, or start the Spring container adapter.
- *Customize a component template*—Seam provides a number of component templates. These are cookie-cutter components that you can customize for your own application domain. Examples include the `EntityManagerFactory` and managed persistence context (and Hibernate equivalents), a Seam Application Framework object (Query, Home, and Controller), a JMS topic publisher or message sender, or a Drools rules manager. These classes don't bear the `@Name` annotation and therefore aren't components until you strike them into action by configuring them in the component descriptor.

Occasionally the distinction between these goals becomes blurry, since you may be activating and configuring a component or service at the same time. The main point to take away is that Seam is highly configurable and the component descriptor is your means of controlling that configuration. As you advance through this book, you'll keep coming back to this means of configuration, particularly to configure Seam's built-in components.

I want to explore Seam's resource bundle management as an example of component configuration in practice. You'll discover that Seam aggregates message keys under a single built-in component. You'll also learn how you can use component configuration to register your own bundles, and use message keys to assign locale-specific property values to a component.

5.5.2 Configuring Seam's internationalization support

When an application needs to output a message, the proper approach is to have it use a message key rather than use a hard-coded message string. The application then looks up a value for that message key in the active resource bundle for the current user at runtime. Typically, the keys are used to select locale-specific message strings. Examples include labels, date and time patterns, and currency units. Resource bundles also have applications that extend beyond locale, such as theme parameters and deployment environment settings.

Unfortunately, resource bundles are one of the most notoriously tedious, yet disproportionally trivial mechanisms to configure in a web application. That's because a Java framework just wouldn't be complete without internationalization (i18n) support. This aspiration has led to a situation where each framework wants to use its own resource bundle and configuration of that bundle for providing i18n messages. As it has done many times, Seam steps in to mop up this mess, giving you an unified map of all the messages contributed by the various frameworks it integrates, making it worth the effort of using i18n messages to your application. In this section, I'll explain how resource bundles work and show you how Seam makes them more accessible.

SEAM'S RESOURCE BUNDLE MANAGEMENT

Resource bundles are an application of the Java properties metadata format (i.e., `java.util.Properties`), which stores metadata in the form of key-value pairs. These pairs are grouped under a common base name, referred to as the bundle name. There are then off-shoots of the bundle name for each locale. Java works from the most specific locale down to the root bundle name to locate a properties file. The name of the file consists of the bundle name, followed by the current locale prefixed with an underscore (_), followed by the .properties extension. If a file for the current locale cannot be located, a file with the name of the bundle followed by the .properties extension is used.[5]

For example, if the bundle were named `messages` and the current locale was US English, Java would use the following search order to locate the key:

- messages_en_US.properties
- messages_en.properties
- messages.properties

---

[5] For a detailed description of how this works, refer to the JavaDoc for `java.util.ResourceBundle`: the `getBundle()` method.

Seam doesn't do anything special here to reinvent the wheel. Instead, it just aggregates contributions from multiple properties files. Seam bundles all of the following resource bundles together under the built-in component name `messages`:

- `messages`—the default message bundle
- `ValidatorMessages`—Hibernate Validator messages (including defaults)
- `javax.faces.Messages`—JSF message keys
- Page-specific bundles defined in a Seam page descriptor

Note that message bundles declared using the `<message-bundle>` element in the faces-config.xml descriptor aren't included in this aggregate bundle. To append to this built-in list, you instead declare your custom bundles in a Seam component descriptor. Let's say that you have a resource bundle named `application` and you want to tie those message keys into Seam's bundle. You register it as follows:

```
<core:resource-loader bundle-names="messages application"/>
```

Notice that I included the bundle named `messages`. If you override the `bundleNames` property, you must restore the default bundle name, which is `messages`, if you want it to be included. As an alternative, you could have declared each bundle name using the nested collection syntax:

```
<core:resource-loader>
  <core:bundle-names>
    <value>messages</value>
    <value>application</value>
  </core:bundle-names>
</core:resource-loader>
```

At this point, the keys from the various bundles are merged into the collection of keys in Seam's aggregate resource bundle, which you can access using the context variable name `messages`. Section 13.6 of chapter 13 shows how to enable multiple languages in your application, how the default locale is chosen, and how to provide the user with control over the locale used for their session. To wrap up this section, I'll explain how to use the message keys from this aggregate bundle.

USING MESSAGE KEYS IN THE APPLICATION LOGIC

The `messages` component can be used via an EL value expression. For instance, instead of hard-coding the labels in the registration form, resource keys could be used. First, define a key-value pair in the messages.properties (or locale-specific) file:

```
registration.firstName=First name
```

Then reference in the UI as follows:

```
#{messages['registration.firstName']}
```

You can also use message bundle keys to create a localized JSF message using the built-in Seam component named `facesMessages`. Earlier, we used the following logic to welcome the new golfer to the club:

```
FacesMessages().instance().add("Welcome to the club, #{newGolfer.name}!");
```

Let's draw on a message key instead. Once again, define a key-value pair in the message.properties (or locale-specific) file:

```
registration.welcome=Welcome to the club, {0}!
```

You then create a JSF message from this key and populate the indexed placeholder:

```
facesMessages.addFromResourceBundle("registration.welcome",
    newGolfer.getName());
```

You also have the option of putting EL notation directly in the message:

```
registration.welcome=Welcome to the club, #{newGolfer.name}!
```

In the next chapter you'll learn how to inject references to Seam component instances into properties of the class using annotations. You make the Seam `ResourceBundle` component available to your class by injecting as follows:

```
@In ResourceBundle resourceBundle;
```

You can also inject the `java.util.Map` of message bundle keys directly:

```
@In Map<String, String> messages;
```

In addition to using the message keys in the application, you can reference them when configuring the properties of a component.

USING MESSAGE KEYS IN COMPONENT CONFIGURATION

As you learned earlier, you can specify initial property values using EL notation. That means you can assign a locale-specific value to a component property by consulting the messages context variable. For instance, you can register the names of the specialty types respective to the current locale:

```
<component name="registerAction">
  <property name="specialtyTypes">
    <key>DRIVE</key> <value>#{messages['specialty.drive']}</value>
    <key>CHIP</key>  <value>#{messages['specialty.chip']}</value>
    <key>PUTT</key>  <value>#{messages['specialty.putt']}</value>
    <key>IRON</key>  <value>#{messages['specialty.iron']}</value>
    <key>LOOKS</key> <value>#{messages['specialty.looks']}</value>
  </property>
</component>
```

These specialty keys would be defined in a properties file loaded by the `ResourceBundle`:

```
specialty.drive=Driving
specialty.chip=Chipping
specialty.putt=Putting
specialty.iron=Iron play
specialty.looks=Lookin' good
```

And with that, you can finally come up for air because you've mastered using the component descriptor for defining and configuring components.

5.6 *Summary*

Seam minimizes the need for XML but doesn't eliminate it. In this chapter, you learned that XML can be useful, and in some cases necessary, for defining and configuring Seam components. XML-based component definitions, which you learned are declared in the Seam component descriptor using the `<component>` element and its namespace-qualified derivatives, are equivalent to those defined using the annotations covered in the previous chapter.

You came to appreciate that Seam's dedication to XML Schema makes configuring built-in components type-safe and gives you an opportunity to define your own component vocabulary. With component XML namespaces, your declarations can be validated against an XML Schema and the IDE can read the XML Schema to provide tag completion. You saw many examples of these custom elements in use, both for defining components and configuring components properties.

In addition to defining components, you learned how to use both XML and Java properties to establish the initial state of an object after it's instantiated by the Seam container. You can now distinguish between an XML component definition and a declaration that merely configures an existing component. If you aren't aware of these differences, you may encounter the error scenario in which two components with the component name and precedence combination are defined.

When you're configuring a component, you can supply property values not only as primitive values, basic Java objects, collections, and maps, but also as references to other components, a process called "component wiring." This chapter showed that component wiring is a form of static dependency injection, where the references are established at the time the component is instantiated, consistent with the dependency injection used in Spring. In the next chapter, you'll learn about dynamic dependency injection provided by bijection, which injects property values each time the component is invoked. You'll also learn about other types of inversion of control, such as outjection (the other half of bijection), just-in-time context variable creation, component events, and interceptors, which round out the foundation of Seam's extensible inversion of control. You'll also get to discover two component descriptor elements left out of this chapter that pertain to inversion of control: `<factory>` and `<event>`.

6
Absolute inversion of control

This chapter covers

- Wiring components together dynamically
- Applying method interceptors
- Raising and observing component events
- Resolving context variables on demand

Inversion of control (IoC) is a pattern in aspect-oriented programming (AOP) that espouses loose coupling, allowing the application to focus on consuming services rather than locating them. Seam embraces the use of IoC not only to "wire" components together but also to produce context variables and to enable components to communicate with one another through event notifications. Often, when people talk about IoC, they're really talking about dependency injection (DI), one use of IoC and the primary focus of this chapter.

Dependency injection is a key concept in POJO-based development that keeps components loosely coupled. In the previous chapter, you learned how static DI can be used to establish references from a component instance to its dependent objects during instantiation. In this chapter, you'll learn about another assembly mechanism

219

in Seam that links a component instance to its dependencies when it's invoked, a device known as injection. To complement injection, outjection facilitates exporting state from a component instance after the component is invoked, effectively producing context variables that can be used elsewhere in the application.

This chapter begins by introducing the four steps of bijection—injection, method invocation, outjection, and disinjection. We then explore several derivatives of bijection. One such variant manages "clickable lists" in a way that's completely transparent to the business component. The key to bijection is that it's dynamic, meaning it happens every time the instance is invoked, not just at creation time. Events, which you'll learn about next, go a step further toward decoupling components by allowing execution logic to jump from notifier to observer without an explicit reference between the participating components. Events let you add features without disrupting well-tested code or relieve a single method from trying to handle too many concerns. Going beyond the built-in behavior that Seam weaves into components, you'll learn how to create custom interceptors to handle your own cross-cutting logic. Shifting back to the subject of context variables, you'll discover how to use factory and manager components to produce variables requiring more sophisticated instantiation, typically with the help of bijection. Let's begin by exploring what makes bijection so unique.

6.1   Bijection: dependency injection evolved

Dependency injection is about as mainstream as MySpace or the iPod. Although it may not be a hot topic at family gatherings (at least not mine), it's the cornerstone of POJO-based development. In DI, the container "injects" dependent objects into the corresponding properties of a target object after instantiating it, establishing references from the object to its dependencies (a process commonly referred to as *bean wiring*). This strategy eliminates lookup logic within the object that might otherwise make it reliant on a particular environment. The object is said to be loosely coupled from the rest of the application. Unfortunately, it's not loose enough.

For as much as DI has been studied, discussed, and presented, it hasn't changed much since its emergence and suffers from several limitations. The first is that the injections are static, meaning they're applied only once, immediately following instantiation of the object. As long as the object exists, it's stuck with these initial references, failing to reflect the changing state of the application over time. Another limitation of DI is that it's focused only on the assembly of objects. It would be just as useful for an object to be able to contribute back to the container by transferring its state to one or more scoped variables.

These limitations highlight a general unawareness of context in the design. The managed objects need to be made more aware of the application's state and become active participants.

6.1.1   Introducing bijection

Seam has responded to this call for change by introducing bijection. Under bijection, the wiring of dependencies is done continuously throughout the lifetime of a component instance, not just when the instance is created. In addition to *inj*ecting values, bijection supports *out*jecting values. *Outject?* Pencil it into your dictionary—it's a new term. Outjecting is the act of promoting the value of a component property to a context variable where it can be picked up by another component or referenced in a JSF view, a page descriptor, or even a jBPM business process definition.

The combination of injection and outjection is known as *bi*jection. Bijection is managed by a method interceptor. Injection occurs prior to the method being invoked, and outjection occurs when the invocation is complete. You can think of the context variables participating in this interaction as flowing through the component as it's invoked. Injection takes context variables from the Seam container and assigns them to properties on the target instance, and outjection promotes the value of its properties to context variables. Figure 6.1 provides a high-level conceptual diagram of this mechanism.

Before you put your dictionary away, I'll mention that Seam also *disinjects* values from a component. In this step, any property that received an injection is assigned a null value. Disinjection is Seam's way of tying up loose ends. Seam can't keep the references up to date while the component instance is idle, so the values are cleared to avoid state from lingering. The injections are restored the next time the component is invoked.

NOTE Bijection modifies the state of the component instance. Therefore, calls to intercepted methods must be synchronized. Fortunately, Seam efficiently synchronizes all components except for those in application scope.

Although bijection may share some similarities with traditional DI, it's genuinely a new approach that makes context a primary concern. As you read through this section, you'll explore, in detail, how the bijection process works, how it affects the relationship between components, and how to put it to use.

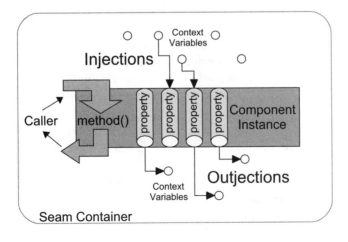

Figure 6.1 **Bijection wraps a method call, performing injection before the call and outjection afterward.**

6.1.2   *Bijection on the golf course*

Before diving into the technical aspects of bijection, I want to start off with an analogy. When you're playing in a golf tournament, you want all of your focus on your game. To help avoid distractions, you are provided a caddy, who acts as your assistant. The role that the caddy plays between each stroke of the ball parallels that of bijection. In this analogy, you are the component, the golf club is the dependent object, and the stroke is the method call.

As you approach your golfball, in whatever context it may be lying—the green, the fairway, a sand trap, on top of a warehouse, or the woods—you aren't holding the golf club that you need to take your stroke. The golf club is your dependency. To satisfy this dependency, your caddy injects the golf club that's appropriate for the context—a wood, iron, wedge, or putter—into your hands. You are now ready to swing. Striking the ball is the action, or, in the case of bijection, the method invocation. After taking your stroke, the ball is outjected and lands in another context on the course—hopefully avoiding bodies of water and sand traps. Outjection occurs as the result of a method call. Once the shot is taken, the caddy disinjects the club, reclaiming the dependency that was previously handed to you, and stores it in your bag for later use. You walk away from the original spot of the ball the way you arrived, empty handed. (You may still hold state, like your scorecard, but not the dependency.)

The caddy lets you concentrate on your golf game, rather than on the routine of carrying the clubs, cleaning them, and remembering not to leave one behind. It's an inversion of control. In the same way, bijection allows you to concentrate on the business logic rather than rounding up dependent objects needed to perform the logic and distributing results afterward. As with DI, bijection makes components easy to test in isolation or reuse since there's no tight coupling to a container-specific lookup mechanism.

With a general understanding of how bijection works, let's dig into the technical details of how you can add this capability to your components.

6.1.3   *Activating bijection*

When Seam instantiates a component, it registers a handful of method interceptors on the instance, an AOP technique for applying cross-cutting concerns. One of those interceptors manages bijection. Like all method interceptors, the bijection interceptor is triggered each time a method is called on the instance, referred to here as the target method. The bijection interceptor wraps the call to the target method, performing injections before the target method proceeds and then outjections, followed by disinjections, after the target method executes—all of which takes place before the method returns to the caller.

The properties that participate in bijection are designated using annotations. The most common bijection annotations are @In and @Out, which define injection and outjection points, respectively. Derivatives of these annotations also exist, but they're processed in fundamentally the same way. For now, we're going to focus on @In and @Out. Here's the first version of the ProfileAction component, which uses both @In and `@Out`. It selects a `Golfer` instance by ID from the injected `EntityManager` and then promotes the instance to a context variable that can be accessed from the view. Assume for now that the golfer ID is passed to the `view()` method defined below by a parameterized expression bound to a UI command button.

```
@Name("profileAction")
public class ProfileAction {
    @In protected EntityManager entityManager;
    @Out protected Golfer selectedGolfer;

    public String view(Long golferId) {
        selectedGolfer = entityManager.find(Golfer.class, golferId);
        return "/profile.xhtml";
    }
}
```

While this component may look straightforward at first glance, upon further examination you may question how the `@In` and `@Out` properties work, knowing that annotations are just metadata. What happens is that Seam scans for `@In` and `@Out` annotations when the component is registered and caches the metadata. The bijection interceptor then interprets this metadata when a method is called on an instance and applies bijection to its properties.

When the bijection interceptor traps a call to a component method, it first iterates over the bean properties on the component marked with an `@In` annotation and helps those properties find the values for which they are searching. If all the required `@In` annotations are satisfied, the method call is allowed to proceed. From within the method, the property values that were initialized via injection can be accessed as if they had been there all along.

If the method throws an exception, bijection is interrupted and control is turned over to the Seam exception handler. If the method completes without exception, the bijection interceptor postprocesses the method call. This time, it iterates over the bean properties marked with an `@Out` annotation and promotes the value of these properties to context variables in the Seam container. Finally, the properties that received injections are cleared, wiping the slate clean for the next invocation. The bijection process just described is illustrated in the sequence diagram in figure 6.2.

That should give you enough technical details to convince your boss that you know what

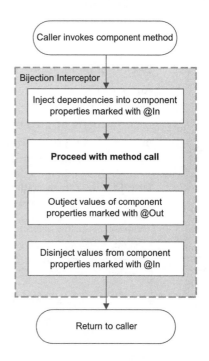

Figure 6.2 The bijection interceptor traps a method call on a component instance and performs the four steps of bijection—injection, method invocation, outjection, and disinjection.

bijection is, but you may need to see some examples to become comfortable using it. You'll also need to figure out how Seam locates a value to inject and which context variable is used when a property is outjected. Without these key details, bijection remains a bit mystical.

Most of the time, you'll be using the injection piece of bijection. Let's put a spin on a well-known phrase by saying "no *component* is an island" and explore how injection is used to "wire" components together dynamically.

6.2   *Dynamic dependency @In-jection*

Implementing business logic typically involves delegating work to other components. A familiar delegate that shows up in nearly every database-oriented application is the persistence manager (e.g., JPA `EntityManager` or Hibernate `Session`), which is used to persist entities or read their state from the database. In the previous chapter, you used component configuration to perform this injection—a form of static DI. That's fine if you're injecting a stateful component into a short-lived component or injecting a stateless component. However, as soon as you start using stateful components that interact with other stateful components, you need a mechanism that keeps the references up to date. Rather than trying to distinguish between the two cases, the recommended way of hooking components together in a Seam application is to use bijection. That way, you can always be sure the component will adapt to changes in the application's state.

6.2.1   *Declaring an injection point*

Annotations come into play when configuring bijection as they did when defining Seam components. The `@In` annotation, summarized in table 6.1, is placed above a bean property of a component—either a field or a JavaBean-style property "setter" method. Seam uses reflection to assign a value to properties marked with `@In` during the first phase of bijection.

Table 6.1   The `@In` annotation

Name:	In
Purpose:	Indicates a dependency on a context variable, which should be satisfied via injection
Target:	METHOD (setter), FIELD

Attribute	Type	Function
value	String (EL)	The context variable name or value expression used to locate a value to inject. If this attribute is not provided, the name of the property is used as the context variable name. Default: the property name.
create	boolean	Indicates that Seam should attempt to create a value if the context variable is missing or null. If the value attribute uses EL notation or is the name of an autocreate component, the create flag is implicitly true. The create flag cannot be used if a scope is specified. Default: false.

Table 6.1 The `@In` annotation *(continued)*

Attribute	Type	Function
required	boolean	A flag that specifies whether or not to enforce that the value being injected is non-null. Default: true.
scope	ScopeType	The context in which to look for the context variable. The scope is disregarded if the value uses EL notation. Default: `UNSPECIFIED` (hierarchal context search).

The `value` attribute on the `@In` annotation can be the name of a context variable or an EL value expression, or it can be omitted. If the `value` attribute is omitted, the most common case, the name of the context variable to search for is implied from the name of the property (according to JavaBean naming conventions). By providing a context variable name in the `value` attribute, the name of the context variable to search for can be different than the name of the property into which it is injected. If the `value` attribute uses EL notation, it is evaluated and the resolved value is injected into the property.

Common use cases for the `@In` annotation include injecting a persistence manager, a JSF form backing bean, or a built-in JSF component. All three types are needed by the `RegisterAction` component, which was created in chapter 4. Listing 6.1 shows the `RegisterAction` component using `@In` to supply all the dependent components needed to perform registration. The `@Logger` and `@In` annotations are placed inline to conserve space.

Listing 6.1   The registration component refactored to use dynamic injection

```
package org.open18.action;

import org.jboss.seam.annotations.*;
import org.jboss.seam.faces.FacesMessages;
import org.jboss.seam.log.Log;
import org.open18.auth.*;
import org.open18.model.Golfer;
import javax.persistence.EntityManager;

@Name("registerAction")
public class RegisterAction {              Injects log at
    @Logger private Log log;      ◁──── component creation

    @In protected FacesMessages facesMessages;
    @In protected EntityManager entityManager;           Injects delegates
    @In protected PasswordManager passwordManager;       at invocation
    @In protected Golfer newGolfer;                      time
    @In protected PasswordBean passwordBean;

    public String register() {
        ...
        entityManager.persist(newGolfer);
        facesMessages.add("Welcome to the community, #{newGolfer.name}!");
        return "success";    ◁──── Activates
    }                              navigation rule
    ...
}
```

With these changes in place, you should be able to run the `RegisterGolferIntegra-tionTest` and verify that the tests pass just as before. The fixture for the test remains the same—only now, Seam wires the context variables into the component under test dynamically using bijection.

There are several permutations for how Seam resolves the context variable to inject. Let's step through the decision process that occurs during the first phase of bijection.

6.2.2   *The injection process*

The decision process for performing an injection is illustrated in figure 6.3. You can see that this process has two main branches: one where the `value` attribute of the `@In` annotation is expressed in EL notation, and one where the `value` attribute is the context variable name or a context variable name is implied. Use this diagram to follow along with the discussion.

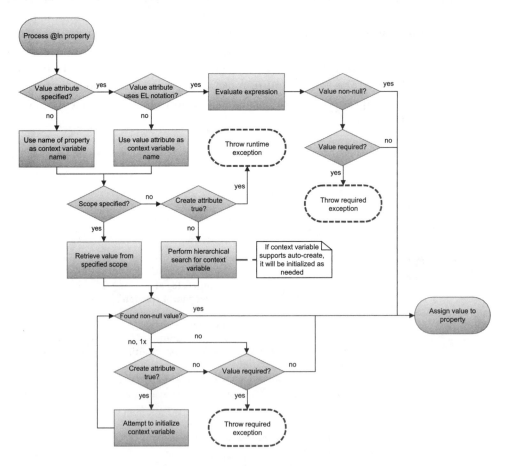

Figure 6.3   The decision process Seam follows when injecting a value into an `@In` property

Let's begin by considering the case where the value attribute of the @In annotation is a context variable name. A few subtle differences exist between this case and when the value attribute of the annotation uses EL notation.

Seam first looks to see if a scope is specified in the annotation. If so, Seam looks for the context variable name in this scope. If a scope isn't provided, Seam performs a hierarchical search of the stateful contexts, starting from the narrowest scope, ScopeType.EVENT,[1] and continuing all the way to the broadest scope, ScopeType.APPLICATION, as illustrated in figure 6.4. The search stops at the first

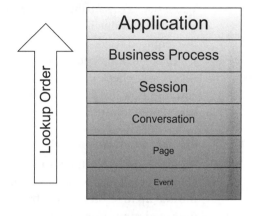

Figure 6.4   The order in which the contexts are scanned when Seam searches for a context variable

non-null value that it finds and assigns that value to the property of the component. Keep in mind that a context variable can hold any value, not just a component instance.

If the hierarchical context search fails to resolve a non-null value for a context variable, Seam attempts to initialize a value, but only if the following two conditions are met:

- The context variable name matches the name of a component.
- The create flag is true on the @In annotation or the matched component supports autocreate.

If these conditions are met, Seam instantiates the component, binds the instance to a context variable, then injects it into the property marked with the @In annotation. Note that the instance may come from a factory component, covered in section 6.7.1. If the context variable name doesn't match the name of a component, there's nothing for Seam to create and therefore the value of the property remains null.

Before finishing its work, Seam validates against the required flag on @In. Requiring a value protects against a NullPointerException. If the required flag is true, and Seam wasn't able to locate a value, the runtime exception RequiredException is thrown. There is one exception to this rule. Required flags are never enforced on lifecycle methods (this is true for both injection and outjection), though bijection does still take place. In any case, if the required flag is false or not enforced, the property remains uninitialized if Seam can't locate a value.

TIP   If you find yourself making heavy use of the required flag to disable required injections (and later outjections), it's an indication that you're trying to make the component do too much. Refactor your monolithic component into smaller, more focused components and use bijection or static injection to allow them to collaborate.

---

[1]   Technically, the narrowest scope is the **METHOD** context, which is discussed in section 6.4.

When the `value` attribute uses EL notation, the semantics are much simpler. The work of locating a value is delegated to the EL variable resolver. The same validation against the required flag is performed as in the non-EL case.

If all such injections for a component succeed, the method invocation proceeds. Before you check the `@In` annotation from your list of Seam concepts mastered, let's consider how the dynamic nature of the injection allows you to mix scopes and properly handle nonserializable data.

6.2.3 *Mixing scopes and serializability*

As you know, every time a method on a component is invoked, Seam performs the lookup to resolve a value based on the information provided in the `@In` annotation. This dynamic lookup allows you to inject a component instance stored in a *narrow* scope into a component instance stored in a *wider* scope. Figure 6.5 shows a narrow-scoped component instance

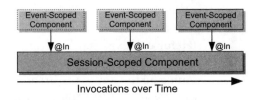

Figure 6.5   A narrow-scoped component is injected into a wider-scoped component.

being injected into a wider-scoped component instance at each invocation. If injection were to only happen when the wider-scoped component instance was created, the injected instance would be retained beyond the lifetime of its scope.

Let's pose this scenario as a question, plugging in actual scope names. What would happen if a request-scoped variable were to be injected into a session-scoped object via static DI? Recall that static DI occurs only once: when the object is created. In this situation, as the request-scoped variable changes between HTTP requests, the session-scoped object retains the original value of the request-scoped variable and never gets updated. This describes the behavior of most other IoC containers in existence today. By using Seam's dynamic DI, the same property on a session-scoped component would always reflect the value of the request-scoped variable from the current request because the injection is reapplied each time the component is invoked. Additionally, the value isn't retained beyond the end of the request since Seam breaks the reference by disinjecting the value once the method call is complete.

Let's consider another difficult scenario that's cleared up thanks to the dynamic nature of Seam's DI: mixing nonserializable objects with serializable objects (a serializable object is an instance of any class that implements `java.io.Serializable`). If a nonserializable object is injected into the property of a serializable session-scoped object, and that property isn't cleared prior to session passivation, the session storage mechanism will get tripped up by the nonserializable data. You could, of course, mark the field as transient so that the value would be automatically cleared, hence allowing the session to properly passivate. However, the real problem is that once the session is restored, the transient field remains null, acting as a land mine in the form of a `NullPointerException` that may be triggered by an unsuspecting block of code.

Applying the `@In` annotation to the field solves both parts of the aforementioned problem. To begin with, the value assigned through the `@In` annotation is cleared in the last phase of bijection, after the method on the component is invoked. Right out of the box, injections are transient without you having to add the `transient` keyword on all the fields marked with `@In`. But the real power of injection is that the injected values are restored prior to the next method call. This continuous injection mechanism allows objects coming out of passivation to be reinflated. Thus, disinjection paired with subsequent injections should alleviate a common, yet trite, pain point that arises when working with both session replication and the reactivation of a session after a server restart.

But the `@In` annotation isn't the only type of injection that Seam supports. Next we look at a couple of domain-specific injection variants.

6.2.4   *Injection variants*

Seam supports several additional annotations for marking dynamic injection points. The two you'll learn about in this section are `@RequestParameter` and `@Persistence-Context`. The first is used to inject an HTTP request parameter and the second an `EntityManager` (JPA). Technically, the Java EE container handles injecting the `EntityManager` into a property annotated with `@PersistenceContext`, but Seam follows that up with a second injection pass. Later on, you'll learn about two more injection annotations in the section covering JSF data model selection. Of all the bijection annotations, `@RequestParameter` is probably the easiest to grasp, so let's start there.

INJECTING A @REQUESTPARAMETER

The `@RequestParameter` annotation is used to inject an HTTP request parameter into the property of a component, retrieved either from the query string or the form data. You either specify a parameter name explicitly in the `value` attribute or let Seam imply the parameter name from the name of the property. Unlike `@In`, however, a value is never required.

You can, of course, inject a request parameter into a string or string array property, since request parameters are inherently strings. Going a step further, if the property's type is not a string or string array, Seam converts the value before injecting it using the JSF converter registered for that type. If no converter is associated with the property's type, Seam throws a runtime exception. As a reminder, JSF converters implement the `javax.faces.convert.Converter` interface and are registered in faces-config.xml or by adding the `@Converter` annotation to a Seam component class.

The `@RequestParameter` annotation is a convenient alternative to page parameters for creating RESTful URLs. In fact, this approach is more "Seam-like" because it uses an annotation rather than XML. The one benefit of page parameters that you lose, however, is Seam rewriting links to propagate page parameters to the next request.

In the Open 18 application, we want to create a page that displays a golfer's profile, which will be prepared by the `ProfileAction` component. Let's design it so that the ID of the golfer to display is passed to the URL using the request parameter `golferId`:

```
http://localhost:8080/open18/profile.seam?golferId=1
```

The `golferId` request parameter can be injected into this component by placing the `@RequestParameter` annotation over a property with the same name. This injection takes place whenever a method on the `ProfileAction` component is invoked.

Therefore, the `golferId` property can be used in the `load()` method to look up the corresponding `Golfer` entity using the JPA `EntityManager`:

```
@Name("profileAction")
public class ProfileAction {
    @In protected EntityManager entityManager;
    @RequestParameter protected Long golferId;

    protected Golfer selectedGolfer;

    public void load() {
        if (golferId != null && golferId > 0) {
            selectedGolfer = entityManager.find(Golfer.class, golferId);
        }
        if (selectedGolfer == null) {
            throw new ProfileNotFoundException(golferId);
        }
    }
}
```

We have the `load()` method invoked when the /profile.seam path is requested by making this method a page action for the corresponding view ID in the page descriptor:

```
<page view-id="/profile.xhtml">
  <action execute="#{profileAction.load}"/>
</page>
```

The motivation for using a page action is to ensure that the profile can be retrieved before committing to rendering the page. If an instance of `Golfer` is found, it's stored in the `selectedGolfer` property. However, if the `golferId` request parameter doesn't produce a `Golfer` instance, a custom runtime exception named `ProfileNotFound-Exception` is thrown. This exception causes Seam to throw up a 404 error page, along with a message stating that the profile could not be found, which happens because the exception class is annotated with `@HttpError`:

```
@HttpError(errorCode = HttpServletResponse.SC_NOT_FOUND)
public class ProfileNotFoundException extends RuntimeException {
    public ProfileNotFoundException(Long id) {
        super(id == null ? "No profile was requested" :
            "The requested profile does not exist: " + id);
    }
}
```

That's as far as we go with this example right now. You still need to learn how to promote the value of the `selectedGolfer` property to a context variable that can be accessed from the view, which the next section covers.

Seam isn't alone in its support for dynamically injecting values into annotated properties. Java EE has its own set of annotations for declaring what the spec terms a "resource injection." For the most part, Seam stays out of the way and lets the container handle the task. But Seam does get its hands dirty with the `@Persistence-Context` annotation.

AUGMENTING THE @PERSISTENCECONTEXT

The `@PersistenceContext` annotation is a Java EE annotation that marks a property on a Java EE component that should receive a container-managed `EntityManager` resource injection. After the `EntityManager` is injected by the Java EE container but before the method invocation proceeds, Seam wraps the `EntityManager` in a proxy object and injects it again. The proxy adds EL value expression support to Java Persistence Query Lanaguage (JPQL) queries. But otherwise, the life cycle of the `Entity-Manager` is controlled by the Java EE container. The `@PersistenceContext` annotation is explained more in chapter 8 and the `EntityManager` proxy in chapter 9. Keep in mind that this annotation is only relevant for Java EE managed components (e.g., JSF managed beans or EJB session beans).

Let's pause for a moment to take a look around because you are now standing at the ridge of where DI ends and bijection continues. Looking behind you, you see that bijection has evolved DI by making the injection dynamic. Looking forward, you see that there's a whole other side of this pattern that has never before been explored. It's the flip side of injection known as outjection. Let's explore it!

6.3   *@Out-jecting context variables*

Outjection is a way of pushing state held by a component out to the Seam container. You can think of a component as the parent and the properties as its children. Outjection is like sending the child off (perhaps kicking it out) to live in the world on its own. The parent (the component) exports the child (the property) to a new address (the context variable). Other people (components) can visit that child at the new address without consulting the parent. The property value is now associated with its own context variable that puts it on equal footing with other components in the Seam container.

An outjection point is declared by adding the `@Out` annotation, summarized in table 6.2, to a bean property—a field or JavaBean-style "getter" method. After a component method is invoked, the value of the property is used to create a context variable or bind to one that already exists. If a name isn't provided in the `value` attribute, the name of the property is used. As with the `@In` annotation, the `value` attribute on the `@Out` annotation can be used to make the name of the context variable different from the property name. Note that the `@Out` annotation doesn't support EL notation as `@In` does.

Table 6.2   The `@Out` annotation

Name:	Out	
Purpose:	Instructs Seam to assign the value of the property to the target context variable after a method on the component is invoked	
Target:	METHOD (getter), FIELD	

Attribute	Type	Function
value	String	The name of the context variable to which the value of the property should be bound. Default: the property name.
required	boolean	A flag that indicates whether to enforce that the value to be outjected is non-null. Default: true.
scope	ScopeType	The context in which to store the context variable. Default: the scope of the target component or the scope of the host component if the context variable name isn't the name of a component.

The outjection process is not as complex as the injection process. However, there are still decisions Seam must make before assigning the value of the property to a context variable.

6.3.1 *The outjection process*

Figure 6.6 shows the outjection process. As you can see, three main decisions are made in this process: the context variable name to use, the scope in which to store the context variable, and whether to permit a null value. Let's step through this process.

The trickiest part to understand is how Seam infers a scope if one is not stated explicitly. If you specify a scope in the @Out annotation, Seam assigns the value of the property to a context variable in that scope. The name of the context variable is either the name of the property or the override specified in the value attribute of the @Out annotation. A context variable can't be bound to the stateless context, so @Out doesn't permit use of this scope.

If a scope isn't specified, Seam first attempts to locate a component with the same name as the target context variable. If one exists, and its type is equivalent to the

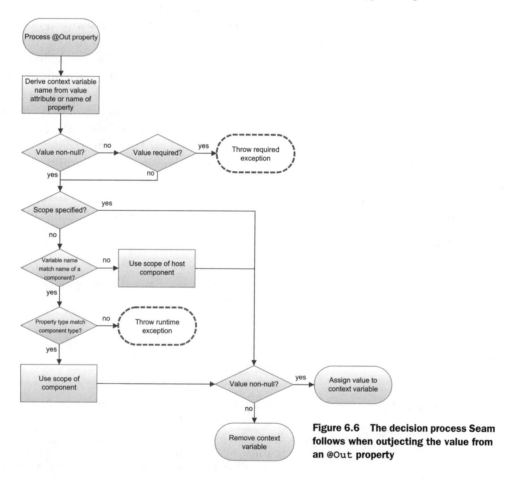

Figure 6.6 The decision process Seam follows when outjecting the value from an @Out property

property's type, the property value is outjected to the scope of that component. Note that the matching component may have been defined using the `@Role` annotation. Roles effectively centralize the target scope of an outjection, rather than defining it at the outjection point. If the context variable name doesn't match the name of a component (or component role), Seam uses the scope of the host component (i.e., the component on which this property resides). If the scope of the host component is stateless, Seam chooses the event scope instead.

In the final step, Seam processes the required flag. If the required flag is true (the default) and the value being outjected is null, Seam throws the runtime exception `RequiredException`. Recall that required flags are implicitly false on life-cycle methods.

Let's look at a couple of use cases where outjection is useful.

6.3.2 Outjection use cases

Outjection is useful for accomplishing two goals. You can use it to expose the model to the view as a result of executing an action method, or you can use it to push data into a longer-term scope so it's available on subsequent requests. Let's look at the two cases in turn.

PREPARING THE MODEL FOR THE VIEW

The view isn't very useful without data to display. Preparing this data is typically the responsibility of the page action or the action method triggered from the previous page. In Struts, you usually pass the model to the view by assigning values to `HttpServlet-Request` attributes in the action. Managing variables in this way can be quite cumbersome and couples your code tightly to the Java Servlet API.

Before abandoning the Servlet API, let's find a compromise that loosens this coupling and makes the code less cumbersome. In chapter 4, you learned that Seam normalizes the servlet contexts under a single API. You can inject one of these contexts directly into a Seam component using bijection. A context behaves like a map, where the keys are the context variable names. You can add a context variable to the event scope with the following setup:

```
@In protected Context eventContext;

public void actionMethod() {
    eventContext.set("message", "Hello World!");
}
```

Although this approach works, there's a cleaner, more declarative way of accomplishing the same task. You simply mark properties with the `@Out` annotation that you want to have placed into the target context and your job is done. Here's the same code taking a declarative approach:

```
@Out(scope = ScopeType.EVENT) protected String message;

public void actionMethod() {
    message = "Hello World!";
}
```

Here you see that outjection decouples the context variable assignment from the business logic in the action. (The `scope` attribute on the `@Out` annotation is only required if the target scope is different from the scope of the host component.) As far as the view is concerned, it doesn't care how the context variable was prepared.

Let's complete the golfer profile example started earlier by making the selected golfer available to the /profile.xhtml view. The goal is to create the output shown in figure 6.7.

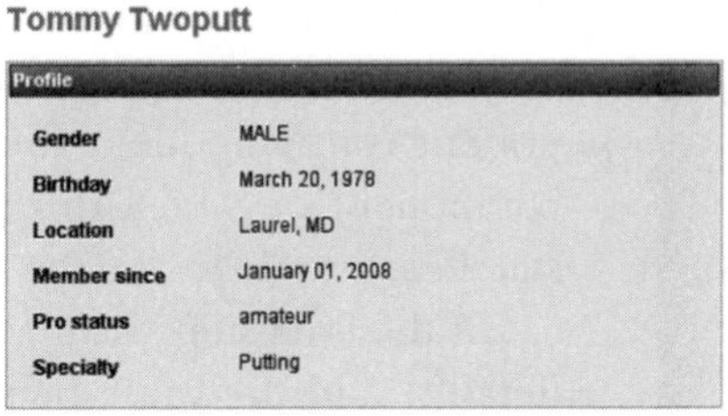

To extract the value of the `selectedGolfer` field from the `ProfileAction` component when the `load()` method is invoked, we add the `@Out` annotation above the field. The value of the field is then assigned to the equivalently named context variable in the event context:

Tommy Twoputt

Profile	
Gender	MALE
Birthday	March 20, 1978
Location	Laurel, MD
Member since	January 01, 2008
Pro status	amateur
Specialty	Putting

Figure 6.7   A golfer's profile page. The data is supplied by an outjected context variable.

```
@Name("profileAction")
public class ProfileAction {
    @Out protected Golfer selectedGolfer;
    ...
    public void load() { ... }
}
```

The `selectedGolfer` context variable can then be referenced in value expressions in the /profile.xhtml page as shown here:

```
<h1>#{selectedGolfer.name}</h1>
<rich:panel>
  <f:facet name="header">Profile</f:facet>
  <s:decorate template="layout/display.xhtml">
    <ui:define name="label">Gender</ui:define>
    #{selectedGolfer.gender}
  </s:decorate>
  <s:decorate template="layout/display.xhtml">
    <ui:define name="label">Birthday</ui:define>
    <h:outputText value="#{selectedGolfer.dateOfBirth}">
      <s:convertDateTime pattern="MMMM dd, yyyy"/>
    </h:outputText>
  </s:decorate>
  ...
</rich:panel>
```

The other use case for outjection is to propagate state.

KEEPING DATA IN SCOPE

Just because a field is outjected doesn't mean it has to be used in the view. It's quite reasonable to outject a value just so that it can be injected into a component on a subsequent request. Say goodbye to hidden form fields and the mentality of having to manually propagate variables from one request to the next. Instead, you simply use outjection to put a context variable on a shelf (a long-term scope such as the page, conversation, or session scope) and pull it down when you need it again. In this case, outjection decouples the mechanism of preserving state from the business logic. This technique is especially useful in conversations, which are covered in chapter 7.

> ### Storing component instances out of Seam's reach
>
> You should not store a reference to a component instance in a place where Seam can't manage it, such as inside a collection. It should only be stored in a context variable.
>
> An object ceases to be an instance of a Seam component when you manage it yourself. While storing it out of Seam's reach won't cause an error, Seam stops intercepting its methods, and thus services such as bijection and events are no longer applied to it.
>
> If you need collection semantics, you should store the name of the component instead, then look up each instance when you need it using Component.getInstance().

When you began reading this chapter, you may have thought bijection a bit mysterious. However, with the information covered up to this point, I doubt you'll forget how bijection works. If for some reason you do, just remember that injections happen before a component method is invoked and outjections happen after the method call is complete. Lastly, the injections are cleared just before the method returns. Repeat it to yourself. That way, when you see the error message "@In attribute requires non-null value" or "@Out attribute requires non-null value," you'll know what Seam is trying to tell you. If all else fails, just ask your golf caddy. Now let's use bijection to make lists in JSF "clickable."

6.3.3 *Built-in @DataModel support*

In JSF, UIData components, such as <h:dataTable>, are backed by a special collection wrapper called a data model. A data model is a way for JSF to adapt various types of collections to the UI component model in a consistent way and to support capturing a row selection made by the user. The collection wrappers extend from the abstract class javax.faces.DataModel and support the major collection types. Seam builds on this set by adding support for the Query component from the Seam Application Framework. The Query component manages the result of a JPQL/HQL query, which Seam retrieves and wraps in a ListDataModel. You'll learn about the Query component in chapter 10. The mapping between the collection types and their wrappers is shown in table 6.3.

Table 6.3 The corresponding JSF data model wrapper for each type of collection

Native Collection	JSF DataModel Wrapper javax.faces.model.*
java.util.List	ListDataModel
Array	ArrayDataModel
java.util.Map	MapDataModel
java.util.Set	SetDataModel
org.jboss.seam.framework.Query	ListDataModel wraps Query#getResultList()

So what do these wrappers have to do with bijection? To properly prepare collection data to be used in a UIData component, you should wrap it in a JSF data model. Why should you have to deal with this drudgery in your business logic? This task sounds like something the framework should handle. Seam developers agree. For this purpose, they created the @DataModel annotation, summarized in table 6.4. The @Data-Model is used in place of the @Out annotation for outjecting one of the collection types listed in table 6.4. Before the value of the @DataModel property is assigned to the context variable during outjection, it's first wrapped in the correct JSF Data-Model implementation.

Table 6.4   The @DataModel annotation

Name:	DataModel	
Purpose:	Wraps a collection in a JSF DataModel and outjects the resulting value	
Target:	METHOD (getter), FIELD; must be one of the collection types in table 6.3	

Attribute	Type	Function
value	String	The name of the context variable under which the value of the wrapped collection should be stored. Default: the property name.
scope	ScopeType	The context in which to place the wrapped collection. The only permissible value is ScopeType.PAGE. Default: inherits scope from component or ScopeType.EVENT if component is stateless.

Let's use Seam's data model support to display a list of newly registered golfers on the home page, which will be made clickable so that a user can view the golfer's profile. The goal of this section is to produce the output shown in figure 6.8.

The business logic is responsible for fetching the list of new golfers. We let Seam handle the details of wrapping that collection in a JSF Data-Model and exposing it to the view by adding the @DataModel annotation, a variant of the @Out annotation, to the newGolfers field:

Figure 6.8   The list of new golfers prepared as a JSF data model as a result of outjection

```
@Name("profileAction")
public class ProfileAction {
    @DataModel protected List<Golfer> newGolfers;
    ...
}
```

Of course, that's not enough for the newGolfers field to be outjected—heck, it's not even populated. First, we need a method that populates this collection. Then, we need to figure out how to activate outjection. Let's reuse the ProfileAction component. We add the method findNewGolfers() to load the list of new golfers from the database. To keep things interesting, we perform a little quick and dirty randomization on the list:

```
@Name("profileAction")
public class ProfileAction {
    protected int newGolferPoolSize = 25;
    protected int newGolferDisplaySize = 5;

    @Out(required = false) protected Golfer selectedGolfer;
    @DataModel protected List<Golfer> newGolfers;
    ...
    public void findNewGolfers() {
        newGolfers = entityManager
            .createQuery(
                "select g from Golfer g order by g.dateJoined desc")
            .setMaxResults(newGolferPoolSize)
            .getResultList();

        Random rnd = new Random(System.currentTimeMillis());

        while (newGolfers.size() > newGolferDisplaySize) {
            newGolfers.remove(rnd.nextInt(newGolfers.size()));
        }
    }
}
```

As you've learned, when a method on a Seam component is executed, such as findNewGolfers(), bijection takes place. That means once the invocation of this method is complete, the value of the newGolfers field is going to be wrapped in a JSF DataModel and outjected to the equivalently named context variable of the event scope. The event scope is chosen since that is the scope of the host component and the scope isn't explicitly specified.

Notice that the required attribute on the @Out annotation above the selected-Golfer property is now set to false. This directive is necessary since the find-NewGolfers() method doesn't assign a value to selectedGolfer and bijection would otherwise complain that it isn't set. This situation often arises when you use the same component for more than one purpose. If you find yourself making excessive use of the required directive, that's an indication that the component is trying to do too much and that you should divide it into smaller, more focused components.

Once the findNewGolfers() method is invoked, the JSF view will have access to the collection of new golfers using the value expression #{newGolfers}. The UIData component that renders the list of golfers (in this case, <rich:dataList>) sees a ListDataModel rather than the java.util.List:

```
<rich:panel>
  <f:facet name="header">Cool New Golfers</f:facet>
  <rich:dataList var="_golfer" value="#{newGolfers}">
    #{_golfer.name}
  </rich:dataList>
</rich:panel>
```

TIP You may notice in this code snippet that I prefix the iteration variable (the golfer) with an underscore (_). I recommend this coding style to make it clear that the variable is local to the iteration loop and to avoid conflicts with existing context variables.

The only remaining question is, "When is the `findNewGolfers()` method invoked?" We want to execute this method eagerly when the home page is requested, not as a result of a user-initiated action. Once again, we use a page action:

```
<page view-id="/home.xhtml" action="#{profileAction.findNewGolfers}"/>
```

Now, whenever the home page is requested, the `findNewGolfers()` method prepares the `newGolfers` context variable for the view. With the `@DataModel` annotation, you never have to think about the JSF `DataModel` interface; it's completely transparent. Seam even takes care of reinitializing the context variable whenever a change is detected in the underlying collection. Your component is free to use properties that are native Java collection types. Your UI component sees the outjected data as the appropriate `DataModel` wrapper class. Where this pays off is in capturing a row selection from the `DataModel`, again without having to tie your component to the JSF API.

MAKING A @DATAMODELSELECTION

Presented with a list of golfers, the user of the application will want to interact with that list. One common use case is "clickable lists." To continue with our example, the user clicks on the name of one of the golfers in the table and the application brings up the golfer's profile. This mechanism is a contrast to using a RESTful URL, though the two can coexist.

In a clickable list, the user is performing an action on the data associated with the row that receives the event. One such action is drilling down, which is demonstrated here. Other actions include deleting and editing. The only limitation is that this mechanism can be applied to only a single row at a time.

How do you know which row was clicked? Seam works in conjunction with JSF to take care of these details. One of the reasons for using a `DataModel` in a `UIData` component is so that JSF can correlate an event triggered from a row in the table with the data used to back that row. Seam can take the data from the selected row and inject it into the component receiving the action using one of two `@In`-style annotations.

Clickable lists are effortless in Seam thanks to the `@DataModelSelection` annotation. The `@DataModelSelection` annotation injects the value of the selected row in a collection previously outjected by the `@DataModel` annotation and assigns it to the corresponding component property. Seam also supports capturing the index of the selected row using the `@DataModelSelectionIndex` annotation. You place either of these two annotations, summarized in table 6.5, on a separate property of the same component in which the `@DataModel` annotation is defined. Of course, the property annotated with `@DataModelSelection` must have the same type as the items held in the collection, while the property annotated with `@DataModelSelectionIndex` must be a numeric type.

Seam will put two and two together and assign the value of the selected row in the UI to the property annotated with `@DataModelSelection`, or the index of the selected row to the property annotated with `@DataModelSelectionIndex`. This selection occurs by triggering an action on a row of a `UIData` component such as `<h:dataTable>`.

Table 6.5 The @DataModelSelection and @DataModelSelectionIndex annotations

Name:	DataModelSelection/DataModelSelectionIndex	
Purpose:	Captures the selected row (or row index) of the corresponding JSF DataModel	
Target:	METHOD (setter), FIELD	

Attribute	Type	Function
value	String	The context variable name of the DataModel. Default: the name of the @DataModel property on the same component, if there is exactly one.

Let's build on the example of the list of new golfers by first making the names clickable. First, we enhance the ProfileAction component to include a method named view() that will be used to select a golfer from the new golfer list. This method will eventually be bound to a UI command component to enable the selection:

```
<h:commandLink value="#{_golfer.name}" action="#{profileAction.view}"/>
```

The implementation of the view() method is shown in listing 6.2, along with several changes to the class that are highlighted in bold to support this new use case. The RESTful logic presented earlier is left intact so that both use cases can be supported.

Listing 6.2 A component that supports a clickable list of golfers

```
package org.open18.action;

import org.jboss.seam.ScopeType;
import org.jboss.seam.annotations.*;
import org.jboss.seam.annotations.web.RequestParameter;
import org.jboss.seam.annotations.datamodel.*;
import org.open18.ProfileNotFoundException;
import org.open18.model.Golfer;
import javax.persistence.EntityManager;
import java.util.*;

@Name("profileAction")
@Scope(ScopeType.CONVERSATION)
public class ProfileAction {
    protected int newGolferPoolSize = 25;
    protected int newGolferDisplaySize = 5;

    @RequestParameter protected Long golferId;

    @DataModelSelection                          Injects selected golfer,
    @Out(required = false)                        stores in conversation
    protected Golfer selectedGolfer;

    @DataModel(scope = ScopeType.PAGE)       ◁──┐ Stores golfers in UI
    protected List<Golfer> newGolfers;             │ component tree

    public String view() {
        assert selectedGolfer != null &&
            selectedGolfer.getId() != null;
        return "/profile.xhtml";
    }
}
```

```
public void load() {
    if (selectedGolfer != null &&
        selectedGolfer.getId() != null) {
        return;
    }

    if (golferId != null && golferId > 0) {
        selectedGolfer = entityManager.find(Golfer.class, golferId);
    }

    if (selectedGolfer == null) {
        throw new ProfileNotFoundException(golferId);
    }
}
public void findNewGolfers() {
    newGolfers = ...;
}
```

Skips RESTful logic when golfer selected ◁——— (annotation pointing to the `if (selectedGolfer != null &&` line)

An important change had to be made to the `ProfileAction` component to support clickable lists. The `@DataModel` property is now scoped to the page context (i.e., `ScopeType.PAGE`) rather than the event context. In order for `@DataModelSelection` to capture the selected row, the original `@DataModel` collection *must* be available on postback. If the collection changes, it may cause the wrong row to be selected. This happens because the row index captured by the event no longer points to the correct row in the collection on postback. If the collection disappears altogether, the result will be a "ghost click" (see the accompanying sidebar). The latter happens because the portion of the JSF component tree that held that event is discarded and thus the event doesn't fire. Regardless of how hard Seam searches, it won't be able to locate the data model selection and the `@DataModelSelection` and `@DataModelSelectionIndex` annotations are helpless. `UIData` components (e.g., `<h:dataTable>`) depend on the underlying data to be stable during subsequent requests. To guarantee that the collection remains stable, you can store it in the UI component tree by scoping `@DataModel` to the page context, as we've done in this example. Always remember this point when dealing with `UIData` components. You have to get your `DataModel` to make the leap from render to postback. In the next chapter you'll learn how conversations are even better suited to deal with this problem since they can carry data across an arbitrary number of postbacks and even non-JSF requests.

Finally, we add an `<h:commandLink>` around the name of each golfer, which will invoke the `view()` method on `ProfileAction` when clicked:

```
<h:form>
  <rich:panel>
    <f:facet name="header">Cool New Golfers</f:facet>
    <rich:dataList var="_golfer" value="#{newGolfers}">
      <h:commandLink value="#{_golfer.name}"
        action="#{profileAction.view}"/>
    </rich:dataList>
  </rich:panel>
</h:form>
```

Ghost clicks

One utterly frustrating problem of JSF that Seam alleviates is the ghost click. A ghost click happens when the portion of the UI component tree that queued a UI event is dropped.

Upon reading this explanation, you might be thinking, "Isn't that a bug?" Sadly, it isn't. Certain branches of the UI component tree are processed dynamically. If the structure of the tree isn't reproducible, there's a chance that the behavior will be lost. An example of where this can happen is in any branch controlled by a component in the UIData family. The UIData components are unique because they are data driven. Let's consider how UIData components are handled and how it can result in portions of the tree being dropped.

JSF walks the UI component tree during rendering. When it encounters a UIData component, it iterates over the collection in the DataModel that's bound to the component to render each row. The component tree is then saved in the session or serialized and sent along with the response. Although the data is a critical part of how UIData components operate, JSF stores only the UIData components themselves, not the underlying data.

When the component tree is restored on postback, JSF walks the UI component tree again, looking for events (among other things). Events triggered on a UIData component are associated with the index of the activated row. When JSF arrives at the UIData component, it again iterates over the data model to process each row, lining up events with the row index. If the data model changes prior to the restore stage, the event may be correlated with the wrong row. Worse, if the data disappears, any event associated with that portion of the tree is silently discarded. The result is a ghost click.

The lesson here is that JSF expects the collection wrapped by the DataModel to remain stable between render and postback. The easiest way to guarantee the stability of the collection is to store it in the UI component tree. In Seam, you store a context variable in the UI component tree by scoping it to the page context. This approach accomplishes the same task as the <t:saveState> tag from the Tomahawk project. As another option, third-party UIData components typically offer a built-in "save state" attribute. The most flexible option is to bind the data model to a long-running conversation.

To truly appreciate how maddening a ghost click can be, you have to be the victim of it. The profile example in this chapter gives you an opportunity to research the problem in a lab environment where your job—or contract—isn't on the line.

When the view() method is invoked, Seam takes the selected row from the @DataModel collection, newGolfers, and injects it into the corresponding @DataModelSelection property, selectedGolfer. Seam makes this association automatically since both properties reside on the same component. If there were more than one @DataModel property on the component, it would be necessary to specify the context variable name used by the @DataModel property in the value attribute of the @DataModelSelection annotation in order for the correlation to be made. Failure to make this distinction results in a runtime exception. The @DataModel property and the @DataModelSelection property must always reside on the same component.

In JSF, you have to use a command link or button to perform a data model selection using the pattern just described. That means a POST form submission occurs. What's worse is that JSF submits the form using JavaScript. If you don't care how the job gets done, the combination of a page-scoped @DataModel, @DataModelSelection, and a JSF command component is a grand slam. However, if you need to allow the user to open the data model selection link in a new tab or window, you may need to take the solution a step further. Currently, if the user right-clicks on the golfer name and tries to open the profile in a new tab or window, the home page will load rather than the profile page. To allow users to achieve the desired result, the data model selection must be passed along with the URL. JSF doesn't support this feature, but Seam does.

DATA MODEL SELECTION WITH SEAM COMMAND COMPONENTS

The command components in the Seam UI component library, <s:link> and <s:button>, support data model selections, despite the fact that they don't submit a form or restore the JSF UI component tree like the JSF command components. In previous chapters, you learned that it's possible to use the Seam command components to execute actions and perform navigation, so you know they are already quite capable. They can also emulate the data model selection feature of JSF through the use of two URL parameters, dataModelSelection and actionMethod, which are processed by the Seam phase listener and used to inject the data from the selected row into a @DataModelSelection or @DataModelSelectionIndex property. An example is provided in a moment.

The Seam command component tags aren't quite a drop-in replacement for the JSF command components. They don't restore the JSF UI component tree, which means that the page-scoped data isn't propagated. For our example, this means that the page-scoped newGolfers data model is left behind. Thus, to allow formless data model selection using the Seam command components, the data model must be stored in a longer-lived scope.

There are two synchronized scopes that you can use as an alternative to the page scope: session and conversation. Generally, I recommend using the conversation scope. But since we haven't explored conversations—and by that I mean long-running conversations—we go with the session scope for now. I encourage you to come back and play with this example after you have mastered conversations in chapter 7.

Your first instinct might be to set the scope of the @DataModel annotation to ScopeType.SESSION. However, that won't work in this case since you can't explicitly outject a data model to the session scope (only to the page scope). Therefore, it's necessary to put the ProfileAction component in the session scope so that the @Data-Model annotation inherits the session scope from the component:

```
@Name("profileAction")
@Scope(ScopeType.SESSION)
public class ProfileAction {
    @DataModel
    protected List<Golfer> newGolfers;
    ...
}
```

You can follow this change with a switch from the `<h:commandLink>` tag to `<s:link>`:

```
<s:link value="#{_golfer.name}" action="#{profileAction.view}"/>
```

An example of a URL generated by this component tag is as follows:

```
/open18/home.seam?dataModelSelection=_golfer:newGolfers[0]
    ➡&actionMethod=home.xhtml:profileAction.view
```

The URL indicates that the first entry in the `newGolfers` collection is to be used as the data model selection and that the `view()` method on the component named `profile-Action` is to be executed. The user is then directed to the view ID returned by `view()`. If `view()` were to return an outcome value rather than a view ID, JSF would consult the navigation rules to determine the next view.

These extra steps to support the Seam command components may seem like too much work, in which case you may just want to stick with the JSF command components. You may want to consider ways to select a row in a `@DataModel` context variable without the use of `@DataModelSelection`.

OTHER APPROACHES TO DATA MODEL SELECTION

As an alternative to using the `@DataModelSelection` annotation, you can pass the context variable of the current row to the action method using a parameterized method expression, supported by the JBoss EL. To use this feature, the data model *must* remain available until the next request, as with the data model selection. Again, the options are page, session, or conversation scope with a long-running conversation. With the scope of the data model set appropriately, you can pass the `_golfer` context variable as an argument to the `view()` action method as follows:

```
<h:commandLink value="#{_golfer.name}"
    action="#{profileAction.view(_golfer)}"/>
```

The signature of the action method would need to change to accept the parameter:

```
public String view(Golfer golfer) {
    this.selectedGolfer = golfer;
    return "/profile.xhtml";
}
```

The benefit of using the parameterized EL is that it allows you to pass a property of the row data rather than the row data itself. For instance, you could pass the golfer's username instead:

```
<h:commandLink value="#{_golfer.name}"
    action="#{profileAction.view(_golfer.username)}"/>
```

To go in a completely different direction, you could use a RESTful URL to select the golfer. In this case, you're using the @DataModel just for rendering purposes, so it doesn't need to survive across the redirect. Instead, the information required to retrieve the golfer is placed directly in the URL using a link parameter:

```
<s:link value="#{_golfer.name}" view="/profile.xhtml">
  <f:param name="golferId" value="#{_golfer.id}"/>
</s:link>
```

After having seen these options, you have to decide for yourself whether you like the convenience of the JSF data model selection or whether you prefer the RESTful URL. Unfortunately, the @DataModelSelection is really just a hindrance when you're trying to create a RESTful URL. My advice is that unless you have a strong use case for supporting a RESTful URL, you should leverage the productivity gain that the page-scoped @Data-Model, @DataModelSelection, and JSF command component combination affords you.

Bijection can be powerful and convenient, but if applied at the wrong time, it can throw a wrench into the works. In the next section, you'll learn how to exert some control over when bijection is used and when Seam applies this reservation automatically.

6.4   *Bypassing bijection*

Bijection is one of the most powerful and compelling features of Seam. But with great power often comes great confusion. It's just as valuable to know when bijection is *not* used as to know when it is. In this section, we look at which method calls do not trigger bijection and also how to disable it when it's getting in your way.

6.4.1   *Internal method calls*

As established earlier, bijection is implemented as a method interceptor. Method interceptors are applied around method calls that are invoked on proxy objects. When you ask the Seam container for a component instance—perhaps through an EL expression or an injection—what you get back is a proxy of the instance. Therefore, any method call invoked on that proxy is going to pass through the method interceptors and, in turn, trigger bijection.

However, method interceptors are blind to what goes on *within* the target method. As far as the interceptor is concerned, the target method is a black box. Inside of the intercepted method, you're dealing with the raw instance of the component when you refer to the implicit variable this. Local method calls (i.e., methods on the same class) aren't observed by the method interceptors, and therefore, bijection isn't wrapped around them. If you have a strong grasp of how method interceptors work, this fact should come as no surprise to you. However, for those with less exposure to method interceptors, the distinction between the two circumstances may not be so obvious.

Let's return to the RegisterAction component to see an example of an internal method call. We want to verify that the username chosen by the new golfer is available. The method isUsernameAvailable() on RegisterAction performs the check and emits an error message if the username is already in use. The modified `RegisterAction` component is shown in listing 6.3 in abbreviated form. Note that the internal call to the `isUsernameAvailable()` method doesn't trigger bijection.

Listing 6.3 An internal method call that checks whether the username is available

```
package org.open18.action;
import ...;

@Name("registerAction")
public class RegisterAction {
    @In protected EntityManager entityManager;
    @In protected FacesMessages facesMessages;
    @In protected Golfer newGolfer;
    ...

    public String register() {
        ...
        String username = newGolfer.getUsername();          ◁── Doesn't trigger
        if (!isUsernameAvailable(username)) {                    bijection
            facesMessages.addToControl("username",          ◁──
                Username is already taken");                 ┐ Attaches message
        }                                                    ┘ to username field
        ...
    }

    public boolean isUsernameAvailable(String username) {
        return entityManager.createQuery(
            "select m from Member m where m.username = :username")
            .setParameter("username", username)
            .getResultList().size() == 0;
    }
}
```

Just remember that when a component is asked to do work by some other part of the system, the communication takes place through the proxy, so bijection will occur before and after the method call. However, any method that the component invokes on itself—an internal method call—isn't going to benefit from or be afflicted by any interceptor-provided functionality, such as bijection.

I chose the words "benefit" and "afflicted" in that last statement for a reason. There are times when you need method interceptors to be applied on a method, even if that method happens to reside on the same component. There are also circumstances when allowing the method interceptors to execute would be problematic. First, I'll explain how to get a reference to the proxy of the current instance to make the method call appear as if it's originating from outside the component. Then, you'll learn why Seam skips bijection if the method is reentered while execution of the target method is still proceeding.

6.4.2 *The mystical method context*

I'll admit that I omitted details earlier when I said that the event scope is the narrowest scope in Seam, but trust that it was for your own good. In truth, it's because the narrowest scope, method, is intended strictly for internal use. So technically, the event scope *is* the narrowest *public* scope and I get to retain my integrity.

If the method scope is part of the internal Seam API, why mention it? I bring it up to raise awareness of its impact and to transition to my next point. Before a method call on a component begins, Seam binds the unproxied instance of the component to the component name in the method context. After the method call, this context variable is cleared. The reason this assignment is done is to avoid invalid behavior in the case of recursive calls. But don't worry about the details; let's look at the consequence.

As you are now fully aware, interceptors aren't applied to internal method calls. For that, you need to invoke the component instance the way the rest of the system sees it (i.e., through the proxy). Recall from chapter 4 that you can look up a component instance using the Seam API as follows:

```
(RegisterAction) Component.getInstance("registerAction")
```

Normally, this call would give you the component instance and its entourage of method interceptors. However, if this call is made from within the RegisterAction component, the unproxied instance is returned instead since it's found in the narrowest scope, method. So even if you invoke the isUsernameAvailable() method on the result of this lookup, the method interceptors won't be applied:

```
((RegisterAction) Component.getInstance("registerAction"))
    .isUsernameAvailable(newGolfer.getUsername())
```

However, you can get the proxied instance by specifying the component's context:

```
(RegisterAction) Component.getInstance("registerAction", ScopeType.EVENT)
```

It's very important to keep this little tool in your emergency kit because I can assure you that a time will come when you need to get a handle on the proxy and, in turn, trigger the interceptors.

With the method context out in the open, it's time to move on to the next point: reentrant method calls. Believe it or not, even if you looked up the RegisterAction component using the trick I just showed you and called the isUsernameAvailable() method on it, bijection still wouldn't be applied. Read on to discover why.

6.4.3   *Reentrant method calls*

A reentrant method call is as simple as it sounds: the component is reentered while it's in use. To be more specific, a method is called on the proxy while a method on the instance is still executing. You just saw an example of this in the previous section. Within the RegisterAction component, the instance of the RegisterAction component was retrieved through the Seam API and a method called on it:

```
(RegisterAction) Component.getInstance("registerAction", ScopeType.EVENT)
    .isUsernameAvailable(newGolfer.getUsername())
```

You might also see this situation if you're implementing a visitor or double dispatch pattern, where the collaborator component reaches back through the proxy to execute a method on the component. So what does all this have to do with bijection? One of the golden rules of bijection reads as follows:

> *At no time during the execution of a component's method is bijection applied to that component a second time.*

This point goes back to the mechanics of bijection, which taught you that bijection encompasses a method call and doesn't do anything while the method is executing. Bijection occurs before and after every method call on a Seam component instance, but *only* if the method call isn't a reentrant method call.

The motivation for skipping bijection on reentrant method calls is twofold:

- It reduces overhead.
- It keeps the state of the component instance stable and consistent.

As for the first point, there's no reason to apply injections again if they've already happened. However, there's hardly any reason to mention the first point in view of how critical the second point is. Bijection alters the state of the instance. Although injection might simply be redundant, or at worse inject a different value than what was injected originally, that's not the biggest impact. The most drastic change occurs in the final step of bijection: disinjection, which wipes away the injections that were applied. If this were to happen while the original method call is still executing, it would have a disastrous effect (i.e., `NullPointerException` mania). So it's important that Seam be cognizant of the reentrant method call and not allow it to trigger bijection. Consequently, this also explains why method invocations on Seam components must be synchronized. Otherwise, two threads calling the same component simultaneously would cause the problem just described. If you can't synchronize the call, don't use bijection.

Let's consider a simple example from Open 18 to illustrate when this situation may occur in a more natural scenario. Before a golfer can register, two validation checks must be performed. The application needs to ensure that the username requested by the registering golfer is available and that the email address entered isn't already in use to avoid a duplicate registration. Let's introduce the `GolferValidator` component, to which these validations can be delegated. However, the `GolferValidator` is just a coordinator. The validation checks just described are hosted on the `Register-Action` component. So we have a double dispatch going on here. Rather than getting bogged down in the code, let's look at a diagram. Figure 6.9 illustrates how three method calls are made to the `RegisterAction` component when the user submits the registration form, yet bijection is only applied to the `register()` method call.

Setting the log level to TRACE reveals that Seam acknowledges the reentrant call:

```
intercepted: registerAction.register
intercepted: golferValidator.validate
intercepted: registerAction.isUsernameAvailable
reentrant call to component: registerAction (skipping bijection)
intercepted: registerAction.isEmailRegistered
reentrant call to component: registerAction (skipping bijection)
```

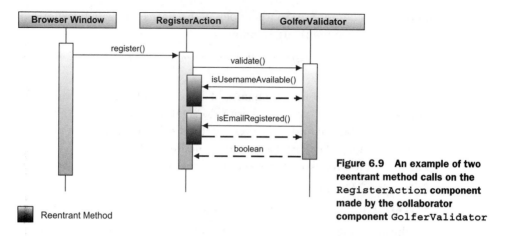

Figure 6.9   **An example of two reentrant method calls on the `RegisterAction` component made by the collaborator component `GolferValidator`**

This discussion of reentrant method calls is technical, but it's important to understand why Seam forgoes the use of bijection even if a method is being invoked on the proxy of the component instance.

With the exception of JPA entity classes, bijection is applied to all Seam components. However, certain isolated components have no use for bijection. In these cases, you likely want to forgo bijection outright. You can tell Seam not to intercept method calls on a component using a special annotation.

6.4.4   *Disabling bijection by disabling interceptors*

Since bijection is provided by a method interceptor, you can avert bijection by disabling the interceptors on a single method or on the entire component. You instruct Seam not to apply interceptors by adding the `@BypassInterceptors` annotation, summarized in table 6.6, at the class or method level. The method-level annotation is a good way to optimize one area of the code without cutting out the benefits of interceptors from the component as a whole.

Table 6.6   **The `@BypassInterceptors` annotation**

Name:	BypassInterceptors
Purpose:	If applied to a method, disables all the interceptors that are wrapped around a single method call. If applied to a component, it has the same effect as applying it to every method on the component.
Target:	TYPE (class), METHOD

Unfortunately, if you disable interceptors, you end up stripping away all the other interceptor-based functionality, not only bijection. Such features include declarative conversation controls, transaction management, and event handling, to name a few. Just be aware that by disabling interceptors, you may get more than you bargained for.

NOTE   Adding `@BypassInterceptors` to a component doesn't disable life-cycle methods. Life-cycle methods are those annotated with `@Create`, `@Post-Construct`, `@Destroy`, or `@PreDestroy` that are covered in section 4.5.5 of chapter 4.

What's the motivation for disabling interceptors? By no means are interceptors punishing to the runtime execution speed of your code, but they do consume extra cycles. If you know that you don't need the functionality provided by interceptors, you might as well disable them. If you're using a Spring bean as a Seam component, explained in chapter 15 (online), disabling Seam's interceptors makes sense if equivalent functionality is already covered by Spring's interceptors.

In the Open 18 application, the `PasswordBean` component has no use for interceptors as it merely holds data and validates its internal state. It's safe to disable interceptors entirely:

```
@Name("passwordBean")
@BypassInterceptors
public class PasswordBean { ... }
```

Another useful place to disable interceptors is on core object methods such as `toString()`:

```
@BypassInterceptors
public String toString() {
    return new StringBuffer()
        .append(getClass().getName()).append("[")
        .append("password=").append(password).append(",")
        .append("confirm=").append(confirm)
        .append("]").toString();
}
```

The `toString()` method, as well as `equals()` and `hashCode()`, don't benefit from the functionality provided by the interceptors. If anything, the interceptors just get in the way. For instance, required values enforced by `@In` and `@Out` might cause the `toString()` method to be aborted, which can mask real problems when you're trying to debug.

While interceptors can sometimes be overzealous, the functionality they provide is essential for decoupling business logic from boilerplate lookup code. One such area where interceptors help to simplify code and cut out tight coupling is when a component wants to send a notification to other components so they have a chance to act.

6.5   *Component events*

Dynamic injection helps decouple components because it eliminates explicit lookups for dependent objects. However, the components still interact with one another directly. This arrangement works well when the components are all working to accomplish a common goal, as is the case with the registration example. However, in cases where tangential logic must be performed, perhaps even to spawn an asynchronous operation, events may be a better option. Events offer a way for components to pass messages to one another. They provide separation of concerns, make components easier to test in isolation, and can even remove a hard dependency on an API such as JSF.

Events can be raised by a component or generated during any page-related activity. These events are passed through the Seam container, which acts as the messaging mediator. Seam's event support works much like a messaging service such as JMS. There are both producers and consumers. When an event is raised, it's posted to the Seam container. Seam then looks for registered observers for that event and notifies them by executing the registered methods.

6.5.1   *Raising an event from a component*

Events can be raised from within a Seam component either using the Seam Events API—the built-in `Events` component—or using an annotation. The Events API offers the most flexibility, but it does tie your code to that API. The annotation `@RaiseEvent`, on the other hand, allows you to control event creation declaratively.

USING THE EVENTS API

The Events API supports passing an arbitrary number of parameters to the observer when an event is raised. Passing data gives the observer a chance to access the data available within the scope of where the event was raised without having to be present.

The default behavior is to notify observers of the event immediately. It's also possible to schedule events. Seam supports both synchronous and asynchronous scheduling. In the synchronous case, you can schedule that an event be fired when a transaction completes or only when it completes successfully. The asynchronous scheduler allows you to supply either an EJB 3 Timer schedule or a Quartz Cron schedule, depending on which asynchronous dispatcher you're using in your application.

Let's consider an example. The marketing department has requested that we gather statistics when members register and when they cancel the registration form so the effectiveness of the registration process can be determined. The requests from marketing are ever-changing. Rather than disrupt our nicely tested registration logic, we want to put this extra logic in an observer. That way, when the next feature request is handed down from marketing, we can just take on another observer, once again avoiding disrupting working code.

Modify the `register()` method of the `RegisterAction` component to raise the `golferRegistered` event once the new golfer has been persisted successfully:

```
public String register() {
    ...
    entityManager.persist(newGolfer);
    Events.instance().raiseEvent("golferRegistered");
    ...
    return "success";
}
```

If we want to ensure that the logic performed by the collateral code operates in a separate transaction (so as not to jeopardize the transaction used to persist the new golfer), we can schedule this event to be fired after successful completion of the current transaction:

```
@In private Events events;

public String register() {
    ...
```

```
        entityManager.persist(newGolfer);
        events.raiseTransactionSuccessEvent("golferRegistered");
        ...
        return "success";
    }
```

You can also pass any number of parameters to the observer:

```
    public String register() {
        ...
        entityManager.persist(newGolfer);
        events.raiseTransactionSuccessEvent("golferRegistered", newGolfer);
        ...
        return "success";
    }
```

The observer could get a handle on the `newGolfer` using bijection, but the event parameter offers more clarity and, thus, it's easier for a fresh set of eyes to understand what's going on with the code—self-documenting code is always a good thing.

One compelling use of the Seam Events API is to develop a mechanism for preparing status messages that's agnostic of UI technology, as opposed to using the Seam `FacesMessages` component. The event would include the message and severity, and the observer would register the message with the UI framework. Before you run off to develop this idea, I should let you know that Seam 2.1 supports creating technology-agnostic status messages.

Before moving on to observers, let's look at how to raise events declaratively.

USING @RAISEEVENT

The `@RaiseEvent` annotation, summarized in table 6.7, offers the most convenient way to raise an event from a component, but you give up control over when the event is raised. Observers are notified of an event raised by the `@RaiseEvent` annotation upon successful completion of the component method on which the annotation resides.

Table 6.7 The `@RaiseEvent` annotation

Name:	RaiseEvent
Purpose:	Raises a component event, which is passed on to registered observers upon successful completion of the component method
Target:	METHOD

Attribute	Type	Function
value	String[]	One or more event names to be raised. Default: the method name.

If you recall, successful completion means either the method is void or it returns a non-null value and no exceptions were thrown. The events are fired after successful completion of the method because, like bijection, it's implemented as an interceptor. This interceptor wraps the transaction interceptor, so if your transaction is configured to complete (commit or roll back) after successful completion of the method, the event will be raised after the transaction completes—though you still don't have the granularity of distinguishing between a commit and a rollback.

With that, let's change the previous example so that the raising of the golfer-Registered event is declared as metadata:

```
@RaiseEvent("golferRegistered")
public String register() {
    ...
    entityManager.persist(newGolfer);
    ...
    return "success";
}
```

The @RaiseEvent annotation can be used to raise an arbitrary number of events. However, it can't be used to pass arguments to the observer (at the time of this writing). Thus, @RaiseEvent is good when you just want to notify observers that something has happened. If information is critical to understanding the event, you'll likely want to use the Events API.

With all of these events floating around out there, you must learn how to observe them.

6.5.2   *Defining an event @Observer*

Events are observed by component methods or EL method expressions that you have registered as observers. An observer can be registered using the @Observer annotation or by attaching an event to an EL method expression in the component descriptor. Let's explore the @Observer annotation first.

The @Observer annotation, summarized in table 6.8, can be added to a method of any Seam component. It can observe one or more events by name, specified in the value attribute. By supplying the create attribute, you can also specify whether to have the observer component created if it doesn't exist at the time the event is raised. This flag is equivalent to the autocreate functionality on components.

Although it's possible to capture multiple events in the same method, you have to remember that an event can pass arguments, thus dictating the signature of the observer. You can't use the same method to observe multiple events if the type and amount of arguments passed by the events vary. You would be much better off refactoring the observation logic into multiple methods in this case.

Table 6.8   The @Observer annotation

Name:	Observer	
Purpose:	Registers a component method to observe events by name. The method can accept arguments if the producer passes arguments along with the event.	
Target:	METHOD	

Attribute	Type	Function
value	String[]	One or more event names to be observed. Default: none.
create	boolean	Controls whether the observer component is created if it doesn't exist at the time the event is raised. Default: true.

Let's observe the `golferRegistered` event and record it for the marketing team's statistics. Instead of going through the exercise of setting up an entity and database table, we just throw in some logging statements:

```
@Name("registrationBookkeeper")
@Scope(ScopeType.APPLICATION)
public class RegistrationBookKeeper {
    @Logger private Log log;
    private int cnt = 0;

    @Observer("golferRegistered")
    synchronized public void record(Golfer golfer) {
        cnt++;
        log.info("Golfer registered - username: " + golfer.getUsername());
        log.info(cnt + " golfers have registered since the last restart");
    }
}
```

Since the `record()` method is a component method, it will trigger bijection, which can be useful for injecting the `EntityManager` when you build the real implementation. You can also register the observer using the component descriptor. The latter is useful if you can't add the `@Observer` annotation to the class—perhaps because it can't be modified—or to have non-Seam components observe events. To do so, you'd add the following declaration in the component descriptor:

```
<event type="golferRegistered">
  <action execute="#{registrationBookkeeper.record(newGolfer)}"/>
</event>
```

You can specify any number of actions to be executed for a single event. Notice that in this case, we're taking advantage of the JBoss EL to pass an argument to the method expression. At the time the event is raised, the `newGolfer` context variable is still in scope, so it's possible to reference it for the purpose of passing it to the observer.

Let's look at another way that events are triggered: tying them to page events.

6.5.3 Raising events on page transitions

Events can be declared in the page descriptor, allowing them to be tied to any page-related activity such as a page render or navigation transition. The `<raise-event>` element can be nested in any of these nodes: `<page>`, `<navigation>`, or `<rule>`. As with the `@RaiseEvent` annotation, it's not possible to pass parameters using this approach.

Let's implement the marketing department's request to capture cases when the registration form is canceled. To do this, we trigger an event on a navigation rule:

```
<page view-id="/register.xhtml">
  <navigation>
    <rule if-outcome="cancel">
      <raise-event type="registrationCanceled"/>
      <redirect view-id="/home.xhtml"/>
    </rule>
  </navigation>
</page>
```

You'll also want to ensure that the cancel button on the registration page, /register.xhtml, is changed to send the `cancel` outcome:

```
<h:commandLink value="Cancel" action="cancel" immediate="true"/>
```

Events are also useful for notifying observers when a page is going to be rendered.

PAGE EVENTS IN PLACE OF PAGE ACTIONS
In chapter 3, you used a page action to preload data before rendering the page. Since the goal is to observe and perform logic for the render event, it would be more appropriate—and self-documenting—to raise an event and have a component method observe it. Let's use this approach to preload the list of facilities on the facility directory page:

```
<page view-id="/FacilityList.xhtml">
  <raise-event type="facilityList.preRender"/>
  ...
</page>
```

Next, the `@Observer` annotation is applied to the `preloadFacilities()` method to watch for this event:

```
@Observer("facilityList.preRender")
public void preloadFacilities() {
    getResultList();
}
```

Even before you start producing your own events, you have a whole slew of built-in events that are raised by the Seam container. You may find that your first steps with events will be observing Seam's built-in events.

6.5.4   *Built-in events*

Events are one of the richest parts of Seam. If you had a nickel for every event that Seam raised, you'd surely be a rich developer. Listing every event that Seam raises would eat a gratuitous amount of space. I encourage you to consult the Seam reference documentation for a comprehensive list. Here's a list of some of the events that Seam raises:

- Seam container initialized
- Context variable assignment (added, removed)
- Component life-cycle events (created, destroyed)
- Scope events (created, destroyed)
- Authentication events
- Transaction events (before complete, commit, rollback)
- Exception events (handled, not handled)
- Conversation, page flow, business process, and task boundaries
- JSF phase transitions (before, after)
- JSF validation failed
- User preference change (theme, time zone, locale)

In certain cases, such as when a context variable is modified, the event raised includes the name of the subject. For instance, when the context variable `newGolfers` is added to the page scope, the name of the events that are raised are

- `org.jboss.seam.preSetVariable.newGolfers`
- `org.jboss.seam.postSetVariable.newGolfers`

In some cases, the subject is also passed as an argument to the event, such as when a component instance is created. When the `profileAction` component is created, the event `org.jboss.seam.postCreate.profileAction` is raised and the `profileAction` instance is sent as an argument. Observing this event allows you to place your post-create logic for a component on a different component entirely:

```
@Name("profileActionHelper")
public class ProfileActionHelper() {
    @Observer("org.jboss.seam.postCreate.profileAction")
    public void onCreate(ProfileAction profileAction) { ... }
}
```

In chapter 11, you'll learn how events can be used to minimize the disruption when requiring users to log in by capturing the current view before sending them to the login page and returning them to the captured page after successful authentication. You'll also use the postauthentication events to tune the HTTP session timeout as a way of managing memory.

Events are one way of separating concerns so that each component can focus on a specialized task, yet those individual tasks can be brought together using the event-observer pattern. Another way to decouple components and apply cross-cutting concerns is to use interceptors. The next section covers how interceptors are handled by both EJB 3 and Seam.

6.6   Custom method interceptors

As you've learned, Seam makes liberal use of method interceptors to weave functionality into components, an application of AOP. While AOP is extremely powerful, concepts such as pointcuts and advice are overly complex for many applications and can overwhelm developers. Seam and EJB 3 truly simplify AOP by making it straightforward to register cross-cutting logic, thus adding to the behavior Seam provides. Seam even aids in stereotyping the cross-cutting concern, allowing it to be applied declaratively. In this section, you'll learn about Seam's interceptor support and how it correlates with EJB 3 interceptors.

6.6.1   Two sides to the interceptor coin

Both Seam and EJB allow you to intercept calls to methods of a component by registering one or more interceptors on the component. Unlike other EJB features that Seam brings to a non-Java EE environment, Seam's interceptor support is not just a clone of what EJB offers. Seam introduces client-side interception, stateless interceptors, and stereotypes. While only Seam's interceptors can be applied to a JavaBean component, its interceptors complement the EJB 3–style interceptors on Seam session bean components. Let's take a quick look at EJB 3 interceptors, and then contrast them with the interceptor support that Seam provides.

EJB 3 INTERCEPTORS

The only requirement for defining an EJB interceptor is that the class have a method with the following signature:

```
@AroundInvoke
public Object methodName(InvocationContext ctx) throws Exception { ... }
```

The name of the method is arbitrary. The `InvocationContext` provides access to information about the intercepted method and component. Within the method, you can invoke the intercepted method using the following call:

```
ctx.proceed();
```

That's pretty much all there is to an interceptor method. The `@AroundInvoke` method intercepts all business methods on the component to which it's applied. You can intercept life-cycle methods of the component by defining additional methods on the interceptor class annotated with the Java EE life-cycle annotations, described in section 4.5.5 in chapter 4. The life-cycle interceptor methods use the same signature as the `@AroundInvoke` method.

Interceptors are applied in an EJB component in one of three ways:

- The EJB component is its own interceptor.
- The interceptor is applied at the class level.
- The interceptor is applied at the method level.

The first option is probably the easiest to understand. The `@AroundInvoke` method is placed on the EJB component that it intercepts. In this case, the component is intercepting itself. You typically only use this solution while prototyping an interceptor, because it provides little in the way of separation of concerns.

The other two options are likely what you will use long term. In this case, the interceptor class is registered on the component using the `@Interceptors` annotation, which accepts a list of interceptor classes. This annotation can be applied at the class or method level. When applied at the class level, every business method is intercepted by the `@AroundInvoke` method on the interceptor class, and the life-cycle methods are intercepted by the corresponding life-cycle method on the interceptor:

```
@Interceptors(RegistrationInterceptor.class)
public class RegisterActionBean implements RegisterAction { ... }
```

When applied at the method level, the `@AroundInvoke` method on the interceptor is only applied to that particular method:

```
public class RegisterActionBean implements RegisterAction {
    @Interceptors(RegistrationInterceptor.class)
    public String register() { ... }
}
```

In either case, the interceptor is external to the component and provides good separation of concerns. Note that the interceptor class doesn't have to be an EJB component itself. As I mentioned, EJB interceptors are pretty straightforward. Let's take a look at how Seam interceptors differ.

SEAM INTERCEPTORS

Seam interceptors differ from EJB interceptors in several ways. The first is cosmetic. Seam provides synonyms for the `@AroundInvoke` annotation and the `Invocation-Context` that can be used when the EJB API isn't available. The synonyms also work in a Java EE environment, so it makes no difference which ones you choose. To intercept life-cycle methods, though, you must use the Java EE life-cycle annotations. Aside from cosmetic differences, a Seam interceptor class appears the same as an EJB interceptor class.

With that out of the way, we can get into the interesting differences:

- Seam interceptors can be stateful or stateless.
- Seam interceptors can be applied on the client or the server.
- Seam interceptors are applied to a component as a stereotype.

The fact that Seam interceptors can be stateful or stateless addresses one of the main shortcomings of EJB interceptors and emphasizes Seam's commitment to stateful components. If the interceptor is stateful, it's bound to the lifetime of the component to which it's applied. Otherwise, Seam registers a singleton instance of the interceptor. The second difference is made possible by the fact that a Seam session bean component is a double proxy. Seam proxies the EJB instance and intercepts method calls before proceeding with the method on the session bean. Then, on the server, EJB applies its set of interceptors before proceeding with the business method. Seam is able to apply its interceptor on either side of the fence because Seam registers itself as an EJB interceptor. The final difference deals with how Seam interceptors are registered. Before we get to stereotypes, let's see how Seam is able to customize the behavior of an interceptor.

6.6.2   Defining a Seam interceptor

I mentioned earlier that, aside from the synonym types, the signature of a Seam interceptor class looks no different than an EJB interceptor class. If that's the case, Seam makes the interceptor stateful and invokes it on the client side. If you want to tune either of these two properties, you need to add the `@Interceptor` annotation to the interceptor class.

CUSTOMIZING YOUR INTERCEPTOR

The `@Interceptor` annotation supports two properties, `stateless` and `type`, which control whether the interceptor is stateless or stateful and whether it's invoked on the client or the server. If the interceptor is applied to a JavaBean component, the value of the `type` attribute isn't relevant. Here's an example of a stateless, client-side interceptor:

```
@Interceptor(stateless = true, type = InterceptorType.CLIENT)
public class StatelessClientSideInterceptor {
    @AroundInvoke public Object aroundInvoke(InvocationContext ctx) {
        ctx.proceed();
    }
}
```

One of the main benefits of using a Seam interceptor is to make it stateful, so I encourage you to take advantage of this feature. This allows you to safely store data in the interceptor between method calls just as you would the stateful component it's intercepting.

The interceptor type you choose depends on the call stack in which you want your interceptor to execute. If you want to short-circuit the call to the EJB component or wrap the work performed in the EJB container, you need to use a client-side interceptor. For instance, you can retry a call to an EJB component (or other remote service) in the event of a failure. On the other hand, if you want the interceptor to execute within the EJB interceptor call stack—duking it out with the other interceptors installed on the EJB session bean—a server-side interceptor is appropriate. The server-side interceptor is sufficient if you're simply adding behavior to the method invocation.

Having decided how to author your interceptor, you need to learn how it's applied to a Seam component. Paying attention here is important because the way Seam interceptors are registered with a Seam component differs from how EJB interceptors are registered with an EJB component. While Seam provides a synonym annotation for @Interceptors, you do *not* apply it directly to the component class as when you're registering EJB interceptors.

INTERCEPTORS AS STEREOTYPES

The @Interceptors annotation is a meta-annotation, meaning it must be added to an annotation, not directly to a class. That annotation is then declared on the component class and the interceptor from the annotation is carried through to the component. Building on the earlier example, we first define an annotation to host the RegistrationInterceptor:

```
@Target(TYPE)
@Retention(RUNTIME)
@Interceptors(RegistrationInterceptor.class)
public @interface RegistrationAuditor {}
```

Next, the annotation is added to RegisterAction JavaBean component:

```
@Name("registerAction")
@RegistrationAuditor
public class RegisterAction { ... }
```

There are two reasons for this level of indirection. First, it's how Seam is able to isolate interceptors so that they can be applied on the client side rather than handled by the EJB container on the server side. If they were registered directly with the class, the EJB container would try to gain control. But there's a more compelling reason, which is design oriented.

Annotations that describe the semantics of a class are known as stereotypes. If you're familiar with UML, the concept is much the same. With the EJB 3 model, the `@Interceptors` annotation placed directly on the class doesn't tell you much about why it is there and what the interceptors do. In Seam, the interceptors are added to a custom annotation. When this annotation is added to the component class, it describes the behavior that it brings without exposing the mechanism by which that behavior is applied. You see this pattern used heavily in JSR 299 (Web Beans).

Just as events and interceptors offer a way to loosely couple sequential logic and apply cross-cutting logic, factory and manager components offer a way to loosely couple the creation of context variables. Let's explore how these special components help to build on Seam's inversion of control principles.

6.7 *Factory and manager components*

Sometimes, there's more to a context variable than first meets the eye. Up to this point, you've learned that requesting a context variable from the Seam container may spawn an instance of a component with the same name. After the instance is resolved, you still have to access its properties or methods to get to the actual data. Factory and manager components allow you to use context variables to produce the underlying data, rather than just a component instance. When the context variable is requested, a data provider is invoked—typically a method on a Seam component—and the return value is bound to the context variable. Thus, the value of a context variable bound to factory or manager components is said to be calculated. A factory component is a generalization of a `@Factory` method, and a manager component is any component that has one, and only one, `@Unwrap` method.

What makes factory and manager components interesting is that they act just like regular components; they use bijection, they can be injected into another component using `@In`, and they can be referenced in EL bindings. Let's begin by exploring the factory component.

6.7.1 *A context variable @Factory*

The factory component is a bit of a misnomer. Technically, it's just a data provider—a component method or EL expression—that can bind a value to a context variable when the context variable is requested. Factory components are useful for creating context variables lazily, such as from a JSF view, as opposed to being outjected from an action method.

WHY FACTORIES ARE NEEDED

Before we dive into factories, I want to clarify the benefit they provide over just using a JavaBean-style "getter" method on a component to retrieve data (such as the list of new golfers). What you must understand is that the EL resolver is *very* persistent about resolving value expressions. If you put logic in a getter method, it may get called a ridiculous number of times in one request. In a JSF view, there are a lot of places where you need to repeatedly access a calculated value to perform such tasks as conditional rendering (checking whether a collection is empty, perhaps), and the branches of the UI component tree where these expressions are located are each visited several times during the JSF life cycle. It's just a natural part of how JSF and the EL work.

There's no harm in using a getter method in a value expression as long as the method simply returns the internal state of an object. However, if that method performs logic, especially logic that accesses the database, this can result in a significant performance problem. A factory component allows you to calculate the value once and bind the result to a context variable. Subsequent requests for that context variable use the previously calculated value rather than running the logic again. This immediately solves the problem just cited. Always be wary of putting heavyweight logic in getter methods and instead use factories. The performance-conscious folks will be thankful to you.

That explanation should get you excited about learning more about factories. Let's see what types of data providers can serve as factories and then dive into the process.

FACTORY DATA PROVIDERS

As we discussed earlier, when a context variable is requested, Seam tries to locate it in one of the available contexts. When that search turns up empty, and the lookup is operating with the create option, Seam turns to initializing a value. I've held back some of the details of how this value is produced. Before looking for a matching component definition to instantiate an instance, Seam first seeks out a volunteer to produce a value. This volunteer is known as a factory. A factory can be implemented using one of the following providers:

- A Seam component method, marked with the `@Factory` annotation
- An EL value or method expression, configured in the component XML descriptor

The reason these delegates are called factories is because they "manufacture" values for the context variables they represent. When a factory is resolved, the factory provider is invoked and the return value is bound to the factory name in the designated scope. If the factory produces a null value, Seam moves on to the next step in the lookup process.

Here's an example of a value expression factory defined in the component descriptor:

```
<factory name="course" value="#{courseHome.instance}"/>
```

When the context variable `course` is requested, this value expression is resolved and the result is bound to the corresponding variable name in the event scope (the event scope is the default scope for `<factory>`). Similarly, the factory product can be resolved from a method expression. Here, the `findNewGolfers()` method populates the `newGolfers` context variable, later defined as an annotation-based factory:

```
<factory name="newGolfers" method="#{profileAction.findNewGolfers}"/>
```

A factory data provider supports autocreate functionality just like a component, allowing it to be resolved even when the corresponding context variable is requested in *lookup only* mode. Unlike a component, factories can create any value, not just component instances. In fact, the result of a factory can be injected into the property of a component using @In:

```
@In(create = true) Course course;
```

In this case, course may be the name of a component or the name of a factory. The injection point doesn't know the difference. It just depends on what's available. Factories support autocreate, so the create attribute on @In isn't necessary if autocreate is enabled on the factory. There are, of course, subtle differences between a component and a factory, but they are small enough that it's reasonable to refer to factories as *components*. Let's consider what happens when a context variable associated with a factory is requested.

THE FACTORY PROCESS

The factory process is illustrated in figure 6.10. While this process can get fairly involved, it essentially follows one of three approaches to produce a context variable:

- Return a value, which Seam then assigns to the context variable
- Outject the context variable
- Assign a value to the context variable in the factory method

To start, you probably just want to have the factory method return a value. You may find, however, that you want to cache the factory result in a property. In that case, you make the factory method return void and outject the property in which the result is stored. Outjection is also useful if you want to wrap the result in a @DataModel. The final option highlights the fact that the factory process ensures that the context variable is still null before assigning a value to it using either of the first two strategies.

Whew! There sure is a lot going on in the factory process. Don't let it overwhelm you, though. There just happens to be many different ways to use a factory, which is why the diagram has so many steps. The best strategy is to pick the variation that works best for you and stick with it.

If you only take away three points about a factory, make them these:

- A factory provider is invoked when the context variable it represents is accessed and the context variable is missing or its value is null.
- A factory can either assign the context variable itself (explicitly or as a result of outjection) or return a value that's to be assigned to the context variable.
- A factory can trigger bijection if the factory provider is a component method (and bijection is not disabled on that method).

One of the side effects of a factory whose data provider is a component method is that it triggers bijection. It's convenient to have access to injected values within the method, but where things get interesting is during outjection. As stated earlier, if the factory method has a void return value, Seam relies on outjection to populate the context variable that the factory represents. However, additional properties may also be outjected at the same time. So when a factory is resolved, other context variables may just suddenly appear.

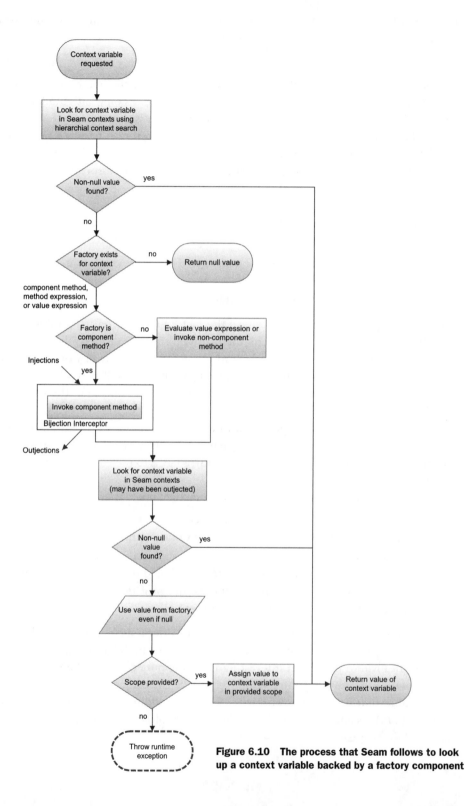

Figure 6.10 The process that Seam follows to look up a context variable backed by a factory component

Once you get the factory process under your belt, you'll find yourself using factories all the time. Let's see how a factory can be used to prepare the list of new golfers on demand.

INITIALIZING CONTEXT VARIABLES ON DEMAND

Earlier, I showed you how to expose the collection of the newest golfers in the form of a JSF `DataModel` using a page action. Page actions are useful in small quantities. Once the page starts to get reasonably complex, the number of page actions can balloon out of proportion if used to prepare context variables needed in the page. A better solution is to allow each variable to be initialized on demand by using a factory.

One way to define a factory is by placing the `@Factory` annotation, summarized in table 6.9, above a component method. This method is called whenever the context variable, whose name is provided in the `value` attribute of the annotation, needs to be initialized.

Table 6.9 The `@Factory` annotation

Name:	Factory	
Purpose:	Marks a method as a factory for a context variable. Used to supply a value when an uninitialized context variable is requested.	
Target:	METHOD	

Attribute	Type	Function
value	String	The name of the context variable that this factory method initializes. Default: Bean property name of method.
scope	ScopeType	The scope where the context variable is set. *The scope should not be used when the factory method is void.* Default: inherited from the host component, or the event scope if the component is stateless.
autoCreate	boolean	Indicates that this factory should initialize the context variable, even when requested in *lookup-only* mode. Default: false.

Let's designate the `findNewGolfers()` method as a factory rather than as a page action. The `@Factory` annotation above the `findNewGolfers()` method in listing 6.4 declares this method as the factory for the `newGolfers` context variable. Seam invokes this method whenever the context variable is null or missing. However, since the method's return type is void, Seam expects the context variable to be populated as a result of outjection.

Listing 6.4 A factory component that produces a list of new golfers

```
@Name("profileAction")
public class ProfileAction {
    protected int newGolferPoolSize = 25;
    protected int newGolferDisplaySize = 5;

    @RequestParameter protected Long golferId;

    @In protected EntityManager entityManager;        ❶

    @DataModelSelection
    @Out(required = false)
```

```
protected Golfer selectedGolfer;

@DataModel(scope = ScopeType.PAGE)          ❷
protected List<Golfer> newGolfers;

public String view() {
    return "/profile.xhtml";
}

@Factory("newGolfers")          ❸
public void findNewGolfers() {
    newGolfers = entityManager.createQuery(
      "select g from Golfer g order by g.dateJoined desc")          ❹
      .setMaxResults(newGolferPoolSize)
      .getResultList();

    Random rnd = new Random(System.currentTimeMillis());

    while (newGolfers.size() > newGolferDisplaySize) {          ❺
        newGolfers.remove(rnd.nextInt(newGolfers.size()));
    }
}
}
```

The first time the #{newGolfers} value expression is encountered in the JSF view, the newGolfers context variable is uninitialized. Seam will turn to the @Factory method ❸ to resolve a value. Before the method proceeds, the EntityManager property ❶ is injected. The method then uses the EntityManager to query the database for the newest golfers ❹, shuffles the result, and pares it down to the configured display size ❺. Outjection is then applied, which initializes the newGolfers context variable as a JSF Data-Model ❷. Seam then returns control to the view renderer, which uses the newly formed data model to render the <rich:dataList>.

Here are some rules that you should be aware of when using a factory method:

- If a scope isn't specified for a factory method that returns a value, the scope of the host component is used, or the event if the host component is stateless.
- A factory method with a defined scope can't allow a value with the same name to be outjected as a result of the call.
- If a factory method doesn't specify a scope, and both a value is outjected and the factory returns a value, the outjected value takes precedence over the value returned by the factory method.

The @Factory annotation on a component method is the only way to designate a factory in Java code. To use a method- or value-binding expression, you must declare the factory in the component descriptor using <factory>. As a quick reminder:

```
<factory name="newGolfers" method="#{profileAction.findNewGolfers}"/>
```

But a more common use of <factory> is for creating component aliases.

FACTORIES AS ALIASES

Factories that are scoped to the stateless context and are mapped to an EL value expression are referred to as aliases. Earlier, you saw an alias that resolves to the get-Instance() method on the CourseHome component, defined here to be stateless:

```
<factory name="course" value="#{courseHome.instance}" scope="stateless"/>
```

Since the stateless context doesn't retain the value after lookup, the alias is resolved each time the factory name is requested, making it a shortcut for a more complex expression.

TIP I prefer to scope aliases to a real context, such as the event scope, to avoid unnecessary, redundant lookups. As long as the target value won't change during the lifetime of the context in which the alias is stored, it's a safe bet.

Another typical use of an alias is to provide a terse name for a fully qualified context variable name. All of the built-in Seam components use namespaces, which make their names very long. You can abbreviate a fully qualified component name using an alias, as I've done here for the built-in FacesMessages component:

```
<factory name="facesMessages"
  value="#{org.jboss.seam.faces.facesMessages}"
  scope="stateless" auto-create="true"/>
```

But guess what? Most of the built-in components, such as this one, can already be referenced by their unqualified names, making this factory unnecessary. Seam sets up this alias by importing the context variable prefix in the component descriptor using the <import> tag, which you learned about in the previous chapter:

```
<import>org.jboss.seam.faces</import>
```

You can declare imports for your own component names as well. As a reminder, imports defined in the component descriptor are applied globally for a project. If you only want to import a context variable prefix in the context of a single Java class or package, you can do so using the @Import annotation, summarized in table 6.10.

Table 6.10   The @Import annotation

Name:	Import
Purpose:	Imports a context variable prefix to allow components having that prefix to be referenced using their unqualified component names
Target:	TYPE (class), PACKAGE

Attribute	Type	Function
value	String[]	A list of context variable prefixes that are used to qualify component names after trying with the unqualified name. Default: none (required).

Let's assume the context variable name of the GolferValidator component is org.open18.validation.golferValidator. We can import its namespace prefix into the RegisterAction component using @Import:

```
@Name("registerAction")
@Import("org.open18.validation")
public class RegisterAction {
    ...
    @In protected GolferValidator golferValidator;
    ...
}
```

We can also import it for all components in the org.open18.action package by applying the @Import annotation to the package-info.java file in that package:

```
@Import("org.open18.validation")
package org.open18.action;
import org.jboss.seam.annotation.Import;
```

Note that just as in the Java package system, it's possible to refer to a context variable in the same namespace as the current component by referring to that variable using its unqualified name. If you named the RegisterAction component org.open18. action.registerAction, you could refer to it from another component whose name is prefixed with org.open18.action using the name registerAction.

So you can see that factories are a powerful and flexible feature of Seam. They help to close gaps when data is needed in an arbitrary location, such as a component buried deep inside a JSF view or as an injected dependency that needs to perform prerequisite work. Factories allow context variables to be dynamic, boasting more meaning than what is observed at first glance. Another type of component that helps make context variables dynamic is the manager component.

6.7.2   *Components that @Unwrap*

The @Unwrap annotation acts like a magician's handkerchief. You see the handkerchief go into the hand, but when the hand opens, you get something entirely different. This trick is called a manager component. A manager component has exactly one method that is marked with the @Unwrap annotation. When a manager component's name is requested from the Seam container, an instance of the component is located or created, and then "unwrapped" before it's returned to the caller, thus beginning the handkerchief trick. During the unwrap stage, the @Unwrap method is executed and the return value of the method is passed on to the requester in place of the component itself. Indeed, the manager component is a slippery little devil. A summary of the @Unwrap annotation is shown in table 6.11.

Table 6.11   The @Unwrap annotation

Name:	Unwrap
Purpose:	Identifies the method whose return value is used in place of the component instance itself when the component name is resolved
Target:	METHOD

The @Unwrap method differs from the @Factory method in that it is stateless, meaning it's invoked every time the host component's name is accessed. Because it's stateless, the return value of the creation method isn't bound to the context variable, as with a factory. Instead, the context variable stores the instance of the manager component, which is the only stateful part. To get to the actual value, the @Unwrap method must be called. Obviously, you have to be careful about what you put into the @Unwrap method since it's going to end up being called many times.

The manager component is more powerful than the factory component for these reasons:

- It's a real component (the factory is only a pseudocomponent).
- Its properties can be configured just like any other component.
- It can have life-cycle methods (`@Create`, `@Destroy`).
- The `@Unwrap` method is called every time the component name is accessed.
- It can hold internal state.
- It can observe events that can trigger updates to its state.

As its name suggests, a manager component is good at managing data. The data stands in for the component when the component is accessed or injected using `@In`, but otherwise it behaves just like any other component. You can think of a manager component as a sophisticated alias, where the `@Unwrap` method is responsible for looking up the value of the alias. What makes the manager component compelling is that it can alias an object that isn't accessible via a value- or method-binding expression. One such example from the Seam API is the manager component that retrieves the JSF `FacesContext` instance, a static method on the `FacesContext` class:

```
@Name("org.jboss.seam.faces.facesContext")
@Scope(ScopeType.APPLICATION)
public class FacesContext {
    @Unwrap public javax.faces.context.FacesContext getContext() {
        return javax.faces.context.FacesContext.getCurrentInstance();
    }
}
```

Another example from the Seam API is a manager component that retrieves the current date:

```
@Name("org.jboss.seam.framework.currentDate")
@Scope(ScopeType.STATELESS)
public class CurrentDate {
    @Unwrap public Date getCurrentDate() {
        return new java.sql.Date(System.currentTimeMillis());
    }
}
```

The manager component offers a convenient way to make Java constants, enum values, and other static method return values accessible via the EL. Manager components are also good for loading resources such as a Hibernate `SessionFactory`, a Java mail session, or a JMS connection. In fact, Seam uses manager components for all of these resources. It would be possible to create regular components for these resources and then register an alias that returns the value of the method that retrieves the runtime configuration, but the `@Unwrap` method saves you the extra step. If you've ever used one of Spring's factory beans, a manager component is the same idea.

Let's put the manager component into practice by using it to maintain the list of new golfers shown on the home page. You see, we're hoping that Open 18 is going to be a big success and as a result, a lot of people are going to be hitting the home page. We don't want every single hit to result in a database query or it could hurt performance. While we could certainly get a faster database server, it's prudent to take the burden off the database, especially since we're repeatedly asking it the same question (who are the new golfers?).

Listing 6.5 shows a manager component that maintains a cache of the new golfers in the application scope. Any time a new golfer registers, it observes the golferRegis-tered event and refreshes the cache.

Listing 6.5   A component that manages the collection of new golfers

```
package org.open18.action;

import org.jboss.seam.ScopeType;
import org.jboss.seam.annotations.*;
import org.open18.model.Golfer;
import javax.persistence.EntityManager;
import java.util.*;

@Name("newGolfersList")
@Scope(ScopeType.APPLICATION)
public class NewGolfersList {
    private int poolSize = 25;
    private int displaySize = 5;

    @In protected EntityManager entityManager;           ❶

    protected List<Golfer> newGolfers;

    public void setPoolSize(int poolSize) {
        this.poolSize = poolSize;
    }

    public void setDisplaySize(int displaySize) {
        this.displaySize = displaySize;
    }

    @Create        ❷
    public void onCreate() {
        fetchNewGolfers();
    }

    @Unwrap        ❸
    public List<Golfer> getNewGolfers() {
        return newGolfers;
    }

    @Observer(value = "golferRegistered", create = false)    ❹
    synchronized public void fetchNewGolfers() {
        List<Golfer> results = entityManager.createQuery(
            "select g from Golfer g order by g.dateJoined desc")
            .setMaxResults(poolSize).getResultList();

        Collections.shuffle(results);

        Random random = new Random();
        while (results.size() > displaySize) {
            results.remove(random.nextInt(results.size()));
        }

        newGolfers = results;
    }
}
```

The golfers are fetched when the component is first created ❷ and whenever a new golfer registers ❹. Manager components support bijection ❶ just like any other component. Every time the component name, `newGolferList`, is accessed, the `@Unwrap` method ❸ is called and the cached list of golfers is returned.

You may notice that this component exposes two configuration properties, `poolSize` and `displaySize`, which control how many golfers are selected from the database and how many are displayed, respectively. To change the defaults, use the following component configuration:

```
<component name="newGolfersList">
  <property name="poolSize">10</property>
  <property name="displaySize">3</property>
</component>
```

If we swapped out the `newGolfers` on the home page with the `newGolfersList`, we'd lose the ability to capture a selection using a command link. It isn't possible to create clickable lists using a manager component alone (without some creative backbreaking). Manager components are designed to maintain data, not to serve as an action bean or data model selector. Therefore, we still need a factory to provide a value for the `newGolfers` property on `ProfileAction` to keep the current functionality. Instead of querying for golfers in the `ProfileAction`, the `newGolfersList` manager component will be consulted to get the list. The relevant changes to `ProfileAction` are shown in listing 6.6.

Listing 6.6 A factory component that uses a manager component as a data provider

```
@Name("profileAction")
public class ProfileAction {
    ...
    @In (create = true) protected List<Golfer> newGolfersList;        ◁────┐
                                                      Uses list maintained by
    @DataModel(scope = ScopeType.PAGE)                manager component
    protected List<Golfer> newGolfers;
    ...
    @Factory("newGolfers")
    public void fetchNewGolfers() {
        newGolfers = newGolfersList;
    }
}
```

The clickable list of new golfers works just as it did before. The only change is that the manager component now provides the list of new golfers rather than performing the entity query directly in the factory method. The best part about this design is that the manager now acts as a data access object (DAO), separating the data access logic from the business logic and making the components easier to test in isolation.

Factory and manager components act as just-in-time variable assignment. Your code references a context variable as if it has already been set and then one of two delegates, either the factory or the manager, creates it, just in time for you to make use of it. But what makes it even better is that the method has access to injected resources to help it create the variable.

6.8   *Summary*

This chapter championed Seam for delivering a much-needed technology update to inversion of control by making injections dynamic and introducing the concept of outjection—the two sides of bijection. You hardly need to be reminded now that bijection occurs every time a method on a Seam component is invoked, so not only are dependency references kept up to date, but it's also possible to inject data from a narrow scope into a component stored in a wider scope.

You learned how you can inject components, request parameters, and value expressions into the bean properties of a Seam component. You also learned that property values can be pushed back out into a Seam context, allowing them to be accessed by other components or in a JSF template. You learned that, when pushing out collections, Seam can wrap them in a JSF DataModel to be used in a UIData component. Seam can also capture the selection from that UIData component and inject it into another property on the component on a subsequent postback.

You discovered that there's a lot more to the component retrieval process than what appears at first glance. Often, context variable names resolve to component instances, but they can also be fed by a factory method or value expression or even resolve to the return value of a delegate method on manager components.

To accomplish the pinnacle of inversion of control, you learned that it's possible to cut the ties between components completely while still being able to establish a linear flow of logic by allowing the Seam container to mediate component event notifications and trigger custom interceptors. Both make it easy to apply cross-cutting concerns to objects without jeopardizing their status as POJOs.

The exchange of context variables in the Seam container is very rich, yet for most uses, is confined to a couple of commonly used annotations. Injecting, outjection, and resolving of context variables is crucial for exchanging data between components and the view. In the next chapter, you'll learn how conversation annotations and page flow definitions help to propagate state across requests. The factory component also gets additional limelight, playing a key role in launching a conversation. The promise of improved state management mentioned in chapter 4 is given substance in the next chapter, so read on because the most exciting parts of Seam are yet to come.

Part 3

Seam's state management

Part 1 presented the motivation for why Seam was created and demonstrated ways it simplifies development of web applications. You used seam-gen to quickly put together a Seam-based application and agile development environment. Part 2 got into the guts of Seam by teaching you to define and configure components and getting them to communicate. What sets Seam apart from other web-oriented frameworks is its focus on state management. This term may not mean much to you right now, but trust that it plays a key role in what you'll learn to master in the next three chapters: conversations, page flows, the extended persistence context, application transactions, and entity home components.

Chapter 7 introduces conversations as a way to effectively string together requests. You define conversation boundaries using a familiar declarative approach. You also learn to orchestrate a conversation with a page flow and to let the user multitask using workspaces.

Chapter 8 puts conversations aside initially to cover Java persistence, the ORM mechanism that translates Java objects to and from database records. The end of the chapter sees a return to state management when the extended persistence context in EJB 3 is introduced. This construct ensures persistent objects remain managed so that updates to the database require no programming, related objects can be fetched on demand, and database reads are kept to a minimum.

In chapter 9, you learn that conversations provide the perfect vehicle for extending the persistence context. This chapter introduces Seam-managed persistence as an alternative to its complement in Java EE, with a number of extensions weaved in. More important, propagation of the persistence context is handled transparently, a relief from complex rules in EJB 3. Seam also offers a unique approach to transactions by wrapping them around each request and facilitating application transactions that span multiple requests.

In chapter 10, you get to bring together everything you have learned about Seam and perform rapid development using the Seam Application Framework. This chapter helps you appreciate how much you have matured as a Seam developer throughout this part.

The conversation:
Seam's unit of work

This chapter covers

- Managing state with a conversation
- Controlling long-running conversations
- Switching between workspaces
- Defining stateful page flows

Seam helps establish a rich user experience by stretching the boundaries of a unit of work to cover a use case—a determinate interchange between the user and the application. In this chapter, you'll learn how Seam's conversation context can host the working set of data needed to support this interchange. Seam's conversation is contrasted with traditional state management techniques, demonstrating how it both relieves the burden of handling this task and gives multipage interactions a formal representation in a web application. Conversations open the door to more advanced state management techniques—such as stateful page flows, nested conversations, and workspaces—that further enrich the user experience.

Conversations are one of Seam's crowning features, touching many areas of the framework and bridging earlier chapters with those that lie ahead. In fact, CRUD applications created by seam-gen use conversations to manage the use case of adding and modifying an entity instance. To witness conversations in action before beginning this chapter, you can study them at work in the Open 18 application. This chapter starts off by defining a use case and then explores how aligning it with a stateful context can improve the user's experience.

7.1   *Learning to appreciate conversational state*

After returning from your golf getaway, you learn that, in your absence, someone has been having fun at your expense, courtesy of your credit card number. To reclaim your assets, you have to endure the disparate customer service process deployed by your bank. I'm sure this exchange will strike a familiar chord.

"How can I help you?"

You take this cue to launch into your rant about being a victim of fraud, your whereabouts during the previous week, and which charges you're disputing.

A brief pause is interrupted by, "Can I have your account number?"

Your momentum is temporarily interrupted as you wait for your call to be logged. The agent then informs you that you need to be transferred to the fraud department, which is properly equipped to deal with this matter. There's no chance to object as the switch happens without delay. A new voice appears on the other end of the line.

"How can I help you?"

Sigh. Time to start over from the beginning.

You began the day a victim of fraud. Now you have become a victim of a stateless process. Critical information about your situation failed to make the leap from the customer service representative to the fraud representative. This mishap could have been avoided had the two representatives engaged in a conversation during the switch to retain a record of your story. Unfortunately for you, they don't see the big picture. As soon as you're handed off, there's another call to answer.

That's exactly how requests are handled in a web application, which rests atop a stateless protocol (HTTP). The result is that data tends to be dropped between page requests, blind to the ongoing use case. Seam acknowledges that all requests occur in the scope of a conversation, that a conversation can span multiple requests, and that conversations are subsets of a user's session, as illustrated in figure 7.1.

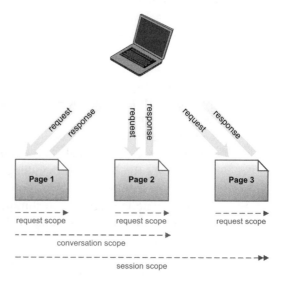

Figure 7.1   The conversation scope ties together individual requests, but is more granular than the session.

Through use of conversations, Seam supports building stateful interactions that bridge the gap between requests. As a result, state can be tracked until the user's goal is accomplished, not just to satisfy an atomic step along the way.

7.1.1 Redefining the unit of work

You may think of a unit of work in terms of a database transaction. The story just told is faithful to this definition at the expense of the caller's time. This short-lived unit of work is problematic because it's not stateful (in the long-running sense). Seam redefines the unit of work by looking at it from the user's perspective, coining what is known as a conversation. During a conversation, database transactions, page requests, and other atomic units of work may come and go, but the overall process isn't deemed complete until the user's goal is accomplished. In a conversation, the state is said to be extended. In the next chapter, you'll learn that the persistence context can also be extended to match this timetable.

The linkage between page requests in a conversation is established through the use of a special token and a partitioning of the HTTP session, which you'll learn about in section 7.2. The conversation's lifetime is controlled by declarative boundary conditions, covered in section 7.3. First, I want to focus on the challenge of establishing a well-defined stateful context in a web application and how this task has been traditionally handled. You could go so far as to say that propagating state in a web application is a downright burden. After studying some of the alternatives, I'll segue into how Seam's conversation provides relief.

7.1.2 The burden of managing state

All applications have state, even those classified as stateless (e.g., RESTful applications). Some applications stash state away in server-side contexts such as the HTTP session scope or the JSF page scope. So-called stateless applications just weave state into the URL or hide it away in hidden form fields. A majority of applications likely use a mix of these strategies. The real question is, as users traverse from one page to the next, how much support do they get from the framework for managing and accessing that state?

I'm sure that in the past you have worked very hard to save data between requests and subsequently prepare it for use in the business logic. Whether you wrote one of those applications that has more hidden form fields than visible ones or one with as many Struts `ActionForm` classes as business components, you have felt the burden of managing state. That's not to say that RESTful URLs, hidden form fields, request parameters, or cookies aren't viable. It's just that when they are means to an end, where the end is to restore the state from the previous request, they cause a lot of work. Seam attempts to make state readily available in contexts that closely represent the life cycle of that state (i.e., a use case). Not only does the conversation context blend state between requests for the duration of a use case, it avoids destroying the identity of objects as a result of serialization, which is the main problem with the traditional approaches.

PASSING DATA THROUGH THE REQUEST

One approach to propagating state is to send it along as part of the request in one of these forms:

- Request parameters (i.e., hidden form fields or the query string)
- As part of the URL (e.g., /course/view/9)
- Browser cookies

All of these options work by disassembling some server-side object into bite-sized chucks, tunneling those parts through the request as string values, then reassembling the objects on the server, as figure 7.2 illustrates. There are times when a RESTful URL, request parameter, or cookie is the right tool for the job. However, if you're working with any decent-size set of data, having to prepare this translation on every request is downright tedious.

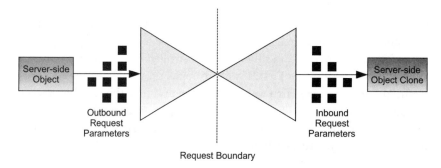

Figure 7.2   Passing an object using request parameters is akin to teleportation.

You learned in chapter 3 that Seam's page parameters offer some relief here by automatically translating objects to and from HTTP request parameters on a per-page basis. The downside to page parameters is that they are hardwired to the page definition. Since a page may be used in more than one set of circumstances, the configuration could result in data being propagated even when you don't need it; or worse, it gets in the way.

The biggest drawback of parameter-based propagation in general is that the server-side object loses its identity when it passes through this funnel. The object that's built on the server, beyond the request boundary, is a clone of the original object, possibly even a partial one. This cloning process makes it impossible to transfer a resource that relies on its identity being maintained, such as a persistence manager or managed entity instance. For an object's identity to be preserved, the object must be stored in a server-side context, such as the JSF UI component tree (which requires server-side state saving), the HTTP session, or as you'll soon learn, the conversation. Then it's only necessary to pass a token to the server to restore the context and the objects it contains.

STASHING STATE IN THE JSF UI COMPONENT TREE

You learned in chapter 4 that the root of the JSF UI component tree has an attribute map that can be used to save data across a JSF postback. Seam's page context and the `<t:saveState>` component tag from the MyFaces Tomahawk library both offer transparent access to this map, among alternatives. As elegant as these abstraction layers may be, it doesn't diminish the fact that this map is merely the JSF equivalent of hidden form fields.

Using the UI component tree as a stateful context has problems that match those cited previously. First, you must reestablish the set of variables in the page context when the UI component tree is rebuilt (which happens during any postback request that issues a redirect or renders a different view). The second problem is that the UI component tree doesn't guarantee that the identity of the objects will be maintained. JSF state saving can be done either on the client side or the server side. When client-side state saving is used, the restored objects are clones of the originals, having the same problem as passing parameters through the request. If you don't have control over the state-saving setting, it's best not to rest an object's identity on such unstable ground.

The challenge of maintaining object identity is often solved by using the HTTP session.

STORING DATA IN THE HTTP SESSION

The HTTP session can be used to store arbitrarily complex objects while preserving their identity. This context is shared by all browser tabs and windows that restore the same session token and typically lasts on the order of hours or days. While this storage mechanism sounds ideal, it's unfortunately too good to be true. The main downfall of the HTTP session is that it quickly becomes a tangled mess of data that consumes excessive amounts of memory and complicates multiwindow application usage. Let's explore these issues.

The HTTP session is well suited for data that you want to retain across all requests made by a given user, such as the user's identity. However, the session isn't a good place to store data for a specific use case. It may seem harmless when the user is accessing the application from a single window—but what happens when the user spawns multiple tabs or windows? Because the session identifier is stored as a cookie in the user's browser, and most browsers share cookies between tabs and windows (herein referred to as tabs), the result is that the multiple tabs naively share the same session data. If the application doesn't recognize this sharing, it can cause data to be manipulated in conflicting ways.

NOTE The session identifier can also be passed through the URL, known as URL rewriting. When URL rewriting is used, links that contain the same session identifier restore the same session, even if opened in a new tab.

Consider the use case of updating a golf course record. Assume that the golf course is stored in the HTTP session while it's being modified. If you select a course to modify in one browser tab and then select a different course to modify in a second tab, the second course selection on the server overwrites the first. When you click Save in the first tab, assuming the changes are applied directly to the record in the session, you inadvertently modify the second course instance. Things get even trickier if you're working with a multipage wizard, since the leakage of data can be less apparent. Yet another problem is that data in the session isn't protected from concurrent use, so if two requests try to access session data simultaneously, it can lead to a race condition.

The most severe problem with the session scope is that it is mostly unmanaged. If objects continue to build up in the session, and there's no application-provided garbage collector to clean it out, memory leaks that impact the performance of the application will occur, thus affecting all of the users.

It's possible to work around the aforementioned problems by using the session with care or by putting in synchronization and locking code to prevent collisions, but that's a burden on you as a developer. In general, heavy use of the session scope is a common source of bugs, and the unexpected behavior it causes is often difficult to reproduce in a test environment.

NOTE   Cookies have the combined problem of request parameters and session data. They only store string data, capped at a fixed size (~4K), and they cannot be partitioned by use case. Their utility is in identifying a repeat visitor or storing basic user preferences.

Although the existing storage options are workable, they aren't well suited for maintaining an isolated working set of data for a use case. Clearly there is room for a better solution. Surprisingly enough, that solution lies in the HTTP session. Despite my having just bashed the session for its weaknesses, it's not all bad. It simply needs to be partitioned and better managed. That's exactly what Seam does. The conversation context is designed to be a well-behaved abstraction layer over the HTTP session.

7.2   *The conversation context*

The conversation context is one of two Seam contexts introduced to serve business-world time frames as opposed to servlet life cycles (the other is the business process context). From reading the previous section, you should have a clear picture as to a conversation's purpose. In this section, you'll learn how it's maintained.

7.2.1   *Carving a workspace out of the HTTP session*

The conversation context is carved out of the HTTP session to form an isolated and managed memory segment, as illustrated in figure 7.3. Seam uses the conversation context as the home for a working set of context variables.

You may shudder at the mention of using the HTTP session to store the conversation, given the problems cited in the last section. However, a conversation doesn't suffer from the same problems as its parentage. First and foremost, the lifespan of a typical conversation is on the order of minutes, whereas a session can last on the order of hours. This difference is made possible by the fact that a conversation has its own distinct life cycle,

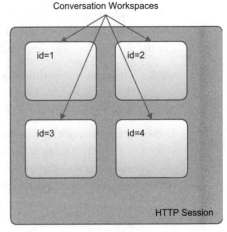

Figure 7.3   Conversation workspaces are isolated segments of the HTTP session, each assigned a unique identifier.

which Seam manages. Each conversation can have its own timeout period, which defaults to the global timeout setting, covered in section 7.3.5. Additionally, concurrent conversations are kept isolated, unlike session attributes, which just get jammed together in a single map.

Since conversations are stored in the session, two requirements must be met:

- Conversation-scoped components must implement `java.io.Serializable`.
- The session timeout, defined in web.xml, must exceed all conversation timeouts.

A conversation has a clear set of life-cycle boundaries that coincide with the boundaries of a use case. When the user triggers a condition that begins a conversation, a new managed area of the HTTP session is sectioned off and dedicated to that conversation. A unique identifier, known as the *conversation id*, is generated and associated with this region of the session. The conversation id is passed on to the next request as a request parameter, hidden form field, or JSF view root attribute. Fortunately, propagation of the conversation id is handled transparently in a Seam application. As a result of the conversation id and session token being sent together to the server, the conversation is retrieved from the session and associated with the request.

NOTE   Although the HTTP session is used as the storage mechanism for a conversation, understand that the memory footprint is strikingly low because conversations are aggressively managed. There's no chance of them lingering on to cause memory leaks.

The conversation context is an ideal place to store data that's needed over the extent of several pages. It leverages the session's ability to store arbitrarily complex objects while preserving object identity, but doesn't suffer from memory leaks or concurrency problems. What makes conversations truly unique is that they remain isolated from one another.

SOLVING THE MULTIWINDOW CONCURRENCY PROBLEM

Let's revisit the scenario in which different golf course records are being edited in separate browser tabs. This time around, we'll assume that a conversation is being used to manage each use case. The user begins by selecting a golf course in the first tab, which starts a new conversation and presents the user with an update form. The user then switches to the second tab and selects a different course, again resulting in a conversation being created and the rendering of an update form. Each tab now has its own conversation. The user then switches back to the first tab and clicks Save. The form values from that tab are sent to the server along with the conversation id. On the server, the conversation context is retrieved from the session using the conversation id. The course instance is pulled out of that conversation, the form values are applied to it, and finally it's synchronized to the database.

Although the two tabs are serving the same use case, with the same context variables, the data is kept isolated. Conversations don't suffer from leaky behavior because they aren't shared across all tabs and windows like the session. Instead, a conversation can be reserved for a single tab and restored on each request by passing the conversation id. As such, activity occurring in one tab doesn't affect other tabs (that use different conversations). Although conversations prevent unwanted sharing of data between separate use cases, sharing data across multiple requests in the same use case is a desirable feature of the conversation.

A BUSINESS TIER CACHE

The conversation context provides a natural caching mechanism that's readily controlled from the application, allowing cached data to be relinquished or refreshed in accordance with the business logic. You can even provide the user with controls that force the data to be refreshed on demand. If the conversation is abandoned, it's not long before this state is cleaned up by Seam (unlike with state stored in the HTTP session).

Caching data is critical because it avoids redundant data inquiries. If you cache database result sets, it means that you don't have to consult the database again when there's no expectation that the data has changed. You should take advantage of this opportunity because, of all the tiers in your application, the database tier is the least scalable. Don't abuse the database by repeatedly asking it to retrieve the same data over and over again. When the application fails to track data that it was already fed, it hurts the performance of both the database and the application.

Reducing load on the database is one of the primary concerns of an ORM. An ORM supports two levels of caching. The first-level cache, known as the persistence context, holds the collection of all entities retrieved by a single persistence manager, which you'll learn about in chapters 8 and 9. If the persistence manager is scoped to the conversation, then the ORM works naturally to reduce database load.

The second-level ORM cache is shared by the persistence managers and holds persistent objects previously loaded through any persistence context. It is used as a way to reduce traffic between the application and the database. Employing an intelligent algorithm, it attempts to keep the cache in sync with the changes made to the database. However, regardless of how good this logic is, within the scope of a use case, it lacks the business-level insight to know exactly when data should be considered stale. Expecting the second-level cache to make up for the application's inability to retain data is a misuse of the technology.

The need for a stateful context acting as an intermediary between the browser and the database is especially important in the world of Web 2.0, where Ajax requests are sent to the server at a rate that far exceeds the previous usage pattern of web applications. Requests that leverage the conversation context save database hits and are faster since they're returning data that's held close at hand. The conversation plays another important role in Ajax: preventing the requests from accessing data concurrently.

PREVENTING CONCURRENCY PROBLEMS

Seam serializes concurrent requests that access the same conversation. This means only one thread is allowed to access a conversation at any given time. In pre–Web 2.0 applications, this might help deal with a double submit, but when Ajax starts firing off requests like they are going out of business, the likelihood of your data entering an inconsistent state as a result of concurrent access dramatically increases. Seam keeps those Ajax requests in line, so you can be confident that conversation-scoped data won't be modified by a second incoming request while the first request is being served.

Conversations fit very naturally with Ajax. The combination of serialized access and stateful behavior drastically minimizes the risk of using Ajax in your application. With these mechanisms in place, you can rest assured that performance and data consistency won't suffer. You'll learn more about how well Seam and Ajax fit together in chapter 12.

Having explored ways in which the conversation context solves the need for a user-focused stateful context, let's examine the types of data you might typically store in a conversation as you prepare to use it.

7.2.2 *What you might store in a conversation*

The conversation provides a way for data to be stashed away during user "think" time—the time after the response is sent to the browser but before the user activates a link or submits a form. Additional information is accumulated in the conversation as the user moves from screen to screen. There are four classifications of data that a working set is used to store, all of which are demonstrated in this chapter:

- *Nonpersistent data*—An example of nonpersistent data is a set of search criteria or a collection of record identifiers. The user can establish the state in one request and then use it to retrieve data in the next. This category also includes configuration data (such as the page flow definition).
- *Transient entity data*—A transient entity instance may be built and populated as part of a wizard. Once the wizard is complete, the entity instance is drawn from the working set and persisted.
- *Managed entity data*—The working set provides an ideal way to work with database-managed entity data for the purpose of updating its fields. The entity instance is placed into the working set and then overlaid on a form. When the user submits the form, the form values are applied to the entity instance that's stored in the working set (whose object identity has been preserved) and the changes are flushed to the database transparently.
- *Resource sessions*—The conversation context offers an ideal mechanism for maintaining a reference to an enterprise resource. For instance, the persistence context (a JPA `EntityManager` or Hibernate `Session`) can be stored in the conversation to prevent entity instances from becoming detached prematurely. The next several chapters focus on how conversations benefit persistence management.

In this section you learned what we mean when we say *conversation*: a context for keeping data in scope for the duration of a use case and a means of enabling stateful behavior in your applications. The next step is to learn about the conversation life cycle and how to control conversations by defining conversation boundaries.

7.3 *Establishing conversation boundaries*

The conversation context is unique from other Seam contexts you have used so far in that it has explicit boundaries dictated by application logic, as opposed to implicit boundaries that correlate with a demarcation in the servlet or JSF life cycle. The boundaries of the conversation context are controlled using conversation propagation directives. This section introduces these directives and demonstrates how they're used to transition the state of a conversation and effectively manage its life cycle.

7.3.1   *A conversation's state*

A conversation actually has two states: temporary and long-running. There is also a third state, nested, which is a characteristic of the long-running state. Nested conversations are covered in section 7.4.2. Right now, I want to focus on the first two states.

Switching the state of a conversation is referred to as *conversation propagation*. When you set the boundaries of a conversation using the conversation propagation directives, you're not initiating and destroying the conversation, but rather transitioning it between a temporary and long-running state.

TEMPORARY VS. LONG-RUNNING CONVERSATIONS

Most of the time, when people talk about Seam conversations, they're referring to *long-running* conversations. The discussion in the early part of this chapter pertains to long-running conversations. A long-running conversation remains active over a series of requests in correlation with the transfer of the conversation id. In the absence of a long-running conversation, Seam creates a *temporary* conversation to serve the current request. A temporary conversation is initialized immediately following the *Restore View* phase of the JSF life cycle and is destroyed after the *Render Response* phase.

You can think of a temporary conversation as achieving the same result as the flash hash in Ruby on Rails: transporting data across a redirect. In Seam, the temporary conversation carries conversation-scoped context variables across a redirect that may occur during a JSF navigation event. This works by maintaining the temporary conversation until the redirect is complete. So to clarify, a temporary conversation is destroyed after the *Render Response* phase ends, even if it's preceded by a redirect. The most popular use of a temporary conversation is to keep JSF messages alive during the redirect-after-post pattern, assuming those messages are registered using Seam's built-in, conversation-scoped FacesMessages component.

The other purpose of a temporary conversation is to serve as a seed for a long-running conversation. A long-running conversation is nothing more than a temporary conversation whose termination has been postponed. This postponement lasts from the time the *begin* conversation directive is encountered up until the *end* conversation directive is met. Instead of just surviving a navigation redirect, a long-running conversation is capable of surviving a whole series of user interactions. Only when the conversation reacquires the temporary state is it scheduled to be terminated. In Seam, every request is part of a conversation. You just have to decide how long you want that conversation to last.

CONVERSATION PROPAGATION DIRECTIVES

Learning to use long-running conversations involves learning the conversation propagation directives, listed in table 7.1, and how they transform a temporary conversation to and from a long-running conversation. You can think of conversation propagation

Table 7.1   A list of the conversation propagation directives

Propagation type	Description
begin	Promotes a temporary conversation to a long-running conversation. An exception is thrown if a long-running conversation is already active.
join	Promotes a temporary conversation to a long-running conversation. No action is taken if a long-running conversation is already active.
end	Demotes a long-running conversation to a temporary conversation.
nest	If a long-running conversation is active, suspends it and adds a new, long-running conversation to the conversation stack. If a long-running conversation is not active, promotes the temporary conversation to a long-running conversation.
none	Abandons the current conversation. The previous conversation is left intact and a temporary conversation is created to serve the incoming request.

directives serving a parallel purpose for a conversation as transaction propagation directives do for a transaction.

The conversation propagation directives can be applied using the following means:

- Method-level annotations
- UI component tags
- Seam page descriptor
- Seam conversation API
- Stateful page flow descriptor (end conversation only)

These variants are provided to accommodate different usage and design scenarios, allowing you to establish conversation boundaries where it makes the most sense in your application. You'll learn to use the conversation propagation directives in the next section.

The conversation propagation directives dictate the life cycle of the conversation. Figure 7.4 diagrams this life cycle, showing how the state of the conversation changes during the request as a result of encountering a conversation propagation directive.

Let's step through the diagram in figure 7.4. At the start of the request, a long-running conversation is restored if the conversation id is detected among the request parameters. If the conversation id is absent or invalid, Seam initiates a new, temporary conversation. At any point during the processing of the request, the conversation may change state as the result of encountering a conversation propagation directive. The begin directive transitions a temporary conversation to long-running. The join directive has the same effect as begin, except that it can enter into an existing long-running conversation, whereas the begin directive raises an exception in this case. The nest directive can also begin a long-running conversation, but if one exists, a new conversation is created, temporarily suspending the existing one. The end directive sends the long-running conversation back to its temporary state. At the end of the request, the temporary conversation is destroyed, whereas the long-running conversation is tucked

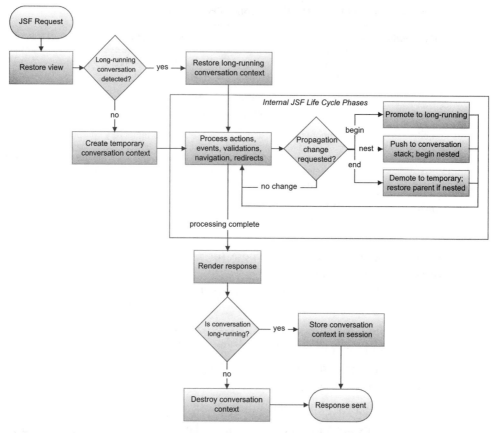

Figure 7.4   How the conversation propagation directives affect the conversation during a request

away in the HTTP session to be retrieved by a subsequent request. Although not shown, if the conversation being restored is invalid or has previously timed out, the user is notified and forwarded to a fallback page if one is configured.

Seam uses a built-in component to keep track of the conversation's state, including its relationships to nested and parent conversations. It's important to know that this component exists as you'll often find that you need to reference it.

THE CONVERSATION COMPONENT

Seam maintains the state of the conversation in an instance of the built-in conversation-scoped component named `conversation`. This component provides a wealth of information about the current conversation in the form of properties and exposes methods for acting on the conversation. These properties and methods are listed in table 7.2.

The most important property on the conversation component is the conversation id, which is typically accessed using the value expression `#{conversation.id}`. The conversation id is used to restore the conversation from the session at the beginning of a request. You'll see this expression used often in this chapter. The properties on the conversation component aid in making decisions about navigation or rendering

Table 7.2 The properties and methods on the built-in conversation component

Property	Type	Description
`id`	`String`	A value that identifies this conversation. This value is typically numeric, though business key identifiers are also supported.
`parentId`	`String`	The conversation id of the parent conversation of this nested conversation.
`rootId`	`String`	The conversation id of the primary (top-level) conversation of this nested conversation.
`description`	`String`	The descriptive name of the conversation evaluated from the expression value specified in the `<description>` node of the page entry.
`viewId`	`String`	The last JSF view ID that was rendered while this conversation was active.
`timeout`	`Integer`	The timeout period that must elapse after its last use for this conversation to be automatically garbage collected.
`longRunning`	`boolean`	A flag indicating whether this conversation is long-running.
`nested`	`boolean`	A flag indicating whether this conversation is nested.

Method	Purpose
`redirect()`	Switch back to the last known view ID for the current conversation.
`endAndRedirect()`	End the current nested conversation and redirect to the last known view ID for its parent conversation.
`endBeforeRedirect()`	End the current conversation and set the before redirect flag to true. Does not trigger an automatic redirect.
`end()`	End the current conversation and set the before redirect flag to false. Does not trigger an automatic redirect.
`leave()`	Step out of the current conversation. A new temporary conversation will be initialized and used for the duration of the request.
`begin()`	Start a new long-running conversation only if one is not already active. This method is equivalent to using the join directive.
`reallyBegin()`	Start a new long-running conversation without checking if one already exists. This method is equivalent to to using the begin directive.
`beginNested()`	Start a nested conversation by branching off the current long-running conversation. If a long-running conversation is not active, an exception will be thrown.
`pop()`	Switch to the parent conversation, leaving the current conversation intact. Does not trigger an automatic redirect.
`redirectToParent()`	Switch to the parent conversation, leaving the current conversation intact, and redirect to the last known view ID for the parent conversation.

Table 7.2   The properties and methods on the built-in conversation component

Method	Purpose
root()	Switch to the root level conversation, leaving the current conversation intact. Does not trigger an automatic redirect.
redirectToRoot()	Switch to the root level conversation, leaving the current conversation intact, and redirect to the last known view ID for the root conversation.

markup conditionally. The methods on the conversation component can change the conversation's state and are often used as page actions or as the action method on links and buttons.

With this component in hand, you're now ready to learn how to define the conversation boundaries. As you read through the next couple of sections, I encourage you to study the options you have for defining these boundaries, decide on a favorite approach, and try to adhere to it a majority of the time. Just because you can define each boundary a handful of ways doesn't mean you should use every single variation, at least not without good reason.

7.3.2   Beginning a long-running conversation

To demonstrate the use of a long-running conversation, let's work through an example of a multipage wizard that captures information about a golf course and adds it to the Open 18 directory. Entering data for a golf course can be quite intimidating, so a wizard is used to break up the form into short, logical steps, shown in figure 7.5. Each box in figure 7.5 represents a screen with a form to fill out. As the user moves from screen to screen, the information from previous screens must be accumulated and stored so that it's available when the final screen is complete and the course is persisted to the database.

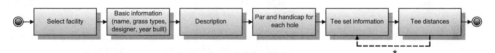

Figure 7.5   The wizard allows the user to enter a new golf course into the directory.

The textbook choice for starting conversations such as the golf course wizard is to add the @Begin annotation to the action method that spawns the wizard. However, there may be times when you need to start a conversation from a GET request, in which case either the <begin-conversation> page descriptor tag or a UI component tag is a more appropriate choice. The latter two may be attractive to you if you prefer to keep your navigation controls out of Java code or you need more fine-grained control over the conversation boundaries. As you read through this section, keep in mind that you need to begin the conversation only once, so these options are mutually exclusive. Let's start by looking at how to use the @Begin annotation.

AN ANNOTATION-BASED APPROACH

One of the method interceptors that Seam wraps around components is the `Conver-sationInterceptor`. This interceptor looks for the `@Begin` annotation on the component method that's being invoked. If it finds one, it converts the temporary conversation to long-running if the method completes successfully. See the accompanying sidebar.

> ### Seam's definition of success
>
> For many of Seam's annotations that designate an action to be performed, such as `@Begin` and `@End`, Seam only performs the action if the method completes successfully according to Seam's definition of success. For Seam to consider a method call successful, it must return without throwing an exception and it must return a non-null value unless it's a void method.

The `@Begin` annotation is outlined in table 7.3. The `pageflow` attribute is used to initiate a stateful page flow and is covered in section 7.6. The `flushMode` attribute is used to switch the flush mode of the persistence context when the conversation begins and can be used to initiate an application transaction as covered in chapter 9.

Table 7.3   The `@Begin` annotation

Name:	Begin
Purpose:	Instructs Seam to convert the temporary conversation to a long-running or nested state after this method is invoked successfully. See the sidebar "Seam's definition of success."
Target:	METHOD

Attribute	Type	Function
join	boolean	A true value allows this method to be invoked even when the conversation is already long-running. If the value is false, and the conversation is long-running, an exception is thrown. If the conversation is temporary, this attribute doesn't apply. Default: false.
nested	boolean	A true value suspends the conversation, if it is long-running, and starts a new, nested long-running conversation. If the conversation is temporary, it is simply converted to long-running. This attribute is mutually exclusive with join. Default: false.
pageflow	String	The name of the page flow descriptor that is to be used to manage the stateful navigation for this conversation. Default: none.
flushMode	FlushModeType	Changes the flush mode of the Seam-managed persistence contexts in this conversation when the conversation begins. Default: AUTO.

Let's use the `@Begin` annotation to initiate a long-running conversation for the course wizard by placing it on the `addCourse()` method. This method is invoked at the start of the course wizard, beginning a long-running conversation. It also outjects the `course` property into the conversation context, making it available throughout the wizard:

```
@Name("courseWizard")
@Scope(ScopeType.CONVERSATION)
public class CourseWizard implements Serializable {
    @In protected EntityManager entityManager;
    @RequestParameter protected Long facilityId;        ⎤ Outjects to
    @Out protected Course course;                    ◁──⎦ conversation context

    @Begin public void addCourse() {    ◁── Begins long-running conversation
        course = new Course();
        course.setFacility(entityManager.find(Facility.class, facilityId));
    }
}
```

To start the course wizard, the user navigates to the detail page of a facility, then clicks a command button that calls the addCourse() method and passes the id of the facility:

```
<s:button action="#{courseWizard.addCourse}" value="Add course...">
  <f:param name="facilityId" value="#{facilityHome.instance.id}"/>
</s:button>
```

The following navigation rule is defined to advance the user to the first screen in the wizard:

```
<page view-id="/Facility.xhtml">
  <navigation from-action="#{courseWizard.addCourse}">
    <render view-id="/coursewizard/basicCourseInfo.xhtml"/>
  </navigation>
</page>
```

The @Begin annotation isn't limited to action methods. You can also add it to a method used as a page action; combine it with a life-cycle annotation, such as @Create; or tie it to a @Factory method. These options allow the long-running conversation to start at various points in the Seam life cycle. Remember, it doesn't matter when the state of the conversation changes during the request, but rather what the state of the conversation is when the request is complete.

Instead of using a UI command button to activate the addCourse() method, you could trigger this method by registering it as a page action on the opening screen in the wizard:

```
<page view-id="/coursewizard/basicCourseInfo.xhtml"
  action="#{courseWizard.addCourse}"/>
```

In this case, when the servlet path /coursewizard/basicCourseInfo.seam?facilityId=3 is requested in the browser, the addCourse() method is invoked and a long-running conversation is started. The benefit of using a page action is that it can start a long-running conversation from a bookmarked page or direct link, rather than waiting for a JSF postback. Starting a conversation from a page request may require additional logic either to prevent excessive conversation creation or to enable conversation joining, both of which are covered later on.

You also have the option of defining a factory method for the course context variable. When the course context variable is looked up by the first screen in the wizard through a factory, a long-running conversation can be started:

```
@Begin @Factory("course")
public void initCourse() {
    course = new Course();
    course.setFacility(entityManager.find(Facility.class, facilityId));
}
```

Factory methods are a good place to start conversations because they don't require user interaction, nor do they require XML to be defined in the page descriptor. The same goes for the @Create life-cycle method. You can also have the conversation begin the very first time the CourseWizard component is accessed:

```
@Begin @Create
public Course initCourse() {
    course = new Course();
    course.setFacility(entityManager.find(Facility.class, facilityId));
}
```

If you fancy those angled brackets, you might instead find the page descriptor to be an ideal place to begin a long-running conversation, which we look at next.

A PAGE-ORIENTED APPROACH

One way to start a long-running conversation in a page-oriented manner is by using a @Begin method as a page action. However, the task of starting a long-running conversation when a page is requested is so common that Seam includes two built-in options. You can either use the method-binding expression #{conversation.begin} in a page action or nest the <begin-conversation> page descriptor tag with a <page> node. The <begin-conversation> tag can also be used during a page transition.

Let's start by applying the <begin-conversation> tag to a page transition. We'll assume that the command button shown earlier is activated, but the action method doesn't have the @Begin annotation. Instead, the following navigation rule will start a long-running conversation, then direct the user to the first screen in the wizard:

```
<page view-id="/Facility.xhtml">
  <navigation from-action="#{courseWizard.addCourse}">
    <begin-conversation/>
    <redirect view-id="/coursewizard/basicCourseInfo.xhtml"/>
  </navigation>
</page>
```

If you want to preclude the use of the command button, you can instead declare the long-running conversation to begin when the /coursewizard/basicCourseInfo.xhtml view ID is requested. This is done either by using the begin() method on the built-in conversation component:

```
<page view-id="/coursewizard/basicCourseInfo.xhtml"
  action="#{conversation.begin}"/>
```

or by nesting the <begin-conversation> tag directly inside the <page> node:

```
<page view-id="/coursewizard/basicCourseInfo.xhtml">
  <begin-conversation/>
</page>
```

If a fine-grained page descriptor is associated with the first screen of the wizard, /coursewizard/basicCourseInfo.page.xml, you could exclude the `view-id` attribute, thus simplifying the declaration to

```
<page>
  <begin-conversion/>
</page>
```

The only downside of using the built-in page action alone is that you can't perform "prep work" in a component method before the first page is rendered. The `addCourse()` method, for instance, initializes and outjects the `course` context variable. The built-in page action is best suited for simply "turning on" a conversation.

The page descriptor offers a lot of control for defining conversation boundaries because you can distinguish between initial requests, postbacks, and even action method outcomes. However, you may want to be able to associate the start of a long-running conversation with a link or button directly. For that, you can use any of the tags from Seam's JSF component library to control the boundaries of the conversation.

A UI COMPONENT TAG APPROACH

As a third option, you can begin a long-running conversation using one of Seam's UI component tags. You can either enhance an existing UI command component with conversation propagation capabilities by adding a nested `<s:conversationPropagation>` tag, or you can use one of Seam's command components, `<s:link>` or `<s:button>`, both of which have native support for conversation propagation. The propagation value, assigned using the `type` attribute on the `<s:conversationPropagation>` tag and the `propagation` attribute on the command tags, can be any of the values listed in table 7.1, and is therefore not limited to beginning a long-running conversation.

Seam reads a request parameter named `conversationPropagation` to decide how to address the current conversation. This request parameter is passed either through the query string of the URL or in the POST data. Rather than having to add this parameter yourself, you can use the component tags cited here to add it for you, which abstracts away the name so that it's not hard-coded in your source code. If you need to use a custom `UICommand` component or submit a JSF form when starting the conversation, you can add a nested `<s:conversationPropagation>` tag to any UI command component tag to give it conversation propagation abilities. Let's assume the facility list page includes a link in each row to start the course wizard for that facility (citing a slightly different use case here), passing the iteration variable, `_facility`, as a parameter:

```
<h:commandButton action="#{courseWizard.addCourse(_facility)}"
  value="Add course...">
  <s:conversationPropagation type="begin"/>
</h:commandButton>
```

Instead of using the `<s:conversationPropagation>` tag as a nested element in a regular JSF component tag, you can use the Seam command tags to specify the conversation propagation using the `propagation` attribute:

```
<s:button action="#{courseWizard.addCourse(_facility)}"
  propagation="begin" value="Add course..."/>
```

In the event that you don't need to submit a form, the command tags are a great way to work with conversations because they have propagation controls built right in and they automatically pass along the conversation token. That adds to the previously mentioned benefits of the command tags to produce bookmarkable URLs (covered in chapter 3).

If you've been experimenting with the begin directive while reading this section, you may have encountered an error message reporting that a long-running conversation can't be created because one is already active. To remedy this problem, you need to know about conversation joining and how to enable it.

ENABLING CONVERSATION JOINING

By default, Seam only begins a long-running conversation if one isn't already in play. A long-running conversation is active if it was restored from a previous request or if a begin directive has already been encountered. In either case, if an attempt to cross the begin threshold happens again in the same request, Seam throws an exception. That's because, by default, conversation joining is disabled.

This restriction could cause undue errors if it's possible for the user to navigate through one of the defined conversation boundaries after having already entered into a long-running conversation. For example, assume that you're using the <begin-conversation> page directive to begin a long-running conversation when the first page in the course wizard is requested. If the user submits the form on that page, and validation errors are found, when JSF attempts to redisplay the page, an exception will be thrown because the <begin-conversation> element is once again encountered, this time in the presence of a long-running conversation.

There are numerous other situations where the user's action attempts to begin a new long-running conversation when one already exists. This situation isn't that rare in applications that use free-form navigation since the possible execution paths are numerous. Unless you have a good reason not to allow conversation joining, always use the join directive to avoid surprising your user with erroneous exceptions. The truth is, the join behavior should probably be the default. In the absence of a long-running conversation, the join directive acts just like the begin directive, without risking an exception.

If you're using the annotation-based approach to setting conversation boundaries, you enable joining of an existing long-running conversation by setting the join attribute on @Begin to true:

```
@Begin(join = true)
public void addCourse() { ... }
```

If you're using the page-oriented approach to mark the boundaries of your conversation, you add the join attribute to the <begin-conversation> element:

```
<page view-id="/Facility.xhtml">
  <navigation from-action="#{courseWizard.addCourse}">
    <begin-conversation join="true"/>
    <redirect view-id="/coursewizard/basicCourseInfo.xhtml"/>
  </navigation>
</page>
```

The `<begin-conversation>` element can be applied conditionally using the `if` attribute. The following declaration has the same effect as a join, made possible by consulting the conversation component to determine whether the conversation is long-running:

```
<page view-id="/Facility.xhtml">
  <navigation from-action="#{courseWizard.addCourse}">
    <begin-conversation if="#{!conversation.longRunning}"/>
    <redirect view-id="/coursewizard/basicCourseInfo.xhtml"/>
  </navigation>
</page>
```

The support for conditions is useful as your pages mature, serving more variant use cases with different entrances and exits. Your only limit is what the EL can tell you.

If you're using the built-in conversation control `#{conversation.begin}` in a page action, you don't have to worry about the join flag since the method called by this expression is already "join safe."

Finally, if you're using the UI component tag approach, you enable conversation joining by setting the value of the `propagation` to `join`:

```
<s:button action="#{courseWizard.addCourse}" propagation="join"
  value="Add course...">
  <f:param name="facilityId" value="#{facilityHome.instance.id}"/>
</s:button>
```

I realize that all of these options may have been a tad overwhelming. My goal was to help you appreciate how flexible Seam is when it comes to setting the boundaries of a long-running conversation. As you might expect, there are just as many options for declaring the end of a long-running conversation. Since they follow the same patterns, learning to use them should be easy.

AUTHOR NOTE   I have determined that controlling conversations using the page descriptor works best for page-oriented applications, whereas the annotations are best suited for single-page, Ajax-based applications. Despite my recommendation, there's no hard-and-fast rule.

All this work of striking up a long-running conversation is only useful if you can keep the conversation going. Let's see how the conversation is carried on to the next request.

7.3.3   *Keeping the conversation going*

Data stored in a long-running conversation is only available to a subsequent request if the long-running conversation holding that data is restored. The secret to restoring a conversation is to pass on its conversation id to the next request using the conversation token. Depending on the style of the request, the conversation token may be passed as a request parameter or tucked away in the JSF component tree. In either case, when Seam detects the conversation token in the request, the value is used to look up the existing long-running conversation from the session context and restore it, thus preventing a new temporary conversation from being spawned.

If passing the conversation token sounds like tedious work, there's good news. This task is handled automatically by any JSF postback or Seam UI command component.

Thus, pages don't even need to be aware of the fact that they're participating in a long-running conversation. We've sure come a long way from managing hidden form fields manually!

Let's consider the two styles of restoring the long-running conversation.

CONVERSATIONS ON POSTBACK

In the presence of a long-running conversation, Seam stores the conversation token in a page-scoped component, leveraging the state-saving feature of JSF. Any subsequent JSF postback gives Seam access to this page-scoped component and thus the conversation token. You don't have to change anything about how you define UI command components to enable this behavior:

```
<h:commandButton value="Next"
  action="#{courseWizard.submitBasicCourseInfo}"/>
```

Notice that there's no indication of the conversation token. In fact, if you view the source of the rendered page, you won't find the conversation token there either. The hand-off takes place completely behind the scenes.

For JSF postbacks, passing the conversation id through the page scope is convenient, but what about non-JSF postbacks that don't carry the page scope? These requests require an alternative means of communicating the conversation token. That brings us to the conversation id parameter, which Seam uses to restore a conversation on a GET request.

RESTORING A CONVERSATION FROM A GET REQUEST

Seam can't read your thoughts, so unless you explicitly pass a conversation token to tell it which conversation to restore, a new temporary conversation is created. Earlier I told you that Seam's UI command components can be used to control the conversation. Knowing that these components are designed to issue a GET request rather than a JSF postback, it's clear that they must send along the conversation id in the URL. Thus, to restore a conversation from a GET request, you can simply use a Seam UI command component.

Let's say that, at any point in the course wizard, you want to allow users to be able to view a summary in a preview window of what they've entered so far. The following link will open the preview window and give it access to the long-running conversation used by the course wizard:

```
<s:link view="preview.xhtml" target="_blank" value="Preview"/>
```

While I'm tempted to tell you not to worry about how this works, I trust that if you've gotten this far, you are one of those developers who wants to know (if you don't, skip on to the next section).

At the beginning of the Seam life cycle, Seam looks for the conversation id in a URL parameter. The default name for this parameter is conversationId. You also know that the current conversation id can be retrieved from the value expression #{conversation.id}. Putting these two facts together, you can manually assemble the link shown previously:

```
<a href="preview.seam?conversationId=#{conversation.id}"
  target="_blank">Preview</a>
```

Alternatively, you can get a little help from JSF to build the link:

```
<h:outputLink value="preview.seam" target="_blank">
  <f:param name="conversationId" value="#{conversation.id}"/>
  <h:outputText value="Preview"/>
</h:outputLink>
```

There's a serious flaw in the previous two links. Seam allows the name of the conversation parameter to be customized, but these links hard-code the default name, conversationId. The name used for the conversation token is set using the conversationIdParameter property on the built-in component named manager. You can override the name of the conversation token using this component configuration:

```
<core:manager conversation-id-parameter="cid"/>
```

With this override in place, any links with a hard-coded conversationId parameter will no longer perpetuate the long-running conversation. Fortunately, Seam provides a special UIParameter component tag, <s:conversationId>, that can be used to add the conversation id parameter to the parent JSF link component:

```
<h:outputLink value="preview.seam" target="_blank">
  <s:conversationId/>
  <h:outputText value="Preview"/>
</h:outputLink>
```

I recommend that you stick to using Seam's UI command components unless you have a good reason not to. Then again, the conversation token is not just useful for creating links and buttons; it also lets you restore the conversation through alternate channels, such as Ajax requests and conversational web services. Remember that the conversation token is the key to the storage locker holding the conversation's working set of context variables.

You have now struck up a long-running conversation and learned how to navigate within its boundaries. Let's consider how to take advantage of this working set by contributing to it on one screen and accessing it from another.

7.3.4   *Enlisting objects in a conversation*

You enlist objects in a conversation by storing them in the conversation context. When you see that a component is scoped to the conversation context, or that a value is outjected to the conversation context, you might think to yourself, "But which conversation?"

FINDING A CONVERSATION TO JOIN

As you've learned, there's always a conversation active during a request, whether it be temporary or long-running—but only one. A request can serve only a single conversation at a time, even though it's possible for concurrent conversations to exist in the background, as you'll discover later on. The conversation to which component instances and outjected context variables are bound is the one that's active for this request.

What you may find interesting—perhaps even surprising—is that a temporary conversation doesn't need to be converted to a long-running conversation before you can start adding objects to it. Any variables added to the conversation while it is temporary remain part of the conversation once it transitions to long-running. The conversation state is simply an indicator that determines whether the conversation should be stored in the session (long-running) or removed (temporary) after the *Render Response* phase.

You should be able to put this knowledge together with what you've learned about component instantiation to conclude that when a conversation-scoped component is requested via its component name, an instance is created and attached to the active conversation. Table 7.4 shows how the conversation is populated as the course wizard is launched, assuming the addCourse() method is annotated with @Begin.

Table 7.4 How the conversation is populated when the course wizard is launched

Step	Description
1. User activates the JSF command button	The JSF life cycle is invoked, the #{courseWizard.addCourse} action is queued, and a temporary conversation is created. The *Invoke Application* phase is entered.
2. Action method is invoked	CourseWizard is instantiated and bound to the courseWizard context variable in the conversation context. The addCourse() method call begins. Course is instantiated and assigned to the protected field course. The addCourse() method call ends. course is outjected into the conversation context and the temporary conversation is promoted to a long-running conversation.
3. Navigation rule fires	The *Render Response* phase is entered and the first screen of the course wizard is rendered. The long-running conversation is stored in the HTTP session and the conversation id is stored in the JSF UI component tree.

When the initial request in the course wizard ends, there are two new context variables in the conversation: courseWizard and course. The course context variable is placed into the conversation scope after the addCourse() method completes as a result of outjection. The conversation scope is used since no scope is specified in the @Out annotation and the component is scoped to the conversation. For the duration of the wizard, the course context variable remains in the conversation and is progressively populated with each form submission as the wizard progresses.

CONVERSATIONS IN ISOLATION

If the user were to open a new browser tab and initiate the course wizard, the process in table 7.4 would occur in a parallel conversation (assuming, of course, that the URL requested didn't include the conversation token from the first tab). The conversation activity taking place in the second tab would happen in an isolated area of the session managing that conversation. With the course wizard under way in both tabs, the same two context variables, courseWizard and course, exist in each of the two conversations, but don't interfere with one another—two conversations, two sets of variables.

TIP   You can see what context variables are stored in each conversation using the Seam debug page. Ensure that debug mode is enabled (see chapter 3) and then visit the servlet path /debug.seam to get the list of conversations. Click on a conversation to inspect it.

Note that the component that hosts the @Begin method doesn't have to be a conversation-scoped component. You could begin the conversation for the course wizard using an event-scoped component and set the scope of the outjection explicitly:

```
@Name("courseWizard")
public class CourseWizard {
    ...
    @Out(scope = ScopeType.CONVERSATION)
    protected Course course;
    ...
    @Begin public void addCourse() { ... }
}
```

In this case, only the course context variable is placed into the conversation after a method is invoked. The scope on the @Out annotation must be set to conversation to override the default of event inherited from the scope of the component.

Instead of beginning or ending a long-running conversation when a component method is invoked, you may simply want to verify that a long-running conversation exists before allowing the method to proceed. Let's see how to enforce this requirement.

MAKING THE CONVERSATION A PREREQUISITE

If you want to enforce that a component or method only be used within the scope of a long-running conversation, annotate the component class or the method with the @Conversational annotation, summarized in table 7.5. Seam verifies that the conversation is long-running before permitting a call to the following method:

```
@Conversational public String submitBasicCourseInfo() { ... }
```

If an attempt is made to execute a @Conversational method outside the presence of a long-running conversation, Seam will raise the org.jboss.seam.noConversation event and then throw the runtime exception NoConversationException.

Table 7.5   The @Conversational annotation

Name:	Conversational
Purpose:	Specifies that this component or method is conversational and the method(s) can only be invoked within the scope of a long-running conversation
Target:	TYPE (class), METHOD

Using this annotation is superficial in most cases since there's likely more to the story than just the existence of a conversation. If you're simply trying to protect a sensitive area of the code, perhaps using this annotation makes sense. You can also enforce the presence of a long-running conversation when a view is rendered. This restriction is configured on the page node that matches the view ID being rendered:

```
<page conversation-required="true"
  no-conversation-view-id="/FacilityList.xhtml"> ... </page>
```

Once again, if a long-running conversation isn't active or has expired when the view ID is requested, the `org.jboss.seam.noConversation` event is raised. However, in this case, the user is redirected to the view ID defined in the `no-conversation-view-id` attribute. In section 7.6 you'll learn that a page flow is a much better way to enforce the existence of a conversation, whether it's at the method or view ID level.

One of the key benefits of conversations is that they can be cleaned up easily. Having learned to fear the session, you may be uneasy about letting data accumulate in the conversation. Let's first consider how to pull context variables out of a conversation and then move on to ending the conversation when the use case is finished.

UNREGISTERING CONVERSATION-SCOPED CONTEXT VARIABLES

Any objects associated with a conversation are held in the conversation context until the conversation ends or the object is explicitly removed from the conversation context. If the conversation is ongoing but there are certain conversation-scoped context variables that you no longer need, you can clear them out of the conversation in one of two ways:

- Set the value of the property annotated with `@Out(required = false)` to null.
- Remove the context variable using the Seam Context API.

Let's consider an example. In the course wizard, the `saveHoleData()` method outjects a temporary `TeeSet` instance to the `teeSet` context variable, which is used by the tee set form to capture information about the tee set. Only when that form is submitted with no validation errors is the `saveTeeSet()` method called, which appends the `TeeSet` to the managed `Course` instance held in the conversation. At that time, the `teeSet` context variable can be cleared from the conversation by assigning the `teeSet` property a null value. The required attribute on the `@Out` annotation is set to false to permit the value to be null:

```
@Out(required = false)
protected TeeSet teeSet;

public void submitHoleData() {
    teeSet = new TeeSet();
}

public void submitTeeSet() {
    course.getTeeSets().add(teeSet);
    teeSet = null;
}
```

Another way to clear a context variable from the conversation is to retrieve the conversation context via the Seam Context API and explicitly remove the context variable:

```
Contexts.getConversationContext().remove("teeSet");
```

The best way to ensure that conversation-scope context variables are cleaned up is to just end the conversation. Leaving conversations active isn't dangerous like letting objects linger in the session because Seam regularly cleans out stale conversations. However, ending a conversation may play an important role in wrapping up the use case.

7.3.5 · Ending a long-running conversation

As you've learned, conversations are a managed region of the HTTP session. Thus, it's possible to terminate a conversation without destroying the entire session. A conversation can either be ended explicitly using an end propagation directive or it can be automatically garbage collected by Seam when its idle time exceeds the timeout value of the conversation.

The end propagation directive is used in the same way as the begin directive. One use case for ending a conversation is to let the user cancel out of a form or wizard. In this case, you discard the conversation and return the user to a screen of your choice, perhaps by using a Seam UI command component:

```
<s:link view="/FacilityList.xhtml" propagation="end" value="Cancel"/>
```

However, if you prefer to keep your conversation directives out of the JSF views, you can use the pages.xml configuration instead:

```
<page view-id="/coursewizard/*">
  <navigation>
    <rule if-outcome="cancel">
      <end-conversation/>
      <redirect view-id="/FacilityList.xhtml"/>
    </rule>
  </navigation>
</page>
```

Pair this navigation rule with the following Seam UI command component:

```
<s:link action="cancel" value="Cancel"/>
```

If you were to instead use a UI command component, you would need to set the immediate attribute to true to prevent the form values from being processed:

```
<h:commandLink action="cancel" value="Cancel" immediate="true"/>
```

Note that the term *end* is deceptive. Ending a conversation merely demotes it from long-running to temporary—it doesn't destroy it outright. It's terminated only *after* the view has been rendered. That means that whatever values were present in the conversation remain available in the *Render Response* phase that immediately follows the demotion.

If you want to part ways with the conversation before the next render, you set the beforeRedirect flag on the end conversation directive and then issue a redirect after demotion has taken place:

```
<page view-id="/coursewizard/*">
  <navigation>
    <rule if-outcome="cancel">
      <end-conversation before-redirect="true"/>
      <redirect view-id="/FacilityList.xhtml"/>
    </rule>
  </navigation>
</page>
```

Having become a temporary conversation, it won't last through the redirect and the next page view will be using a fresh conversation. Be careful using the `before-Redirect` flag, though, because you'll lose any JSF status messages that you added in the action method. An alternative is to use a confirmation page that displays the status messages. Navigating away from the confirmation page leaves behind the conversation that ended.

Assume that the user made it all the way through the wizard and is ready to save the new course. This case is perfect for showing the use of the `@End` annotation. Let's place a command button on the last page that invokes the `save()` method:

```
<h:commandButton action="#{courseWizard.save}" value="Save"/>
```

Next, add the `@End` annotation to the `save()` method so that the conversation is demoted to temporary when the method call is complete:

```
@End public String save() {
    try {
        ...
        entityManager.persist(course);
        FacesMessages.instance().add(
            "#{course.name} has been added to the directory.");
        return "success";
    } catch (Exception e) {
        FacesMessages.instance().add("Saving the course failed.");
        return null;
    }
}
```

The `course` context variable is available to the confirmation page since the conversation isn't ended prior to the redirect. If an exception is thrown, the conversation isn't ended at all and the previous page is redisplayed. The `@End` annotation is summarized in table 7.6.

Table 7.6 The @End annotation

Name:	End	
Purpose:	Instructs Seam to convert the long-running conversation to a temporary state after this method is invoked successfully	
Target:	METHOD	

Attribute	Type	Function
beforeRedirect	boolean	If set to true, instructs Seam to terminate the conversation prior to issuing a redirect. The default is to propagate the conversation across the redirect and terminate it once the response is complete. Default: false.

Alternatively, you may want to end the conversation using the `<end-conversation>` element in the page descriptor rather than using the `@End` annotation:

```
<page view-id="/coursewizard/*">
  <navigation from-action="#{courseWizard.save}">
    <rule if-outcome="success">
      <end-conversation/>
```

```
        <redirect view-id="/coursewizard/summary.xhtml"/>
      </rule>
    </navigation>
  </page>
```

In this case, the conversation is maintained across the redirect. You can set the before-Redirect attribute on the <end-conversation> element to true to have the conversation terminated before the redirect.

CONVERSATION TIMEOUTS

The other, less graceful way of terminating a conversation it to allow it to expire. The default timeout period of the conversation is stored in the built-in component named manager. The timeout is specified in milliseconds. The following component configuration overrides the default timeout of ten minutes, setting it instead to a period of one hour:

```
<core:manager conversation-timeout="3600000"/>
```

You can customize this value by setting the timeout attribute on the <page> node in the page descriptor. This lets you modify the timeout period per view ID, so you can give the user more time to fill out a more complex form:

```
<page view-id="/coursewizard/holeData.xhtml" timeout="7200000"/>
```

You also have the option of assigning a timeout value for a particular conversation by calling the setTimeout() method on the built-in conversation component.

A conversation will eventually time out if the user walks away from the computer. It's also possible for the current long-running conversation to be abandoned as the result of ad hoc navigation, at which point it's also subject to timeout. Let's consider how conversations get abandoned and why it's not necessarily a bad occurrence. You'll also see how to suspend a conversation, just as a transaction might be suspended, to allow the user to perform more granular work in a nested conversation. The parent conversation is restored when the nested conversation ends.

7.4   *Putting the conversation aside*

So far we have talked about how to begin, restore, and end a long-running conversation, but what happens to the conversation when it's not propagated to the next request? In that case, the conversation simply sits idle in the background. You can think of it as stepping outside of the conversation. It's also possible to step out of a conversation by spinning off a nested conversation. Let's explore these two cases.

7.4.1   *Abandoning a conversation*

It's understandable why a conversation is abandoned when the user leaves the application. But there's also good reason to intentionally abandon a conversation. Although the stateful behavior that conversations provide for have nice benefits, sometimes the conversation just needs to be set aside to do something else. This section explores how to get away from the current long-running conversation to move on to a separate use case, regardless of whether there is intention of returning to it. Note, however, that once a conversation is abandoned, it may eventually time out if not restored in a timely manner.

Suppose we want to give the user the option to pick up other tasks while in the midst of using the course wizard, perhaps even to start a second wizard process. When transitioning to the start of the wizard, you don't want to go into it using the existing conversation. You can break ties with that conversation by using the propagation directive none. For now, don't worry about how to get back to the partially complete wizard (that comes later when you study conversation switchers).

To disable propagation, you can use either the `<s:conversationPropagation>` component tag inside a UI command component or the `propagation` attribute if you're using a Seam command component tag. The none directive is necessary in both cases since the conversation token is added automatically by these tags. This directive prevents the conversation token from being appended, effectively warding off the conversation. The following link is used from within the wizard to start a new instance of the course wizard reusing the same facility:

```
<s:link action="#{courseWizard.addCourse}" propagation="none"
  value="Add course...">
  <f:param name="facilityId" value="#{course.facility.id}"/>
</s:link>
```

Another way to get away from the current long-running conversation is to use the `leave()` method on the conversation component as an action listener. This method can be used as an action listener thanks to the Seam EL, which makes the Action-Event parameter optional. This method has the same effect as the none propagation directive:

```
<s:link action="#{courseWizard.addCourse}"
  actionListener="#{conversation.leave}"
  value="Add course...">
  <f:param name="facilityId" value="#{course.facility.id}"/>
</s:link>
```

Links created by `<h:outputLink>` have no awareness of the current long-running conversation, so abandoning a conversation in those cases is just a matter of leaving off the nested `<s:conversationId>` tag.

If you get to the end of the use case and no longer need the current long-running conversation, it's usually best to end the conversation properly rather than abandon it. However, if you're not ready to call it quits, then abandoning the conversation is the appropriate choice. Before deciding to abandon a conversation to allow the user to go off on a tangent, consider whether it's more appropriate to suspend the current long-running conversation by nesting a new long-running conversation within it.

7.4.2 Creating nested conversations

Nested conversations allow you to suspend a long-running conversation, isolating context variables within the scope of a new, self-contained conversation. A nested conversation maintains a reference to its parent conversation and can even access its context variables. When the nested conversation ends, the parent conversation is automatically restored.

BRANCHING OFF THE MAINLINE

Nested conversations share similar semantics with child processes in an operating system. When you begin a nested conversation, you're effectively suspending the state of the current long-running conversation and starting a new long-running conversation with its boundaries. This branching process is illustrated in figure 7.6. As you can see, more than one nested (child) conversation can exist concurrently within a parent conversation. When the nested conversation is terminated, the parent conversation is popped back into place. When that happens, Seam may even redirect the user back to the page where the branch occurred, depending on the configuration. If the parent conversation is terminated, so are all of its children. Conversations can be nested to arbitrary depth, so a nested conversation can itself be a parent to another nested conversation. Seam maintains a stack of these nested conversations, which you learn about later in the section.

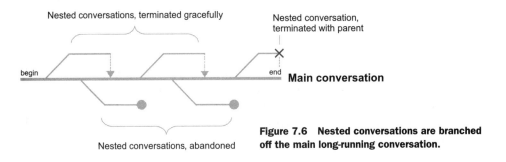

Figure 7.6   Nested conversations are branched off the main long-running conversation.

Context variables in the parent conversation are visible to the nested conversation, but the nested conversation cannot alter this set. In fact, if the nested conversation sets a context variable with the same name as one in the parent conversation, the result is that the variable in the nested conversation shadows its namesake in the parent conversation. Although it appears that the context variable has been reassigned, when the nested conversation ends, the shadowed value of the context variable is once again revealed.

NOTE   Although the nested conversation cannot alter the set of context variables in the parent conversation, the objects bound to those variables are mutable.

It's time to start branching! Let's consider cases when nested conversations are useful.

WHEN TO USE NESTED CONVERSATIONS

You typically use a nested conversation when you want to allow users to maintain their proverbial spot in line while they go do something else. Keeping that spot in line means not destroying the existing conversation and perhaps sharing its position (its state).

NOTE When an isolated conversation is required, you should think hard about whether it's more appropriate to branch the current conversation (`prop-agation="nest"`) or abandon it (`propagation="none"`) and begin a brand-new conversation. Both have pluses and minuses.

Let's say that, while working through the course wizard, the user realizes the information about the course's facility is incorrect. While the error is fresh in the user's mind, you want the user to be able to pause the course wizard and go update the facility. As it stands now, editing a facility joins the existing conversation. When the user saves the facility, the conversation ends. However, you don't want the conversation for the course wizard to end too. Instead, you want to return users to the course wizard and let them continue as though they never left. Keeping the use cases isolated, yet linked, calls for a nested conversation.

A nested conversation is started whenever the nested propagation directive is encountered and is ended the same way as a regular conversation. To use a nested conversation for the facility editor, we need to change the FacilityEdit.page.xml descriptor so that a nested conversation is started upon entry to the page:

```
<begin-conversation nested="true"/>
```

If there's no long-running conversation available at the time, the nested directive has the same effect as the begin directive. However, you can't join and nest at the same time. If the current conversation is long-running, Seam begins a nested conversation, even if the current conversation is itself a nested conversation. That means each time the user performs a postback, it's going to spawn yet another nested conversation. We prevent Seam from beginning a nested conversation if one already exists by using a conditional on the `<begin-conversation>` element in the FacilityEdit.page.xml descriptor:

```
<begin-conversation nested="true" if="#{!conversation.nested}"/>
```

Now, when the user clicks Save on the facility editor screen, the nested conversation is ended and the long-running conversation that manages the course wizard is restored.

WARNING Page flows, covered in section 7.6, enforce a strict navigation path. To spawn a nested conversation from a page flow, it must be configured as part of the page flow definition. Another option for initiating a parallel task is to abandon the page flow's conversation.

However, we're not quite done yet. The most critical part of letting users go off on a tangent is to return them to where they left off. If the navigation is unpredictable, users will be hesitant to branch out for fear they cannot easily get back to the current page. Let's see how to let users restore their place in line when the nested conversation is closed.

RETURNING TO THE BRANCH POINT
When a long-running conversation begins, Seam initializes a conversation stack and adds the conversation to the base of the stack. This first entry is known as the root conversation. Each time a branch occurs, Seam adds the nested conversation onto the stack. Thus, each entry added to the stack is a child of the previous. When a nested

conversation is ended, using the end propagation directive, Seam "pops" the conversation stack, restoring the previous entry—the parent conversation—into the foreground as the current conversation.

By maintaining the conversation stack, Seam relieves the burden on the developer of tracing the user's steps. But it does more than that. As part of this conversation stack, Seam keeps track of the last view ID visited by each conversation (at the branch point). This makes it possible to redirect the user back to the branch point when the nested conversation ends. However, Seam doesn't automatically perform this routing—it requires some work on your part. Fortunately, Seam offers assistance.

To get the user back on track, you can use the endAndRedirect() method on the conversation component (i.e., #{conversation.endAndRedirect}). This method ends the nested conversation and, if the view ID where the nested conversation was spawned is known, redirects the user back to that page. For instance, this method can be used as the action of the cancel button to get the user back to the current page in the course wizard:

```
<s:button action="#{conversation.endAndRedirect}" value="Cancel"
  rendered="#{conversation.nested}"/>
```

Combining this functionality with a form submission, such as the Save operation, requires calling the endAndRedirect() method from within the action method. This ensures that the end and redirect only occurs if the business logic completes. It also bypasses the navigation rules. For instance, you could weave this logic into the update() method on the FacilityHome component:

```
@In private Conversation conversation;

public String update() {
    String outcome = super.update();
    if (conversation.isNested()) {
        conversation.endAndRedirect();
    }
    return outcome;
}
```

This feature also comes in handy when you're developing breadcrumb-link navigation. For instance, suppose you want to allow users to spawn a nested conversation from the course page to view a related course. From there, the cycle may continue. To allow the user to back up to the previous course—without needing to use the browser back button—you can use the end-and-redirect behavior. Let's assume that the context variable nearbyCourses holds a list of courses in close proximity to the current course. To allow the user to navigate to one of these courses using a nested conversation, you create a link for each related course:

```
<ui:repeat var="_course" value="#{nearbyCourses}">
  <s:link view="/Course.xhtml" value="#{_course.name}" propagation="nest">
    <f:param name="courseId" value="#{_course.id}"/>
  </s:link>
</ui:repeat>
```

When the user navigates to a nearby course, the conversation is nested. On the course detail page, a link is provided to return the user to the previously viewed course if a nested conversation is active:

```
<s:link action="#{conversation.endAndRedirect}"
    value="Return to previous" rendered="#{conversation.nested}"/>
```

This nested conversation example is the first you have seen of shuffling conversations. Having suspended or idle conversations might make you nervous about the possibility of leaking memory. Although I've assured you that conversations are cleaned up when they time out, you may not be comfortable with the idea of having all these idle conversations lying around. Fortunately, Seam provides a way to allow the user to rediscover lost conversations and either return to them or end them manually. In the next section, you'll discover that leaving a long-running conversation and later switching back to it can be a natural part of how the application works.

7.5   *Switching between conversations*

Abandoning a conversation may sound remiss, but it can be a powerful tool. Keep in mind that your user is a person and people like to multitask. The popularity of browser tabs reflects this fact. When a conversation is abandoned, you don't have to consider it lost forever. It's just sitting behind the scenes waiting to be rediscovered, just like a background tab in a browser. Unless the abandoned conversation reaches its timeout period, it's possible to restore it using a conversation switcher widget. Switching between existing long-running conversations in the same browser window is referred to as *workspace management*. Think of it as switching tabs in a browser. In this section, you're introduced to workspaces, how they're defined, and how you can provide a way for the user to jump between them.

7.5.1   *The conversation as a workspace*

A conversation is more than just a context. It also represents the user's workspace within the application. Not just any conversation can be a workspace, though. To be a workspace, a conversation must have a description, which you'll learn to assign in the next section.

If there were only one workspace (per user), there wouldn't be much need to assign it a description. We'd simply call it *the conversation*. The term *workspace* is significant because it's possible for a user to have multiple, parallel conversations. Since the browser window can only focus on one workspace at a time, the remaining workspaces exist in the background.

Workspace support is useful for two reasons. First, it allows the user to pause the current task and pick up something else with the intention of returning to the original task later. You have already seen an example of this in the nested conversation section. What you are about to learn is that the user can switch back to the original task without having to end the nested conversation. Workspace switching sanctions multitasking as a natural part of the application, rather than requiring the user to turn to browser tabs to get this feature.

Keeping conversations natural

Conversations can use a natural business key as the conversation token, supplied by an EL value expression, rather than a surrogate key generated by Seam. This configuration provides several benefits. First, since the key is derived from a business object, restoring the conversation happens automatically as a result of the user making the same selection in the UI, instead of the user needing to use a conversation switcher. This channeling minimizes the number of conversations created—another benefit. Finally, the conversation token is meaningful to both the user and the application. The trade-off is that it's no longer possible to have parallel conversations that operate on the same business object.

A natural conversation token configured for the course editor page might use this URL:

/open18/CourseEdit.seam?courseId=9

No much different, you say? Well, notice that the awkward `cid` parameter is absent. In this case, the `courseId` parameter serves as the conversation token. A natural conversation token is defined in the global page descriptor, assigned a name, and then assigned to the `<page>` node corresponding to the view ID on which it is used:

```
<conversation name="Course" parameter-name="courseId"
  parameter-value="#{courseHome.instance.id}"/>
```

```
<page view-id="/CourseEdit.xhtml" conversation="Course" ...</page>
```

When a page with a natural conversation is requested, and that page begins a long-running conversation, Seam sets the URL parameter accordingly. The only oddity with natural conversations is that you must educate JSF and Seam UI command components about the natural conversation, using the `<s:conversationName>` component tag and `conversationName` attribute, respectively. Here is an example of a JSF command button that joins into a natural conversation:

```
<h:commandButton action="#{courseHome.update}" value="Save" ...>
  <s:conversationName value="Course"/>
</h:commandButton>
```

By applying the UrlRewrite configuration described in chapter 3, you can get friendly URLs and stateful behavior at the same time, without having to worry about that pesky `cid` parameter. You can find several examples of natural conversation in the book's source code. For additional information, consult the Seam reference documentation.

A workspace is also useful for limiting the number of active long-running conversations. Because users are going to inevitably perform ad hoc navigation, conversations will be inadvertently abandoned. By presenting users with a widget that lets them restore abandoned workspaces, you encourage users to finish what they started.

As you've learned, the application tracks and restores conversations using a conversation token, which passes along the value of the conversation id. The task of switching workspaces will be lost on users if you require them to specify a numeric ID to continue a conversation. You need to provide users with a workspace switcher component that can be used to select a conversation. The options in the switcher should consist of friendly descriptions so that users can recognize the workspace and have motivation to return to it.

7.5.2 *Giving conversations a description*

A conversation is assigned a description, thus promoting it to a workspace, when the user navigates to a page with a description during a long-running conversation. A description is assigned to a page by populating the <description> element within the <page> node in either the Seam page descriptor (the stateless navigation model) or jPDL page flow descriptor (the stateful navigation model). When the current view ID matches that <page>, the value of the <description> element is assigned to the conversation. An example of a page with a description, defined in a Seam page descriptor, is shown here:

```
<pages>
  ...
  <page view-id="/CourseList.xhtml">
    <description>
      Course search results (#{courseList.resultList.size})
    </description>
  </page>
</pages>
```

The same element is used in the stateful navigation model:

```
<pageflow-definition name="Course Wizard">
  ...
  <page name="basicCourseInfo"
      view-id="/coursewizard/basicCourseInfo.xhtml" redirect="true">
    <description>
      Course wizard (New course
      @ #{course.facility.name}): Basic information
    </description>
    ...
  </page>
</pageflow-definition>
```

Assigning a description to a conversation by way of assigning a description to a page may strike you as odd. Why not just assign a description to the conversation directly? Well, if you think about it, the state of a conversation changes over the course of its use. By describing the conversation only when it's created, the description quickly becomes outdated, failing to reflect the current state of the conversation. Conversations are shaped by their most recent page visit and the state of the system at the time the page is viewed. Therefore, it makes sense that the description is frequently updated. If the conversation is abandoned, the description reflects the last known state of the conversation and gives users an idea of where they'll be taken when the workspace is restored.

What makes the descriptions even more contextual and descriptive is that they can leverage EL value expressions. That might get you wondering when these descriptions are evaluated. The description of a page is evaluated just prior to the page being rendered. You can see where this happens in the Seam life cycle by looking at table 3.2 in chapter 3.

By giving a conversation a description, it becomes a workspace (at least in the eyes of the user). It's one prerequisite for allowing it to appear in a conversation switcher component. The other prerequisite is that the conversation must be "switch enabled." Let's explore how a conversation is assigned this status.

ALLOWING THE SWITCH TO OCCUR

Just as the description of the conversation is updated as each page in the conversation with a description is requested, the view ID is updated as well. When a background conversation is restored using a switcher component, the conversation comes into the foreground and the user is redirected to the last view ID recorded for that conversation.

However, the view ID is only registered with the conversation if the corresponding <page> node supports switching, which is the default behavior. If switching is explicitly disabled, the conversation isn't made aware of the visit to the view ID:

```
<page view-id="/FacilityList.xhtml" switch="disabled">
  <description>Facility List</description>
  ...
</page>
```

The description and the view ID can be assigned to the conversation independently of one another. For instance, if switching is disabled, yet the <page> has a description, then the description of the conversation is still updated. Likewise, if the <page> supports switching, but there is no description, then only the view ID is recorded, leaving the conversation description as it was. If none of the pages the user visits support switching, then the workspace can't be restored because there's nowhere for the switcher component to redirect the user to. Thus, for a conversation to support switching, at least one view ID with switching enabled must be requested.

All that is left to enable conversation switching is to provide the user with a menu of available workspaces and a command to select one. Seam includes a handful of built-in components that aid in creating such a control.

7.5.3   *Using the built-in conversation switchers*

Workspaces are a new concept in web applications. To promote their use, Seam provides several built-in conversation switchers that you can drop into your application with little effort. Seam offers a simple select menu switcher, a more advanced table-based switcher, and a conversation stack that can be used for breadcrumb navigation. The first two components are used to switch between parallel conversations, while the latter is constrained to the ancestry of the current conversation. Let's start with the select menu.

THE BASIC CONVERSATION SWITCHER

Seam's built-in conversation switcher component, named `switcher`, is a ready-made component intended to be used with a `UISelectOne` component, such as `<h:selectOneMenu>`. This conversation switcher is a great place to start because it's simple and unobtrusive. What's more important about it is that it helps raise awareness of the workspace construct. Users can see which workspace is currently active and get an inventory of the other active workspaces in their session, as figure 7.7 shows.

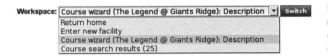

Figure 7.7   A basic conversation switcher that includes static outcomes for returning home and entering a new course.

Here is the markup that creates a switcher control that includes the list of workspaces:

```
<h:form id="switcher"> Workspace:
  <h:selectOneMenu value="#{switcher.conversationIdOrOutcome}">
    <f:selectItems value="#{switcher.selectItems}"/>
  </h:selectOneMenu>
  <h:commandButton action="#{switcher.select}" value="Switch"/>
</h:form>
```

The #{switcher.selectItems} value expression prepares a set of select menu items from the list of long-running conversations that support switching (i.e., workspaces). The value of the options are the conversation ids and the labels are the conversation descriptions. When the action #{switcher.conversationIdOrOutcome} is invoked, Seam uses the value of the selected option to locate the background conversation. The user is then redirected to the last view ID used by that conversation. When the switch occurs, the current conversation is abandoned.

TIP   Notice that I used a standard UI command component to invoke the action method of the switcher component. In order for this component to work, it must submit the form so that the value selected in the UISelectOne component is captured. Seam UI command components would not work since they *do not* submit the form.

This component allows you to tack on your own options to the menu, which is where the OrOutcome part of the action method becomes relevant. If the selected value isn't numeric, the action method returns the selected value as a logical outcome and allows the JSF standard navigation rules to take effect. Let's add an outcome that returns the user to the home page and one to add a new facility:

```
<h:form id="switcher"> Workspace:
  <h:selectOneMenu value="#{switcher.conversationIdOrOutcome}">
    <f:selectItem itemLabel="Return home" itemValue="home"/>
    <f:selectItem itemLabel="Enter new facility" itemValue="addFacility"/>
    <f:selectItems value="#{switcher.selectItems}"/>
  </h:selectOneMenu>
  <h:commandButton action="#{switcher.select}" value="Switch"/>
</h:form>
```

You then need to define navigation rules that match the new outcomes. If the switcher is displayed on every page, the navigation rule must be global (match the view ID *). The navigation rule that matches the addFacility outcome is shown here:

```
<page view-id="*">
  <navigation from-action="#{switcher.select}">
    <rule if-outcome="addFacility">
      <redirect view-id="/FacilityEdit.xhtml"/>
    </rule>
  </navigation>
</page>
```

The auxiliary outcomes in this switcher have to be fairly rudimentary since they can't pass additional information and don't execute a dedicated action.

WARNING   The only downside of switching to a background conversation is that any nonsubmitted form data on the foreground page is lost. You can work around this issue by using an Ajax component library, such as Ajax4jsf, to periodically synchronize the form values with the properties on the model.

As you can see, the basic conversation switcher component is straightforward. Although it gets the job done, it leaves a little to be desired. For one thing, it can only show the conversation description, even though a conversation entry has a lot more useful information. It doesn't let the user terminate background conversations either. Both of these features are supported by the built-in conversation list component.

A MORE POWERFUL CONVERSATION SWITCHER

Seam maintains a list of all long-running conversations and metadata about each one in the built-in Seam component named `conversationEntries`. These conversations are exported to the session-scoped context variable `conversationList` as a list of `ConversationEntry` objects, whose properties are shown in table 7.7. This list excludes all entries that aren't displayable by default. You can use the `conversation-Entries` component to export a custom list.

Table 7.7 The properties on a conversation entry

Property	Type	Description
id	String	A value that identifies this conversation. The value is typically numeric, though "natural" identifiers are also supported.
description	String	The conversation description resolved from the EL value expression specified in the `<description>` nodes in the page descriptor.
current	boolean	A flag indicating whether this conversation entry is the current conversation.
viewId	String	The view ID that was rendered when this conversation was last used.
displayable	boolean	A flag indicating whether this entry is displayable, meaning it must be active and it must have a description.
startDatetime	Date	The timestamp when this conversation began.
lastDatetime	Date	The timestamp when this conversation was last restored.
lastRequestTime	long	The timestamp when this conversation was last restored.

Table 7.7 The properties on a conversation entry (continued)

Property	Type	Description
timeout	Integer	The timeout period that must elapse after its last use for this conversation to be automatically garbage collected.
nested	boolean	A flag indicating whether this conversation is nested.
ended	boolean	A flag indicating whether this conversation has ended.
removeAfterRedirect	boolean	A flag indicating that this conversation will be removed immediately after a redirect.

You may not want to use all of these properties in the display, but the information they provide can be useful for deciding how to render the list of conversations. In addition to these properties, each conversation entry has several built-in action methods, which are listed in table 7.8.

Table 7.8 The methods on a conversation entry that operate on the selected conversation

Action method	Purpose
select()	Selects the conversation entry, making it the current conversation, and redirects to the last-rendered view ID when that conversation was active. The previous conversation is abandoned.
destroy()	Selects the conversation entry and ends that conversation. The previous conversation is abandoned, so it's necessary to select it again, if it still exists.

Armed with these properties and action methods, you're ready to construct your advanced workspace control. We'll be using a `UIData` component to present a list of workspaces, as shown in figure 7.8.

Workspaces				
Id	**Is nested?**	**Current page**	**Last used**	**Action**
55	no	Course search results (1)	08:07 PM	Select | Destroy
54	yes	Course wizard (Talon Course @ Grayhawk Golf Club): Description	08:07 PM	Select | Destroy

Figure 7.8 A list of workspaces in a user's session. The user can switch to one of the workspaces or destroy it.

The conversations in this table are sorted based on the last time they were used, with the most recent conversations appearing first. The JSF markup to produce this table is shown in listing 7.1.

Listing 7.1 A table-based conversation switcher component

```
<h:form id="workspaces">
  <rich:panel><f:facet name="header">Workspaces</f:facet>
    <s:span rendered="#{empty conversationList}">No workspaces</s:span>
```

```
    <rich:dataTable value="#{conversationList}" var="_entry"
      rendered="#{not empty conversationList}">
      <h:column><f:facet name="header">Id</f:facet>
        #{_entry.id}
      </h:column>
      <h:column><f:facet name="header">Is nested?</f:facet>
        #{_entry.nested ? 'yes' : 'no'}
      </h:column>
      <h:column><f:facet name="header">Description</f:facet>
        <h:commandLink action="#{_entry.select}"
          value="#{_entry.description}"/>
      </h:column>
      <h:column><f:facet name="header">Last used</f:facet>
        <h:outputText value="#{_entry.lastDatetime}"
          rendered="#{not _entry.current}">
          <s:convertDateTime type="time" pattern="hh:mm a"/>
        </h:outputText>
        <h:outputText value="current" rendered="#{_entry.current}"/>
      </h:column>
      <h:column><f:facet name="header">Action</f:facet>
        <h:commandLink action="#{_entry.select}" value="Select"/> |
        <h:commandLink action="#{_entry.destroy}" value="Destroy"/>
      </h:column>
    </rich:dataTable>
  </rich:panel>
</h:form>
```

When a UI command link in one of the rows is activated, the appropriate action method, either select() or destroy(), is called on the conversation entry associated with that row. JSF is able to locate the appropriate conversation entry to invoke because the conversationList is a page-scoped component and is therefore available on a JSF postback (it is stored in the UI component tree).

The select() action method on the conversation entry works just like the basic switcher shown in the previous section. Seam issues a redirect to the last-used view ID in that conversation. When the destroy() method is invoked, Seam switches to the selected conversation and ends it. Recall that if you destroy a conversation, all of its descendants are terminated as well.

DEALING WITH DESTROY

While destroying a conversation appears straightforward, it carries with it some complexities. The destroy() method on the conversation entry restores the background conversation before terminating it, which means the terminated conversation remains available—along with all of its context variables—while the current view ID is rendered again. To get around this problem, you may want to add a navigation rule that terminates the conversation before redirect and issues a redirect back to the current view ID:

```
<page view-id="*">
  <navigation from-action="#{_entry.destroy}">
    <end-conversation before-redirect="true"/>
    <redirect/>
```

```
  </navigation>
</page>
```

There is another, more serious problem, though. If the user destroys a background conversation while working in the context of a long-running conversation, the current long-running conversation is abandoned. The navigation rule just implemented makes matters worse since the current page is now rendered without a long-running conversation. If that page requires a long-running conversation (i.e., the conversation-required attribute on <page> is true), the user would be issued a warning and redirected to a fallback page.

I don't mean to scare you off by presenting these complications. It just leads to the following advice. Only allow background conversations to be destroyed from a page dedicated to displaying workspaces. Another way to let users destroy a workspace is to have them switch to it and then end the conversation in the normal way for that conversation, such as by clicking a cancel button. While you could develop a more intelligent destroy method than the one on the conversation entry, it's probably best to follow this advice.

TIP The table-based conversation switcher is a great way to test conversation timeouts. Open two tabs in your browser, one that you're using to test the application and one that displays the list of workspaces. You can destroy the active conversation in the workspace tab to see how the application behaves when the conversation lapses.

The conversation switcher just shown displays both top-level and nested conversations. It's also possible to create a switcher that moves solely along the ancestral chain of the conversation stack component.

TRACING YOUR STEPS WITH BREADCRUMBS

Breadcrumb navigation complements switching between parallel conversations. Each breadcrumb represents a point where the conversation was branched to create a nested conversation. Since conversations can be nested to arbitrary depth, it's possible to have a long chain of breadcrumbs. Seam exports a list of generational conversation entries to the session-scoped context variable conversationStack.

Your application must support a nested conversation model for the conversation stack to be populated with more than one entry. The example of navigating related golf courses presented earlier is a perfect use case for this component. The conversationStack context variable can be used in an iteration component to lay out the chain as a delimited list:

```
<h:form id="breadcrumbs" rendered="#{conversation.nested}">
  <s:span rendered="#{not empty conversationStack}">Trail:
    <ui:repeat value="#{conversationStack}" var="_entry">
      <h:outputText value=" > " rendered="#{_entry.nested}"/>
      <h:commandLink action="#{_entry.select}"
        value="#{_entry.description}"/>
    </ui:repeat>
  </s:span>
</h:form>
```

Here's an example of the output produced by this component. Each item is a link that restores the appropriate nested conversation:

```
Trail: Course search results (25) > Talon Course @ GrayHawk Golf Club >
    Raptor Course @ GrayHawk Golf Club
```

The entries in the conversation stack are selected in the same way as the table-based conversation switcher. In fact, the only difference is that this list consists of hierarchical entries rather than parallel conversations.

You've now seen a couple of examples of how to use Seam's built-in conversation switchers. Once you're comfortable using them, you may decide to create more sophisticated or context-sensitive switchers to suit your needs. Recall that conversation switchers aren't the only way to control conversations. The built-in conversation component, whose properties and methods are summarized in table 7.7, can be used in both action methods and views to navigate between conversations related to the current one.

Workspaces and conversation switching offer a new, yet surprisingly refreshing, experience for the user. They can cut down on the proliferation of tabs in the user's browser because users never fear they are "losing their place" by taking a temporary detour. Instead, you can bring the power of tabs into the application.

There's one important aspect of conversations that has yet to be addressed: navigation. You probably agree that the course wizard could benefit from improved navigation control. I want to introduce you to how Seam combines conversations and page flows to provide stateful navigation. In the next section, we bolt Seam's page flow support onto the course wizard to ensure the user stays on the right track while populating the course data.

7.6 Driving the conversation with a page flow

There are two types of navigation models in Seam: stateless and stateful. Up to this point you've worked solely with the stateless navigation model. The stateless model is ideal if you don't want to enforce order on the user's actions. When the navigation's state carries meaning in the use case, as in the course wizard example, driving the conversation with a page flow is a good fit.

In Seam, page flows are implemented using a special integration with the jBPM library. It may seem like overkill to use a Business Process Management (BPM) library to control a page flow. Understand that Seam is leveraging jBPM for its process definition language (jPDL) and interpreter, which together serve as a framework for building flow-based software modules. In this section you'll see how Seam uses the page flow module in jBPM. In chapter 14 (online), you'll learn to use jBPM to drive business processes.

TIP   The JBossTools project includes a GUI page flow editor that can help visualize and maintain page flows like the one presented in this section.

A jPDL descriptor defines the page flow for a single conversation. The conversation and the page flow share the same life cycle. When we discuss page flows, you'll encounter references to a *process token*. During the conversation, a process token tracks the user's place within the page flow. The process token always coincides with the currently rendered page. Navigations resulting from a user interaction are applied relative to the node at which the process token is positioned.

7.6.1 Setting up a page flow

The course wizard presented earlier is going to be refactored so that it's driven by a page flow named Course Wizard, following the steps in figure 7.5. The flow is defined in the jPDL descriptor courseWizard-pageflow.jpdl.xml. Rather than just dump the page flow on your lap at one time, I'm going to step through it in phases. The complete descriptor is available in the sample code at the book's website.

NOTE Page flows descriptors (*.jpdl.xml) are not hot deployable.

First things first: it is necessary to create and "install" the page flow for this example. The page flow descriptor must reside on the classpath. (For seam-gen projects, it should be placed in the resources folder.) Next, declare it in the Seam component descriptor:

```
<bpm:jbpm>
  <bpm:pageflow-definitions>
    <value>courseWizard-pageflow.jpdl.xml</value>
  </bpm:pageflow-definitions>
</bpm:jbpm>
```

As of Seam 2.1, files ending in .jpdl that reside on the classpath are detected by the deployment scanner and registered automatically, making this declaration unnecessary. With the page flow descriptor in place, you're ready to start populating it.

7.6.2 Learning your way around a page flow

The root tag of a page flow is `<pageflow-definition>`. The name of the page flow is defined in the `name` attribute on this node. Seam provides an XSD schema for the page flow descriptor so that you get all of the tag completion goodness that you enjoy with the other Seam descriptors. Here's the outer shell of the page flow descriptor for the course wizard:

```
<pageflow-definition xmlns="http://jboss.com/products/seam/pageflow"
  xmlns:xsi="http://www.w3.org/2001/XMLSchema-instance"
  xsi:schemaLocation="
    http://jboss.com/products/seam/pageflow
    http://jboss.com/products/seam/pageflow-2.0.xsd"
  name="Course Wizard">
</pageflow-definition>
```

To put the page flow in motion, you have to create a process instance that manages it. Fortunately, Seam makes this task extremely easy.

STARTING THE FLOW

You begin a page flow using the same directive that you use to begin the conversation. Regardless of whether you're using the `@Begin` annotation, the `<begin-conversation>` page descriptor tag, or the Seam UI component tags, you specify the page flow definition in the `pageflow` attribute. The value of this attribute is the name of the page flow, which was defined above. When the conversation begins, an instance of the page flow definition is created and the process token is advanced to the start node.

Here, the `@Begin` annotation has been augmented to initiate the Course Wizard page flow when the `addCourse()` method on the `CourseWizard` component is invoked:

```
@Begin(pageflow = "Course Wizard")
public void addCourse() {
    course = new Course();
    course.setFacility(entityManager.find(Facility.class, facilityId));
}
```

When the process instance that tracks the page flow is created, it immediately looks for a start node. There are two options: `<start-state>` or `<start-page>`. If you're starting a page flow from an action, you choose the `<start-state>` node. This approach has been chosen for the course wizard. An example of using the `<start-page>` node is shown later. The `<start-state>` of the course wizard page flow is defined as follows:

```
<start-state>
  <transition to="basicCourseInfo"/>
</start-state>
```

Let's now look at how navigation events are handled.

NAVIGATING TO A PAGE

The `<transition>` node is analogous to the `<rule>` node in the page descriptor. In this case, it's the `name` attribute that is matched against the outcome value—the return value—of the action method. If there's no outcome value, as is the case with the `addCourse()` method, the `<transition>` element without a `name` attribute is selected.

A transition implies a target. The `to` attribute specifies the name of the node to which to advance. There are four main nodes that can appear in the page flow definition after the start state. These nodes are summarized in table 7.9.

Table 7.9   The main nodes in the page flow descriptor

Node name	Purpose
page	Renders a JSF view and declares transitions that are used upon exiting that view
decision	Evaluates an EL expression and follows a declared transition based on the result
process-state	Used to spawn a subpage flow
end-state	Terminates the process instance without ending the long-running conversation; typically used to end a subpage flow

The jPDL `<page>` node indicates which view ID should be rendered when the process token arrives. The `<page>` node is the "wait" state in the page flow process.

NOTE   Don't confuse the `<page>` node from jPDL with the one used in the Seam page descriptor. They are not the same.

The following <page> node stanza renders the first screen in the course wizard, which is called on by the start state:

```
<page name="basicCourseInfo"
  view-id="/coursewizard/basicCourseInfo.xhtml" redirect="true">
  <transition name="cancel" to="cancel"/>
  <transition name="next" to="description"/>
</page>
```

Notice the nested <transition> elements. Since <page> is a "wait" state node, it means that these transitions don't apply until an action is invoked from the view ID. You can think of them as *exit* transitions. We'll get back to those shortly.

If the redirect attribute is included on the <page> node and has a value of true, then Seam performs a redirect prior to rendering the page. Doing so resets the URL in the browser so that it reflects the current page. The redirect also prevents the situation where the user hits the refresh button and is prompted with a confusing message about resubmitting post data. More about browser buttons in a moment.

AUTHOR NOTE The redirect functionality can also be declared using a nested <redirect/> element. I prefer the redirect attribute; I find it more intuitive since it is adjacent to the view-id attribute to which it applies.

Let's put this page flow configuration aside for now and look at how to start the flow the other way, beginning with the <start-page> node.

INITIALIZING A PAGE FLOW LAZILY

If the conversation that manages the page flow begins in the *Render Response* phase, perhaps by a factory, it isn't possible to invoke a navigation event at the start of the flow. Therefore, the start of the page flow must be declared using a <start-page> node.

Let's say that we want to start the course wizard by navigating the user directly to the first page. To support this starting point, the course context variable referenced on that page is created by a @Factory method, which also begins the long-running page flow:

```
@Out private Course course;
...
@Begin(pageflow = "Course Wizard")
@Factory("course")
public void initCourse() {
    course = new Course();
    course.setFacility(entityManager.find(Facility.class, facilityId));
}
```

In this scenario, the start of the page flow is declared using a <start-page>. The value of the view-id attribute must match the view ID of the first page in the course wizard:

```
<start-page name="basicCourseInfo"
  view-id="/coursewizard/basicCourseInfo.xhtml">
  <transition name="next" to="description"/>
  <transition name="cancel" to="cancel"/>
</start-page>
```

Note that aside from the use of <start-page>, this element is equivalent to the <page> element configured in the first scenario. Now, on to the transitions.

7.6.3   *Advancing the page flow*

As mentioned earlier, page flow transitions work just like JSF navigation rules, chosen based on the outcome of the action method. In lieu of using an action method, the outcome can be specified as a literal value in the action attribute of the command component tag, which is the approach often used in page flows. Here are the buttons on the first page of the wizard:

```
<s:button id="cancel" action="cancel" value="Cancel"/>
<h:commandButton id="next" action="next" value="Next"/>
```

When either button is activated, Seam locates the matching <transition> node and advances the token to the node whose name matches the value in the to attribute. In this case, the targets nodes are named description and cancel:

```
<page name="description"
  view-id="/coursewizard/description.xhtml" redirect="true">
  <transition name="cancel" to="cancel"/>
  <transition name="next" to="holeData">
    <action expression="#{courseWizard.prepareHoleData}"/>
  </transition>
</page>

<page name="cancel" view-id="/CourseList.xhtml" redirect="true">
  <end-conversation before-redirect="true"/>
</page>
```

Now things are starting to get interesting. Let's begin with the cancel transition.

ENDING SO SOON?

The cancel transition advances to the <page> node named cancel. There, we see another familiar element, <end-conversation>. This element ends the conversation upon entering the <page> node. In this case, the conversation is ended prior to the redirect, which immediately follows. As a result, the conversation that served the page flow is wiped out before CourseList.xhtml is rendered. At this point, the process instance is effectively terminated (no <end-state> is needed).

The transition to holeData is unique in that it executes an action before advancing to the target node. Let's see what that is all about.

INVERTING THE CONTROL

Using an <action> node in a page flow is an inversion of the typical navigation mechanism in JSF. Rather than declaring an action method expression on a UI command component and following it with a navigation rule based on the action method's outcome, the outcome comes first and then an action method is invoked. What's nice about the inverted approach is that it abstracts the action method expression from the view. All the UI command component says is "next." The page flow descriptor takes it from there. You can use either approach.

Now it's decision time. Page flows can consult a component's state to determine which navigation path to follow, thus enabling conditional navigation.

PERFORMING LOGIC IN A TRANSITION

Although the game of golf is designed to level the playing field by giving men and ladies different par and handicap values, many courses don't make that distinction. Therefore, when the user is presented with the form to enter the men's par and handicap data, a checkbox appears to indicate whether it's necessary to provide a different set of data for the ladies. The checkbox's state is consulted in the page flow to determine whether it's necessary to return to the holeData.xhtml page to capture the additional data:

```
<h:selectBooleanCheckbox rendered="#{gender == 'Men'}"
  value="#{courseWizard.ladiesDataUnique}" /> Unique data for ladies?
<h:commandButton action="Men" value="Next"
  rendered="#{gender == 'Men'}"/>
<h:commandButton action="Ladies" value="Next"
  rendered="#{gender == 'Ladies'}"/>
```

The decision of whether to return to the holeData.xhtml page is handled by the decide-HoleData node. The value of the expression attribute on the <decision> node, which is a value expression, is resolved immediately upon entry and its value is used to determine where to transaction next:

```
<page name="holeData"
  view-id="/coursewizard/holeData.xhtml" redirect="true">
  <transition name="cancel" to="cancel"/>
  <transition name="Men" to="decideHoleData">
    <action expression="#{courseWizard.submitMensHoleData}"/>
  </transition>
  <transition name="Ladies" to="teeSet">
    <action expression="#{courseWizard.submitLadiesHoleData}"/>
  </transition>
</page>

<decision name="decideHoleData"
  expression="#{courseWizard.ladiesHoleDataRequired}">
  <transition name="true" to="holeData"/>
  <transition name="false" to="teeSet"/>
</decision>
```

Once all of the data has been collected for the course, the user arrives at the review screen. The final two <page> nodes that wrap up the wizard are defined as follows:

```
<page name="review" view-id="/coursewizard/review.xhtml" redirect="true">
  <transition name="cancel" to="cancel"/>
  <transition name="success" to="end">
    <action expression="#{courseHome.setCourseId(course.id)}"/>
  </transition>
  <transition to="review"/>
</page>

<page name="end" view-id="/Course.xhtml" redirect="true">
  <end-conversation/>
</page>
```

The review screen assumes the use of an action method in the UI command button, since the transitions are set up to handle the outcome of that method:

```
<h:commandButton id="save" action="#{courseWizard.save}" value="Save"/>
```

By putting the method-binding expression in the UI, we can leverage the transition action to set the newly established ID of the course so that the course can be displayed once the page flow is complete.

You've now completed your very first page flow! While page flows are fresh in your mind, I want to address two additional features. First, let's talk about those pesky browser buttons, back and refresh.

7.6.4   *Addressing the back button*

If you've heard it asked once, you've heard it a hundred times: "Can the back button be disabled?" Lucky are those who are so blissfully unaware. It's a stateless world and we have to learn to live in it. Fortunately, Seam addresses the back button "problem" not by disabling the back button, but by being smart enough to know what to do when it's used.

BACKING UP IN THE FLOW

If, during a page flow, users attempt to return to an earlier page and resubmit the form, Seam will gracefully redirect them to the current page—the <page> node where the process token is positioned. The same goes for when users click the refresh button and the browser attempts to resubmit the form. Of course, the refresh problem has already been solved by performing a redirect during the transition, but it's still nice to know that Seam prevents the double submit anyway.

Holding the user to the current page is the default behavior for a page flow. You may decide that it's permissible for users to back up in the flow to modify or review their work. If you want to sanction this behavior, you need to bake it into the page flow. You enable use of the back button by setting the back attribute on the <page> node to enabled:

```
<page name="review" view-id="/coursewizard/review.xhtml"
    redirect="true" back="enabled"> ... </page>
```

This setting lets the user return to any page leading up to this page and step through the flow again. The only downside is that once you open this door, you have to deal with the possibility of the user executing parts of the page flow over again.

WHAT'S DONE IS DONE

The back button can be used to do more than just move around in the current conversation. Its most troubling aspect is that it allows the user to back up into an old conversation and attempt to interact with it again. Fortunately, Seam takes notice and scorns this behavior.

Let's say that the user previously posted a transaction that ends a conversation (perhaps submitting an order). If the user backs up to the form and tries to submit it again, Seam detects that the conversation has already ended and raises a warning. If a no-conversation-view-id is configured in the page or page flow descriptor, Seam also redirects the user to this fallback page. This check is applied to both regular conversations and conversations managed by a page flow.

That wraps up our introduction to page flows. Page flows have a wealth of additional features, including the ability to define subflows, set the timeout per page, end tasks, initiate a business process, and even tap into the native extension points of the jPDL. You can seriously micromanage the user's interaction with your system using page flows. It's a lot to configure, but then again, if power is what you're after, it may be worth the trouble.

The course wizard is an example of a well-defined conversation, having explicit begin and end points and a logical progression in between. A conversation can also be combined with free-form interaction to let the user mold the state and direction of the user interface. An example of this type of conversation is presented in the next section.

7.7 Ad hoc conversations

While there are standard use cases that are modeled best using a page flow, such as a store checkout process or wizard-based form, the most popular web-based applications don't try to enforce a structure on the user. Instead, they let the user see and do everything at once. To support these nonlinear interactions, the state of the application needs to be tracked and managed. Once again we look to a conversation to handle this task. In this case, an ad hoc conversation is used, which is identified by its omission of a well-defined flow.

7.7.1 Open for business

I like to think that when an ad hoc conversation begins, it becomes open for business. Any widget on the page can offer to let the user engage in that conversation, to contribute, modify, or reduce its state. As before, this activity occurs independently of other conversations in the background or in other tabs.

A good example of an ad hoc conversation from the real world is a flight search engine. The conversation begins with a form that captures the most elemental criteria: the origin and destination cities and dates of travel. The initial search brings back a list of all matching flights. From that point, the user can tune a slew of additional criteria and watch the results change. But that's just the beginning. Other possible interactions include expanding the details about a flight, marking a flight for comparison, seeing flight trends for the current trip, or changing the currency displayed.

The conversation provides several benefits in this situation:

- Keeps track of the state of the data in the UI: selected, visible, or expanded
- Acts as a near cache to avoid database hits
- Maintains the persistence context to ensure entity instances remained managed

Although the JSF UI component tree was designed to support the first two cases, a conversation can supplement the UI component tree to give the state more longevity. The final point is covered in detail in the next two chapters.

To see these benefits in action, the comparison feature will be distilled from the flight search example and used in the golf course directory. An ad hoc conversation will host a collection of courses that the user marks. The selections are then compared side by side on a comparison page. A page action is used to begin (or join) a conversation when the /CourseList.xhtml page is requested:

```
<begin-conversation join="true"/>
```

Next, a link is added to each row in the courses table that lets the user mark the course for comparison:

```
<s:link action="#{courseComparison.mark}" value="Mark">
  <f:param name="courseId" value="#{_course.id}"/>
</s:link>
```

Although it's not shown here, you could also add a link to unmark a previously marked course. A minimal version of the component that manages the comparison, named `courseComparison`, is shown in listing 7.2.

Listing 7.2   A conversation-scoped component used for comparing courses

```
package org.open18.action;
import ...;

@Name("courseComparison")
@Scope(ScopeType.CONVERSATION)
public class CourseComparison implements Serializable {
    @In protected EntityManager entityManager;

    @RequestParameter protected Long courseId;

    @Out("readyToCompare")
    protected boolean ready = false;

    @DataModel("comparedCourses")
    protected Set<Course> courses = new HashSet<Course>();

    public void mark() {
        Course course = entityManager.find(Course.class, courseId);
        if (course == null) return;
        courses.add(course);
        ready = courses.size() >= 2;
    }
}
```

Each time a course is marked, both the `readyToCompare` and `comparedCourses` context variables are outjected to the conversation scope. Once at least two courses have been marked, the `readyToCompare` context variable will be set to true and a button can be added that takes the user to the comparison screen:

```
<s:button value="Compare" view="/CompareCourses.xhtml"
    rendered="#{readyToCompare}"/>
```

All that's left is to create the course comparison screen and show the courses.

7.7.2   *Show me what you've got*

The courses to be compared reside in the conversation once a course has been marked. When the user is taken to the course comparison page, it's just a matter of iterating over this collection to render the comparison.

```
<h:panelGrid columns="#{comparedCourses.rowCount + 1}">     ⟵  Adds extra
  <rich:panel>                                                  column for
    <f:facet name="header"> </f:facet>                     labels
```

```
      <div>Location:</div>
      . . .
    </rich:panel>
    <c:forEach items="#{comparedCourses.wrappedData}" var="_c">
      <rich:panel>
        <f:facet name="header">#{_c.name}</f:facet>
        <div>
          #{_c.facility.city}, #{_c.facility.state}          Loads facility
        </div>                                                on demand
        . . .
      </rich:panel>
    </c:forEach>
  </h:panelGrid>
```

The reference to facility from course is a lazy association. It can be loaded here since the persistence context is scoped to the conversation and therefore the course entities remain managed. You'll learn the importance of persistence context scoping in the next two chapters.

Since the CompareCourses.xhtml page requires that you have a conversation active, you may want to enforce this restriction in the page descriptor:

```
<page view-id="/CompareCourses.xhtml" conversation-required="true"
  no-conversation-view-id="/CourseList.xhtml"/>
```

In this section, you've learned how to use an ad hoc conversation that is capable of accumulating state until it's time for the user to act on it, such as to produce a report. This style of conversation is useful in situations where the possible interactions are numerous.

7.8 Summary

Users become frustrated when their story is forgotten, a far too frequent occurrence in call centers and web applications. If the application fails to track state, kicking the user back to the starting point as a result, the user will be ready to hang up on your application. Seam's conversation remedies this situation by propagating state held in one request to the next.

This chapter introduced the conversation as a stateful context in which context variables for a use case are stored. You learned two important things about a conversation: that it's a managed and isolated segment of the HTTP session, identified by its conversation id, and that it represents a unit of work from the perspective of the user. At times, a unit of work may span only one request, which you learned is modeled as a temporary conversation, ensuring that conversation-scoped variables are maintained until the view is rendered. To extend the unit of work across a sequence of pages, you learned that you must use a propagation directive that begins a long-running conversation. Toward the end of the chapter you learned that a long-running conversation can either be managed by a page flow descriptor or left open to be used in an ad hoc manner.

Much of the chapter was spent going over various options for switching a conversation between its three states: temporary, long-running, and nested. The options include annotations, page descriptor elements, UI component tags, and methods on the built-in conversation component and conversation entry. The propagation directives are what set the conversation apart from other contexts covered so far in the book.

The discussion turned from singular to plural as you learned that you can have multiple conversations going at once, either sharing a nested relationship or as isolated background conversations. Seam acknowledges multitasking through the use of workspaces, providing several built-in conversation switchers that allow the user to restore previously abandoned conversations.

This chapter established a foundational knowledge of conversations, but it's really just the beginning. One of the primary uses of a conversation is to manage the persistence context. Before you can learn about Seam's pioneering work with the persistence context, you need to learn about Java persistence, which is where the next chapter picks up.

Understanding
Java persistence

8

Java persistence is the mechanism by which object-based entities are translated between the Java runtime environment and a relational database. It's undoubtedly the most popular feature of the Java EE platform, perhaps even the Java language. This popularity can be attributed to the fact that persisting data is central to nearly all enterprise applications. For that reason, persistence is a core part of Seam. In fact, you can't get very deep into a Seam application without encountering it. As you're probably aware, you've been using Java persistence in the sample application since chapter 2—though solely the Java Persistence API (JPA) variety.

This chapter provides a crash course in Java persistence and prepares you to use it in Seam. The two frameworks covered are JPA—the standard persistence mechanism in Java EE—and Hibernate—the popular open source persistence framework–turned–JPA implementation, both of which Seam support out of the box. Given the fact that these APIs, and Seam's built-in components to support them, are so similar, this chapter establishes a persistence terminology that can be used to address them both in a general way. At the end of this chapter, I compare JPA and Hibernate and you'll learn whether it's worth adhering to the Java EE standard or better to venture onto the bleeding edge with Hibernate, or if it's possible to have it both ways. Since you can't get far persisting data in the absence of explicit transaction boundaries, this chapter also covers the role transactions play in the Java persistence mechanism.

One important point missing from the discussion in the previous chapter is the role that the persistence context plays in the conversation. In this chapter, you're introduced to the persistence context, and I show you how to extend it across multiple HTTP requests. In the next chapter, you'll discover how Seam offers to manage the extended persistence context, using the conversation as a vehicle, so you can align the lifetime of the persistence context to the boundaries of a use case.

Trying to cover all aspects of Java persistence in a single chapter would be impossible, so the focus here is on understanding the concepts you need to know when using it with Seam. Besides, a number of books are available that explain the fundamentals of transactions and persistence using either JPA or Hibernate in tremendous detail. I highly recommend *Java Persistence with Hibernate* (Manning 2007) to start, as well as *EJB 3 in Action* (Manning 2007), *JPA 101 Java Persistence Explained* (SourceBeat 2008), and *Spring in Action, Second Edition* (Manning 2007). That only scratches the surface of what's available.[1] By the end of this chapter, you'll be ready to decide which persistence API to use and learn what Seam brings to the table with its own transaction and persistence management.

8.1   *Java persistence principles*

Persisting data, and doing it consistently and reliably, is vital to enterprise business applications. But transactions and persistence are complex subjects. They are both technically challenging—to the point of being academic—and they can be difficult to manage and tune. The complexity is magnified by the fact that a lot of misinformation exists out there. Once you start down the wrong path, it can be expensive and time consuming to correct your approach. The goal of this section is to "reset" your view of Java persistence and examine its architecture.

8.1.1   *Establishing expectations*

Developers shouldn't expect to sprinkle magic pixie dust on POJOs in hopes they will become persistent. You have to understand the underlying mechanisms and spend a respectable amount of time dedicated to getting the mappings to the database right. Java persistence is intended to make the process of persisting objects to the database easier, but the impression you get from reading many developer blogs is that Java persistence is expected to do all the work. This shallow, magic pixie dust approach is what got folks who spread fear, uncertainty, and doubt (FUD) about the capabilities of Hibernate and JPA into such hot water in the first place.

---

[1] How many Hibernate books do we need? (See http://in.relation.to/Bloggers/MyStackOfHibernateBooks.)

In contrast to what may have been reported in blogs, these frameworks are stunningly adept at handling and optimizing persistence operations. Sadly, developers are doomed from the start because of problems that stem from the stateless architecture of the frameworks that try to manage the persistence resources, not from poor or careless application code. For instance, the persistence context is often scoped to the thread-based (or database) transaction, or worse, each persistence operation. This usage scenario is the nexus of the most frequently reported "bug" in Hibernate: the unnerving `LazyInitializationException`. In this chapter and the next, you'll learn why this exception happens and how not to fear it anymore. In the process, you'll discover that the persistence context was intended to represent a unit of work (i.e., use case) and should therefore be held open until that work is complete.

Throughout this chapter, you can expect to learn about not only Java persistence but also the principles behind its design and how it is supposed to work. You'll then appreciate the vital enhancements that Seam weaves into Java persistence, introduced in the next chapter. The definitions I present here are going to be integral to the remainder of the book, where I'll assume you know how to use the persistence mechanism.

Fortunately for you, seam-gen sets up the persistence configuration so that you can focus on learning the core Seam concepts right out of the gate. The basic seam-gen configuration includes a data source connection pool, a persistence unit, a persistence manager, and a transaction manager. In chapter 2, you used seam-gen to build a set of entity classes and transactional components to manage the database by reverse-engineering the database schema. But you won't always have seam-gen to do all the work for you, so you need to take the time to learn how to get started with Java persistence in a more hands-on manner and understand its moving parts.

8.1.2 *The four pillars of Java persistence*

From the perspective of the database, Java persistence is no different than any other database client. It performs read and write queries—nothing more, nothing less. However, from the developer's perspective, Java persistence is so much more than that. In fact, the whole reason that Java persistence was created (and when I say Java persistence I am referring to object-relational mapping [ORM]) is to extract the SQL out of the code and replace it with object manipulation. The database operations take place transparently to reflect the changes in the state of the objects.

Don't assume, though, that Java persistence was meant to shun SQL as an inferior technology. Rather, the goal is to take the burden of performing that SQL off you, the developer, a majority of the time and allow you to form an object representation of the database that fits more cleanly with the rest of the object-oriented application. The four pillars of Java persistence that form this abstraction over SQL are as follow:

- Entities (entity classes)
- The persistence unit (represented at runtime by a persistence manager factory)
- The persistence manager
- Transactions

NOTE Java persistence encompasses both JPA and the native Hibernate API. Hibernate shares a close resemblance to JPA and therefore the persistence terminology introduced in this section applies to both frameworks. When I present code, only the JPA classes are shown.

Figure 8.1 illustrates the relationship between these constituents. The persistence unit organizes and manages metadata, which maps entities to the database. The persistence manager factory obtains the mapping metadata from the persistence unit and uses that information to create persistence managers. The persistence managers are responsible for moving entities between the Java runtime and the database, a process known as the entity life cycle. Operations performed by the persistence manager should always be wrapped within the scope of a transaction. A transaction can also encompass operations performed by two or more persistence managers as a single atomic unit.

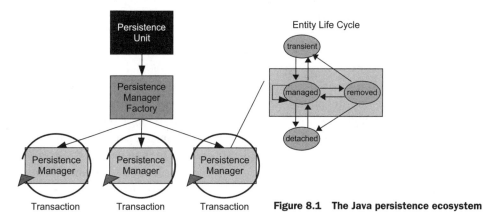

Figure 8.1   **The Java persistence ecosystem**

The fundamental goal of Java persistence is to move data between entity instances and the database. You've already used entities quite extensively throughout this book. Let's quickly shed some light on what has already been at play.

8.2   *Entities and relationships*

Entities in an ORM tool, such as JPA or Hibernate, are the join point between the application and the underlying database, transporting data between them, as illustrated in figure 8.2. Because they are such a central piece of the application, the entities should be treated as more than just dumb data holders. Seam allows you to bind entity classes directly to a JSF view to capture form data, establish prototypes for new

Figure 8.2   **Managed entities are used to exchange data between the application and the database.**

transient instances, and lazy-load data in the view. These objects transcend the layers of a Seam application.

While the entities serve as a representation of the data stored in the database tables, they don't have to mimic the database schema. That gap is filled by the mapping metadata.

8.2.1 *Mapping metadata*

The ORM tool gives you free reign to assemble your entity graph as you choose, perhaps by following domain-driven design or other common object-oriented principles. You then use the mapping metadata of the ORM tool to form-fit the classes to the database schema. The flexibility that the mapping provides includes, but is not limited to, preventing certain properties in the entities from being persisted to the database (using `@Transient`), using different names for the properties that are mapped to their respective columns (using `@Column`), organizing tables along an inheritance hierarchy (using `@Inheritance`), subdividing a table across multiple entities (using `@SecondaryTable`), or molding data from a single table into composite objects (using `@Embedded`). Naturally, there are limits to how far you can stretch the mappings. If the mapping requirements are too steep and the object model is rigid, you have to question whether the database schema is serving its purpose of representing the domain of the business or whether ORM is the right solution to your problem.

One of the benefits of having mapping metadata is that it can be used to export the schema at runtime and have it build the database tables, foreign keys, and constraints automatically. You've taken this approach for each entity that was added to Open 18 since running `seam generate` in chapter 2. You might recall the following two questions from the seam-gen questionnaire:

- Are you working with tables that already exist in the database?
- Do you want to drop and re-create the database tables and data in import.sql each time you deploy?

Had you answered no for the first question and yes for the second, you could've started your application from existing entities alone. You'd generate the user interface using the command `seam generate-ui` and Hibernate would build the database each time the application starts. You should appreciate that mapping metadata can either be the result of bottom-up development or consulted for top-down development (to follow up on a point made back in chapter 2).

Let's next explore how entities help make the task of managing persistence data simpler, particularly related data.

8.2.2 *Transitive persistence*

One of the core benefits of entities in ORM is transparent association handling. There are two sides to this feature. The first side is the read operations. Managed entities can load associated entities on demand (a feature known as lazy loading) by traversing them within the confines of an active persistence context (and ideally within a transaction). The other side is the write operations. When an entity is flushed to persistence storage, modifications to any associated objects are also processed and synchronized with the database. When a managed entity is removed, the removal may cascade into child entities, depending on the attributes in the mapping. This process is referred to as transitive persistence.

Entities can save you a lot of time, not because they shield you from SQL but because they handle the majority of the grunt work necessary to store related objects in a database. However, to use ORM effectively, you must manage the persistence context and transactions appropriately—or confusion reigns.

8.2.3   *Bringing annotations to the persistence layer*

If you've bought into the benefits of annotations, you'll likely use them to configure your entities. The standard Java persistence annotations (in the package `javax.persistence.*`) work in both JPA and Hibernate. In addition to the standard JPA annotation set, Hibernate has its own "vendor" annotations to support additional mapping features and association types that aren't part of the JPA specification. Hibernate strives to be the prototype for future versions of the JPA specification, so some of these annotations represent early versions of what may become available in JPA. Seam also takes advantage of some of Hibernate's other vendor extensions, such as manual flushing of the persistence context, covered in the next chapter.

The `@Entity` annotation is used to declare a Java class as an entity. You've seen this annotation used many times throughout this book, often accompanying the `@Name` annotation to allow the class to serve a dual purpose as persistence entity and Seam component. Listing 8.1 shows an excerpt of the `Course` entity, which is used to store information about a golf course. Several key mapping annotations are shown in this listing that define how the class maps to the table in the database.

Listing 8.1   A Java persistence entity class

```
package org.open18.model;
import ...;

@Entity
@Table(name = "COURSE")
public class Course extends Serializable {
    private Long id;
    private Facility facility;
    private String name;
    private Set<Hole> holes = new HashSet<Hole>(0);
    ...

    @Id @GeneratedValue
    @Column(name = "ID", unique = true, nullable = false)
    public Long getId() { return this.id; }
    public void setId(Long id) { this.id = id; }

    @ManyToOne(fetch = FetchType.LAZY)
    @JoinColumn(name = "FACILITY_ID", nullable = false)
    public Facility getFacility() { return facility; }
    public void setFacility(Facility facility) {
```

```
            this.facility = facility; }

        @Column(name = "NAME", nullable = false, length = 50)
        public String getName() { return this.name; }
        public void setName(String name) { this.name = name; }

        @OneToMany(cascade = CascadeType.ALL,
            fetch = FetchType.LAZY, mappedBy = "course")
        public Set<Hole> getHoles() { return this.holes; }
        public void setHoles(Set<Hole> holes) { this.holes = holes; }
        ...
    }
```

It is also possible to define all of the entity metadata in XML mapping files, regardless of whether you're using JPA or Hibernate. In JPA, all of the XML mappings are declared in the file META-INF/orm.xml. Hibernate reads XML mappings from individual *.hbm.xml files. Consult the reference document for Hibernate[2] or the Hibernate EntityManager (JPA)[3] for details on using the mapping descriptors in the respective frameworks.

The metadata alone is not enough to allow these classes to be persisted. They must be associated with a persistence unit.

8.3   The persistence unit

The persistence unit groups the entities to be managed and determines how they are to be associated with a database runtime. It also indicates which transaction type is to be used when the database operations occur. The persistence unit consists of three main parts:

- *Entity metadata*—A set of all annotated classes or XML mappings to be managed, containing instructions for how Java classes and bean properties are mapped to relational database tables. It also indicates the relationships between entities and defines the global fetching strategy used to traverse relationships.

- *Persistence unit descriptor*—Specifies which persistence provider to use (not applicable for native Hibernate), database connection information, transaction type and lookup, and vendor extensions.

- *Persistence manager factory*—The runtime object representing the configuration of the persistent unit as a whole. The factory is used to create individual persistence managers that provide the services for managing entity instances.

It's important to understand the distinction between application-managed and container-managed persistence managers. The former is where the application bootstraps the persistence unit and is responsible for creating its own persistence managers. The latter, which only applies to JPA, is where the container loads the persistence unit and dishes out persistence managers as requested. Regardless of which style of Java persistence you're using, you must first set up a persistence unit.

---

[2] http://www.hibernate.org/hib_docs/reference/en/html_single/
[3] http://www.hibernate.org/hib_docs/entitymanager/reference/en/html_single/

8.3.1   *Defining a JCA data source*

There is one prerequisite for setting up a persistence unit: a data source. After all, the goal of persistence is to talk to a database, and the data source provides the channel to that resource. Application servers employ JCA to allow a database resource adapter to integrate with the server connection pooling. What that basically means is that it's possible to stick a database connection configuration into JNDI and have it managed as a connection pool. Data sources can be of the nontransaction, local transaction, or XA transaction variety. Up until now, you've been using a local transaction, but you'll get a chance to play with XA transactions in chapter 14 (online).

In JBoss AS, files that end in *-ds.xml are used to install a data source. seam-gen sets up one of these deployment artifacts for each profile, dev and prod, and puts it in the resources folder of the project. When the build runs, the file is shipped off to JBoss AS. If you're using a different application server, such as GlassFish, you may set up the data source in the administration panel instead. As an alternative, you can define your database connection (JDBC) configuration directly in the persistence unit. In the case of JPA, this is done with vendor-specific JDBC properties (supported in Hibernate, TopLink Essentials, and OpenJPA).

Once the data source is in place, you're ready to configure the persistence unit. The persistence unit descriptor hosts the only XML required in Java persistence.

8.3.2   *The persistence unit descriptor*

The persistence unit descriptor brings all the entity classes together under a single persistence unit and hitches them to an actual database. For JPA, the persistence unit descriptor is META-INF/persistence.xml, and for Hibernate it is hibernate.cfg.xml. Each has a distinct XML schema. Listing 8.2 shows the JPA persistence unit descriptor used in the Open 18 directory application.

Listing 8.2   A JPA persistence unit descriptor

```
<persistence xmlns="http://java.sun.com/xml/ns/persistence"
  xmlns:xsi="http://www.w3.org/2001/XMLSchema-instance"
  xsi:schemaLocation="
    http://java.sun.com/xml/ns/persistence
    http://java.sun.com/xml/ns/persistence/persistence_1_0.xsd"
  version="1.0">
  <persistence-unit name="open18" transaction-type="JTA">        ❶ ❹
    <provider>org.hibernate.ejb.HibernatePersistence</provider>  ❷
    <jta-data-source>open18Datasource</jta-data-source>          ❸
    <properties>
      <property name="hibernate.hbm2ddl.auto" value="validate"/>
      <property name="hibernate.dialect"
        value="org.hibernate.dialect.H2Dialect"/>
      <property name="hibernate.show_sql" value="true"/>
      <property name="hibernate.transaction.manager_lookup_class"
        value=
        "org.hibernate.transaction.JBossTransactionManagerLookup"/>  ❺
```

```
      </properties>
    </persistence-unit>
  </persistence>
```

The file in listing 8.2 identifies several key pieces of information that tell the container how to operate. The fact that there is only one `<persistence-unit>` node ❶ indicates that we're connecting to a single database. There's a one-to-one mapping between the persistence unit and the database. Therefore, if you're working with several different databases, or one or more read-only replicas of a master database, you'll need multiple persistence units, and hence multiple `<persistence-unit>` nodes.

The persistence unit configuration ❶ creates a persistence unit with the name open18, ❷ identifies Hibernate as the JPA provider, ❸ indicates which JNDI data source the persistence manager should use to obtain connections to the database, ❹ configures the persistence manager to use JTA transactions, and ❺ specifies which class maintains the JNDI names of the `UserTransaction` and `TransactionManager` objects. The `TransactionManager` lookup is only relevant for application-managed persistence. You can also use resource-local transactions—often referred to as entity transactions—in environments where JTA isn't available or if you'd rather not use it. The remaining properties in the descriptor are specific to the Hibernate provider.

NOTE   The data source defined in the `<jta-data-source>` node (or optionally the `<non-jta-data-source>` node) of the persistence unit descriptor refers to a `javax.sql.DataSource` in JNDI. seam-gen creates applications that use this configuration. Alternatively, you can configure a JDBC connection using vendor-specific persistence unit properties. The JNDI data source is typically a better choice to offload management of this resource. Note that Seam uses the Embedded JBoss container to provide a local JNDI registry in which to store the data source in a testing environment.

So why use annotations for the mappings and XML for the persistence unit configuration? After all, they both represent metadata about how entity classes tie in to database columns and tables. The answer involves the essence of ORM.

One of the core principles of Hibernate and JPA is to abstract vendor-specific database information from the Java code. The entity mappings are generally fixed, regardless of which database you use, so annotations are appropriate. It's still possible to override the entity mappings in XML if you really need to, perhaps because a different table-naming convention is used in a given database. This setup gives you the rapid development of using annotations without losing the flexibility of configuration provided by an XML descriptor. Where XML is best suited, though, is in defining the SQL dialect, transaction manager, connection URL, and credentials, which are practically guaranteed to change when you switch among databases or deployment environments. These property values can even be tokenized so that a build can sweep through and apply the appropriate replacement values.

There are important differences in how JPA handles the persistence unit descriptor in comparison to Hibernate. In JPA, the following rules apply:

- The persistence unit descriptor must be located at META-INF/persistence.xml.
- Annotated classes are automatically discovered unless indicated otherwise in the descriptor by declaring the `<exclude-unlisted-classes>` element.[4]
- In a Java EE environment, if META-INF/persistence.xml is present, the persistence units in this descriptor will automatically be loaded.[5]

As you can see, some optimizations in JPA allow it to follow configuration-by-exception semantics. The fact that you can't change the location and name of the persistence unit descriptor may leave you scratching your head as to how to define multiple persistence units. Unlike the Hibernate configuration, JPA supports multiple persistence units within the same descriptor, so you don't need separate files.

Hibernate does less work for you when setting up a persistence unit, perhaps as a trade-off for giving you more control. If you're using JPA annotations, you must explicitly define each class in the Hibernate configuration file. You also need multiple Hibernate configuration descriptors (hibernate-database1.cfg.xml, hibernate-database2.cfg.xml) if you need multiple persistence units. Finally, Hibernate isn't automatically loaded into the Java EE environment. If you want to stay away from the proprietary API and configurations of native Hibernate, you're better off using Hibernate as a JPA provider. Putting JPA in front of Hibernate permits you to switch to a different JPA vendor more easily if you feel the need to do so.

Reading the persistence unit descriptor, interpreting the XML mappings, and scanning the classpath for entity annotations are expensive operations. They should be done only once, when the application boots. That's the role of the persistence manager factory.

8.3.3   *The persistence manager factory*

When the persistence unit is loaded, either by the container or by the application, its configuration is stored in a runtime object known as the persistence manager factory. In JPA, the persistence manager factory class is `EntityManagerFactory`. The equivalent class in Hibernate is `SessionFactory`. Once the configuration is loaded into this object, it is immutable. For each persistence unit (either a single `<persistence-unit>` in a JPA persistence unit descriptor or the `<session-factory>` in a Hibernate configuration file), there's a persistence manager factory object to manage it.

When the persistence unit is managed by the container, within a Java EE environment, the persistence manager factory can be injected into a bean property of a Java EE component (a JSF managed bean or an EJB component) using the `@Persistence-Unit` annotation:

```
@PersistenceUnit
private EntityManagerFactory emf;
```

---

[4] In TopLink Essentials, you must set this property to false to enable automatic detection of entity classes.

[5] In Java AS 4.2, this only happens if META-INF/persistence.xml is packaged in an EJB JAR within an EAR.

In the absence of container-managed persistence, you must load the persistence unit in application code using the `Persistence` class. For instance, you could load the `open18` persistence unit using a call to a static method on the `Persistence` class in JPA:

```
EntityManagerFactory entityManagerFactory =
    Persistence.createEntityManagerFactory("open18");
```

The term persistence manager factory reflects its primary function: to create persistence managers. It's a thread-safe object designed to be loaded once when the application starts and closed when the application ends for the sole reason that it's very *expensive* to create. Therefore, it's almost always stored in the application scope, the longest-running scope in the Servlet API.

That wraps up our discussion of the persistence unit. As you've learned, the persistence unit defines which entity classes are to be managed by the persistence API and specifies the resources involved, such as the database dialect and the transaction lookup mechanism. You're now aware that the persistence unit can be loaded by the container or by the application. With the persistence runtime established, we can move on to the persistence manager, the real workhorse of Java persistence.

8.4   *The persistence manager*

The persistence manager is the API that you use to move entity instances to and from the database. It's also used to track changes to the state of the entity instances that it manages to ensure those changes are propagated to the database. In JPA, the persistence manager class is `EntityManager`; in Hibernate, it is the `Session` class.

8.4.1   *Obtaining a persistence manager*

A persistence manager is created from a persistence manager factory. In contrast to the persistence manager factory, persistence managers are very *inexpensive* to create. In fact, they don't even allocate an underlying JDBC connection until a transaction begins. Assuming you've managed to obtain a reference to an `EntityManagerFactory`, you'd use it to create an `EntityManager` instance as follows:

```
EntityManager entityManager =
    entityManagerFactory.createEntityManager();
```

When container-managed persistence is being used (available in a Java EE environment), a persistence manager can be injected into a bean property of a Java EE component using the `@PersistenceContext` annotation, saving you from having to create it yourself:

```
@PersistenceContext
private EntityManager em;
```

You also have the option of creating your own persistence manager in a container environment by injecting a persistence manager factory, as shown earlier. Outside the container (such as in a Java SE environment or JavaBean component), you have no other choice but to create the persistence manager manually from a persistence manager factory. But that doesn't mean you can't delegate this task to Seam. As you'll learn in the next chapter, Seam provides its own version of container-managed persistence so that you can inject a Seam-managed persistence manager into any component using @In. Seam's solution also allows you to work with Hibernate in the same way.

8.4.2   *The management functions of a persistence manager*

The persistence manager is more than just a database mapper and query engine. It takes care of its entities from the moment they're loaded until they're kicked out the door. To that end, the persistence manager has three main responsibilities:

- *Manage entity instances within the scope of a single use case*—Entities are managed via the persistence manager API. This API has methods to create, remove, update, find by id, and query entity instances. It also manages the life cycle of an entity instance as it moves between four possible states: transient, persisted, detached, and removed.
- *Maintain a persistence context*—The persistence context is an in-memory cache of all entity instances that have been loaded into memory by this manager. It is the key to optimizing performance and enabling write-behind database operations (queued SQL statements). It's often referred to as the "first-level" cache. The terms persistence context and persistence manager are often used interchangeably.
- *Perform automatic dirty checking*—The state of managed objects that reside in the persistence context are monitored throughout the lifetime of the persistence context. When the persistence manager is flushed, the pending changes in the entity instances are sent to the database as a batch of SQL statements. Once an object becomes detached, changes to it are no longer monitored.

The persistence manager works at a higher level than SQL. It understands that data going to and from the database has a structure (the entity) and that this structured data has a life cycle, shown in figure 8.3. Entity instances start off as unmanaged, the transient state. They then become managed, allowing them to be synchronized with the database. If they are removed, that synchronization becomes a deletion. When a removal occurs, or the persistence context is closed, the entity instance becomes detached, which means it has been abandoned by the persistence manager and changes to it are no longer monitored.

The most significant aspect of the persistence manager is its persistence context. In

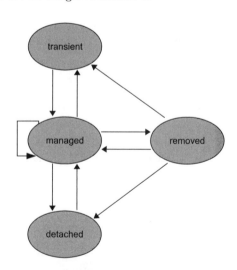

Figure 8.3   The entity life cycle in a Java persistence (ORM) framework

fact, you could argue that the persistence context is what makes using Java persistence worthwhile. The persistence manager will forgo trips to the database when it recognizes that the requested instance has already been loaded into the persistence context. What's more important is that the persistence manager guarantees uniqueness of each instance in the persistence context according to its identifier and the object identity of those instances is preserved. As a result, the persistence manager can monitor the state of the entity instances and will propagate changes made to them to the database, even cascading into related entities, whenever the persistence context is flushed. As long as the persistence manager remains open, you can traverse lazy associations and the persistence manager will go back to the database to load the data without requiring you to assemble a query. These features are what make it a persistence *manager*, not just a database access layer. But to use these features, the persistence context must be scoped appropriately.

8.4.3 *Persistence context scoping*

The persistence manager (and accordingly the persistence context) is often misrepresented as being bound to either a database connection or transaction. This misguided information was brought about by the persistence manager being misused as a means to an end in stateless architectures, popularized by the Spring Framework. The result is that many developers now fear keeping the persistence manager open for an extended period of time or believe that it isn't supposed to remain open beyond the scope of a transaction. The persistence manager was actually designed to serve a use case, for however long that use case may last. The persistence manager will reestablish database connections as needed, and by no means does it leave connections open just because it lives on.

The truth of the matter is that when the persistence manager is scoped incorrectly, Java persistence can become more of a hindrance than a help. When the lifetime of the persistence manager is cut short, perhaps because it's tied to a transaction, it leads to detached entity instances, a topic discussed in depth in section 8.6. By putting the persistence context on such a short leash, you're stripping out all of its value as a manager of entity instances. The persistence manager was designed so that it could outlive a transaction and later be re-associated with a new transaction, informing that transaction, and the database, of the changes to the entities while it was away (a process known as dirty checking). Without this ability, the persistence manager is reduced to a mediator for accessing the database.

What you want to do is treat the persistence manager as a stateful object. That means letting it live through the request and beyond, a need filled by the conversation context. You have to be careful that you don't put it in a shared scope, though, because the persistence manager is not thread safe. In section 8.6, you'll learn how to extend the persistence context's scope by letting a stateful session bean manage it. In the next chapter, you'll see that the conversation is best suited for managing the persistence context, which is exactly how a Seam-managed persistence context is handled.

That covers how entities are formed and how they're used to move data between the Java runtime and the database. But, as you know, data consistency is paramount to persisting data. A brief discussion of the purpose of transactions and how they're controlled wraps up this crash course in Java persistence.

8.5   *Transactions*

Transactions are about as important as the persistence operations themselves. Without transactions, you're risking corrupted or inconsistent data. It is crucial that whenever you perform work against a database, you ensure that the boundaries of a transaction are well defined and that all work is conducted within the scope of such a well-defined transaction.

8.5.1   *Sorting out the transaction APIs*

A database transaction is a grouping of SQL statements that perform an atomic unit of work. This grouping is demarcated by special database statements (e.g., BEGIN, COMMIT, or ROLLBACK). An alternative to issuing these statements explicitly is to use one of various Java transaction APIs responsible for handling this task. You have three choices:

- JDBC transactions
- Resource-local transactions
- JTA transactions

At the most basic level, the JDBC API provides a thin wrapper around these statements. However, when you're working with ORM, you want to work at a higher level to allow the ORM to involve the persistence context in the transaction commit. Resource-local transactions, represented by the RESOURCE_LOCAL constant in the JPA persistence unit descriptor, are those controlled via the persistence manager API (Hibernate or JPA). This is a descriptive term that can be translated as "database focused."

When working with more than one persistence manager, you need an API that can facilitate a transaction across several resources. Java Transaction API (JTA) provides a comprehensive transaction manager that can handle several resources in a single transaction. JTA transactions are therefore referred to as global or system transactions.

JTA is a standard Java EE API and is favored when working in a Java EE–compliant environment. JTA is also used behind the scenes by EJB components that use container-managed transactions. Resource-local transactions are typically used in Java SE environments or servlet containers. If available, JTA is the best choice because it simplifies the task of obtaining an active transaction and issuing rollbacks. It can also enlist multiple resources into the transaction, so if you're partway through development you don't have to change your existing code if you must add a new transactional resource. Seam makes working with the various transaction APIs simple by providing a wrapper that can delegate to the configured transaction API.

Let's now look at the guarantees that a transaction provides.

8.5.2 *Atomic units of work*

From the standpoint of the application, a transaction is an atomic unit of work. An atomic unit of work is a set of operations, or tasks, that you want to perform on the database. Since you're working with Java persistence, you perform these operations against the persistence manager rather than the database. When you reach the point when you want to commit the changes to the database, you're guaranteed by the transaction that either they all happen or none of them happen.

KEEPING DATA CONSISTENT

Rather than rehash the overused bank account scenario to explain transactions, we're going to talk golf! Consider that you use a tee-time reservation system to secure your time slot at your favorite golf course. As a user, you browse through the available times for your course and find one that fits best with your schedule. You pick one and then submit the form. The action method is then tasked with performing an atomic unit of work. The following code shows several operations that are performed within a resource-local transaction using JPA. Proper exception handling is excluded for clarity, but certainly not optional:

```
entityManager.getTransaction().begin();
Course course = entityManager.find(Course.class, courseId);
TeeTime teeTime = new TeeTime(course, selectedDate);
course.reserveTeeTime(teeTime);
Golfer golfer = entityManager.find(Golfer.class, currentGolfer.getId());
golfer.addTeeTimeToSchedule(teeTime);
entityManager.flush();
entityManager.getTransaction().commit();
```

The operations involve marking the time as occupied in the COURSE_SCHEDULE table and then adding a row to the GOLFER_SCHEDULE table so that you don't forget about your obligation. The transaction guarantees that information in these two tables remains consistent—meaning they tell the same story. It ensures that if the insert operation were to fail on the GOLFER_SCHEDULE table, the slot would open back up on the COURSE_SCHEDULE table, and vice versa. You certainly don't want tee times blocked off without anyone intending to show up. You also don't want to show up to the golf course to find a foursome of golfers chatting at the first tee at your scheduled time.

INFO It's often necessary to handle data exchange between two or more persistence managers (and in turn, two or more databases). This scenario calls for a distributed transaction that involves XA-compliant data sources. The XA transaction has the same guarantees but works using a Java-based transaction manager rather than delegating the establishment of transaction boundaries to the database.

The previous example mirrors the classic credit-debit account scenario often cited. Let's consider another source of inconsistency that transactions can protect against.

IT'S ALL OR NOTHING

Assume that you're adding a new golf course to the directory. You spent a good half hour collecting all the data for the course and populating the form. You click Submit to save your work. Once again, the action method is tasked with performing a unit of work. It must save the main information to the course table, a row for each hole in the HOLE table, a row for each tee set in the TEE_SET table, and finally a row for each tee (the number of tee sets times the number of holes) in the TEE table. Assume that somewhere along the line, one of the inserts chokes and the database kicks back an error. If a transaction wasn't active, partial course information could be left spread across the tables. If you tried to submit the form again, it would bail out because the top-level record already exists in the database, even though its related data is incomplete. If the application is smart enough to handle incomplete course data, you may be able to start the form over by editing the data that was inserted, but programming for that situation is complicated. You have a mess on your hands. The damage is magnified if thousands of users are encountering the problem at once.

These two scenarios should give you a compelling reason to use transactions when interacting with the persistence manager. However, even if you're not performing write operations, transactions are still important. In fact, for databases that support transactions, it's impossible to execute a SQL statement without a transaction. It's just that it doesn't last longer than this one statement, behaving the same as auto-commit mode.

READS NEED PROTECTING TOO

The database will open and close a transaction on every operation if explicit transaction boundaries are not set. This mechanism is referred to as an *implicit transaction*. When you forgo the use of transactions, you're just letting the database handle it for you, one SQL statement at a time. These repeated processes of opening and closing transactions incur an unnecessary performance cost (even if optimized). Therefore, even when you're just reading data, you should do so within explicit transaction boundaries.

Using a transaction for successive read-only operations guarantees you the isolation that transactions provide. If the database were to change in the middle of the rendering process, for instance, a transaction could guarantee that you won't end up showing some of the old and some of the new data. If you use Seam's transaction management, you get at least two transactions per request: one that covers the execution of the actions and one that covers the rendering of the response (which you'll learn about in the next chapter).

8.5.3 *ACID abridged*

A proper database transaction adheres to the ACID criteria. This acronym stands for Atomicity, Consistency, Isolation, and Durability. Each criterion is essential to ensuring the integrity of the database and the operations executed against it. However, from the standpoint of the business logic, worrying about the details of each criterion is too low-level. You can instead group them into two key guarantees, which, as an application developer, you want your business logic to adhere to:

- All logically grouped operations succeed or the database remains untouched.
- Your data isn't intermixed with the data from other concurrent operations.

Although some may criticize this as an oversimplification of transactions, if it helps to bring along those developers who merely view transactions as something that makes JPA and Hibernate work, I will have done my job. If you're interested in learning about the specifics of the ACID principle, consult the resources listed at the beginning of the chapter. To go deeper into the topic of transactions and concurrency, check out chapter 5 of Martin Fowler's *Patterns of Enterprise Application Architecture* (Addison-Wesley Professional, 2002).

You're now familiar with the four pillars of Java persistence and how they work together to exchange data between the database and object-based entities while at the same time ensuring that the integrity of the data is upheld. Although the operations on the database form the foundation of Java persistence, the state maintained by the persistence manager is the value added by this abstraction. That's because any time you can avoid hitting the database, the more scalable your application will become (based on the assumption that the database is the least scalable tier). In the next section, you'll learn about a lesser-known feature of Java persistence: using the persistence manager as a stateful context that extends the lifetime of managed entity instances over a series of requests, thus making database-oriented web applications more scalable and less cumbersome to develop and use.

8.6 *Managing persistence in the enterprise*

The servlet environment, an abstraction over the HTTP protocol, is a less-than-ideal setting for performing transactional data processing. The lack of continuity between the stateless HTTP requests means that database connections and persistence managers are constantly being turned over. To further disrupt continuity, a web application is typically partitioned into layers, relying on a data layer to perform Java persistence operations, then shut down connections afterwards. When a persistence manager is closed, the entities it manages become detached and no longer support lazy loading (at least they shouldn't) or automatic dirty checking, two valuable features of ORM.

You can instill continuity by reusing the same persistence manager throughout the duration of a use case. That's the design goal of the extended persistence context. In this section, we put Hibernate aside and focus on using JPA in a standard Java EE environment to implement an extended persistence context and explore the benefits of doing so. In the next chapter, you'll learn how Seam mirrors this pattern using either JPA or Hibernate operating independently of Java EE.

8.6.1 *Introducing the extended persistence context*

Java EE 5 introduced the concept of an extended persistence context by marrying JPA and stateful session beans, both residents of the EJB 3 specification. The persistence manager in JPA is capable of managing a set of entity instances, but it also must be managed. Although it's possible to place the persistence manager directly into a stateful scope (e.g., session or conversation), thus making it available across an arbitrary number of requests, it gets lost there with no dedicated watchman to close it when the stateful scope ends and nothing to provide thread safety, security, or transactions. All of these concerns are what EJB components were designed to handle. Given that the persistence manager is a stateful resource, it makes sense to have it managed by a stateful EJB component.

A stateful session bean (SFSB) is allocated by the EJB container for a single client and remains active (and managing state) until it's removed by the client, potentially spanning multiple thread-based (or database) transactions. In a web application, this type of session bean is typically stored in the HTTP session, allowing it to span multiple requests. In the next chapter, you'll learn that the most suitable context for an SFSB is the conversation, making a stateful session bean conversational as it was intended.

An SFSB is a fitting solution for enclosing the persistence manager and shielding it from the disturbance of HTTP requests being opened and closed during a use case. The only problem is that the default behavior of EJBs is to tie the persistence manager to the scope of the transaction, which typically lasts for the duration of a call to a transactional method (the exact duration depends on the propagation behavior of the transactions). This guarantees that the persistence manager will only be available for a single request; a new one is allocated on the next go-around. The result is that the persistence manager fails to serve the needs of this stateful component or the use case. The lifetime of the persistence manager needs to be aligned with that of the SFSB rather than the transaction—precisely the definition of an extended persistence context.

When the entity manager is injected into a stateful session bean using the Java EE 5 `@PersistenceContext` annotation, you have the choice of using a transactional or extended persistence context, defined by the annotation's `type` attribute. The transaction-scoped persistence context, which is the default type, binds the `EntityManager` to the scope of the JTA transaction. An *extended persistence context*, on the other hand, keeps the `EntityManager` open for the lifetime of the SFSB, delaying the call to the persistence manager's `close()` method until the SFSB is destroyed. Here's an example showing how to inject an extended persistence context into an SFSB:

```
@PersistenceContext(type = PersistenceContextType.EXTENDED)
private EntityManager em;
```

Transactions and requests may come and go, but as long as the SFSB exists, the injected `EntityManager` remains open and manages the entity instances it has loaded. Let's see what benefits this brings and how it simplifies database-oriented web development.

8.6.2   *The benefits of an extended persistence context*

Why would you want to use an extended persistence context? Simple: to prevent detached entities. An entity becomes detached when the `EntityManager` that loaded it is closed. Don't get me wrong; detached entities are useful in that they erase the need for data transfer objects (DTOs). But you generally want to prevent entities from entering this state if you intend to return them to the persistence manager to be updated, you want to use them to load related objects, or you need to repeatedly access the same database records.

When the persistence manager is closed prematurely, it is being abused and so is the database. I use the term *abused* because instead of the persistence manager helping to save you time, it ends up getting in your way. As you wrestle with it, the database gets queried excessively, even though one of the main goals of ORM is to reduce the number of database reads. If you're committed to using ORM, and seeing a return on your investment, it pays to learn to use it correctly. Using an extended persistence context

- Allows safe lazy loading of entity associations and uninitialized proxies
- Eliminates merging to synchronize detached entity instances to the database
- Ensures only one object reference exists for a given entity identifier
- Works in conjunction with optimistic locking to support long-lived units of work

I will walk you through the use case of updating a golf course to shed light on these benefits, showing how an extended persistence context remedies problems caused by use of a transaction-scoped persistence context. Here are the steps involved in that use case:

1 A list of golf courses stored in the database is presented to the user.
2 The user clicks on a course to be modified.
3 An editor form is presented, populated with the course's information.
4 The user makes modifications to the course and clicks the Save button.
5 The modified course is synchronized with the database.

This use case appears simple enough, but because of challenges of working with Java persistence in a web application, presented earlier, programming for this scenario can be made unnecessarily complex without proper treatment of the persistence manager. The good news is that the persistence manager practically handles the work for you if extended throughout the use case. Once you learn to wield the persistence context properly, you will be ready to take on tougher challenges than the one presented here. Let's begin by looking at what lazy loading is and how it's affected by the scoping of the persistence context.

CROSSING LAZY ASSOCIATIONS IN THE VIEW

Lazy loading of entity associations has unfortunately established a bad reputation. The first thing that comes to mind in most developers' minds when you talk about lazy loading is Hibernate's `LazyInitializationException`. The culprit is the detached entity instance.

The associations between entities are represented as an object graph that mimics the relationships of the corresponding database tables. When you fetch an entity, you typically only want to grab a fraction of the total graph or risk loading a significant portion of the database. For example, if you retrieve a `Course` object, it would be very expensive to eagerly load its facility and all of its holes, tee sets, and tees. (It gets worse if the same eager load were to occur when performing a query for multiple `Course` objects.)

The alternative to eager fetching is to mark the associations as lazy. When you traverse the association on the Java object, the uninitialized object or collection of objects is loaded transparently. Although you need to be aware of when this type of loading is

> ## Batch fetching
>
> JPA can be optimized to perform additional eager fetching when lazy loading is triggered to avoid the classic n+1 select problem. Consider what happens when you iterate over the items in a lazy collection. Without optimization, each item is fetched from the database individually. If the number of items in the collection is n, then the database is consulted once to load the parent and n additional times to retrieve each of the children. The persistence frameworks can be configured to batch-fetch the children when the iterator on the collection is accessed to reduce the number of database hits. In Hibernate, this behavior is controlled globally using the `hibernate.default_batch_fetch_size` property. It can also be set at the entity or association level.

occurring, it's neither risky nor a bad practice. See the accompanying sidebar to learn how the classic n+1 select problem can be averted when using Java persistence.

Let's see what the hang-up is about lazy loading. When the user selects a course to edit, the `editCourse()` method on a Seam session bean component is invoked. This method retrieves the `Course` entity instance using a transaction-scoped persistence manager:

```
@Stateful
@Name("courseAction")
public CourseActionBean implements CourseAction {
    @PersistenceContext private EntityManager em;

    @Out private Course course;

    @Begin public void editCourse(Long id) {
        course = em.find(Course.class, id);
    }
    ...
}
```

When the `editCourse()` method is called, the following events occur:

1 A long-running conversation begins.
2 A transaction is started.
3 A new persistence manager is created and bound to the transaction.
4 The `Course` entity instance is retrieved from the persistence manager by its identifier.
5 The transaction is committed (and terminated).
6 The persistence manager is closed.

The last step presents a problem. If the persistence manager is closed after the action method is invoked, the `Course` instance is detached when the view is rendered. Reading the scorecard data from the `Course` instance requires crossing several associations, including the collection of holes, tee sets, and tees, all of which are configured to use a lazy fetching strategy. These associations are sitting ducks for a `LazyInitializationException`. One such traversal may happen when accessing the holes:

```
<ui:repeat var="hole" value="#{course.holes}">
  <th>#{hole.number}</th>
</ui:repeat>
```

A call to the method `getHoles()` triggers an exception because the `EntityManager` that loaded the `Course` instance is no longer available to further communicate with the database. The same problem arises on postback, even if a lazy association wasn't hit in the view.

NOTE In my tests, Hibernate complains about lazy loading on detached entities, whereas TopLink Essentials (another JPA provider) doesn't exhibit this behavior because it proactively creates a new `EntityManager` as needed. While you can avoid this exception by switching to TopLink Essentials, it doesn't mean you've escaped the problem. It's not semantically correct to allow an entity to load data from different persistence managers. The persistence manager should guarantee uniqueness for an entity of the same type and identifier. When you violate this assumption, you're asking for conflicts.

You can avoid problems with lazy loading (properly) in one of two ways:

- Touch all the lazy associations needed in the view while the transaction is active.
- Ensure that the persistence manager stays open for the duration of the request.

The first solution is similar to eager fetching, and thus has the same problems. You may be able to inflate the related objects on the `Course` entity instance in this case, but this is laborious for everyone involved. Eventually you're going to encounter a case where this eager fetch strategy puts too many objects in memory, puts too much unnecessary load on your database, or is simply impossible. Either way, you're going to quickly grow tired of constantly trying to tiptoe around these association boundaries—I know I have. Lazy associations were designed to be traversed, so why can't we traverse them?

The best solution is to set the type of the `EntityManager` that's injected to EXTENDED. That way, the persistence manager remains open for the lifetime of the SFSB and you can cross lazy associations in the view and on subsequent requests to your heart's content. With the editor rendering successfully, let's now explore capturing the changes on postback.

JUST SAY NO TO MERGING

Throughout this book, you've seen how JSF is used to bind input fields to properties of an object. While JSF takes care of updating the property values when the form is submitted, those changes still need to get propagated to the database if the object is an entity instance. Continuing with the current example, let's assume that an instance of the `Course` entity is bound to input fields in the course editor. We consider what happens when the form is submitted depending on whether the entity instance is detached or managed. Let's start by assuming that it is detached (and no lazy-load exceptions occurred during view rendering).

As you know, the persistence manager tracks the state of entity instances bound to it. Outside of the persistence manager's realm, though, changes are not recognized.

When the entity instance is introduced to a new persistence manager, the entity instance is treated like a stranger. Even though the entity instance has an identifier, and perhaps pending updates, the new persistence manager can't vouch for it. To get the changes into the database, you must force those changes onto the EntityManager by passing the detached instance to the merge() method:

```
@PersistenceContext private EntityManager em;

@End public void save() {
    em.merge(course);
}
```

Merging is a crude operation and should be avoided if possible. It first loads an entity instance with the same identifier as the detached instance into the current persistence context, resulting in a database read. Then, the property values from the detached instance are copied onto the properties of the managed instance. The main problem with this operation is that merging clobbers any changes that may have been made to the database record since the detached instance was retrieved (unless object versioning is used). There are other problems as well. If an entity instance with the same identifier as the detached instance has already been loaded into the current persistence context, a non-unique object exception is thrown because the uniqueness contract of entities in a persistence context is violated. You may also run into a lazy loading exception if you hit an uninitialized association on the detached instance during the merge. Avoid merging if at all possible.

By using an extending persistence context, entity instances don't become detached. Therefore, the persistence manager continues to track changes that are made to the entity. When it comes time to synchronize the entity with the database, calling the flush() method will do the trick within the scope of any transaction.

```
@PersistenceContext(type = PersistenceContextType.EXTENDED)
private EntityManager em;

@End public void save() {
    em.flush();
}
```

As you can see, the save() method just instructs the EntityManager to push any dirty state to the database. The persistence manager pays its dues in the following two ways:

- You aren't required to write code to tell the EntityManager to save the changes.
- If no changes are made to the entity instance, no database writes occur.

The coolest part is that no matter how deep down in the object graph changes were made, those changes are pushed to the database on a flush() wherever cascading is enabled. You just don't even have to think about how to write a SQL update statement anymore. The first benefit might get you home from work sooner, but it's the second benefit that takes a step toward relieving the database and making the application more scalable. Reads and writes should occur only when *different* data needs to be exchanged with the database, not data that the application should already be tracking. That brings us to our next topic: the persistence context acting as a first-level cache.

HEY ENTITY, HAVE I SEEN YOU HERE BEFORE?

When you retrieve an entity instance from the persistence manager by its identifier (the value of @Id property), the persistence manager first looks to see if that instance has already been loaded into the persistence context. If so, it returns that instance and the database is spared a read. The persistence context can be combined with the conversation to maintain that "natural cache" of data that was introduced in the previous chapter.

There's another benefit to the persistence context's in-memory cache in addition to saving the database some cycles. If you keep the persistence manager open, it can guarantee that for as long as you work with it, you'll never end up with two different objects with the same identifier in the persistence context. Simply put, you don't have to implement your own equals() method (and thus the hashCode() method) to get the result of two equivalent lookups to be equal in the eyes of Java.

Let's assume that you've defined the following method on your SFSB:

```
public Course findCourseById(Long id) {
    return em.find(Course.class, id);
}
```

If the SFSB uses a transaction-scoped entity manager, the following assertion will fail, whereas if it uses an extended entity manager, it will pass:

```
assert courseAction.findCourseById(9L) == courseAction.findCourseById(9L);
```

Thus, by using an extended persistence context, you don't have to put effort into achieving object equality for the duration of the use case. Trust that this prevents a lot of headaches.

OPTIMISTIC LOCKING

The world doesn't stand still while the user is thinking about what changes to make to the course. It's possible that another user could have gone into the application and chosen to modify the same course. While you could instrument a locking routine on the record, there's a better way that doesn't inconvenience everyone when someone with a record "checked out" goes on a coffee break. The solution is to check for conflicts when the entity instance is being saved, termed optimistic locking.

JPA provides the @Version annotation, which accompanies the @Column annotation on a field intended to maintain the version of an object. The version is simply an integer (though it can also be a timestamp) that increments each time the entity is updated:

```
@Version
@Column(name = "obj_version", nullable = false)
public int getVersion() { return version; }
```

When an update occurs, the version in the database is checked against the version in the entity instance. If they differ, the write is aborted and an application exception is thrown, which can be caught to notify the user of the situation.

This type of locking is termed "optimistic" because it hopes for the best and only aborts the update if the database record was changed externally. Pessimistic locking, which is a formal database lock, prevents anyone else from accessing the record while it's being updated. Holding long-term locks on database resources is a bad idea for performance reasons, especially when it relies on a user interaction to be released. You're far better off using optimistic locking and designing a UI to deal with conflicts when they occur.

Throughout this section, you've witnessed how hairy things can get when you use a transaction-scoped persistence manager and how easy persistence operations become, in contrast, when you switch to an extended persistence manager. Although there are cases when entity instances aren't needed outside of a transactional method, the resounding argument here is "down with the transaction-scoped persistence manager."

Although the SFSB appears promising as the steward of the external persistence context, it has several limitations, most notably that it relies on a Java EE environment. In the next chapter, you'll discover that the Seam-managed persistence context can emulate and improve upon the extended persistence context in Java EE. In addition, a Seam-managed persistence context can be easily shared with Java EE and JavaBean components alike, gets around complex persistence context propagation rules in EJB, and brings an extended persistence context solution to Hibernate. You'll also learn how the extended persistence context is aligned with a conversation to make it available for an entire use case.

8.7   *Choosing between JPA and Hibernate*

There's been a lot of talk in this chapter about JPA and Hibernate, but I haven't formally addressed how they relate to each other or discussed the benefits of choosing one over the other. Seam supports both persistence APIs out of the box, though seam-gen sets up applications to use JPA, implicitly making it the default in Seam. Even so, for every feature in Seam that involves JPA, there's also a Hibernate complement. Before you begin developing your application, you need to decide which API you're going to use.

To choose between native Hibernate and JPA, you need to know a little about the history they share. There's a common misconception that Hibernate and JPA are the same thing. They are not. They do have many similarities, though. This section sets the record straight about how Hibernate relates to JPA and gets you thinking about which API might offer the best choice for your application.

8.7.1   *How Hibernate relates to JPA*

Hibernate served as one of several references when the JPA specification was being developed and can now be used as a JPA provider as an alternative to its native API. But, given that JPA is a specification, it encompasses an agglomeration of other persistence providers, which include Oracle TopLink Essentials (and its derivative, EclipseLink), BEA Kodo, OpenJPA (the open source version of Kodo managed by Apache), and JPOX, to name a few.[6] While Seam can theoretically support any JPA provider, truth be told, there are advantages to choosing the Hibernate implementation (Hibernate `EntityManager`), which will be summarized in the next section.

Many of the JPA interfaces mimic those of Hibernate, differing only in name. Although the two APIs mostly overlap, as figure 8.4 illustrates, there are several features that Hibernate boasts that weren't included in the JPA specification or that have been added since. On the other hand, some concepts were introduced in JPA that aren't available in Hibernate.

Figure 8.4   The overlap between JPA and Hibernate. Hibernate can be used natively or as a JPA provider.

Now that you understand the common history that Hibernate and JPA share, let's consider what differentiates them.

8.7.2   *What sets Hibernate and JPA apart*

Hibernate has been around a lot longer than the JPA specification and has the advantage of being a self-directing open source project, not held back by the (sometimes very slow) Java Community Process (JCP). JPA, on the other hand, has the advantage of leveraging the standard Java EE environment. While that word *standard* carries a great significance, you're always going to get more features using the Hibernate APIs. The most important feature, and the one that the Hibernate developers felt should have been in JPA from the start, is manual flushing of the persistence context. This feature allows you to defer updates to the database until an explicit flush is issued, such as when the use case ends. Manual flushing is essential to implementing an application transaction (called an atomic conversation when managed in the context of a Seam conversation). You'll learn about application transactions and how they're related to conversations in the next chapter.

> **INFO**   It's likely that manual flushing will make it into a future version of the JPA specification. By using Seam, you don't have to wait. Seam offers declarative control over the flush mode of the persistence context. You define the boundaries, and Seam instruments the Hibernate extension for you. You must be using Hibernate to take advantage this feature.

Aside from manual flushing, I'd like to mention a couple of other unique features in Hibernate. One exciting feature is Hibernate Search, a recent extension that supports full-text searching using the Lucene search engine. There's also an extensive set of association mappings that Hibernate supports over JPA, such as indexed collections. And who can forget Gavin's most revered feature: postquery filters. Hibernate can also save keystrokes by allowing you to use shorthand for JPQL in the style of Hibernate's HQL (e.g., "from Course" instead of "select c from Course c") and generally has a more intelligent query parser. If you're a person who thrives on bleeding-edge features, you'll probably be most comfortable with Hibernate. One of the unique features of

---

[6]   A more complete list can be found at http://en.wikibooks.org/wiki/Java_Persistence/Persistence_Products.

Hibernate, to give it credit, is its ability to use JPA annotations. So you take a hybrid approach, which Seam builds on further.

8.7.3 Seam's hybrid approach

Does choosing JPA mean that you have to sacrifice features? What if you want to use JPA but still take advantage of what Hibernate has to offer? I have good news for you. By choosing Hibernate as the JPA provider and using Seam-managed persistence, which you'll learn about in the next chapter, Seam allows you to get the best of both worlds. Seam does some fancy footwork behind the scenes to give your JPA EntityManager access to several of Hibernate's extensions. The best part is that, for the most part, you can stick to using the standard JPA interfaces in your code. Seam distills the best features of both frameworks so that, with little or no casting, you get the following benefits:

- Manual flushing of the persistence context (application transaction)
- Postquery filters (defined in the component descriptor)
- Vendor-specific query hints[7] (defined in the component descriptor)
- Full-text searching (using the Lucene search engine)
- Hibernate Validator (enforced when the persistence context is flushed)

Seam's philosophy is to let you keep the standards close at hand and feed you with the extra features that the standard isn't ready to dish out. If maintaining strict JPA portability is important to you, you'll likely want to avoid using extensions that aren't common across the persistence providers. However, my advice is that you shouldn't let your choice to use JPA hold back your application. Take advantage of the capabilities of the JPA provider.

> ### What about designing to interfaces?
>
> If you're an advocate of interface-based design, you may be shouting that the best way to abstract the persistence framework choice is to hide it behind an interface that uses the object repository pattern (as suggested in Eric Evans's Domain-Driven Design: Tackling Complexity in the Heart of Software [Addison-Wesley, 2003]). A data access layer would absolutely fit into the Seam component model. You're simply moving the dependency injections down a layer. Understand, though, that you still have to consider which persistence framework is going to get you to a working implementation faster. An interface is but an interface. You still have to implement it.

The Seam reference documentation sends a clear message regarding which persistence framework to choose. It recommends that you use JPA with Hibernate as the provider. Making this pairing allows you to adhere to JPA until you decide that it's necessary to leverage Hibernate-specific features. If you discover along the way that you

---

[7] http://www.hibernate.org/hib_docs/entitymanager/reference/en/html_single/#d0e797

need Hibernate to make your application successful, you can easily tap into it. It also recommends that you use Seam-managed persistence, which you'll learn about in the next chapter. As for the basics of Java persistence, I trust that you have what you need to get started and to understand the resources I recommended. You can also correct your colleagues when they make the claim that JPA and Hibernate are the same.

8.8 *Summary*

This chapter gave you the crash course in Java persistence that you need to use Seam's managed persistence and transactions, covered in the next chapter. The four main elements of Java persistence were explored: entities, the persistence unit, the persistence manager, and transactions. I then explained the distinction between a transactional and extended persistence context, and expounded the benefits of having an extended persistence context. Finally, you learned how JPA differs from Hibernate, and I presented reasons why you would choose one over the other. I recommended that you use Hibernate as a JPA provider rather than the native Hibernate API so that you're able to take advantage of Java EE standards while still having access to the extensions offered by Hibernate.

In the next chapter, you're going to learn how Seam supplements Java persistence and how it does a better job of managing the persistence context than what's provided by the Java EE container alone. You'll also discover how Seam offers the same declarative transaction behavior for regular JavaBeans that EJB 3 session beans enjoy. Read on to see how Seam makes creating transactional applications a truly pleasant experience.

Seam-managed persistence and transactions

This chapter covers
- Handling the persistence context properly
- Bootstrapping Java persistence in Seam
- Applying a multifaceted transaction strategy
- Implementing an application transaction

Most web frameworks remain agnostic of persistence rather than recognize it as vital to the overall state of the application. Stateless architectures, especially, have depleted the persistence manager of its true value—to monitor a set of managed entities and transparently migrate changes made to them to the database. Seam seeks to restore Java persistence (i.e., ORM) to its full potential by recognizing it as a core part of the application. In addition to adeptly managing the persistence context, Seam ensures that a transaction is always active, commits the transaction when appropriate, and broadcasts transaction synchronization events to improve transparency of persistence operations. In the previous chapter, you learned the fundamentals of Java persistence and how persistence is used both inside and out of a Java EE container. In this chapter, you'll discover how Seam's involvement with transactions and persistence helps make these services truly manageable.

The conversation is also revisited in this chapter, which combines with persistence to form the core of Seam's state-management architecture. Seam hosts the persistence manager in the conversation context, giving it refuge from the confines of a stateless design. The true benefit of this union is realized at the end of the chapter when you learn about an *application* transaction, a special type of transaction that allows modifications made to managed entities to be queued across requests until the end of the use case, at which time the changes are committed to the database within a *database* transaction.

This chapter also prepares you to use the Seam Application Framework, covered in the next chapter, which enables rapid development of create, read, update, delete (CRUD)-based applications and embodies the design goal of properly handling the persistence context, a theme that continues through this chapter. Let's pick up with this theme where the previous chapter left off.

9.1 Getting persistence context management right

To realize the true value of Java persistence, the persistence manager—a general term for a JPA `EntityManager` or Hibernate `Session`—must be scoped properly. In chapter 8, you learned that if you treat the persistence manager as a stateful component, it can do a lot for you; if you don't, it can lead to a lot of pain. The transaction-scoped persistence context inhibits the capabilities of Java persistence and is generally discouraged in Seam.

The challenge of using an extended persistence context is deciding how long to extend it without overdoing it. If it's not held open long enough, your entities become detached prematurely. If it's held open for too long, it can result in an overzealous cache and memory leaks. As it turns out, the persistence manager was intended to serve a use case, making the conversation context the ideal host for an extended persistence context. In this section, I explain how a conversation-scoped persistence manager gets to the heart of the problems that many developers encounter using ORM. I then show you two ways to bind the persistence manager to a conversation in a Seam application.

9.1.1 Respecting the persistence manager

It's true that using Java persistence in a web application can be a challenge. Unfortunately, some developers have made it harder than it has to be. I want to educate you about the shortcomings of the so-called "patterns" that have been developed to solve Hibernate lazy-loading exceptions. The purpose in raising this issue is to emphasize that this exception is really a symptom of incorrect usage, which these shortsighted fixes fail to address.

THE OPEN SESSION IN VIEW REMEDY

Recognizing that Hibernate wasn't going to allow lazy loading in the view unless the `Session` remained open, developers created the Open Session in View pattern,[1] which controls the `Session` from the outer rim of the application using a servlet filter. It works by preventing the data layer from closing the `Session` and instead the filter closes it at the end of the request. (There is a parallel implementation for JPA that also applies here.)

The problem with this fix is that a filter is too far removed from the application to know what it's doing. It blindly tries to determine whether it should open one `Session` or whether several are needed. Complications also arise because now the `Session` has two masters, the application framework and the filter, which may not always be in agreement.

The filter may make a mess of things, but at least it allows lazy loading in the view, right? Sure, but the benefits end there. By waiting until the end of the request to flush and close the persistence context, the application doesn't know if the database writes succeeded or failed until after the view is rendered, a problem addressed in section 9.4.1. Once the page is rendered, all of the entity instances stored in stateful scopes become detached. Thus, the lazy-loading problems are merely deferred until postback, where you no longer benefit from the persistence cache or automatic dirty checking of entities. In addition, having detached entities around during a postback can introduce the `NonUniqueObjectException`. A far better solution is to respect the persistence manager by scoping it to the conversation.

THE OPEN SESSION IN CONVERSATION SOLUTION

As you learned in chapter 7, conversations last for at least the entire request, including redirects. By associating the persistence manager with the conversation, you get the Open Session in View pattern for free. But now, you aren't allowing a filter to make arbitrary decisions about how the persistence manager should be managed. If the conversation is long-running, then the persistence manager stretches to match it, termed the Open Session in Conversation pattern. As a result, entities aren't detached prematurely, which means you can avoid merging and instead benefit from automatic dirty checking. In fact, to propagate an entity instance between requests, you only have to keep track of the entity's identifier since the same instance can be retrieved again out of the persistence context.

Placing the persistence manager directly into the conversation introduces the problem that no one tends to it. Who will close it? How will it be enlisted in transactions? I present two options for tying the persistence manager to a conversation in a way that it is still managed.

9.1.2   *Managing an extended persistence context*

Seam has two strategies for managing an extended persistence context, contrasted in figure 9.1. In chapter 8, you learned that a container-managed persistence manager

---

[1] http://www.hibernate.org/43.html

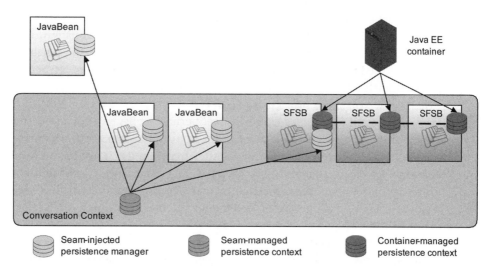

Figure 9.1   Contrasts the independence of a Seam-managed persistence context with the coupling of the container-managed persistence managers to their stateful session bean components.

can latch onto a stateful session bean (SFSB) for the duration of its lifetime. By scoping the SFSB to the conversation, Seam can indirectly manage the extended persistence context. Alternatively, Seam can take full control of the extended persistence context by creating its own persistence manager and storing it directly in the conversation. The benefit of the Seam-managed persistence manager is that it can be injected into any Seam component.

Picking up from the previous chapter, I reiterate the inherent limitations of using an SFSB to host the extended persistence context and segue into Seam's more flexible solution.

SCOPING THE PERSISTENCE CONTEXT INDIRECTLY

When an SFSB becomes a Seam component, Seam doesn't control how a container-managed persistence manager is bound to the SFSB. Thus, Seam can only tune the lifetime of the extended persistence context by managing the lifetime of the SFSB. (Keep in mind that this has no effect on a transaction-scope persistence context on the SFSB.) However, there are several problems with this solution:

- It can only be used in an EJB environment (EJB session bean and JPA).
- There are complex propagation rules[2] for sharing the extended persistence context across loosely coupled Java EE components.
- The extended persistence context on an SFSB cannot be accessed easily from JavaBean components.
- Seam can't control the flush mode of the persistence context on an SFSB (no manual flushing).

---

[2] http://www.hibernate.org/hib_docs/entitymanager/reference/en/html_single/#architecture-ejb-persistctxpropagation

I'm not saying that you can't make the conversation-scoped SFSB work. It may sufficiently suit your needs. But if any one of these issues gets in your way, it calls for a more flexible solution. Seam can assume the task of managing the persistence manager, a feature known in Seam as a Seam-managed persistence context. Seam can even go a step further by managing Java persistence end to end.

LETTING SEAM MANAGE THE PERSISTENCE CONTEXT

A Seam-managed persistence context is a Hibernate or JPA extended persistence manager operating in isolation of Java EE. It's application managed, which means that Seam is responsible for instantiating it. After that, you use it just as you would a container-managed persistence context in a Java EE component, except that it's injected using @In rather than @PersistenceContext. To give Seam control of creating the persistence manager, you have to feed it a persistence unit, which you'll learn to do in section 9.3.

The Seam-managed persistence context is scoped to the conversation, which means you tune its lifetime using the conversation propagation controls you learned about in chapter 7. What sets the Seam-managed persistence context apart from its container-managed counterpart is that it's stored directly in the conversation, making it a first-class citizen of the application, rather than being bound to the lifetime of a single component. Consider that if an SFSB hosting an extended persistence context is removed, the persistence context goes along with it. In contrast, a Seam-managed persistence context remains available as long as the conversation is active, regardless of which components come and go. The best part is that you can share the persistence context between Java EE and non–Java EE components alike without having to worry about complex (and tricky) propagation rules. Although the extended persistence context in EJB 3 is a good start, Seam is better at handling this task.

Another nice feature of the Seam persistence infrastructure is that the support for JPA and native Hibernate is parallel. The classes and configurations differ, of course, but the overall architecture is the same, making it easy to switch between the two APIs across different projects. This parallel support extends into the Seam Application Framework, covered in the next chapter, which wraps the persistence manager and provides additional built-in functionality to support persistence tasks.

Regardless of who controls the persistence manager, the conversation is the key to giving the persistence manager the respect it deserves. It's really a perfect marriage. Seam's persistence strategy goes beyond just scoping the persistence manager. When used in a Seam application, your persistence manager gets some upgrades. If you're using native Hibernate or Hibernate as the JPA provider, you get yet another set of enhancements.

9.2   *Enhancing the capabilities of the persistence manager*

Seam proxies the persistence manager when it's injected into a Seam component and decorates it with extra functionality (i.e., the Decorator pattern). This section presents these upgrades, starting with standard enhancements and then those specific to Hibernate.

9.2.1 Seam's standard enhancements

Given that Seam and Hibernate are both JBoss-supported frameworks, it should come as no surprise that Hibernate gets special treatment in Seam. If you're already using Hibernate, this is good news. But Seam also offers some standard enhancements that are available to any persistence provider:

- EL notation in persistence queries
- Entity converter that allows entities to be used in UI select menus
- Managed entity identity across session passivation

Only the first two items will be covered in detail. The last item is a low-level feature and it's not necessary to concern yourself with the details. Let's start with the crowd favorite: the EL.

EL IN THE QL

As you have come to expect by now, Seam lets you use the EL all over a Seam application. With persistence, the EL is back again. Seam supports the use of EL value expressions within a JPQL or HQL query just as it does in JSF messages and log messages. This holds true regardless of which persistence provider or API you're using.

The value expressions provide an alternative to supplying positional or named parameters in your queries and are evaluated when the query is executed. Let's say that in the registration process, you want to check to make sure that a username isn't taken:

```
assert entityManager.createQuery(
    "select m from Member m where m.username = #{newGolfer.username}")
    .list() == 0;
```

Using the EL in a query provides a number of benefits. First, it serves as shorthand for creating a named query parameter and assigning it a value. Also, since the value of the expression is assigned using a query parameter (i.e., `setParameter()`), it's properly escaped, protecting the query from SQL injection. And any value that can be resolved via the EL can be used as a parameter. That includes contextual variables as well as factory and manager components. You see this combination used in the restriction clauses of the Query component, covered in chapter 10. Finally, the inline EL syntax moves all parameters into a string, making it possible to define the query in a string constant or externalize it to a configuration file, where it can be assigned using component configuration.

PICK ME OUT AN ENTITY

I bet that at one point or another, you've needed to present a list of entities in a form field and let the user select one or more of them. This is one of those tasks JSF doesn't support out of the box (or most frameworks for that matter). It's your job to convert the instances into a string representation and then reinterpret the selections when the form is submitted. Well, guess what? Seam offers to take care of it for you! The only catch is that you must be using a Seam-managed persistence context and, ideally, a long-running conversation.

Let's assume that you need to assign a member a list of roles and you've prepared a factory named `availableRoles` that returns a list of `Role` entity instances. (You cannot use a `Set` with a `UISelectMany` component, only a parameterized `List` or an array.) You can assign roles to a member as follows, nesting the `<s:convertEntity>` UI component tag to let Seam know to handle the conversion:

```
<h:selectManyListbox size="10" value="#{member.roles}">
  <s:selectItems var="r" value="#{availableRoles}" label="#{r.name}"/>
  <s:convertEntity/>
</h:selectManyListbox>
```

That's all there is to it! When the view is rendered, the id of each entity (as defined by its `@Id` property) is used in the value of a select option. On postback, the entity instance is restored by passing the id to the persistence manager. For the selection to be valid, its object identity must be equivalent to an instance in the collection. The best way to guarantee this condition is to use a conversation-scoped collection and a long-running conversation.

The component that handles the conversion for `<s:convertEntity>` is named `org.jboss.seam.ui.EntityConverter`. This component looks for a JPA persistence manager according to a standard naming convention, described at the end of section 9.3.2. It's possible to override the JPA persistence manager that the converter uses, or configure the converter to use a Hibernate persistence manager. However, the configuration changed between Seam 2.0 and 2.1. Let's start with Seam 2.0.

In Seam 2.0, you can establish the persistence manager that the converter uses by setting its `entityManager` property (for JPA) or `session` property (for Hibernate). Here's an example of an override when using JPA:

```
<component name="org.jboss.seam.ui.EntityConverter">
  <property name="entityManager">#{em}</property>
</component>
```

If you only want to override the persistence manager for a single conversion, you first define a new component for the converter class in the component descriptor:

```
<component name="customEntityConverter"
  class="org.jboss.seam.ui.converter.EntityConverter">
  <property name="entityManager">#{em}</property>
</component>
```

The name of this component is a valid JSF converter id, which you then supply to a JSF converter tag that takes the place of `<s:convertEntity>` within the select component:

```
<f:converter converterId="customEntityConverter"/>
```

In Seam 2.1, a layer of indirection was introduced. Instead of the entity converter using a persistence manager directly, it uses an entity loader component. In addition, two configuration elements in the component namespace http://jboss.com/products/seam/ui, prefixed as ui, were introduced to simplify the configuration. The entity loader elements are `<ui:jpa-entity-loader>` and `<ui:hibernate-entity-loader>` for JPA and Hibernate, respectively. Here's the same global override for JPA in Seam 2.1:

```
<ui:jpa-entity-loader entityManager="#{em}"/>
```

To define a custom entity converter, you must also define a custom entity loader:

```
<ui:jpa-entity-loader name="customEntityLoader" entityManager="#{em}"/>
<ui:entity-converter name="customEntityConverter"
  entity-loader="#{customEntityLoader}"/>
```

If all of this configuration is stressing you out, just remember that you can be configuration free if you stick to the defaults. These overrides are just there if you need them.

NO THANKS, HIBERNATE

Before moving on to the Hibernate extensions that Seam exposes, I want to discuss Seam's JPA extension manager and how it affects using alternate JPA providers. Seam uses a built-in component named `persistenceProvider` to transparently tap into vendor-specific JPA extensions, such as Hibernate's manual flushing, allowing Seam to leverage the strengths of the persistence provider while respecting your choice to use JPA. As its JavaDoc states, "The methods on this class are the TODO list for the next revision of the JPA specification."

The only trouble with this component is that in Seam 2.0, it has a strong affinity for Hibernate. If the Hibernate JARs are present on the classpath, Seam automatically assumes that Hibernate is the JPA provider. To reverse this assumption and prevent Seam from trying to use Hibernate extensions, add the following configuration to the component descriptor:

```
<component name="org.jboss.seam.persistence.persistenceProvider"
  class="org.jboss.seam.persistence.PersistenceProvider"/>
```

Seam 2.1 switched to using runtime detection of the JPA provider by consulting the persistence manager, thus making this override unnecessary. Let's check out what extensions are used if it is Hibernate.

9.2.2 *Letting Hibernate shine through*

As I mentioned in chapter 8, Hibernate has several nice extensions that Seam can elegantly expose to your application even if you're using JPA. Here are the most notable extensions:

- Postquery filters
- Hibernate Search
- Manual flushing of the persistence context

This section focuses on the first two features, as well as how to elegantly expose the Hibernate `Session`. An entire section, section 9.4, is dedicated to the last feature and how it relates to application transactions.

FILTERING THE QUERY RESULTS

Although it's perhaps not the first feature you'll use in Hibernate, if the need arises, it's nice to know that Hibernate supports filtering of the query results for a given `Session`. This feature is useful for regional filtering and redacting sensitive data. Best of all, you can apply it without touching Java code. Instead, you define filters using XML in the component descriptor. This feature is only available if you're using a Seam-managed

persistence context. Consult the Hibernate reference documentation for details on
how to define filters.

But why filter when you can search? That's what Hibernate Search is all about.

CALLING ON HIBERNATE SEARCH

For more sophisticated searching, and to take load off the database, you can use
Hibernate Search, a Hibernate extension that can perform Lucene-based full text
search queries against the domain model. When the Hibernate Search libraries are
present on the classpath (consisting of hibernate-search.jar, hibernate-commons-
annotations.jar, and lucene-core.jar), Seam proxies the persistence manager, wrapping it with Hibernate Search capabilities. If you're using Hibernate, the `Session` is
wrapped in a `FullTextSession`; if you're using JPA, the `EntityManager` is wrapped in
a `FullTextEntityManager`. Hibernate Search is available even when you're using a
Java EE container-managed `EntityManager` (i.e., `@PersistenceContext`).

To use Hibernate Search, you either downcast to the full-text variant when you
need its features or, if you're using a Seam-managed persistence context, just inject it
directly using the appropriate property type. Here, we search for golf courses using a
Lucene query:

```
@Name("courseSearch")
public class CourseSearchAction {
    @In private FullTextEntityManager entityManager;
    @Out private List<Course> searchResults;

    public void search(String searchString) {
        org.apache.lucene.query.Query luceneQuery =
            new MultiFieldQueryParser(new String[] {"name", "description"},
            new StandardAnalyzer()).parse(searchString);
        javax.persistence.Query query = entityManager
            .createFullTextQuery(luceneQuery, Course.class);
        searchResults = (List<Course>) query.getResultList();
    }
}
```

Of course, to query entities with Hibernate Search, you need to apply the Hibernate
Search annotations to your entity classes and add the indexer settings to the persistence unit descriptor. A minimal configuration consists of an index storage provider
and index location, shown here for JPA (/META-INF/persistence.xml):

```
<properties>
    ...
    <property name="hibernate.search.default.directory_provider"
        value="org.hibernate.search.store.FSDirectoryProvider"/>
    <property name="hibernate.search.default.indexBase"
        value="/home/twoputt/indexes/open18-index"/>
</properties>
```

There's no way to do Hibernate Search justice in this small amount of space. Besides,
Seam simply handles the task of wrapping the full-text search persistence manager
around the native one. From there, it's out of Seam's hands. I encourage you to grab a
copy of *Hibernate Search in Action* (Manning, 2008) to learn how to use this extremely
powerful feature of Hibernate.

While Seam's role as liaison between JPA and the underlying Hibernate API is a desirable abstraction and usually fishes what you need out of Hibernate, there may be times when you have to work directly with the Hibernate `Session`. Fortunately, Seam offers a neat trick.

GETTING DOWN TO HIBERNATE

When you're using JPA, you can always get down to the provider interface by calling the `getDelegate()` method on the `EntityManager` instance. But you have to perform a cast that makes an assumption about the underlying JPA provider:

```
Session session = (Session) entityManager.getDelegate();
```

You can define a factory in Seam to hide the cast:

```
<factory name="hibernateSession" value="#{entityManager.delegate}"
    auto-create="true"/>
```

You then use the `@In` annotation to inject the value of this factory into your component:

```
@In private Session hibernateSession;
```

One reason you might need the Hibernate Session is to check if there are modified entities in the persistence context:

```
boolean dirty = hibernateSession.isDirty();
```

Hopefully these upgrades motivate you to use the Seam-managed persistence components. In the next section, you'll learn to set up a persistence unit and persistence manager in Seam. I present the JPA configuration followed by Hibernate configuration. If you're only interested in one of the frameworks, you can skip over its complement.

9.3   *Setting up a persistence unit in Seam*

In the previous chapter, you learned how to prepare a persistence unit descriptor for JPA (META-INF/persistence.xml) and one for Hibernate (hibernate.cfg.xml), which you'll use in this section to load JPA and Hibernate, respectively. While the Java EE container can find the JPA persistence unit descriptor on its own, Seam requires some direction in locating a persistence unit. Seam's persistence management is capable of bootstrapping the persistence unit, but it's not required. You can also configure Seam to use the persistence unit runtime managed by the Java EE container, which only applies to JPA, or, as you'll learn in chapter 15 (online), Seam can retrieve a persistence unit runtime that's managed by the Spring container.

I start by introducing you to Seam's built-in components that load and manage either a JPA or Hibernate persistence unit, then move on to configuring them.

9.3.1   *Seam's persistence manager factories*

Seam provides manager components for bootstrapping JPA and Hibernate persistence units. I refer to these components, which wrap the runtime configuration object of the persistence unit, as Seam-managed persistence units. Table 9.1 shows the mapping between each Seam-managed persistence unit and the persistence manager factory it manages.

Table 9.1 The Seam-managed persistence units

Persistence framework	Seam component `org.jboss.seam.persistence.*`	Persistence configuration it manages
JPA	`EntityManagerFactory`	`javax.persistence.EntityManagerFactory`
Hibernate	`HibernateSessionFactory`	`org.hibernate.SessionFactory`

The Manager design pattern allows Seam to tie the life cycle of the underlying persistence manager factory to that of an application-scoped Seam component. Each of the two components listed in table 9.1 has a `@Create` method, which starts the persistence manager factory, and a `@Destroy` method, which closes it. The components initialize on application startup as directed by the `@Startup` annotation.

Since the Seam-managed persistence units are manager components, they resolve to the value they manage, which is the persistence manager factory. Thus, when a Seam-managed persistence unit is injected into a property of a Seam component, the property's type must be that of the persistence manager factory. Assuming the name of the JPA persistence unit component is `entityManagerFactory`, it's injected as follows:

```
@In private EntityManagerFactory entityManagerFactory;
```

For Hibernate, if the component is named `sessionFactory`, the injection looks like this:

```
@In private SessionFactory sessionFactory;
```

The Seam-managed persistence unit components are actually just component templates, meaning that neither has a `@Name` annotation. To actualize them as Seam components, you must declare them in the component descriptor. Only then will the persistence manager factory be loaded.

As with all of the built-in Seam components, Seam provides a component namespace to ease the XML configuration burden. Seam's persistence components fall under `http://jboss.com/products/seam/persistence`, aliased as `persistence` throughout this section. With the namespace declaration in place, let's see how this component is configured in the case of JPA and Hibernate.

BOOTSTRAPPING A JPA ENTITYMANAGERFACTORY

The component definition for the Seam-managed persistence unit must include both a name and a reference to a persistence unit. Let's assume you have a JPA persistence unit named `open18` defined in META-INF/persistence.xml as follows:

```
<persistence-unit name="open18" transaction-type="JTA">
    ...
</persistence-unit>
```

For that, you declare the following declaration in the component descriptor:

```
<persistence:entity-manager-factory name="entityManagerFactory"
    persistence-unit-name="open18"/>
```

If the `persistence-unit-name` attribute is excluded from the component definition, the name of the component is used as the persistence unit name, which in this case would be `entityManagerFactory`.

That's pretty much all there is to it! Internally, Seam uses the persistence unit name to create an `EntityManagerFactory` as follows:

```
EntityManagerFactory entityManagerFactory =
    Persistence.createEntityManagerFactory("open18");
```

To have Seam defer loading of the persistence unit until it's needed, perhaps for a quicker deployment turnaround, you can disable the startup behavior of this component:

```
<persistence:entity-manager-factory name="entityManagerFactory"
  persistence-unit-name="open18" startup="false"/>
```

JPA can accept vendor-specific properties for a persistence unit. Typically these properties are defined inside the `<properties>` element in the persistence unit descriptor. In Seam, you have the option of defining these properties on the manager component itself:

```
<persistence:entity-manager-factory name="entityManagerFactory"
  persistence-unit-name="open18">
  <persistence:persistence-unit-properties>
    <key>hibernate.show_sql</key><value>true</value>
  </persistence:persistence-unit-properties>
</persistence:entity-manager-factory>
```

Supplying these properties using Seam's component configuration feature gives you the flexibility to tune them for a specific environment by using a replacement token or value expression as the property's value. See chapter 5 for more details.

The component that loads the Hibernate configuration is a touch more sophisticated.

BOOTSTRAPPING A HIBERNATE SESSIONFACTORY

Hibernate is configured in much the same way as JPA, only instead of providing a persistence unit name, you indicate the location where the Hibernate configuration resides on the classpath. If the configuration file is named according to Hibernate's convention, you don't even need to specify the file's location. Hibernate automatically looks for hibernate.cfg.xml (as well as hibernate.properties) at the root of the classpath when it loads, unless told otherwise. In this default case, the component definition is specified as follows:

```
<persistence:hibernate-session-factory name="sessionFactory"/>
```

Internally, Seam loads the Hibernate `SessionFactory` as follows:

```
SessionFactory sessionFactory =
    new AnnotationConfiguration().configure().buildSessionFactory();
```

If the name of the configuration file doesn't follow the Hibernate convention, perhaps because you're loading a second Hibernate persistence unit, you must specify the location of the Hibernate configuration file:

```
<persistence:hibernate-session-factory name="teetimeSessionFactory"
  cfg-resource-name="hibernate-teetime.cfg.xml"/>
```

In this case, the load performed internally changes to

```
SessionFactory sessionFactory =
    new AnnotationConfiguration().configure(cfgResourceName)
    .buildSessionFactory();
```

With Hibernate, you have the option of configuring the persistence unit entirely in the component descriptor, specifying the Hibernate configuration properties[3] using component configuration properties:

```
<persistence:hibernate-session-factory name="sessionFactory">
  <persistence:cfg-properties>
    <key>hibernate.connection.driver_class</key>
    <value>org.h2.Driver</property>
    <key>hibernate.connection.username</key>
    <value>open18</value>
    <key>hibernate.connection.password</key>
    <value>tiger</value>
    <key>hibernate.connection.url</key>
    <value>jdbc:h2:/home/twoputt/databases/open18-db/h2</value>
  </persistence:cfg-properties>
</persistence:hibernate-session-factory>
```

You have to decide you want whether to define the Hibernate configuration properties in the Hibernate persistence unit descriptor or the Seam component descriptor. If the cfg-resource-name attribute is present, the <cfg-properties> element is ignored.

The Hibernate persistence unit component offers a rich set of configuration properties for supplying the location of mapping artifacts. The properties are defined using the <mapping-classes>, <mapping-files>, <mapping-jars>, <mapping-packages>, and <mapping-resources> elements. Consult the Hibernate documentation for information on using these settings.

Seam's components are just one option you have for loading a persistence unit. In section 9.3.3, you'll learn how to work with a persistence manager factory stored in JNDI, a less Seam-centric approach. We'll forge ahead for now using the Seam-managed persistence unit as the source from which a Seam-managed persistence context is created.

9.3.2   *Seam-managed persistence contexts*

Having just registered a persistence manager factory, you could use it to create your own application-managed persistence manager. But why manage this resource yourself when Seam can take the burden off your shoulders? Once again, Seam uses a manager component to handle this task. However, in this case the persistence

---

[3] For a full list of properties available to Hibernate, please refer to the Hibernate reference documentation.

manager is allocated when the Seam-managed persistence context is retrieved from the Seam container rather than being initialized at application startup like the persistence manager factory.

When the Seam-managed persistence context is created, it's stored in the active conversation context—regardless of whether the conversation is temporary or long-running. The life cycle of the underlying persistence manager is then bound to the lifetime of the conversation. When the conversation ends, Seam calls the `close()` method on the persistence manager to close the persistence context. Table 9.2 shows the persistence manager that Seam creates for each persistence framework.

Table 9.2 The Seam-managed persistence contexts

Persistence framework	Seam component `org.jboss.seam.persistence.*`	Persistence manager it creates
JPA	`ManagedPersistenceContext`	`javax.persistence.EntityManager`
Hibernate	`ManagedHibernateSession`	`org.hibernate.Session`

Once the Seam-managed persistence context is defined (which will be covered shortly), you can inject it into the property of another Seam component using the `@In` annotation. The target property's type is expected to be that of the persistent manager. Assuming the name of the JPA component is `entityManager`, it's injected as follows:

```
@In private EntityManager entityManager;
```

Remember that this injection can occur at any layer in your application, not just on a JSF action bean component as you see in many of the examples in this book.

For Hibernate, where application-managed persistence contexts are your only option, the injection is performed as follows, assuming the component is named `hibernateSession`:

```
@In private Session hibernateSession;
```

If a JTA transaction is active when the Seam-managed persistence context is injected, the persistence manager is enlisted in that transaction. In addition, if you're using Hibernate, either as a provider for JPA or natively, and Hibernate filters are defined on the component, they're applied to the persistence manager at this time.

Like the Seam-managed persistence units, the Seam-managed persistence contexts are component templates. To make them available to the application, they must be activated using the component descriptor. Let's see how they're defined.

DEFINING A MANAGED PERSISTENCE CONTEXT

When you declare the Seam-managed persistence context, you must supply a name and a reference to a persistence manager factory. If you've configured a Seam-managed persistence unit named `entityManagerFactory` that loads the JPA persistence unit, you inject a reference to it as a value expression into the Seam-managed persistence context:

```
<persistence:managed-persistence-context name="entityManager"
  entity-manager-factory="#{entityManagerFactory}" auto-create="true"/>
```

Likewise, if you've configured a Seam-managed persistence unit named `session-Factory` to load the Hibernate persistence unit, you inject the corresponding value expression:

```
<persistence:managed-hibernate-session name="hibernateSession"
  hibernate-session-factory="#{sessionFactory}" auto-create="true"/>
```

In the previous two declarations, the `auto-create` attribute is set to true. By default, the Seam-managed persistence context components are defined with the autocreate feature disabled. By enabling this feature, you can inject these components using an `@In` annotation without having to supply the `create` attribute.

TIP   If you assign the name `entityManager` to the JPA persistence manager and `session` (or `hibernateSession` as of Seam 2.1) to the Hibernate persistence manager, you can save yourself a couple of keystrokes. Seam uses these names in several of its modules to look up the Seam-managed persistence context, unless an override is specified.

So far you've established Seam-managed persistence contexts for both JPA and Hibernate, letting Seam handle the entire process. Although there are times when this is the most convenient approach, Seam won't always be in command. Fortunately, Seam is able to look to JNDI and use a persistence unit waiting there, loaded and ready.

9.3.3   *Sharing the persistence manager factory through JNDI*

Seam's JPA persistence manager component is capable of obtaining a reference to a JPA persistence unit loaded by the Java EE container, if made available through JNDI. Seam can also retrieve a Hibernate `SessionFactory` stored in JNDI for use in its Hibernate persistence manager component. We explore how to make these resources available in JNDI and how to get Seam to use them, starting with the native Java EE integration.

PERSISTENCE UNIT REFERENCES

There's no use loading a JPA persistence unit if one's already available, which is the case in a standard Java EE environment. However, the Java EE container doesn't expose the `EntityManagerFactory` by default, which means it's not published to JNDI. This isn't necessary for using the `@PersistenceContext` annotation on a Java EE component. But now, you need to allow Seam to obtain the persistence manager factory from the Java EE container. That requires the extra step of declaring it as a resource reference.

The persistence unit reference can be defined in either the web.xml descriptor using the `<persistence-unit-ref>` element or in a `@PersistenceUnit` annotation on a Java EE component. I cover only the XML-based configuration here. The reference associates a JNDI name in the `java:comp/env` namespace with the persistence unit name, as follows:

```
<persistence-unit-ref>
  <persistence-unit-ref-name>open18/emf</persistence-unit-ref-name>
  <persistence-unit-name>open18</persistence-unit-name>
</persistence-unit-ref>
```

In order for this reference to be usable, the persistence unit descriptor and entities must be on the classpath of a WAR or packaged as a persistence archive[4] (PAR) and placed in the lib directory of an EAR. When a PAR is in the lib directory of an EAR, its persistence units are visible to the WAR and the EJB JAR. If the persistence unit is packaged inside an EJB JAR, it's private and therefore not visible to the web context or Seam (JBoss AS is an exception).

A reference to the `EntityManagerFactory` for this persistence unit is obtained by looking up the qualified JNDI name `java:comp/env/open18/emf` in the `Initial-Context`. Of course, you don't have to perform this lookup yourself since Seam can accept a JNDI name in the configuration of the persistence manager, replacing the `entity-manager-factory` attribute:

```
<persistence:managed-persistence-context name="entityManager"
  persistence-unit-jndi-name="java:comp/env/open18/emf"
  auto-create="true"/>
```

This whole setup assumes you're working in a Java EE 5–compliant environment, and JBoss AS 4.2 is not. Until JBoss AS 5.0 is rolled out, the means of binding to JNDI and the JNDI naming convention are different.

DEALING WITH JNDI IN JBOSS AS

JBoss AS 4.2 doesn't implement the entire Java EE 5 specification, coming up short in the area of persistence archives. It doesn't support the use of persistence unit references, as described earlier. Your only option is to instruct Hibernate to bind the `EntityManagerFactory` to JNDI at runtime by adding a special JNDI Hibernate property to the persistence unit configuration:

```
<persistence-unit name="open18" transaction-type="JTA">
  ...
  <properties>
    <property
      name="jboss.entity.manager.factory.jndi.name" value="open18/emf"/>
  </properties>
</persistence-unit>
```

This trick only works, however, if Hibernate is the persistence provider. It also depends on Hibernate being able to write to JNDI at runtime, which isn't supported in all environments (see the accompanying sidebar). Also note that this JNDI name isn't placed in the `java:comp/env` namespace[5] but rather in the global JNDI namespace, so the reference to the `EntityManagerFactory` is obtained by looking up the JNDI name verbatim:

```
<persistence:managed-persistence-context name="entityManager"
  persistence-unit-jndi-name="open18/emf" auto-create="true"/>
```

Unfortunately, the situation with JBoss AS is even grimmer. JBoss AS 4.2 only loads persistence units if they're packaged as an EJB JAR inside an EAR and declared as an EJB

---

[4] The persistence archive is detailed in this blog entry: http://in.relation.to/Bloggers/PartitionYourApplication.

[5] On most Java EE application servers, the java:comp/env namespace can't be modified at runtime.

> ## Writing to the JNDI registry is not so easy
>
> JNDI namespaces, and the rules regarding which namespaces can be modified at runtime, vary widely across application servers. For instance, JBoss AS supports the namespace `java:/`, which isn't available on any other server. GlassFish doesn't permit the application to modify the java:comp/env namespace. Tomcat disables writing to the JNDI registry at runtime entirely. Keep in mind that writing to the JNDI registry is only necessary if the application server doesn't support persistence unit references or if you want to bind a Hibernate `SessionFactory` to JNDI.

module in the EAR's application.xml descriptor. If your configuration is different, you need to have Seam bootstrap the persistence unit before it can be bound to JNDI. The same goes if you deploy your application to a servlet container such as Tomcat or Jetty. A Hibernate `SessionFactory` is bound to JNDI using the same runtime technique.

GETTING THE HIBERNATE SESSION INTO JNDI

Hibernate at least has an excuse for JNDI tricks since it doesn't answer to a standard. The way that Hibernate is configured to bind to JNDI is so subtle that it's often overlooked. You simply add the `name` attribute to the `<session-factory>` node in the Hibernate configuration, and that value is used as the global JNDI name to which to bind:

```
<hibernate-configuration>
  <session-factory name="open18/SessionFactory">...</session-factory>
</hibernate-configuration>
```

Since the mechanism of binding to JNDI is the same as when Hibernate is used as the JPA provider, the lookup follows the same rules. Namely, the JNDI name is passed verbatim to the Seam-managed persistence context component for Hibernate:

```
<persistence:managed-hibernate-session name="hibernateSession"
  session-factory-jndi-name="open18/SessionFactory" auto-create="true"/>
```

Because a Hibernate configuration isn't going to be picked up by the Java EE container, you must use Seam (or an alternative) to load the persistence unit. In that regard, JNDI really doesn't provide much benefit in this scenario.

The downside of relying on a persistence unit in JNDI is that you don't know whether it's available until the first time you attempt to retrieve it. This presents an opportunity for you to be proactive and validate the configuration when the application starts.

9.3.4   *Validating the persistence context at startup*

To remedy the uncertainty of relying on a JNDI lookup, you can register an application-scoped `@Startup` component, shown in listing 9.1, to perform a sanity check by verifying that a managed persistence context can be successfully created.

Listing 9.1 Verifies the persistence configuration at startup

```
package org.open18.persistence;
import ...;

@Name("persistenceContextValidator")
@Scope(ScopeType.APPLICATION)
@Startup
public class PersistenceContextValidator {
    private ValueExpression<EntityManager> entityManager;

    @Create
    public void onStartup() {
        if (entityManager != null) {
            try {
                EntityManager em =
                    entityManager.getValue();
                entityManager.setValue(null);
            } catch (Exception e) {
                throw new RuntimeException("The persistence context "
                    + entityManager.getExpressionString()
                    + " is not properly configured.", e);
            }
        }
    }
    public void setEntityManager(
        ValueExpression<EntityManager> entityManager) {
        this.entityManager = entityManager;
    }
}
```

Triggers JNDI lookup

Closes temporary entity manager

Accepts unevaluated EL expression

The reference to the Seam-managed persistence context is supplied as a value expression:

```
<component name="persistenceContextValidator">
  <property name="entityManager">#{entityManager}</property>
</component>
```

A conversation context is active during container initialization, allowing the conversation-scoped `EntityManager` to be created at that time.

That gives you a handful of options for setting up Java persistence in Seam. Seam does just as much to aid with transactions, which is the topic of the next section.

9.4   Seam's transaction support

Seam's transaction support makes your persistence operations robust and the transaction APIs more accessible. Three services comprise Seam's transaction support (all optional):

- Global transactions
- Transaction abstraction layer
- Application transactions

Seam recognizes that transactions are not only useful at the business layer, but also around the entire request, making them truly global. As part of providing this service, but also to make transaction APIs more accessible, Seam introduces a transaction abstraction layer built around the JTA interface. Seam's transaction API makes switching between different transaction platforms a matter of configuration. Finally, Seam works with the Seam-managed persistence context and Hibernate to facilitate application transactions. This section shows how these services support you in creating robust database-oriented applications.

9.4.1   Global transactions

The JSF life cycle grants Seam granular control over a request through the use of a phase listener. Seam takes advantage of this visibility to manage the persistence context, manipulate transaction boundaries, catch exceptions, and issue transaction rollbacks. During the Seam life cycle, Seam applies two key aspects of its global transaction strategy:

- Wraps each request in two (or three) distinct transactions
- Disables flushing of the persistence context during view rendering

To safeguard persistence operations, regardless of when they occur, Seam uses two global transactions per request (three, if page actions are triggered). The initial transaction begins either before the *Restore View* phase or before the *Apply Request Values* phase, depending on whether JTA or resource-local transactions are being used, respectively. Another distinct transaction wraps page actions, if they are used. These initial transactions allow transactional operations performed through the *Invoke Application* phase (i.e., event listeners, action listeners, page actions, and the action method) to complete their work before advancing to rendering. That way, a rendering exception doesn't cause business logic that completed successfully to be rolled back after the fact. If the business logic does fail, it can be handled using a transaction rollback and subsequent navigation to an error view.

The final transaction ensures that database reads occurring in the *Render Response* phase—as a result of lazy loading and other on-demand fetch operations—remain isolated to protect against interim database changes as defined by the transaction isolation level. Seam also disables flushing of Seam-managed persistence contexts during the *Render Response* phase if Hibernate is the persistence provider, effectively making the transaction read-only. This measure ensures that the view can't inadvertently cause the database to be modified. Figure 9.2 illustrates these transaction boundaries by shading each distinct life-cycle region.

The transaction manager that Seam uses to originate the global transaction is determined by the transaction component, which you'll learn to configure in the next section. Use of Seam's global transactions is optional. You are free to use transactions at the boundaries of your service layer methods (or wherever you have them defined). To disable Seam's global transactions, you set the following configuration in the component descriptor:

```
<core:init transaction-management-enabled="false"/>
```

As a word of warning, taking away Seam-managed transactions leaves the view rendering without a transaction. Let's consider the consequences of this choice.

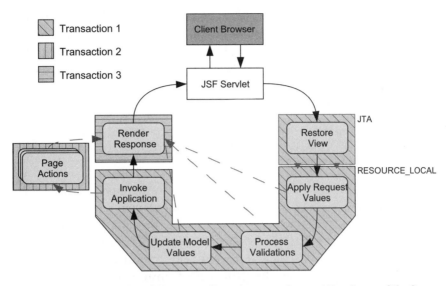

Figure 9.2 The boundaries of the transactions are wrapped around the phases of the Seam life cycle by Seam's transaction management. The `RESOURCE_LOCAL` transaction is delayed until the start of a conversation.

LAZY LOADING IN ISOLATION
Do you need a transaction to use lazy loading? No. Lazy loading is made possible by extending the persistence context for as long as you need to cross the boundary of an uninitialized collection or proxy (the lazy-fetching strategy). But even with a conversation-scoped persistence manager, you still face the problem that without explicit transaction boundaries defined, lazy-load operations execute in autocommit mode, opening and closing a transaction for every query. Not only is this expensive, it also lacks isolation guarantees. Each lazy-load operation could execute more than one query, and you may hit more than one lazy association in a given view. Some queries may take a long time to run. Regardless of how many external transaction commits occur in the interim, you want your reads to return data as if all the queries executed in an instant. Thus, it's a good idea to use an explicit transaction, even when the operations are read-only. And the global transaction guarantees that they are.

Transactions are another area of turf that is highly contested. The Java EE container offers JTA, the standard transaction manager in Java EE, the persistence frameworks provide resource-local transactions, and Spring has its own platform for transaction management. Which solution should you use? Seam reduces this decision to a mere configuration detail.

9.4.2 Seam's transaction abstraction layer

Seam normalizes all of the transaction implementations just mentioned under its own abstraction layer. But here's the kicker: Seam molds this abstraction out of the standard Java EE transaction API by extending JTA's `UserTransaction` interface. Calls to this interface are delegated to the underlying transaction manager. That means you can take advantage of Seam's transaction management without committing to yet another transaction platform. Seam also weaves in a number of convenience methods that ease the task of managing the transaction from the application code. When control of transactions is out of Seam's hands—which is the case with container-managed transactions on EJB components—Seam still participates by performing a narrower set of operations and listening for transaction synchronization events raised by the EJB container.

NOTE Container-managed transactions can't be controlled by the application, so `begin()`, `commit()`, and `rollback()` are disallowed. `setRollback-Only()` is permitted.

Table 9.3 shows the transaction managers that are supported by Seam's abstraction layer. The namespace alias `tx` used by the XML elements in this table resolves to `http://jboss.com/products/seam/transaction`. Your job is to connect Seam to a transaction manager so that it can create transactions as needed.

Seam's transaction managers are mutually exclusive. Seam uses application-managed JTA, retrieved from the JNDI registry, in non–EJB environments. If you'd rather have Seam use resource-local transactions, perhaps because JTA isn't available, you configure the one that corresponds with the persistence API you're using. To use the resource-local transaction manager with JPA, define the following component configuration:

```
<tx:entity-transaction entity-manager="#{em}"/>
```

You activate the resource-local transaction manager from Hibernate as follows:

```
<tx:hibernate-transaction session="#{hibernateSession}"/>
```

The persistence manager only needs to be specified if its name doesn't adhere to Seam's standard naming conventions for the respective Seam-managed persistence context.

Table 9.3 Transaction managers supported by Seam's abstraction layer

Seam transaction manager `org.jboss.seam.transaction.*`	How installed	Native transaction manager
`UTtransaction`	Default in non-EJB environment	Application-managed JTA `UserTransaction`
`EntityTransaction`	`<tx:entity-transaction>`	JPA `EntityTransaction`
`HibernateTransaction`	`<tx:hibernate-transaction>`	Hibernate `Transaction`
`CMTTransaction`	Default in EJB environment	Container-managed JTA `UserTransaction` available via the `EJBContext` object
`NoTransaction`	`<tx:no-transaction>` or when JTA is not available	Used when no transaction managers are available

If your components rely on container-managed transactions, available in an EJB environment, Seam works alongside the `UserTransaction` on the `EJBContext` to capture transaction synchronization events. Since Seam isn't in control of container-managed transactions, it's necessary to register Seam to be notified of the transaction boundaries:

```
<tx:ejb-transaction/>
```

This configuration activates a stateful session bean that implements the `Session-Synchronization` interface to capture transaction events from the EJB container. This SFSB is packaged in jboss-seam.jar, which must be bundled in the EAR. From this SFSB, Seam passes on the following two events to other Seam components using its own internal event mechanism, the same events Seam raises for Seam-managed transactions:

- `org.jboss.seam.beforeTransactionCompletion`
- `org.jboss.seam.afterTransactionCompletion` (raised on commit or rollback)

The second event passes a `boolean` parameter to the observer indicating whether the transaction was successful (i.e., commit or rollback). As a word of warning, mixing Seam's global transactions with CMTs is complex since the transactions themselves are not shared.

If you disable the Seam transaction manager (i.e., `<tx:no-transaction>`), you must also disable Seam's global transactions. Otherwise, Seam throws an exception when it attempts to look up a transaction.

Using distributed transactions in a Seam application

One of the main reasons for using JTA transactions is to take advantage of distributed transactions. Despite Seam wrapping global transactions around each request, only the JTA implementation can support distributed transactions. In that case, you can work with multiple persistence managers and get two-phase commits as long as the underlying data source is configured as an XA resource. Chapter 14 (online) demonstrates how to set up XA data sources in the sample application.

When using EJB components, you have the option of declaring transaction boundaries using the standard Java EE mechanism, using either `@TransactionAttribute` annotations or the ejb-jar.xml descriptor. Seam brings this declarative approach to JavaBean components by providing the `@Transactional` annotation. The next section focuses on using Seam-managed transactions on non-EJB components.

9.4.3 *Controlling Seam-managed transactions*

Transactions controlled in the business logic are referred to as *bean-managed transactions* (BMTs). While BMTs offer more granular control, their use mixes up transaction management with business logic. As with persistence, Seam volunteers to play the role of the "bean" in this equation by taking on management of the transactions, delivering the same value proposition as container-managed transactions (CMTs). The key benefit of this approach is that JavaBean and EJB components can share the same strategy. If necessary, you can still use the Seam transaction API (i.e., the `Transactional` component) to get more fine-grained control of the transaction.

Seam provides the `@Transactional` annotation to control the propagation of a Seam-managed transaction around a method call. The `@Transactional` annotation, summarized in table 9.4, is a synonym for the Java EE `@TransactionAttribute` annotation. Seam's annotation supports a set of propagation types that mirror those in the Java EE API. Seam wraps a built-in method interceptor around components that contain the `@Transactional` annotation, which interprets this annotation and drives the transaction accordingly. Note, however, that the `@Transactional` annotation is irrelevant during a JSF request when using Seam global transactions.

Table 9.4   The `@Transactional` annotation

Name:	Transactional
Purpose:	Specifies the transaction propagation that should be used for a method call
Target:	TYPE (class), METHOD

Attribute	Type	Function
value	`TransactionPropagationType`	Indicates how the transaction should be handled around the method call. Default: `REQUIRED`.

The `@Transactional` annotation can be applied at the class or method level. When it's applied at the class level, it's inherited by all methods unless the method overrides this setting with its own `@Transactional` annotation. The propagation values that are permitted are summarized in table 9.5. Note that Seam doesn't support suspending or nesting transactions.

Consider that you want to apply a transaction to all of the public methods of a Seam component. For that, you define the `@Transactional` annotation at the class level:

Table 9.5   The transaction propagation types supported by the `@Transactional` annotation

Propagation type	Purpose
REQUIRED	Indicates that a transaction is required to execute the method. If a transaction isn't active, Seam will begin a new transaction. This is the default type.
SUPPORTS	Indicates that the method is permitted to execute in the presence of an active transaction, but it won't begin a transaction if one isn't active.
MANDATORY	Indicates that an active transaction is required to execute the method. A runtime exception is thrown if a transaction isn't already in progress.
NEVER	Indicates that a transaction shouldn't be active when this method is called. A runtime exception will be thrown if a transaction is active.

```
@Name("courseAction")
@Transactional
public class CourseAction {
    @In private EntityManager entityManger;
    public void addCourse(Course course) {
        entityManager.persist(course);
    }
}
```

Now assume you want to delegate work to a method on another component. To ensure that the helper method only executes in the presence of an existing transaction, you declare the propagation type to be mandatory, declared here using a method-level annotation override:

```
@Name("courseAuditManager")
@Transactional
public class CourseAuditManager {
    @In private EntityManager entityManager;
    @Transactional(TransactionPropagationType.MANDATORY)
    public void storeAuditInfo(Course course) {
        entityManager.persist(new CourseAudit(course));
    }
}
```

At the end of any method call that begins a transaction, the transaction is committed. When using Seam global transactions, though, a transaction will already be active, so the transaction commits at the boundaries of the phases illustrated in figure 9.1 instead. But what happens when the method call is disrupted by an exception? That where rollbacks come in.

ROLLING BACK WHEN THINGS GO WRONG

Seam mimics the rollback behavior employed by the EJB container for transactional method calls. In fact, when using Seam session bean components, Seam steps in and issues the rollback even before the exception gets to the EJB container in certain cases. The rules for rollback are as follows:

- Roll back if a system exception is thrown. A system exception is a `Runtime-Exception` not annotated with @ApplicationException.
- Roll back if an application exception with rollback enabled is thrown. An application exception is defined by the @ApplicationException annotation, which indicates whether a rollback should be issued when the exception is thrown.
- Don't roll back if an application exception with rollback disabled or a checked exception is thrown.

Seam can process the @ApplicationException from the Java EE API and its synonym in Seam, which is summarized in section 3.6.3 of chapter 3. If the exception bubbles out of the application logic, Seam's exception-handling facility picks it up and issues a rollback on the transaction if it's still active. The rollback characteristics on the exception just give you control over when the rollback happens and allow you to handle it more gracefully. Whenever a transaction fails, Seam also adds a JSF warning message to the response from the message key `org.jboss.seam.TransactionFailed`.

The transactional methods exhibited thus far use atomic database transactions. We're now going to look at another type of transaction, the application transaction, which is more of a design pattern than a service.

9.4.4 *Application transactions*

The *application transaction* (also called an atomic conversation, optimistic transaction, or long-running application transaction) is the pinnacle of Seam's Java persistence support. It requires coordination from several different aspects of Seam, but it is without a doubt the key to ensuring data consistency in a web-based application.

THE GOAL OF AN APPLICATION TRANSACTION

A persistence context is flushed by calling the `flush()` method on the persistence manager. When that happens, modifications made to managed entities (dirty entities) are propagated to the database using a series of Data Modification Language (DML) statements (i.e., INSERT, UPDATE, and DELETE), a strategy referred to as *write-behind*. When operating within the scope of a database transaction, it doesn't matter when the DML statements are executed since they're part of the same transaction and can be rolled back if something causes the transaction to fail (i.e., they are atomic).

However, an extended persistence context can span many requests and therefore many database transactions. Flushes that occur in different transactions aren't part of the same atomic unit of work. Therefore, it's not possible to ask the database to roll back to the state it was in when the conversation began. One workaround is to use compensating transactions (i.e., "undo"), but they are laborious and error prone, and don't address the fact that these interim commits allow data (which is only partially complete from the standpoint of the use case) to enter the database, thus effectively breaking the conversation. Sending modifications to the database prematurely is analogous to charging your credit card as you add items to an online shopping cart. What's worse is that other parts of the system see these incomplete records as committed, the very situation isolated transactions are intended to prevent.

What you want to be able to do is group all DML statements in a use case together so they can be applied or rolled back uniformly as an atomic unit of work. I can assure you that I'm not proposing the use of a long-term database lock. Holding a database lock during user "think" time would introduce a tremendous bottleneck into the system. The trick is to use an application transaction, which leverages the persistence context as a database intermediary.

You already know that a conversation-scoped persistence context can queue changes throughout a use case, which you can think of as instructions for creating DML statements. In an application transaction, flushing the persistence context is deferred until the final step of the use case and executed within a database transaction. Since the DML statements for the entire use case are applied together, the conversation (i.e., use case) is atomic. An application transaction relies on optimistic locking, presented in the previous chapter, to guarantee that the statements only execute if the database records that map to the managed entities in the persistence context haven't been modified externally since the use case began.

Let's consider how an application transaction is implemented according to the JPA specification and the alternate solution that Hibernate provides. The difference is the product of a heated debate. The extension in Hibernate that facilitates an application transaction (manual flushing) was forced out of the specification because several decision makers didn't understand it. Hopefully, this section will make you one of the enlightened ones.

A WRINKLE IN THE SPECIFICATION

The flushing behavior of the persistence context is controlled using the flush mode setting on the persistence manager. The JPA specification only defines two flush modes, AUTO and COMMIT. In AUTO flush mode, a flush occurs when the persistence manager deems it necessary. The COMMIT flush mode instructs the persistence manager to hold off flushing until the transaction commits.

The specification states that if you want to perform an application transaction, you should set the flush mode to COMMIT and work *outside* of explicit transactions until you're ready to perform the flush. At the end of the use case, you call a transactional method, which results in the changes being flushed to the database when the transaction commits.

Following this proposed approach means completely avoiding the use of transactions in the interim, which is a very bad design. You are once again tiptoeing through your own application (reminiscent of the lazy-initialization exception). You're also operating in autocommit mode, which as you learned earlier doesn't provide isolation for a sequence of database operations. Finally, it completely rules out the use of Seam's global transaction strategy, which uses at least two transactions per request. For these reasons, Hibernate adds the MANUAL flush mode as an extension to the JPA specification.

HIBERNATE'S MANUAL FLUSH MODE

Hibernate's MANUAL flush mode ensures that the persistence context is only flushed when a call is made to the flush() method on the persistence manager API (bean-managed flushing). This mode gives you the flexibility to take your persistence context in and out of transactions as you please without risking a premature flush.

WARNING   If the entity identifier is generated during an insertion (i.e., auto-increment column), then even with manual flushing, a flush occurs after a call to persist(). This is necessary since each managed entity in the persistence context must be assigned an identifier. To avoid the flush, you need to set the id-generation strategy to sequence (not identity).

Application transactions using Hibernate's MANUAL flush mode extension are controlled at the boundaries of the conversation. Fortunately, Seam can manage the flush mode extension transparently. By setting the flushMode attribute on the @Begin annotation to MANUAL (or the flush-mode attribute on the <begin-conversation>

page descriptor tag), Seam switches the persistence manager to manual flushing when the conversation begins:

```
@Begin(flushMode = FlushModeType.MANUAL)
public void beginApplicationTransaction () { ... }
```

As of Seam 2.1, you can set the default flush mode globally in the component descriptor:

```
<core:manager default-flush-mode="MANUAL" .../>
```

If you want to use application transactions in your application (and don't want to use the workaround of avoiding transactional methods), you must be using a Seam-managed persistence context and the native Hibernate API or Hibernate as the JPA provider. MANUAL flush mode isn't supported by any other JPA 1.0 provider. Let's take a look at a complete example that uses an application transaction.

AN APPLICATION TRANSACTION IN PRACTICE

Two compelling use cases for an application transaction are a wizard-based form and an editor preview screen. In both cases, the user has the opportunity to verify the data is correct before it's committed. We'll put the first use case into practice.

Building on the golf course wizard example from chapter 7, the `CourseWizard-Action` component, shown in listing 9.2, supports adding a new course as well as updating an existing one, initiated by the action listener methods `addCourse()` and `editCourse()`, respectively. Notice that these methods switch to a MANUAL flush mode while initiating a long-running conversation. This opens a Seam-style application transaction. Interim method calls don't flush changes to the `Course` entity to the database. Instead, all changes are deferred and sent in an atomic commit when the `save()` method is called. (Note, however, that the `persist()` method forces a flush if the entity's identifier is generated on insert.)

Listing 9.2   A component that supports an application transaction

```
package org.open18.action;
import ...;

@Name("courseWizardAction")
@Scope(ScopeType.CONVERSATION)
@Transactional
public class CourseWizardAction implements Serializable {
    @In private EntityManager entityManager;
    @RequestParameter private Long facilityId;
    @Out private Course course;

    @Begin(flushMode = FlushModeType.MANUAL)       ◁── Begins application transaction
    public void addCourse() {
        course = new Course();
        course.setFacility(
            entityManager.find(Facility.class, facilityId));
        entityManager.persist(course);            ◁── Doesn't flush changes to database
    }

    @Begin(flushMode = FlushModeType.MANUAL)       ◁── Begins application transaction
```

```
    public void editCourse(Long id) {
        course = entityManager.find(Course.class, id);
    }                                        ┌── Doesn't flush
    public String submitBasicInfo() {   ◁────┘   changes to database
        return "next";
    }
    ...
    @End public String save() {   ┌── Flushes changes
        entityManager.flush();  ◁──┘   to database
        return "success";
    }
}
```

What's important is that you aren't forced to sidestep transactional methods to implement an application transaction. The MANUAL flush mode instructs the persistence context not to take action until it hears your command, ensuring that the conversation isn't broken by a premature flush. In the interim, you're free to use transactions to get proper read isolation or for any other purpose.

Application transactions demonstrate the resourcefulness of the persistence context when treated as a first-class citizen of a use case and not relegated to the handyman of a transaction. For more in-depth coverage of application transactions, consult chapter 11 of *Java Persistence with Hibernate* (Manning, 2007).

9.5 *Summary*

This chapter introduced Seam's managed persistence and transactions as an alternative to the container-managed counterparts in Java EE. I hope you were able to conclude that using Java persistence in Seam is quite compelling. You saw how the persistence context is often mishandled and that by hosting the persistence manager in the conversation, Seam makes these problems melt away, letting you realize the true value of Java persistence. In fact, Seam makes it hard *not* to get persistence right.

In addition to scoping the persistence manager properly, you discovered that Seam gives it some nice upgrades. We examined the general enhancements and ones specific to Hibernate. To give Seam control of the persistence context, you have to feed it a persistence unit at runtime. You learned how to configure Seam to bootstrap a JPA or Hibernate persistence unit itself or grab one already loaded from JNDI. You also saw how to define a Seam-managed persistence context for either persistence API.

I then unveiled Seam's transaction support. You saw that global transactions extend the guarantees that transactions provide across the whole request, that Seam's transaction abstraction layer makes the transaction APIs far more accessible, and that application transactions are the key to ensuring data consistency in a stateful application—enhanced by Hibernate's MANUAL flush mode extension.

You're ready to use Seam's Application Framework to rapidly throw together CRUD applications and gain some experience using Seam-managed persistence contexts and transactions at the same time.

Rapid Seam development

This chapter covers

- The Seam Application Framework
- Building CRUD screens for an entity
- Paginating and sorting a query result set
- Assigning restrictions to queries

If you think back to when you first learned golf—perhaps you are still learning—you were probably overwhelmed with all of the things you have to concentrate on at once. To start, you have to judge the distance you want to hit the ball and choose the right club for it. This "design decision" is a tough call even for the best golfers. Once your aim is set and you're ready to take your swing, you have to position your stance, set your grip, align the clubface, keep your head down, your shoulders level, and your eye on the ball. It's all so mechanical that even a good swing feels unnatural.

Then, one day, it all clicks. You stop thinking about every last detail and you just swing. It's hard to explain how you know—it just becomes natural to you, like walking or riding a bike. When you look down the fairway, accounting for the obstacles in front of you, you just get that sense of how far you want to send the ball and which club to use to get it there. You are no longer "designing" your decisions based on some prescribed distance chart, nor do you feel uncomfortable when you swing.

This chapter is the culmination of everything you've learned so far about Seam, and it's your chance to make things click. You'll be combining components, component instances, conversations, page parameters, page actions, navigation rules, managed persistence, and transactions to implement several new features in the Open 18 application. By the end of this chapter, developing with Seam should feel so natural that you'll be able to assemble a custom application and still enjoy the fresh air. The key to increasing your productivity with Seam is learning about the component templates in the Seam Application Framework and knowing how to put them to use. These templates enable you to develop rapidly by handling repetitive and mundane tasks and putting Seam services close at hand. You'll discover that these classes can be put to use by extending them in Java, configuring them in the component descriptor, or both. Let's begin by exploring what this framework has to offer.

10.1 A framework within a framework

As you are well aware by now, Seam is an application framework for Java EE. It provides a container that manages components and leverages those components to tie the layers of an enterprise Java application together. Nestled within the Seam code base lies a handful of classes that comprise the Seam Application Framework. This "framework within a framework" is a specialized collection of component templates that effortlessly blanket the programming requirements of garden-variety web applications. Such tasks include performing create, read, update, and delete (CRUD) operations on entity instances; querying for data; and developing JSF page controllers. You may be hesitant to give this spattering of classes much notice, but I assure you that they'll carry you a long way.

NOTE The Seam reference documentation refers to this grouping of classes as the *Seam Application Framework*. The title is a potential cause of confusion, as it resembles the name of the broader Seam framework in which it resides. Therefore, whenever I talk about this set of classes and the functionality they provide, I address it using the proper noun *Seam Application Framework* to remain consistent with the documentation. I define it as *a framework of classes for quickly building page controllers that perform CRUD and query operations on entities.*

At the end of chapter 2, you had a CRUD application in place that you could use to impress your boss. Since then, you've made enhancements to the application to further demonstrate that your investment in Seam is paying off (hopefully convincing your boss to buy copies of this book for your coworkers). The trouble is, most of the inner workings of those original CRUD screens, which are powered by the Seam Application Framework, remain a mystery. You've learned how to manage the view-edit-save sequence correctly using conversations and the extended persistence context. You'll now learn how this framework helps facilitate that use case. You'll also discover that it can generate status messages that keep the user informed along the way.

You'll see how the framework aids in creating pages that list entities of a particular type retrieved from the database. But it doesn't just dump all the records at once, which could potentially be a costly operation. Instead, it provides support for truncating the list into pages. The component that manages the query responds to pagination and sorting commands, and helps you develop a search filter to allow the user to pare down the result set.

In this chapter, you'll mirror the behavior and design of the screens created in chapter 2 to incorporate a new entity into the application, Round, which represents a round of golf. This time, you'll build the functionality from the ground up and then take it several steps further. This exercise allows you to become familiar with the Seam Application Framework and shows you how to build on it. It should come as no surprise that the cornerstone of this framework is persistence.

10.1.1   *Wrapping the persistence API*

Database-oriented applications live and die by their ability to read and write relational database tables. In the previous two chapters you've seen how easy it is to manage persistent entities in a Seam application, thanks in large part to the ability of JPA and Hibernate to transparently map objects to relational database tables and to move them back and forth through use of a persistence manager. These object-relational mapping (ORM) frameworks do away with verbose JDBC/SQL code sprinkled throughout the objects in the data access layer (or worse, directly in the view).

Despite the convenience of using an ORM tool over straight JDBC, you must still perform repetitive tasks. The general belief is that ORM operations need to be wrapped in a data access object (DAO) to eliminate boilerplate code and remove code duplication across projects. There's a number of DAO frameworks that take care of this tedious work either by generating code or by providing template classes to isolate data operations and exceptions from the business logic. Here's a small sampling of these frameworks:

- AppFuse: http://www.appfuse.org
- Crank: http://code.google.com/p/krank
- EL4J: http://el4j.sourceforge.net
- OpenXava: http://www.openxava.org

DAO frameworks such as these are capable of handling the following tasks:

- Create or obtain a reference to the persistence manager
- Manage CRUD operations and transactions with parameterized template classes
- Reduce casting by using generic types or generated code
- Provide a facility to define queries declaratively and help manage the result set

There's nothing stopping you from using a data access layer in a Seam application. In fact, for large-scale projects, I might be inclined to encourage such a design. But Seam dispels the myth that the persistence manager must be trapped inside a DAO. Instead, Seam proposes that the persistence manager *is* the DAO. But the persistence manager isn't a page controller—that's where your Seam component fits in. It negotiates with the persistence manager to perform data access operations. Not only does this design collapse layers, it also introduces a stateful component. The data access layer has become so ingrained in our minds that it seems we can't just let it go and try to justify its existence by convincing ourselves that it protects us from technology change (the same goes for the service layer).

While Seam can manage the persistence context and allows it to be easily shared among components, which you learned about in the previous chapter, the Seam developers recognized that you still need to write a page controller. The Seam Application Framework is a variation on the generic DAO framework, except it gets the persistence manager and the page controller to work as a single unit rather than introducing an additional layer of stacking. In addition, the classes in the Seam Application Framework are aware of the state of the entities being exchanged (making it stateful), rather than just blindly passing on operations to the persistence manager. The framework includes two categories of persistence controllers, which you'll learn about in the next section: one that manages a single entity and one that manages a result set. These controllers cover the following tasks:

- Act as a JSF form bean and action bean (page controller)
- Create prototype instances, either to be persisted or used as part of a query
- Assist in managing the state of the entity instance or query result set
- Retrieve the entity instance or query result set on demand
- Monitor the parameters to determine when the managed data needs to be refreshed
- Use Java 5 generics to provide type-safe checking and eliminate casting for operations performed on the entity instance or query result set
- Define transactional boundaries around persistence operations
- Prepare status messages and raise events when the transaction wrapping the operation commits successfully

Thus, the classes that comprise the Seam Application Framework don't purposelessly wrap the persistence API. Instead, they foster rapid development of database-oriented applications by handling many of the auxiliary concerns required to manage persistent entities. Let's take a look at what classes are available and how they interact with the persistence manager.

10.1.2 *The persistence controllers*

The Seam Application Framework is a hierarchical set of classes, all extending from the `Controller` base class. `Controller` contains convenience methods for accessing the Seam contexts and component instances, interacting with the Servlet API and JSF life cycle, logging messages, registering JSF messages, and raising events. The classes in this hierarchy make extensive use of Java 5 generics to provide strong typing.

These classes are intended to be used as JavaBean components. If you wanted to extend one to create an EJB component, you'd need to define an interface for the class since one is not provided. Even then, the `PersistenceController`, which is the primary descendent in the class hierarchy, is designed to be used with a Seam-managed persistence manager. In particular, it provides generic access—of the Java 5 variety—to the persistence manager as part of its class definition, shown here:

```
public abstract class PersistenceController<T> extends Controller { ... }
```

In this declaration, the generic type parameter T is a placeholder for the persistence manager. Extending from the PersistenceController are three branches of classes that facilitate interaction with the persistence manager. Each branch has an implementation for JPA and one for Hibernate. For JPA, T is replaced with EntityManager and for Hibernate it is replaced with Session. The controller classes in the Seam Application Framework are summarized in table 10.1. In each of these classes, the generic type parameter E is a placeholder for the entity class.[1]

Table 10.1   The three branches of parent classes in the Seam Application Framework

Type/Purpose	JPA	Hibernate
Home<T, E> Manages a single entity instance and supports CRUD operations.	EntityHome<E>	HibernateEntityHome<E>
Query<T, E> Manages a JPQL/HQL query result set. Supports restrictions, ordering, and pagination.	EntityQuery<E>	HibernateEntityQuery<E>
PersistenceController Parent class for developing JSF page controllers. Has convenience methods for interacting with the persistence manager, Seam, and JSF.	EntityController	HibernateEntityController

The JPA implementation of this class hierarchy is diagrammed in figure 10.1.

So what's the benefit of wrapping the persistence manager? There are in fact two: transaction boundaries and generics. Although the persistence manager can control or participate in a transaction, it can't dictate transaction boundaries. The methods on the persistence controller, on the other hand, are decorated with the @Transactional annotation to guarantee that the persistence operations are nestled within an explicit transaction. In

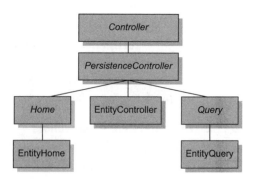

Figure 10.1   The Seam Application Framework hierarchy for JPA. There's an equivalent one for Hibernate.

---

[1] According to http://java.sun.com/docs/books/tutorial/java/generics/gentypes.html, T is the common parameter name for a **Type**. E is common for **Element**, though here you can think of it as **Entity**.

the previous chapter, you learned that Seam uses global transactions around a JSF request, so this is only a concern outside that environment. Generics allow these classes to be form-fitted to a persistence manager implementation and an entity class. Let's focus on the benefits of generics.

A GENERIC APPROACH

It's no secret that Seam embraces the language extensions introduced in Java 5 in order to simplify the Java EE programming model. You've already seen that Seam makes extensive use of annotations as a means of providing declarative behavior. Seam builds on this adoption of Java 5 by using generics throughout the Seam Application Framework. Generics help cut down on casting,[2] thus removing a lot of unnecessary clutter from your code. For example, you can adopt the `EntityHome` to the Round entity using a parameterized type:

```
EntityHome<Round> roundHome = new EntityHome<Round>();
```

You can then initialize a new instance of the entity without the need for a cast:

```
Course newRound = roundHome.newInstance();
```

The generics support is only relevant if you extend the framework classes in Java. You also have the option of declaring your framework components entirely in XML. In that case, the generic type parameters don't play a role since the instances are only referenced using the dynamically typed (or "duck-typed") EL. Let's consider when each is the appropriate choice.

10.1.3 *Two ways to play*

The classes in the Seam Application Framework aren't components themselves—meaning they don't bear the `@Name` annotation. They are component templates, akin to the Seam-managed persistence classes covered in the previous chapter. As you learned, one way to commission a template class as a Seam component is by declaring and configuring it in the component descriptor, as shown here for the roundHome component, which you'll encounter later in this chapter:

```
<framework:entity-home name="roundHome"
  entity-class="org.open18.model.Round"/>
```

This component declaration falls under the built-in component namespace `http://jboss.com/products/seam/framework`, prefixed as `framework` throughout this chapter. Like the persistence framework classes, the application framework classes are designed to be controlled entirely through configuration. The XML-based approach is amazingly flexible, in large part due to the capabilities of the Seam component model and the ubiquitous EL. When defined in this way, the component is fully capable of preparing an entity instance to bind to the JSF form inputs and handling the form's actions. All of the necessary functionality is built right into the Home class.

---

[2] For a more detailed discussion of generics and how they help eliminate casting, please refer to the technical article on generics at http://java.sun.com/developer/technicalArticles/J2SE/generics/.

If the feature you're looking for isn't already covered by the framework class, the configuration-only approach is going to come up short. Fortunately, these classes are designed to be extended. You can extend them in Java or Groovy to build your own custom components. This option gives you the most flexibility for all the reasons class extension is useful. As an added bonus, you can fulfill the generic type parameters on the parent class to get type-safe checking. Here's the same `roundHome` component defined in Java:

```
@Name("roundHome")
public class RoundHome extends EntityHome<Round> { ... }
```

Don't feel that you have to make the decision between Java or XML up front. From the standpoint of the rest of the application, the end result is the same, a Seam component. You can comfortably mix the two styles in your application, or even on the same component. In fact, the most flexible approach is to define properties in XML and the methods on a subclass, referencing the subclass in the component descriptor. This flexibility is the essence of the unified component model in Seam. You're now ready to swing away by implementing CRUD screens to manage instances of the `Round` entity using a Home component.

10.2   *Stateful CRUD using the Home component*

Managed persistence has a history of being at odds with sound object-oriented design. EJB 2 championed the use of distributed objects. As a consequence, developers quickly resorted to using data transfer objects (DTOs) to push aggregated data over the wire as a way to reduce network traffic. These domain objects were void of behavior. Unfortunately, the intelligence in domain objects didn't get restored once "lightweight" DAO frameworks replaced EJB 2 because the same flawed architecture was adopted. Treating domain objects as buckets for holding data, without giving them real behavior, is an anti-pattern known as the Anemic Domain Model.[3] As is the fate of all things out of balance, a change was imminent.

10.2.1   *Remedying the Anemic Domain Model*

In an attempt to swing the pendulum away from the Anemic Domain Model, as illustrated in figure 10.2, some contemporary frameworks, such as Ruby on Rails, promote the use of the Active Record design pattern as a way of making domain objects active participants in an object-oriented design. In the Active Record pattern, the domain object is mapped directly to a database record, just like with ORM. But this relationship is pushed

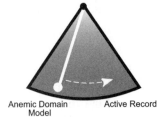

Anemic Domain   Active Record
Model

Figure 10.2   An industry trend toward adding more behavior to domain model objects. The Anemic Domain Model only holds state, whereas the Active Record pattern encapsulates state and performs data access logic.

---

[3] Martin Fowler first presented the concept of an Anemic Domain Model on his bliki: http://martinfowler.com/bliki/AnemicDomainModel.html.

further by allowing the domain object to save and retrieve *itself* from the database. Thus, in addition to encapsulating data, it encapsulates data access logic.

Seam, being a progressive framework itself, supports the Active Record pattern, right? Absolutely not. For one, the Active Record pattern has been attempted once in J2EE and failed miserably. Entity beans from the EJB 2 era—not to be confused with JPA entity *classes* in EJB 3—bear a close resemblance to the Active Record pattern since they internalize data access logic. This interaction is particularly evident in bean-managed persistence (BMP) entity beans, which embed SQL statements directly in the life-cycle methods. Just like domain objects in the Active Record pattern, EJB 2 entity beans can create, update, load, and remove the database records to which they map.

One of the main factors in the failure of entity beans is the hard link between the domain object and the persistence framework. There is no separation of concerns. To put it simply, entity beans are not POJOs. In fact, it's difficult to implement the Active Record pattern using POJOs. Hopefully, by now, we are in agreement that POJOs are indicators of a sound design. They are easy to test and they are reusable. The main reason Seam doesn't support the Active Record pattern is because it has a better solution based on POJOs that strikes a nice balance between the fading Anemic Domain Model and the overeager Active Record pattern.

10.2.2 *Giving the domain object a Home*

Entity classes *are* POJOs. This trait is good for reasons just mentioned, but limiting because they can't set transaction boundaries and can't manage their own persistent state (1 for POJOs, 0 for active domain models). But history has taught us that entity classes shouldn't handle this work anyway since it's not a good separation of concerns. Ideally, we want a solution that provides a competent domain model without introducing tight coupling between the domain object and the persistence framework.

INTRODUCING THE HOME COMPONENT

Seam answers this challenge by introducing the Home component (herein referred to as a Home). A Home manages an entity instance by caching it and coordinating CRUD operations on it with the persistence manager, all completely transparent to the entity instance. Each Home is represented by the Home class, which extends from PersistenceController, or any subclass of Home. As I've alluded to throughout this chapter, the framework classes, such as Home, are abstract classes that are, in reality, just component templates. They are also agnostic of the persistence framework. Seam provides two implementations of Home: one for JPA, EntityHome, and one for Hibernate, HibernateEntityHome. The class diagram for EntityHome is shown in figure 10.3. This section teaches you how to use the Home component, focusing on the JPA implementation.

A Home is a keeper of an entity instance, hence the term (in case you were wondering). You can use the following analogy to give more meaning to the term. The entity class is like a family, and an instance of that class is a member of the family. The Home,

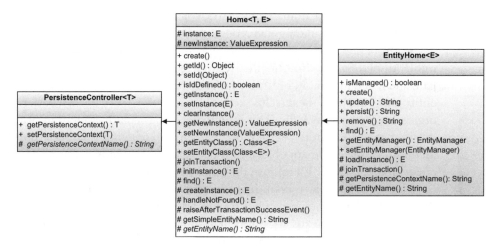

Figure 10.3   The class diagram of `EntityHome`. Several supplemental operations have been excluded.

illustrated in figure 10.4, is where you go to find a family member. The only restriction is that at any given time, a Home can only accommodate a single family member. (The whole house to yourself! Wouldn't that be nice?) The entity instance is said to be the Home's *context*.

Figure 10.4   A Home manages an entity instance, negotiating with the persistence manager to retrieve it.

You use a Home to manage an existing record by supplying an identifier value to the `setId()` method on Home. The identifier value represents a unique entity instance and is mapped to the database table through the `@Id` property on the entity class. The `getInstance()` method on Home uses this identifier to look up the entity by calling the `find()` method on the persistence manager. Figure 10.5 shows the lookup process.

When a different identifier is assigned to a Home, the ensuing call to `getInstance()` performs a fresh lookup to retrieve the entity instance associated with

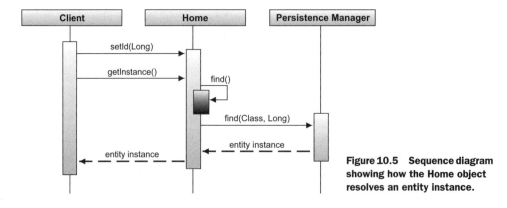

Figure 10.5   Sequence diagram showing how the Home object resolves an entity instance.

that identifier. If an identifier isn't assigned when `getInstance()` is called, a new entity instance is created internally by a call to the `createInstance()` method. Another method, `isManaged()`, reports whether the entity instance maintained is transient or persistent. The three operations that change the entity instance managed by the Home are listed in table 10.2.

Table 10.2   The methods on `Home` that are used to set the instance that is managed

Method	Description
`setId()`	Assign the id. Supplied to the persistence manager to retrieve the instance.
`setInstance()`	Manually establish the instance, bypassing the lookup by id mechanism.
`clearInstance()`	Forcefully clear both the id and the instance.

The Home serves as the main interface of the domain model object in this design, which is now an aggregate of classes rather than a single "active" class like with Active Record.

A DOMAIN MODEL COALITION

A Home encapsulates the entity instance and the persistence manager, facilitating communication between them without making them aware of each other, as shown in figure 10.6. To the outside world, this domain object appears as a single unit, allowing the domain model to be "active" without contaminating the entity class with data access logic.

This design most closely resembles the Mediator Design pattern. In the words of the Gang of Four (*Design Patterns: Elements of Reusable Object-Oriented Software*, Addison-Wesley Professional, 1994):

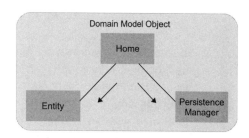

Figure 10.6   A Home acts as a façade for the domain object, delegates operations to the entity instance and the persistence manager, and facilitates communication between them.

> *A mediator serves as an intermediary that keeps objects in a group from referring to each other explicitly.*

A Home uses the persistence manager to manipulate the persistence state of the entity instance it manages, seeing it through its entire life cycle, as shown in figure 8.3 in chapter 8. To coordinate these state transitions, the Home performs the well-known CRUD operations by delegating the work to the persistence manager. This encapsulation and delegation is what makes the Home pattern a good object-oriented design. These façade methods on the Home class are listed in table 10.3.

What the Mediator pattern brings to the table, and how it sets the Home apart from the entity instance itself, is that the Home is both transactional and stateful.

Table 10.3 The methods on `Home` dedicated to interacting with the persistence manager

Method	Description
getInstance()	Retrieves the instance managed by this Home object
isManaged()	Reports whether the instance is in a transient or persistent state
persist()	Saves the transient instance to the database
update()	Synchronizes the persistent instance with the database
remove()	Makes the instance transient by removing it from the database

CONTROLLING TRANSACTIONS AND STATE

The `Home` class provides transactional boundaries around the methods on the persistence manager, declared using Seam's `@Transactional` annotation. An excerpt of the `persist()` method on `EntityHome` is shown here:

```
@Transactional
public String persist() {
    getEntityManager().persist(getInstance());
    getEntityManager().flush();
    ...
    return "persisted";
}
```

In this method, you can see how the Home is mediating between the entity instance and the persistence manager. But the Home's work extends far beyond the boundaries of a transaction. By default, an instance of Home is scoped to the conversation context, allowing it to maintain the entity instance throughout the use case. When combined with an extended persistence context, that translates into not having to retrieve the entity instance on each page transition or having to merge it when changes need to be sent to the database. Instead, the persistence manager can be responsible for tracking the changes in the entity instance. That brings us to the update operation.

Assume that you retrieved an entity instance using a Home and overlaid it on a form in a web page. You would bind the action of the form to the `update()` method on Home to have those changes pushed to the database when the form is submitted. An excerpt of the `update()` method on the `EntityHome` is shown here:

```
@Transactional
public String update() {
    joinTransaction();
    getEntityManager().flush();
    ...
    return "updated";
}
```

As you can see, the `update()` method performs two operations on the persistence manager, neither of which issues an explicit update. It ensures the persistence manager is enlisted in the active transaction, which is only applicable if Seam is configured to use

JTA transactions, and then flushes the persistence context to synchronize changes to the database. The changes become permanent when the transaction commits.

NOTE The `update()` method doesn't need to perform a merge operation, even if the entity instance isn't stored in a long-running conversation. The reason is because the entity instance is fetched from the database in the *Update Model Values* phase prior to the values from the form being applied to it. Thus, the instance is guaranteed to be managed when the `update()` method is called. Any changes made during the *Update Model Values* phase are detected and synchronized to the database.

This transparent management of the entity instance is the quintessence of stateful behavior and is arguably more "active" than what the Active Record pattern affords you. It's certainly a more sound object-oriented design than EJB 2 entity beans with data transfer objects. With the transactional boundaries established at the fringes of the methods on the Home class, you are free to give your entity classes behavior, even if it necessitates a transaction. However, logic that requires direct interaction with the persistence manager is better placed on the Home object itself.

That's enough practical discussion about the Home component. Let's put it to work by using it to develop a data-entry screen for a round of golf in the Open 18 application. We will task it to see if it lives up to its design goals.

10.2.3 *Putting Home to work*

After taking a leisurely stroll through 18 holes on the golf course—leaving plenty of work for the groundskeepers in your wake—you'll want to record your golf score to track your improvement—or lack thereof. Eventually, this data can be used to calculate a golf handicap value. Let's put together logic to manage this data by following the same design used in a seam-gen project. We need to create the entity class, a Home object to manage it, and the JSF templates for rendering the view and edit screens. Mimicking the layout that seam-gen uses, the edit screen should appear like figure 10.7. The view screen only differs in that the data is displayed as read-only.

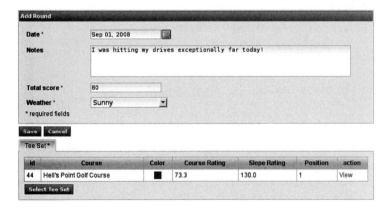

Figure 10.7 The form for adding a new round, the final product of this section's tutorial

A golf round is represented by the `Round` entity class, shown in listing 10.1, which establishes the O/R mapping to the `ROUND` table where the data is persisted. Note that an entity class must implement `Serializable` if it's to be stored in a stateful context (e.g., conversation) or passed through a remote interface.

Listing 10.1   The `Round` entity class

```
package org.open18.model;
import ...;

@Entity
@Table(name = "round")
public class Round implements Serializable {
    private Long id;
    private Integer version;
    private Date date;
    private String notes;
    private Golfer golfer;
    private TeeSet teeSet;
    private Integer totalScore;
    private Weather weather;

    @Id @GeneratedValue
    public Long getId() { return id; }
    public void setId(Long id) { this.id = id; }              ⟵── Permits use of
                                                                   optimistic locking
    @Version
    public Integer getVersion() { return version; }
    private void setVersion(Integer version) { this.version = version; }

    @Temporal(TemporalType.DATE)                        ⟵──── Tells JPA how to
    public Date getDate() { return date; }                    handle the date
    public void setDate(Date date) { this.date = date; }

    @Lob                                                ⟵──── Prepares
    public String getNotes() { return notes; }                database
    public void setNotes(String notes) { this.notes = notes; }   to accept
                                                                  large
    @ManyToOne(fetch = FetchType.LAZY)                            strings
    @JoinColumn(name = "GOLFER_ID", nullable = false)
    @NotNull
    public Golfer getGolfer() { return golfer; }
    public void setGolfer(Golfer golfer) { this.golfer = golfer; }

    @ManyToOne(fetch = FetchType.LAZY)
    @JoinColumn(name = "TEE_SET_ID", nullable = false)
    @NotNull
    public TeeSet getTeeSet() { return teeSet; }
    public void setTeeSet(TeeSet teeSet) { this.teeSet = teeSet; }

    @Column(name = "total_score")
    public Integer getTotalScore() { return totalScore; }
    public void setTotalScore(Integer score) { this.totalScore = score; }

    @Enumerated(EnumType.STRING)
    public Weather getWeather() { return weather; }
    public void setWeather(Weather weather) { this.weather = weather; }
}
```

Note the `@ManyToOne` mappings to `Golfer` and `TeeSet`. The fetch type declared in this annotation is the global fetch strategy, which in this case is lazy. Later on, you'll learn how to temporarily change the fetch strategy to eager for a single JPQL/HQL query to optimize the data retrieval. As you've learned, though, it's perfectly safe to cross lazy associations in the view thanks to Seam's proper scoping of the persistence context.

A round is associated with a tee set—the area on the golf course where you begin each hole. (A tee set isn't a collection, but rather a singular entity that represents the position and color of the tee box on each hole.) The relationship between a round and a golf course is implied indirectly through the tee set relationship. A round is also associated with a golfer, which we assume is the golfer using the application when a new round is being entered. You will see how a Home can be used to establish these two relationships. Let's start by looking at the declaration of the Home object that manages the `Round` entity.

DECLARING A HOME

The `Home` implementation class is typically quite sparse. The purpose of the implementation class is to fulfill the generic type parameter for the `Home` type and yield a Seam component. It can also provide custom routines that the template class doesn't cover. The following class definition shows a bare-minimum implementation subclass of `Home`:

```
package org.open18.action;
import org.jboss.seam.annotations.Name;
import org.jboss.seam.framework.EntityHome;
import org.open18.model.Round;

@Name("roundHome")
public class RoundHome extends EntityHome<Round> {}
```

Believe it or not, this declaration is capable of performing CRUD for a `Round` entity! All of the necessary logic is inherited. The `Round` entity class is passed as a generic type parameter in the `extends` clause to make the `EntityHome` class aware of the type of entity it is managing. The `@Name` annotation makes it a Seam component. The scope isn't declared, so it defaults to the conversation context, inherited from the superclass.

By extending `EntityHome`, we are implicitly selecting JPA as the persistence framework to manage the `Round` entity. `EntityHome` feeds `EntityManager` to the generic type parameter T in `Home<T, E>`:

```
public class EntityHome<E> extends Home<EntityManager, E> { ... }
```

If you're using Hibernate natively, define the `RoundHome` component by extending the `HibernateEntityHome` class instead:

```
@Name("roundHome")
public class RoundHome extends HibernateEntityHome<Round> { ... }
```

The Hibernate implementation of the `Home` superclass has exactly the same methods as the JPA implementation, so switching between the two has a low impact on the application.

RETRIEVING THE PERSISTENCE MANAGER

As with all the persistence controllers in the Seam Application Framework, the persistence manager is retrieved by the method `getPersistenceContext()`. In the JPA implementation, this method looks for a Seam-managed persistence context named `entityManager` and in the Hibernate implementation, `session` (or, `hibernate-Session` as of Seam 2.1). If you aren't able to adhere to this naming convention, you have three options to customize it:

- Override the method `getPersistenceContextName()` method and supply an alternative component name for Seam to use:

  ```
  public String getPersistenceContextName() { return "em"; }
  ```

- Override the `getPersistenceContext()` method and look up the persistence manager explicitly:

  ```
  public EntityManager getPersistenceContext() {
      return (EntityManager) Component.getInstance("em");
  }
  ```

- Use component configuration to wire in a persistence manager:

  ```
  <framework:entity-home ... entity-manager="#{em}"/>
  ```

You can also override the `getEntityManager()` method if you're using JPA or `getSession()` if you're using Hibernate. These methods are the delegates of the `getPersistenceContext()` method in the respective class hierarchy.

TAKING THE XML ROAD

As mentioned in section 10.1.3, you have the option of defining the Home component in the component descriptor using XML. Since generic types are not available in this case, you have to specify the entity class explicitly:

```
<framework:entity-home name="roundHome"
  entity-class="org.open18.model.Round"/>
```

The equivalent XML element for Hibernate is `<framework:hibernate-entity-home>`. Using XML works for simple cases, but as you'll soon discover, there's more value in extending the `Home` class in Java (or Groovy) to create a more intelligent domain model. As another option, you can use XML to configure a Java component that is a subclass of `Home`.

BINDING A HOME TO A FORM

The Home component plays a dual role in a JSF form. It exposes the entity instance, whose properties are bound directly to the inputs in the form. It also responds to the form actions. This direct binding cuts out the "middleman" so you can get right down to business. The JSF form used in the RoundEdit.xhtml template is shown in listing 10.2. We analyze this form in the remainder of this section. Note that the `<s:decorate>` tags simplify the markup for each field, as described in chapter 3. The possible enum constants for the weather select menu are retrieved by a factory named `weatherCategories`, which isn't shown here.

Listing 10.2   The editor form for a golf round

```
<h:form id="roundForm">
  <rich:panel>
    <f:facet name="header">
      #{roundHome.managed ? 'Edit' : 'Add'} Round
    </f:facet>
    <s:decorate id="dateField" template="layout/edit.xhtml">
      <ui:define name="label">Date:</ui:define>
      <rich:calendar id="date" datePattern="MM/dd/yyyy"
        value="#{round.date}"/>
    </s:decorate>
    <s:decorate id="notesField" template="layout/edit.xhtml">
      <ui:define name="label">Notes:</ui:define>
      <h:inputTextarea id="notes" cols="80" rows="3"
        value="#{round.notes}"/>
    </s:decorate>
    <s:decorate id="totalScoreField" template="layout/edit.xhtml">
      <ui:define name="label">Total score:</ui:define>
      <h:inputText id="totalScore" value="#{round.totalScore}"/>
    </s:decorate>
    <s:decorate id="weatherField" template="layout/edit.xhtml">
      <ui:define name="label">Weather:</ui:define>
      <h:selectOneMenu id="weather" value="#{round.weather}">
        <s:selectItems var="_weather" value="#{weatherCategories}"
        label="#{_weather.label}" noSelectionLabel="-- Select --"/>
        <s:convertEnum/>
      </h:selectOneMenu>
    </s:decorate>
    <div style="clear: both;">
      <span class="required">*</span> required fields
    </div>
  </rich:panel>
  <div class="actionButtons">
    <h:commandButton id="save" value="Save"
      action="#{roundHome.persist}"
      rendered="#{!roundHome.managed}" disabled="#{!roundHome.wired}"/>
    <h:commandButton id="update" value="Update"
      action="#{roundHome.update}"
      rendered="#{roundHome.managed}"/>
    <h:commandButton id="delete" value="Delete"
      action="#{roundHome.delete}"
      rendered="#{roundHome.managed}"/>
    <s:button id="discard" value="Discard changes" propagation="end"
      view="/Round.xhtml"
      rendered="#{roundHome.managed}"/>
    <s:button id="cancel" value="Cancel" propagation="end"
      view="/#{empty roundFrom ? 'RoundList' : roundFrom}.xhtml"
      rendered="#{!roundHome.managed}"/>
  </div>
</h:form>
```

The input elements are bound to an instance of Round managed by RoundHome through the value expression root #{roundHome.instance}. Since the #{round-Home.instance} is used so frequently in this template, it makes sense to create an alias for it. As you learned in chapter 6, aliases are defined using a factory component. The factory can be defined in Java using the `@Factory` annotation on a method or as a `<factory>` element in the component descriptor. Let's define it in XML:

```
<factory name="round" value="#{roundHome.instance}"/>
```

You can now use the expression root #{round} in place of #{roundHome.instance} throughout the template. Not only does it save a couple of keystrokes, it also hides the implementation details of the Home pattern, making it appear as though you are working with the entity itself! When choosing an alias, make sure the name isn't already in use or doesn't conflict with the name of an existing component. Otherwise, you may be surprised when you don't get the object you're expecting.

Two questions are raised by the form in listing 10.2 that are integral in understanding how the Home object works:

- When is the instance referenced by #{roundHome.instance} initialized?
- What is the purpose of #{roundHome.managed}?

Let's answer each in turn.

INITIALIZING AN INSTANCE FROM A PROTOTYPE

The `RoundHome` component is instantiated the first time its component name is referenced on the RoundEdit.xhtml page. Most references are to the method `get-Instance()`, the most frequently used method on Home. It serves the underlying entity instance, whether it be transient—not yet saved—or persistent.

As mentioned earlier, when the `getInstance()` method is first called, it either looks up an existing entity instance using the `find()` method on the persistence manager or creates a new transient instance, depending on whether an identifier has been established on the Home, a determination which is made by a call to the `isIdDe-fined()` method. Since we don't yet have any rounds to manage, we focus on creating a new instance.

One of the Home's functions is to create an entity instance from a prototype. It can do more than just instantiate the entity class, though that's the default case. The `getInstance()` method delegates to the `createInstance()` method when a new instance needs to be created. The Home figures out which entity class to instantiate in one of two ways. If the Home was defined through class extension, and an entity class was passed as a parameterized type, the Home uses reflection to determine the type. In this case, the `createInstance()` method instructs the entity class to create a new instance of itself:

```
protected E createInstance() {
    ...
    return getEntityClass().newInstance();
}
```

You can override the `createInstance()` method to provide a more sophisticated prototype. Since the round must be associated with the current golfer, this method provides the perfect opportunity to establish this relationship.

Let's assume that the current user is a golfer and the corresponding `Golfer` instance is stored under the context variable `currentGolfer`. The initialization of this variable is part of the authentication routine implemented in the next chapter. To get by with the stub authentication prepared by seam-gen, you can use the following XML-based configuration:

```
<framework:entity-query name="currentGolferQuery"
  ejbql="select g from Golfer g where g.username = #{identity.username}"/>
<factory name="currentGolfer" scope="conversation" auto-create="true"
  value="#{identity.loggedIn ? currentGolferQuery.singleResult : null}" />
```

The `currentGolfer` is injected into `RoundHome` using `@In` and wired to the `Round` instance in the overridden `createInstance()` method. The injection point shown here is marked optional to allow the Home to be used in the absence of an authenticated golfer:

```
@In(required = false)
Golfer currentGolfer;

@Override
protected Round createInstance() {
    Round round = super.createInstance();
    round.setGolfer(currentGolfer);
    round.setDate(new java.sql.Date(System.currentTimeMillis()));
    return round;
}
```

If you're using the XML-based approach, you instead supply a prototype instance as a value expression to the `new-instance` attribute of `<framework:entity-home>` (or `<framework:hibernate-entity-home>`). To support declaring a Home component in XML, we create a prototype named `roundPrototype`, wire the authenticated golfer instance and built-in current date component to it, and then assign it to the `new-instance` property of the `RoundHome` component in the XML definition:

```
<component name="roundPrototype" class="org.open18.model.Round"
  scope="stateless">
  <property name="golfer">#{currentGolfer}</property>
  <property name="date">#{currentDate}</property>
</component>

<framework:entity-home name="roundHome" class="org.open18.action.RoundHome"
  new-instance="#{roundPrototype}"/>
```

You can also use the XML definition to configure the `newInstance` property of a Home component defined in Java. Note that the `#{roundPrototype}` value expression isn't resolved when assigned to the `newInstance` property. That's because `newInstance` property is of type `ValueExpression`. The expression is resolved in the `createInstance()` method instead of calling `getEntityClass().newInstance()`.

WHAT'S THE STATUS?

The entity instance held by the Home object can be in either a persistent or a transient state. The `contains()` method on the persistence manager is used to check the state of an entity instance. The `isManaged()` method on `EntityHome` performs this check, shown here:

```
@Transactional
public boolean isManaged() {
    return getEntityManager().contains(getInstance());
}
```

There is an equivalent method on `HibernateEntityHome`. Looking back at listing 10.2, you'll notice that different buttons are rendered based on the status returned by this method. The editor only permits the user to persist the round if the instance isn't currently managed by the persistence context. Conversely, the user can only delete or update the instance if it's managed by the persistence context. This UI restriction doesn't avert an attempt to enter a duplicate record. You still need to implement that logic. It just makes the form cognizant of whether it's being used to create or update a record.

Let's focus on the use case of saving a new round. When the user clicks the Save button, the `#{roundHome.persist}` action method is activated and the create operation (the *C* in *CRUD*) is delegated to the `persist()` method of `EntityManager`. However, we can't save an instance of a round until the association to a tee set is satisfied. Let's consider strategies to allow the user to make this selection.

WIRING IN A TEE SET

One logical place to start when adding a new round is the detail page of the tee set played, rendered by the TeeSet.xhtml template. At the bottom of the page, a button can be added that lets the user enter a new round. The button will pass the identifier of the tee set using the `teeSetId` request parameter. The return page is also maintained using the `roundFrom` request parameter in the event the user decides to cancel. The button is defined as follows:

```
<s:button value="Add round" view="/RoundEdit.xhtml">
  <f:param name="teeSetId" value="#{teeSetHome.instance.id}"/>
  <f:param name="roundFrom" value="TeeSet"/>
</s:button>
```

The `TeeSetHome` component, named `teeSetHome` and created in chapter 2 by seamgen, manages a `TeeSet` instance in the same way that `RoundHome` manages a `Round` instance. Assuming the tee set has an identifier of 10, the following URL is created by this button:

```
http://localhost:8080/open18/RoundEdit.seam?teeSetId=10&roundFrom=TeeSet
```

On the RoundEdit.xhtml page, `TeeSetHome` can once again be used to retrieve the tee set instance using the value of the `teeSetId` parameter. The `TeeSet` is then wired into the new `Round` instance. The identifier of the tee set is established on `TeeSetHome` using a page parameter, defined in the RoundEdit.page.xml page descriptor, which is adjacent to RoundEdit.xhtml. The other page parameter copies the value of the `roundFrom` request parameter to the page-scoped `roundFrom` variable:

```
<page>
  <param name="teeSetId" value="#{teeSetHome.teeSetId}"/>
  <param name="roundFrom"/>
</page>
```

The `setTeeSetId()` and `getTeeSetId()` methods on `TeeSetHome` delegate to `setId()` and `getId()` on the superclass, performing a conversion to `Long`, the identifier's type.

The next step is to wire the `TeeSet` instance managed by `TeeSetHome` to the `Round` instance. This logic is handled in the `wire()` method on `RoundHome`. The `TeeSetHome` component must be injected into `RoundHome` so we can access the managed tee set:

```
@In(create = true)
private TeeSetHome teeSetHome;

public void wire() {
    TeeSet teeSet = teeSetHome.getDefinedInstance();
    if (teeSet != null) {
        getInstance().setTeeSet(teeSet);
    }
}
```

The method `getDefinedInstance()` on `TeeSetHome` is a custom method that strictly attempts to retrieve a `TeeSet` instance from the persistence manager if the id is established, as determined by the `isIdDefined()` method.

The final step is to call the `wire()` method from a page action defined in Round-Edit.page.xml so that the association is established prior to the editor being rendered:

```
<page>
  <param name="teeSetId" value="#{teeSetHome.teeSetId}"/>
  <param name="roundFrom"/>
  <action execute="#{roundHome.wire}"/>
</page>
```

To prevent users from clicking the Save button if they haven't yet selected a tee set , we can add the convenience method `isWired()` to `RoundHome` that is used to toggle the `disabled` attribute of the Save button:

```
public boolean isWired() {
    if (getInstance().getTeeSet() == null) {
        return false;
    }
    return true;
}
```

The page fragment in listing 10.3 renders the tee set associated with the round below the editor form. Information about the tee set is read from the `teeSet` property on `Round`.

> **Listing 10.3 The panel showing the tee set associated with the round**

```
<rich:tabPanel>
  <rich:tab label="Tee Set">
    <div class="association">
```

```
        <h:outputText value="Tee set not selected"
          rendered="#{round.teeSet == null}"/>
        <rich:dataTable var="_teeSet" value="#{round.teeSet}"
          rendered="#{round.teeSet != null}">
          <h:column>
            <f:facet name="header">Course</f:facet>
            #{_teeSet.course.name}
          </h:column>
          <h:column>
            <f:facet name="header">Color</f:facet>
            <div title="#{_teeSet.color}" class="colorSwatch"
              style="background-color: #{_teeSet.color}"/>
          </h:column>
          ...
          <h:column>
            <f:facet name="header">Position</f:facet>
            #{_teeSet.position}
          </h:column>
        </rich:dataTable>
      </div>
    </rich:tab>
  </rich:tabPanel>
```

Everything's in place for a new round to be persisted! Although there was a lot of explaining, the work boiled down to creating a Home implementation class, a page parameter, a page action, and a JSF template. The rest of the work is handled by JSF and the Home component working together. JSF binds the values from the form to the properties on the Round entity instance, and the Home component delegates to the persistence manager to save the record.

Now that a round is stored in the table (assuming you were brave enough to click the Save button), we can move on to the other letters in the CRUD acronym. Let's tackle *R* by creating a page to display the round just entered.

PULLING UP A ROUND

The template Round.xhtml, shown in listing 10.4, handles the task of displaying the details of a round. It's identical to the RoundEdit.xhtml template except that the input fields are replaced with read-only output.

> **Listing 10.4   The panel that renders the details of a round**

```
<rich:panel><f:facet name="header">Round</f:facet>
  <s:decorate id="date" template="layout/display.xhtml">
    <ui:define name="label">Date:</ui:define>
    <h:outputText value="#{round.date}">        ◁──── Formats date
      <s:convertDateTime type="date"/>                 according to locale
    </h:outputText>
  </s:decorate>
  <s:decorate id="golfer" template="layout/display.xhtml">
    <ui:define name="label">Golfer:</ui:define>
    #{round.golfer.name}
  </s:decorate>
  <s:decorate id="totalScore" template="layout/display.xhtml">
```

```
        <ui:define name="label">Total score:</ui:define>
        #{round.totalScore}
      </s:decorate>
      <s:decorate id="weather" template="layout/display.xhtml">
        <ui:define name="label">Weather:</ui:define>
        #{round.weather}
      </s:decorate>
      <s:decorate id="notes" template="layout/display.xhtml">
        <ui:define name="label">Notes:</ui:define>
        #{round.notes}
      </s:decorate>
    </rich:panel>
```

To render the data of an existing round, the getInstance() method needs to return the record in the database. That means the identifier of the round must be assigned to the RoundHome component prior to the getInstance() method being called. This assignment is a good fit for a page parameter. However, the id property on Home is of type java.lang.Object, which doesn't provide JSF with enough information to convert the incoming parameter to the identifier's type, which is java.lang.Long. We could create a typed "getter" method that passes the converted value to setId(). But a better solution is to leverage the converter feature of page parameters. The javax.faces.Long converter is registered on the page parameter for roundId in the Round.page.xml descriptor to instruct JSF to convert the string-based request parameter to a java.lang.Long:

```
    <param name="roundId" value="#{roundHome.id}"
      converterId="javax.faces.Long"/>
```

That's all there is to it! When the Round.xhtml template is requested, the corresponding entity instance is loaded from the database according to the request parameter value.

As an alternative to using a page parameter to assign the identifier request parameter to Home, you can inject the parameter into the component directly by using the @RequestParameter annotation. In the case of RoundHome, you create a setRoundId() method to receive the injected request parameter and then set the identifier on the superclass. JSF converts the value to the method parameter's type:

```
    @RequestParameter
    public void setRoundId(Long id) {
        super.setId(id);
    }
```

The option of using the @RequestParameter annotation or the XML-based page parameter is up to you. Keep in mind, though, that page parameters also outject values back to the query string in addition to injecting request parameter values. Let's consider how the presence of the page parameter affects the Edit button:

```
    <div class="actionButtons">
      <s:button id="edit" view="/RoundEdit.xhtml" value="Edit"/>
    </div>
```

Notice that there are no parameters nested in the button component. Thanks to page parameters, the `roundId` is automatically added to the generated URL, saving you the trouble of having to use `<f:param>` to include it explicitly. When thinking about how the URL is built, keep in mind that the page parameters are read from the page descriptor corresponding to the target view ID, which in this case is RoundEdit.xhtml. Thus, the page parameters are read from the RoundEdit.page.xml descriptor. That means the `roundId` page parameter must be added there as well.

```
<page>
  <param name="roundId" value="#{roundHome.id}"/>
  <param name="roundFrom"/>
  <param name="teeSetId" value="#{teeSetHome.teeSetId}"/>
  <action execute="#{roundHome.wire}"/>
</page>
```

Before we move on, there's one last thing to consider. Recall that the `getInstance()` method retrieves the entity instance using the persistence manager's finder method:

```
getEntityManager().find(getEntityClass(), getId());
```

This default lookup is naïve because it leaves all lazy associations uninitialized. Although the conversation-scoped persistence context makes worrying about loading lazy associations a thing of the past, it's a good idea to eagerly fetch data when you know you'll be traversing associations or collections in the view. Eager fetching is paramount to preventing the n + 1 select problem.

TIP   When using Hibernate, you can detect n + 1 select problems by observing the log output or by producing a report from the return value of the `get-Statistics()` method on `SessionFactory`. These two features require the properties `hibernate.show_sql` and `hibernate.generate_statistics` to be enabled in Hibernate, respectively.

On the round detail page, we know we need to render the tee set, course, and golfer, so we might as well initialize these associations in the finder query. This is done by temporarily promoting the fetching strategy from lazy to eager using the `join fetch` JPQL operator. You customize the loading behavior by overriding the `loadInstance()` method on `EntityHome`:

```
protected Round loadInstance() {
    return (Round) getEntityManager.createQuery(
        "select r from Round r " +
        "join fetch r.golfer g " +
        "join fetch r.teeSet ts " +
        "join fetch ts.course c " +
        "where r.id = :id")
        .setParameter("id", getId())
        .getSingleResult();
}
```

Consult a JPA reference for more information on the `join fetch` operator. The `load-Instance()` method can also be used to postprocess the instance after it's loaded. For instance, if you store XML in one of the columns and need to unmarshal that data to a Java structure, you can take this opportunity to perform such logic.

With the detail page out of the way, things start to get interesting in the case of editing an existing entity. That brings us to the *U* and *D* in *CRUD*, which we cover in the next section.

10.2.4 *Venturing away from home*

A Home can only maintain state for as long as it lives. To stretch out the lifetime of a Home, which is scoped to the conversation by default, you need to activate a long-running conversation. This ensures that the `RoundHome` component, the entity instance, and the persistence manager remain in scope while the user is working on modifying the round, even if it means departing the editor screen to go find a tee set.

SWITCHING TO A LONG-RUNNING CONVERSATION

As you learned in chapter 7, there are many ways to begin a long-running conversation. Since we already have the RoundEdit.page.xml descriptor setting up the entity instance, we might as well keep it busy by having it begin the long-running conversation as well:

```
<page>
  <begin-conversation join="true"/>
  <param name="roundId" value="#{roundHome.id}"/>
  <param name="roundFrom"/>
  <param name="teeSetId" value="#{teeSetHome.teeSetId}"/>
  <action execute="#{roundHome.wire}"/>
</page>
```

Depending on how the round editor ties into the application, you may decide that nesting the conversation is more appropriate. With the long-running conversation in place, the `Round` instance being edited remains managed by both the Home and the persistence context between the time the editor is first rendered to when the user submits the form successfully. You can tell that the `Round` instance is managed (it's in the persistent entity state) because the buttons that call the `update()` and `remove()` action methods on `Home` are displayed below the form.

But keeping the entity managed involves more than just showing the right controls. As you learned in the previous two chapters, using an extended persistence context yields important benefits. First, the database only has to be asked once for a record during the use case since the application does its part to "remember" what the database retrieved for it. The other benefit is that the update statement only executes *if the entity instance changes.* If the entity instance hasn't changed, there's nothing to ask the database to do.

OFF TO FIND A TEE SET

With a long-running conversation active, the user is not stuck on the editor screen. You can allow users to roam freely throughout the application, as long as the conversation token is restored when they return. In the case of the round editor, this allows the user to traverse to the tee set listing page, search for, and select a new tee set to link to the round. This step is necessary when the user wants to change the tee set for the round being edited or when a tee set identifier wasn't provided when the user began creating a new round.

We add a button to the bottom of the editor that takes the user to the tee set listing page, where the user can select a tee set to associate with the round:

```
<s:button value="Select Tee Set" view="/TeeSetList.xhtml">
  <f:param name="from" value="RoundEdit"/>
</s:button>
```

The `from` parameter is used by the tee set listing page to know where to send the user after a tee set is selected. (You could also store this information in the conversation context.) The default behavior is to show the detail page of the tee set, which we don't want in this case. Recall that the `<s:button>` component passes the conversation token automatically, thus preserving the long-running conversation.

On the tee set listing page, each row has a Select link, which appends the `teeSetId` request parameter to the URL with the value of the identifier for the tee set in the current row. The tee set for the current row is bound to the iteration variable `teeSet`. The Select link is defined as follows:

```
<s:link view="/#{empty from ? 'TeeSet' : from}.xhtml"
  value="#{empty from ? 'View' : 'Select'}">
  <f:param name="teeSetId" value="#{teeSet.id}"/>
</s:link>
```

Once again, the `<s:link>` component takes care of passing along the conversation token. The `RoundHome` is still active in the conversation and awaiting the user's return, which happens when the user clicks one of the Select links. When the Round-Edit.xhtml page is requested, the `teeSetId` is assigned to the `TeeSetHome` component, and the `wire()` method uses `TeeSetHome` to retrieve the selected `TeeSet` instance and assign it to the `Round`. These steps are exactly the same as those I described earlier when we were creating a new round. The only difference is that now the tee set is being wired to an instance of `Round` that's managed by the persistence context (and is therefore in the database).

The benefit of navigating to the tee set listing page is that the user can use the search form to locate a tee set. However, this page flow presents a problem. If the user has made any changes to the values of the inputs in the form, those changes are lost when the user navigates away to select a tee set. That's because the `<s:button>` component issues a GET request to navigate to the next page and *does not* submit the form, a point that I've raised many times in this book. You have two options for preserving the pending changes:

- Submit the form before navigating
- Periodically push the form values to the model using Ajax

The first option requires that you replace `<s:button>` with a UI command component:

```
<h:commandButton value="Select Tee Set" action="selectTeeSet"/>
```

When a UI command button is used, the `from` parameter must be appended to the URL using a navigation rule in the RoundEdit.page.xml page descriptor:

```
<navigation from-action="selectTeeSet">
  <redirect view-id="/TeeSetList.xhtml">
    <param name="from" value="RoundEdit"/>
  </redirect>
</navigation>
```

The second option requires that you use an Ajax-enabled JSF component library such as Ajax4jsf or ICEfaces, which you'll learn more about in chapter 12. Here's an example of using the `<a:support>` component tag from Ajax4jsf to synchronize the changes in one of the fields with the component on the server when the field loses focus:

```
<s:decorate id="scoreField" template="layout/edit.xhtml">
  <ui:define name="label">Total score:</ui:define>
  <h:inputText id="score" value="#{round.totalScore}">
    <a:support event="onblur" reRender="scoreField" ajaxSingle="true"/>
  </h:inputText>
</s:decorate>
```

There's a side effect to proactively pushing changes onto the managed entity (which occurs in the *Update Model Values* phase). The changes are flushed to the database before the user has finished editing the record. To avoid that situation, we need to switch to manual flushing.

HOLDING BACK CHANGES

As you'll recall from the previous two chapters, the persistence manager flushes the persistence context when the transaction is closed, or possibly sooner. To hold off the changes until the user explicitly requests that they be flushed to the database, we need to enable manual flushing of the persistence context. You can have Seam handle the switch by declaring a flush mode on the `<begin-conversation>` element in page descriptor (e.g., RoundEdit.page.xml) or on the @Begin annotation. Remember that to use manual flushing, you must be using Hibernate natively or as the JPA provider:

```
<begin-conversation join="true" flush-mode="manual"/>
```

With this configuration in place, database transactions may come and go, but the changes to the entity instance aren't migrating to the database until the `flush()` method on the persistence manager is called. The right time for these changes to be made is when the user clicks the Save, Update, or Delete button, signaling the end of an application transaction. Fortunately, you don't have to worry about calling `flush()`. The `persist()`, `update()`, and `remove()` methods on Home take care of flushing the persistence context.

SELECTING A TEE SET IN PLACE

After examining the navigation routine to select a tee set, you may be thinking that it would make more sense to have the user choose the tee set from a select menu within the editor form. That's certainly a reasonable approach. The challenge is how to assign a value to a property whose type is an entity class using a JSF form input. As you learned in chapter 9, Seam's entity converter, registered using the `<s:convert-Entity>` tag, takes care of converting entity instances to and from their identifier values when used as options in a select menu. Keep in mind that this negotiation relies on the Seam-managed persistence context. Here's how you define the form input for selecting a tee set in the round editor:

```
<h:selectOneMenu value="#{round.teeSet}">
  <s:selectItems var="_teeSet" value="#{teeSets}"
    label="#{_teeSet.course.name} - #{_teeSet.color}"/>
  <s:convertEntity/>
</h:selectOneMenu>
```

The request-scoped context variable teeSets supplies the collection of tee sets, something you learn to create with ease using the Query component in section 10.4. Note that it's no longer necessary to wire in a tee set in the wire() method. With the form fields in the round editor populated, let's take a look at the user's exit strategies.

REVERTING CHANGES

There is one caveat to watch out for when working with an extended persistence context. If the user makes changes to the entity instance but doesn't follow up with a save, update, or delete operation, the changes remain on the instance (i.e., it's dirty) for the duration of the conversation, unless it's refreshed from the database. The dirty instance will also be used in a result set retrieved in the same conversation if its identifier matches one of the results.

Consider the case when the user clicks Cancel and is redirected to the detail page by a navigation rule, but the navigation rule doesn't end the conversation prior to the redirect, perhaps to avoid dropping JSF messages. Now there's a chance that the data shown doesn't coincide with the record in the database. This doesn't jeopardize the data's integrity, but it can mislead the user. What you want to do in this scenario is revert the managed entity back to its old self. There may be other use cases when you want to "reset" the pending changes.

Fortunately, the persistence manager includes a method that handles this task. The refresh() method synchronizes from the database to the entity instance, overwriting any changes that might have been made to the instance since being retrieved from the database. (Any collections containing transient entity instances must be first cleared.) This method is the exact opposite of persist(). First, we need to add a method to RoundHome that delegates to refresh() and clears the selected tee set:

```
@Transactional
public String revert() {
    getEntityManager().refresh(getInstance());
    teeSetHome.clearInstance();
    return "reverted";
}
```

Next, this method is attached to the Cancel button at the bottom of the round editor:

```
<s:button id="revert" value="Discard changes"
  action="#{roundHome.revert}" rendered="#{roundHome.managed}"/>
```

Finally, we need a navigation rule:

```
<navigation from-action="#{roundHome.revert}">
  <end-conversation/>
  <redirect view-id="/Round.xhtml"/>
</navigation>
```

When the user clicks the Discard Changes button, any changes are washed away and the data shown on the round detail page reflects the current values stored in the database.

It's a good idea to provide the user with the ability to cancel cleanly like this on all CRUD forms. As an alternative, users always have the option of abandoning the conversation.

NUKING AN INSTANCE

Although it would certainly fit, the *D* in *CRUD* doesn't stand for *Discard changes*. As you know, the *D* stands for *Delete*. Fortunately, there's nothing you have to do to implement the delete operation. The user can already click the Delete button that we added to the form in listing 10.2. This button activates the remove() method on Home, which delegates to the remove() method on the persistence manager to remove the instance from the database, putting the instance of Round back into the transient entity state. The only work required from you is to navigate the user somewhere afterward, such as the previous page or the listing of rounds:

```
<navigation from-action="#{roundHome.remove}">
  <end-conversation/>
  <redirect view-id="#{roundFrom != '/Round.xhtml' ?
    roundFrom : '/RoundList.xhtml'}"/>
</navigation>
```

That segues us into the next task, which is to fill in the remainder of the navigation rules to ensure the user is returned to an appropriate page after each CRUD operation is complete.

WRAPPING THINGS UP

All that's left is to add the remaining navigation rules, secure the page, and deal with exceptions. The navigation rule for the persist and update operations follows the same pattern used by the navigation rule for the remove operation. The navigation rule for the persist operation is shown here:

```
<navigation from-action="#{roundHome.persist}">
  <end-conversation/>
  <redirect view-id="#{roundFrom != null ?
    roundFrom : '/Round.xhtml'}"/>
</navigation>
```

The long-running conversation is terminated by the <end-conversation> element following the execution of each CRUD operation since these methods define the boundaries of our use case. Although the conversation is ended, the status messages queued by the CRUD methods still carry over to the next page since we aren't ending the conversation before the redirect. You'll learn how to configure the messages that the Home component produces in section 10.3.1.

We need to add the login-required restriction to the <page> node to ensure that the user is authenticated before creating or editing a round. In the next chapter, you'll learn how to create more restrictive security rules.

```
<page login-required="true">
  ...
</page>
```

If an existing entity can't be located in the database, the Home component raises the exception org.jboss.seam.framework.EntityNotFoundException, which results in a 404 error page being displayed as declared by the @HttpError annotation on the exception class. If a persistence exception is thrown, you can handle it in one of two ways. You can override the CRUD methods on Home and implement a try/catch block, or you can register an exception handler in the global page descriptor to direct the user to an error page as follows:

```
<exception class="javax.persistence.OptimisticLockException">
  <redirect view-id="/error.xhtml">
    <end-conversation/>
    <message>The record was modified by another user.</message>
  </redirect>
</exception>
<exception class="javax.persistence.PersistenceException">
  <redirect view-id="/error.xhtml">
    <message>The operation failed. Please try again.</message>
  </redirect>
</exception>
```

You've now seen the key aspects of the Home component and how it's used to implement a CRUD scenario. Although there wasn't a lot of Java code, you did have to write code to make it work (the wiring of the tee set and the revert logic). If you're one of those people who would rather "program in XML"—you know who you are—you'll be excited to hear that you can commission a Home while steering clear of Java. To demonstrate, we add a new feature that lets a golfer add a review to a golf course.

10.2.5   *CRUD a la XML*

A Home component is "programmed" in XML by declaring and configuring it in the component descriptor. You primarily interact with its instances using the EL. If you do intend on injecting the instance into another component, the receiving property's type must be EntityHome (or HibernateEntityHome) parameterized with the entity class since there's no application-specific subclass:

```
private EntityHome<RoundHome> roundHome;
```

As you might imagine, defining a component entirely in XML is best suited for relatively straightforward use cases. In this case, you are merely the Home's puppeteer. You can pull its strings in different ways, but your options are limited. Fortunately, the EL and the component descriptor give us enough flexibility to establish relationships for the entity instance that the Home manages. This wiring is done by creating a prototype for the entity using component configuration, then passing that prototype to the newInstance property on Home, the approach followed in this next example.

From the course detail page you'll provide a form to let users comment on a course. The course detail page was built by seam-gen in chapter 2. All we need to do in this section is define the CourseComment entity class, create a Home component to manage it, and add a new form to the bottom of the course detail page where the comment is entered. We assume that the author of the comment is the current golfer.

Let's start with the CourseComment entity class, shown in listing 10.5.

Listing 10.5 The entity class representing a comment on a course

```
package org.open18.model;
import ...;

@Entity
@Table(name = "course_comment")
public class CourseComment implements Serializable {
    private Long id;
    private Integer version;
    private Date datePosted;
    private String text;
    private Course course;
    private Golfer golfer;

    @Id @GeneratedValue
    public Long getId() { return id; }
    public void setId(Long id) { this.id = id; }

    @Version
    public Integer getVersion() { return version; }
    private void setVersion(Integer version) { this.version = version; }

    @Temporal(TemporalType.TIMESTAMP)
    public Date getDatePosted() { return datePosted; }
    public void setDatePosted(Date date) { this.datePosted = date; }

    @Lob
    public String getText() { return text; }
    public void setText(String text) { this.text = text; }

    @ManyToOne(fetch = FetchType.LAZY) @NotNull
    @JoinColumn(name = "COURSE_ID", nullable = false)
    public Course getCourse() { return course; }
    public void setCourse(Course course) { this.course = course; }

    @ManyToOne(fetch = FetchType.LAZY) @NotNull
    @JoinColumn(name = "GOLFER_ID", nullable = false)
    public Golfer getGolfer() { return golfer; }
    public void setGolfer(Golfer golfer) { this.golfer = golfer; }
}
```

Next, we configure a prototype that initializes a transient instance of CourseComment, inject the value expression for the prototype into the Home component that manages this entity, and finally define an alias for the getInstance() method:

```
<component name="courseCommentPrototype"
  class="org.open18.model.CourseComment">
  <property name="datePosted">#{currentDatetime}</property>
  <property name="course">#{courseHome.instance}</property>
  <property name="golfer">#{currentGolfer}</property>
</component>

<framework:entity-home name="courseCommentHome"
  entity-class="org.open18.model.CourseComment"
  new-instance="#{courseCommentPrototype}"/>

<factory name="courseComment" value="#{courseCommentHome.instance}"/>
```

The expression #{currentDatetime} references a built-in component provided by the Seam Application Framework that resolves to a SQL-compliant timestamp representing the time it is resolved. Seam also has built-in components that resolve to the current SQL-compliant date and SQL-compliant time, currentDate and currentTime, respectively.

All that's left is to define the form for creating a comment. The form is only rendered if the user is logged so that there's someone to blame for the comment.

```
<h:form id="commentForm" rendered="#{currentGolfer != null}">
  <rich:panel><f:facet name="header">Leave a comment</f:facet>
    <s:decorate id="textField" template="layout/edit.xhtml">
      <ui:define name="label">Comment:</ui:define>
      <h:inputTextarea id="text" value="#{courseComment.text}"/>
    </s:decorate>
    <div class="actionButtons">
      <h:commandButton id="save" value="Post"
        action="#{courseCommentHome.persist}"/>
    </div>
  </rich:panel>
</h:form>
```

You're done! With all the time you saved, you can spend the rest of the day making the application prettier for your boss. Granted, not all forms are going to be this simple, but that's why you can mix and match the XML configuration with Java at the component or application level. When the forms are this simple, you should be glad to know you can simply whip out the component descriptor and get the job done in no time flat. When things are more complex, you can use the Java API and earn your living. If complex coding is required, your best bet may be to use Groovy!

Amid all the CRUD that has taken place, we've overlooked one very important detail. We're pleased that data is being persisted to the database, but we aren't letting the user know how things are going. Let's see how to keep the user informed after the submit.

10.3   Providing feedback

Communication is important. That's why the Home component supports two ways of providing feedback. The first is a success message that's displayed to the user. The second is a set of internal events that notify other components of the transaction's completion. This section explores these two communication mechanisms.

10.3.1   Customizing the status messages

The Home component prepares a generic, info-level status message after successful completion of any CRUD operation. At the time of this writing, the messages generated are specific to JSF, though in the future, the controller classes in the Seam Application Framework will produce status messages appropriate for the UI framework being used. All you have to do is display the message on the ensuing page:

```
<h:messages globalOnly="true"/>
```

But who wants generic messages? I'm sure you want to give the users lots of good information so that it's very clear to them what happened. Let's customize the CourseHome component generated by seam-gen in chapter 2 to give the user personalized messages rather than the canned responses that Seam provides.

As you've learned, Seam is very flexible when it comes to message handling, especially since you can use EL notation in message templates to reference contextual data. Messages are added to the response using the built-in FacesMessages component. One way to access this component is by calling the getFacesMessages() method on any Controller component. The FacesMessages component allows you to

- Use EL notation in message templates to take advantage of context variables
- Load message templates from a Seam-managed resource bundle for i18n support
- Configure a fall-back message string to use if a key isn't found in the resource bundle

There are two ways to override the message templates used by the Home component. You can either define them directly on the component or you can place them in a resource bundle. Listing 10.6 shows the CourseHome component, which sets up custom message templates in the create() method. This method is called immediately after the component is instantiated, as indicated by the @Create annotation inherited from the overridden method. The message templates all use the value expression #{course}, which is satisfied by the @Factory method on the same component.

Listing 10.6 The CourseHome component configured to use custom messages

```
package org.open18.action;
import ...;

@Name("courseHome")
public class CourseHome extends EntityHome<Course> {         Inherits @Create
    @Override                                                from superclass
    public void create() {                       <─────
        setCreatedMessage("You've successfully added #{course.name}. " +
            "Thanks for contributing!");
        setUpdatedMessage("Thanks for updating #{course.name}. " +
            "Your careful eye is appreciated!");
        setDeletedMessage("#{course.name} has been removed. " +
            "We never liked it anyway.");
    }

    @Override
    @Factory(value = "course", scope = ScopeType.EVENT)
    public Course getInstance() {
        return super.getInstance();
    }
}
```

Alternatively, you could set these messages using component configuration:

```
<framework:entity-home name="courseHome"
  class="org.open18.action.CourseHome"
```

```
created-message="You've successfully added #{course.name}.
➥Thanks for contributing!"
updated-message="Thanks for updating #{course.name}.
➥Your careful eye is appreciated!"
deleted-message="&#8205;#{course.name} has been removed.
➥We never liked it anyway."/>
```

NOTE Notice the use of ‍ at the start of the deleted-message attribute. Seam evaluates strings that begin with the character sequence #{ at the time they're assigned to the property. This XHTML entity reference, a zero-width space, offsets the first character, allowing the evaluation to be deferred until the status message is created.

The limitation of configuring the message templates directly on the component is that, even though the templates have dynamic parts, only a single language is supported. Let's see how to define message templates that can be selected according to the user's locale.

10.3.2 Creating i18n-compliant messages

To enable internationalization (i18n) support for the success messages, you define them in the Seam resource bundle. Refer back to section 5.5.2 in chapter 5 to see how to configure the Seam resource bundle. Fortunately, you don't have to establish a connection between the Home component and the resource bundle since logic is built-in to the Home class to consume messages in this bundle.

Before consulting the messages defined on its own message properties, Home looks for message bundle keys associated with the entity class being managed. It assembles the message key by combining the simple name of the entity class (as returned by the getSimpleName() method on the class object) with the operation being performed, separated by an underscore (_), as illustrated in figure 10.8.

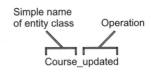

Figure 10.8 The way Home assembles a message bundle key for a CRUD operation.

Here are the English message bundle keys for the CourseHome component that were configured previously, now defined in messages_en.properties:

```
Course_created=You've successfully added #{course.name}.
  ➥Thanks for contributing!
Course_updated=Thanks for updating #{course.name}.
  ➥Your careful eye is appreciated!
Course_deleted=#{course.name} has been removed.
  ➥We never liked it anyway.
```

If the message key can't be found in the Seam resource bundle, the Home component falls back to using the message templates configured on the component or, if those aren't set, the built-in messages. In section 13.6.1 in chapter 13 you'll learn how the default language is selected and how to create a UI control that allows users to change the language for their session. In addition to keeping the user informed, Seam broadcasts the success of the CRUD operations to other components using its event facility.

10.3.3 *Transaction success events*

When a CRUD operation completes successfully, so does a transaction. The Home component schedules two events to be raised when the transaction is committed, using the `raiseAfterTransactionSuccessEvent()` method. The first is a generic event indicating the success of the transaction, duplicating the `org.jboss.seam.afterTransactionCompletion` event raised by the Seam transaction infrastructure. The second event is customized to the simple name of the entity class whose persistence state is being modified. Unfortunately, neither event tells you which operation was performed. If this were the `RoundHome` component, the events would be as follows:

- `org.jboss.seam.afterTransactionSuccess`
- `org.jboss.seam.afterTransactionSuccess.Round`

The second event can be used to refresh a result set which may now hold a stale reference to the modified entity. Assuming the result set is managed by a `roundList` component, introduced in the next section, you can bind its refresh methods to the transaction success event using the component descriptor:

```
<event type="org.jboss.seam.afterTransactionSuccess.Round">
  <action execute="#{roundList.refresh}"/>
  <action execute="#{roundList.getResultList}"/>
</event>
```

What's unique about these events is that they aren't raised immediately, but only after the transaction completes. If you're using Seam's global transactions, the commit happens at the end of the *Invoke Application* phase. This scheduling is handled by registering these events using transaction synchronization, an interface that allows callback code to be executed by the transaction. You learned in the previous chapter that Seam allows transaction synchronizations to be used even when using resource-local transactions.

In this section, you've learned to appreciate that the Home class is much more than a generic CRUD interface. It can be a stateful component and active domain model object that wraps an entity instance, manages its state, and provides declarative transaction boundaries around the CRUD operations performed on it. It can also coordinate with other Home components to establish associations to other entity instances. To add polish, it even prepares success messages for the user and raises transaction completion events to notify other components when the transaction completes.

While the Home component manages a single entity instance, the component template we look at next manages the result set of a JPQL or HQL query. You can even create stateful lists just as you've created stateful domain objects.

10.4 *Smarter queries with the Query component*

When you introduce queries into your application, you're immediately faced with the decision of how to manage the result set. Knowing the right time to execute the query can be difficult to determine. If you execute the query every time you need to present the results, you put undo pressure on the database. At the other extreme, if you hold onto the results for too long, you end up feeding users with stale information that may confuse them, or worse, cause them to make wrong decisions. Once again, you need a strategy.

Fortunately, the Seam Application Framework includes a class that helps you manage the results of a query, appropriately named Query. As you soon discover, the Query component manages contextual queries, which means that the query can change dynamically as its parameters (which are mapped to context variables) change. Just like the Home component template, there are implementations of the Query class for both JPA and Hibernate, EntityQuery and HibernateEntityQuery, respectively. The class diagram for the EntityQuery component is shown in figure 10.9. This section shows you how to use the Query component, focusing on the JPA implementation.

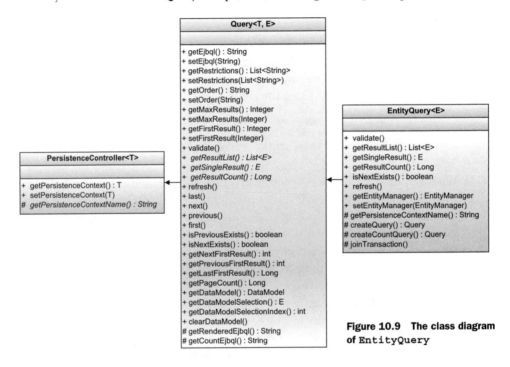

Figure 10.9 The class diagram of EntityQuery

As with the Home component, you can use the Query component either by extending the Query class, configuring it directly in the component descriptor, or a combination of the two. Query is a sufficiently flexible component template, so typically there isn't a need to write custom Java code. Let's build on the example in the previous section by creating a page that lists all the Round instances stored in the database. We use a Query component to manage the result set.

10.4.1 *Creating a result set listing*

To use the Query component, at a minimum, you must supply it with an entity query, written in JPQL (when using JPA) or in HSQL (when using native Hibernate). You assign the query to the component's ejbql property (despite the name of the property, it isn't specific to JPA).

The declaration of the Query component used to manage the list of rounds is shown here:

```
<framework:entity-query name="roundList" ejbql="select r from Round r"/>
```

The `ejbql` property holds the static portion of the query. This fragment includes the `select` clause, join operators, and static conditions. The contextual restrictions are added in a later section. Rather than pulling all of the rounds, let's set a limit of 15 using the `maxResults` property of the Query class, which you'll eventually bind to a UI control:

```
<framework:entity-query name="roundList" ejbql="select r from Round r"
    max-results="15"/>
```

Preparing and executing the query is handled entirely by the Query class, which delegates the work of running the query to the persistence manager. Three operations are supported by the query: You can query for a list of results, a single result, or the result count. If you're only expecting one result and more than one result is found, a `NonU-niqueResultException` is thrown. The Query class also includes a convenience method for wrapping the result set in a JSF `DataModel`. The methods for retrieving the result set data are shown in table 10.4.

Table 10.4   The methods on `Query` that execute JPQL/HQL queries

Method	Description
getResultList()	Executes the query if a local result set isn't available. The result set is stored to avoid redundant queries. Returns the result set as a `java.util.List`.
getSingleResult()	Executes the query if a local result value isn't available. The result value is stored to avoid redundant fetches. Returns the result as an object.
getResultCount()	Executes the count equivalent of the query if a result count isn't available. The count is stored to avoid redundant fetches. Returns the row count as a `java.lang.Long`. May require customization if the query is complex.
getDataModel()	Wraps the return value of `getResultList()` in the appropriate `javax.faces.DataModel` type and stores it until the query is executed again. Returns the wrapped value.

The query methods listed in table 10.4 avoid redundant database queries by caching the results in a private property on the class. The query isn't executed again until the component considers the state of the results to be "dirty," as defined by any of the following conditions:

- A query restriction parameter changes.
- The sort order changes.
- The maximum result value changes.
- The first result offset changes.
- The results are manually cleared by a call to `refresh()` on Query.

The retention of the query results is especially important for components that are used in JSF templates since the encoding and decoding process of a JSF component tree can cause methods in table 10.4 to be executed *many* times. Ensuring that the query only executes when necessary avoids taxing the database.

By default, an instance of Query is scoped to the event context. If you scope it to the conversation context instead, the caching of the result is able to span multiple requests:

```
<framework:entity-query name="roundList" scope="conversation"
  ejbql="select r from Round r" max-results="15"/>
```

Caching the result does run the risk of stale data, but thanks to the aforementioned dirty checks the Query class ensures that the query is executed at the appropriate time. An event can also be used to refresh the query, as demonstrated earlier.

The roundList component is now ready to be used to display the collection of Round instances in a data table. The relevant portions of the RoundList.xhtml JSF template that renders these results are shown in listing 10.7.

Listing 10.7   A table showing the results of the query that fetches the list of rounds

```
<rich:panel><f:facet name="header">Round search results</f:facet>
  <h:outputText value="No rounds were found"
    rendered="#{empty roundList.resultList}"/>
  <rich:dataTable var="_round" value="#{roundList.resultList}"
    rendered="#{not empty roundList.resultList}">
    <h:column>
      <f:facet name="header">Golfer</f:facet>
      #{_round.golfer.name}
    </h:column>
    <h:column>
      <f:facet name="header">Date</f:facet>
      <h:outputText value="#{_round.date}">
        <s:convertDateTime type="date"/>
      </h:outputText>
    </h:column>
    <h:column>
      <f:facet name="header">Course</f:facet>
      #{_round.teeSet.course.name}
    </h:column>
    <h:column>
      <f:facet name="header">Tee set (color)</f:facet>
      <div title="#{_round.teeSet.color}" class="colorSwatch"
        style="background-color: #{_round.teeSet.color};"/>
    </h:column>
    ...
    <h:column>
      <f:facet name="header">action</f:facet>
      <s:link id="round" view="/Round.xhtml" value="View">
        <f:param name="roundId" value="#{_round.id}"/>
      </s:link>
    </h:column>
  </rich:dataTable>
</rich:panel>
```

Notice in listing 10.7 how the lazy associations on the `Round` entity are casually traversed. Once again, it's a good idea to optimize the initial query to prevent excessive querying in the view. The first optimization is to tune the persistence manager to anticipate lazy fetches and batch fetch the data. In Hibernate, this behavior is configured by setting the default batch fetch size in the persistence unit configuration:

```
<property name="hibernate.default_batch_fetch_size" value="16"/>
```

Play around with the batch size while monitoring the SQL statements logged by Hibernate to see how it affects the number of queries that are executed. The other approach you can take is to modify the query to fetch associations eagerly. If the association mapping is marked as `FetchType.LAZY`, it can be temporarily promoted to eager by using the `join fetch` clause. The following query grabs all the information needed on the round list page in one aggregate query:

```
select r from Round r
   join fetch r.golfer
   join fetch r.teeSet ts
   join fetch ts.course
```

I recommend always using lazy associations in the mapping and enabling eager fetching at the query level. For other ways of cutting down on lazy-loading queries, consult the reference documentation for your persistence provider. To help your DBA find the source of a SQL statement, you can add a comment to the query using a query hint:

```
<framework:entity-query ...>
  <framework:hints>
    <key>org.hibernate.comment</key>
    <value>Query for rounds used on RoundList.xhtml</value>
  </framework:hints>
</framework:entity-query>
```

The `hints` property accepts any hint that the persistence provider supports. Let's see what else we can do with the query.

10.4.2 *Paging the result set*

The RoundList.xhtml page has one serious flaw at the moment. If there are more than 15 results, there's no way to see beyond the first page. The UI needs to give the user a way to paginate to other regions of the query. It should come as no surprise that the `Query` class has built-in support for pagination. Query paging is controlled by the `firstResult` and `maxResults` properties on this component, which alter the underlying JPQL/HQL to load the corresponding region of the result set. Anytime either of these properties change, the result set is refreshed. Table 10.5 lists the methods on the `Query` class that assist in creating UI controls to manipulate the value of these two properties.

The logic in the `Query` class is able to extract the pagination offset information without having to use a second query. While most of the methods are simple calculations based on the current offset value, `isNextExists()` is a special case. The `Query`

Table 10.5   The methods on `Query` that provide information about pagination

Method	Description
isNextExists()	Indicates whether more results exist beyond the current page
isPreviousExists()	Indicates whether results exist before the current page
getNextFirstResult()	Returns the offset of the first result on the next page
getPreviousFirstResult()	Returns the offset of the first result on the previous page
getLastFirstResult()	Returns the offset of the first result on the last page
getPageCount()	Returns the number of pages in the result set, using the maximum results setting as the page size

class avoids using an extra query by always fetching one more record than the page size (i.e., the `maxResults` value). If the extra record is present in the result set, the `Query` class knows another page is available. It then truncates the result set back to the page size to remove trace of this "feeler" record. The `getPageCount()` is the one method that requires an extra query to be executed, but only if the page size is non-null, because it needs to know the total number of records in the database.

With the pagination information in hand, there's still the matter of keeping track of pagination offset between requests. If you aren't using a long-running conversation on the listing page, then the offset must be passed as a request parameter. This strategy is accomplished by combining a page parameter with links that include the offset in the query string. Begin by declaring a page parameter in the RoundList. page.xml descriptor:

```
<page>
  <param name="firstResult" value="#{roundList.firstResult}"/>
</page>
```

Next, add links for the user to navigate between pages. The following link advances the user to the next page in the result set, if it's available:

```
<s:link id="next" value="Next Page" rendered="#{roundList.nextExists}">
  <f:param name="firstResult" value="#{roundList.nextFirstResult}"/>
</s:link>
```

You can see examples of this approach in the listing pages generated by seam-gen in chapter 2. Page parameters are great because they create RESTful URLs. However, they break down when the user has to navigate away from the page because they get dropped. Another way to maintain the state of the offset is to use a long-running conversation.

The benefit of using a long-running conversation with a conversation-scoped Query component is that the user is free to roam the application without losing the current position in the result set. If the user manages to abandon the conversation, it can be restored using a conversation switcher, revealing that the result set is in the exact state the user left it in.

You have to determine whether it's more important to you to produce RESTful URLs or for the state of the query to be maintained. While it's possible to implement both simultaneously, it takes some work. For the remainder of the chapter, we work within the context of a long-running conversation to demonstrate the stateful approach.

The first step to creating a stateful Query component is to begin a long-running conversation when the round list page is rendered, which is defined in the Round-List.page.xml descriptor. The page is also given a description to allow the user to return to this conversation using a conversation switcher:

```
<page>
  <description>
    Round List: #{roundList.resultList.size} of #{roundList.resultCount}
  </description>
  <begin-conversation join="true"/>
</page>
```

Now that the `roundList` is maintained in a long-running conversation, it's no longer necessary to set the pagination offset explicitly. Instead, it's possible to use the built-in pagination methods on the `Query` class, listed in table 10.6. These actions take care of setting the `firstResult` property internally and also resetting the cached result set when called.

Table 10.6   The methods on `Query` that paginate the result set

Method	Description
next()	Advances the first result value to the offset of the next page
previous()	Reverts the first result value to the offset of the previous page
last()	Advances the first result value to the offset of the last page
first()	Reverts the first result value to the offset of the first page, which is always 0

All that's left is to add command links that execute the pagination action methods. The links must be nested within a JSF form as required by the JSF specification. Between the links is a select menu to change the page size. A value change listener is used on the select menu to reset the pagination offset when the page size is changed:

```
<div id="tableControl">
  <h:form id="pagination">
    <h:commandLink id="first" action="#{roundList.first}"
      value="First Page" rendered="#{roundList.previousExists}"/>
    <h:commandLink id="previous" action="#{roundList.previous}"
      value="Previous Page" rendered="#{roundList.previousExists}"/>
    <h:selectOneMenu id="pageSize" value="#{roundList.maxResults}"
      valueChangeListener="#{roundList.first}"
      onchange="this.form.submit();">
      <f:selectItem itemValue="25"/>
      <f:selectItem itemValue="50"/>
    </h:selectOneMenu>
    <h:commandLink id="next" action="#{roundList.next}"
      value="Next Page" rendered="#{roundList.nextExists}"/>
```

```
    <h:commandLink id="last" action="#{roundList.last}"
       value="Last Page" rendered="#{roundList.nextExists}"/>
   </h:form>
 </div>
```

Now that the user has access to all the rounds in the database and the list remains stable on postback, it's the perfect opportunity to implement multirow deletions.

10.4.3   *Deleting multiple records at once*

Let's steer slightly off topic for a moment to implement a CRUD feature that wasn't possible earlier in the chapter. Any operation on multiple records at once is typically done from the listing page. Fortunately, the process is straightforward. First, add a transient boolean property to the Round class that indicates whether the record is selected:

```
private boolean selected;

@Transient public boolean isSelected() { return this.selected; }
public void setSelected(boolean selected) { this.selected = selected; }
```

Next, add a new column to the listing table with a checkbox for selecting a record:

```
<h:column>
  <h:selectBooleanCheckbox value="#{_round.selected}"/>
</h:column>
```

Then, add a button below the list that invokes the delete() method when clicked:

```
<h:commandButton action="#{multiRoundAction.delete}"
  value="Delete selected"/>
```

Finally, implement the delete() method on the new MultiRoundAction component. For fun, we implement the component in Groovy, naming the file MultiRoundAction.groovy.

```
@Name("multiRoundAction")
class MultiRoundAction {
    @In private def entityManager
    @In private def roundList
    void delete() {
        roundList.resultList.findAll { r -> r.selected }
            .each { r -> entityManager.remove r }
        roundList.refresh()
        "/RoundList.xhtml"
    }
}
```

The types on the properties are not required since Seam uses name-based injections. Let's return to managing the query by giving the user the ability to sort the results by clicking on the column headers.

10.4.4   *Putting the results in order-*

The Query class has built-in support for sorting the result set. The sort order is maintained in a property named order, which holds both the sort column and sort direction, and is appended to the managed JPQL/HQL query. Whenever the order property changes, the cached result set is invalidated and the query is executed again.

Keep in mind that the `Query` class sanitizes the `order` property to check for SQL injection. Seam 2.1 increases the resilience to SQL injection by splitting the `order` property into `orderColumn` and `orderDirection`, which I strongly encourage you to use.

Let's start by establishing a default sort by assigning a value to the `order` property:

```
<framework:entity-query name="roundList" scope="conversation"
  ejbql="select r from Round r
    join fetch r.golfer g
    join fetch r.teeSet ts
    join fetch ts.course c"
  max-results="15" order="r.date desc"/>
```

The result set of this query will be sorted by the date of the round in descending order. The `date` property on `Round` is qualified in this query as `r.date` to distinguish it from a property named `date` on any other entity in the query. It's always a good idea to qualify the name of the property by prefixing it with the alias defined in the `select` clause. The aliases in this query are `r` for `Round`, `g` for `Golfer`, `ts` for `TeeSet`, and `c` for `Course`. These aliases will be used throughout the remainder of this chapter. To sort on the name of the golfer, you'd set the `order` property to `g.lastName asc, g.firstName asc`.

Once again, your job is to provide the user with a UI control, this time to assign the `order` property of the Query component. As is standard practice, we make each column header a sort link. In our case, the link will pass the `sort` clause to the `Query` class's `setOrder()` method using a parameterized method expression in the action of the UI command component. Here's the link in the column header for the course name column:

```
<s:link value="Course Name"
  styleClass="#{roundList.order == 'c.name asc' ? 'asc' :
    (roundList.order == 'c.name desc' ? 'desc' : '')}"
  action="#{roundList.setOrder(roundList.order eq
    'c.name asc' ? 'c.name desc' : 'c.name asc')}"/>
```

Two bits of logic are performed by this component tag. In the parameter of the action method, a check is performed to determine if the sort needs to be reversed or the default sort applied, depending on whether the column is currently sorted. In the `styleClass` attribute, a similar check is performed to determine if this column is sorted and, if so, the direction of the sort. The work of rendering a sort indicator is left up to two CSS classes, shown here:

```
th a.asc {
    background-image: url(../img/sort_asc.gif);
}
th a.desc {
    background-image: url(../img/sort_desc.gif);
}
```

Since this markup has to be reproduced for every column, it's just screaming to be converted to a Facelets composition template,[4] which you learned about in chapter 3.

---

[4] For more information regarding how to define and use Facelets composition templates, please refer to the Facelets reference documentation at https://facelets.dev.java.net/nonav/docs/dev/docbook.html.

Let's push this logic into the template layout/sort.xhtml to encapsulate the complexity of this link:

```
<ui:composition ...>
  <h:commandLink value="#{name}" action="#{query.setOrder(param.order)}"
    styleClass="#{query.order == property.concat(' asc') ? 'asc' :
    (query.order == property.concat(' desc') ? 'desc' : '')}">
    <f:param name="order" value="#{query.order ==
      property.concat(' asc') ? property.concat(' desc') :
      property.concat(' asc')}"/>
  </h:commandLink>
</ui:composition>
```

Now, the logic of the sort link is only defined in one place. However, some changes had to be made to accommodate Facelets: We are now using a standard UI command link and there's extensive use of parameterized EL. But all of that is behind you now. All you have to do is fill in the template parameters. Here's the sort link for the course name column again:

```
<s:decorate template="layout/sort.xhtml">
  <ui:param name="query" value="#{roundList}"/>
  <ui:param name="name" value="Course Name"/>
  <ui:param name="property" value="c.name"/>
</s:decorate>
```

That takes care of sorting! The Query class handles the task of applying the order clause to the JPQL/HSQL query. If you need features like multicolumn sort or column reordering, I recommend using an advanced table component from a JSF component library instead.

Query paging and sorting only scratches the surface of the Query component's capabilities. The most powerful feature is conditional restrictions. Let's explore this feature by implementing a form that allows the user to search for rounds.

10.4.5 *Placing restrictions on the result set*

Paging through hundreds of results can take its toll on your user. To make for a better experience, you need to let users help themselves to the data by giving them a way to supply criteria that pares down the result set. Searching is one of those tasks that has been long dreaded by developers because it almost always means building dynamic queries. If you've ever had to maintain code that uses a custom SQL builder to implement a search page, you can appreciate how much pain is involved. That's why effort was put into establishing an intelligent restriction mechanism for the Query component.

RESTRICTIONS AS A BUILT-IN QUERY BUILDER

Restrictions are assigned to the Query component as a collection of conditions, each having exactly one embedded value expression. At runtime, the restrictions are adjoined to the where clause of the JPQL/HQL query using the AND operator. Thus, each restriction works to limit the result set. Here's an example restriction that searches by the golfer's last name:

```
g.lastName = #{roundExample.golfer.lastName}
```

We're going to get to the `roundExample` context variable in a moment. What's important to recognize is that the condition is derived from an EL value expression. Each restriction must have exactly one value expression embedded in it. That value expression is the equivalent of a query parameter, but with one crucial enhancement. If the expression resolves to null or an empty string value, the restriction is *omitted* from the query. That's how Seam is able to formulate dynamic queries using restrictions.

Aside from the obvious benefit of being able to reference context variables in your queries, using the EL gives Seam the opportunity to prepare the values as query parameters so they're properly escaped. That way, your application isn't vulnerable to SQL injection attacks. What's nice about the restriction facility in general is that query building is just a matter of configuration, rather than yet another hand-built solution.

The restrictions are stored as a collection of strings on the `restrictions` property of `Query`. You can initialize the collection in Java or assign the values using component configuration. The remainder of this section explores various ways to apply the restrictions.

QUERY BY EXAMPLE

Restrictions are a way to make a JPQL/HQL query contextual. The context—or state, in this case—is the criteria the user has entered in the search form. To get the criteria values from the form to the query, they need to be bound to the properties of a component instance. The Query by Example (QBE) pattern lends itself nicely to this problem. In QBE, you pass a criteria object to the query engine and tell it to "find results like this." The object that you pass to the query engine is a partial representation of the objects in the result set. Since the results in the listing page are instances of an entity class, in this case `Round`, then the example object must be an instance of `Round`.

Let's create a new component role for `Round` named `roundExample` that's fed as the example criteria for the round search. It's scoped to the conversation, the default scope for an entity class, so that the criteria doesn't get lost when the user paginates or sorts the result set or navigates away from the listing page.

The properties on this criteria object will be referenced in the restriction clauses on the Query component for the round list page. However, just searching on the properties of the `Round` entity is going to be limiting. Thus, we need to build up a hierarchical example object that can be fed into the join query introduced in the previous section. We create several additional component roles and wire instances of them together using component configuration:

```
<component name="teeSetExample" class="org.open18.model.TeeSet"/>
<component name="golferExample" class="org.open18.model.Golfer"/>
<component name="roundExample" class="org.open18.model.Round">
  <property name="golfer">#{golferExample}</property>
  <property name="teeSet">#{teeSetExample}</property>
</component>
```

With the example object ready to go, let's put it to use building restriction clauses. We start small by allowing the user to perform a case-insensitive wildcard search on the name of the golfer and the color of the tee set played:

```
<framework:entity-query name="roundList" ...>
  <framework:restrictions>
    <value>
      lower(g.firstName) like
        concat(lower(#{roundExample.golfer.firstName}),'%')
    </value>
    <value>
      lower(g.lastName) like
        concat(lower(#{roundExample.golfer.lastName}),'%')
    </value>
    <value>
      lower(ts.color) like
        concat(lower(#{roundExample.teeSet.color}),'%')
    </value>
  </framework:restrictions>
</framework:entity-query>
```

The restrictions comprise the where clause of the JPQL/HQL query. The entity properties in the restriction must be qualified to the entity alias to which they belong. For instance, in the first restriction, the g prefix in g.firstName is an alias to the Golfer entity. When defining a restriction, you have the full power of JPQL at your disposal. That means you can use built-in JPQL/HQL functions (not SQL functions) such as concat() and lower() to customize the condition, as shown earlier. Unfortunately, you can't apply two different value expressions in the same restriction. In that case, you probably need to rethink the problem or consider if you've outgrown the intentionally focused restriction facility, perhaps graduating to Hibernate Search.

The restrictions are one half of the equation. The other is the search form. The properties of the example object are bound to the inputs in the search form to capture the criteria values from the user:

```
<h:form id="roundSearch">
  <rich:panel><f:facet name="header">Round search parameters</f:facet>
    <s:decorate id="firstNameField" template="layout/display.xhtml">
      <ui:define name="label">First name:</ui:define>
      <h:inputText id="firstName"
        value="#{roundExample.golfer.firstName}"/>
    </s:decorate>
    <s:decorate id="lastNameField" template="layout/display.xhtml">
      <ui:define name="label">Last name:</ui:define>
      <h:inputText id="lastName"
        value="#{roundExample.golfer.lastName}"/>
    </s:decorate>
    <s:decorate id="colorField" template="layout/display.xhtml">
      <ui:define name="label">Tee set color:</ui:define>
      <h:inputText id="color" value="#{roundExample.teeSet.color}"/>
    </s:decorate>
  </rich:panel>
  <div class="actionButtons">
    <h:commandButton id="search" value="Search"
      actionListener="#{roundList.first}"/>
  </div>
</h:form>
```

Notice the #{roundList.first} method expression used in the action listener of the UI command component that submits the form. This action listener ensures that the pagination offset is reset before the search is performed. Although the Query class clears the result set when it detects a change to the restrictions, it doesn't reset the pagination offset. It's important to rewind the offset back to the first page because it ensures that if the search criteria were to reduce the size of the result set, the pagination offset wouldn't be left beyond the last result. If that happened, no results would be displayed, even though results might have been returned by the query. To avoid putting the user in this confusing situation, we introduce the minor inconvenience of resetting the pagination.

Since restrictions are joined using the AND operator, if the user fills in a value for first name, last name, and tee set color, a record must match all of these conditions to be included in the result set. Query doesn't have built-in support for the OR operator, though you can find an insider trick in the example code to get partial support.

So far, we've only used string-based properties in the restriction clause. In addition to primitive types, JPQL and HQL support complex types. Let's start with dates.

Do you speak calendar?

It's possible to use a value expression that resolves to a java.util.Date object directly in the JPQL/HQL query, and hence the restriction clause, just like any other primitive type. This will be demonstrated by allowing the user to filter the rounds within a date range. However, the Round entity class doesn't have a way to represent a date range. Alas, we've outgrown the basic QBE use case. We introduce a new criteria object, RoundCriteria, that can host property values that cannot be captured by the entity:

```
@Name("roundCriteria")
@Scope(ScopeType.CONVERSATION)
public class RoundCriteria {
    private Date beforeDate;
    private Date afterDate;

    public Date getBeforeDate() { return this.beforeDate; }
    public void setBeforeDate(Date date) { this.beforeDate = date; }

    public Date getAfterDate() { return this.afterDate; }
    public void setAfterDate(Date date) { this.afterDate = date; }
}
```

Next, add the restrictions to the roundList component definition:

```
<value>r.date &gt;= #{roundCriteria.afterDate}</value>
<value>r.date &lt;= #{roundCriteria.beforeDate}</value>
```

If either date filter resolves to null, the date range will be open ended on that side. Notice that when you're defining restrictions in the component descriptor, less-than and greater-than signs must be escaped. Finally, add the date input fields on the search form:

```
<s:decorate id="afterDateField" template="layout/display.xhtml">
  <ui:define name="label">From:</ui:define>
  <rich:calendar id="afterDate" datePattern="MM/dd/yyyy"
```

```
      value="#{roundCriteria.afterDate}"/>
  </s:decorate>
  <s:decorate id="beforeDateField" template="layout/display.xhtml">
    <ui:define name="label">To:</ui:define>
    <rich:calendar id="beforeDate" datePattern="MM/dd/yyyy"
      value="#{roundCriteria.beforeDate}"/>
  </s:decorate>
```

The date filter example helps emphasize how convenient it is to attach a value from a nonprimitive UI input component to a query with little effort. The converting and formatting is handled for you and it just works. Next, you discover the same is true for collections.

ANY OF THESE WILL DO

Like SQL, JPQL/HQL queries support the IN operator to find rows with a column value that matches any one of a collection of parameter values. This feature is often combined with "pick lists" where the user is presented with a set of options from which the search values can be selected. Searching on collections of simple types such as strings and numbers is fairly straightforward. What makes JPQL/HQL, and in turn the restriction clauses, so powerful is that the values in this collection can be entity instances, not just primitive values.

In the next example, the user is presented with a list of courses that can be used to filter the rounds by the courses selected. As you know, you can use entity instances in the options of a UI select menu when combined with the <s:convertEntity> converter tag. So far, we have used this technique to "wire" one entity instance to another. Now, we take this a step further by combining <s:convertEntity> with <h:selectManyListbox> to assign a collection of selected entity instances to the collection bound to the input. That collection will then be used in a restriction clause of the roundList component. To support these search criteria, a new java.util.List property is added to RoundCriteria to capture a collection of selected Course entity instances:

```
private List<Course> courses;

public List<Course> getCourses() { return this.courses; }
public void setCourses(List<Course> courses) { this.courses = courses; }
```

Note that JSF can only process a multivalue selection that is bound to an array property or a parameterized collection property that extends java.util.List. You cannot bind to a java.util.Set property, for instance.

Next, we add a restriction that uses the courses property within an IN operator:

```
<value>c IN(#{not empty roundCriteria.courses ?
  roundCriteria.courses : null})</value>
```

NOTE An explicit check for an empty collection must be performed or an empty IN() clause is generated, resulting in a SQL error.

You may wonder how JPA manages to stuff a whole entity instance into a SQL query. Actually, it doesn't. When entities are compared in a JPQL/HQL query, the query is rewritten to compare the identifier values of the records.

Two steps remain: We need to prepare a collection of courses from which the user can select and render the pick list. Let's start by defining a Query component that fetches the courses. An alias is defined for the result set and scoped to the conversation to prevent redundant fetches (though request-scoped would also work here):

```
<framework:entity-query name="coursesQuery" ejbql="select c from Course c"
  order="c.state asc, c.name asc"/>
<factory name="courses" value="#{coursesQuery.resultList}"
  scope="conversation"/>
```

The courses context variable can now be used to back the `<h:selectManyListbox>` component. Here is the form fragment that renders the course pick list:

```
<s:decorate id="coursesField" template="layout/display.xhtml">
  <ui:define name="label">Courses:<ui:define>
  <h:selectManyListbox id="courses" value="#{roundCriteria.courses}">
    <s:selectItems var="_course" value="#{courses}"
      label="#{_course.state} - #{_course.name}"/>
    <s:convertEntity/>
  </h:selectManyListbox>
</s:decorate>
```

Seam also has parallel support for converting enum constants, activated by nesting the `<s:convertEnum>` tag within any form input. You can use it with a text field, in which case the user has to enter the enum constant, or a select menu, in which case the select items need to map to a collection of enum constants.

Thus far, you've seen restrictions that bind a property value to a query parameter through the use of a value expression. The restriction is enabled if that property value is non-null or non-empty. You may instead want to use a `boolean` property in the value expression to create a switched restriction.

SWITCHED RESTRICTIONS

To incorporate a dynamic parameter value in a restriction clause, you place decision logic in the value expression using the ternary operator. In this case, the criteria value is acting as a controller rather than the value of the parameter. This adds a shade of gray to the Query component's black-and-white view of the restriction clauses.

As an example, we will add a checkbox to the criteria form that allows the user to toggle between all rounds and just the ones the user has played. First, a `boolean` property is added to the `RoundCriteria` class to capture the vanity flag:

```
private boolean self = false;

public boolean isSelf () { return this.self; }
public void setSelf (boolean self) { this.self = self; }
```

Next, a restriction is added that checks the value of the `self` property and, if true, returns the `currentGolfer` context variable. If the value is false, or the `current-Golfer` is null because the user isn't authenticated, the restriction is excluded:

```
<value>g = #{roundCriteria.self ? currentGolfer : null}</value>
```

The search criteria appears in the form as a check box:

```
<s:decorate id="selfField" template="layout/display.xhtml"
   rendered="#{currentGolfer != null}">
   <ui:define name="label">My rounds:</ui:define>
   <h:selectBooleanCheckbox id="self" value="#{roundCriteria.self}"/>
</s:decorate>
```

Having seen this example, you should now recognize the added power that the EL gives you to make the restrictions contextual and to control whether the restriction is used through the use of a conditional.

When you're all done, assuming you haven't made any customizations, the round search page should look like figure 10.10.

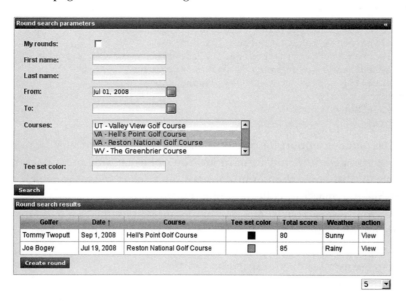

Figure 10.10   The round search screen supported by a Query component

Before we close the books on query restrictions, I want to highlight one final scenario.

JUST GIVE ME THE NUMBERS
Throughout this section, the focus has been on displaying a result set. But what if you want to use all of this great restriction functionality but in the end just retrieve a single number? Well, guess what? There's really nothing to show. You simply change your JPQL/HQL to fetch a single result and then use the `getSingleResult()` method instead of `getResultList()` on the `Query` class. Let's say the user wanted to get an average score of all rounds. You just define a new Query component, specify an aggregate query, and then find a place on the page to place the result:

```
<framework:entity-query name="averageScore" scope="conversation"
   ejbql="select avg(r.totalScore) from Round r join r.golfer g">
   <framework:restrictions>
      <value>g = #{roundCriteria.self ? currentGolfer : null}</value>
   </framework:restrictions>
</framework:entity-query>
```

The Query component is convenient because it allows you to get information up on the screen without having to hassle with boilerplate result set logic and unnecessary layers. It's especially helpful when the feature requests come flying in. Storing the instance of Query in a long-term scope combined with its intelligence about when to execute a query can ensure minimal load on the database and thus good performance. I'll leave it as an exercise for you to list the top rounds played at a course and for a golfer on the respective detail pages.

10.5 Summary

This chapter brought together everything you've learned about Seam. You used the component template classes in the Seam Application Framework to create screens for managing and listing golf rounds. The editor and detail screens were powered by a Home component, allowing the current golfer to create, read, update, and delete rounds. The editor screen used a long-running conversation to establish the tee set association and an application transaction to prevent changes from being made to the database prematurely. The listing screen was powered by a Query component, allowing the user to paginate, sort, and filter the rounds in the database. All of this functionality has traditionally been time consuming to implement, but with the Seam Application Framework component templates, you find yourself going for extra credit before the day is through.

The Seam Application Framework exemplifies how to create active domain models in Seam. The Home component, in particular, wraps an entity instance and the persistence manager into one cohesive unit, making it appear as though the entity is capable of reading and writing itself from the database. The Query component infuses behavior into a JPQL/HQL query and result set. From a design perspective, the tight coupling between the managed object and the persistence framework, present in the Active Record pattern and EJB 2, is avoided. You don't have to use the template classes in the Seam Application Framework, but you may want to study them as a reference if you plan on implementing your own solution.

At this point you should be comfortable enough with Seam to start using it day to day. But there's still a critical part missing from your knowledge, which I mentioned several times in this chapter: proper authentication of the user. In the next chapter, you finally get to fill out the stub authentication component installed by seam-gen and discover how to lock down the application at both the component and page levels.

Part 4

Sinking the
business requirements

Seam goes well beyond being simply a web application framework. It gives you support to cover all the business requirements, which you'll learn to appreciate in this part of the book.

Chapter 11 shows how quickly you can weave security into a Seam application. A single method on a POJO gives you both authentication and role-based authorization. You use annotations and the EL to define restrictions. Going deeper, you'll get a crash course in the Drools rule engine and use it to create fine-grained, contextual restrictions. Finally, you'll learn to keep out pesky spammers and bots using CAPTCHA, a nearly zero-effort integration.

Though critical, security can often be a dry topic. But everyone loves Ajax! Chapter 12 highlights the two flavors of Ajax in a Seam application. First you'll study Ajax-enabled UI components, which honor the JSF life cycle and let you avoid the JavaScript and CSS nightmares that typically come with adopting Ajax. If you prefer the low-level control, the JavaScript Remoting library lets you interact directly with server-side components from JavaScript, stepping outside of the JSF life cycle. The latter approach opens the door to alternative front ends such as GWT.

If this book is a full-course meal, then chapter 13 is definitely dessert. This is the chapter where you'll learn to make your application pop. It begins by showing how to accept file uploads using a JSF input binding. You'll then discover the versatility of Facelets templates to create and serve PDF documents, compose and send email messages with attachments, and produce RSS. Finally, you'll learn to use themes and i18n to customize the application.

That's where the book ends and the online chapters pick up. Chapter 14 eases you into Seam's business process integration and shows that a business process is simply a multiuser conversation, controlled using the same declarative approach as a single-user conversation. Chapter 15 reveals how Seam taps into the Spring container. The Spring integration is vital because it allows Spring to leverage Seam's proper management of the persistence context.

The underlying theme of this final part is that Seam's programming model remains consistent, regardless of which integration you use, making the technologies accessible.

11
Securing
Seam applications

This chapter covers

- Developing an authentication routine
- Enforcing role-based authorization
- Writing permission rules with Drools
- Adding a CAPTCHA challenge to a form

While winding down after a round of golf, I came across a magazine ad for Microsoft Visual Studio 2005 that serves as an example of how *not* to treat security. The ad shows side-by-side shots of a software development scene in which two developers are discussing a web application, one before the product is introduced and one after. The developer paraphernalia and the to-do list on the whiteboard reflect the state of the project, with the before scene being far more cluttered and laden with stress. But the contrast reveals a critical oversight in the after scene. An outstanding item on the to-do list reads "TEST CODE FOR SECURITY!!" The items crossed off are personalization features, consistency review of UI, accessibility, and breadcrumbs. At least the application will look pretty while it's being hacked.

433

Just because this chapter is in the final part of this book doesn't mean you should wait until the last minute to implement or test for security. A common misconception is that security can be tacked onto the application when it's ready to be sent off to QA, or worse, production, as if it's just polish. A complex application can't be made secure after the fact. Security must be present from the beginning and weaved into every layer of the application, from the view down to the database. That's why security is such an integral part of Seam.

Seam helps you secure your application without spending a lot of time on the details. In this chapter, you'll learn how to implement an authentication routine and how to protect areas of the application from unauthorized access across all layers. The foundation of Seam's security model is a role-based system that ensures a quick start. Obviously, some applications require a more granular approach. To meet these needs, Seam builds on this foundation by leveraging the Drools rule engine to support contextual, rule-based permissions. The possibilities opened up by a rules system are limitless. Seam 2.1 introduces an identity and permissions management module to make administering security even easier. The best part of Seam's security model is that you don't have to stomach a single line of XML, a breath of fresh air for those who have used other Java security frameworks.

Seeing is believing, so I want to start by showing you the quickest way to secure your application after first defining some basic security terminology and how a user's identity is represented. As the chapter progresses, the security becomes more sophisticated.

11.1   *Authentication jump-start*

Why do you think security often gets the back seat in the design and development process? My reasoning is that security frameworks, such as the Java Authentication and Authorization Service (JAAS) and Spring Security (formally Acegi), are just too hard to implement. The first is too cryptic and, let's face it, primitive, and the second buries you deep in XML Hell.

The goal of a security layer is to prevent hackers, nonprivileged users, and rogue client endpoints from accessing sensitive areas of the application, and not scare off developers from implementing it. Given its importance, security should be easy to configure and use, and it should be integrated into the core of the application framework rather than split off as an extension. Both are true in Seam. What's more important is that this ease of use is accomplished without compromising the ability of Seam's security model to scale in accordance with security requirements. I start by presenting authentication, the foundation of security, and show you how to tie it into a Seam application in three simple steps.

11.1.1   *Giving the user an identity*

Authentication is just a fancy way of saying "login." The login routine, which you are about to implement, prefaces nearly every action we perform in today's online world. But it's not just about making you ransack the piles of papers on your desk to find the

scribbled characters that get you past the
login challenge. Authentication is about
giving an anonymous user a face, as depicted in figure 11.1.

**Figure 11.1   By authenticating (signing in), the
user is revealing his or her identity to the application.**

SHOW ME YOUR FACE

The transformation in figure 11.1 sym-
bolizes the user establishing an identity.
During authentication, Seam assembles
an instance of `Subject` from the JAAS API and associates it with the user's session,
allowing the server to recognize the user until the session expires or the user explicitly
logs out.

The `Subject` instance is a digital representation of the user. It consists of a collection of principals, filling in the user's facial features. A principal implements the
`Principal` interface from the JAAS API. There can be an unbounded set of principals,
but Seam limits it to just two. The first principal holds the username of the authenticated user and is called the *user principal*. The second principal, known as the *roles
group*, implements the `Group` interface and holds a collection of roles. Each role is a
`Principal` as well, though distinct from the user principal and roles group and appropriately referred to as a *role principal*.

But the details about the structure of the `Subject` don't really matter because Seam
provides a simple abstraction layer that you use to establish a user's principals during
authentication and to access those principals when performing authorization checks.

JAAS A LA CARTE

Seam uses JAAS, but only select parts of it. Don't panic when you see that four-letter
word because, by and large, Seam's JAAS integration is completely transparent to you.
Behind the scenes, Seam relies on JAAS to handle the authentication handoff, which
delegates to one of your components to give the approval, and also uses the identity
portion of the API as mentioned above. The only time you even come in contact with
JAAS is to assert a user's role using Servlet security (e.g., `isUserInRole()`). Seam
ignores the permission and policy piece of JAAS, instead offering its own multifaceted
authorization strategy. We cover authorization after we finish with authentication.
Let's take it one *A* at a time.

LOCATING THE USER ACCOUNTS

To implement authentication, you need to decide where the user accounts for your
application are stored. Seam leaves this task entirely up to you. If you do want Seam to
help out, you have the option in Seam 2.1 of letting the identity manager consult your
database or LDAP to find an account, though it requires that you follow a standard, yet
flexible, model.

In Open 18, the accounts are mapped to a table in the database through the `Mem-
ber` entity and retrieved using the `EntityManager`. The `Member` entity, introduced in
chapter 4, has fields to store the member's username and hashed password, but
doesn't have a field to hold the member's roles. Though not mandatory, you may want

to assign roles to the user during authentication, which are pulled from the database. First, you need a `Role` entity:

```
@Entity
@Table(name = "ROLE", uniqueConstraints =
  @UniqueConstraint(columnNames = "name"))
public class Role implements Serializable {
    private Long id;
    private String name;

    @Id @GeneratedValue
    public Long getId() { return id; }
    public void setId(Long id) { this.id = id; }

    public String getName() { return name; }
    public void setName(String name) { this.name = name; }
}
```

Next, you add a `Role` collection to the `Member` entity, related through a join table:

```
private Set<Role> roles = new HashSet<Role>();

@ManyToMany(fetch = FetchType.LAZY)
@JoinTable(name = "MEMBER_ROLE",
  joinColumns = @JoinColumn(name = "member_id"),
  inverseJoinColumns = @JoinColumn(name = "role_id"))
public Set<Role> getRoles() { return this.roles; }
public void setRoles(Set<Role> roles) { this.roles = roles; }
```

While roles are optional for authentication, they are essential when it comes to implementing authorization. In a sense, authentication is the binary part of security: The user is either authenticated or the user is not authenticated. Only after establishing the user's identity can we begin talking about authorization. Let's find out, in three steps, how a 0 becomes a 1.

11.1.2 Implementing authentication in three steps

The three steps for setting up authentication in Seam are as follow:

1 Switch on authentication by configuring an authentication method.
2 Verify the user's credentials in the authentication method.
3 Create a JSF login form.

When these steps are complete, your application will support form-based authentication. Later on, you'll learn that in Seam 2.1, you can let Seam's identity manager handle the second step for you. If you would rather not bother with the login form, you can plug in Seam's support for HTTP authentication, in which case the credentials are negotiated by the browser. Let's put these alternatives aside for now and continue with the steps laid out here.

STEP 0: ZERO PREREQUISITES
The first step isn't a step at all but simply a fact. You don't need any extra libraries to implement authentication and role-based security in Seam. Only when you branch out to Seam's rule-based security, covered in section 11.4, are additional dependencies needed.

In fact, projects created using the seam-gen tool already have the authentication routine configured. It just leaves out one critical detail. The default configuration accepts any username and password. To heighten security (to put it lightly) and keep out the imposters, the user's login credentials need to be validated against the database of registered members.

STEP 1: SWITCHING ON AUTHENTICATION

Enabling security in Seam is a bit of a misnomer. Security is enabled by default, unless you purposely disable it (perhaps in a test). However, out of the box, there's no way for users to authenticate themselves. To make that possible, you first need to tell Seam which method handles the authentication logic (i.e., the authentication delegate). This method is provided by one of your components. Three requirements must be met by the authentication method:

- It must take no arguments.
- It must return a `boolean` indicating whether the credentials could be verified.
- It must be accessible via the EL (which isn't much of a problem in Seam).

The authentication method can have any name, it can reside on any class, and that class doesn't have to implement any special security interfaces. Seam plugs your authentication method into JAAS, but hides the complexity of JAAS in the `SeamLogin-Module`. Internally, JAAS invokes your authentication method and adds the appropriate principals to the security subject if the method returns `true`. This authentication routine is activated through Seam's `identity` component, freeing you from having to interact with the colossus that lies beneath.

The built-in `Identity` component, named `identity`, maintains a reference to the authentication method as a method-binding expression. The `identity` component lives in the component namespace `http://jboss.com/products/seam/security`, declared in the component descriptor using the prefix `identity`. The authentication method can be assigned to the `identity` component using component configuration:

```
<security:identity
    authenticate-method="#{authenticationManager.authenticate}"/>
```

Here, the authentication method is provided by the `authenticationManager` component. The next step is to implement this method.

STEP 2: AUTHORING AN AUTHENTICATION METHOD

As I mentioned earlier, the authentication method can reside on any class. We use a JavaBean component in this example. Here's a naïve, but valid, implementation of the method:

```
@Name("authenticationManager")
public class AuthenticationManager {
    public boolean authenticate() {
        return true;
    }
}
```

To get serious, we need credentials to validate. If the `authenticate()` method doesn't take any arguments, where do the credentials come from? One of the roles of the identity component, which is scoped to the session context and instantiated when the user's session begins, is to capture the credentials being challenged. The credentials are stored in the username and password properties on this component, and are typically populated by a JSF form. Thus, you get to the credentials by obtaining a reference to the identity component.

NOTE   If your authentication routine requires additional credentials, you can extend Seam's security infrastructure to capture them. In Seam 2.0, you extend the Identity class and register it using the component name org.jboss.seam.security.identity. In Seam 2.1, you extend the Credentials class and register it using the component name org.jboss. seam.security.credentials. The credentials component was introduced in Seam 2.1 to hold the credentials. Although the credentials can still be accessed using the identity component, the credentials component is the preferred means of access.

To pull the credentials into the authentication method, you simply inject identity (or credentials in Seam 2.1) into the authentication component using @In:

```
@Name("authenticationManager")
public class AuthenticationManager {
    @Logger private Log log;
    @In private Identity identity;

    public boolean authenticate() {
        log.info("username: #0, password: #1",
            identity.getUsername(), identity.getPassword());
        identity.addRole("member");
        return true;
    }
}
```

As you see here, the role of the identity component in the authentication method is twofold. It delivers the login credentials and it's used to store a set of roles. In this implementation, we assign all users the member role. JAAS transfers the roles to the security subject during the post login routine. Let's consider how that works.

When the authentication method is called, the user principal and roles group haven't yet been established on the Subject instance (because the user hasn't been authenticated). That initialization takes place inside the JAAS login module *after* the authentication method returns true. In the interim, the identity component provides temporary storage for roles—appended using the addRoles() method—that need to be transferred to the user's group identity. During the post-authentication routine, Seam converts the role names into role principals and adds them to the roles group on the Subject instance.

NOTE   Seam doesn't impose a naming convention for roles, so feel free to use your own scheme.

The authentication routine produces a standard Java security principal, meaning Servlet security just works. You can use the HttpServletRequest#isUserInRole() method to check if a user has been granted a role, and it enables transparent integration with libraries that depend on this method. To get all of this, you only have to write a couple lines of code (even counting the XML). That number grows when you add the authentication logic.

The authentication logic for Open 18 is presented in listing 11.1. The username on the `identity` component is used to look up a matching `Member` entity in the database using the `EntityManager`. If an instance is found, the password is validated by comparing its hash to the hashed password from the database. If both checks succeed, the roles are added and the method returns `true`, returning control to JAAS to establish the security principals. If either check fails, a return value of `false` sends the user back to the login page with a failure message. We examine the details of the failure scenario a bit later.

Listing 11.1 An authentication component that plugs into Seam's JAAS login module

```java
package org.open18.action;
import org.jboss.seam.security.Identity;
import ...;

@Name("authenticationManager")
public class AuthenticationManager {
    @In private EntityManager entityManager;
    @In private Identity identity;
    @In private PasswordManager passwordManager;
    @Out(required = false) Golfer currentGolfer;

    @Transactional public boolean authenticate() {
        try {
            Member member = (Member) entityManager.createQuery(
                "select m from Member m where m.username = :username")
                .setParameter("username", identity.getUsername())
                .getSingleResult();

            if (!validatePassword(identity.getPassword(), member)) {
                return false;
            }

            identity.addRole("member");
            if (member.getRoles() != null) {
                for (Role role : member.getRoles()) {
                    identity.addRole(role.getName());
                }
            }

            if (member instanceof Golfer) {
                currentGolfer = (Golfer) member;
                identity.addRole("golfer");
            }
            return true;
        } catch (NoResultException e) {
            return false;
        }
    }
}
```

```
    public boolean validatePassword(String password, Member m) {
        return passwordManager.hash(password).equals(m.getPasswordHash());
    }
}
```

If the member is a golfer, `currentGolfer` is outjected for convenience. To ensure it hangs around for the duration of the session, we define a role for it on the `Golfer` class:

```
@Role(name = "currentGolfer", scope = ScopeType.SESSION)
```

All that's left is to create a form for the user to enter credentials and attempt a login.

STEP 3: CREATING THE LOGIN FORM
You'll be thrilled to discover that the `j_username` and `j_password` request parameters and the `/j_security_check` servlet path, defined in the Servlet specification for implementing form-based logins, have finally been retired under Seam. And for those of you who have had to invent a custom handoff to get a JAAS login module to play nicely with JSF, you'll be happy to know that you can use a native JSF form on the login page. The login form boils down to two value-binding expressions, `#{identity.username}` and `#{identity.password}`, which capture the user's login credentials (in Seam 2.1, you use the `credentials` component for this purpose) and one method-binding expression, `#{identity.login}`, which invokes the built-in action method that kicks off the authentication routine. Here's an example of a basic login form:

```
<h:form id="login">
  <h:panelGrid columns="2">
    <h:outputLabel for="username">Username</h:outputLabel>
    <h:inputText id="username" value="#{identity.username}"/>
    <h:outputLabel for="password">Password</h:outputLabel>
    <h:inputSecret id="password" value="#{identity.password}"/>
  </h:panelGrid>
  <div class="actionButtons">
    <h:commandButton value="Login" action="#{identity.login}"/>
  </div>
</h:form>
```

Each time an attempt is made to authenticate, the password is cleared before the `login()` method returns. If the login fails, this method returns `null`, causing the login page to be redisplayed. If the login succeeds, this method returns the value `loggedIn`, which you can plug into a navigation rule to redirect the user somewhere besides the login page:

```
<navigation from-action="#{identity.login}">
  <rule if-outcome="loggedIn">
    <redirect view-id="/home.xhtml"/>
  </rule>
</navigation>
```

This rule applies to when a user requests the login page directly. In section 11.2.2, you'll learn how to configure Seam to restore the user's original request if it was interrupted by a request to login.

That's all there is to it! You can finally wipe your hands clean of low-level JAAS details, which Seam keeps hidden so the work you have to do is minimal. In fact, you don't even need the JSF form to perform authentication. Let's say that you want to authenticate the user automatically, perhaps following registration or in response to a remote method invocation. You just register the credentials on `identity` and invoke the `login()` method:

```
@In private Identity identity;

public String register() {
    ...
    identity.setUsername(newGolfer.getUsername());
    identity.setPassword(passwordBean.getPassword());
    identity.login();
    return "success";
}
```

Don't fear that as your requirements become more complex, you'll outgrow Seam's security model. Throughout this chapter, you'll learn that Seam gives you all the power you need without compromising simplicity or extensibility.

BONUS ROUND: LOGGING OUT

If authenticating the user is so easy, you probably expect the logout to be the same. You guessed right. Just as the #{identity.login} method-binding expression is attached to a UI command component to log in, the #{identity.logout} method-binding expression is used to log out. To create a login/logout control, you can use the value expression #{identity.loggedIn} to check whether the user is authenticated and, if so, you can personalize the page by displaying the username credential, which is retained by the session-scoped `identity` component:

```
<h:outputText value="You are signed in as: #{identity.username}"
  rendered="#{identity.loggedIn}"/>
<s:link view="/login.xhtml" value="Login"
  rendered="#{not identity.loggedIn}"/>
<s:link view="/home.xhtml" action="#{identity.logout}" value="Logout"
  rendered="#{identity.loggedIn}"/>
```

Before calling the authentication process a done deal, we need to address what happens when authentication fails. As I mentioned earlier, the user is returned to the login page and presented with a failure message. As it turns out, a message is created either way. There are also a plethora of events surrounding authentication. Let's explore this flurry of activity.

AUTHENTICATION MESSAGES AND EVENTS

While Seam assumes control of authentication, it doesn't keep other parts of the application in the dark. This transparency is accomplished through the use of events. Table 11.1 lists the events that are most relevant. The first event listed signals when the user is being directed to the login page to authenticate, a process that we discuss in section 11.2.2.

In addition to raising events, Seam adds a global `FacesMessage` to the response whenever the user is directed to the login page or the user makes an authentication attempt.

Table 11.1   A list of events related to authentication

Event name	When it is raised
org.jboss.seam.security.notLoggedIn	When a nonauthenticated user encounters a restriction
org.jboss.seam.security.preAuthenticate	Prior to delegation to the JAAS login module
org.jboss.seam.security.postAuthenticate	At the end of the authentication process, when the security subject is fully initialized
org.jboss.seam.security.loginFailed	Before the login() method on the identity component returns and the authentication failed
org.jboss.seam.security.loginSuccessful	Before the login() method on the identity component returns and the authentication was successful
org.jboss.seam.security.loggedOut	Before the logout() method on the identity component returns, after the session has been invalidated
org.jboss.seam.security.initCredentials	The first time the getUsername() method is called on the credentials component for a given session (Seam 2.1 only)
org.jboss.seam.security.quietLogin	Before a restriction is checked to give an observer the opportunity to log in the user automatically (Seam 2.1 only)

Following multilingual best practices, Seam resolves the authentication message from a message key in the Seam resource bundle. Table 11.2 lists the message keys and severities for each event. The Seam resource bundle was covered in section 5.5.2 of chapter 5. You render the authentication messages using the following component tag:

```
<h:messages globalOnly="true"/>
```

In order for the user to see the login success message, this tag must be included on any page the user is taken to after login. In section 11.2.2, you'll learn how to redirect the user back to the intercepted request, widening this pool of target pages. If you don't want one of the messages to be used, just assign an empty value to the message key.

Table 11.2   The message keys that Seam uses following an authentication event

Message key	FacesMessage severity	When it is used
org.jboss.seam.loginFailed	SEVERITY_INFO	Authentication fails
org.jboss.seam.loginSuccessful	SEVERITY_INFO	Authentication succeeds
org.jboss.seam.NotLoggedIn[a]	SEVERITY_WARN	Authentication is requested

a. The "N" in the **org.jboss.seam.NotLoggedIn** key is intentionally uppercase.

With the user being scolded or praised accordingly, the authentication routine is complete. Looking back on the work you've done, the most complex part was implementing the authentication method, which involved locating an account, validating the password, and adding the roles. Granted, the authentication logic in your own application may be different. But if you are simply retrieving the accounts from the database using JPA or from LDAP, you can let Seam's identity manager (introduced in Seam 2.1) handle this work for you. While both JPA and LDAP providers exist, only the JPA one is covered here. At the time of this writing, this feature was still under active development, so I won't go into too much detail. However, the next section should be enough to get you started.

11.1.3 *A glimpse at Seam's identity management*

Seam's new identity management module, introduced in 2.1, stretches Seam's declarative services to cover authentication. The module consists of a handful of annotations and a bunch of glue code that work collectively to authenticate the user and set up the user's roles. All you have to do is put the annotations where they belong and do some component configuration. Once that is done, your authentication method becomes history.

The first step is creating entities to represent a user and a role. In Open 18, these entities are `Member` and `Role`, respectively. The next step is to identify the fields that store the user's account information using the following annotations:

- `@UserPrincipal`—Identifies the field on the user class that stores the username.
- `@UserPassword`—Identifies the field on the user class that stores the password. Both plain-text and hashed passwords are supported. The hashing algorithm is specified in the `hash` attribute. The hashed password must be Base64 encoded.
- `@UserRoles`—Identifies the collection field on the user class that stores the roles. The collection must map to a class that has a field annotated with `@RoleName`.
- `@RoleName`—Identifies the field on the role class that stores the name of the role.

There are a couple additional annotations not listed here for tracking additional information about the user. Abbreviated versions of `Member` and `Role` are shown here with the identity management annotations applied:

```
@Entity
public class Member implements Serializable {
    @UserPrincipal
    public String getUsername() { return this.username; }
    @UserPassword(hash = "SHA")
    public String getPasswordHash() { return this.passwordHash; }
    @UserRoles
    public Set<Role> getRoles() { return this.roles; }
    ...
}
@Entity
public class Role implements Serializable {
```

```
    @RoleName
    public void String getName() { return this.name; }
    ...
}
```

Next, you need to configure an identity store in the component descriptor and indicate which classes represent the user and role. The authentication method on `identity` is no longer needed:

```
<security:identity/>
<security:jpa-identity-store
  user-class="org.open18.model.Member" role-class="org.open18.model.Role"/>
```

The identity manager uses the JPA identity store by default if it's available. The JPA identity store assumes that the name of the Seam-managed persistence context is `entityManager`. If it's not, you must assign it to the `entityManager` property using EL.

Using the `identity` component to authenticate the user is no different in this case. Behind the scenes, the `SeamLoginModule` delegates to the identity manager to validate the credentials. If you need to execute custom logic during authentication, you can use a method that observes the postauthentication event, listed in table 11.1.

Although you never interact with the identity manager directly during authentication, you can use its API to manage accounts. It supports full CRUD capabilities for users and roles and has additional methods for performing tasks such as changing a user's password, enabling an account, and granting and revoking roles. To complement the identity manager, Seam 2.1 provides a permission manager for maintaining persistent user permissions, which is mentioned in section 11.4. Check out the seamspace example from the Seam distribution to see both in action.

Now that you know how to implement form-based authentication, let's explore an alternative that leverages the browser's ability to negotiate credentials with the server.

11.1.4 *Even more "Basic" authentication*

You mean that what you've seen so far isn't basic enough for you? Okay, I understand. Sometimes you just want to block off an application from the public eye without making any changes to the user interface. To accomplish that, HTTP Basic or HTTP Digest (RFC 2617) authentication may be sufficient for your needs. Guess what? Seam has that covered. However, it doesn't get you totally off the hook. You still need to implement and configure the authentication method as before. You just no longer need a login page (and you don't have to worry about navigation, a concern addressed later on).

As you learned in chapter 3, the Seam filter uses a delegation model to wrap each request in a chain of Seam-configured filters, each declared using the `@Filter` annotation. One of Seam's built-in filters, `AuthenticationFilter`, handles HTTP authentication. However, this filter isn't installed by default (i.e., `@Install(false)`). To use it, you must make sure it's activated in the component descriptor. Seam's built-in filters reside in the component namespace `http://jboss.com/products/seam/web`, prefixed as `web`. When activating the `AuthenticationFilter`, specify whether you want to use Basic or Digest (digest) authentication, controlled by the `auth-type` attribute. Let's start with Basic:

```
<web:authentication-filter url-pattern="*.seam" auth-type="basic"/>
```

Now, any URL that matches the value of the `url-pattern` attribute is protected by Basic authentication. To protect only JSF requests, the `url-pattern` attribute should match the pattern configured for the JSF servlet in web.xml. If the `url-pattern` attribute is excluded, the filter is applied to all requests captured by Seam's main filter. During authentication, Seam invokes the authentication method you configured in steps 1 and 2 of section 11.1.2.

If you're content with Basic authentication, your work is done. However, HTTP Basic authentication is extremely weak because the password is sent with each request only slightly obfuscated using the well-known Base64 encoding (i.e., not encrypted or hashed), making it easy to pick off by network sniffers. A better choice is Digest authentication, in which the browser hashes the credentials before sending them to the server.

NEGOTIATING CREDENTIALS USING A MESSAGE DIGEST

Digest authentication is more secure than Basic authentication, but that security comes at the cost of some additional setup. Start by changing the value of the `auth-type` attribute on the `<web:authentication-filter>` element to digest. Then, add two additional properties: `key` and `realm`. The value of the `key` property can be any string. Its purpose is to reduce the predictability of the digest created (i.e., the salt). The value of the `realm` property is used in the prompt that captures the user's credentials. A typical prompt reads something like this:

```
Enter username and password for "Open 18" at http://localhost:8080
```

The realm is the text in quotes, which in this case is the title of the application. You can pull the realm from a message bundle using EL notation, making it i18n-friendly. The result of these configuration changes is shown here:

```
<web:authentication-filter url-pattern="*.seam" auth-type="digest"
    key="g0!f15f#n" realm="#{messages['application.title']}"/>
```

Seam provides the `DigestAuthentication` base class to handle the digest computation and validation. Thus, the next step is to change the authentication component to extend `DigestAuthentication` and delegate the work of validating the digest to the inherited `validatePassword()` method. Listing 11.2 shows a simplified example. Unfortunately, to use Digest authentication, you must store the passwords in the database unhashed. This change is necessary because the authentication routine must generate a digest from the original password to compare it against the digest sent by the client.

Listing 11.2 An authentication component used for HTTP Digest authentication

```
package org.open18.action;
import org.jboss.seam.security.digest.DigestAuthenticator;
import ...;
```

```
@Name("authenticationManager")
public class AuthenticationManager extends DigestAuthenticator {
    @In private EntityManager entityManager;
    @In private Identity identity;

    @Transactional public boolean authenticate() {
        try {
            Member member = (Member) entityManager.createQuery(
                "select m from Member m where m.username = :username")
                .setParameter("username", identity.getUsername())
                .getSingleResult();
            return super.validatePassword(member.getPassword());
        } catch (NoResultException e) {
            return false;
        }
    }
}
```

Having seen the configuration for both form-based and HTTP authentication, you'll likely agree that the form-based approach is no more difficult to implement in Seam than its HTTP counterpart. Given the fact that the gap in effort has been eliminated, three limitations of HTTP authentication now make it a less desirable option:

- The login prompt doesn't appear to be part of the application.
- The user isn't given an alternative when the login prompt appears (it is modal).
- There is no standard way for the user to log out.

Of the three, the lack of a standard logout mechanism is its most significant downfall. This fact is acknowledged by the W3C in the User Agent Authentication Forms specification:

> *HTTP Authentication has the additional problem that there is no mechanism available to the server to cause the browser to "logout"; that is, to discard its stored credentials for the user.*

However, in HTTP authentication, the credentials are sent by the browser with each request, so it's really the browser's responsibility to provide a logout button that lets the user signal when to stop sending the credentials. Unfortunately, no major browser supports this feature natively. One hack developers have discovered is that sending a 401 response causes some browsers to clear the authentication cache for the realm. But this trick isn't reliable.

In light of all these complications, I strongly recommend using form-based authentication. The only catch with form-based authentication is that you have to worry about navigation (unless authentication is done using Ajax). In the next section, you'll learn how to implement basic page security and how navigation to the login page gets tied into it.

11.2 Securing pages

The most common form of security in a web application is page-level security. Even when we get into securing components later on, the web layer still needs to be involved to direct the user to the login page or an error page when the user is denied access to a resource. In this section, you'll learn why page-level security has traditionally been so difficult to enforce in JSF and the solution that Seam offers. You'll then explore a couple of Seam's page-level security features and how to use them to protect pages and serve them securely.

11.2.1 *The challenge with JSF security*

The biggest challenge in dealing with security in JSF is that there isn't any. JSF has absolutely *no* notion of security anywhere in its design. Presumably, a decision was made that security is the concern of another layer, such as the EJB container or a servlet filter. This stance has made the task of implementing security (specifically page-level security) in a JSF application a real pain, again opening the door for Seam to step in and provide a solution. Seam has both page- and component-level security covered. In fact, you could even argue that security is Seam's most significant and compelling enhancement to Java EE.

WHY SERVLET FILTERS DON'T WORK

At first glance, a servlet filter appears to be perfect for implementing page-level security. It can trap an incoming request and make a decision about whether to let the request through or divert the user to another page. The main limitation with this approach is that it operates at too high a level, unable to track what's going on inside the JSF life cycle. While the high-level view may work brilliantly for some applications, others require more insight.

When a URL is requested initially, the default behavior in JSF is to render the template for the corresponding view ID (ignore page actions for right now). So you set up the security filter to restrict access to a URL based on some rule. That restriction works as designed. Let's say that the page has a JSF form with a UI command component that calls an action method. When the user clicks the button, the same URL is requested using a postback and the same restriction is evaluated. After the action method is called, JSF invokes a navigation event, which may result in a different view ID being rendered. The security framework has absolutely no knowledge of this switch and therefore can't verify whether the user should be allowed access to the destination page. Figure 11.2 illustrates how the security filter is kept out of the loop when the navigation occurs.

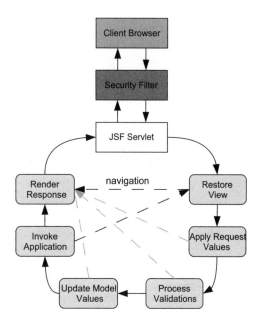

Figure 11.2 The security filter isn't aware of a navigation event that happens inside the JSF life cycle.

If you're using JSP as the view handler, the navigation is performed using an internal forward handled by the servlet request dispatcher. It's possible to get the filter involved by wrapping the filter around internal forwards, configured in the web.xml descriptor as follows:

```
<filter-mapping>
  <filter-name>Third-party security filter</filter-name>
  <url-pattern>/*</url-pattern>
  <dispatcher>REQUEST</dispatcher>
  <dispatcher>FORWARD</dispatcher>
</filter-mapping>
```

However, this mapping only applies to view handlers that use the servlet request dispatcher. Facelets, for instance, uses its own mechanism for selecting the next view to render. Therefore, if your application uses Facelets, the security filter is once again left in the dark.

A CONTEXTUAL SECURITY WRAPPER

Another limitation of a third-party security filter is that it's not part of the JSF application and thus doesn't have insight into the application's context. We talked about this problem back in chapter 3 with regard to the stateless navigation model. The same limitation exists here. Can you decide if users should be granted access to a page based on the URL? Where did they come from, where are they going, and what is the current state of their session? These are questions you need to know the answers to in order to make a viable decision. The only way you're going to get all of this information is if the security framework is integrated into JSF. That's exactly what Seam offers.

Instead of operating before and after each request, like a security filter, Seam applies page-level security before and after the two page-oriented phases in the JSF life cycle, *Restore View* and *Render Response*. Thus, Seam can apply restrictions directly to a view ID (as opposed to a URL). When access to a resource is denied, Seam can route the user to an error page, but not before giving the user the opportunity to authenticate, a process we look at next.

11.2.2 *Requiring authentication*

If a nonauthenticated user tries to access a protected resource, Seam redirects the user to the login page, giving the user a chance to reveal his or her identity. Once the user authenticates, the authorization check is evaluated to determine if the user can access the protected resource. That describes how the application will work once you complete this section. For any of this to work, you first have to tell Seam where to direct a nonauthenticated user when a login is required.

SINGLING OUT THE LOGIN PAGE

One way a user can initiate the authentication routine is by navigating directly to the login page. While some users may navigate to this page willingly, most of the time you have to give them a little push. In Seam, you can protect a page (i.e., view ID) by requiring a nonauthenticated user to log in before accessing it, a security feature I like to call binary authorization. It's like hanging signs throughout the application that read "Members Only." This prerequisite is declared by adding the login-required attribute to the <page> node in the corresponding page descriptor:

```
<page login-required="true"/>
```

Only Seam isn't going to know where to direct a nonauthenticated user when this page is requested because you haven't specified a login page. If a login page hasn't been set, Seam throws a NotLoggedInException. We get to this exception shortly. For now, it can be avoided by simply configuring a login page. The view ID that hosts the login form is designated using the login-view-id attribute on the root node of the global page descriptor:

```
<pages login-view-id="/login.xhtml"/>
```

Some applications require the user to be authenticated before doing anything else, in which case the login page *is* the home page. To accommodate this scenario, you can blanket the application with the authentication prerequisite by using the login-required attribute on a <page> node that matches all of the view IDs (though I don't recommend it):

```
<pages login-view-id="/login.xhtml">
  <page view-id="*" login-required="true"/>
</pages>
```

There's at least one page you do want to serve to nonauthenticated users: the login page, which you declare in the login-view-id attribute on the <pages> node. Seam understands the function of a login page and automatically excludes it from the list of restricted pages. It's very important that you specify it to ensure the user always has a way to log in.

Even with the login page accessible, I don't recommend declaring the site-wide login requirement using a wildcard because it can break the delivery of resources (e.g., JavaScript or CSS) sent through the JSF servlet. It's far better to restrict only what's necessary, perhaps grouping views into directories and securing them as needed (e.g., /admin/*).

PLEASE SHOW SOME IDENTIFICATION

Instead of requiring the user to start at the login page, applications can use deferred authentication as a way to be more welcoming to new users and to avoid scaring them off by throwing up the dreaded login page too soon. In this model, the user is allowed to poke around the application anonymously until running into a protected resource. When that happens, the user is escorted to the login page and asked to show some identification before being allowed to proceed. This describes how the native JAAS login routine works. Seam, on the other hand, supports both up-front and deferred authentication.

You've already learned how to configure Seam to protect a page from being accessed by a nonauthenticated user, in which case Seam redirects the user to the login page. However, there are other ways to restrict access to resources, which you'll learn about in the next two major sections. If a nonauthenticated user encounters any of the following scenarios, Seam throws the `NotLoggedInException` as a way to require the user to log in:

- A view ID with a restriction is requested.
- A method with a restriction is invoked.
- A view ID that requires a login is requested (and the login view ID isn't set).

As experience tells you, throwing an exception is certainly not going to bring up a login page—that is, unless you handle the exception. Deferred authentication relies on the use of Seam's exception-handling facility, covered in chapter 3, to route the user to the appropriate view ID. The following exception handler catches the `NotLoggedInException` and mimics the behavior of Seam when protecting pages that require login:

```
<exception class="org.jboss.seam.security.NotLoggedInException">
  <redirect view-id="/login.xhtml">
    <message
      severity="warn">#{messages['org.jboss.seam.NotLoggedIn']}</message>
  </redirect>
</exception>
```

Now, any time a nonauthenticated user encounters a restricted resource, the user is escorted to the login page. You can raise the `NotLoggedInException` in your own code to require the user to authenticate.

WARNING   When Facelets is running in development mode, it intercepts exceptions thrown in the *Render Response* phase. In that case, Seam's exception-based routing will not kick in.

The only danger in all of this redirecting is that it risks losing the user's spot in the application. Whenever you design an application that uses deferred authentication, you want to keep the disruption caused by asking the user to authenticate to a minimum. One of the most obvious ways of ensuring minimal disruption is to redirect the user back to the page that was originally requested once authentication is successful.

KEEPING THE INTERRUPTION TO A MINIMUM

To get the user back to the page that was originally requested, you have to capture the current URL before the user is directed to the login page. After successful authentication, you need to retrieve the saved URL and redirect the user back to it. Given that Seam manages the authentication interlude, you may wonder how you're going to get in there and change the course of action. The key is observing the authentication events.

Seam has a built-in component, named `redirect`, that is capable of capturing the current view (as well as the request parameters) and redirecting back to that view. You just need to connect this component to the event that's raised when the user is being directed to the login page and the event that's raised when authentication is successful. You can register the `redirect` component to observe these events in the component descriptor:

```
<event type="org.jboss.seam.security.notLoggedIn">
  <action execute="#{redirect.captureCurrentView}"/>
</event>
<event type="org.jboss.seam.security.postAuthenticate">
  <action execute="#{redirect.returnToCapturedView}"/>
</event>
```

You may ask yourself how the redirect component manages to store the captured view ID while the user is authenticating. The little-known secret is that redirect, which is a conversation-scoped component, begins a long-running conversation when the captureCurrentView() method is called, if one isn't already active. That conversation is ended when the returnToCapturedView() method is called, if it was started by the redirect component. Thus, the captured view is preserved in a long-running conversation that surrounds the login process. See the accompanying sidebar for another important use of authentication events.

Keeping memory consumption in check

One of the boldest claims that Seam makes is that it helps eliminate the problem of HTTP sessions consuming excessive memory. However, this statement doesn't account for the fact that too many sessions, no matter how small, can cause leaks. If your site receives a lot of anonymous traffic, you end up paying for each visit long after the visitor has left.

Fortunately, there's an elegant solution using events. Start by making the default session timeout very short. This value is configured (in minutes) in the web.xml descriptor:

```
<session-config>
  <session-timeout>10</session-timeout>
</session-config>
```

Then, grant authenticated users a more comfortable timeout period in an action or method that observes the postlogin event. To change the timeout, you explicitly assign a new value (in seconds) to the active HTTP session object, shown here in an event action:

```
<factory name="currentSession" scope="stateless"
  value="#{facesContext.externalContext.request.session}"/>
<event type="org.jboss.seam.security.loginSuccessful">
  <action execute="#{currentSession.setMaxInactiveInterval(3600)}"/>
</event>
```

Always restrict anonymous users from consuming system resources in excess. After all, they may not even be valid guests.

Another way to make the login page less of an annoyance is to remember the user on subsequent visits. Authenticating is a chore, so you want to make it as pleasant as possible.

RECOGNIZING THE REGULARS WITH "REMEMBER ME"

If you visit the same coffee shop every morning on your commute to work, after a while, the baristas start remembering you. The really good ones just say "Hi," perhaps calling you by your name, and start brewing your drink of choice. You can do the same for the users of your application by using a feature known as *Remember Me.*

Remember Me is the check box that often accompanies the username and password fields on login forms. Although the developer's intention for putting it there is to help the user, it often causes confusion. I'll admit that it has confused me at times. The source of this confusion is the fact that applications interpret this check box in two very different ways:

- *Username only*—Populate the username field with the value from the previous visit.
- *Auto-login*—Automatically authenticate the user with the credentials last used.

Both implementations work by storing a persistent cookie in the user's browser. (A persistent cookie is a cookie that isn't removed when the browser closes.) The cookie is assigned a value during the postauthentication routine, and that value is read in the next time the user is sent to the login page. In the *username only* scenario, the username is stored in the cookie and is used to populate the username field whenever the login page is displayed. In the *auto-login* scenario, an authentication token is stored in the cookie, which is used to log in the user quietly, thus bypassing the login page altogether.

Seam 2.0 provides the *username only* implementation out of the box. You enable it by setting the `rememberMe` property on the `identity` component to true, as shown here:

```
<security:identity
  authenticate-method="#{authenticationManager.authenticate}"
  remember-me="true"/>
```

By default, the Remember Me cookie is set to expire after one year of inactivity. You can assign an override value, in seconds, on the built-in `facesSecurityEvents` component:

```
<security:faces-security-events cookie-max-age="604800"/>
```

Seam 2.1 provides both Remember Me implementations and also makes it easy to implement your own solution. The "Remember Me" switch was moved to the `rememberMe` component. This component has a property named `mode` that controls which implementation is used. The possible values are `usernameOnly` and `autoLogin`, with `usernameOnly` being the default. Here's the same configuration as shown earlier for Seam 2.1:

```
<security:rememberMe enabled="true" cookie-max-age="604800"/>
```

To implement your own solution, you observe the postauthentication event and the `org.jboss.seam.security.quietLogin` event. The latter event is raised just before the user is sent to the login page. If the security principal is established by a method observing this event, the user won't be taken to the login page (and hence won't be disrupted).

Once the cookie has been created, regardless of implementation, the last username that the user entered is always accessible from the `username` property on the `identity`

The danger of using auto-login

Although convenient for the user, auto-login using a persistence cookie is dangerous. Any cross-site scripting (XSS) vulnerability in the application can be exploited by an attacker to send the user's authentication token outside of the application. The attacker can then use this token to authenticate as the user. A bigger risk with auto-login is cross-site request forgery (XSRF). In this case, the attacker knows that the user is always logged in and can "remote control" the user's session by getting the user to request a URL that performs an action on the site. In neither case is the application aware of the trickery.

Browser vendors recognized the danger of application-initiated logins and the motivation for using them, so they introduced a feature known as "Remember Passwords." In this case, the browser takes care of remembering the username and password credentials for a given website and fills out the login form for the user automatically. This approach is almost as convenient as auto-login but it's inherently much safer because the browser's keychain is not accessible to XSS or XSRF attacks, nor can it be read by local users.

In general, auto-login is a bad practice and you should avoid the temptation of using it. The *username only* Remember Me implementation doesn't pose this risk.

component (and the `credentials` component in Seam 2.1). Since the username field on the login form is bound to this property (e.g., #{identity.username}), this explains how this field gets autopopulated. You may question how this helps the user, since most browsers offer to fill in the credentials anyway. To see the benefit, you must think outside the login page, so to speak. Knowing the last username entered lets you pull nonsecure information out of the database, such as the user's preferences. If the user tries to perform a secure action, you can make them log in at that time.

Regardless of which implementation you use, my advice is to choose a label that fits. If you're using *username only*, make the label "Remember my username" and if you're using *auto-login*, make the label "Don't make me log in again." That should clear up the confusion.

There's another dimension of security to consider. In addition to protecting pages from being accessed by nonauthenticated users, you may want to secure the communication channel to protect a request from network sniffers. In production applications, you almost always want to serve the login page securely, and perhaps other pages as well. Seam can ensure the proper switch is made on a page-by-page basis or across the whole application.

11.2.3 *Serving pages securely*

When a high-ranking official makes a top-secret call to the Pentagon, it's not done over a regular telephone line. Instead, the official makes a request to get a "secure line." The equivalent in web applications is an HTTPS request. The HTTPS protocol encrypts the traffic sent to and from the server using the Secure Sockets Layer (SSL).

In development it's easy to forget about SSL security. Developers tend to stick with the HTTP protocol when testing locally since SSL is typically only configured in the production environment (hopefully this section encourages you to make the effort). However, just as the high-ranking official doesn't want to risk leaking information over a nonsecure telephone line, you don't want the users of your application to expose their sensitive data over an insecure web transmission. Failure to capture users' credentials over the HTTPS protocol makes them vulnerable to sniffing and jeopardizes the security of your application.

GETTING A SECURE LINE

In some infrastructures, the entire application is served over HTTPS and the protocol is handled by the web server. If that's the case, you can safely skip over this section. However, if your application uses a mixed environment, and it's up to the application to decide when to switch between secure and nonsecure requests, you need to pay attention here.

The URL prefix, which determines whether the request is secure (https) or nonsecure (http), is known as the scheme. The scheme is configured at the page level by specifying the scheme attribute on a <page> node in the page descriptor. The acceptable values are http and https. You can configure Seam to serve the login page over HTTPS as follows:

```
<page view-id="/login.xhtml" scheme="https"/>
```

Now, when authentication is necessary, Seam routes the user to the secure URL for the login page. If the user requests the login page directly using the HTTP protocol, Seam issues a redirect to the HTTPS equivalent URL. You can configure additional pages this way. Note that Seam's UI command components and the page descriptor's redirect rule are also aware of the scheme setting and will build the URL for the target view ID accordingly.

FINDING THE RIGHT PORT

If a scheme isn't specified for a view ID, Seam sticks with the scheme from the previous request. Therefore, if you mark the login page to be served securely, and no other pages have a scheme set, the user becomes permanently stuck in HTTPS after a trip to the login page. If your application doesn't require SSL across the board, it's better for performance to revert back to HTTP to serve low-risk pages. Since Seam issues a redirect to the scheme defined for a page if the wrong scheme is requested, this setting can be used to switch back to a nonsecure line. Use the following configuration to have all pages without a scheme defined served over HTTP:

```
<page view-id="*" scheme="http"/>
```

You may wonder how Seam knows how to modify the URL. In the default configuration, it's quite simple. Going from nonsecure to secure, Seam simply changes the beginning of the URL from http to https, and vice versa. That works as long as the server uses the standard scheme-to-port mapping (port 80 for HTTP and port 443 for HTTPS). If you're using different ports, then you need to let Seam know what the port numbers are. First, add the component namespace `http://jboss.com/products/` `seam/navigation`, prefixed as `navigation`, to the component descriptor. Next, configure the built-in component named `pages` to set the ports:

```
<navigation:pages http-port="8080" https-port="8443"/>
```

As one final measure, if the data in your application is particularly sensitive, you may want to consider invalidating the HTTP session when the scheme changes. This feature is controlled by the built-in component named `session` in the `web` namespace setup earlier. You configure this component to invalidate the session when the scheme is changed as follows:

```
<web:session invalidate-on-scheme-change="true"/>
```

Keep in mind that if you destroy the session on a scheme change, you also terminate any of the user's conversations or session-scoped data. This setting is designed to be used when the security requirements are stringent and loss of state is acceptable.

You've seen how to implement authentication, how to keep nonauthenticated users from accessing protected pages by requiring them to log in, and how to send data over a secure channel. But there's plenty more to learn about securing your application. Next up, you'll learn to enforce restrictions based on roles from the user's identity to determine where the user can go in the application and what actions the user can perform. Restricting access according to role membership is known as role-based authorization.

11.3 *Role-based authorization*

Authentication and authorization are easily confused with each other. Authentication is about establishing the user's identity. Authorization, the second *A*, is about checking to see whether the user is permitted to access a restricted resource or perform a restricted action. The restriction is based on a fact. In the previous section, you used binary authorization, which separates the members from the guests. In that case, the fact reads "the user is authenticated." If that fact can be verified, the user is permitted access. However, once the user is authenticated, you need more facts to check (otherwise, everyone would be an administrator).

If you recall, one of the user's principals is a collection of roles. So you can create facts that separate users that have a role from those that don't, known as role-based authorization. In this case, the fact reads "the user has role X." Once again, if the fact can be verified, the user is permitted access. For instance, you can require that a user be a member of the admin role in order to enter the administration section of the application. In section 11.4, you'll learn about rule-based authorization, which consists of fine-grained, contextual facts of arbitrary complexity. Rule-based authorization can be used in cases where roles alone are too broad.

In this section, you'll learn how to express a restriction and add it to a page, component, or method. Seam takes a declarative approach to security by using annotations, and it relies heavily on the EL, a constant theme throughout this book and throughout the framework. The focus of this section is on role-based authorization, though the infrastructure presented here also applies to rule-based authorization.

11.3.1 *Expressing restrictions*

It should come as no surprise to you that the universal way of checking whether a user has been granted a role in Seam is to use an EL value expression. What you may find puzzling, though, is how to perform such a check using EL notation. That's because to check if the user has a role, you have to pass in the role name as an argument. In standard EL notation, a value expression can only access JavaBean properties of a context variable. But you learned in chapter 4 that Seam incorporates the JBoss EL, which allows you to invoke methods with parameters. Brilliant! So you can seek out the component in Seam that performs security checks and invoke it using a parameterized value expression. Ah, but Seam has yet another solution based on EL functions. Let's start there first.

SEAM'S EL SECURITY FUNCTIONS

The Unified EL, introduced into Java EE through the JSP 2.1 specification and the foundation of Seam's EL support, provides a function mapper capable of linking an EL function name to a static method on a Java class. Seam registers two security-related EL functions: `s:hasRole` and `s:hasPermission`. The `s:hasRole` function is used to perform role-based checks, and the `s:hasPermission` function performs a rule-based check using the Drools rule engine, as shown in figure 11.3. The prefix `s` is a hardcoded namespace that prevents naming conflicts with other EL functions. The syntax of EL functions resembles that of JSP functions, but there's no dependency on JSP. You don't even have to do anything to enable them—Seam

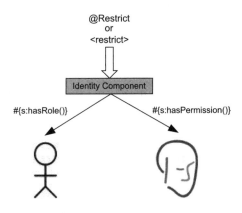

Figure 11.3 Seam supports two authorization models. Role-based authorization compares role names to the user's role principals. Rule-based authorization delegates the decision to Drools.

takes care of that for you. In fact, these functions can be used anywhere in Seam that EL is accepted. However, they merely delegate to equivalently named methods on the `identity` component, so you may want to consider just using the parameterized EL to invoke this component directly to remain consistent with the rest of your codebase.

You'll learn how to use rule-based security in the next section. For now, we focus on the role-based check, the left-hand path in figure 11.3. The mechanics of how these two functions are treated from the security API is consistent.

NOTE In Seam 2.0, if you attempt to perform an authorization check using `s:hasPermission` and the Drools library is not available on the classpath, the check will return false. Even with Drools on the classpath, a user won't be granted permission if the corresponding rule is missing. Seam 2.1 relaxes the coupling with Drools by making the permission resolver pluggable.

The function `s:hasRole` maps to the static method defined here. This method uses the `identity` component to verify whether the authenticated user is a member of the given role:

```
public static boolean hasRole(String name) {
    return Identity.instance().hasRole(name);
}
```

The function `s:hasPermission` has a similar mapping. Given that the work is delegated to the `identity` component, you could just invoke its `hasRole()` method directly:

```
#{identity.hasRole('admin')}
```

But to save a couple of keystrokes, you can use the `s:hasRole` function instead:

```
#{s:hasRole('admin')}
```

Internally, both expressions invoke the `hasRole()` method on the `identity` component, which returns a `boolean` indicating whether the supplied role is present in the user's group identity. You can use either form, but again, the first choice has the benefit of being consistent with the rest of your codebase.

NOTE   The delimiter in `s:hasRole` is a colon (:) not a dot (.), signaling a function call.

The `s:hasRole` function can be used multiple times in the same expression or combined with other EL logic. This expression checks two roles to verify the administrator is a golfer:

```
#{s:hasRole('admin') and s:hasRole('golfer')}
```

Unlike other security checks in Seam, the `s:hasRole` function doesn't throw an exception, raise an event, or attempt to redirect the user when the verification fails. Thus, it's perfect for rendering UI elements or controlling navigation according to what roles the user is granted.

ROLE-BASED DECISIONS

One way to use the `s:hasRole` function is to tie it to the rendered attribute of a UI component as a way to hide page elements that unauthorized users should not see:

```
<s:link view="/admin/GolferList.xhtml" value="Administer Golfers"
  rendered="#{s:hasRole('admin')}"/>
```

It can also be used to redact sensitive data, using it as the condition in a ternary operation:

```
<h:outputText value="#{s:hasRole('admin') ? golfer.emailAddress : 'XXX'}"/>
```

You can also use it to route the user according to role, a form of contextual navigation:

```
<navigation from-action="home">
  <rule if="#{s:hasRole('admin')}">
    <redirect view-id="/admin/home.xhtml"/>
  </rule>
```

```
    <rule if="#{not s:hasRole('admin')}">
      <redirect view-id="/home.xhtml"/>
    </rule>
</navigation>
```

Optionally, you can move this navigation logic to the action method, injecting the `identity` component and invoking it directly:

```
@In Identity identity;

public String action() {
    if (identity.hasRole('admin')) return "/admin/home.xhtml";
    else return "/home.xhtml";
}
```

That should stir up your thinking about how to use the security-related functions and their counterparts on the `identity` component. But so far, we've only determined whether or not the user has a role. To get the actual authorization part, you need to place this check somewhere that Seam can use it to enforce the restriction and take appropriate action when the criteria isn't met. For that, Seam provides declarative restrictions.

11.3.2 *Declaring role-based restrictions*

Restrict declarations are like having security guards at various places in your application. To pass by, the user must be authenticated and must satisfy the restriction. If the user is denied access, the user is either sent to the login page or an exception is thrown.

   Seam provides two restriction labels: one for securing JSF views and one for securing components. They are both capable of performing a role-based authorization check as well as a rule-based one. While this section focuses on role-based security, keep in mind that these labels are designed for any type of restriction.

SECURING JSF VIEWS

Hiding a link that leads to a restricted page keeps the user from wandering down the wrong path, but we need to do more than hide links to secure pages. You learned earlier that you can require a user to log in before accessing a page. To get page-level security for authenticated users, you add the `<restrict>` element to a `<page>` node in the page descriptor. Seam enforces the authorization criteria in the `<restrict>` element prior to restoring (JSF postback) and prior to rendering (both an initial request and postback) the view ID(s) defined in the `<page>` node. If a restriction fails, both an event and an exception are raised. Table 11.3 lists the event and exceptions that are used, depending on whether or not the user is authenticated at the time the restriction fails.

Table 11.3   The event and exception that Seam raises when an authorization restriction fails

Authenticated?	Event raised	Exception raised `org.jboss.seam.security.*`
No	`org.jboss.seam.security.notLoggedIn`	`NotLoggedInException`
Yes	`org.jboss.seam.security.notAuthorized`	`AuthorizationException`

The `AuthorizationException` can be handled using a similar configuration as earlier to direct the user to an error page. The following exception configuration catches authorization errors and directs the user to a security error page:

```
<exception class="org.jboss.seam.security.AuthorizationException">
  <redirect view-id="/securityError.xhtml">
    <message
      severity="warn">You've been denied access to the resource.</message>
  </redirect>
</exception>
```

Let's continue with the example of securing the administration section of the Open 18 application to demonstrate use of the `<restrict>` tag. To keep nonadministrators away from pages in the /admin/ folder, you declare a `<restrict>` tag as follows:

```
<page view-id="/admin/*">
  <restrict>#{s:hasRole('admin')}</restrict>
</page>
```

Notice that the body of the `<restrict>` tag contains an EL expression. That EL expression must return a `boolean` value, but otherwise it can be as complex as you need it to be, as explained in the previous section. If the body of the `<restrict>` tag is empty, Seam performs a rule-based permission check following a convention covered in section 11.4.4. The rule-based permission check has the benefit of being able to distinguish between the restore phase and the render phase. A rule is capable of checking for a role, so you can use a rule as a way to get both flavors of security. Either way, to have Seam apply authorization at the page level, whether it be role- or rule-based, you have to use the `<restrict>` tag.

Securing pages is only half the battle. If, by some chance, the user finds his or her way through the page-level restrictions or accesses the component through some other channel (i.e., web service), you want to be sure that your classes and methods are also locked down. Seam allows for declarative restrictions on all Seam components.

SECURING COMPONENTS

Components are secured by adding the `@Restrict` annotation at the class or method level. The restriction is expressed using an EL string in the value of the annotation, which can accept the `s:hasRole` and `s:hasPermission` functions, or just check that the user is authenticated using `#{identity.loggedIn}`. Once again, if the value is omitted, Seam performs a rule-based check following the convention covered in section 11.4.4. If the check fails, the same event and exception are thrown as with the `<restrict>` tag.

Let's assume that there is an action method that is called in the administration area that grants pro status to a golfer. The `@Restrict` annotation can enforce that only users with the `admin` role can invoke this method:

```
@Restrict("#{s:hasRole('admin')}")
public void grantProStatus() { ... }
```

Having to specify this restriction for every method of a class can be tedious, so you can opt to blanket the component by specifying the restriction at the class level:

```
@Name("golferAdminAction")
@Restrict("#{s:hasRole('admin')}")
public class GolferAdminAction {
    public void grantProStatus() { ... }
    public void anotherAdminAction() { ... }
}
```

Any method that doesn't have a `@Restrict` annotation will inherit the requirement from the class-level annotation. You can override the class-level restriction by applying the `@Restrict` annotation to an individual method. One way to restore anonymous access is to use an EL expression that invariably returns true:

```
@Restrict("#{true}")
public void safeToExecute() { ... }
```

Table 11.4 gives an overview of the `@Restrict` annotation.

Table 11.4   The `@Restrict` annotation

Name:	Restrict
Purpose:	Used to define a security restriction that is enforced before a method or all methods on a component can be invoked
Target:	TYPE (class), METHOD

Attribute	Type	Function
value	String (EL)	An EL value expression that is evaluated to determine whether the user has permission to execute the method. The EL functions `s:hasRole` and `s:hasPermission` are typically used to build the restriction. If the expression evaluates to false, Seam directs an anonymous user to the login page or throws an authorization exception if the user is authenticated. Default: an automatic rule-based permission check.

In addition to being used on Seam components, the `@Restrict` annotation can be used on entity classes and enforced prior to persistence events, which is covered later.

ASSERTING AN AUTHORIZATION

When Seam enforces a restriction, it does more than just give a thumbs up or thumbs down. As I mentioned, Seam takes action if the check fails. The declarative restrictions we just covered delegate to the `checkRestriction()` method on the `identity` component. For example:

```
Identity.instance().checkRestriction("#{s:hasRole('admin')}");
```

This is one of several methods on the `identity` component that assert a condition, rather than just check for it, where assert means to take action if the check fails. The other two methods that assert are `checkRole()` and `checkPermission()`, which complement the `hasRole()` and `hasPermission()` functions, respectively. You can assert that the user has a role in Java as follows:

```
Identity.instance().checkRole("admin");
```

Whether you decide to check or assert depends on whether you're prepared to turn over control to Seam if the condition fails. For instance, you might want a chance to record the incident if the user isn't authorized. In that case, you just want to check, not assert:

```
if (!Identity.instance().hasRole("admin")) {
    AuthorizationViolation violation =
        new AuthorizationViolation(Golfer.class, currentGolfer.getId());
    entityManager.persist(violation);
    throw new AuthorizationException(
        "You must have the admin role to perform this action. " +
        "This incident has been reported.");
}
```

Even if you aren't in control of the authorization, you can record a failed restriction in a method that observes the `org.jboss.seam.security.notAuthorized` event. The downside is that you lose the context in which it was raised.

KING FOR A THREAD

After defining a restriction on a method, you may have a scenario where that method needs to be used even though the user doesn't have the appropriate authorities. The goal here is not to restrict the user, per se, but to secure a component so that it can only be invoked by another component under a known set of circumstances (i.e., a use case).

One way to solve this problem is to use contextual security rules, which are covered in the next section. But when role-based security is all you have, you can execute a method using elevated privileges. Seam supports this feature through the `RunAsOperation` class. For those of you who know Unix, this is the equivalent of the `sudo` command. You instantiate the class and override the `execute()` method, which is where you put the privileged code that you want to run, then pass the instance to `Identity.runAs()` to be executed. You can set a new `Subject`, `Principal`, or set of roles to set the identity of the "current" user. If you don't specify a subject or roles, then the code executes as if the user isn't authenticated. In Seam 2.1, you can set the code to run as a system operation, which bypasses all restrictions. Here's an example that grants the admin role for the operation:

```
new RunAsOperation() {
    public String[] getRoles() {
        return new String[] { "admin" };
    }
    public void execute() {
        facilityAction.setOwner(golfer);
    }
}
```

As this section has demonstrated, role-based authorization is straightforward to implement in Seam. However, it's also very coarse. That's great for securing entire sections of the site, such as the administration section, but it becomes difficult to meet all the security requirements of a multiuser application. These requirements demand more sophisticated authorizations based on contextual rules.

11.4   *Rule-based authorization using Drools*

This section covers authorization decisions made by the right-hand path in figure 11.3. Following this path, a permission is fed into a rule to decide whether to grant access. A permission consists of a target and the action to be performed on that target. In that sense, permissions are like access control lists (ACLs). Unlike with role-based authorization, Seam doesn't just inspect the user's identity to decide whether to allow access. Instead, logic of arbitrary complexity "crunches the context" and out comes the verdict. In this section, you'll learn how to define a permission and how to implement the logic to support it using Drools rules. Let's first look at how rule-based authorization differs from role-based authorization.

11.4.1   *Rules vs. roles*

Averting security is a common theme in action movies. Getting past the security guards is never much of a problem for the assailants. A mere bump on the head is usually enough to thwart that obstruction. What hangs up the intruders is a dense network of lasers crisscrossing the room that hosts the artifact they're after. Maneuvering through this web of barricades would require breaking the laws of physics.

Role-based authorization can be equated to the defense provided by the feeble security guards. It's predictable and naïve. It performs its rounds, giving attention to known weak spots, but it's completely unaware of the threat that looms. Although this line of defense has its uses, it can't measure up to complex security requirements. Rule-based authorization, on the other hand, provides much tighter security. It knows exactly what it's protecting and can activate itself under a certain set of conditions. It's also known as contextual security.

Consider the security requirement that a record can only be modified by the user that created it. Role-based authorization isn't sufficient in this case since the best the restriction can do is ensure that the current user has permissions to modify records (e.g., the edit role). If the system holds records from different customers, and the role-based authorization granted the user access, that user might be allowed to modify a record owned by a different customer. Yikes! The role restriction can't make a decision based on the relationship between the user and the record. It's blind to the context.

Naturally, the first thing that comes to mind is to craft custom logic that verifies the owner of the record is the current user before granting access. Although you may not realize it, by doing so, you are implementing rule-based authorization (it's just not pretty). The problem with this custom approach is that the restrictions are no longer declarative. They're hardcoded into the business logic. You want to be able to assign rule-based restrictions in the same way as you specify the role requirements. That's exactly what Seam's rule-based authorization allows you to do.

11.4.2   *Setting up Drools*

In Seam, rule-based authorization checks are handled by Drools. Drools is a rule engine that supports declarative programming. You define a set of rules that must be matched in order for the user to have access to a resource. These rules allow for separation of restriction logic and business logic. More importantly, the restrictions can be modified without affecting the business logic. They can even be swapped out dynamically at runtime if set up appropriately.

NOTE The name Drools is derived from the term "dynamic rules." The rules are dynamic because they're compiled and interpreted at runtime.

Seam's rule-based authorization is considered the advanced security mode in its security model. The reason for this label is that it requires a few extra libraries and configuration. It also requires knowledge of how to author rules using the Drools rule language. The fact that basic security mode can be implemented without any add-ons or special knowledge is an important aspect of Seam's security model. Regardless, the power of rule-based authorization is worth the extra effort.

Permission management in Seam

The design of Seam's authorization mechanism was improved considerably in Seam 2.1. While the rule-based authorization covered in this section remains, it's not the only way to implement permissions. Permission checks are now delegated to a chain of resolvers, one of which is a new persistent permission resolver that reads permissions from a database and another to support rule-based permissions. You can also implement and register your own resolver.

Storing permissions in the database is convenient because they can easily be granted and revoked from the user interface. To help manage these permissions, Seam provides a permission manager, complementing the identity manager introduced earlier. A permission is mapped to the database using annotations on entity classes, allowing Seam to search them. The focus of this chapter is on rules, but feel free to explore persistent permissions as an alternative to writing a rule.

Both the permission manager and identity manager require that you have the permissions to invoke the methods in either API.

The good news is that if you used seam-gen to prepare your project, there's no additional work you must do to set up rule-based security using Drools. You're all set! If you're going at it alone, you first need to get the required libraries, drools-core.jar, drools-compiler.jar, core.jar (Eclipse JDT), antlr-runtime.jar, janino.jar, and mvel14.jar. The second step is to activate the set of security rules. Don't worry about the actual rules right now. We get to them once the configuration is in place.

Security rules are registered using the built-in `RulesBase` component, named `rulesBase`, specified as one or more rules files. Typically, the rules are defined in a file named security.drl at the root of the classpath. First, add the component namespace for Drools to the component descriptor, `http://jboss.com/products/seam/drools`, prefixed as `drools`. Then, declare the `securityRules` component:

```
<drools:rules-base name="securityRules" rules-file="/security.drl"/>
```

The `identity` component assumes that the `RuleBase` for security is named `security-Rules`, so its best to use this name.

You're now ready to start adding rules! There's only one problem, though. How do you write rules? It's time for your crash course in Drools. I promise that it's a lot simpler than it first appears, and you'll be glad you invested the time to learn it because it's so powerful.

11.4.3   *Creating rules with Drools*

I don't know about you, but I like crash courses. Who wants to go through a whole semester when you can learn it all in one sitting? The good news is that rules are such a simple concept that you can probably learn how to write them in the time it takes to drink your coffee. Which cup are you on now?

THE MOTIVATION FOR CREATING RULES

Let's start with the end in mind. That way, we'll know when we've covered just enough to get by. I alluded earlier to the fact that the complement to the s:hasRole EL function is s:hasPermission and that it's capable of performing rule-based permission checks. You can use s:hasPermission in lieu of s:hasRole in both the <restrict> page descriptor tag and the @Restrict annotation. However, it's more than just changing the function name. The s:hasPermission function consults the security rules to determine whether the executing thread should be granted permission to perform the action on the given target.

The s:hasPermission function takes three arguments. The first is a resource name, the second is an action, and the third is a context variable that is inserted into the working memory. (If you invoke the hasPermission() method on identity directly, you can pass any number of additional arguments, which get added to the working memory.) These values define the permission that needs to be verified. The permission is sent off to the rule engine, which looks for a matching rule that will grant the user access. If a match isn't found, Seam presumes that the current user doesn't have access and takes the appropriate action.

Let's consider an example scenario, which can be used to understand the purpose of a rule. Private golf facility owners are particular about the information that's made available about their facility. Therefore, they ask that only administrators be able to modify private facilities (e.g., country clubs). The first thing we want to do is place this restriction on the update method of FacilityHome using the @Restrict annotation:

```
@Restrict(
    "#{s:hasPermission('facilityHome', 'update', facilityHome.instance}")
public String update() {
    return super.update();
}
```

The restriction is examined in figure 11.4. This permission check attempts to determine whether an instance of Facility can be modified by the current user.

s:hasPermission accepts the conditions. The decision is handled by the rule engine. That brings us to rule engines and how they process conditions to arrive at a decision.

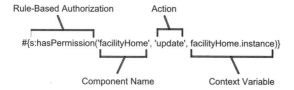

Figure 11.4 The set of conditions that are passed into a rule-based authorization check

DROOLS 101

Drools is an inference engine. It matches conditions against facts. When a matching condition is located, the rule is activated and action is taken. This type of rule processing is known as a forward-chaining. Facts are checked to arrive at a conclusion. You can think of it as a glorified if-then statement. The crucial distinction is that rules aren't executed sequentially. The order of the rule processing is optimized using the Rete algorithm.[1] That's part of what makes evaluating them so efficient. As a general rule, it's a good idea not to count on the rules firing in any particular order and try and author the rules without worrying about a particular "flow." (But don't be afraid to have lots of rules because they are cheap.)

Facts are the objects present in the working memory. You can think of the working memory as similar to the persistence context. It holds data in a runtime cache. You can query (match conditions) and perform operations (execute actions) on the objects that it maintains. The working memory is also referred to as a session.

As with EJB components, Drools supports both stateful and stateless sessions. A stateful session is maintained over multiple invocations of the rules, whereas a stateless session is discarded after the rules are done firing. An invocation ends when all of the permutations of each rule have been tested.

Seam uses a stateful session and populates it with the security principals, which are the primary principal and the set of roles associated with the current user. Since the primary principal and the principals that represent the roles are both instances of the same class, `Principal`, Seam inserts the roles into the working memory as `Role` objects to distinguish them. Seam also inserts objects into the working memory specific to the permission check, which it later cleans up when the check is complete.

So far, you know that there's a working memory that stores objects, that rules are fired in some optimized order to match facts in the working memory, and that the purpose of the rules is to execute actions as the result of drawing a conclusion. The next step is to understand the anatomy of a rule.

CREATING A PERMISSION CHECK RULE

A rule consists of two parts: a premise and a conclusion. The premise is known as the left-hand side (LHS) and the conclusion is known as the right-hand side (RHS). To support these two sides, Drools uses a custom syntax for defining rules, known as the Drools Rule Language (DRL). Its syntax is reminiscent of Java. In fact, the code in the conclusion *is* Java. The premise uses a shorthand that's focused on matching, though it may look confusing the first time you see it.

---

[1] The Rete algorithm was designed by Dr. Charles L. Forgy. See http://en.wikipedia.org/wiki/Rete_algorithm.

Each rule must be given a unique name (for a given session). The name you choose is arbitrary and isn't referenced anywhere in the code. Let's begin creating a rule by assigning it a name:

```
rule ModifyPrivateFacility
...
```

Next, we need to define a premise. Each line in the when statement consists of a condition. All of the conditions must evaluate to true for the rule to fire. For this rule, we want to ensure that if the golf facility is private, the current user has the admin role. However, we don't just want this rule to fire at any old time. We only want it to fire when the restriction #{s:hasPermission('facilityHome', 'update', facilityHome.instance)} is consulted. How do we know which restriction check kicked off the rules? Seam creates an instance of the PermissionCheck class and stores it in the working memory prior to executing the rules. The PermissionCheck holds the first two arguments to s:has-Permission the target and the action. It also maintains a flag that determines whether permission should be granted, which starts off as false. The purpose of the rules is to determine whether permission should be granted. The final argument to s:has-Permission, the context variable, is inserted directly into the working memory. Continuing to build out our rule incrementally, the condition clause can now be added:

```
rule ModifyPrivateFacility
when
    $perm: PermissionCheck(name == "facilityHome", action in ("update",
    ➡"remove"), granted == false)
    Role(name == "admin")
    Facility(type == "PRIVATE")
...
```

Before you reach to scratch your head, I'll help you make sense of this syntax. Recall that a rule is intended to match facts in the working memory. The class names in the previous snippet are being used to locate objects of those types in the working memory. What looks like a constructor is actually shorthand for running the instanceof operator against all objects in the session. The arguments used between the brackets is another shorthand for checking property values against expected values. The name on the left side of the operator is the name of the bean property. The value of the property is being compared against the test value on the right-hand side of the operator. Unlike with Java, two objects are equal when compared with the == operator as long as their equals() and hashCode() methods return the same value. The Java syntax equivalent of Role(name == "admin") is as follows:

```
objectInWorkingMemory instanceof Role &&
    "admin".equals(((Role) objectInWorkingMemory).getName())
```

This check is performed against every object in the working memory. I'm sure you'll agree that the rule DRL syntax is simpler. You may be wondering what the prefix $perm: at the start of the first condition is all about. Any time you see a name followed by a colon, it's a declaration. The purpose of a declaration is to create an alias. The name of the alias can be any valid Java variable name. The dollar sign ($) is not specific to Drools—it's a legal character. Beginning alias names with $ is a convention used to help distinguish between aliases and bean property names.

An alias establishes a back reference. It's created either for use in subsequent conditions or in the action of the rule. In the case of the `PermissionCheck`, an alias must be created so that the `grant()` method can be called on it if the rule's condition is true. With that said, let's conclude the rule:

```
...
then
  $perm.grant();
end
```

You can put any Java code you want in the conclusion (it gets compiled at runtime). Here, it's limited to granting permission. We aren't done just yet. Any time you modify an object in the working memory, rule execution stops and all the rules are fired again. To prevent the rule from being evaluated more than once, you can add the no-loop operator. The no-loop operator, highlighted in bold, is placed in the rule's options section:

```
rule ModifyPrivateFacility
  no-loop
when
...
```

Since all users are denied access until granted permission by a rule, only users with the admin role can modify private facilities. However, at this point, nobody is allowed to modify a nonprivate facility. Time to add some context!

CONTEXTUAL RULES

While the private facility owners have asked us to only allow administrators to modify private facilities, we don't want to lock facility owners out from their own facilities, and we want to grant access to any member to modify nonprivate facilities. Thus, in one case, the rule must be aware of the absence of an object in the working memory, and in the other, it must be able to correlate objects in the working memory to the authenticated user. The rules for these two cases are shown in listing 11.3:

Listing 11.3 Rules that allow a user to modify a facility under certain conditions

```
rule ModifyNonPrivateFacility
  no-loop
when
  $perm: PermissionCheck(name == "facilityHome", action in ("update",
  ➥"remove"), granted == false)
  Role(name == "member")          ❶
  not Facility(type == "PRIVATE")        ❷
then
  $perm.grant();
end

rule OperateOnOwnFacility
```

```
     no-loop
  when
     $perm: PermissionCheck(name == "facilityHome", granted == false)    ❸
     Role(name == "member")
     Principal($username: name)      ❹
     Facility($golfer: owner)     ❺
     Golfer(username == $username) from $golfer     ❻
  then
     $perm.grant();     ❼
  end
```

There are a couple of things to point out in these two new rules. The ModifyNon-PrivateFacility rule is almost identical to the ModifyPrivateFacility rule except that the role is downgraded to member ❶ and the check for the private facility type is negated ❷.

The second rule is more interesting. The PermissionCheck doesn't look at the action property ❸, so this condition applies to any permission triggered from the facilityHome component. The relationship between Principal and Facility is interesting. The Principal condition merely checks for the presence of Principal in the working memory. If present, the value of its name property is aliased to $username ❹. The Facility condition verifies that a Facility instance is present in the working memory and creates the alias $golfer that references the owner of the facility ❺. In the final statement, the $username alias is compared to the username of the owner using a nested condition ❻. If all of the checks pass, the current user is assumed to be the owner of the facility ❼.

Now we just need to get the rules to compile. DRL files are just like Java source files in that they can have a package declaration and import classes.

WARNING   Be sure to import any class that's referenced by a rule definition. Otherwise, the rules won't compile and therefore won't be fired (and no error will be displayed in the UI). You can get instant validation using the Drools plug-in for Eclipse or by writing unit tests. This step prevents security holes caused by syntax errors.

The complete DRL file for the example in this section is shown in listing 11.4.

Listing 11.4 Security rule definitions for securing access to Facility entities

```
package org.open18.permissions;

import java.security.Principal;
import org.jboss.seam.security.PermissionCheck;
import org.jboss.seam.security.Role;
import org.open18.model.Facility;
import org.open18.model.Golfer;

rule ModifyPrivateFacility
  no-loop
when
  $perm: PermissionCheck(name == "facilityHome", action in ("update",
```

```
➥"remove"), granted == false)
    Role(name == "admin")
    Facility(type == "PRIVATE")
then
    $perm.grant();
end

rule ModifyNonPrivateFacility
    no-loop
when
    $perm: PermissionCheck(name == "facilityHome", action in ("update",
➥"remove"), granted == false)
    Role(name == "member")
    not Facility(type == "PRIVATE")
then
    $perm.grant();
end

rule OperateOnOwnFacility
    no-loop
when
    $perm: PermissionCheck(name == "facilityHome", granted == false)
    Role(name == "member")
    Principal($username: name)
    Facility($golfer: owner)
    Golfer(username == $username) from $golfer
then
    $perm.grant();
end
```

If your rules file becomes too large, you can break it up into multiple files. You register the additional files to the `<drools:rule-base>` component declaration.

Using rule-based authorization in Seam is simple because you don't have to concern yourself with managing the RuleBase or the working memory. You just author the rules file, plug it into the securityRules component, and the laser beams light up the room. For more examples of security rules, check out the seamspace example in the Seam distribution.

With your newfound ability to write and understand rules, let's return to the restrict clauses and learn how to cut out some of the work.

11.4.4 *Automatic context detection*

One of the reasons that Seam's rule-based security is so powerful is that, through the use of interceptors, Seam is able to automatically detect the context at the spot of the permission check. Earlier, you defined the restriction using an explicit call to either s:hasRole or s:hasPermission. However, all this manual work takes away the benefit of using declarative security. Seam allows you to use these two declarations in their no-arguments form and creates and evaluates an implicit s:hasPermission check.

When the `<restrict>` tag or @Restrict annotation is used without a value, a default permission is created. The format of the permission is always name:action. When used with the @Restrict annotation, the name part is the component's name and the `action` part is the name of the method. When dealing with page-based security, the `name` is the view ID and the `action` is the page-oriented JSF life cycle phase—either render or restore. These mappings are shown in table 11.5.

Table 11.5   The mapping defining how a rule-based restriction is interpreted

Source	Applies to	Name part	Action part
`<restrict>`	JSF view IDs	View ID	JSF life cycle phase (restore or render)
`@Restrict`	Methods	Component name	Method name

The downside of using the restrict declarations without arguments is that they don't allow you to put a context variable into the working memory. As you saw in the example rules, knowing which instance of `Facility` is in scope is critical for deciding whether to let the user perform the action. But don't be discouraged. There is a way to have this information passed on. To have that happen, you need to use entity restrictions.

SECURING ENTITIES

When you want to restrict CRUD operations, you can generalize the restriction to securing the entity that's being persisted. Seam leverages the entity life-cycle annotations to apply rule-based security at the spot of the operation. If the `@Restrict` annotation is added at the class level, the restriction will be enforced on each CRUD operation. If you want to secure an individual operation, you can use it alongside one of the entity life-cycle annotations.

The first argument to `s:hasPermission` is always the context variable name of the entity class, if it has been assigned one, or the fully qualified class name. The name of the action corresponds to the CRUD operation being performed. The names of the actions that Seam uses as the second argument to the `s:hasPermission` call are mapped to the entity life-cycle annotations in table 11.6.

Table 11.6   The mapping between the entity life-cycle event and the permission action

Entity life cycle annotation	Action	When applied
`@PostLoad`	read	After the entity instance is loaded from the database
`@PrePersist`	insert	Before a transient instance is persisted to the database
`@PreUpdate`	update	Before a dirty instance is flushed to the database
`@PreRemove`	delete	Before a managed instance is deleted from the database.

The final argument is always the current entity instance that's the subject of the CRUD operation. What that means is that the entity instance will be available in the working memory when the rule is fired.

Let's assume that we only want to allow users to update or delete their own rounds. The first step is to secure the update and remove operations of the `Round` entity class:

```
@Entity
@Table(name = "ROUND")
@Name("round")
public class Round implements Serializable {
    ...

    @PreUpdate @PreRemove
    @Restrict
    public void restrict() {}
}
```

The name of the method on which the @PreUpdate, @PreRemove, and @Restrict annotations are applied is arbitrary. It's a means to an end. The next step is to put a rule in place in the security.drl file:

```
rule ModifyOwnRound
    no-loop
when
    $check: PermissionCheck(name == "round", action in ("update",
➡"delete"), granted == false)
    Role(name == "member")
    Principal($username: name)
    Round($golfer: golfer)
    Golfer(username == $username) from $golfer
then
    $check.grant();
end
```

That's all there is to enforcing the restriction! One last bit of configuration remains: the security framework must be hooked into the life cycle of the entity.

REGISTERING THE SECURITY LISTENER

Like many other cross-cutting features provided by Seam, entity-level security is applied using a life-cycle listener. However, Seam doesn't have the same level of control over entities that it does over the other components in its container. The entities call the persistence manager their master. To allow Seam to tap into the life-cycle events of JPA entities, it's necessary to register Seam's entity security listener with the persistence unit using the following META-INF/orm.xml descriptor:

```
<entity-mappings xmlns="http://java.sun.com/xml/ns/persistence/orm"
  xmlns:xsi="http://www.w3.org/2001/XMLSchema-instance"
  xsi:schemaLocation="
    http://java.sun.com/xml/ns/persistence/orm
    http://java.sun.com/xml/ns/persistence/orm_1_0.xsd"
  version="1.0">
  <persistence-unit-metadata>
    <persistence-unit-defaults>
      <entity-listeners>
        <entity-listener
          class="org.jboss.seam.security.EntitySecurityListener"/>
      </entity-listeners>
    </persistence-unit-defaults>
  </persistence-unit-metadata>
</entity-mappings>
```

If you're using Hibernate natively, you don't have to reach for your text editor. Seam automatically registers an equivalent listener with the Hibernate `SessionFactory`.

You can now add either role-based or rule-based restrictions to pages (view IDs), component methods, and entity operations. Your application is locked down. Or is it? What about those public-facing pages? They should get some attention as well, not so much from humans but from malicious computers. In the final section of this chapter, you'll learn how to protect your public-facing pages from abuse.

11.5   Separating the computers from the humans

Most of the time when we talk about security, the focus is on keeping intruders out of the application. But public resources can also be abused. An evildoer could write a bot that uses a public registration form on your site to register random users, filling up your database with bogus records and potentially leading to denial of service for genuine users. How do you tell computers apart from humans to keep out the bots? That's the purpose of CAPTCHA.

11.5.1   An overview of CAPTCHA

CAPTCHA stands for **C**ompletely **A**utomated **P**ublic **T**uring Test to Tell **C**omputers and **H**umans Apart.[2] It is a challenge-response system that attempts to determine whether the user operating on the client side is a human or a computer. There are a variety of ways this test can be conducted, but the general idea is as follows. The application poses a challenge, typically rendered as an image. The user is then required to solve the challenge and send the response back to the server. Only when the response is correct is the remaining data in the form submitted. While the challenge only requires basic comprehension for the human to solve, even the most sophisticated computer algorithms get stopped dead in their tracks. Thus, a user who enters a correct response is assumed to be human.

If you have never implemented CAPTCHA before, your first reaction might be to say, "Forget it. This seems too hard. Image generation? Eek!" On the contrary, implementing CAPTCHA using Seam is so easy, it's just wrong not to use it.

11.5.2   Adding a CAPTCHA challenge to forms

Seam implements CAPTCHA by rendering a basic arithmetic problem using a Java 2D image. The complete interaction is managed by Seam, so you don't have to do anything other than add it to your form. The image is served using the `SeamResource-Servlet`, so be sure to have that installed. You can find information on how to set it up in chapter 3, section 3.1.3.

Let's return to the registration form example from chapter 4 to protect it from being abused. All you need to do to secure your form using CAPTCHA is render the dynamically generated CAPTCHA image at /seam/resource/captcha and provide the

---

[2] CAPTCHA is a trademark of Carnegie Mellon University.

user with a text field, bound to the #{captcha.response} property, in which to enter a response. The rest is up to Seam. Here's an example of a CAPTCHA field:

```
<s:decorate id="verifyCaptchaField" template="layout/edit.xhtml">
   <ui:define name="label">Security check</ui:define>
   <h:graphicImage value="/seam/resource/captcha"/>
   <h:inputText value="#{captcha.response}" required="true"/>
</s:decorate>
```

Seam's built-in component named captcha handles the logistics of the challenge. Validation of the response is enforced by the Hibernate Validator annotation @CaptchaResponse, which is defined on this component's response property. The @CaptchaResponse validator uses the following message when the response is incorrect:

```
input characters did not match
```

Believe it or not, that's all there is to it! No XML configuration files, custom components, or custom servlets. You simply incorporate the captcha component into your JSF form. If you want to customize the challenge, create a custom component named captcha that extends org.jboss.seam.captcha.Captcha. Seam can still assume the responsibility of proctoring the challenge. Consult the Seam reference documentation for details.

CAPTCHA security helps to keep the abusers away today, but in general, the fight against wrongdoers is a perpetual battle. But, at the time of this writing, CAPTCHA is still holding the lines, so it's worth adding to all of your public-facing forms—it provides the protection you need from bogus data and denial-of-service attacks.

11.6 Summary

The more accessible the security API is, the more likely you will be to use it—that's Seam's stance. Security is critical to an application's success, and implementing security in Seam is easy. There's no prize for putting a single restriction in place that covers the security requirements for the entire application. You should put security in the view, in your components, and in your entities. That way, when the front line comes down, the next line can pick up the swords and maintain the guard.

I used the word "easy" quite liberally in this chapter, but each time I backed it up with proof. You started off by adding authentication to the application with little more than a single method on a POJO. That method validates the credentials provided by the identity component. Seam and JAAS work together to handle the low-level details of establishing the user's identity. You learned that the identity component can accept roles that are transferred to the user's identity. This gave you two forms of authorization, binary and role-based, which brought you a long way toward locking down the application. Where role-based authorization falls short is in enforcing contextual restrictions. That led you to Seam's rule-based authorization powered by Drools. I provided a crash course in Drools, then showed you how to create rules to make permission decisions based on facts that Seam places in the working memory. Finally, you learned that securing public-facing forms with CAPTCHA is just as important as protecting internal ones and implemented a CAPTCHA challenge in Seam in just one step.

With security in place, it's safe to move on to Ajax and JavaScript remoting, both of which are exciting parts of the Web 2.0 movement and benefit from security as a prerequisite. In the next chapter, you'll see the "easy" theme extend to Ajax, giving your application a rich upgrade without the effort typically associated with this modern approach to web interactions.

12

Ajax and
JavaScript remoting

This chapter covers

- Combining Ajax and JSF
- Validating form inputs instantly
- Invoking components from JavaScript
- Using Seam as a GWT service

When applications are ported to the web environment, something is often lost in translation: the user experience. Even nontechnical users understand the need to wait for a page to load after each action, evidence of the lack of continuity that plagues many web applications. Ajax provides a way to bring the rich, interactive application (RIA) user experience to the web.

In the previous chapter, you learned how the mission-critical and sometimes daunting task of securing your application is dramatically simplified thanks to Seam. By filling in a few blanks, you're able to blanket your application with basic security and then fine-tune it with contextual security rules. In this chapter, you'll witness another example of how Seam helps you transform your application with a handful of keystrokes by leveraging its multifaceted Ajax support. This news is especially promising, since moving to Ajax has proven to be a more costly investment than many product managers first anticipated. One reason is that cross-browser JavaScript is not for the faint of heart, and its problems can put the brakes on your development schedule. Another is that JavaScript code quickly becomes spaghetti, making it difficult to comprehend and even harder to test.

In this chapter, you'll discover that Ajax-based JSF component libraries and Seam's JavaScript remoting API offer a refreshed approach to Ajax by putting separation between the application and the low-level XMLHttpRequest object, significantly reducing the risk of letting Ajax through the door. The Ajax-enabled JSF component libraries covered in this chapter, Ajax4jsf and ICEfaces, execute the JSF life cycle asynchronously in response to user interactions, resulting in partial page updates that don't disrupt the user's activity. Even better, this exchange is transparent to the developer, who doesn't have to touch a line of JavaScript. Rather than wait for the user's next move, ICEfaces has a mechanism for pushing presentation changes to the browser in response to changes in the application state. JavaScript remoting cracks the door open to JavaScript slightly, while still managing to hide the interaction with the server, by allowing server-side components to be executed through JavaScript function calls. Seam's remoting can also give alternate front ends like GWT access to the Seam component model.

Although simplicity remains the underlying theme in the final part of this book, the key word in this chapter is transparency. The investment you have made in learning about the JSF life cycle, Seam components, and the EL throughout this book pays off and helps you get your application rich quick. We begin by looking at how Ajax is transparently weaved into the JSF component model and the types of interactions this enables.

12.1   Using Ajax with JSF

JSF beat Ajax mania to the scene by nearly a year. The order of events was unfortunate because Ajax would have fit perfectly with the design of JSF as an event-driven framework backed by a server-centric model. Although Ajax wasn't included in the JSF specification (and still isn't as of JSF 1.2), innovators recognized the potential of Ajax to close the gap in the JSF vision and adapted it to JSF in an intelligent and efficient manner. This section talks about the right and wrong ways of using Ajax with JSF, the two main component libraries that brought Ajax to JSF, and Seam's role in Ajax-based JSF requests.

12.1.1   Embracing a server-centric application model

JSF uses a server-side model to handle client-side events. The server then responds with an updated view. Unfortunately, the standard mechanism in JSF for propagating an event from the UI to the server is to use a regular form submit followed by a full-page refresh. This makes for a disruptive and costly event notification, in stark contrast with the goal of Ajax and the rich web.

JSF developers with Ajax-envy (myself being one of them) initially attempted to use Ajax in their JSF applications by stepping outside the JSF component model. User interactions would be trapped by custom JavaScript and the HTML in the rendered page manipulated without JSF's knowledge. To invoke the JSF life cycle from an Ajax request, form data had to be fabricated to trick JSF into thinking the user had initiated the event. When the response arrived, the rendered HTML would once again be manipulated without JSF's knowledge.

The trouble you get into when attempting to use ad hoc Ajax in JSF is that the rendered page gets out of sync with the server-side UI component model. The next authentic JSF postback is utterly confused, often resulting in unexpected behavior. Frustrated developers pointed the finger at JSF for being too rigid. The real problem, though, is the developer not appreciating JSF's server-centric application model and the benefits it provides.

The intent of JSF is to let you develop enterprise applications primarily in Java, with a reasonable amount of declarative markup for connecting Java components to user interface components (a linkage known as *binding*). Ajax, on the other hand, tempts you to become involved in the low-level concerns of hand-coded Dynamic HTML (DHTML) and JavaScript.

Programming models aside, JSF was designed to manage the UI. When it gets left out of the loop, an impedance mismatch develops. The proper way to use Ajax with JSF is to put JSF in charge of the Ajax communication, thus embracing JSF's server-centric model. This approach extends the value proposition of JSF to cover the development of *rich* Java-based applications without needing to introduce the complexity of JavaScript to the process. Both Ajax4jsf and ICEfaces position Ajax so that it honors the JSF model.

12.1.2 *Ajax4jsf and ICEfaces open a communication channel to JSF*

The main draw of Ajax is that it allows communication between the browser and the server to proceed in the background without disrupting the user. In a JSF application, it's just as important to keep an open channel of communication between the rendered page and the server-side UI component tree. That's because, as soon as an Ajax request is issued, the rendered page is at risk of becoming stale. It must be synchronized with the server-side UI component tree as soon as possible to prevent its integrity from being compromised.

Although the outlook for the JSF and Ajax marriage may seem grim from this description, Ajax4jsf and ICEfaces each provide a lightweight Ajax bridge that keeps the lines of communication open. Even better, it's mostly transparent to the developer. Although the first ICEfaces release (August 2005) came six months earlier than Ajax4jsf (March 2006), I want to start by discussing Ajax4jsf because it enables you introduce Ajax into JSF incrementally.

AJAX-ENABLING JSF WITH SUPPORT FROM AJAX4JSF

The challenge of introducing Ajax into JSF is that the standard UI components, and plenty of third-party UI components, have no awareness of Ajax. Rather than mandating that you switch to an Ajax-based UI component set, RichFaces developer Alexander Smirnov developed a way to weave Ajax into JSF transparently, a solution now

Ajax4jsf or RichFaces—which is it?

RichFaces is a visual JSF component set that's based on the Ajax4jsf concept and APIs. Ajax4jsf was once its own project, but now it's bundled with RichFaces. The Ajax4jsf tags are geared specifically toward adding Ajax capabilities to non-Ajax components, such as the standard JSF palette. RichFaces components natively support the Ajax4jsf interaction. The *rich* in RichFaces credits both its support for Ajax and its attractive look and feel.

known as Ajax4jsf. The mechanism he invented is so transparent, in fact, that it can be used to "Ajax-enable" any JSF page without the UI components having any awareness they're participating in an Ajax request. This one library took JSF from being Ajax-inept to being one of the most compelling approaches to Ajax.

While the Ajax4jsf component library contains a broad set of UI component tags, the tag that gets the heaviest use, almost disproportionately so, is `<a:support>` (often written as `<a4j:support>`). It's used to bind a user-initiated JavaScript event to a server-side action invoked via Ajax and to designate regions of the page that get rerendered from the Ajax response, encompassing the essence of Ajax4jsf.

A PATCHWORK OF UPDATES

The Ajax4jsf process is depicted in figure 12.1. When a request is sent out by Ajax4jsf, the JSF life cycle is invoked, just like with a standard JSF request. However, since the

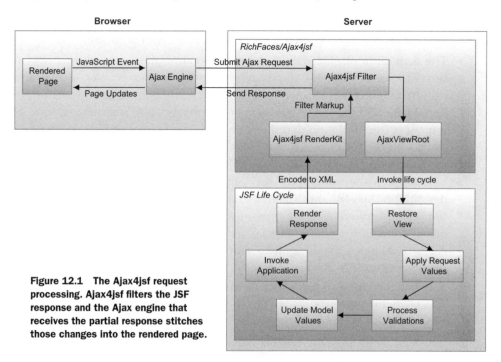

Figure 12.1   The Ajax4jsf request processing. Ajax4jsf filters the JSF response and the Ajax engine that receives the partial response stitches those changes into the rendered page.

request occurs using Ajax, the page doesn't change, at least not immediately. To ensure that the rendered page doesn't become stale, Ajax4jsf lets you declaratively control which areas of the UI to synchronize. Prior to the rendered page being sent back to the Ajax engine, Ajax4jsf extracts the corresponding markup and returns only a set of "patches" (i.e., XHTML fragments) to the browser. The Ajax engine cuts out the dead areas of the UI and stitches in the replacements. Since the state of these areas remains consistent with the server-side UI component tree, any JSF-related actions triggered in those areas behave as expected.

Let's put this process into practice on the golf course search screen. Right now, when the user clicks the Search button to filter the results, it causes a full-page refresh. It would be faster and less disruptive to simply replace the results table, the area of the page we want to rerender. First, we need to assign an id to the results panel, giving it a "handle":

```
<rich:panel id="searchResultsPanel">
  <f:facet name="header">Course search results</f:facet>
  <rich:dataTable var="course" value="#{courseList.resultList}" ...
</rich:panel>
```

Next, we nest the `<a:support>` tag within an input field in the search form, tying a JavaScript event triggered by this field to an invocation of the JSF life cycle. To ensure that the search runs as soon as possible but not before the user is done typing, we choose to bind to the input field's onblur event (i.e., when it loses focus). We also tell Ajax4jsf which area of the page to rerender by declaring a component id in the reRender attribute:

```
<h:input value="#{courseList.course.name}">
  <a:support event="onblur" reRender="searchResultsPanel"/>
</h:input>
```

When the user tabs or clicks away from the input field, an Ajax request is sent, invoking the JSF life cycle just as though the user had clicked the Search button. But in this case, the response is filtered by Ajax4jsf and only the results panel is sent back. The page is then updated incrementally to reveal the new search results.

The search is able to execute without an explicit action because the Query component automatically detects when the search criteria has changed. You may have a situation that requires an explicit action to be called in order for the search to execute. Ajax4jsf lets you specify either an action or an action listener on the `<a:support>` tag, using the `action` and `actionListener` attributes, respectively. This turns the `<a:support>` tag into a UI command component, which isn't triggered by a click but rather a JavaScript event:

```
<a:support event="onblur" reRender="searchResultsPanel"
  action="#{hypotheticalSearchAction.search}"/>
```

If we were to continue Ajax-enabling every input field in the search form, the only problem would be having to specify the `reRender` attribute each time. Fortunately, Ajax4jsf supports a way to make certain branches of the tree support "autografting." By wrapping the `<a:outputPanel ajaxRendered="true">` tag around a region of the page, it tells Ajax4jsf to automatically rerender that region whenever an Ajax request passes through the Ajax engine. Let's apply this to the search results panel:

```
<a:outputPanel ajaxRendered="true" layout="none">
  <rich:panel>
    <f:facet name="header">Course search results</f:facet>
    <rich:dataTable var="course" value="#{courseList.resultList}"...
  </rich:panel>
</a:outputPanel>
```

With the autografting output panel in place, the `<a:support>` tags no longer have to specify the reRender attribute. If you're doing other Ajax operations on the page, you can localize the Ajax activity that triggers automatic rerendering by wrapping a portion of the page in `<a:region>`. In this case, you might wrap the search form and results panel.

Although it may seem like a lot of work to merge the changes back into the UI, this work is far outweighed by the benefits. It ensures the integrity of the page is maintained, it makes Ajax transparent to the developer, and, since the response contains only necessary updates and not a full HTML document, JSF can behave like an efficient event-driven framework and the user's activity isn't disrupted by a page refresh.

Ajax4jsf lets you adopt Ajax without having to write JavaScript or replace your existing components, but it still requires that you do a fair amount of work to configure the Ajax interactions. Depending on what you're trying to accomplish, this can be either a good or a bad thing. One of the limitations of Ajax4jsf is that the marked regions of the page are synchronized even if the markup hasn't changed. Regions that aren't specified are prone to falling out of date. What you are basically missing is intelligent synchronization of the UI, a central concern in ICEfaces.

INTELLIGENT UI SYNCHRONIZATION WITH ICEFACES

ICEfaces is an Ajax extension for JavaServer Faces that regards Ajax as a framework concern rather than a developer concern. Ajax-based JSF applications using ICEfaces are virtually indistinguishable from non-Ajax JSF applications. The key lies with the ICEfaces rendering process. Rather than rendering to a stream that's sent directly to the browser, each view is rendered into a Document Object Model (DOM) on the server, another progression of the UI component tree. The changes to the DOM are detected after each invocation of the JSF life cycle and only the corresponding markup is sent to the browser. As with Ajax4jsf, an Ajax bridge resident in the browser is responsible for merging these updates into the page, as illustrated in figure 12.2.

There are two key benefits to the ICEfaces approach (which is known as Direct-to-DOM [D2D] rendering). First, it reflects an efficient use of the network, making it especially suitable for mobile applications. Second, the developer doesn't need to decide which areas of the page need to be rerendered when an event is triggered—that's something the framework decides at runtime. In fact, the developer doesn't have to do anything to Ajax-enable the UI components on the page. Ajax is baked in at a much deeper level so that every interaction is channeled through an Ajax request.

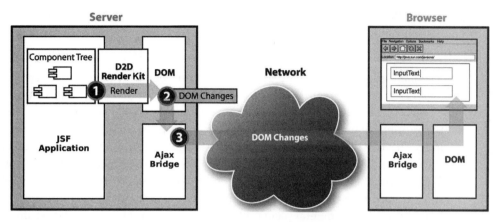

Figure 12.2   An illustration of how changes in the UI component tree are channeled through the ICEfaces Ajax bridge and merged back into the rendered page in the browser. The numbers indicate the sequence of events

TIP   If a long-running conversation isn't active, the conversation id changes during the Ajax request. Since Seam automatically appends the conversation id to Seam UI command components, this confuses ICEfaces into thinking that areas of the page have changed, resulting in a much larger Ajax response than necessary. To remedy this problem, you either need to ensure that the conversation id isn't rendered somewhere in the HTML markup or operate within the context of a long-running conversation.

Let's look at the course search example again, this time augmenting it using ICEfaces. Since it's not necessary to declare which areas of the page are synchronized, we're only concerned with the search form. Here's one of the input fields and the submit button:

```
<h:inputText value="#{courseList.course.name}"/>
<h:commandButton value="Search"/>
```

Hmm. That's interesting—no special Ajax tags. As I mentioned, ICEfaces transparently adds Ajax interactions to the page. It does so by replacing the standard JSF component renderers with renderers cognizant of the D2D mechanism. In order for the page to be updated in place, you simply forgo use of a JSF navigation event, guaranteed in this case since an action isn't specified in the UI command button. That raises an important point. Although requests are made over Ajax, JSF navigation rules are still honored. The same goes for Ajax4jsf.

There is a key improvement that can be made in the ICEfaces example. Currently, the Ajax request only happens when the Search button is activated, whereas in the Ajax4jsf example, the search occurs when the input field loses focus. This behavior is accomplished in ICEfaces using a feature known as partial submit. While it's possible to trigger a partial submit using a built-in JavaScript function, in the spirit of transparency we use the ICEfaces input component tag to hide this JavaScript behind declarative markup. This tag also brings the benefit of component styling.

```
<ice:inputText value="#{courseList.course.name}" partialSubmit="true"/>
```

The `partialSubmit` attribute activates the same behavior as the `<a:support event="onblur">` tag in Ajax4jsf. Partial submit is explored in more depth in section 12.2.

Ajax4jsf and ICEfaces are about more than just Ajax. They are about letting you perform incremental page updates synchronized from the state on the server. You no longer have to design pages around the full-page refresh model. Instead, you can consider fine-grained manipulation of the page to achieve rich effects in the application. The patchwork of updates that are merged back into the rendered page behave as though they'd been there all along (meaning when the page was initially rendered). In addition to incremental page updates, RichFaces and ICEfaces offer styling of components, rich widgets, drag and drop, visual effects, and many more features that set your application apart from a classic web application.

The big question at this point is, what's Seam's role in all of this Ajax stuff? That's the real beauty of it. Seam just keeps doing what it does best.

12.1.3 Seam's role in Ajax-based JSF requests

While the Ajax requests allow the page to continuously interact with Seam, there's nothing that Seam has to do differently. The JSF life cycle is still invoked and therefore Seam treats each request just as it would any other postback. That doesn't mean Seam has nothing to add, though. On the contrary, you find that Seam's stateful design lends itself perfectly to the Ajax-enabled JSF environment. Here are a few ways Seam adds value:

- *Maintain server-side state*—Seam can connect the state from one Ajax request to the next, avoiding the negative impact of pounding the server's resources. Both the page scope and a long-running conversation work well here. Seam can even facilitate an application transaction performed entirely over Ajax.
- *Contribute outjected context variables*—Any action invoked during an Ajax request can trigger bijection. The outjected context variables are available to the regions of the view being rerendered.
- *Dry-run the JSF life cycle*—Ajax4jsf can ask JSF to run through the life cycle without performing actions or navigations to verify that form data is acceptable. Seam's integration with Hibernate Validator is of most interest here.
- *Notify changes in application state*—Seam's event/observer model, its asynchronous dispatcher, and its integration with JMS offer ways to notify components of a change in the application's state. When combined with ICEfaces' Ajax Push, presentation changes can be sent to browsers with having to wait for interaction from the user.

Aside from the last point, covered in detail in section 12.3, the items in this list remain consistent with points made throughout the book. The only difference now is that everything is happening in closer to real time and the browser isn't spinning its wheels reloading the page. You do need to be aware that Ajax requests occur more frequently, so there's a greater chance that multiple requests in the same conversation will arrive at the server simultaneously. See the accompanying sidebar on the topic of conversation contention.

No configuration is necessary to use RichFaces/Ajax4jsf with Seam. As long as the RichFaces JAR files are present on the classpath and the SeamFilter is registered in the web.xml descriptor, Seam automatically activates the Ajax4jsf filter. Seam doesn't automatically configure ICEfaces because it requires more than just a filter. Consult the output of the ICEfaces version of seam-gen or the ICEfaces reference documentation for instructions.

Concurrent Ajax requests contending for ownership of the conversation

Seam serializes access to conversations, requiring requests to obtain a lock in order to restore a long-running conversation. A common problem encountered when using Ajax4jsf with Seam is contention for a conversation lock, reported by the error message "The conversation ended, timed out or was processing another request." This problem can happen when multiple Ajax requests requesting the same conversation arrive at the server simultaneously. If the amount of time that a request has to wait exceeds the concurrent request timeout, Seam will abort the request.

One solution is to ensure that Ajax4jsf requests are serialized so that they never contend for a conversation. Related requests are placed into a named sequence using the eventsQueue attribute on RichFaces and Ajax4jsf component tags:

```
<a:support event="onblur" eventsQueue="nameOfSequence" .../>
```

For information about eventsQueue, see the RichFaces reference documentation.[1]

There is still the problem of Ajax and non-Ajax requests contending for the same conversation. To minimize the chance of a timeout occurring as the result of a lock contention, you can increase the timeout period. The timeout value (in milliseconds) is set by configuring the built-in component named manager in the component descriptor:

```
<core:manager concurrent-request-timeout="5000" .../>
```

You should try to eliminate concurrent requests for a conversation before increasing this timeout since leaving threads waiting on the server can impact performance.

Contention for the conversation isn't seen when using ICEfaces since the ICEfaces framework automatically synchronizes requests from the same page to ensure that the server-side DOM remains uncorrupted.

I walk you through more examples showing how the abstraction offered by Ajax4jsf and ICEfaces can be leveraged to enhance the user experience. We first explore live form

---

[1] http://www.jboss.org/file-access/default/members/jbossrichfaces/freezone/docs/devguide/en/html/index.html

validation using partial submit and then look at how ICEfaces can push changes in application state to the client without having to wait for the user to perform an action.

12.2 *Partial form submits*

One of the most frequently requested features in JSF is client-side form validation. Although there are certainly benefits to the performance and near real-time execution of client-side validation, there are equal benefits to having these validations performed on the server instead. Even if the validation passes in the UI, it's still necessary to validate on the server since JavaScript validation can't be trusted (execution of JavaScript is voluntary). In addition, validations often need access to server-side resources to arrive at a decision. Thus, client-side validation doesn't provide that much value. What developers are really asking for is instant, or "live," validation. That doesn't mean it has to happen strictly on the client.

12.2.1 *Live validation*

Both Ajax4jsf and ICEfaces accommodate live form validation using a feature known as partial submit. You have seen this feature used once already with ICEfaces as a way to trigger an Ajax-based form submit from a JavaScript event. What you may not realize is that this flag also enables intelligent form processing, resulting in only partial validation of the form. Ajax4jsf separates the two concerns by letting you control whether one or all of the inputs are validated when an Ajax form submit is triggered from a user-initiated event.

Before getting into the details of how live validation is set up, I want to briefly discuss how server-centric validation, based primarily on Hibernate Validator constraints, centralizes validation concerns, reduces duplication of effort, and ensures that validations are consistent across the application. This discussion sets the stage for the examples that follow.

END-TO-END CONSTRAINTS USING HIBERNATE VALIDATOR

Using partial form submits, it's possible to enforce Hibernate Validator constraints instantly, as well as other JSF validators registered on a field, without having to duplicate the effort of writing client-side validators. It's pretty easy to branch out from there and apply business validations as well. In the end, all the validation work is done in one place, at one time.

As a reminder, Hibernate Validator annotations define constraints on properties of a model object. You first saw these annotations in chapter 2 when they were translated by seam-gen from constraints on database fields and added to the properties of the entity classes. A wealth of constraints are provided for you out of the box. For instance, the `@Email` annotation on the `emailAddress` property of the `Member` entity ensures that the syntax of the email address is valid:

```
@Column(name = "email_address", nullable = false)
@Email @NotNull
public String getEmailAddress() {
    return emailAddress;
}
```

You can also write your own constraint by defining a custom annotation, implementing the Hibernate `Validator` interface, and declaring the implementation in the `@ValidatorClass` meta-annotation on your custom annotation. For a list of built-in constraints and information about how to author your own, see the Hibernate Validator reference documentation.[2]

In chapter 3, you learned that it's possible to stretch Hibernate Validator constraints all the way to the view by using a Seam model validator tag (`<s:validate>` within an input component or `<s:validateAll>` around a set of input components). To take it a step further, constraints can be enforced in response to a user-initiated event using the partial submit feature in either Ajax4jsf or ICEfaces. Let's first look at the ICEfaces approach.

INTELLIGENT FORM PROCESSING USING ICEFACES

The partial submit in ICEfaces is more accurately described as intelligent form processing and partial validation rather than an incomplete form post, as the name implies. Before explaining how it works, let's first consider the problem to be solved.

If you submit a form while the user is still working on it, it's likely that there are required fields that the user hasn't gotten to yet. When the *Process Validations* phase of the JSF life cycle runs, it would normally flag these required fields as invalid and the page would be sprinkled with validation errors. As a result, the application appears impatient with the user's progress. ICEfaces circumvents this issue by temporarily marking required fields as optional during a partial submit. This allows the validation process to focus on the fields the user has already filled out, for which the user will welcome validation feedback.

As you saw earlier, partial submit is enabled using the ICEfaces input component. From there, getting the Hibernate Validator constraints to be enforced when the field loses focus is just a matter of registering the Seam model validator on the input:

```
<ice:inputText id="emailAddress" value="#{newGolfer.emailAddress}"
  required="true" partialSubmit="true">
  <s:validate/>
</ice:inputText>
```

If you're using a seam-gen application, you can decorate the input component with the provided composition template to preclude the use of the model validator tag:

```
<s:decorate id="emailField" template="layout/edit.xhtml">
  <ui:define name="label">Email address</ui:define>
  <ice:inputText id="emailAddress" value="#{newGolfer.emailAddress}"
    required="true" partialSubmit="true"/>
</s:decorate>
```

That's pretty much all there is to it. Let's try this with Ajax4jsf.

SINGLING OUT A FIELD USING AJAX4JSF

The way that Ajax4jsf defines partial submit is more true to the name. You instruct Ajax4jsf to process a single field by enabling the `ajaxSingle` attribute on `<a:support>`,

---

[2] http://www.hibernate.org/hib_docs/validator/reference/en/html/validator-defineconstraints.html

overriding the default behavior of submitting the entire form. Once again, this prevents overeager validation of form fields. However, instead of temporarily marking
fields as optional, like ICEfaces, Ajax4jsf pretends as though the form has only one field,
the one that triggered the event. The benefit is that the user only sees a validation error
for that field, no matter what state the other fields are in. The downside is that this feature cannot be used if you need to do interfield validation.

To add instant validation of the email address using the Hibernate Validator constraint with Ajax4jsf, you nest both `<a:support>` and `<s:validate>` in the input
component:

```
<h:inputText id="emailAddress" value="#{newGolfer.emailAddress}"
  required="true">
  <a:support id="emailAddressCheck" event="onblur" reRender="emailAddress"
    ajaxSingle="true" bypassUpdates="true"/>
  <s:validate/>
</h:inputText>
```

You can use the component template included in the seam-gen project as before to
isolate the markup and incorporate the validation error message. Figure 12.3 shows
an email address validation error in the registration form.

Figure 12.3   Live
validation in the UI
performed using
partial submit

Notice in this example I snuck in another new attribute, `bypassUpdates`. This attribute tells Ajax4jsf to short-circuit the JSF life cycle as soon as the *Process Validations* JSF
life-cycle phase is complete. The motivation for doing this is to get the validation done
quicker and to prevent the partial form submit from making changes to the model. If
a managed entity is loaded in the editor, and you aren't using manual flushing, updating the model would result in the database being updated at the end of the request.
You can leave off `bypassUpdates` if you do want the model to be updated, perhaps to
allow the user to switch between conversations without losing the values entered.

In addition to applying conversion and model validations on the trip to the server,
you can weave in some business-savvy validations in an action or event listener
method.

12.2.2 *Business-savvy validations*

The Hibernate Validator annotations focus primarily on constraints. To perform validations that are driven by business rules or contextual state, you need to turn to an action
component, which is better equipped to handle these "business-savvy" validations.

Once again, you'll be using partial form submit, but this time you need to register
a method that executes custom validation logic (or delegates the work to another
component). You have a wide variety of options for associating a method with an

input. My preference is to listen for the component's value change event. Let's consider an example where a business-savvy validation is needed in the Open 18 registration form.

Choosing a unique username can often be a challenge, especially on a popular site. Therefore, we want to validate not only that the username is syntactically correct but also that it isn't already taken. The first step is to define a value change listener method on the `RegisterAction` component that performs the check and warns the user if it's taken. When you're writing a method that listens for a value change event, it's important to understand that the submitted value is in a transient state on the component and hasn't yet been transferred to the property bound to the input. You access the submitted value by calling the `getNewValue()` method on the `ValueChangeEvent` object passed as an argument to the method. From there, you can check for a duplicate username:

```
public void verifyUsernameAvailable(ValueChangeEvent e) {
    String username = (String) e.getNewValue();
    if (!isUsernameAvailable(username)) {
        facesMessages.addToControl(e.getComponent().getId(),
            "Sorry, username already taken");
    }
}

public boolean isUsernameAvailable(String username) {
    return entityManager.createQuery(
        "select m from Member m where m.username = ?1")
        .setParameter(1, username).getResultList().size() == 0;
}
```

The next step is to register this method as a value change listener on the username field:

```
<h:inputText value="#{newGolfer.username}"
    valueChangeListener="#{registerAction.verifyUsernameAvailable}"...>
```

Let's now shift the focus from slapping the user's wrist to playing the role of a helping hand.

12.2.3 *Working alongside the user to fill out a form*

Since Ajax4jsf and ICEfaces have the ability to rerender areas of the page, it's possible to assign values to form inputs or alter the composition of the form (i.e., add, remove, or modify elements). These changes become visible when the presentation changes are delivered to the browser. Let's consider a simple example.

Each U.S. zip code maps to a city and state. We can save the user time by automatically populating the city and state fields when the user enters a zip code. To accomplish this task, a value change listener is registered on the zip code field. Any time the value of that field changes and the value is considered valid, a value change event is fired and the listener called. Within the listener, the zip code is used to look up the city and state, and those values are assigned to the values of the city and state input components.

Before implementing the logic, we need to determine how to get a handle on the city and state input components from within an event listener method. A UI component is located by passing its key to the `findComponent()` method on any other UI component. Seam provides a map named `uiComponent` that's used for the same purpose, except it searches from the root of the UI tree. That brings us to the key that's used as the lookup value.

JSF stores each component in the tree under a *client id*, which is a qualified path to the component. This path is built by combining the component's ID with the ID of each ancestor component that is a `NamingContainer`, delimited by colons. For instance, the client id of the city component is `facility:cityField:city`, where `facility` is the ID of the form, `cityField` is the ID of the field decorator, and `city` is the ID of the input. To start the search from the root of the UI component tree, you add a leading colon to the path.

You can also get a reference to a UI component by binding it to a property of a Seam component using the `binding` attribute on the component tag. This works just like binding an input value to a property, only in this case, you're binding the UI component itself.

Let's get back to work. For the purpose of this demonstration, the value change method uses a canned response, but you can just as easily consult a database, web service, or service layer to get real values. This code also shows two ways to locate a UI component:

```
@In Map<String, UIComponent> uiComponent;
public void updateCityAndState(ValueChangeEvent e) {
    String zipCode = (String) e.getNewValue();
    UIComponent city = e.getComponent()
        .findComponent(":facility:cityField:city");
    UIComponent state = uiComponent.get("facility:stateField:state");
    if ("20724".equals(zipCode)) {
        ((EditableValueHolder) city).setSubmittedValue("Laurel");
        ((EditableValueHolder) state).setSubmittedValue("MD");
    }
}
```

The final step is to register this method to listen for the value change event on the zip field. The Ajax4jsf version, shown here, marks the fields to be rerendered, which isn't necessary when using ICEfaces:

```
<h:inputText id="zip" size="5" value="#{facilityHome.instance.zip}"
    valueChangeListener="#{facilityHome.updateCityAndState}">
    <a:support event="onblur" bypassUpdates="true" ajaxSingle="true"
        reRender="zipField,cityField,stateField"/>
</h:inputText>
```

Most of this section has focused on features that are supported in both Ajax4jsf and ICEfaces, highlighting the slightly different approach taken by the two frameworks. In the next section, we look at Ajax Push, a feature pioneered by ICEfaces that allows server-initiated asynchronous presentation updates.

12.3 *Ajax Push with ICEfaces*

The other distinguishing feature of ICEfaces is its Ajax Push (aka "Comet") capability. The *A* in *Ajax* stands for *asynchronous*, and ICEfaces is truly asynchronous. Not only is the page updated in the background in response to user events, but the page can also be updated from the server at any time, independently of user events. One use for this is to send users notifications (for instance, to notify a user when it's his or her tee time), but what is really interesting is to use Ajax Push for collaboration between multiple users.

Adding Push features to your ICEfaces application is straightforward: first, update the model with the current state; then, notify those users interested in the current state. Updating the model is a basic function of a JSF application; how do we update the users? Let's jump into an example to find out.

In chapter 10, you developed a module that allows golfers to enter their score for a round of golf. One of the driving factors for a golfer to publish a round is to get ranked on the leaderboard (i.e., best scores per tee set). For simplicity of demonstration, let's assume that the leaderboard is managed "in-memory" in an application-scoped component, shown in listing 12.1. Each time a round is entered by a golfer, an event named `roundEntered` is raised, which broadcasts the `Round` instance. The leaderboard manager observes this event and attempts to rank the round. This is where Ajax Push comes in. If the round gets ranked, ICEfaces is instructed to immediately rerender the pages associated with the corresponding leaderboard group as a result of a call to the `SessionRenderer.render()` method. The page changes are calculated by ICEfaces and are pushed to the user's browsers.

> **Listing 12.1 A component that manages and renders the leaderboards**

```
package org.open18.action;
import ...;
import org.icefaces.x.core.push.SessionRenderer;

@Name("leaderboardManager")
@Scope(ScopeType.APPLICATION)
public class LeaderboardManager {
    private Map<Long, List<Round>> topRoundsByTeeSet =
        new ConcurrentHashMap<Long, List<Round>>();

    public List<Round> getTopRoundsForTeeSet(Long id) {
        return Collections.unmodifiableMap(topRoundsByTeeSet.get(id));
    }

    @Observer("roundEntered")                          ◁——┐ Observes insertion
    public synchronized void checkRank(Round rnd) {        │ of new round
        Long teeSetId = rnd.getTeeSet().getId();
        String leaderboard = "leaderboard-" + teeSetId;
        if (!topRoundsByTeeSet.containsKey(teeSetId)) {
            topRoundsByTeeSet.put(teeSetId, new ArrayList<Round>());
        }
        List<Round> topRounds = topRoundsByTeeSet.get(teeSetId);
        for (int i = 0, len = topRounds.size(); i < len; i++) {
            if (rnd.getTotalScore() <= topRounds.get(i).getTotalScore()) {
                topRounds.set(i, rnd);
```

```
                SessionRenderer.render(leaderboard);        ◁─┐
                return;                                          │
        }                                                        │   Forces
    }                                                            │   leaderboard
    if (topRounds.size() < 10) {                                 │   to refresh
        topRounds.add(rnd);                                      │
        SessionRenderer.render(leaderboard);          ◁─────────┘
    }
}
}
```

So how does a user become a member of the group for a leaderboard? First, the user is presented with a select menu of tee sets. After making a selection, the user clicks a UI command button, which binds the tee set selection to the teeSet property of an action component and invokes the followLeaderboard() method on that same component:

```
public void followLeaderboard() {
    SessionRenderer.addCurrentSession("leaderboard-" + teeSet.getId());
}
```

Once the user is a member of a leaderboard group, whichever page the user is currently viewing will be updated incrementally as soon as that group is rendered. For instance, if a user is viewing a leaderboard for a tee set when a new round becomes ranked, the score appears immediately in the list.

Using just two methods on SessionRenderer, we've transformed our application into a new communication tool that lets users keep up with their favorite golfers in real time. The development methodology is also natural: build a conventional JSF application with Seam; turn it into an Ajax application by including the ICEfaces JAR files; then make it into a multiuser application by invoking server-side rendering in response to a specific application event.

The possibilities of what you can do with an Ajax-based JSF component palette are virtually endless. Unfortunately, this chapter is not, so the story must end here. To get the most out of these libraries, I recommend consulting a dedicated resource on the topic. Max Katz, one of the developers of RichFaces, provides in-depth coverage of RichFaces in his book *Using RichFaces* (Apress, 2008). For more information on ICE-faces, check out icefaces.org[3] or *Ajax in Practice* (Manning, 2007), featuring Ted Goddard from the ICEfaces project. You may be tempted to mix Ajax4jsf and ICEfaces, or any Ajax-enabled component set for that matter, but it's not recommended. The Ajax engines collide with each other while attempting to manipulate the rendered page. Expect this situation to improve once JSF 2.0 is finalized, which will define a standard Ajax mechanism for JSF components. There's no such restriction for incorporating additional non-Ajax component sets.

As cool as declarative Ajax using JSF sounds, you may be looking for a way to do Ajax in Seam without JSF, perhaps using a high-level JavaScript library such as Dojo or jQuery. The Seam developers recognized that there is value in being able to talk to a

---

[3] The developer guides for ICEfaces are located at http://www.icefaces.org/main/resources/documentation.
iface.

Seam component directly from JavaScript and therefore introduced the JavaScript remoting module.

12.4   JavaScript remoting to Seam

JavaScript remoting is an alternative to Ajax-based JSF requests for establishing a channel of communication between the browser and the server. It supports using JavaScript to invoke a method on a server-side object as if it were local to the browser. Seam's JavaScript remoting library is inspired by the Direct Web Remoting (DWR) project,[4] but designed specifically for accessing Seam components. The interaction with the server-side object is performed using Ajax requests, but the requests are encapsulated within dynamically generated JavaScript proxy objects, so you never have to interface with the XMLHttpRequest object directly.

In JavaScript remoting, the client (browser) and the server (Seam container) are fused together as one, establishing a continuity between local and remote operations. The interchange between the client and server during a remoting request resembles a conventional remote procedure call (RPC) over Java RMI or SOAP, except that JavaScript remoting is far more lightweight and mostly transparent to the developer.

Here's a sampling of tasks that are well suited as JavaScript remoting tasks:

- Facilitating a user interaction that's tangential to the rendered page
- Persisting entities that don't have a visual representation
- Starting and completing tasks in a business process
- Sending an email in response to a user-triggered event
- Transmitting a user interface error or statistic to the server to be logged
- Monitoring or polling for a value maintained on the server

This section provides an overview of the JavaScript remoting technique, explains how to expose your Seam components as endpoints, and presents examples that use this style of browser-to-server communication.

12.4.1   Transparent Ajax

Throughout this book, I've demonstrated the ability of Seam's component model to manage state and provide access to a wide range of technologies. By incorporating Seam's remoting library into your application, you enable JavaScript to tap into that server-side model and reap its benefits. In the same way that the @Name annotation on a component makes that component accessible to JSF and the EL, the @WebRemote annotation on a component method makes that method accessible to JavaScript, effectively binding JavaScript code to server-side components with little effort.

COMMUNICATING THROUGH STUBS

In order for this transparency to be possible, Seam dynamically generates JavaScript classes[5] that represent the server-side components. These classes are known as stubs. As far as JavaScript is concerned, the stub object *is* the remote object.

---

[4]   http://getahead.org/dwr

[5]   A JavaScript class is a misnomer since JavaScript is technically a prototype-based language. However, it's possible to pretend that the prototype construct is an actual class if you treat it as one.

The stub is responsible for carrying out method execution on the server-side component instance. When a method is invoked on the stub, a new Ajax request is prepared and sent across the wire to the server. The request communicates the method to execute and carries with it parameters that need to be passed to the remote method. If the method has a return value, that value is encoded into the response of the Ajax request. As the response comes back across the wire, it's received by the remoting framework, which converts the return value, if present, into a JavaScript object. This process is illustrated in figure 12.4.

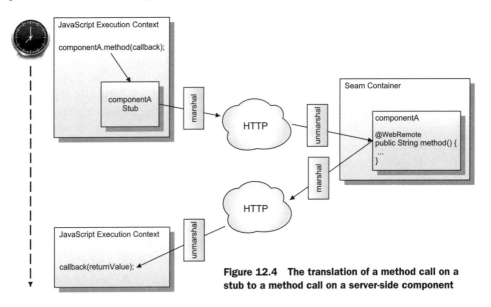

Figure 12.4   The translation of a method call on a stub to a method call on a server-side component

What it comes down to is that JavaScript remoting enables the browser to speak the native tongue of the server. Although it may seem like the execution is happening in the local lingo—JavaScript—in reality the server is executing the code and the stub objects are marshaling the data back and forth.

CUTTING COSTS BY SIDESTEPPING JSF

JavaScript remoting is about cutting out the middleman and giving JavaScript access to Seam components without the overhead of restoring the JSF component tree and venturing through the JSF life cycle. The product is a much smaller request. It also gives the browser direct access to the return value of the method invoked, which is not straightforward in JSF.

Seam remoting requests target the `SeamResourceServlet` rather than the JSF servlet, effectively sidestepping the JSF life cycle. Of course, you never interface with this servlet directly since the negation with the servlet is handled by the stub. When the method is invoked, it has full access to components and context variables. What's not present, though, is the JSF component tree. That means you can't access page-scoped or UI components during a remoting request.

Let's see how to get Seam to generate the stubs, how they're used to perform remote method invocations, and how the return value can be captured in your JavaScript code.

12.4.2 *Giving the browser access to Seam components*

The reason acronyms like RPC and SOAP give developers the chills is because they require a lot of commitment. Surely, Seam remoting would suffer the same fate if it were difficult to set up. The good news is that it's not. In fact, it's shockingly easy. Only two steps are involved in making your server-side component accessible to your JavaScript code:

- Declare one or more methods on the component as accessible via remoting.
- Import the JavaScript remoting framework and stub objects into the browser.

The first step is a necessary formality. Seam could allow remote access to methods across all components, but there is an element of security to be concerned about. Therefore, remoting is disabled for a method unless made exempt from this constraint. If this discussion worries you, realize that remoting just adds a new path to the method, not a more insecure one. You can use the restrictions you learned about in chapter 11 to lock down methods from unauthorized users, regardless of how they're called.

The second step is what builds the JavaScript stubs and other auxiliary types. Fortunately, Seam makes this a one-liner. Let's consider how each step is accomplished.

DECLARING A REMOTING METHOD

You declare methods that you want to be involved in remoting requests using the `@WebRemote` annotation, summarized in table 12.1. The `@WebRemote` annotation is placed differently depending on whether you're exposing a method on an EJB component or a JavaBean. To provide access to a method on an EJB component, you add the `@WebRemote` annotation to the method declaration on the local interface annotated with `@Local`. The remote EJB interface isn't supported. To provide access to a Java-Bean, you simply add the annotation to a method on the JavaBean class.

There's nothing special about a remoting method. It can accept any number of parameters of any type and can have a return value. For the most part, the type conversions are handled as you'd expect. The main difference is how the call to the

Table 12.1 The `@WebRemote` annotation

Name:	WebRemote
Purpose:	Declares that the method is allowed to be invoked through the JavaScript remoting library. The JavaScript stub object that Seam generates for this component will include this method.
Target:	METHOD

Attribute	Type	Function
exclude	String[]	A list of dot-notation paths that dictate which properties of the return object should be filtered out. Only relevant if a value is returned. Default: none.

method is handled. If the method returns a value, it's received by the browser asynchronously. The @WebRemote annotation can declare certain properties on the return object, using dot notation, that should be filtered out (nullified) before the object is returned to the browser.

Once the return object is transferred into the JavaScript context, it's accessed using the same methods that you'd use in Java. That includes maps, collections, and built-in Java types like java.util.Date. Transparency is the key here.

> **NOTE**   If you add a @WebRemote method to a hot deployable class, you need to restart the application for the change to be picked up. The stub generator caches the available methods and is not aware of the hot deployable activity.

Let's consider an example. Members of the Open 18 community can keep their golf trivia skills sharp by quizzing themselves. The Trivia component, shown in listing 12.2, manages a set of golf trivia questions, which are retrieved when the component is instantiated. It has two remoting calls: one to draw a question from the list and one to verify the response.

Each trivia question is represented by an instance of the TriviaQuestion class, which is a simple JPA entity class with three properties: id, question, and answer. Here's where things get interesting. When the trivia question is sent to the browser, you only want to send the question and the id, not the answer. Otherwise, those tech-savvy members could use Firebug[6] to inspect the Ajax request and steal the answer. This filtering is accomplished by declaring answer in the exclude attribute in the @WebRemote annotation. You can also use the exclude attribute to nullify large text or binary fields on the return object that make the response unnecessarily large. You can reach nested properties using dot notation just as you would with the EL. It's also possible to exclude a property from a type regardless of where it is in the hierarchy using the syntax [type].property. In this expression, type can be a component name or the qualified class name of a noncomponent.

> **Listing 12.2   A JavaScript remoting-capable JavaBean component**

```
package org.open18.action;
import ...;
import org.jboss.seam.annotations.remoting.WebRemote;

@Name("trivia")
@Scope(ScopeType.SESSION)
public class Trivia implements Serializable {
    @In private EntityManager entityManager;
    private List<TriviaQuestion> questions;

    @Create public void init() {
        questions = entityManager.createQuery(
            "select q from TriviaQuestion q").getResultList();
```

---

[6]   A web development add-on for Firefox, Firebug is available at http://www.getfirebug.com.

```
        }

        @WebRemote
        public boolean answerQuestion(Long id, String response) {
            TriviaQuestion questionInstance = findQuestion(id);
            if (questionInstance == null){
                return false;
            }
            return questionInstance.getAnswer().equals(response);
        }

        @WebRemote(exclude = "answer")
        public TriviaQuestion drawQuestion() {
            if (questions.size() == 0) {
                return null;
            }
            return questions.get(new Random().nextInt(questions.size()));
        }

        public TriviaQuestion findQuestion(Long id) {
            return entityManager.find(TriviaQuestion.class, id);
        }
    }
}
```

Makes method accessible to JavaScript (annotation for `answerQuestion`)

Applies filtering to object returned (annotation for `drawQuestion`)

Once the server-side component is prepared, it needs to be forged into JavaScript.

IMPORTING COMPONENT STUBS

Upon importing the JavaScript remoting framework, Seam doesn't automatically generate stubs for every Seam component that has a @WebRemote annotation. Instead, you instruct Seam to prepare a fixed set of component stubs that you need access to on a given page.

You can use the <s:remote> component tag to import the remoting framework and the component stubs. This tag produces HTML <script> tags, which request the remoting framework and stubs from the SeamResourceServlet. This tag's include attribute accepts a comma-separated list of component names to import. To import the components named trivia and componentA, you add the following declaration to your JSF view:

```
<s:remote include="trivia,componentA"/>
```

This declaration produces the following HTML markup, which you'd need to declare manually if you aren't using JSF:

```
<script type="text/javascript"
  src="seam/resource/remoting/resource/remote.js"></script>
<script type="text/javascript"
  src="seam/resource/remoting/interface.js?trivia&componentA"></script>
```

The first <script> tag imports the remoting framework, a static JavaScript file. The remoting framework amounts to a handful of JavaScript objects, such as Seam.Component and Seam.Remoting, that are used to access and create instances of stubs. The second <script> tag imports the executable stubs that Seam generates as well as type stubs for any Java type used as a parameter or return value by a @WebRemote method. Seam creates these additional stubs to marshal and unmarshal parameters and return values from the XML payload. There are three stub varieties.

THE THREE STUB VARIETIES

Not all stubs are created equal. There are stubs responsible for communicating with the server, and there are stubs that act as the payload exchanged with the server. A stub can't serve both roles. There is further distinction between nonexecutable stubs, or local stubs, depending on whether the Java class is a Seam component. The three stub varieties are

- Executable stub
- Local component stub
- Local type stub

When the remoting interface generator prepares the stub, it determines which stub to create based on the characteristics of the server-side component. Executable stubs are created for any component that has a `@WebRemote` method. Recall that for EJB session bean components, the `@WebRemote` annotation must be applied to methods on the local interface. As far as JavaScript knows, the server-side component represented by the executable stub has no other methods aside from the ones marked as `@WebRemote`. JavaScript can't distinguish what type of Seam component it is, either. Local stubs are covered in section 12.4.4. Right now, let's look at how to get a handle on an executable stub to invoke it.

12.4.3 *Making calls to a server-side component*

The `Seam.Component` JavaScript object acts as a mini-client-side version of the Seam container. The relationship between a component and a component instance, discussed in chapter 4, still applies. However, in the JavaScript remoting environment, the instance is an instance of a stub, not the instance from the server. You state your intent to execute a method on a component instance by invoking the equivalently named method on the stub. Only after the request is shipped off to the server is the actual instance retrieved from the Seam container and invoked.

GETTING A HANDLE ON AN EXECUTABLE STUB

You retrieve an instance of a stub using the `Seam.Component.getInstance()` method, which takes the component name as an argument. For example, you can get an instance of the stub for the component named `trivia` by executing

```
var trivia = Seam.Component.getInstance("trivia");
```

NOTE   The `newInstance()` method would also return an instance of an executable stub, but that method is intended for creating new local stub instances. The `getInstance()` method returns a singleton JavaScript object, which is sufficient for executable stubs.

The next step is to invoke a method on the executable stub and capture the return value. The only thing you have to wrap your head around is that the Ajax call is asynchronous.

EXECUTING A REMOTE METHOD ASYNCHRONOUSLY

You execute methods on an executable stub just as you would on a server-side instance of the component—well, not quite. There are two important differences. You already know that the stub only contains the methods that are marked as `@WebRemote`. The stub for the `Trivia` component only has the methods `drawQuestion()` and `answerQuestion()`, but not `findQuestion()`. The other difference is that the method on the stub doesn't return a value, at least not right away. Let's find out why.

Every method call made to the server-side component is done asynchronously, which means that it is nonblocking. After all, freezing the browser would defeat the purpose of Ajax. What that means, though, is that the result of the remote method call isn't available immediately to the executing thread. As such, the method on the stub doesn't have a value to return, even if the matching server-side method has one. When a method on the remote stub is executed, it is effectively saying, "I'll get back to you on that. Do you have a number where I can reach you?" The number you provide is a "callback" JavaScript function.

The callback function is a standard construct in asynchronous APIs. It's executed by the remoting framework when a response from an Ajax request arrives back at the browser. If the method on the server-side component has a nonvoid return value, that value is passed into the callback function as its only argument. If the method on the server-side component has a void return type, the callback function takes no arguments. (Actually, the final argument is always the Seam remoting context, which is covered in section 12.5.2.)

Let's begin with the quizzing. We add a link on the page that encourages members to challenge themselves with a trivia question:

```
<a href="javascript: void(0);" onclick="askQuestion();">Quiz me!</a>
```

The `askQuestion()` JavaScript function captures a question from the `Trivia` component:

```
function askQuestion() {
    var trivia = Seam.Component.getInstance("trivia");
    trivia.drawQuestion(poseQuestion);
}
```

As you can see, the call to `drawQuestion()` only starts the process. A callback JavaScript function, `poseQuestion()`, is used to capture the `TriviaQuestion` instance when it arrives and to prompt the user with the question:

```
function poseQuestion(triviaQuestion) {
    if (triviaQuestion == null) {
        alert("Sorry, there are no trivia questions.");
    }
    else if (triviaQuestion.getAnswer() != undefined) {
        alert("This quiz has been compromised!");
    }
    else {
        var response = window.prompt(triviaQuestion.question);
```

```
        if (response) {
            var trivia = Seam.Component.getInstance("trivia");
            trivia.answerQuestion(
                triviaQuestion.getId(), response, reportResult);
        }
    }
}
```

After receiving the `TriviaQuestion` instance, we verify that the `answer` property has been nullified, which was declared in the `@WebRemote` annotation as an excluded property. Without this exclusion, the integrity of the quiz is drawn into question. If all goes well, the member is prompted with the question using a JavaScript prompt, shown in figure 12.5.

Figure 12.5   The trivia question prompt in which the member enters a response

If the member responds, we initiate another method invocation, this time to verify whether the response is correct. In the call to the `answerQuestion()` method, the callback function is moved to the third slot. The callback function is always the n+1 parameter, where n is the number of parameters in the remote method. The `reportResult()` callback JavaScript function handles the verdict (in a crude fashion):

```
function reportResult(result) {
    alert(result ? "Correct!" : "Sorry, wrong answer. Keep studying!");
}
```

The only major architectural change brought about by using JavaScript remoting over executing calls in Java is that you have to shift to thinking about every interaction in terms of asynchronous communication. This takes some getting used to, both for the developer and the user. Let's see what the impact is on the user.

WHAT'S THE STATUS?

The browser uses a spinner, typically appearing in the upper-right corner of the window, that notifies the user when a page is loading. However, an Ajax-based application "breaks" this feedback mechanism because the browser interacts with the server without a page being formally requested. To reinstate the feedback, Ajax frameworks typically render a spinner in the page while an asynchronous request is in progress. Seam follows this pattern.

Seam's JavaScript remoting library renders a loading message in the upper-right corner of the page during a remoting call. The message is defined in the property `Seam.Remoting.loadingMessage`. You can override it like this:

```
Seam.Remoting.loadingMessage = "Request in progress";
```

If you're using Ajax because you don't want to bother the user, you can disable the message by overriding the methods that toggle the message with empty functions:

```
Seam.Remoting.displayLoadingMessage = function() {};
Seam.Remoting.hideLoadingMessage = function() {};
```

Rather than disabling the feedback mechanism, you can use these two functions to customize it.

As a developer, you may want to track the remoting call. Seam remoting includes a debug window that shows the status of the Ajax request. You can call `Seam.Remoting.setDebug(true)` to enable the window for a given page or activate it for all pages in the component descriptor. First, import the component namespace `http://jboss.com/products/seam/remoting`, prefixed as `remoting`. Then, enable debug mode on the built-in `remoting` component:

```
<remoting:remoting debug="true"/>
```

The debug window appears whenever an Ajax request goes out and you can follow its progress. Despite having this debug window, I strongly urge you to use Firebug instead.

Let's get back to remoting. As you know, the EL notation plays an important role in every Seam module. No module would be complete without it. JavaScript remoting is no exception.

EVALUATING EL FROM THE CLIENT

JavaScript remoting can tap into the Seam container via EL, whether it is to access values (value expressions) or execute methods (method expressions). You use the `Seam.Remoting.eval()` function to execute an EL expression, giving you a way to perform a remote operation without a `@WebRemote` method. Keep in mind that the resolved value is sent to a callback function asynchronously.

The `eval()` method (don't confuse this with JavaScript's `eval()` function) is ideal for fetching objects stored in the Seam container. This differs from executable stubs, which ask a component to perform work and return the result.

The only thing you have to be aware of when using `eval()` is that if the value expression resolves to an object of a custom type, you need to explicitly import that type using the `<s:remote>` tag. This problem doesn't come up when using executable stubs

---

Escaping the EL

If you intend to use the Seam remoting `eval()` function from within a JSF page, you have to escape the EL notation. The JSF view handler gets a first pass at the template and will resolve any value expressions it finds. You must escape the EL to delay the evaluation.

You make an expression unrecognizable to the view handler by either escaping the pound sign (#) with a leading backslash (\):

```
"\#{contextVariable}"
```

or by assembling the expression using string concatenation:

```
"#" + "{contextVariable}"
```

Personally, I prefer the backslash syntax.

since Seam automatically generates the necessary type stubs. Because the EL can resolve any type, it would be difficult for Seam to know what type stubs to prepare. If you're only using the EL to resolve primitive values or built-in types (strings, dates, collections), you don't need any extra imports.

Let's try an example to get a feel for using the EL with remoting. In the Java world, we care a great deal about language support, but as soon as we move to JavaScript we seem to forget about this lofty goal. Having the ability to evaluate EL from JavaScript opens up the possibility of pulling down the message bundle map so that it can be referenced from JavaScript. In this case, we don't want to execute a method but instead just retrieve the map:

```
var messages = null;
Seam.Remoting.eval("\#{messages}", function(value) {
    messages = value;
});
```

Keep in mind that the call is asynchronous, so there's a brief period of time before the messages arrive, but it's likely to execute fast enough so that you don't have to worry about the lapse.

With access to the locale-specific message bundle, we can reward or shame members in their language of choice in the reportResult() callback function:

```
alert(result ? messages.get("response.correct") :
   messages.get("response.incorrect"));
```

As you can see, evaluating EL is a great way to pull down reference data needed in the UI. Next up, you'll learn how to push data the other way by creating instances of local stubs and sending them off to the server through methods on executable stubs.

12.4.4 *Local stubs*

A local stub is a JavaScript version of a JavaBean class. It shares all of the same properties as its server-side counterpart. The properties on the local stub are addressed using JavaBean-style accessor methods or direct field access, as shown here:

```
triviaQuestion.setAnswer("The Masters");
triviaQuestion.answer = "The Masters";
"The Masters" == triviaQuestion.getAnswer();
```

The fundamental difference between a local stub and an executable stub is that when a method on a local stub is called, it doesn't trigger a remote execution (an Ajax request).

SORTING OUT THE LOCAL STUBS

There are two categories of local stubs: component and type. A Seam component with no @WebRemote methods becomes a local component stub when imported through the remoting framework. (The Seam component must be declared using @Name. It's not enough to declare it in the component descriptor.) All other classes become local type stubs.

A local component stub is instantiated by passing its component name to the Seam.Component.newInstance() JavaScript method from the remoting framework, whereas a local type stub is instantiated by passing its qualified class name to the `Seam.Remoting.createType()` method:

```
var favorite = Seam.Component.newInstance("newFavorite");
var golfer = Seam.Remoting.createType("org.open18.model.Golfer");
```

Apart from how they're instantiated, the two local stub varieties are identical. The benefit a component stub has over a type stub is that the component stub gets addressed by its component name, which is typically shorter than the class name and doesn't tightly couple the qualified class name to the client (the JavaScript).

A local stub is intended to be used as a data structure that's passed as a parameter to a method on an executable stub or mapped to the method's return value. When an instance of a local stub reaches the server, it's translated into a real Java object. Local stubs aren't needed to create primitives and strings since there's an implied mapping between JavaScript and Java for simple types.

So why do these objects need to be passed to the server? Well, the primary reason for using JavaScript remoting is to get the server to perform work that JavaScript can't do. One example is persisting an object to the database. Local stubs are a perfect complement for this operation. The client can seed a transient entity instance from a local stub, which is then shipped off to the server to be persisted.

PERSISTING ENTITIES FROM JAVASCRIPT

Let's work through an example to see how a transient entity instance can be persisted via remoting. In this example, the entity class named `Favorite` is introduced to capture an item that the user has selected to be in his or her list of favorites. The essential parts of this entity are shown here:

```
@Entity
@Table(name = "FAVORITE")
@Name("newFavorite")
public class Favorite implements Serializable {
    private Long id;
    private Long entityId;
    private String entityName;
    private Golfer golfer;
    // getters and setters hidden
}
```

Since the entity class is annotated with @Name, it becomes a local component stub and can be referenced by its component name, `newFavorite`. The `FavoritesAction` component, shown in listing 12.3, is responsible for persisting instances of the `Favorite` entity. It also has a method to check for a duplicate entry.

Listing 12.3 A remoting-capable component for working with `Favorite` entities

```
package org.open18.action;
import ...;

@Name("favoritesAction")                      Declares methods
@Transactional                          ◁──┘  as transactional
public class FavoritesAction {
    @In private EntityManager entityManager;
```

```
@WebRemote
public Favorite addFavorite(Favorite favorite) {
    try {
        entityManager.persist(favorite);
        return favorite;
    } catch (Exception e) {                ◁─────┐ Catches exceptions
        return null;                             │ for a clean response
    }
}

@WebRemote
public boolean isFavorite(Long entityId, String entityName) {
    try {
        entityManager.createQuery("select f from Favorite f " +
            "where f.entityId = :id and f.entityName = :name")
            .setParameter("id", entityId)
            .setParameter("name", entityName)
            .getSingleResult();
        return true;
    } catch (Exception e) {
        return false;
    }
}
}
```

Notice the @Transactional annotation on the class. Since remoting requests operate outside the JSF life cycle, they aren't wrapped in Seam's global transaction. Therefore, @WebRemote methods must declare transaction boundaries.

If an exception is thrown during the execution of a @WebRemote method, no result is returned. Thus, it's important to catch any exceptions and handle them gracefully. To expose the status of the exception, you can either return it or save it, then access it on a subsequent remoting call.

The next step is to create a JavaScript function that invokes the method to add the current entity to the golfer's favorites, shown in listing 12.4. You place this JavaScript function on any entity detail page (since this design is agnostic to entity type).

Listing 12.4   Remoting logic used to add an entity as a favorite

```
function addToFavorites(entityId, entityName, golferId) {
    var favoritesAction =
        Seam.Component.getInstance("favoritesAction");       ❶
    favoritesAction.isFavorite(
        entityId, entityName, function(exists) {             ❷
        if (exists) {
            alert("This " + entityName + " is already a favorite");
        }
        else {
            var favorite = Seam.Component.newInstance("newFavorite");   ❸
            favorite.setEntityId(entityId);
            favorite.setEntityName(entityName);
            var golfer =
                Seam.Remoting.createType("org.open18.model.Golfer");     ❹
            golfer.setId(golferId);
            favorite.setGolfer(golfer);
```

```
                favoritesAction.addFavorite(favorite, notify);      ⑤
            }
        });
    }

    function notify(favoriteInstance) {
        if (favoriteInstance == null) {
            alert(messages.get("favorite.addFailed"));
        }
        var message = messages.get("favorite.addSucceeded");
        message = message.replace("{0}", favoriteInstance.getEntityName());
        message = message.replace("{1}", favoriteInstance.getId());
        alert(message);
    }
```

The addToFavorites() method accepts the information to create and persist an
instance of Favorite. The first step is to get a handle on the stub for Favorites-
Action ❶. Rather than jumping right into the call, we verify that the favorite doesn't yet
exist by invoking the isFavorite() method. This deals with a race condition to the
server. Like all remoting methods, the isFavorite() method runs asynchronously, so
it's necessary to jump into a callback method to continue with the operation ❷.

  If the favorite doesn't already exist, a transient instance of Favorite is constructed
by passing its component name to newInstance() ❸. The Golfer entity is not a Seam
component. Therefore, it's necessary to use createType() to create a transient
instance ❹. Here's where things get interesting. To satisfy the foreign key relationship
from Favorite to Golfer, an identifier is assigned to the transient instance of Golfer.
The persistence manager understands how to link the records in the database. Once
the transient instance of Favorite is built, it's sent off to the server ❺ to be persisted.

  All that's left is to add a link to the entity detail page that invokes the JavaScript
method:

```
<a href="javascript: void(0);" onclick=
  "addToFavorites(#{facilityHome.id}, 'Facility', #{currentGolfer.id});">
  Add to favorites</a>
```

The EL value expressions in the link definition is interpreted when the page is rendered,
resolving to the numeric identifiers of the current golfer and facility, respectively.

  This example uses the persistence manager to perform a duty in response to a
user-triggered event. As you may recall from chapter 7, Ajax requests occur with a
much greater frequency than traditional page requests and it's a good idea to leverage
conversations to avoid unnecessary load from being placed on vital resources such as
the database. Let's explore how you give JavaScript remoting requests access to stateful components in a long-running conversation.

12.5 *Conversational remoting calls*

There are two ways for JavaScript remoting requests to partake in conversations. They
can join the conversation associated with the current page, or they can go off and
establish their own conversation, isolated from and transparent to the rendered page.
Let's consider these two scenarios for using conversations with JavaScript remoting.

12.5.1 *Joining the conversation in progress*

Remoting requests maintain a special context for holding the "active" conversation id. You can access this context using the JavaScript method `Seam.Remoting.getContext()`. The context has two methods: `getConversationId()` and `setConversationId()`. Once the conversation id is established on this context, it remains set until it's explicitly changed.

If a long-running conversation is active at the time the page is rendered, the remoting context can join it. The technique is to use an EL value expression to resolve the current conversation id and pass it as an argument to the `setConversationId()` method:

```
Seam.Remoting.setConversationId(#{conversation.id});
```

The expression is resolved when the page is rendered, leaving behind the numeric conversation id. This call should be placed in the window's `onload` handler. Once the conversation id is established, remoting requests are able to "see" all objects in the long-running conversation in progress (objects related to the rendered page). You can pull references to these objects using `Seam.Component.getInstance()` or `Seam.Remoting.eval()`. For instance, if a list of data were retrieved and stored in the conversation, the remoting request could talk to the server and ask it to hand over that data set rather than asking the database to retrieve it again. You could also invoke a method on a conversation-scoped component, manipulating the state of the data held in the conversation. Seam offers parallel support for conversations in web service calls.

Remoting requests can also work in their own conversation context. Let's consider how this differs from participating in the page's conversation.

12.5.2 *Striking up a conversation*

A remote method call can start a new long-running conversation and then participate in that conversation on subsequent calls. When it's time to say goodbye, another remoting method can end the conversation. This style of conversational Ajax is great for single-page applications where the page flow concept doesn't apply. It's even possible to get multiple conversations going at the same time. You swap between them by changing the active conversation id on the remoting context prior to issuing a call.

Let's return to the trivia example and make it a cohesive quiz. We also give the user a choice of category and three chances to get each answer right. The member is first presented with a list of topics. Once a topic is selected, the quiz is started, which in turn begins a long-running conversation. Each time a question is answered correctly or the user fails all three attempts, it's removed from the pool. When members reach the last question, they get their score and the conversation ends. We stick to pseudocode since the method implementations aren't important to understanding the concept. The following shows the conversation component with the method stubs:

```
@Name("trivia")
@Scope(ScopeType.CONVERSATION)
public Trivia implements Serializable {
    @In private EntityManager entityManager;
    private Double score;
```

```
        private List<TriviaQuestion> questions;

        @WebRemote
        public List<String> getCategories() { ... }

        @Begin @WebRemote
        public boolean selectQuiz(String category) { ... }

        @WebRemote(exclude = "answer")
        public TriviaQuestion drawNextQuestion() { ... }

        @WebRemote
        public boolean answerQuestion(Long id, String response) { ... }

        public TriviaQuestion findQuestion(Long id) { ... }

        @End @WebRemote
        public Double endQuiz() { ... }
    }
```

Things kick off with a call to the getCategories() method:

```
    Seam.Component.getInstance("trivia").getCategories(showCategories);
```

This call happens outside a long-running conversation. When the response comes back from the server, it contains the conversation id of the temporary conversation. The next remoting call, which is to the selectQuiz() method, sends this conversation id along with the request:

```
    Seam.Component.getInstance("trivia").selectQuiz(startQuiz);
```

The selectQuiz() method queries the database for the questions associated with the category and stashes them in the questions property of the component. When the response comes back from the selectQuiz() call, it contains the conversation id of the long-running conversation that was started as a result of executing this method. However, it will *not* overwrite the conversation id on the remoting context since one has already been established. There are two ways to force the conversation id to be updated:

- Clear the conversation id before executing the method on the stub.
- Explicitly overwrite the conversation id with the value returned from the server.

The second option is typically the best approach to take. I mentioned earlier that the callback function accepts a remoting context as the last argument. This context contains the conversation id that was assigned by the server. By accepting this parameter in your callback function, you can transfer the conversation id to the page's remoting context:

```
    function startQuiz(ready, context) {
        Seam.Remoting.setConversationId(context.getConversationId());
        askQuestion();
    }
```

The remoting context is now participating in the long-running conversation. Questions are drawn and answered until no more questions remain. When the questions are exhausted, the endQuiz() method is called to end the conversation and report the member's score:

```
    Seam.Component.getInstance("trivia").endQuiz(reportScore);
```

The `setConversationId()` method can also be used to switch between parallel conversations. In some ways, JavaScript remoting is more capable of dealing with conversations than regular JSF navigation because you have fine-grained control over the active conversation.

There's one final form of conversation I want to mention before closing this chapter. This one has to do with batching communication between the browser and the server.

12.5.3 *Storing up requests for a shipment*

Ajax is chatty. While it may be a lot of little requests, they can take their toll on the server. Studies have shown that the metric that matters most in server load is not the size of the request, but rather the quantity of requests.[7] Therefore, if possible, it's a good idea to try to stockpile the requests and send them all at once. By doing so you'll see a significant performance boost by reducing both server load and network traffic. A good way to know if you have such a use case is to use Firebug to monitor the Ajax requests being fired. If they're occurring in rapid succession, you could benefit from bundling them together.

To begin queuing requests—executable stub method invocations and EL evaluations—you call `Seam.Remoting.startBatch()`. You still use callback functions just as you always would, only there is going to be a longer delay before those functions are executed by the response. When you're ready to have the pending requests sent off, you call `Seam.Remoting.executeBatch()`. The requests are fired off in the order that they were queued. Rest assured that the callback functions are also executed in this order. If you decide at some point after opening the queue that you want to discard the pending requests, simply call `Seam.Remoting.cancelBatch()` and exit batch mode. The cancel batch feature is useful for letting the user discard pending changes in the UI.

Having Ajax requests participate in conversations minimizes the load that Ajax requests would otherwise impose on the server. Conversely, remoting requests add a new dimension to how conversations are able to serve the application, enabling you to take advantage of Seam's conversation model for single-page applications. If you're committed to single-page applications, you may even want to consider switching to GWT.

12.6   *Responding to GWT remoting calls*

As you lean more toward the single-page application, you may reach a point where JSF just doesn't fit any longer. If that's the case, you are probably better off moving to a UI framework that's designed around the use of remoting calls. One such library is the Google Web Toolkit (GWT). A move from JSF to GWT doesn't mean that you have to leave Seam behind. GWT is intended for creating the user interface, which means it must delegate work to transactional components on the back end. Seam remoting can establish that bridge.

---

[7] For "Best Practices for Speeding Up Your Web Site," see http://developer.yahoo.com/performance/rules.html.

This section is focused on the integration of Seam and GWT, not on GWT fundamentals. If you are a novice to GWT and are seeking in-depth information on the subject, I encourage you to pick up a copy of *GWT in Action* (Manning, 2007). Once you're comfortable with GWT, or if you're just interested in finding out how the integration works, forge ahead.

12.6.1 *A quick introduction to GWT integration*

GWT is an Ajax-based framework that allows you to develop your web application purely in Java, without having to write HTML or JavaScript. It offers a similar value proposition as Ajax-based JSF libraries, but replaces the declarative UI with Java constructs. The toolkit compiles your Java code down to JavaScript, which means that you don't have to go through the pain of coding JavaScript and you can be confident that the JavaScript is delivered to the browser in the most efficient manner possible.

GWT's remote procedure call (RPC) mechanism is designed to allow a GWT client application to access server-side business components via Ajax. In the GWT tutorials, you are told to use a Java servlet to handle the request. However, in this section, I show you how to hook one of these RPC calls to a `@WebRemote` method on a Seam component. We refactor the `Trivia` component so that it can act as a remote service to GWT, giving GWT access to the trivia questions in the database. Seam's GWT integration uses Seam remoting, so be sure to have the Seam resource servlet installed when using this integration.

12.6.2 *Preparing the remoting service*

To make a Seam component accessible to GWT, you first have to convert it to a GWT service. This step involves implementing GWT's `RemotingService` interface. You will end up with three Java classes. First, you define a synchronous interface that declares the public methods of the Seam component. `Trivia` is now an interface:

```
public interface Trivia extends RemotingService {
    public TriviaQuestion drawQuestion();
    public void answerQuestion(Long id, String response);
}
```

All return values and parameters in a GWT service must be primitive or serializable. That means the `TriviaQuestion` class must be declared as serializable using the `IsSerializable` interface from GWT:

```
public class TriviaQuestion implements IsSerializable {...}
```

NOTE Although GWT 1.4 and above supports the `java.io.Serializable` interface, at the time of this writing, Seam's GWT integration doesn't support it. Also, to make a collection serializable, you need to specify the type it contains using the special JavaDoc annotation `@gwt.typeArgs`. See the GWT reference documentation for details.

GWT makes asynchronous calls to the remote service. But, as you learned earlier, asynchronous methods can't have return types. Instead, when an asynchronous call is made, the status code and return value are directed to a callback object. The `Trivia` interface can't accommodate such a call. That means it's necessary to define an asynchronous version of the service interface that can be called on by the GWT application. You must use the following list of conventions when developing the asynchronous interface:

- It must be in the same Java package as the synchronous interface.
- Its name must be the name of the synchronous interface plus the suffix `Async`.
- It must have the same methods as the synchronous interface, except the return types must be `void` and each method must accept `AsyncCallback` as the final argument.

Here's the asynchronous interface for the trivia service that satisfies these requirements:

```
public TriviaAsync implements RemotingService {
    public void drawQuestion(AsyncCallback callback);
    public void answerQuestion(Long id, String response,
        AsyncCallback callback);
}
```

Although you have a pair of interfaces for the GWT service, you only have to provide an implementation class for the synchronous interface. The asynchronous interface is implemented at runtime by GWT and its method calls delegate to the implementation of the synchronous interface. The `AsyncCallback` is an interface that defines two methods: `onSuccess()` and `onFailure()`. The first accepts the return value of the synchronous method, and the second accepts the `Throwable` object that reports the nature of the failure.

To complete the contract, the `Trivia` class from the earlier example is renamed to `TriviaImpl` and now implements the synchronous interface. In addition, the name of the component must match the qualified name of this interface. The component is scoped to the session because conversations aren't supported in the GWT integration at the time of this writing:

```
@Name("org.open18.action.Trivia")
@Scope(ScopeType.SESSION)
public class TriviaImpl implements Trivia, Serializable { ... }
```

If you need to access a conversation, pass the conversation id as an argument to a `@WebRemote` method. Within the method, manually restore the conversation using the `switchConversation()` method on the built-in `manager` component. After switching to (or restoring) the conversation, you can retrieve a conversation-scoped component using the Seam API (i.e., `Component.getInstance()`).

With the implementation of the `Trivia` service interface, you now have a bona fide GWT service. Let's see how it is called from GWT.

12.6.3 *Making a GWT service call through Seam remoting*

After looking up the GWT service in a GWT client application, you set the service entry point to a URL that's handled by the Seam resource servlet and subsequently the Seam remoting library. The lookup for the trivia service is handled in the `getTrivia-Service()` method on the GWT application class (shown here):

```
private TriviaAsync getTriviaService() {
    String endpointURL = GWT.getModuleBaseURL() + "seam/resource/gwt";
    TriviaAsync service = (TriviaAsync) GWT.create(Trivia.class);
    ((ServiceDefTarget) service).setServiceEntryPoint(endpointURL);
}
```

Notice that this lookup casts to the asynchronous interface, which lets you provide a callback to handle the response from the server. To use the Seam integration while debugging a GWT application in hosted mode, start the application server that hosts the Seam application as usual and then hardcode the absolute URL in the Java GWT client code. You can use `GWT.isScript()`, which returns true in deployment mode and false in hosted mode, thus making the code portable.

Let's use the endpoint in the GWT application that presents the trivia challenge. Since the focus of this section is not on creating a full GWT application, only a small excerpt is shown here. The method that sends the user's response to be validated is bound to a button named `Guess`:

```
final Button guess = new Button("Guess");
guess.addClickListener(new ClickListener() {
    public void onClick(Widget w) {
        getTriviaService().answerQuestion(question.getId(),
            answerInput.getText(), new AsyncCallback() {
            public void onFailure(Throwable t) {
                Window.alert("The call didn't go through");
            }
            public void onSuccess(Object data) {
                boolean result = ((Boolean) data).booleanValue();
                Window.alert(result ? "Correct!", "Wrong, try again.");
            }
        });
    }
});
```

This example demonstrates that using a Seam component as a GWT RPC service is relatively straightforward. The best part is that you can back GWT with the power of Seam rather than a clunky servlet. Seam remoting is very powerful because not only does it allow you to call server-side methods from JavaScript, it also serves as the foundation to integrate with other rich-client frameworks. This section presents GWT, but parallel integrations are available for Laszlo, Flex, and Java FX. To assist with this integration, Exadel has developed a seam-gen clone called Flamingo,[8] which uses Maven 2 to generate projects that use either Flex or Java FX as a front end to Seam. Also check out Granite Data Services' GraniteDS,[9] another framework that bridges Flex to Seam.

12.7 Summary

In this chapter, you learned to use two types of Ajax without having to get your hands dirty with the `XMLHttpRequest` object. You began by using Ajax4jsf and ICEfaces to execute Ajax requests that honor the JSF life cycle and perform partial rerendering of

---

[8] http://exadel.com/web/portal/flamingo
[9] http://graniteds.org

the page by grafting on updated branches of the JSF component tree. ICEfaces intelligently calculates the portions of the UI component tree that need to be rerendered, whereas Ajax4jsf relies on declarative hints. To give credit to Ajax4jsf, it's capable of creating Ajax interactions between components not designed with Ajax in mind.

Although Ajax-based JSF components are powerful, there are times when you need something leaner. As an alternative, you learned to bypass the JSF life cycle and let JavaScript invoke server-side components as if they were local to the browser. The only challenge is that you have to think in terms of asynchronous return values. You discovered that Seam remoting allows JavaScript to speak the language of EL notation and tap into conversations, two paramount features of Seam that are particularly useful for single-page applications. Finally, you used Seam remoting to connect GWT to a Seam component acting as a GWT RPC service.

The two styles of Ajax presented in this chapter each have their own purpose. Ajax-based JSF component libraries are critical when you want to alter areas of the page under JSF's control, such as a form or data table, while keeping in sync with the server's view of the page. JavaScript remoting is for lightweight calls that don't involve UI components. Both styles get you thinking in terms of incremental pages updates rather than full-page refreshes.

In the next chapter, you'll escape the well-worn groove of HTML and JavaScript and explore file uploading, dynamic graphic generation, PDF creation, multipart emails, and themes. After taking in the lessons from the next chapter, you'll find that the applications you create become far more 3D, to play on the name of one of the topics that await.

File, rich rendering, and email support

This chapter covers

- Handling file uploads
- Creating PDF documents and charts
- Sending emails with attachments
- Customizing the UI with resource bundles

Many people playing their first round of golf question why anyone would want to torture themselves with such a maddening game, concluding that those who play it are simply masochistic. But anyone who has experienced the triumph of sinking the ball in the hole from the tee box, clearing a large water hazard, or just taking a great swing understands that there's something extremely gratifying about golf once you get the hang of it. The same can be said about an application framework. There's a lot to learn at first and it can seem overwhelming. Then things click. Your newfound ability makes the experience enjoyable and you get to do things you've never experienced before.

You saw in the last chapter how Seam and JSF component libraries take the pain out of using Ajax, making Ajax more accessible than ever. That's just one example

511

of how Seam provides features that are both rewarding to develop and rewarding for your customers and clients to use. In this chapter, you'll learn how to do more fun and enjoyable tasks in Seam, including handling file uploads, creating PDF documents, rendering dynamic image data and charts, sending emails that include attachments, and adding themes to your application. This sampling represents the set of features that are quite often tossed out in the name of budget and time constraints. With Seam, you discover that performing these tasks is a breeze. They're all just variations on what you have done so many times throughout this book.

Because several of the examples covered in this chapter work with raw file and image data, you'll begin by learning how to accept file uploads and how to serve them back to the browser.

13.1   *Uploading files and rendering dynamic images*

How many times have you cringed at the requirement of processing an image upload and having it rendered on a page in the application? The problem isn't that the task is impossible, but that it isn't as straightforward as dealing with plain form data. In fact, accepting file uploads in Java has a well-founded reputation for being notoriously difficult. With Seam, it's almost too easy. In this section, you'll learn how to bind an upload form element to a Seam component to accept an image and persist it to the database. Then you'll use Seam's enhanced graphic component to turn that raw data back into a dynamically rendered image.

13.1.1 *Accepting file uploads*

Seam practically sacrifices itself to protect you from the nastiness of file uploads in Java, reducing the task to a simple EL value binding expression—it's that dramatic. There are no buffers, stream reading, or multipart boundaries to worry about. All of that is handled for you transparently by the `MultipartFilter` and the `MultipartRequest` it wraps around the incoming servlet request. If you already have the `SeamFilter` configured, you don't have to do anything else to enable Seam's file upload support.

SEAM'S FILE UPLOAD UI COMPONENT

Seam provides a UI input component, `<s:fileUpload>`, for receiving file uploads from a JSF form. The file data is passed through an EL value binding that references a `byte[]` or `InputStream` property on a Seam component. The upload component can also capture the content type of the file, the filename, and the file size and apply that information to a Seam component along with the file data.

To demonstrate a file upload, we augment the registration form to allow members to upload a profile image, or avatar. Two properties have to be added to the `Golfer` entity, `image` and `imageContentType`, to capture the image data and content type, respectively. The relevant parts of the `Golfer` entity class are shown here:

```
@Entity
@PrimaryKeyJoinColumn(name = "MEMBER_ID")
@Table(name = "GOLFER")
public class Golfer extends Member {
```

```
...
private byte[] image;
private String imageContentType;

@Column(name = "image_data")
@Lob @Basic(fetch = FetchType.LAZY)
public byte[] getImage() { return image; }
public void setImage(byte[] image) { this.image = image; }

@Column(name = "image_content_type")
public String getImageContentType() { return imageContentType; }
public void setImageContentType(String imageContentType) {
    this.imageContentType = imageContentType;
}
}
}
```

I've decided to accept the file data as a byte[]. The lazy-fetch strategy prevents the data from being loaded until the image data is requested, slightly reducing the memory footprint.

The only remaining step is to add the upload field to the registration form and wire it to the image and imageContentType properties on the Golfer entity. You also need to set the enctype attribute on the <h:form> component tag to multipart/form-data.[1] This setting tells the browser to send the form data using multipart data streams. Failure to make this adjustment will prevent the browser from sending the file data. An excerpt of the registration form with these changes applied is shown here:

```
<h:form id="registerActionForm" enctype="multipart/form-data">
  ...
  <s:decorate id="imageField" template="layout/edit.xhtml">
    <ui:define name="label">Profile image / avatar</ui:define>
    <s:fileUpload id="image"
      accept="image/png,image/gif,image/jpeg"
      data="#{newGolfer.image}"
      contentType="#{newGolfer.imageContentType}"/>
  </s:decorate>
  ...
</h:form>
```

You don't have to make any changes to the RegisterAction class to accept the uploaded image and have it stored in the database. The image data is bound to the entity instance named newGolfer and automatically persisted to the database along with the other fields on this entity. If you're content with the image as it's uploaded, your work is done. However, it's likely that you'll want to put some limits on what the user can upload.

CONTROLLING WHAT GETS UPLOADED

The accept attribute on <s:fileUpload> is used to specify a comma-separated list of standard Multipurpose Internet Mail Extensions (MIME) types that can be uploaded. The upload field in the registration form limits the acceptable file types to graphic formats that Seam is capable of rendering dynamically. The use of wildcards is also

---

[1] See http://www.w3.org/TR/html4/interact/forms.html#h-17.13.4.2 for information about this setting.

permissible. You could accept all image MIME types, for instance, using the pattern image/*. Even with this restriction in place, though, you should still validate the file type in the action method.

Seam exposes two global settings on the built-in component named multipart-Filter to control file uploads. The maxUploadSize property allows you to cap the size (in bytes) of the file being uploaded. There's no limit in the default configuration. You use the createTempFiles property to control whether Seam uses a temporary file to store the uploaded file data or whether the file data is held in memory, which is the default. These two properties can be adjusted using component configuration as follows:

```
<web:multipart-request max-upload-size="5242880" create-temp-files="true"/>
```

While the maxUploadSize property puts a limit on file size of the uploaded profile image, it doesn't put restrictions on its dimensions. Once the profile image has uploaded, it's a good idea to scale it so that it doesn't steal too much space on the page when rendered.

PROCESSING AN UPLOADED IMAGE

The uploaded image can be resized in the action method before the newGolfer instance is persisted. The class org.jboss.seam.ui.graphicImage.Image, which is bundled with the jboss-seam-ui.jar file, makes resizing and scaling images a cinch. Listing 13.1 shows the code added to the register() action method that manipulates the uploaded image. This code is just a starting point. If you use it in your application, you'll likely want to make it more configurable by eliminating the hardcoded values you see used here.

Listing 13.1   Resizing the profile image

```
if (newGolfer.getImage() != null) {
    try {
        Image image = new Image();                          Reads in
        image.setInput(newGolfer.getImage());        ◁─┘   image data
        if (image.getBufferedImage() == null) {
            throw new IOException("The profile image data is empty.");
        }

        if (!image.getContentType().getMimeType()        ◁─┐  Validates
            .matches("image/(png|gif|jpeg)")) {           │  MIME type
            facesMessages.addToControl("image",
                "Invalid image type: " + image.getContentType());
        }
        if (image.getHeight() > 64 || image.getWidth() > 64) {
            if (image.getHeight() > image.getWidth()) {
                image.scaleToHeight(64);
            }
            else {
                image.scaleToWidth(64);
            }                                              Restores
            newGolfer.setImage(image.getImage());   ◁─┘  resized image
        }
    } catch (IOException e) {
```

```
                    log.error("An error occurred reading the profile image", e);
                    facesMessages.addToControl("image", FacesMessage.SEVERITY_ERROR,
                        "An error occurred reading the profile image.");
                    newGolfer.setImage(null);
                    newGolfer.setImageContentType(null);
                    return null;
                }
        }
```

Once you've accepted the raw file data into the database, you need to render it. After all, what good would it be? Seam can render raw file data in addition to static files read from the classpath and input streams, in any of the following ways:

- As an image in a web page
- As an image in a PDF document
- Pushed to the browser to be downloaded
- As an inline image in an email or as an email attachment

Let's begin by exploring how to render the raw image data in a web page using Seam's enhanced graphic UI component. As the chapter progresses, you'll learn about the other ways to use the raw file data listed here. These additional options build on this initial lesson in that they're merely variations on the graphic UI component.

13.1.2 *Rendering images from raw data*

The Seam UI component set includes an enhanced graphic component capable of operating on a dynamically generated image. Seam's graphic component, `<s:graphicImage>`, is an extension of the standard JSF graphic component, `<h:graphicImage>`. In addition to the features supported by the standard component, Seam's version has support for rendering raw image data and performing image transformations.

RENDERING DYNAMIC IMAGES WITH SEAM'S ENHANCED GRAPHIC UI COMPONENT

The standard `<h:graphicImage>` tag only accepts a string value or an EL value expression that resolves to a string value. This value is used to serve a static graphic resource from the web application context (e.g., /img/golfer.png). The `<s:graphicImage>` tag supports a much broader range of Java types resolved from an EL value expression. Table 13.1 lists the supported dynamic Java types from which the `<s:graphicImage>` can read image data and the image MIME types that the component can handle.

Like the `<h:graphicImage>` component, the `<s:graphicImage>` produces a standard HTML `<img>` element. The difference is that Seam generates a random filename for the image, which is used in the src attribute of the `<img>` tag and served by the

Supported Java types	Supported MIME types

`String` (any classpath resource)
`byte[]`
`java.io.File`
`java.io.InputStream`
`java.net.URL`
	image/png
	image/jpeg (or image/jpg)
	image/gif

Table 13.1 The Java types and MIME types supported by `<s:graphicImage>`

SeamResourceServlet. If you don't want the filename to be random, you can specify a fixed filename in the `fileName` attribute. You don't need to put the extension of the image in the filename; Seam appends the extension automatically according to image type.

You should recognize that one of the supported Java types listed in table 13.1 is `byte[]`, which is the property type that holds the golfer's profile image. Let's use the `<s:graphicImage>` component tag to display the profile image uploaded during the registration process on the golfer's profile page. The image data is specified in the `value` attribute. A fallback image is used if the golfer doesn't have a profile image. The golfer's username is used as the filename of the image to produce a URL that remains stable and thus allows the browser to cache the image. Finally, alternate text is provided for browsers that can't render images:

```
<s:graphicImage value="#{selectedGolfer.image ne null ?
    selectedGolfer.image : '/img/golfer.png'}"
  fileName="#{selectedGolfer.username}"
  alt="[profile image]"/>
```

In this example, we display image data retrieved from the database. However, you can also use a Seam component to create an image using Java 2D. The image can be prepared in a Seam component, converted to one of the accepted Java types listed in table 13.1, and then bound to the `<s:graphicImage>` tag. But before you venture into Java 2D, you may be able to leverage one of the basic image transformations that Seam provides.

IMAGE TRANSFORMATIONS

Given that the `<s:graphicImage>` component loads image data into memory, it stands to reason that the image can be transformed prior to being rendered. One of three transformation component tags can be nested within `<s:graphicImage>` to apply transformations to the image using Java 2D, which are listed in table 13.2. Each component tag accepts one or more parameters that control how the transformation is applied. These transformations are the same as those provided by the `Image` class from the Seam API introduced in section 13.1.

The golfer's profile image is reduced to a reasonable size when it's initially uploaded. But it may be necessary to scale it even further to create a thumbnail for personalizing a review or comment that the golfer posts somewhere on the site, as shown here:

Table 13.1 Transformation components that can be used with `<s:graphicImage>`

Component tag	What it does...	Parameters

`<s:transformImageSize>`	Resizes the image to a specific height, width, or both. The aspect ratio can be fixed if scaling is performed on a single dimension.	`width`
		`height`
		`maintainRatio`
		`factor`

`<s:transformImageType>`	Converts the image to either PNG or JPEG.	`contentType`
`<s:transformImageBlur>`	Performs a blur on the image.	`radius`

```
<s:graphicImage value="#{_review.reviewer.image ne null ?
    _review.reviewer.image ? '/img/golfer.png'}"
  fileName="#{_review.reviewer.username}-36-thumbnail"
  alt="[thumbnail of profile image]">
  <s:transformImageSize width="36" maintainRatio="true"/>
</s:graphicImage>
```

You can easily create your own transformation component by implementing the interface `org.jboss.seam.ui.graphicImage.ImageTransform`. This interface has one method, `applyTransform()`, which accepts the `Image` type from the Seam API that you worked with in section 13.1. To make your component available to JSF, you have to go through the song and dance of setting up a JSF component. If you're going to do so, check out the source code in the Seam UI module and have a good JSF reference close by such as *JavaServer Faces in Action* (Manning, 2004) or *Pro JSF and Ajax* (Apress, 2006). To save yourself time, take advantage of the Ajax4jsf Component Development Kit (CDK).

You'll have the opportunity to visit the `<s:graphicImage>` tag again when you learn how to send emails with Seam in section 13.4. There's an equivalent graphic component for embedding dynamic images in a PDF document. Speaking of PDF, it's time to move away from HTML and explore how to create PDF documents dynamically.

13.2 *PDF generation with iText*

You may be wondering, "What can an application framework do to help me create PDF documents?" After all, most other frameworks provide a halfhearted integration attempt by only helping you serve the PDF to the browser, leaving the work of creating the PDF up to you. Well, with Seam, the answer to this question is *plenty*.

You see, Seam goes well beyond just playing matchmaker between the browser and the PDF renderer. In Seam, creating and serving a PDF is handled just like any other JSF view. Seam provides a set of UI component tags that generate PDF content. When the template is processed, the view handler serves a PDF document to the browser, generated by the open source (LGPL/MPL) iText Java-PDF library, rather than an HTML document.

The PDF component tags extend from the tag handler in the Facelets API, so you must use Facelets to generate PDF documents in this way. To enable PDF support in your application, you need to add two files to the application classpath: itext.jar and jboss-seam-pdf.jar (both of which you'll find in the lib folder of projects generated with seam-gen). You can then begin using the PDF component tags in your Facelets templates.

13.2.1 *Laying out a PDF with UI components*

A Facelets template that renders a PDF document uses `<p:document>` as the root tag. Aside from the new root tag and the accompanying palette of PDF tags, there's no difference in how you develop it compared to any other Facelets template. You can use Facelets and Seam composition tags (e.g., `<ui:composition>`, `<s:decorate>`), non-rendering JSF component tags (e.g., `<h:panelGroup>`, `<s:fragment>`), and JSF component tags that produce HTML to build the JSF UI component tree. Since the PDF template is rendered by JSF just like any other JSF view, you can front-load the request with Seam's page-oriented controls (page actions, page parameters, and page restrictions). That's a pretty powerful combination. Notice that nowhere in that description did I mention Java. In this scenario, we want to avoid the use of Java to reuse our Facelets knowledge to create dynamic views. There's no need to step into a Java API to perform this work.

For the most part, the PDF component tags map one to one with the functionality provided by iText. An iText PDF document rendered through Seam consists of paragraphs, images, headers, footers, chapters, sections, tables, lists, bar codes, and even Swing components. You can customize the font size, font color, and background color on most elements. Some limitations exist, but the PDF component tags should be sufficient for all but the most complex requirements.

Rather than itemize each and every tag in the PDF component palette, I provide a comprehensive example that puts many of the tags to use. This approach will give you real-world experience with the PDF tags, which you can supplement by consulting the reference documentation for the specifics of each tag. In this example, we generate a scorecard in PDF format for a golf course. The scorecard is the grid of holes and tee sets that you use to record the number of strokes you took on each hole. It's fairly complex to render, but also aesthetically pleasing. Thus, I guarantee that this will be a rewarding experience.

SETTING UP FOR THE SCORECARD

To display the full scorecard for a course, it's necessary to use all the entities in the golf course model: `Facility`, `Course`, `Hole`, `TeeSet`, and `Tee`. The associations between these entities are configured to be lazy loaded. However, as you've learned, it's best to avoid lazy loading in cases when using it wouldn't be efficient. For instance, rendering the scorecard would cause a large number of lazy associations to be crossed, in turn causing a lot of queries. To optimize, we want to use a page action to eagerly fetch all the necessary data in a single query and then make that data available to the Facelets template. The `Scorecard` component, shown in listing 13.2, handles this preload logic in the `load()` method. The abundance of `join fetch` clauses in the JPQL that's executed in this method represents the eager fetching of the associations.

The `Scorecard` component also provides a handful of utility methods needed to render portions of the scorecard. The implementation details aren't important to this discussion, so the method bodies are hidden (you can see them in the book's source code). The use of the terms *out* and *in* represent the two halves of the golf course. *Out* is the first nine holes, leading away from the clubhouse. *In* is the back nine holes, returning to the clubhouse. The methods `getTeesOut()` and `getTeesIn()` are invoked from the Facelets template using a parameterized value expression.

Listing 13.2   The component that eagerly fetches the scorecard data

```
@Name("scorecard")
public class Scorecard extends EntityController {
    private static final String JPQL =
```

```
            "select distinct c from Course c " +
            "join fetch c.facility join fetch c.holes " +
            "join fetch c.teeSets ts join fetch ts.tees " +
            "where c.id = #{scorecard.courseId}";

    @RequestParameter private Long courseId;

    @Out private Course course;

    public void load() {
        course = (Course) createQuery(JPQL).getSingleResult();
    }

    public List<TeeSet> getTeeSets() { ... };
    public List<TeeSet> getMensTeeSets() { ... };
    public List<TeeSet> getLadiesTeeSets() { ... };
    public List<Integer> getHoleNumbersOut() { ... };
    public List<Integer> getHoleNumbersIn() { ... };
    public List<Hole> getHolesOut() { ... };
    public List<Hole> getHolesIn() { ... };
    public List<Tee> getTeesOut(TeeSet teeSet) { ... };
    public List<Tee> getTeesIn(TeeSet teeSet) { ... };
}
```

A scorecard is complex and so is the Facelets template needed to generate it. We get there in two phases. In the first phase, we get our feet wet with a simple PDF report.

A BASIC PDF REPORT

The first step is to create the Facelets template exportCourseInfo.xhtml, shown in listing 13.3. This template renders basic information about a course and the facility logo. Notice that the root of the template is `<p:document>` and that the template declares the following namespace, which imports the PDF UI component tags:

```
p:xmlns="http://jboss.com/products/seam/pdf"
```

Next, we connect a page action to this view ID to preload the scorecard data, defined in the exportCourseInfo.page.xml descriptor:

```
<page action="#{scorecard.load}"/>
```

The page action isn't a prerequisite for rendering a PDF, but it's relevant in this scenario.

Listing 13.3   A simple PDF template that renders text, an image, and a list

```
<p:document xmlns="http://www.w3.org/1999/xhtml"          ❶
  xmlns:p="http://jboss.com/products/seam/pdf"
  xmlns:ui="http://java.sun.com/jsf/facelets"
  xmlns:s="http://jboss.com/products/seam/taglib"
  title="#{course.name}"
  creator="Open 18"
  pageSize="LETTER"                   ❷
  type="#{not empty param.type ? param.type : 'pdf'}">     ❸
  <p:image value="#{course.facility.logo}"                 ❹
    rendered="#{course.facility.logo != null}">
    <s:transformImageSize height="96" maintainRatio="true"/>
  </p:image>
  <p:font size="18">
```

```
          <p:paragraph>#{course.name}</p:paragraph>
      </p:font>
      <p:font size="8" color="darkgray">
          <p:paragraph>Designed by #{course.designer}</p:paragraph>
          <p:paragraph spacingAfter="4">
            <p:font style="bold">#{course.numHoles}</p:font> HOLES #{' - '}
            <p:font style="bold">PAR</p:font> #{course.totalMensPar}
          </p:paragraph>
          <p:list listSymbol="-">                    ⑥
            <ui:repeat var="ts" value="#{scorecard.teeSets}">      ⑦
              <p:listItem>#{ts.name} (#{ts.totalDistance} yds)</p:listItem>
            </ui:repeat>
          </p:list>
      </p:font>
  </p:document>
```

As you can see in listing 13.3, it doesn't take much to create a PDF document. The `<p:document>` tag ❶ notifies the view handler to initialize a new iText PDF document. If used alone, this tag will produce an empty document and push it to the browser. A wide range of optional attributes are available on the `<p:document>` tag that you can use to adjust the properties of the PDF document, such as `title`, `subject`, `author`, `keywords`, and `creator`. You can also change the orientation and size of the page. The default page size is A4, but here it has been changed to LETTER ❷.

iText documents are optimized to be rendered as PDF, the default, but can also produce RTF or HTML. You can set the output format using the `type` attribute ❸, which accepts three values: `pdf`, `rtf`, and `html`. Here, the output format is controlled by the request parameter `type`, if present.

NOTE   The RTF and HTML output formats support the same features as PDF with the exception of tables, images, and inline HTML. If any of these features are present in the template, they're ignored when the document is rendered.

Moving on to the content of the document, the template includes one image ❹, three paragraphs ❺, and one bulleted list ❻. The `<p:image>` tag works just like the `<s:graph-icImage>` tag. It can read images from the Java types in table 13.1 and can apply image transformations. The `<p:image>` tag is used here with `<s:transformImageSize>` to reduce the height of the image to 96 pixels, but the tag also has built-in scaling functionality. The `<p:font>` tag applies font settings to all descendent tags until another `<p:font>` tag is encountered that alters those settings. All inline text *must* be enclosed in a `<p:paragraph>` tag or strange things occur (exceptions include `<p:header>`, `<p:footer>`, and `<p:listItem>`). You can also use a `<p:font>` tag within a span of paragraph text to change the font characteristics for a single word or phrase.

NOTE   There are some cases when the font settings aren't inherited by a nested `<p:font>` tag. For instance, if you use a `<p:font>` around a `<p:list>` and then use the `<p:font>` to customize the contents of a `<p:listItem>`, the font settings from the outer tag—such as font size—aren't inherited, forcing you to have to apply them again on the nested tag. Expect this to be fixed in the future.

It's possible to use the Facelets iteration component tag ❼ to generate branches of the component tree dynamically. In this case, we iterate over the tee sets on the course and display the tee set name and total distance in yards of each set as list items. The final result is shown in figure 13.1.

The Pointe Golf Club
Designed by Russell Breeden
18 HOLES - PAR 71

- Gold (6343 yds)
- Blue (5911 yds)
- White (5426 yds)
- Red (4862 yds)

As you can see, creating a report in PDF format is no more difficult than creating a web page. But you aren't done yet. Most reports that you have to build probably require some sort of tabular data. Seam offers a set of component tags for creating PDF tables that make it no more difficult than using the JSF panel grid component for rendering HTML tables. We put these PDF table tags to the test by rendering a complete course scorecard, which shows the tee sets as well as the distances for each hole in a tee set.

Figure 13.1   A PDF document showing basic course and tee set information

13.2.2   Working with tables and cells

PDF tables are created in Seam using the `<p:table>` and `<p:cell>` component tags. The `<p:table>` tag works in precisely the same way as the `<h:panelGrid>` tag from the standard JSF component palette, except that the child components must be wrapped in a `<p:cell>` tag. You explicitly state how many columns the table has by using the columns attribute. Once an equivalent number of `<p:cell>` tags have been encountered, a new row is started. The contents of a `<p:cell>` tag can be another table, giving rise to nested tables. A single cell can be made to span multiple columns using the colspan attribute on `<p:cell>`. It's not possible, however, for a cell to span more than one row (i.e., rowspan).

TIP   As an alternative to PDF tables, you can use HTML tables. You can use other HTML elements as well, including JSF component tags that produce HTML. To add HTML to the PDF, you nest it within a `<p:html>` element. Keep in mind that the HTML is converted to iText objects internally, so you are limited to what iText can produce. You can also use `<p:swing>` for rendering a Swing component and `<p:barcode>` to create a bar code. The `<p:barcode>` tag can also be used in an HTML page.

To demonstrate the table component tag in action, we use it to help render the scorecard for a golf course. This use case offers enough complexity to show off many of the advanced capabilities of the table tag, rather than having me list them in a table. Before jumping into the template, though, I briefly explain the goal.

The scorecard consists of a single table that's logically partitioned into two halves. The left side of the card has information about the course's front nine holes (Out), and the right side of the card has information about the course's back nine holes (In). The first row displays the hole numbers. Following that row are rows for each tee set.

The tee set rows consist of distance values that correspond with each hole number. Finally, there's a row that displays the par for each hole. The template that produces this markup, exportScorecard.xhtml, is shown in listing 13.4.

Listing 13.4   The PDF template that renders the course scorecard

```
<p:document xmlns="http://www.w3.org/1999/xhtml"
  xmlns:ui="http://java.sun.com/jsf/facelets"
  xmlns:f="http://java.sun.com/jsf/core"
  xmlns:p="http://jboss.com/products/seam/pdf"
  title="#{course.name} Scorecard"
  orientation="landscape">            ❶
  <p:font size="8">
    <p:table columns="22" widthPercentage="100" headerRows="1"      ❷
      widths="3 1 1 1 1 1 1 1 1 1 1 1 1 1 1 1 1 1 1 1 1 1">
    <f:facet name="defaultCell">      ❸
      <p:cell padding="5" noWrap="true"
        horizontalAlignment="center" verticalAlignment="middle"/>
    </f:facet>
    <p:font size="8" color="white" style="bold">      ❹
      <p:cell horizontalAlignment="left" grayFill=".25">      ❺
        <p:paragraph>Hole</p:paragraph>
      </p:cell>
      <ui:repeat var="_holeNum" value="#{scorecard.holeNumbersOut}">      ❻
        <p:cell grayFill=".25">
          <p:paragraph>#{_holeNum}</p:paragraph>
        </p:cell>
      </ui:repeat>
      <p:cell grayFill=".25"><p:paragraph>Out</p:paragraph></p:cell>
      <ui:repeat var="_holeNum" value="#{scorecard.holeNumbersIn}">
        <p:cell grayFill=".25">
          <p:paragraph>#{_holeNum}</p:paragraph>
        </p:cell>
      </ui:repeat>
      <p:cell grayFill=".25"><p:paragraph>In</p:paragraph></p:cell>
      <p:cell grayFill=".25"><p:paragraph>Total</p:paragraph></p:cell>
    </p:font>
    <ui:repeat var="_ts" value="#{scorecard.mensAndUnisexTeeSets}">
      <p:font size="8">
        <p:cell horizontalAlignment="left"
          backgroundColor="#{_ts.color}">      ❼
          <p:paragraph>#{_ts.name}</p:paragraph>
        </p:cell>
        <ui:repeat var="_tee" value="#{scorecard.getTeesOut(_ts)}">
          <p:cell backgroundColor="#{_ts.color}">
            <p:paragraph>#{_tee.distance}</p:paragraph>
          </p:cell>
        </ui:repeat>
        <p:cell backgroundColor="#{_ts.color}">
          <p:paragraph>#{_ts.distanceOut}</p:paragraph>
        </p:cell>
        <ui:repeat var="_tee" value="#{scorecard.getTeesIn(_ts)}">
          <p:cell backgroundColor="#{_ts.color}">
            <p:paragraph>#{_tee.distance}</p:paragraph>
          </p:cell>
```

```
        </ui:repeat>
        <p:cell backgroundColor="#{_ts.color}">
          <p:paragraph>#{_ts.distanceIn}</p:paragraph>
        </p:cell>
        <p:cell backgroundColor="#{_ts.color}">
          <p:paragraph>#{_ts.totalDistance}</p:paragraph>
        </p:cell>
      </p:font>
    </ui:repeat>
    <p:font size="8" style="bold">
      <p:cell horizontalAlignment="left" grayFill=".9">
        <p:paragraph>Par</p:paragraph>
      </p:cell>
      <ui:repeat var="_hole" value="#{scorecard.holesOut}">
        <p:cell grayFill=".9">
          <p:paragraph>#{_hole.mensPar}</p:paragraph>
        </p:cell>
      </ui:repeat>
      <p:cell grayFill=".9">
        <p:paragraph>#{course.mensParOut}</p:paragraph>
      </p:cell>
      <ui:repeat var="_hole" value="#{scorecard.holesIn}">
        <p:cell grayFill=".9">
          <p:paragraph>#{_hole.mensPar}</p:paragraph>
        </p:cell>
      </ui:repeat>
      <p:cell grayFill=".9">
        <p:paragraph>#{course.mensParIn}</p:paragraph>
      </p:cell>
      <p:cell grayFill=".9">
        <p:paragraph>#{course.totalMensPar}</p:paragraph>
      </p:cell>
    </p:font>
  </p:table>
  </p:font>
</p:document>
```

The default layout for a document is portrait, but the layout of this document is set to landscape ❶ to make room for the scorecard. If a table is wider than the document, the text in each cell is forced to wrap. If wrapping is required but the noWrap attribute on <p:cell> is false, the text in the cell may overrun the cell borders (and look ugly).

The table is declared using the <p:table> tag. The scorecard table has 22 columns and is configured to span the width of the page ❷. The first row is treated as a header, as defined by the headerRows attribute. This row is repeated if the table is divided across a page boundary. The widths attribute dictates the width ratios of the cells. In this example, the first column is three times as wide as the other columns in the table. If the widths attribute isn't specified, the cells are evenly distributed. As an alternative to using the widths attribute, we could have used 24 columns and added colspan="3" to the first <p:cell> tag in each row to achieve the same effect.

The content of the table is created by repeating the <p:cell> across columns and rows, either explicitly ❺ or indirectly using an iteration component ❻. To help with the task of defining cells, the <p:table> tag supports "Don't Repeat Yourself" (DRY) semantics by offering a cell prototype, declared in the defaultCell facet ❸. You can place all of the attributes you would like to have applied to each <p:cell> in this prototype cell. You can, of course, override these settings as needed in the <p:cell> tag. Here we establish the default padding, wrap behavior, and alignments. You can also surround the whole table, or a series of cells, in a <p:font> tag to have font settings applied to descendent cells.

NOTE   The <p:cell> must have a <p:paragraph> tag as its first and only element. Although the text will still render without being wrapped in <p:paragraph>, the font settings will not be applied to it.

The final result of the scorecard is shown in figure 13.2.

The Pointe Golf Club
Designed by Russell Breeden

Hole	1	2	3	4	5	6	7	8	9	Out	10	11	12	13	14	15	16	17	18	In	Total
Gold	528	429	194	347	339	454	151	459	361	3262	537	179	348	372	152	353	377	144	619	3081	6343
Blue	493	397	188	330	325	386	137	447	346	3049	512	163	344	350	125	328	347	137	556	2862	5911
White	433	372	186	289	308	349	116	422	316	2791	483	134	328	312	114	301	325	125	513	2635	5426
Par	5	4	3	4	4	4	3	5	4	36	5	3	4	4	3	4	4	3	5	35	71

Figure 13.2   A PDF document showing a golf course scorecard

The scorecard makes liberal use of color and grayscale shading. To apply a grayscale background to a cell, you set the grayFill attribute on <p:cell> ❺ to a value between 0 and 1 (lower is darker). You can also apply colors to text, cell backgrounds, tables, sections, and image borders. The scorecard example makes use of color for the header row text ❹ and most of the cell backgrounds ❼. Color is important for making an attractive document, so let's take a closer look at what types of color values are accepted.

13.2.3 *Adding a splash of color*

The iText library uses the AWT Color object for applying color to a PDF document or a chart, covered later. Given that you are working in a Facelets template, you need a translation layer. Fortunately, Seam provides one. Seam lets you choose from several color code sets that you can use to specify a color value in a component tag attribute. That value is then translated into a Color object and passed to the iText API. The possible value types you can enter are shown in table 13.3. If you enter an invalid color value, an exception will be thrown when the document is rendered.

The AWT color constant names are the most convenient approach and should be sufficient if basic colors will do. If you've spent a lot of time with Cascading Style Sheets (CSS), you may be fluent in hexadecimal color codes and may choose to use

Table 13.2 Possible color values used in the PDF or chart components

Type	Identified by	Examples
`java.awt.Color` constant	Lowercase constant name	red, green, blue
Hexadecimal number	Leading #, 0x, or 0X	#FF0000, 0x00FF00, 0X0000FF
Octal number	Leading 0	077600000, 0177400, 0377
`UIColor`	JSF client identifier	`<p:color id="maroon" color="#8B0000"/>`

those instead. For those of you who can even comprehend octal numbers, you'll be glad to know they're supported too.

You've seen many of the features offered by Seam's PDF component palette in this section. You'll be excited to hear that equivalent support for creating Microsoft Excel documents is coming your way soon, as part of Seam 2.1. Although the Excel tags aren't covered in this book, you have the background knowledge you need to be able to use them.

There are some limitations with the template-based approach, but remember that if you find yourself pushing the envelope of what these tags can handle, you can always switch to using the iText API directly. If you do make that switch, you'll be glad to know that, in addition to the component tags, Seam's PDF module includes an API for serving PDF documents to the browser. We first look at customizing the document store servlet to handle missing documents and serve friendly file extensions, and then dig deeper into how to use it to serve your own documents.

13.2.4 *Graceful failures and friendly file extensions*

Seam serves PDF documents from the JSF phase listener `DocumentStorePhaseListener`. After a document is created from a Facelets template, it's stored in the built-in component named `documentStore` under a unique id. Seam redirects to a servlet path that begins with /seam-doc, passing the id in the request parameter `docId`. The phase listener traps requests matching this path, reads the id from the request parameter, and pushes the document with this id to the browser. Here's an example of the servlet path for a document:

```
/seam-doc.seam?docId=10&cid=3
```

Notice the conversation token in the URL. The `documentStore` component is scoped to the conversation. Thus, documents exist for the lifetime of the conversation that created them. If a long-running conversation isn't active, the document lasts for a logical request (i.e., a temporary conversation). It's likely that if the user bookmarks the URL of the PDF document, he or she will encounter an error when trying to retrieve the document again because the URL is stale and the document no longer exists. To help the user understand why the request doesn't work, you can configure a custom error page. First, add the component namespace `http://jboss.com/products/seam/pdf`, prefixed with `pdf`, to the component descriptor. Then, configure the `documentStore` component as follows:

```
<pdf:document-store error-page="/missingDoc.seam"/>
```

It's also possible to configure this built-in component to switch from using a JSF phase listener to a servlet to serve the PDF document. The benefit of using a servlet is that users won't see a cryptic /seam-doc.seam?docId=4, but rather a friendly one that ends in the .pdf file extension. There are two steps to making this change. First, add the `org.jboss.seam.pdf.DocumentStoreServlet` to the web.xml descriptor to trap servlet paths that end in .pdf or .rtf:

```
<servlet>
  <servlet-name>Document Store Servlet</servlet-name>
  <servlet-class>org.jboss.seam.pdf.DocumentStoreServlet</servlet-class>
</servlet>
<servlet-mapping>
  <servlet-name>Document Store Servlet</servlet-name>
  <url-pattern>*.pdf</url-pattern>
</servlet-mapping>
<servlet-mapping>
  <servlet-name>Document Store Servlet</servlet-name>
  <url-pattern>*.rtf</url-pattern>
</servlet-mapping>
```

Then let the document store component know that this servlet is available and can be used by adding the `use-extensions` attribute to the component configuration:

```
<pdf:document-store use-extensions="true" error-page="/missingDoc.seam"/>
```

When extensions are enabled, Seam prepares the document URL by removing the default suffix from the view ID and replacing it with the file extension of the document. A redirect is then issued to the new path. Here's an example of the servlet path for the scorecard:

```
exportScorecard.pdf?docId=10&cid=3
```

The filename in the path is completely irrelevant to Seam. The only piece of information that matters is the `docId` request parameter. However, the friendly URL is extremely relevant to an end user because the document id doesn't carry any semantic value. For this reason, I highly recommend that you use the file extension feature.

Although the document store component was designed to serve documents generated using the `<p:document>` tag, you can also use it to serve your own binary documents (e.g., PDF, Word, Excel), either served from a database or that you generate using a document builder API such as iText or Apache POI. On the other hand, if you're happy using Seam's PDF support to create documents using Facelets templates, you can skip this next section.

13.2.5 *Serving dynamic documents*

I promised earlier that you would see other ways to serve a binary document. One option is to create a custom servlet. Seam makes this easy by allowing any Seam component that extends `AbstractResource` to be used as a servlet. You override the method `get-ResourcePath()`, which is appended to /seam/resource, to indicate the URL that your servlet handles. You then override the `getResource()` method to serve the resource. But that still puts a lot of burden on you to prepare the file. There's an easier way.

In addition to the template-based approach to creating PDF documents, Seam has support for managing a file download, which is tricky to do on your own, especially in a JSF application. The built-in `documentStore` component handles the dirty work of preparing and serving a file to the browser. You simply inject `documentStore` into your component, use it to store the file data under a unique id, and then redirect the user to a URL that is processed by the `DocumentStorePhaseListener` (or `DocumentStore-Servlet`). Seam takes over from there. Listing 13.5 shows an example of this process using raw PDF data. Note that Seam doesn't import the context variable prefix `org.jboss.seam.pdf` by default, so you must import it in order to use the unqualified component name `documentStore`.

Listing 13.5   A component that pushes a dynamic document to the browser

```java
package org.jboss.seam.report;
import ...;

@Name("reportGenerator")
@Import("org.jboss.seam.pdf")
public class ReportGenerator() {
    @In private Manager manager;
    @In private DocumentStore documentStore;
    @In private FacesContext facesContext;

    public void generate() {
        byte[] binaryData = ...;
        DocumentData data = new DocumentData("report"          ◁─── Wraps binary
            new DocumentData.DocumentType("pdf", "application/pdf"),    data as Seam
            binaryData);                                                document
        String docId = documentStore.newId();         ┌─ Stores document
        documentStore.saveData(docId, data);       ◁──┘  using unique id
        String documentUrl =
            documentStore.preferredUrlForContent(    ◁───┐
                data.getBaseName(),                      │  Builds URL to
                data.getDocumentType().getExtension(),   │  serve document
                docId);
        redirect(documentUrl);
    }

    protected void redirect(String url) {           ┌─ Adds
        try {                                        │  conversation
            facesContext.getExternalContext().redirect(  │  token to URL
                manager.encodeConversationId(url));  ◁──┘
        }
        catch (IOException ioe) { throw new RedirectException(ioe); }
    }
}
```

As you can see, Seam provides a convenient way to push binary documents to the browser, comparable to what other frameworks offer. In most cases, though, you won't use this approach unless you absolutely need the extra power of creating documents in Java. Instead, you'll take advantage of Seam's template-based approach, which goes well beyond where other frameworks leave off.

So far you have learned to render dynamic images and PDF documents. Next up is charts, another type of dynamic image. Charts can be rendered in both an HTML page and a PDF document. Not to spoil the excitement, but after the next section, you'll learn to include images, PDFs, and charts in an email with almost no additional work.

13.3   *Quick and easy charting with JFreeChart*

Creating charts in Seam is, you guessed it, just another Facelets template—only this time, it's just a fragment of a template. Learning to use Seam's charting module is simply a matter of learning how to use the chart-related UI component tags.

Charts provide a visual representation of data sets. In technical terms, that means dynamic graphic generation. Seam's charting module is based on the open source (GNU General Public License, or GPL) JFreeChart chart library. JFreeChart offers a wide variety of chart types and can render them in several image formats. At the time of this writing, Seam only offers a subset of the JFreeChart functionality, but the idea is to eventually bring most of the chart types under the wings of Seam's Facelets-based infrastructure. Seam currently supports bar charts, pie charts, and line plots, all of which are rendered in JPEG format.

To enable charting support in your application, you add jfreechart.jar and jcommon.jar to the application's classpath. Then, it's just a matter of hooking the UI component tags up to data. Seam's charting support is bundled in Seam's PDF module, and the component tags share the same UI component set. That doesn't mean you can only use charts in PDF documents, though. They can be rendered in HTML pages too!

13.3.1   *Chart basics*

To add a chart to your Facelets template, you first register the UI component library in the root element of the template using the same namespace as for the PDF component tags:

```
xmlns:p="http://jboss.com/products/seam/pdf"
```

The charts that Seam supports, along with the corresponding component tag, are as follow:

- Bar chart—`<p:barchart>`
- Pie chart—`<p:piechart>`
- Line chart—`<p:linechart>`

Each chart consists of several common configuration elements, including title, legend, orientation, width, height, and a wide variety of paint, stroke, gridline, and border display options. If you're a fan of cool graphics, your favorite display option might be the 3D feature, which gives the chart visual depth. Appearances aside, the most important aspect of every chart is the data.

A chart consists of one or more sets of data, represented by the `<p:series>` tag, and one or more nested data points in each series, represented by the `<p:data>` tag. The tags can map one to one with the data displayed, or you can nest either of them in a repeating component, such as `<ui:repeat>`, to render a dynamic collection of data.

The crowning feature of charts is that they are eye-catching. Otherwise, tabular data would do just fine. That means adding a splash of color. There are attributes on each component tag that allow you to specify the color for various regions of the chart. These attributes all end in `Paint`. The JFreeChart library also uses the AWT `Color` object for defining colors. Thus, Seam offers the same translation for color values in charts as it does for PDF documents. Refer back to table 13.3 for the possible color values.

I now take you through each chart type, demonstrating how to use the `<p:series>` and `<p:data>` tags, as well as several of the aesthetic configurations. The examples shown pertain to golf rounds, which were added to the application in chapter 10. Let's start with bar charts.

13.3.2 *Bar charts*

A bar chart can be viewed as a series of buckets. Each bucket is filled proportionally to the value being represented. The purpose of a bar chart is to compare one or more values. A complete set of the different buckets is referred to as a series. There can be more than one series on the same chart, each representing some data variation. For instance, if the buckets represented golf pro shop sales, there would be buckets for balls, shirts, and shoes. The series could represent a single day's sales.

In Seam's charting component palette, each bucket is represented by a `<p:data>` tag. The `key` attribute on this tag represents the name of the bucket (the sale item), and the `value` specifies how much it is filled (how many sold). The `<p:data>` tags are grouped in a series as children of the `<p:series>` tag. The `key` attribute on the `<p:series>` tag is the data variation (the date of sale). The `<p:series>` tag is the child of the chart tag, in this case `<p:barchart>`.

Taking an example from the Open 18 application, we look at the average score (average number of strokes taken) versus par (the number of expected strokes for a given hole) for a round. We group all of the holes with the same par together and look at what the golfer scored on average. The title of the chart is "Average Score vs. Par." In this case, the bucket is the par value and how much the bucket is filled is the average score. A very basic version of this chart is shown here:

```
<p:barchart title="Average Score vs. Par" rangeAxisLabel="Avg Score">
  <p:series key="#{round.date}">
    <p:data key="Par 3" value="#{roundHome.getAverageScore(3)}"/>
    <p:data key="Par 4" value="#{roundHome.getAverageScore(4)}"/>
    <p:data key="Par 5" value="#{roundHome.getAverageScore(5)}"/>
  </p:series>
</p:barchart>
```

The default size of the chart in pixels is 400x300, which can be overridden using the `width` and `height` attributes. Don't worry right now how the average scores are calculated because that's tangential to how the bar chart works. This chart has one series, named after the date that the round was played. You must always provide at least one series. If you have only one series, and the name isn't relevant, you can hide its presence by keeping the legend disabled. If you have more than one series, the legend is used for the purpose of identifying each series according to its color.

Let's add another series by comparing the golfer's round with the average of all of that golfer's rounds to date. In this case, there are two series, so the legend is needed to distinguish them from one another.

```
<p:barchart title="Average Score vs. Par" rangeAxisLabel="Avg Score"
    legend="true" is3D="true" plotForegroundAlpha=".9">
  <p:series key="#{round.date}" seriesPaint="series1">
    <p:data key="Par 3" value="#{roundHome.getAverageScore(3)}"/>
    <p:data key="Par 4" value="#{roundHome.getAverageScore(4)}"/>
    <p:data key="Par 5" value="#{roundHome.getAverageScore(5)}"/>
  </p:series>
  <p:series key="#{round.golfer.username}'s rounds" seriesPaint="series2">
    <p:data key="Par 3" value="#{golferRounds.getAverageScore(3)}"/>
    <p:data key="Par 4" value="#{golferRounds.getAverageScore(4)}"/>
    <p:data key="Par 5" value="#{golferRounds.getAverageScore(5)}"/>
  </p:series>
  <p:color id="series1" color="#FFBF4F"/>
  <p:color id="series2" color="#A6C78E"/>
</p:barchart>
```

The rendered output of the Average Score vs. Par chart is shown in figure 13.3.

There are now two series in this chart, a legend, and some flare, the later provided by the 3D flag, the alpha transparency, and the custom bar colors. Although not shown in these examples, I tend to use the following options as a starting point to clear the default canvas (border and background) that's applied to the charts:

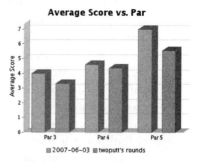

Figure 13.3   A bar chart with two series generated using the Seam chart component tags

```
borderVisible="false"
borderBackgroundPaint="white"
plotOutlinePaint="white"
legendOutlinePaint="white"
```

(legendOutlinePaint applies to bar and line charts only.)

Many other properties are available for customizing the look of a chart. At this point, you have enough to run with. In fact, with bar charts under your belt, we can cruise through the next two chart types because they are much the same, starting with line charts.

13.3.3   *Line charts*

Line charts are similar to bar charts except that the points in a series are connected together rather than filled from the base. If you've ever had to work on a spreadsheet assignment in a subject like economics, you've probably created at least one if not a hundred line charts. Fortunately, creating them in Seam is no more difficult than creating them in a spreadsheet.

Line charts are ideal for showing trends. In the Open 18 application, trends can be used to show a golfer's progress from one round to the next, such as putting average and strokes over par. First, we need to retrieve the golfer's rounds. Assuming the context variable `selectedGolfer` is available on the current page, we can use it in a restriction clause of a Query component, defined in the component descriptor, that fetches the golfer's rounds:

```
<framework:entity-query name="golferRounds"
  ejbql="select r from Round r join fetch r.scores" order="r.date asc">
  <framework:restrictions>
    <value>r.golfer = #{selectedGolfer}</value>
  </framework:restrictions>
</framework:entity-query>
```

The statistics for each round are represented as a series (a line) on the chart. The individual data points are taken from each round and plotted progressively over time according to the date the round was played. To plot the points for each round, we use an iteration component to loop through the rounds for a golfer and read the data points from each `Round` instance:

```
<p:linechart title="Game Analysis" domainAxisLabel="Date of round"
  legend="true">
  <p:series key="Putting average">
    <ui:repeat var="_round" value="#{golferRounds.resultList}">
      <p:data key="#{_round.date}" value="#{_round.averagePutts}"/>
    </ui:repeat>
  </p:series>
  <p:series key="Strokes over par">
    <ui:repeat var="_round" value="#{golferRounds.resultList}">
      <p:data key="#{_round.date}" value="#{_round.strokesOverPar}"/>
    </ui:repeat>
  </p:series>
</p:linechart>
```

The rendered output of the game analysis chart is shown in figure 13.4. In this example, the labeling of the chart is reversed from what it was in the bar chart. The range axis is unlabeled since the purpose of the values varies according to the series, making

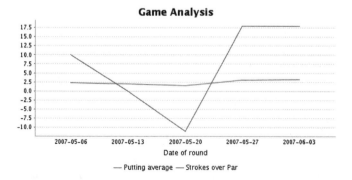

Figure 13.4 A line chart with two series generated using the Seam chart component tags

the legend very important. If you're plotting series that represent the same type of data, it makes sense to label the range axis. The domain axis is labeled to indicate that the dates represent the date the round was played. As the range of data changes, the chart automatically scales itself accordingly. While automatic scaling is sometimes desirable, there may be times when you need to fix the range. Unfortunately, the component tags don't provide a way to customize the default behavior.

All that's left is the simplest and most universal of all the charts: the pie chart.

13.3.4 *Pie charts*

No matter how you divide it up, a pie chart adds up to 100 percent. Each slice represents the percentage of the whole an item accounts for. The slices are each assigned a unique color and identified by a label. You can have as many wedges as you want, but over a certain point you start to get diminishing returns because the chart becomes too difficult to read.

Pie charts, by nature of design, only represent a single series of data. Therefore, you only need to use `<p:data>` tags. (If a `<p:series>` tag is present, it's ignored.) Each `<p:data>` tag represents one slice of the pie. The value of each slice is treated as a weight, not a percentage. The percentage is assigned to each slice automatically, calculated by dividing the slice's value by the total value of all of the slices. (It's impossible to exceed 100%.)

In the Open 18 application, we provide users with a pie chart to help them analyze their putting. Each wedge in the pie chart represents the number of strokes it took the user to get the ball in the hole, and the size of the wedge is how often that number of strokes was taken. The value expression `#{roundHome.puttFrequencies}` returns a collection of `PuttFrequency` objects. The `PuttFrequency` class has two properties, `numPutts` and `count`, which are used as the key and value of the data point, respectively. Since the user can take any number of putts, and some numbers may not be used, we use an iteration component to render the data points:

```
<p:piechart title="Putt Analysis" legend="false"
  circular="true" is3D="true" plotForegroundAlpha="0.9">
  <ui:repeat var="_freq"
    value="#{roundHome.puttFrequencies}">
    <p:data key="#{_freq.numPutts} putt" value="#{_freq.count}"/>
  </ui:repeat>
</p:piechart>
```

The rendered output of the putt analysis chart is shown in figure 13.5. Because a pie chart uses labels for each of the slices, there's no need for a legend, so it's disabled.

You've seen several examples of how you can create dynamic graphics and documents simply by using JSF component tags. You can make the graphics even more dynamic by using the Ajax-driven partial page rendering covered in the previous chapter.

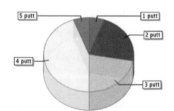

Putt Analysis

Figure 13.5   A pie chart generated using the Seam chart component tags

Then you can manipulate the settings in one part of the page and see the image, such as a chart, update instantly. That's one of the main benefits of using JSF component tags to create graphics.

Up to this point, everything in this chapter has catered to the browser, either to upload a file, render a graphic, or to serve a file to the browser as a download. But guess what? You can generate and send emails following this philosophy. In fact, you can even send dynamic graphics and documents along with the email as attachments. You are practically there already. There's just a little bit of additional knowledge to fill in.

13.4   Composing email the Seam way

To send an email in Seam, you can use a Facelets template just as you do to create a PDF document. Once again, it's just like any other JSF view; however, once the template is processed, the view handler sends an email using a JavaMail Session rather than serving an HTML response to the browser. To support this feature, there's another set of UI component tags oriented toward email composition. These tags extend from the tag handler from the Facelets API, so you must be using Facelets to send email this way. Let's try it out.

13.4.1   Sending your first message

An email template differs slightly from its PDF counterpart—it doesn't send any response to the browser. Instead, the root email component tag, `<m:message>`, is treated like a utility tag in that it performs an action. Although it does render its children, that result is buffered into an email message.

When the start tag is encountered during the rendering process, a new email message object, `MimeMessage`, is instantiated. The tags nested within `<m:message>` contribute to the `MimeMessage` object. When the end tag is encountered, the object is passed to the JavaMail `Transport` object, which sends the message off to the recipients.

It's possible to embed the `<m:message>` tag in any Facelets template, which would result in an email message being sent when that page is rendered. In practice, however, you typically create a stand-alone template reserved for composing an email and then call on that template from Java when the message needs to be sent. We'll get to that in a moment.

Let's consider an example to demonstrate how the process of composing and sending an email works. After new golfers register, we want to send them an email welcoming them to the community and encouraging them to participate. Listing 13.6 shows a plain-text email containing the welcome message and authentication credentials for new golfers.

Listing 13.6   A plain-text email message template

```
<m:message xmlns="http://www.w3.org/1999/xhtml"        ❶
   xmlns:m="http://jboss.com/products/seam/mail"
   importance="normal">
   <m:header name="X-Composed-By" value="JBoss Seam"/>       ❷
   <m:from name="Open 18" address="members@open18.org"/>       ❸
   <m:replyTo address="noreply@open18.org"/>
```

```
    <m:to name="#{newGolfer.name}">#{newGolfer.emailAddress}</m:to>      ❹
    <m:subject>Open 18 - Registration Information</m:subject>       ❺
    <m:body type="plain">#{newGolfer.name},       ❻
```

Welcome to the Open 18 community!

Thank you for registering. On behalf of the other members, I would
like to say that we look forward to your participation in the Open
18 community.

Below is your account information. Please keep it for your records.

Username: #{newGolfer.username}
Password: #{passwordBean.password}

Your password has been encrypted in our database...

Open 18
...a place for golfers
Member Services</m:body>
</m:message>

The <m:message> tag ❶ indicates that this component tree fragment is responsible
for producing and sending an email message. The <m:message> tag supports the configuration of a number of standard email headers using the attributes importance,
precedence, and requestReadReceipt. Additional headers can be added using the
<m:header> tag ❷. All email messages must specify a sender ❸, a recipient ❹, a sub-
ject ❺, and a body ❻. Any number of <m:cc> or <m:bcc> tags can be included to add
Cc and Bcc recipients to the message, respectively.

The body of the message is assumed to be HTML unless specified as plain text
using the type attribute on <m:body>. You can send both an HTML and plain-text
body so that the email client has a choice of which one to render, shown here. The
HTML part is placed directly inside the <m:body> tag and the alternative part, assumed
to be plain text, is placed within a facet named alternative.

```
    <m:body>
      <html>
        <body>
          <p>#{newGolfer.name},</p>
          <p><b>Welcome to the <span style="color: green;">Open 18</strong>
community!</b></p>
          ...
        </body>
      </html>
      <f:facet name="alternative">#{newGolfer.name},
Welcome to the Open 18 community!
      ...
      </f:facet>
    </m:body>
```

The rendered HTML version of the welcome email is shown in figure 13.6. You'll see
later on how the inline image gets inserted.

The email template appears simple enough, but we haven't addressed when the
template is activated and how it gains access to the context variables newGolfer and
passwordBean. This is where Seam's email support shows its uniqueness.

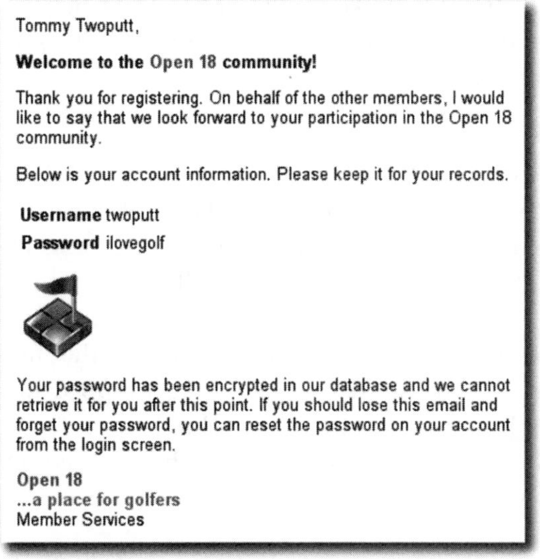

Tommy Twoputt,

Welcome to the Open 18 community!

Thank you for registering. On behalf of the other members, I would like to say that we look forward to your participation in the Open 18 community.

Below is your account information. Please keep it for your records.

Username twoputt
Password ilovegolf

Your password has been encrypted in our database and we cannot retrieve it for you after this point. If you should lose this email and forget your password, you can reset the password on your account from the login screen.

Open 18
...a place for golfers
Member Services

Figure 13.6   An HTML email created by Seam's mail component that includes an inline image

GETTING THE EMAIL TO GO THROUGH

If you've worked with JSP in the past, you may shudder at the idea of embedding email logic in a view template, as we are doing here. It's not that drafting an email using a template is inherently bad; it's that without some back-breaking effort, it's not possible to have the application code render a JSP template on demand. It *is* possible to do this with a Facelets template, though. That's exactly how you "send" an email: you render it.

The rendering is handled by Seam's `Renderer` component, named `renderer`, which is typically invoked from within an action method. The template can access any context variables that are in scope at the time the renderer is invoked. The `Registra-tionMailer` component, shown here, can be injected into the `RegisterAction` component and invoked from the `register()` method. The `newGolfer` and `passwordBean` components are still in scope, so they can be accessed from the email template. The `render()` method doesn't return anything because the rendered content is swept away to the email transport.

```
package org.open18.action.mail;
import ...;
import org.jboss.seam.faces.Renderer;

@Name("registrationMailer")
public class RegistrationMailer() {
    @In private Renderer renderer;

    public void sendWelcomeEmail() {
        renderer.render("/email/welcome.xhtml");
    }
}
```

You may worry that if the mail server is on a coffee break when the user submits the registration form, the user's browser will hang until the mail server comes back. To avoid this scenario, you can have the email sent asynchronously. Creating an asynchronous method in Seam is so trivial you almost feel like you're cheating. Asynchronous tasks aren't covered in this book, but I want to give you a glimpse of how they're initiated. You just add the `@Asynchronous` annotation to the method:

```
@Asynchronous void sendWelcomeEmail() { ... }
```

That's it! There's nothing else to set up. By default, Seam uses the Java 5 concurrent library to execute the method in a background thread. The only caveat is that, in Seam 2.0, you *cannot* use JSF component tags (other than the mail tags) in the template since the rendering occurs in a mock JSF environment. This feature will be available in Seam 2.1.

If the mail server can't be contacted, or otherwise fails to send the message, the `render()` method throws a `javax.mail.MessagingException` wrapped in a `javax.faces.FacesException`. Notice, however, that there's absolutely no reference to the JavaMail API (or email helper library) in the code that sends the message. This makes email very noninvasive and easy to test.

TESTING EMAIL MESSAGES

Because the life cycle leading up to the email being rendered is the same as with a normal JSF page, you can test an email using `SeamTest`. In fact, `SeamTest` even includes the convenience method `getRenderedMailMessage()`, which parses the email template passed in as a parameter and returns the resulting `MimeMessage` object. You can use this object to verify the headers and structure of the message. Keep in mind that in Seam 2.0, `SeamTest` has the same limitation as sending email asynchronously: the JSF components aren't rendered. Thus, you can't fully test the rendered output of the email.

To avoid spending a lot of time sending messages to yourself to verify the contents, I recommend that you make the body of the message a separate Facelets composition template. Then include it in a normal JSF page and inspect the result in the browser. You can even use a tool like Selenium[2] to validate the output. When you're happy with what it produces, just include it inside the `<m:body>` tag in the email template. You may still have to do manual testing, but at least this trick gets you most of the way there.

What's great about using Seam's email integration is that you don't even have to think about the mechanics of sending the email. Seam is your administrative assistant. You just say, "Go send that email" and it's done. With all the extra time on your hands, you may want to get more mileage out of your messages by adding attachments, using inline images, and leverage all of the Facelets composition techniques you've learned to appreciate.

13.4.2 *Adding an entourage to the message*

Nothing puts the unnecessary complexities of technology in perspective like having a requirements meeting with a non-tech-savvy client. You've been there. A client asks for something that is, logically, a very simple task. Yet, for one reason or another, implementing it costs you a solid day's work or more. Knowing that, your response is "No

---

[2] Selenium is a browser-based testing tool. It can be downloaded from http://selenium.openqa.org.

way" or "That's going to be expensive." One such scenario is email attachments. In theory, it should be so simple. Here's the file, here's the email address. Put them together. But there are so many subtle complexities that it never is quite that simple.

STATIC ATTACHMENTS

You saw an example of how Seam erases complexity in the "Accepting file uploads" section. Seam does it again with email attachments. Attaching a static file to an email using Seam's email support is as simple as mashing two components together. Let's assume that marketing wants to attach a flyer to the welcome email that gives an overview of Open 18. It can be added by placing the <m:attachment> tag just above the <m:body> tag:

```
<m:attachment value="/open18-flyer.pdf" contentType="application/pdf"
  fileName="About Open 18.pdf"/>
<m:body>Dear #{newGolfer.name}, ...
```

The structure of the <m:attachment> tag is almost identical to the <s:graphicImage> tag, covered earlier. In fact, the value attribute accepts all of the Java types shown in table 13.1. The only catch with <m:attachment> is that you must specify the content type and append the file extension to the alternate filename.

DYNAMIC ATTACHMENTS AND EMBEDDED IMAGES

Let's send the golfer's profile image to demonstrate creating an attachment from raw file data (i.e., byte[]). First, add a convenience method to Golfer to get the image extension:

```
@Transient
public String getImageExtension() {
    return Image.Type.getTypeByMimeType(imageContentType).getExtension();
}
```

Next, reference the image data in the value of the attachment and specify the content type:

```
<m:attachment value="#{newGolfer.image}"
  contentType="#{newGolfer.imageContentType}"
  fileName="#{newGolfer.username}#{newGolfer.imageExtension}"
  rendered="#{newGolfer.image != null}"/>
```

How about instead of sending the golfer his or her own profile image, we send the profile images of other recently registered golfers? You can call on the newGolfers context variable prepared in chapter 6 and iterate over it using the Facelets iteration component:

```
<ui:repeat var="_golfer" value="#{newGolfers}">
  <m:attachment value="#{_golfer.image}"
    contentType="#{_golfer.imageContentType}"
    fileName="#{_golfer.username}#{_golfer.imageExtension}"
    rendered="#{_golfer.image != null and _golfer != newGolfer}"/>
</ui:repeat>
```

Adding an image as an attachment is not enough for most email readers to render it automatically. Even if it's rendered, it is grouped at the bottom of the email with all of the other attachments. It would better to have the image displayed within the body of the message. To do this, you start by setting the disposition of the attachment to inline and designating a status variable that holds information about the inline attachment:

```
<m:attachment value="#{newGolfer.image}"
  contentType="#{newGolfer.imageContentType}"
  fileName="#{newGolfer.username}#{newGolfer.imageExtension}"
  disposition="inline" status="profileImageAttachment"/>
```

You then embed an `<img>` tag in the body of the message that references the inline attachment using a special URL scheme. The URL consists of the scheme `cid:` followed by the attachment's content id, which is read from the status variable of the attachment:

```
<p><img src="cid:#{profileImageAttachment.contentId}"/></p>
```

You can even use the `<m:attachment>` in the body of the message so that you can render images in a loop. The only requirement is that you declare the attachment before trying to access its status variable:

```
<ui:repeat var="_golfer" value="#{newGolfers}">
  <m:attachment value="#{_golfer.image}"
    contentType="#{_golfer.imageContentType}"
    fileName="#{_golfer.username}#{_golfer.imageExtension}"
    rendered="#{_golfer.image ne null and _golfer ne newGolfer}"
    disposition="inline" status="profileImageAttachment"/>
  <p><img src="cid:#{profileImageAttachment.contentId}"/></p>
</ui:repeat>
```

If all of this inline disposition stuff seems like too much trouble, or you are concerned it will make the size of the email message too large, you have the option of serving images (and other assets such as style sheets) as linked resources just like in a web page. Let's say you want to include the logo for Open 18 in the message. First, add it somewhere in the body:

```
<h:graphicImage value="/img/logo.png"/>
```

At this point, the email client isn't going to know how to find the image based on this relative path, so you have to give it some context. You set the absolute base URL for linked resources using the `urlBase` attribute on the email message component tag:

```
<m:message ... urlBase="http://open18.org">...</m:message>
```

The value of `urlBase` is used *before* the application's context path (e.g., /open18). In this example, the URL of the logo image is `http://open18.org/open18/img/logo.png`. You can use EL notation to calculate a base URL instead of hardcoding it, as I do here.

ATTACHMENTS USING COMPOSITIONS
But wait! There's more to attachments. You can supply a body to the `<m:attachment>` tag. Within that body you can put plain text, HTML, or even a PDF document. And since these are Facelets templates, that means you can easily insert the contents of another template into this spot. Let's give the user the ability to send a course's scorecard to a friend. The scorecard is rendered within the attachment tag and then attached to the email:

```
<m:message xmlns="http://www.w3.org/1999/xhtml"
  xmlns:m="http://jboss.com/products/seam/mail"
  xmlns:ui="http://java.sun.com/jsf/facelets">
```

```
<m:from name="Open 18 Notifications" address="notification@open18.org"/>
<m:replyTo address="#{currentGolfer.emailAddress}"/>
<m:to>#{recipient.emailAddress}</m:to>
<m:subject>#{currentGolfer.name} sent you a scorecard</m:subject>
<m:attachment fileName="scorecard.pdf" contentType="application/pdf">
  <ui:include src="/exportScorecard.xhtml"/>
</m:attachment>
<m:body type="plain">While browsing the Open 18 course directory,
I came across a golf course that I thought might interest you.

#{course.name}

The scorecard for this course is attached to this message.

Cheers,

#{currentGolfer.name}</m:body>
</m:message>
```

This Facelets template provides a glimpse at using Facelets compositions to construct a message. The component named `recipient` is used to capture the target email address from a JSF form. The `sendScorecard()` method of the `Notifications` component preloads the scorecard data and then renders the email template. When that happens, the scorecard PDF is rendered and attached to the message. As a courtesy, the user is informed that the email went through. This method can't be asynchronous in Seam 2.0 because the email template uses nonemail JSF component tags.

```
@Name("notifications")
public class Notifications {
    @In private Recipient recipient;
    @In private Renderer renderer;
    @In private FacesMessages facesMessages;
    @In(create = true) private Scorecard scorecard;

    public void sendScorecard() {
        scorecard.load();
        renderer.render("/email/scorecard-notification.xhtml");
        facesMessages.add(
          "The scorecard has been sent to #{recipient.firstName}.");
    }
}
```

The chain reaction of one Facelets template invoking the next is a powerful concept. Table 13.4 provides a list of other common email tasks and how they can be accomplished.

Table 13.3 Solutions to common email composition tasks

Goal	How to achieve...
Conditional logic	Use the `rendered` attribute on a component tag to toggle a single component or a grouping of components.
Email templates	Design a composition template that uses `<ui:insert>` placeholders within an `<m:message>` region; call on this template from a content template and fill in the placeholders using `<ui:define>` and `<ui:param>`.

Table 13.3   Solutions to common email composition tasks *(continued)*

Goal	How to achieve...
Send multiple messages	Nest the `<m:message>` tag in an iteration component (i.e., `<ui:repeat>`).
Send to multiple recipients	Nest the `<m:to>`, `<m:cc>`, or `<m:cc>` tag in an iteration component.
Customize the language or theme of a message	Use the resource bundle map `messages` or `theme` to insert the value of a message key for the current locale or theme in the message; set charset using the `charset` attribute on the `<m:message>` tag.

I'd like to be able to say that you don't have to lift another finger to send emails with Seam. Sadly, the task of configuring an email transport is a necessary evil. I can assure you that Seam makes this task just about as simple as it can be.

13.4.3 Setting up JavaMail in Seam

Setting up email for a project tends to be one of those black magic tasks that you do on the first day of employment and dare not touch again. Even then, someone is usually dictating the email settings over your shoulder, so it's not much of a learning experience. In this section, I give you a clear understanding of what you need to do to configure a mail session.

To start, you need Seam's mail module, jboss-seam-mail.jar, and the JavaMail API and implementation on the classpath of your application. The latter requirement is satisfied by the mail.jar and activation.jar libraries, both present in the lib directory of a seam-gen project. But guess what? You don't need them if you're deploying to a Java EE–compliant application server because they're already provided. If you're deploying to a servlet container, on the other hand, you need to bundle these libraries in your application or place them in the servlet container's classpath. Let's see how to use Java-Mail in Seam.

HOOKING UP JAVAMAIL TO A TRANSPORT

Seam provides a built-in component named `mailSession` that initializes and provides access to a JavaMail session (`javax.mail.Session`). But setting up the mail session is only half the story. The mail session is just a mediator between the application and the Mail Transport Agent (MTA). While the mail session negotiates with the MTA to send an email over the SMTP protocol, in the end it's the MTA that actually sends the message. Thus, to configure a mail session, you must have access to an SMTP server.

Typically, the SMTP server is provided by your internet service provider (ISP) or your company. In Seam, you have two options for connecting a JavaMail session to an SMTP server. You can configure the connection information directly in the Seam component descriptor, or you can point Seam at a JavaMail session bound to JNDI. Seam also ships with an embedded mail server called Meldware that you deploy to JBoss AS, which is especially useful for development. Meldware can be controlled within the application using another set of built-in Seam components. You'll find a step-by-step

> **Save time by using an externally hosted SMTP server**
>
> To avoid time messing around with an email transport, your best bet is to take advantage of the wide array of free SMTP mail servers available on the web. One such example is Gmail, the example that is used in this section. Google allows messages to be sent over SMTP/TLS after proper authentication.[3] First, you must enable either POP or IMAP access on the Gmail account to use the Gmail SMTP server, and then configure Seam to use it.

tutorial for configuring Meldware in the Seam reference documentation. The focus here is on using an externally hosted SMTP server because configuring Seam to use it is straightforward and it gets your emails out the door with the least amount of effort.

CONFIGURING A SEAM-MANAGED JAVAMAIL SESSION

Although you never interact with the mail session component directly, it must be configured in order for the messages rendered by the message templates covered earlier to be sent. The mail session component is configured in the component descriptor just like many of the other Seam integrations, such as persistence. To start, add the component namespace `http://jboss.com/products/seam/mail`, typically prefixed as `mail`, to the component descriptor. Next, supply the connection information to the `mailSession` component. Here's an example configuration that uses Gmail's SMTP/TLS server.

```
<mail:mail-session host="smtp.gmail.com" port="587"
    username="example@gmail.com" password="secret"/>
```

Of course, you need to fill in the correct username and password values for your account. The messages originate from the account's email address. If the messages aren't being sent, enable the `debug` property to diagnose the problem. Note that Gmail requires the `tls` property to be true, which is the default value. Placing connection information directly in the component descriptor isn't very secure, nor can the values be customized for different environments. I recommend using replacement tokens, which were covered in chapter 5. An even more elegant approach, though, is to use an externally configured JavaMail session.

CONFIGURING SEAM TO USE A JAVAMAIL SESSION FROM JNDI

The mail session component can consume a JavaMail session stored in JNDI. In this section, I demonstrate how to configure the mail service in JBoss AS to bind a JavaMail session to JNDI, and show you how to configure the mail session component to use it. If you're using an alternate application server, you can configure a JavaMail session using the server's admin console. For GlassFish, see the note about SMTP authentication in the accompanying sidebar.

---

[3] See configuration instructions for Gmail: http://mail.google.com/support/bin/answer.py?answer=78799.

SMTP authentication and GlassFish JavaMail sessions

SMTP authentication is an automated login that occurs prior to sending an email message. If your ISP uses SMTP authentication, the JavaMail session fed to the Seam mail component must be configured to use an SMTP authenticator with the proper credentials already set. Unfortunately, it's not possible to set the SMTP authentication credentials for a JavaMail session configured through GlassFish. JBoss AS, on the other hand, accommodates this configuration.

To register a JavaMail session in JBoss AS, open the mail-service.xml descriptor in the server's hot deploy directory and replace the contents with listing 13.7.

Listing 13.7   Mail service configuration for JBoss AS

```xml
<?xml version="1.0" encoding="UTF-8"?>
<server>
  <mbean code="org.jboss.mail.MailService" name="jboss:service=Mail">
    <attribute name="JNDIName">java:/Mail</attribute>
    <attribute name="User">example@gmail.com</attribute>
    <attribute name="Password">secret</attribute>
    <attribute name="Configuration">
      <configuration>
        <property name="mail.transport.protocol" value="smtp"/>
        <property name="mail.smtp.host" value="smtp.gmail.com"/>
        <property name="mail.smtp.port" value="587"/>
        <property name="mail.smtp.auth" value="true"/>
        <property name="mail.smtp.starttls.enable" value="true"/>
      </configuration>
    </attribute>
    <depends>jboss:service=Naming</depends>
  </mbean>
</server>
```

Next, supply the Seam mail component with the JNDI name assigned in this service:

```xml
<mail:mail-session session-jndi-name="java:/Mail"/>
```

Restart your application and you should be able to send mail using Gmail. If you need to use a different SMTP server, simply fill in the appropriate values in the mail service configuration.

The JNDI name in this example uses the proprietary `java:/` namespace for JBoss AS. The standard JNDI subcontext for JavaMail sessions is `java:comp/env/mail`. If you configured a JavaMail session named `mail/Session` in a Java EE–compliant server like GlassFish, you feed the value `java:comp/env/mail/Session` to the Seam mail component. You also have to declare a JNDI resource reference of type `javax.mail.Session` in web.xml.

You now have the full range of multipart email capabilities at your fingertips, sent into the great wide open using your ISP's SMTP server. Just remember to use this power wisely, for fools are called spammers!

While email may not go away anytime soon, the email is mostly dead. Instead, people opt to keep up with the latest news using a newsfeed reader. That way, when you want the news to stop, all you have to do is unsubscribe (and it actually works!). At the risk of sounding mundane, creating newsfeeds in Seam is yet another Facelets template.

13.4.4 Publishing newsfeeds

What better way to produce XML than with XML. Don't worry, I'm not talking about that scary XSLT pseudolanguage. I'm talking about Facelets. Seam does it again by making it extremely simple to publish newsfeeds, such as RSS or Atom, using a Facelets template. I'll prove to you how simple it is by making this second extremely short.

Newsfeeds are delivered using XML, each type having its own schema. In this section, we work with an Atom feed. The only trick in serving XML through a Facelets template is setting the content type header appropriately. By default, Facelets assumes you're generating HTML (text/html). But in order for the feed readers to digest the feed, the header must be an XML type. For an Atom feed, that type is application/xml+atom. You set the content type on the `<f:view>` tag, which can be placed anywhere in the document. As for the remainder of the document, you simply use the XML tags specific to the feed type. Facelets doesn't care what markup it's producing.

Let's publish the latest golf rounds that have been entered by the golfers, a list provided by the context variable `latestRounds`. From that list, we create the feed template named latestRounds.xhtml, shown in listing 13.8.

Listing 13.8 An atom feed reporting scores from the latest rounds

```
<?xml version="1.0" encoding="UTF-8"?>
<feed xmlns="http://purl.org/atom/ns#" version="0.3" xml:lang="en"
  xmlns:ui="http://java.sun.com/jsf/facelets"
  xmlns:f="http://java.sun.com/jsf/core"
  xmlns:h="http://java.sun.com/jsf/html"
  xmlns:s="http://jboss.com/products/seam/taglib">
<f:view contentType="application/atom+xml">
<title>Open 18: Latest Rounds</title>
<link rel="alternate" type="text/html"
  href="http://localhost:8080/open18"/>
<tagline>A place for golfers</tagline>
<updated><h:outputText value="#{latestRounds[0].date}">
    <s:convertDatetime pattern="yyyy-MM-dd'T'HH:mm:ss'Z'"/>
  </h:outputText></updated>
<ui:repeat var="_round" value="#{latestRounds}">
<entry>
  <title>#{_round.golfer.name} @ #{_round.teeSet.course.name}</title>
  <link rel="alternate" type="text/html"
    href="http://localhost:8080/open18/Round.seam?roundId=#{_round.id}"/>
  <id>http://localhost:8080/open18/Round.seam?roundId=#{_round.id}</id>
  <summary type="text/plain">#{_round.totalScore}</summary>
  <published><h:outputText value="#{_round.date}">
      <s:convertDatetime pattern="yyyy-MM-dd'T'HH:mm:ss'Z'"/>
    </h:outputText></published>
  <updated><h:outputText value="#{_round.date}">
```

```
                <s:convertDatetime pattern="yyyy-MM-dd'T'HH:mm:ss'Z'"/>
            </h:outputText></updated>
        </entry>
        </ui:repeat>
        </f:view>
    </feed>
```

Despite all the fancy Java-based newsfeed creators, nothing beats writing the newsfeed in its native tongue, with some enhancements provided by JSF UI components to iterate over and format the data. The user simply requests the path /latestRounds.seam in the browser or feed reader to monitor the latest scores entered.

Throughout this chapter, you've added a lot of wealth to the application. But the richest applications are those that allow users to customize the UI to suit their needs. Seam provides a means of empowering your users to control internationalization, time zone, and theme settings for their sessions, with intelligent defaults to start.

13.5   *Customizing the UI with resource bundles*

Seam follows a consistent approach for providing customization of the UI by using resource bundles. As you learned in section 5.5.2 in chapter 5, Seam aggregates the i18n message bundles under a unified map named `messages`. When the application logic needs a message to be rendered, it supplies a message key rather than embedding the message string directly in the code. Seam then retrieves the actual message at runtime from the resource bundle, taking note of the user's preference, whether it be a locale, time zone, or theme. Seam assembles a separate map named `theme` to support the active theme, prepared using a similar configuration (which is covered later in this section).

While chapter 5 examines the details of how to prepare a message bundle and use it in your components and pages, what you haven't learned yet is how Seam decides which locale, time zone, and theme to use and how to give the user control over these selections. This section covers the three selector components that Seam provides, which are controlled by the UI, and also goes into detail about what themes are and how they fit into the resource bundle picture. Let's begin by telling Seam how to speak the right language.

13.5.1   *Getting Seam to speak the right language*

In Java, a regional language is known as a locale. Locale selection has long been a standard part of the communication between the browser and the Java Servlet API, and is equally well supported in JSF. The negotiation works as follows. The browser sends a header named `Accept-Language` as part of the request, itemizing the languages understood by the user, weighted by preference. The server then sets the preferred locale accordingly, falling back to the server's default locale if the `Accept-Language` header is empty or absent.

Granted, the user's preferred locale setting doesn't do much good if the application doesn't support it. Thus, JSF goes a step further by comparing the user's preferred languages against a list of locales the application claims to support and selecting the best possible match. If there are no matches, the server's default locale is chosen. While Seam aggregates the i18n resource bundles in your application, it relies on JSF to handle the negotiation of the user's locale.

You declare the supported locales and override the server's default locale using the `<locale-config>` element in the JSF configuration file, /WEB-INF/faces-config.xml:

```
<faces-config>
  <application>
    <locale-config>
      <default-locale>en</default-locale>
      <supported-locale>en</supported-locale>
      <supported-locale>fr</supported-locale>
    </locale-config>
  </application>
</faces-config>
```

Of course, if you indicate that you support a locale, make sure you have a localized resource bundle to support it. Otherwise, the user is going to see the message key. To prevent the message key from being displayed, you can set fallback messages in the base bundle file (the bundle name followed immediately by the `.properties` extension).

That covers the standard language negotiation. Seam also provides built-in support for allowing the user to choose the effective locale from within the application (as opposed to changing the browser setting). This feature is particularly useful for internet terminals where the user can't modify the browser's setting. In that case, the `Accept-Language` header may not reflect the user's true language preference.

LETTING THE USER SELECT THE LOCALE

Seam makes it simple to throw together a UI selector that controls the locale associated with the user's session. The user's locale is stored in a built-in component named `localeSelector`, which Seam consults whenever it needs to look up a message key. This component also has action methods that can be called to change the locale.

The typical way to use the `localeSelector` component is to bind its `localeString` property to a `UISelectOne` component and supply a list of locale keys in the options. The user can select an option to change the value of this property and in turn the effective locale. To apply the change, you bind the action of the form to the component's `select()` method:

```
<h:form id="settings">
  <span>Language: </span>
  <h:selectOneMenu value="#{localeSelector.localeString}">
    <f:selectItem itemValue="en" itemLabel="English"/>
    <f:selectItem itemValue="fr" itemLabel="Francais"/>
  </h:selectOneMenu>
  <h:commandLink action="#{localeSelector.select}" value="[ Select ]"/>
</h:form>
```

You can do away with the UI command link by having JavaScript submit the form when a new option is selected. The selection is applied on the server using a value change listener:

```
<h:form id="settings">
  <span>Language: </span>
  <h:selectOneMenu value="#{localeSelector.localeString}"
    valueChangeListener="#{localeSelector.select}" onchange="submit()">
    <f:selectItem itemValue="en" itemLabel="English"/>
    <f:selectItem itemValue="fr" itemLabel="Francais"/>
  </h:selectOneMenu>
</h:form>
```

As you can see, I'm having to manually input the language choices in the select menu. But we've already supplied the supported locales once in the JSF configuration. Thankfully, Seam can consult the JSF context and prepare a ready-made list of SelectItem objects holding the locale strings and labels for use in the options of a UISelectOne component:

```
<f:selectItems value="#{localeSelector.supportedLocales}"/>
```

Instead of using a select menu, you can iterate over this list to create links that select a locale, passing the locale string to a parameterized action method:

```
<ui:repeat var="_locale" value="#{localeSelector.supportedLocales}">
  <s:link action="#{localeSelector.selectLanguage(_locale.value)}"/>
</ui:repeat>
```

Seam's default behavior is to store the selected locale for the duration of the user's session. To make the selection more long term, it can be persisted as a cookie.

GETTING THE LOCALE SELECTION TO STICK

You can configure Seam to persist the locale setting in a browser cookie. First, add the component namespace http://jboss.com/products/seam/international, prefixed as i18n, to the component descriptor. Next, configure the localeSelector component to store the locale using a cookie:

```
<i18n:locale-selector cookie-enabled="true"/>
```

The default lifetime of the cookie is one year, which you can change in the cookie-max-age attribute. You can also use this component to set the default locale, as with the JSF configuration file, but you can't use it to specify the supported locales.

If you want to make the locale setting permanent, you can persist it to the database in a user preferences table. You then use the localeSelector in the authentication routine to transfer that setting to the user's session:

```
@In LocaleSelector localeSelector;

localeSelector.setLocaleString(userPreferences.getLocale());
localeSelector.select();
```

When the user changes the locale, Seam raises the org.jboss.seam.localeSelected event. You can observe this event to persist the selection back to the database:

```
@Observer("org.jboss.seam.localeSelected")
@Transactional
public void localeChanged(String localeString) { ... }
```

Often forgotten about, but just as important as the language, is the time zone.

MANAGING THE TIME ZONE

Seam offers parallel support for selecting a time zone using the `timeZoneSelector`. Here's a UI component for switching time zones that mirrors the structure of the locale switcher:

```
<span>Time zone: </span>
<h:selectOneMenu value="#{timeZoneSelector.timeZoneId}"
  valueChangeListener="#{timeZoneSelector.select}" onchange="submit()">
  <f:selectItem itemValue="GMT-08:00" itemLabel="Pacific Time"/>
  <f:selectItem itemValue="GMT-07:00" itemLabel="Mountain Time"/>
  <f:selectItem itemValue="GMT-06:00" itemLabel="Central Time"/>
  <f:selectItem itemValue="GMT-05:00" itemLabel="Eastern Time"/>
</h:selectOneMenu>
```

You can access the list of time zones known to the Java runtime from the `timeZone` context variable, which can be used to build the options for the time zone switcher:

```
<s:selectItems var="_timeZoneId" value="#{timeZone.availableIDs}"
  label="#{timeZone.getTimeZone(_timeZoneId).displayName}"/>
```

Unfortunately, the result isn't even close to being normalized. Your best bet is to retrieve the available time zones from a database. This list may be available in Seam in the future.

The time zone selector also has support for persisting the time zone selection in a cookie, having the same two property names as the `localeSelector` component:

```
<i18n:time-zone-selector cookie-enabled="true"/>
```

When the time zone is changed, Seam raises the `org.jboss.seam.timeZoneSelected` event, passing the time zone id as an argument. Thus, the advice I gave earlier about storing the user's locale preference in the database applies for the time zone as well.

TIME ZONE REPAIRS

Seam adds a bandage to another wound in JSF with regard to how time zones are used, or not used, for that matter. The JSF specification says that when using the `<f:convert-DateTime>` converter, the date and time values should be assumed to be UTC (coordinated universal time) unless a time zone is explicitly specified in the tag. I can name at least two QA people who would strongly disagree that this is acceptable behavior. One way to override the default in Seam is to reference the `timeZone` context variable:

```
<f:convertDateTime timeZone="#{timeZone}"/>
```

But rather than having to specify this override every time you use the converter, you can save a couple of keystrokes by using the `<s:convertDateTime>` converter from the Seam UI palette, which automatically applies the user's time zone preference.

There's another glitch in the way JSF handles time zones that Seam fixes. JSF doesn't support setting a default time zone, using the time zone of the server instead. The default value can be customized using the `timeZoneSelector` as follows:

```
<i18n:time-zone-selector time-zone-id="America/New_York"/>
```

Time zones are one of those things you need to synchronize from your database to your front end, so I advise that you spend some time thinking about and testing them.

While Seam certainly improves on the accessibility of locale and time zones, both for the developer and for the user, you've probably used these features before. Where Seam open new doors with resource bundles is in the area of themes—often referred to as skins.

13.5.2 *Themes*

Themes add another dimension to message bundles, as shown in figure 13.7. Just as locales allow you to switch between locale-specific variants of the same bundle name, themes allow you to switch between different bundle names that have the same set of key-value pairs. In the end, the idea of using a message key as a replacement token is still the same. The coolest part is that each theme can support multiple languages, providing i18n branding.

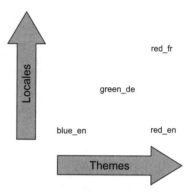

Figure 13.7   **Themes add an extra dimension to resource bundle selection.**

For each theme that you want to support, you must create a resource bundle whose name is that of the theme. For instance, to create a blue theme, you'd create the file blue.properties and place it on the application classpath (adjacent to your message bundle files). You'd then tell Seam about the themes by configuring the built-in Seam component named themeSelector in the component descriptor:

```
<theme:theme-selector cookie-enabled="true" theme="blue">
  <theme:available-themes>
    <value>red</value>
    <value>green</value>
    <value>blue</value>
  </theme:available-themes>
</theme:theme-selector>
```

Here, three themes have been defined, with blue being the default. You can allow the user to switch themes using the same approach that was used for locale and time zone selection:

```
<span>Theme: </span>
<h:selectOneMenu value="#{themeSelector.theme}"
  valueChangeListener="#{themeSelector.select}"
  onchange="submit()">
  <f:selectItems value="#{themeSelector.themes}"/>
</h:selectOneMenu>
```

Without additional configuration, the bundle name of each theme is shown in the label of the options in the select menu. If you want to give the themes fancy names, you must add message keys in your Seam message bundle (e.g., messages.properties) that use the prefix org.jboss.seam.theme. followed by the theme name:

```
org.jboss.seam.theme.blue=Sky
org.jboss.seam.theme.green=Eco
org.jboss.seam.theme.red=Ruby
```

Now that you have a theme, how do you use it? Well, just like any other message bundle. Only, rather than using a map named `messages`, you use a map named `theme`. You can tie a style sheet, logo, and master template to the theme using the following three message keys:

```
stylesheet=#{request.contextPath}/stylesheet/sunnyday.css
logo=noclouds.png
template=layout/outside.xhtml
```

You can reference the first two keys in the master Facelets template:

```
<link href="#{theme['stylesheet']}" rel="stylesheet" type="text/css"/>
<h:graphicImage value="#{theme['logo']}" alt="Logo"/>
```

and then select the master template for the specific page using the last key:

```
<ui:composition xmlns="http://www.w3.org/1999/xhtml" ...
  template="#{theme['template']}">
  ...
</ui:composition>
```

If you want to tie the colors used in PDF documents and charts into your theme, you first define `<p:color>` tags that each have a semantic name and bind to a theme's key:

```
<p:color name="series1" value="#{theme['series1Color']}"/>
```

You then associate the semantic name with a color by assigning a value to the theme's key:

```
series1Color=#FF0000
```

If you want to skip creating the theme message keys, you can just reference the theme name directly in a value expression:

```
<h:graphicImage value="#{themeSelector.theme}.png" alt="Logo"/>
```

Themes can be used to control just about anything that accepts an EL value expression. Check out the sample code to see how you can tie the theme to a RichFaces skin. I have no doubt you'll think of other creative ways to use these special resource bundles.

13.6 Summary

I hope the promise I made that you'd have fun in this chapter held true. Looking back on what you've learned, you can now handle file uploads, render dynamic images, generate PDFs, create charts, compose emails with attachments, publish news feeds, and customize the UI with resource bundles. These features can take your application from good to great.

The constant theme throughout this chapter has been ease and accessibility. Software development is rarely easy. But it doesn't have to be unnecessarily difficult either. Many of the areas of functionality covered in this chapter have been huge pain points for Java developers in the past, particularly file uploads and multipart email messages. Seam's UI component tags make these problems just melt away.

Seam is able to accomplish this feat in two ways. First, Seam extends the EL value binding concept to transport binary data in addition to strings. Going the other way, Seam renders raw file data as a dynamic graphic in a web page, in a PDF document, or as a file attachment in an email. The other key is the Facelets template. Facelets is powerful because it is a stand-alone rendering technology, but with access to all the power of JSF components. One way to leverage this tool is to render a Facelets template within an action method to send an email. Another is to serve a Facelets template that generates a PDF to the browser, allowing the user to download the result. Yet another is to publish a newsfeed. If the Facelets template is being served directly to the browser, you can even take advantage of Seam's page-oriented controls. The focus is to give you the same XHTML-based approach backed by the EL and Seam components no matter what format is being produced.

That brings this book to a close, but not your journey with Seam. There are additional chapters online to broaden your Seam knowledge. Chapter 14 takes you into the world of business processes and shows how they follow the same declarative approach as conversations. Chapter 15 details how to integrate Seam and Spring using Seam's Inversion of Control (IoC) bridge. For those of you who won't pick up another framework if it means letting go of Spring, that chapter should definitely be of interest.

Before you close the book, I want to say that I hope both Seam and this book change your life as they have for me. Thanks for reading and good luck with your next application!

appendix A:
Seam starter set

This appendix explores the set of libraries and tools you need to develop with Seam. Seam consists of just a handful of JAR files, listed in section A.2.1. Once these libraries are added to your application's classpath, they open the door to a wealth of integrations and a consistent programming model. To get started with Seam, you can create a new project using seam-gen (see chapter 2), adopt an example application from the Seam distribution, or add the Seam libraries to an existing project by mining the JAR files from the Seam distribution or registering the Seam modules as Maven 2 or Ivy dependencies.

Given that Seam is often described as an "integration framework," you'd expect it to rely on a wide variety of external libraries. While that's true, it's nothing to get worried about. Both the Seam distribution and the Maven 2 configuration provided by Seam include compatible libraries that are verified to work with a given Seam version. Thus, Seam truly lives up to its title as an integration framework, both at the API and distribution levels.

Before swinging away, you need to check the prerequisites for using Seam and the seam-gen tool, which extend beyond just extracting the Seam distribution on your hard drive.

A.1 Stepping through the prerequisites

Chapter 2 makes the recommendation of using seam-gen as your first step into Seam. Thus, the prerequisites presented in this section are geared toward using seam-gen to create and deploy the database-oriented application that accompanies this book. Let's have a look at what software is needed to follow along with the tutorial in chapter 2:

- Java SE (JDK) (5.0 or greater) from Sun, IBM, BEA, Apple, or RedHat (IcedTea)
- JBoss Application Server (4.2 or greater)
- JBoss Seam (2.0 or greater)

- A database and JDBC driver (the book source code uses the H2 database)
- Seam in Action source code (needed for the database schema and seed data)

While you can get by using the seam-gen tool with the software listed here, you may find the following optional dependencies valuable as well:

- Apache Ant (1.7.0 or greater)
- Alternate application server (GlassFish Application Server V2 or greater)

I'll step through each of these prerequisites in turn. Any time you see a reference to /home/twoputt, replace it with the location of your software development directory. The folders under this directory referenced in this appendix are consistent with the book's source code and are described further in the introduction. Don't get too worked up over the JBoss AS requirement. It just happens to be the application server supported by seam-gen out of the box. Any Java EE application server can stand in its place. Java 5 is required, which hopefully will not turn you off Seam if you're still using Java 1.4 or lower. I begin with the reasoning behind the Java 5 requirement.

A.1.1   *Java 5 compliance*

A Java 5–compliant JDK (Java SE Development Kit) is required to develop Seam applications, and the applications must be run under a Java 5–compliant JVM (Java virtual machine). It's also strongly recommended that applications be deployed to a Java EE 5–compliant application server. This recommendation becomes a requirement if you want to take advantage of Seam's EJB 3 integration.

The dependency on Java SE 5 and Java EE 5 accounts for a large part of Seam's success and works to your advantage. Instead of having to tiptoe around the enhancements that came with the release of Java 5, as some other frameworks do, Seam embraces annotations and generics to eliminate unnecessary XML configuration and ugly casting. Seam is sending the message to the industry that it's time to move on. The productivity gains afforded by using a Java 5–compliant language are too valuable to put off any longer. Although it may be possible to use a tool like Retrotranslator[1] to port a Seam application to a J2SE 1.4 JVM, it still doesn't eliminate the requirement of using a Java 5–compliant JDK for development, nor does it get you any closer to using EJB 3.

If you haven't yet moved to JDK 5 (or better), you'll need to download it from the vendor of your choice. I recommend using Sun's JDK 6 since, in my gut-feeling tests, it's the fastest JVM for development. Once you've downloaded the Java distribution, you need to add the `java` binary to your PATH environment variable. It's also good practice to set the JAVA_HOME environment variable to point to the extracted Java distribution, as some tools rely on it. Here are the shell commands (for Linux and Mac OS X) for setting these variables:

```
export JAVA_HOME=/home/twoputt/opt/jdk1.6.0_03
export PATH=$JAVA_HOME/bin:$PATH
```

---

[1] Retrotranslator (http://retrotranslator.sourceforge.net/) is a Java bytecode transformer that translates Java classes compiled with JDK 5.0 into classes that can be run on JVM 1.4.

If you're using Debian/Ubuntu Linux, it's even easier. You simply type `sudo apt-get install sun-java6-jdk` and the Sun Java distribution is downloaded from the multiverse apt repository and configured for you. This channel is available since Java has finally been released under a distributable license.[2] Other Linux distributions offer similar packages. Mac OS X 10.5 (Leopard) is distributed with Java 5 and it's already available in the default `PATH`. If you're on Windows, I strongly recommend using Cygwin or a VMWare image of Linux.

Your next stop is the JBoss labs, where you'll pick up the JBoss Application Server (JBoss AS). Following that, I discuss two alternate servers: GlassFish and Tomcat.

A.1.2   *Java EE 5 application servers*

Seam is designed to make the standard Java EE 5 services more accessible, not to reinvent them. Throughout this book, I emphasize why deploying to a Java EE 5 application server is a "Good Thing." You may be inclined to assume that Tomcat, JBoss AS without EJB 3, and integration tests are left out in the cold. This is not the case. Seam applications just fit more naturally in a Java EE 5 environment. Rest assured that the Embedded JBoss runtime can be added to the classpath of a non–Java EE environment to "enlighten" it with Java EE 5 capabilities. It's also possible to configure a Seam application to run in a Java SE environment, independent of any Java EE 5 features. For instance, you can use resource-local transactions and an application-managed persistence manager as alternatives. But to get going quickly, you'll find that using JBoss AS is the most convenient option.

JBoss APPLICATION SERVER

You can download the JBoss Application Server (AS) from its project page in the JBoss labs: http://labs.jboss.org/jbossas. You'll be directed to the SourceForge.net site, where you can download the zip file. The recommended version of JBoss AS to use with Seam 2.0.x is 4.2.2.GA.[3] After the download completes, extract the archive into the opt folder in your home directory. The location of the extracted archive is referenced as the placeholder ${jboss.home} in chapter 2. Chapter 2 also provides instructions on how to start JBoss AS. Recall that you must run the application server using a Java 5–compliant JVM. If you plan on accessing the server from another computer, you need to add the `-b 0.0.0.0` argument to the `run` command. This tells the server to accept connections from all IP addresses. The default is to only allow local connections.

The 4.2.x series of JBoss AS is a partial implementation of Java EE 5, with support for EJB 3, allowing you to take advantage of all of Seam's features. I encourage you to move to JBoss AS 5 when it's finalized to get all the Java EE 5 features. The benefit of using a Java EE 5 environment is discussed in the remainder of this section.

---

[2] For information on the announcement regarding the release of the full Java stack on Debian/Ubuntu, see http://www.linuxplanet.com/linuxplanet/newss/6380/1/.

[3] The versions used by JBoss may seem confusing at first glance, many ending in "GA." This abbreviation stands for General Availability, a fancy way of saying that it is the final release. A product is labeled as GA when all the outstanding bugs have been resolved in the candidate release version that preceded it.

No love for JBoss?

I expect that some of you will grumble about the required JBoss AS download. Perhaps you fear vendor lock-in or find the hefty 100 MB-plus download painful. You can unfold your arms and put your hands back on the keyboard. *JBoss AS is not required to use Seam*. However, having it around makes getting started a heck of a lot easier since JBoss AS is the target application server for projects created by seam-gen. Remember, sticking with the defaults cuts down on work—and hassle.

ALTERNATE APPLICATION SERVERS

If you're developing an off-the-shelf application, it's important to test it on alternate application servers to ensure portability. Covering the interoperability of Seam applications among different application servers here would duplicate the focused effort done by the Seam development team and logged in the Seam reference documentation. Although theoretically Seam can run on any Java EE application server, the officially tested platforms are JBoss AS 4.2, IBM WebSphere 6.1, WebLogic 10, GlassFish version 2, Oracle OC4J 11g, and Tomcat 5 and 6. I want to contrast two of the options, GlassFish and Tomcat, to help you put the choice of where to deploy a Seam application in perspective.

GLASSFISH

One of the application servers to which I am partial is GlassFish,[4] the open source Java EE 5–compliant server sponsored by Sun Microsystems. It's the reference implementation for Java EE–compliant servers and passes the Java EE 5 Technology Compatibility Kit (TCK) 100 percent, unlike JBoss 4.2. It also sports an attractive and intuitive administration console, making it user-friendly and easy to adopt.

I put strong emphasis on the word *compliant* in the last paragraph. What's so great about compliance? It's about the rule of least surprise. If every application server had its own set of guidelines, then moving your application from one server to another would require a lot of reconfiguring in the best-case scenario. If the services provided by a server behave differently or don't line up, the changes might even be more drastic, perhaps requiring you to modify your code. Any work spent making such changes provides zero value to your application and is pure overhead from a monetary standpoint, definitely something you want to avoid. That brings us to Tomcat, which is many miles from being compliant.

TOMCAT

Once upon a time, the industry flocked to Tomcat while fleeing a bad relationship with J2EE application servers. Developers wrote them off because they were expensive, slow, and heavyweight, and led to vendor lock-in. Tomcat represented the grassroots

---

[4] You can download GlassFish from the GlassFish Community site: https://glassfish.dev.java.net/. Look for the direct download links on the right side of the page. The recommended version of GlassFish is V2 or greater.

movement and let developers feel more free. Today, Tomcat is the most widely used "application server."[5]

The main problem with Tomcat is that it isn't a Java EE–compliant application server—it's a servlet container. Although it made sense to cut corners at the time when J2EE servers had grown fat and expensive, times have changed. The Java EE 5 application servers have escaped their legacy and are now fast and cheap (GlassFish, for instance, is open source and starts in under a second). Furthermore, application servers adhere to a stack of successful and progressive specifications and offer all the services that you need to support transactional applications right out of the box. In my opinion, Java EE application servers offer a much better development experience than a servlet container like Tomcat.

You can even argue that Tomcat is now the culprit of vendor lock-in. It requires you to bend your application over backward to get it to work in this nonstandard environment, whereas all other application servers can theoretically share applications with little effort. That's why the preferred solution for deploying an application that uses EJB 3 or JTA to Tomcat is to make Tomcat act like a Java EE 5 application server rather than forcing the application to fit Tomcat's expectations. In this scenario, Seam 2.0 relies on Embedded JBoss to be configured directly in the Tomcat container (a change from packaging the Embedded EJB 3 runtime in the application, the strategy used in Seam 1.2). You can find instructions for setting up Embedded JBoss on Tomcat in the Seam reference documentation.

It's certainly possible to deploy Seam applications to a vanilla Tomcat installation. However, you have to either change the application so that it doesn't rely on container-provided services such as JCA and JTA, or you need to register these services using Tomcat's proprietary configuration descriptors. Either way, EJB 3 gets tossed out the window. Are you starting to see why I claim that servlet containers are more proprietary, and more of a hassle, than a Java EE–complaint application server? My advice is to rethink why you are considering Tomcat.

A.1.3 *Absent (JavaServer) Faces*

As you know, Seam uses JavaServer Faces (JSF) as the preferred user interface (UI) framework. Thus, you may be wondering why JSF isn't listed as a dependency. Once again, Seam applications are intended to be deployed to a Java EE 5–compliant application server and since JSF 1.2 is a part of Java EE 5, it's already available. If you aren't using a standard Java EE 5 environment, you need to download JSF and package it with your application. You should grab a JSF 1.2–compliant implementation, which is required by Seam's JSF support.

Seam developers recommend the Sun implementation of JSF (Mojarra) over Apache MyFaces. The reason for this preference is that Sun's implementation has succeeded in keeping up with the latest JSF specification and because it too is an open

---

[5] http://www.infoq.com/news/2007/12/tomcat-favorite-container

source project. Both JBoss AS and GlassFish now bundle the Sun implementation in their respective application servers. Despite this move, I'm sure this is not the last we'll hear of this debate.

With your deployment environment ready, it's finally time to grab Seam and the example source code so that you are ready to go through the tutorial in chapter 2.

A.2   *Downloading the Seam distribution*

You can download the latest version of the Seam 2.0 distribution from the Seam project page in the JBoss labs: http://labs.jboss.org/jbossseam. Feel free to upgrade as new versions become available, but know that this book's source code is developed for Seam 2.0.3.GA. Extract the Seam distribution archive into the opt folder in your home directory. The location of the extracted archive is referred to as the Seam distribution directory throughout this book.

> ### Why is the Seam distribution so large?
>
> You may consider the Seam distribution to be unnecessarily large (greater than 100 MB) and for this reason conclude that Seam is bloated. The reality is that the Seam JAR files amount to less than 2 MB. The distribution is large for the benefit of the developer. It contains all of the source code, seam-gen, the reference documentation, dependent JAR files, and 30-plus examples. You can always get the essential artifacts from the JBoss Maven 2 repository.[6]

A.2.1   *Seam's modules*

Seam 2.0 consists of seven JAR files, each representing one Seam module. Table A.1 lists the artifact ID of each module and its purpose. The JAR files, whose names are derived by appending .jar to the artifact ID, are found in the lib folder of the Seam distribution.

Table A.1   A listing of Seam's modules and their purposes

Artifact ID	Purpose
jboss-seam	Provides the Seam container, Seam annotations, bijection, extended JSF life cycle, CRUD framework, security, jBPM integration, Drools integration, web services, page flows, asynchronous support, conversations, extended EL, managed transactions and persistence, and the integration test framework
jboss-seam-remoting	Supports invoking Seam components using Ajax requests and allows JavaScript to listen for messages on JMS queues and topics
jboss-seam-ui	Includes the Seam JSF components, file upload capability, graphics generation, Facelet integration, and conversation controls

---

[6]   http://repository.jboss.org/maven2

Table A.1 A listing of Seam's modules and their purposes *(continued)*

Artifact ID	Purpose
jboss-seam-debug	Activates the hot deployment classloader and provides a Seam debug page and developer-oriented error page
jboss-seam-ioc	Provides integration with Spring and other IoC containers
jboss-seam-pdf	Has support for generating PDF files using Facelet templates and a document storage mechanism for pushing binary files
jboss-seam-mail	Provides email integration and supports creating emails from Facelet templates

Take note that the presence of the Seam debug module on the classpath activates hot deployment of components and the Seam development pages. I recommend that you remove this module from the classpath when deploying to production.

A.2.2 *A wealth of documentation and examples*

Second to this book (sorry, I'm biased), the best resource you have for using Seam is the Seam reference documentation, which weighs in at 500-plus pages. We always want documentation to be better, but my feeling is that the Seam developers have done a great job of documenting Seam, especially in the area of application server interoperability. In fact, there are several places in this book where I point you to the reference documentation because, for certain topics, it will always provide the most updated information.

The reference documentation can be found in both HTML and PDF format on the Seam project page. To ensure that you always have the resources you need, keep the PDF of the Seam documentation and the eBook of Seam in Action on your hard drive at all times. If you've exhausted these resources and are still looking for more information, consult the Seam in Action link feed, http://del.icio.us/seaminaction.

The Seam distribution includes a plethora of example applications. Although this book has its own example application, the examples in the Seam distribution give you additional exposure to how Seam is used. They also exercise many different deployment environments. To deploy an example, you must specify the location of the target application server in the build.properties file at the root of the Seam distribution using either the jboss.home or tomcat.home property. I encourage you to explore the example applications early on because they'll give you context when you read about the features of Seam in this book.

A.2.3 *Finding seam-gen amid the noise*

The seam-gen tool is easily lost within the busy root folder of the Seam distribution. The tool consists of two parts: the seam-gen script and the template folder. Unless you're planning to customize seam-gen, you're likely only interested in the seam-gen script. On Unix (or Cygwin), the script is named seam, and on Windows it's named seam.bat.

To use seam-gen, you must navigate to the root of the Seam distribution directory. Before you can run the seam-gen script on Unix, you have to make it executable. To do that, execute chmod 755 seam (or chmod +x seam). When you run the seam script in Unix, you always prefix the shell command with a dot followed by a forward slash, ./seam, to let the shell know that the script is in the current directory. To run the script on Windows, you simply type seam. Following the script name, you enter the seam-gen command to execute.

You are now ready to begin using seam-gen. The next section covers a couple more resources that are useful for running the example application in this book.

A.3   seam-gen and the Open 18 example application

The example application used in this book is titled Open 18. It's a golf directory and community site. It begins its life as a seam-gen CRUD application and is customized throughout the book. Several additional applications are also provided.

A.3.1   The source code

This book's source code can be downloaded or checked out from the SVN repository of the Google Code project: http://code.google.com/p/seaminaction. The source code is organized in stages so that you can pick up with the application anywhere in the book by using the result from the previous chapter. However, you should also be able to get there without using the source code. You can find more information on the project page about how the source code is organized and how to build the staged projects. You can also find instructions on how to modify a seam-gen project so that it can be deployed to GlassFish.

Chapter 2 walks you through creating the initial application by reverse-engineering an H2 database, which you'll need to set up to follow along with the tutorial. Instructions for building the database are provided in the download. Note that all of the example applications for the book use the H2 database for persistent storage.

A.3.2   H2 database

The seam-gen tool specializes in setting up database-oriented applications. Thus, in chapter 2, you feed it an H2 database to get started. H2 is a SQL database written entirely in Java. It's much faster than other low-end databases for reasons cited on the H2 project website. H2 is the successor of the HSQL Database Engine (HSQLDB), both developed by Thomas Mueller.

The example application leverages H2's embedded mode, which allows the database to be bootstrapped directly from the file system. One major limitation of using embedded mode is that the database files can only be accessed by one JVM at a time. To avoid locking errors, you may want to consider using client-server mode, which allows several processes to connect to it over TCP/IP (or SSL/TLS over TCP/IP for improved security). Another option to circumvent locking problems is to add the flag FILE_LOCK=no to the JDBC URL, which disables H2's file locking. Beware that if you disable locking, you risk corruption of the database if writes occur from more than one client. For more information about client-server mode and the H2 database in general, visit the H2 project website: http://h2database.com.

The H2 JAR file is bundled with the source code. You can also download it from the H2 project website. The tutorial in chapter 2 assumes that it resides in the lib folder in your home directory. seam-gen takes it from there and installs it into the JBoss AS domain.

A.3.3   *Apache Ant, turning the wheels of seam-gen*

As chapter 2 explains, the workhorse behind seam-gen is Apache Ant. While you don't need Ant to run seam-gen, you need Ant to execute the build in a project that seam-gen creates.

You can download Ant from the Apache Ant project site: http://ant.apache.org. The recommended version is 1.7.0. Extract the Ant distribution into the opt folder in your home directory. You'll also need to add the ant binary to your PATH environment variable:

```
export PATH=/home/twoputt/opt/apache-ant-1.7.0/bin:$PATH
```

Once again, if you're using Debian/Ubuntu Linux, you can simply type sudo apt-get install ant to have Ant installed and configured for you automatically. Mac OS X 10.5 (Leopard) is distributed with Ant 1.7 and it's already available in the default PATH.

A.3.4   *RichFaces or ICEfaces—take your pick*

The seam-gen tool offers a choice of using either RichFaces or ICEfaces to build the user interface. Both libraries, covered in depth in chapter 12, are extensions to JSF that provide Ajax-based interactivity, an elegant look and feel, and rich UI components. By using either one, you eliminate a lot of custom CSS, graphics, and JavaScript that would otherwise have to be developed and maintained as part of your application. This abstraction and shift of responsibility is the whole value proposition of JSF components.

So how do you configure one or the other? That's the good news. If you use seam-gen to create your project, you just need to answer "y" or "n" in response to the question "Do you want to use ICEfaces instead of RichFaces?" when you run seam setup. The appropriate JAR files and configurations are then used. If you're using ICEfaces, you can optionally provide a local directory as an override.

A.4   *Managing libraries in a seam-gen project*

Both the structure and build of a seam-gen project are rather eclectic. On the one hand, this is justifiable because it's optimized for the most efficient turnaround during development. On the other hand, it's atypical build requires some explanation of how libraries are managed.

In a seam-gen project, libraries are stored in the lib folder at the root of the project. All libraries in this folder are included on the compile classpath. Which libraries are selected to be packaged with the deployment archive is controlled by the deployed-jars.list file at the root of WAR projects (split up as deployed-jars-war.list and deployed-jars-ear.list files in EAR projects). Each entry in this file, one per line, corresponds to the name of a JAR file in the lib folder to be packaged. You can use an asterisk character (*) for wildcard matching.

   To add a new JAR file to the project, you first add it to the lib folder. To have it packaged, you append it to the deployed JARs file. That still leaves the IDEs in the dark. You need to point the IDE at the JAR file and tell it to add the JAR to the classpath. In Eclipse, right-click on the JAR file in the Project Navigator and select Build Path > Add to Build Path. In NetBeans, select Project Properties and add the library to each classpath in the Java Source Classpath panel (NetBeans differentiates between src/model, src/action, and src/test).

   If this configuration isn't appealing, you can add Seam to a standard Maven 2 project.

A.5   *Adding Seam as a Maven 2 dependency*

If you're only interested in the bare minimum of what you need to use Seam, or you want to add Seam to an existing build, pulling the artifacts from the JBoss Maven 2 repository is your best bet. But using the Maven 2 artifacts doesn't mean you have to use Maven 2 as the build tool. Other tools, such as Ant, can also take advantage of the artifacts in the Maven 2 repository. You can point Ant at the Maven 2 repository using either the Maven 2 Ant tasks or Ivy. This section introduces the Seam artifacts in the JBoss Maven 2 repository by showing you how to add them to a Maven 2 build.

   A Maven 2 dependency follows the convention groupId:artifactId:version. The Seam artifacts are classified under the org.jboss.seam group ID. The artifact IDs were listed in table A.1. If you always want to use the recommended library versions with Seam, declare the Seam root artifact as the parent in your project's pom.xml as follows:

```
<parent>
  <groupId>org.jboss.seam</groupId>
  <artifactId>root</artifactId>
  <version>2.0.3.GA</version>
</parent>
```

Using the Seam root Maven 2 POM precludes the need to declare the JBoss repository or any versions of Seam artifacts and their respective transitive dependencies in your pom.xml. The only version that must be specified is the one in the <parent> stanza to indicate which version of Seam you want to use (adjust the version as needed). Once the parent POM is configured, you can add a Seam module inside the <dependencies> node as follows:

```
<dependency>
  <groupId>org.jboss.seam</groupId>
  <artifactId>jboss-seam</artifactId>
</dependency>
```

You can also add other artifacts declared in the parent dependency management without specifying versions. For instance, if you want to add the Drools libraries (which are marked as optional dependencies), use these declarations:

```
<dependency>
  <groupId>org.drools</groupId>
  <artifactId>drools-core</artifactId>
</dependency>
<dependency>
  <groupId>org.drools</groupId>
  <artifactId>drools-compiler</artifactId>
</dependency>
```

Since Seam is designed to work with a Java EE 5 environment, any artifact that's provided by a Java EE 5–compliant application server is marked as provided. Provided artifacts include the Servlet API, JSF, and the unified EL. If you need these to be included in the archive, you can declare them as compile-time dependencies. Here, JSF is included:

```
<dependency>
  <groupId>javax.faces</groupId>
  <artifactId>jsf-api</artifactId>
  <scope>compile</scope>
</dependency>
<dependency>
  <groupId>javax.faces</groupId>
  <artifactId>jsf-impl</artifactId>
  <scope>compile</scope>
</dependency>
```

As is typical with Maven 2 builds, you'll likely need to spend time getting all the dependencies configured just right (though the root POM helps out a lot). Consult the resources regarding the use of Maven 2 with Seam listed in the Seam in Action link feed mentioned earlier. If you're interested in exactly which libraries are required for each Seam module or integration, consult the last chapter of the Seam reference documentation.

resources

Allen, Dan. 2007. "Seamless JSF, part 1: an application framework tailor-made for JSF."
http://www-128.ibm.com/developerworks/java/library/j-seam1/.
2007. "Seamless JSF, part 2: conversations with Seam."
http://www-128.ibm.com/developerworks/java/library/j-seam2/.
2007. "Seamless JSF, part 3: Ajax for JSF."
http://www-128.ibm.com/developerworks/java/library/j-seam3/.

Bauer, Christian, and Gavin King. 2006. *Java Persistence with Hibernate*. Greenwich, CT: Manning
Publications.

Bergsten, Hans. 2003. *JavaServer Faces*, 3rd ed. Sebastopol, CA: O'Reilly.

DeMichiel, Linda, and Michael Keith. 2006. JSR 220: Enterprise JavaBeans, Version 3.0.
http://jcp.org/en/jsr/detail?id=220.

Evans, Eric. 2003. *Domain-Driven Design: Tackling Complexity in the Heart of Software*. Boston: Addison-
Wesley Professional.

Gamma, Erich, Richard Helm, Ralph Johnson, and John Vlissides. 1994. *Design Patterns: Elements of
Reusable Object-Oriented Software*. Boston: Addison-Wesley Professional.

Hightower, Richard. 2005. "JSF for nonbelievers: the JSF application lifecycle."
http://www.ibm.com/developerworks/library/j-jsf2/.

Hoeller, Juergen. 2005. "Implementing transaction suspension in Spring." http://www.oracle.com/
technology/pub/articles/dev2arch/2005/07/spring_transactions.html.

ICEsoft Technologies Inc. 2008. ICEfaces Developer's Guide.
http://www.icefaces.org/docs/v1_7_1/htmlguide/devguide/DevelopersGuideTOC.html.

Jacobi, Janos, and John R. Fallows. 2006. *Pro JSF and Ajax: Building Rich Internet Components*. New York:
Apress.

JBoss.org. 2008. "Drools documentation." http://downloads.jboss.com/drools/docs/4.0.7.19894.GA/
html_single/index.html.
2008. "jBPM jPDL User Guide." http://docs.jboss.com/jbpm/v3.2/userguide/html_single/.
2008. "Seam—contextual components: a framework for Enterprise Java."
http://docs.jboss.com/seam/latest/reference/en-US/html_single/.

Katz, Max. 2007. "Happy birthday, Ajax4jsf! A progress report." *Java Developer's Journal* 12:9.
http://java.sys-con.com/read/430975.htm.

Lubke, Ryan. 2006. "Web tier to go with Java EE 5: a look at resource injection."
http://java.sun.com/developer/technicalArticles/J2EE/injection/.

Richards, Norman. 2006. "Seam: the next step in the evolution of web applications." *Java Developer's
Journal* 11(2): 24–30. http://java.sys-con.com/read/issue/730.htm.

Srivastava, Rahul. "XML schema: understanding namespaces."
http://www.oracle.com/technology/pub/articles/srivastava_namespaces.html.

Walls, Craig, with Ryan Breidenbach. 2007. *Spring in Action*, 2nd ed. Greenwich, CT: Manning
Publications.

index

MORE TITLES FROM MANNING

Java Persistence with Hibernate
Second Edition of Hibernate in Action
by Christian Bauer and Gavin King

  ISBN: 1-932394-88-5
  880 pages
  $59.99
  November 2006

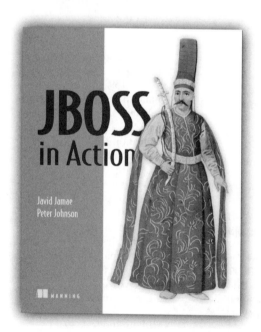

JBoss in Action
Configuring the Jboss Application Server
by Javid Jamae and Peter Johnson

  ISBN: 1-933988-02-9
  476 pages
  $49.99
  September 2008

For ordering information go to www.manning.com